中外语言文学学术文库

中西对比语言学
——历史与哲学思考（上）

Contrastive Linguistics in
China and the West
——Historical and Philosophical

潘文国　谭慧敏　著

华东师范大学出版社
East China Normal University Press

图书在版编目（CIP）数据

中西对比语言学：历史与哲学思考/潘文国，谭慧敏著.—上海：华东师范大学出版社，2017
（中外语言文学学术文库）
ISBN 978-7-5675-6879-2

Ⅰ.①中… Ⅱ.①潘… ②谭… Ⅲ.①对比语言学—中国、西方国家 Ⅳ.①H0

中国版本图书馆CIP数据核字（2017）第218806号

中西对比语言学——历史与哲学思考

著　　者	潘文国　谭慧敏
策划编辑	王　焰
项目编辑	曾　睿
特约审读	汪　燕　纪超然
责任校对	龚海燕
封面设计	金竹林　华君伟
责任印制	张久荣
出版发行	华东师范大学出版社
社　　址	上海市中山北路3663号 邮编 200062
网　　址	www.ecnupress.com.cn
电　　话	021-52713799 行政传真 021-52663760
客服电话	021-52717891 门市（邮购）电话 021-52663760
地　　址	上海市中山北路3663号华东师范大学校内先锋路口
网　　店	http://hdsdcbs.tmall.com
印　刷　者	上海商务联西印刷有限公司
开　　本	710×1000　16开
印　　张	40.75
字　　数	727千字
版　　次	2018年5月第1版
印　　次	2018年5月第1次
书　　号	ISBN 978-7-5675-6879-2/H.946
定　　价	158.00元（上下册）
出版人	王　焰

（如发现本版图书有印订质量问题，请寄回本社客服中心调换或电话021-52717891联系）

《中外语言文学学术文库》编委会

成员：（按姓氏音序）

辜正坤　何云波　胡壮麟　黄忠廉

蒋承勇　李维屏　李宇明　梁　工

刘建军　刘宓庆　潘文国　钱冠连

沈　弘　谭慧敏　王秉钦　吴岳添

杨晓荣　杨　忠　俞理明　张德明

张绍杰

总　序
GENERAL PREFACE

改革开放以来，国内中外语言文学在学术研究领域取得了很多突破性的成果。特别是近二十年来，国内中外语言文学研究领域出版的学术著作大量涌现，既有对中外语言文学宏观的理论阐释和具体的个案解读，也有对研究现状的深度分析以及对中外语言文学研究的长远展望，代表国家水平、具有学术标杆性的优秀学术精品呈现出百花齐放、百家争鸣的可喜局面。

为打造代表国家水平的优秀出版项目，推动中国学术研究的创新发展，华东师范大学出版社依托中国图书评论学会和南京大学中国社会科学研究评价中心合作开发的"中文学术图书引文索引"（CBKCI）最新项目成果，以中外语言文学学术研究为基础，以引用因子（频次）作为遴选标准，汇聚国内该领域最具影响力的专家学者的专著精品，打造了一套开放型的《中外语言文学学术文库》。

本文库是一套创新性与继承性兼容、权威性与学术性并重的中外语言文学原创高端学术精品丛书。该文库作者队伍以国内中外语言文学学科领域的顶尖学者、权威专家、学术中坚力量为主，所收专著是他们的代表作或代表作的最新增订版，是当前学术研究成果的佳作精华，在专业领域具有学术标杆地位。

本文库首次遴选了语言学卷、文学卷、翻译学卷共二十册。其中，语言学卷包括《新编语篇的衔接与连贯》、《中西对比语言学——历史与哲学思考》、《语言学习与教育》、《教育语言学研究在中国》、《美学语言学——语言美和言语美》和《语言的跨面研究》；文学卷主要包括《西方文学"人"的母题研究》、《西方文学与现代性叙事的展开》、《西方长篇小说结构模式研究》、

《英国小说艺术史》、《弥尔顿的撒旦与英国文学传统》、《法国现当代左翼文学》等;翻译学卷包括《翻译理论与技巧研究》、《翻译批评导论》、《翻译方法论》、《近现代中国翻译思想史》等。

  本文库收录的这二十册图书,均为四十多年来在中国语言学、文学和翻译学学科领域内知名度高、学术含金量大的原创学术著作。丛书的出版力求在引导学术规范、推动学科建设、提升优秀学术成果的学科影响力等方面为我国人文社会科学研究的规范化以及国内学术图书出版的精品化树立标准,为我国的人文社会科学的繁荣发展、精品学术图书规模的建设做出贡献。同时,我们将积极推动这套学术文库参与中国学术出版"走出去"战略,将代表国家水平的中外语言文学学术原创图书推介到国外,构建对外话语体系,提高国际话语权,在学术研究领域传播具有中国特色、中国高度的语言文学学术思想,提升国内优秀学术成果在国际上的影响力。

《中外语言文学学术文库》编委会
2017年10月

双语修订版序
Authors' Note to the Revised Bilingual Edition

　　本书初版以《中西对比语言学：历史与哲学思考》的名称于2006年在国内出版，一时颇受欢迎。谬赞之馀，也有读者感到有些不足，遗憾此书的外文引文没有提供英文文本，因而引用起来颇不方便，特别是需要撰写英文论文的时候。此书其实早在2007年就有英文本问世，与中文本相隔不到一年，由英国著名学术出版社The Continuums出版了，只是那个时候国内一般不容易找到而已。为便于读者使用，我们决定将两书合成一本，以双语对照形式出版。这一想法得到了王焰社长及华东师范大学出版社的支持，今日得以实现。

　　The original manuscript, first published in China in 2006 under the title *Contrastive Linguistics: History, Philosophy and Methodology*, has met with a warm reception and a wide welcome. Nonetheless, many readers looked forward to having original texts to quotations on foreign articles provided in order that many of the worthy inputs could be easily cited in their own papers in English. In fact, it was little known, due to limited accessibility to publications abroad then, that the original manuscript did have an English version published alongside in Britain in 2007, barely less than a year after its Chinese version, by the well acclaimed academic publisher The Continuums. To address readers' feedback, we decided to combine the two versions into the present bilingual edition. The thought comes true with the blessings of the East China Normal University Press and its President, Ms. Wang Yan.

　　由于原来的英文本不是中文本的逐字对译，因此这次统成一本，我们在文字疏通和版面调整上下了不少功夫，使之读起来更像"对照"读物，便于读者在阅读过程中找到自己需要的东西。囿于时间，我们仅能在内容上作微小的调整和补充，增加了一些我们认为不得不增加的事件、观点等，例如历史发展进程的补充、沈家煊的名动包含说。因为这不仅对于对比研究有意义，对于中国语言学建设乃至普通语言学研究也有意义。

The English version of 2007, though in many ways similar to the Chinese one, was not meant to be an exact English translation per se. Efforts have been made to rearrange and reformat the text and the wordings so that the two language versions run more or less "parallel" to the convenience of readers. In the interest of time, we have to live with minor revisions and supplements to include only some critical events, figures or viewpoints. Additions take into account a more complete picture of historical development as well as Shen Jiaxuan's Super-Noun Category Hypothesis. These are significant to the study of contrastive linguistics, and impactful on the grounding of Chinese linguistics and furthering general linguistics.

值此双语版出版，我们感激为当时中、英文版出版付出辛勤劳动的编校人员唐发铙、Jennifer Lovel, Rebecca Simmonds, Joanna Taylor, Judy Napper等，也感激这次双语版的特约审读汪燕和纪超然。

At the publication of the present bilingual edition, we remember the hard work put in by the editors of the previous monolingual versions Tang Fanao, Jennifer Lovel, Rebecca Simmonds, Joanna Taylor, Judy Napper among others, for their incredible patience and professionalism; we are of course greatly indebted to Wang Yan and Ji Chaoran, the editor of the present bilingual edition.

最后，中国对比语言学的领军人物之一、为本书撰写导论的杨自俭先生已于2009年辞世，他生前为此书的写作倾注过很多心血，他的精神一直激励着我们，谨以此书的双语出版作为本书作者对他最好的纪念！

Last but not least, this bilingual edition is dedicated to Professor Yang Zijian, a great champion in contrastive linguistics in China and author of the introduction to this book who passed away in 2009. Professor Yang had shaped and contributed to ideas in the course of writing and he will always be a constant inspiration to us. This book is a living tribute to his memory.

Pan Wenguo
Tham Wai Mun
November 2017

目录
CONTENTS

导论：对比语言学的新进展　/ 1

第一章　西方对比语言学研究　/ 35

    1.1　越过拉多和沃尔夫　/ 36

    1.2　对比语言学起源与西方对比语言学史　/ 39

    1.3　第一期（19世纪20年代至20世纪40年代）：
　　　　对比哲学思想的奠基　/ 52

    1.4　第二期（20世纪40—70年代）：
　　　　在主流语言学理论转向中寻求立足点的开拓　/ 87

    1.5　第三期（1980年至今）：走向宏观和注重理论建构　/ 111

第二章　中国对比研究简史（上）　/ 165

    2.1　研究中国对比语言学史的意义　/ 165

    2.2　汉外对比研究发展史再探　/ 196

    2.3　第一期（1898—1921）：
　　　　比较与对比之间：《马氏文通》及其意义　/ 197

    2.4　第二期（1922—1955）：
　　　　旨在建立汉语自身语法体系的对比研究　/ 224

导论：对比语言学的新发展
Introduction: Fresh Developments in Contrastive Linguistics

杨自俭　中国英汉语比较研究会会长
Yang Zijian　President, China Association for Comparative Studies Between English and Chinese

　　读了潘文国、谭慧敏的这本新作使我想起了1996年4月我为潘文国《汉英语对比纲要》写序的时候，现已近10年了。当时我正在筹备中国英汉语比较研究会第2次全国大会，想请徐通锵先生来会上讲讲汉语"字本位"问题，他因忙于修改《历史语言学》，没能成行。但文国为大会提交的两篇有重要理论价值的论文起到了补救作用，一篇讲对比语言学理论与学科体系问题，另一篇是《换一种眼光如何？——关于汉英对比研究的宏观思考》。就是这篇文章尖锐地批评了英汉对比研究和汉语研究都严重地依赖英语，以英律中，明确提出摆脱"印欧语的眼光"。他说从地道的汉语出发，就是"语言观和方法论的根本改观"，同时转述了徐通锵先生关于"字本位"和英语句子封闭性与汉语句子开放性的思想，并指出只有从汉语出发才能使对比研究"达到真正的深度和广度"。后来我们学会讨论学科史和"两张皮"的问题，文国都带头做出了成绩。他在2000年第1期《语言研究》上刊载了长达27页的《汉语研究：世纪之交的思考》，2001年4月在青岛翻译学科建设专题讨论会上发表了史论结合的关于当代西方翻译学研究的长篇论文（《中国翻译》2002年1—3连载3期），同年10月在大连教授沙龙讲了"两张皮"的由来及对策，2002年第1期《世界汉语教学》刊登了他的又一篇长文（26页）《汉英对比研究一百年》，同年他还出版了专著《字本位与汉语研究》，《华东师范大学学报》2004年第3期发表了他的《语言哲学与哲学语言学》。近期他在与谭慧敏合作完成这本著作的同时，还在和徐通锵先生共同主编"汉语字本位研究丛书"（暂定8本，详见徐通锵先生写的总序，载于《语言教学与研究》2005年第6期），并亲自撰写其中的《字本位和普通语言学》一书。另一方面，慧敏还在读大学本科时就对对比语言学感兴趣。作为班上的尖子学生，她以一篇关于汉语中的虚拟语气论文获得了荣誉学位。当时她还不是个语言学者，却已开始挑战汉语虚拟语气说的理论基础，无意中踏进了哲学语言学领域。在她关于汉语量词的硕士论文中，她从历史和微观的角度进行了深入的对比。后来她致力于机器翻译和中文计算语言学，尤其是董振东的知网模式，这激起了她对字本位理论和词汇语义学的思考。她与文国的学术背景完全不同，而在对比语言学理论探索方面居然想到一起去了，这也是件有趣的事情。我之所以罗列这些，主要想探讨：（1）这些年他们，尤其是文国，在对比语言学这个领域所思考的问题、所做的研究、所追求的目标，也就是他们这本新作产生的基础和条件。（2）在此基础上总结一下他治学的道路和学科建设的经验。文国他们的这本新作的确做了许多创造性的研究，不论是中国的和西方的学科理论史的研究，还是对比语言学的本体论和方法论的探索，都提出了许多新的看法，可以说，这本新作的出版标志着国内外对比语言学理论建设和学科理论史研究进入了一个新的历史时期。我之所以有这样的认识主要基于我读后有几个感受很深的问题，现简述如下：

Reading this book, I cannot help recalling the time I penned a foreword for Wenguo's *Chinese-English Contrastive Study*. Let me invite you to travel ten years back with me to April 1996. At that time, the China Association for Comparative Studies Between English and Chinese (CACSEC) was occupied with organizing the second national conference for the Association, held at Qingdao Ocean University. Originally I wished Professor Xu Tongqiang (徐通锵) to share his thoughts on sinogram-based theory and issues; however, he was preoccupied with the revision of his work on *Historical Linguistics*. Fortunately, two other important papers by Wenguo filled the gap. One dealt with the theoretical construction and disciplinary system of contrastive linguistics; the other was entitled "How about changing a viewpoint?—Thoughts on the macro-perspectives of Chinese-English contrastive study". It is this paper that questions the prevailing emphasis on and imposition of the English rudiments that are common in English-Chinese contrastive studies as in Chinese language studies. The paper has no reservations in its call for Chinese language studies to diverge from the shadowy "Indo-European viewpoint": the new respect for the Chinese language would necessarily signify "a fundamental change in linguistic views and methodology", in his words. In addition, the paper also relates the sinogram-based approach of Xu Tongqiang and discusses the closed nature of English sentence structures against the openness of the Chinese language to drive home the point that we will never achieve much in contrastive studies without taking a first step in studying Chinese in its own right and making that a basis for contrastive studies. Since 2000 Wenguo has again led the historical research of contrastive linguistics as well as the discussion of the "two-skin" phenomenon. *Yuyan Yanjiu* (*Language Review*) (2000: 1) contains his detailed retrospective study of the past century's Chinese linguistics; *Zhongguo Fanyi* (*Journal of the Chinese Translator*) (2002: 1—3) carries three articles containing his survey of the Western translation theories from a historical perspective, presented at a national conference on translatology in April 2001. In October 2001, he explained the origin of and discussed solutions to the "two-skin" phenomenon at the professorial salon held at Dalian; *Shijie Hanyu Jiaoxue* (*Teaching Chinese in the World*) (2002: 1) published, at length, his study of Chinese-English contrastive studies of the last century; also in 2002, his work *On Sinogram-based Chinese Studies* arrived on the shelves and the *Journal of East China Normal University* (2004: 3) included his Linguistic Philosophy and Philosophical Linguistics. As he prepares this book with Tham Wai Mun, he is at the same time co-editing with Xu Tongqiang a book series on sinogram-based Chinese language research (a planned-for eight books at this stage, with a series prefaced by Xu Tongqiang published in *Yuyan Jiaoxue yu Yanjiu* (*Language Teaching and Research*) (2005: 6) which he will write on sinogram-based approach and general linguistics. On the other hand, Wai Mun's interest in contrastive studies was first aroused in her undergraduate days, when she was top of her class with a thesis that discusses the subjunctive mood in Chinese, leading to an honours degree. Not yet quite a linguistics student at that time, she began challenging the theoretical and typological grounds for the subjunctive mood in Chinese, totally unaware that she had unknowingly broken early into the territory of philosophical linguistics. In her master's research on "quantifiers" in Chinese, Wai Mun delved deep into the historical and micro-contrastive perspectives. Later, her involvement in machine translation and Chinese computational linguistics, particularly the How-net model by Dong Zhendong (董振东), excited more thoughts on sinogram-based theory and lexical semantics. Since they were not treading exactly the same research path, and particularly as they did not come from the same research background, it is even more interesting that the two should share similar scholastic thoughts. I mention these to illustrate the following. First, the foundation of the production of this book—all the pondering, research and pursuit on the part of the authors, particularly Wenguo. Second, I wish to summarize the research path of Wenguo and his experiences in constructing the contrastive linguistic discipline. As you read this book, you will find that it is full of creativity, filled with novel ideas, in terms of both the survey of the historical development path of the discipline in China and the West and the discussion on the ontology and methodology of contrastive linguistics. Be it within China or in the rest of the world, efforts in theoretical study, in particular theoretical development in contrastive linguistics, would, as I may safely put, now advance to the next milestone in history following the release of this benchmark volume. I base my argument on what struck me most deeply upon reading the draft, and which I may share only briefly below.

1. 立意高远
Far and deep insights

我之所以说此书立意高远，主要有以下四个方面的根据。

On account of the following grounds, I must say that the book is planned with a far-reaching foresight.

（1）它把对比语言学看成是普通语言学的基础

Grounding general linguistics on contrastive linguistics

它挖掘和继承了西方洪堡特（W. Von. Humboldt）、沃尔夫（B. L. Whorf）、叶斯柏森（O. Jespersen）和中国赵元任、王力、吕叔湘、林语堂等人关于对比语言学和普通语言学关系的思想，比如洪堡特说："从哲学观念上看，人们还几乎只是停留在普遍语法的贫乏境地。甚至对普遍语法，也极少视之为一门纯理性的科学，更未把它看作一种普遍的比较语法。"赵元任说：

"所谓语言学理论，实际上就是语言的比较，就是世界各民族语言综合比较研究得出的科学结论。"文国评论赵元任这句话说："据我们所知，在洪堡特之后，中外语言学家中还没有一个人把语言对比提到这么高的地位的。这句话也成了1990年以后中国对比研究的主旋律，许多有成就的学者、有影响的著作都是本着这个精神来进行对比研究的。"其实文国他们这本书各部分都贯穿着这个精神：对比语言学的理论目标就是做普通语言学的支柱。

The work took pains in unearthing from both the East and the West on the relations between contrastive linguistics and general linguistics by such great linguists as Wilhelm von Humboldt, Benjamin Lee Whorf, Otto Jespersen, Chao Yuen-ren (赵元任), Wang Li (王力), Lü Shuxiang (吕叔湘) and Lin Yutang (林语堂). For example, Humboldt (1810-11: 7) remarks that: "From the philosophical perspective, people are still resting themselves on the poor state of universal grammar. They don't even regard universal grammar as a pure rational science, not to say to regard it as a universal comparative grammar." Chao Yuen-ren concludes that: "Theoretical linguistics is in reality the comparing of languages, i.e. the scientific conclusion arises out of the consolidated comparison of ethnic languages in the world." On this postulation, Wenguo says: "In so far as we know, no one else on Planet Earth apart from Humboldt has ever accorded such high status to contrastive study of languages. This remark of Chao was taken as the principle for China's contrastive studies after 1990." That underpinning general linguistics is the theoretical goal of contrastive linguistics has been the ground upon which many prominent scholars have produced their works. It is that same spirit that runs throughout this work.

（2）中国汉外对比研究的另一个目标是建立汉语自身的语言学

The alternative objective of Chinese-foreign-language contrastive studies in China: towards a real Chinese linguistics

马建忠、章炳麟、王国维、赵元任、李方桂、陈望道、罗常培、黎锦熙、王力、吕叔湘、高名凯、朱德熙、张志公等为代表的前辈语言学家，大都学了外语来研究汉语，为的是建立我们自己的汉语语言学，这是他们终生奋斗的目标。在古代世界上有三大语言研究中心，中国的训诂，希腊的语法，印度的音韵，各有特长。中国从先秦到1898年《马氏文通》出版在历史上形成了自己的语言学研究传统，即研究文字、训诂、音韵的小学传统。宋代晁公武（《郡斋读书志》卷一）称小学为"文字之学"，这说明中国古代语言学以文字为研究对象，研究字形（文字学）、字义（训诂学）、字音（音韵学），而不是以语言为研究对象，所以不研究语法。西方语言学以语言为研究对象，不重视研究文字，很重视研究语法。和西方语言学研究传统相比这两点就是我们语言研究传统的最突出的特点。《马氏文通》改变了这个传统。印欧语言学的理论引进来以后，特别在语法理论中引进了汉语中找不到恰当对应物的两个重要范畴：词（word）和句子（sentence），还有其他一些语法范畴，比如性（gender）、数（number）、格（case）、时（tense）、体（aspect）、态（voice）、人称（person）、语气（mood）以及名（noun）、动（verb）、形（adjective）、代（pronoun）、副（adverb）、连（conjunction）、介（preposition）和主（subject）、谓（predicate）、宾（object）、表（predicative）、定（attributive）、状（adverbial）等等以后，我们的语言研究发生了重大变化，而且语法学成了最重要也是最主要的学科。所以《马氏文通》就成了中国现代语言学时期开端的标志。一个世纪过去了，我们积累了很多经验和教训，但大家都感到中与外的关系和古与今的关系都处理得不够好。文国分析说，中国古人的语言研究走的是另一条路，19世纪末我们急于学西方走富国强兵现代化之路，中国语言学家心怀民族振兴的重任，孜孜追求建立西方式的汉语语法体系，"这恐怕是他国的对比语言学家们所想象不到的。西方对比语言学的鼻祖们，即使是洪堡特、叶斯柏森和沃尔夫，大约也没有想到过对比语言学可以成为一个民族语言学建立的基础。"我们的语言研究在处理中与外、古与今之间的关系上存在什么问题呢？潘文国把这个问题放在普通语言学的观照下，先引证评述了洪堡特、高本汉（Bernhard karlgren）、叶斯柏森等对汉语特点的论述，后又引证评述了陈承泽、赵元任、黎锦熙、王力、吕叔湘、何容、高名凯、张志公、徐通锵等人的思想观念与困惑，得出结论说汉语和印欧语是两大不同类型的语言，其本质差别在于语义和语法形式的关系不同，也就是有没有"形态"，汉语没有印欧语词类和句法那样对应的关系。张志公说"印欧语都是形态语……汉语本身是'非形态语言'。形态语和非形态语是明显不同的两种语言体系，我们应当理直气壮、明白无误地确认汉语'非形态'这一事实，从而有勇气打破印欧语的语法框架，探索和建立汉语自己的语法体系。"（1990年）潘文国说："否定'形态说'和否定'词'的概念是语言对比研究带有全局性的大问题，牵一发而动全身，对普通语言学理论是个相当大的冲击。"他分析了研究汉语的9类学者之后说："我们有必要研究中国的汉外对比发展史,从中来观察汉语研究和中国普通语言学研究的真正进展。"汉语的研究必须走中外和古今两个结合的道路,中国语言学百年历史证明,中断自己的传统、跟着外国的理论转是没有出路的。

That forerunners such as Ma Jianzhong (马建忠), Zhang Binglin (章炳麟), Wang Guowei (王国维), Chao Yuen-ren, Li Fanggui (李方桂), Chen Wangdao (陈望道), Luo Changpei (罗常培), Li Jinxi (黎锦熙), Wang Li, Lü Shuxiang, Gao Mingkai (高名凯), Zhu Dexi (朱德熙) and Zhang Zhigong (张志公) chose to learn foreign language(s), they did it for an ultimate aim harboured for Chinese-language research. They were truly bilinguals or multilinguals having a lifelong commitment to the construction of a linguistic system true to the Chinese language. Far back in those old days, there were three centres of linguistic research: in China, exegesis (训诂); in Greece, grammar and in India, phonology. Each specializes in a field. Spanning from pre-Qin to the release of *Mashi Wentong* (Ma's grammar) in 1898, the Chinese have long shaped and owned a tradition of philology that was termed "primary learning" (小学), involving the graphical and etymological study of sinograms (文字学), phonology and phonetics (音韵学) and exegetic semantics (训诂学). Chao Gongwu (晁公武) of the Song Dynasty defines "primary learning" as the study about sinograms. (*Jun Zhai Du Shu Zhi*《郡斋读书志》vol. 1). In itself, the definition is illustrative of the nature of linguistic studies in ancient China, which focuses on the various aspects of sinograms, or Chinese characters, as the pictography (字形) or the science of sinogram construction; the meaning as well as the sound or phonology and prosody. Clearly, language *per se* never falls within the research scope, so, as such, grammar has no place. Western linguistics, on the other hand, looks at language itself instead of the writing signs, so grammar is important. We thus see that the outstanding characteristics of the linguistics tradition of the Chinese are different from those of the West. *Mashi Wentong* twisted this course of tradition. The introduction of Indo-European linguistic theories introduces, in particular, two significant grammatical categories that have no equivalent in Chinese: word and sentence, following a string of other categories such as gender, number, case, tense, aspect, voice, person, mood, noun, verb, adjective, pronoun, adverb, conjunction, preposition, subject, predicate, object, predicative, attributive, adverbial, and so on. Armed with the new tool, linguistic research in China took a major shift, with grammar becoming the star discipline. We could well attribute the formation of modern linguistics in China to *Mashi Wentong*. One century has passed, and enough experiences drawn and lessons learnt. And the concerns have been the proper integration of the Chinese and foreign linguistic traditions as well as the proper inheritance of past linguistic legacy within modern Chinese. In this light, the authors shared and evaluated the path taken by Chinese linguists of the nineteenth century. Chinese intellectuals, mindful of their mission to empower China with tools that will lead the country to modernization signified by military might and economic strength, have wasted no time in taking their cue from the West. Shouldering the task of revitalizing the Chinese ethnicity, linguists at the time looked hard to establish a Chinese linguistic system based on the Western model. "It would never occur to any linguist in the world that a linguistic discipline in contrastive studies could be tied to the fate of the nation, not even Humboldt or Jespersen or Whorf could ever imagine laying foundation of linguistics for a nation through contrastive linguistics." (Chapter 2). What are the issues concerning our handling of tradition and current development, and the way we manage Chinese and foreign linguistic systems? Guided by general linguistics, the authors discuss the above questions with illustrative quotations, first from Humboldt, Karlgren and Jespersen on their views of the characteristics of the Chinese language, and further from Chen Chengze (陈承泽), Chao Yuen-ren, Li Jinxi, Wang Li, L Shuxiang, He Rong (何容), Gao Mingkai, Zhang Zhigong and Xu Tongqiang of their perceptions and perplexities. The conclusion distinguishes the typology of Chinese and Indo-European languages, as evident in how semantic and grammatical forms are connected, which boils down to the existence of "morphology". One does not find the kind of mapping word classes and sentence patterns of Indo-European languages in the Chinese language. Zhang Zhigong remarked that Indo-European languages are morphological languages... whereas the Chinese language is a "non-morphological language. Obviously, morphological and non-morphological languages are two systems of language. We shall confidently and unequivocally uphold the fact that Chinese is non-morphological, only then do we have the courage to break free from the grammatical frame of the Indo-European languages in search of a grammatical system genuine to Chinese." (1990) The authors warn: "The dismissal of morphology and the concept of word are two big issues in language contrast relating to the big picture, a slightest change would create great repercussions. These are great challenges to the validation of language universal" (Chapter 3). The observation of nine types of linguists prompted Wenguo's comment that "Looking into the research history of contrasting Chinese with foreign languages, we get to realize the true development in Chinese language research as well as general linguistics research in China" (Chapter 2). Without doubt, research in Chinese language and linguistics must advance along a path that integrates Chinese-foreign efforts and unites past traditions with modern theories. Lessons from the past hundred years clearly suggest that severing the Chinese tradition to jump on the bandwagon of foreign theories leads to no through road.

（3）正确运用历史和逻辑相统一的方法

Correct integration of history and logic

历史决定逻辑，逻辑反映和修正历史，二者是对立统一的关系。恩格斯说："历史从哪里开始，思想进程也应当从哪里开始，而思想进程的进一步发展不过是历史过程在抽象的、理论上前后一贯的形式上的反映；这种反映是经过修正的，然而是按照现实的历史过程本身的规律修正的。"（《马恩选集》第2卷第122页）这是学科理论体系建设的科学而有效的方法，因为它遵循以下三个原则：理论范畴的建立与转化必须以揭示历史发展规律的历史材料为依据的原则；历史发展的内在动力在逻辑上要用范畴内涵的自身矛盾来表达的原则；历史进程中过去、现在与将来之间的内在联系要体现在比较完整而成熟的范畴体系中的原则。我读完文国的书稿深深感到他努力按照这三条原则在思考和研究学科的发展规律、理论系统、研究方法等重大理论问题。

Historical events determine the logic behind developments, which in turn reflect and moderate history as we know it. History and logic are antithetical. Friedrich Engels says: "Thought process shall advance from where history happens. The further development in thoughts merely reflects the development of history in its abstract but theoretically-consistent-throughout form. Such reflection is being adjusted and the adjustment due to the pattern of historical development per se." (*Collected Works of Karl Marx and Friedrich Engels*, vol. 2:122) This can be deemed as an effective and scientific method for establishing theoretical basis in any discipline. First, it is necessary that theoretical categories be built and transformed based on historical facts that are revealing historical development patterns. Next, the inner drive of historical development must logically be grounded upon the contradictions found within the logical categories. Finally, the internal linkage of the past, present and future of historical progress has to be organized within a relatively complete and mature categorical system. As I read this manuscript, I was convinced that all major theoretical issues—the developmental trend, theoretical system and research methodology—were discussed in accordance to the above three principles.

（4）用高层理念来观照学科全局
An overall view of the discipline with lofty ideals

人文学科和其他学科的最大不同在于前者对人类的命运有着强烈的终极关怀，它关心过去与现在，但更关心未来。当然在这一点上哲学是排头兵。但吕叔湘（1988）说："说到底，语言学本质上仍然是一门人文科学。"所以它也有这种品质。不过以前很少有人关注语言学的高层理念问题。文国在这本书中多次讲到中国语言学问题要让外国学者有更多的了解和参与，外国语言学家应主动关注中国的语言学，因为语言是人类的生存方式，我们应该存异求同，他重申了《论语》中"和而不同"的思想，说只有这样人类才能友好而和谐的共生，不然"就意味着语言世界的纷争和人类社会的不太平"，在书的结尾处他画龙点睛地宣告："对比语言学的终极目标是求'和'，这也是本书的最终结论。"由此足可以看出他思考和研究问题的境界之高，我读后大有登上泰山极顶一览众山小之感。每个学科都有自己的高层理念，实际就是学科的灵魂，它观照和统帅着学科的全局与各个层面，所以任何一个学科的建设都不应把"灵魂"的位置放错。

Humanistic disciplines differ from other disciplines in that there exist here burning ultimate concerns for the fate of humankind—about its past and present and not least its future. Of course, philosophy, more than any other humanistic discipline, would be the most passionate in this respect. However, Lü Shuxiang (1988) remarked that: "At the end of the day, Linguistics is essentially very much a humanistic discipline still." Given this humanistic nature of linguistics, it shares the ultimate concern of any other disciplines of humanities. Nevertheless, few ever thought about the lofty ideal of linguistic studies. In this particular work, Wenguo mentions time and again the need for greater understanding and participation by foreign scholars in the discussion of issues relating to Chinese linguistics. Foreign linguists should take an initiative regarding the development of linguistics in

China, because it is in language that human being exists. Repeating after *Analects of Confucius* the ideal of "seeking harmony instead of sameness", Wenguo felt this is the way for human races to coexist and flourish in harmony, otherwise, disputes and discord in the linguistic world and the society will prevail. The book expresses the concern that "the ultimate aim of contrastive linguistics is to seek harmony out of differences, which is also the final conclusion of the present book" (Chapter 5). As I read the last page, I felt as if I were standing at the peak of Mount Taishan overseeing the lower ranges. In every discipline there exists this lofty ideal, which really is the soul of the discipline governing the whole as well as the parts. For this matter, no discipline should ever misplace its "soul".

2. 理论研究更加深入系统
Digging deep into the theoretical system

　　此书在研究了中西对比语言学理论史的基础上抓住三个重大问题进行了深入探讨。

The book focuses on three major issues that emerged from studying the theoretical history of the contrastive linguistics of the East and West.

　　第一，在学科基础论层面上提出了一个新的语言定义。

A new definition for language grounded on the fundamentals of the discipline

　　他在波兰对比语言学家菲齐亚克（Jacek Fisiak）"元理论"的基础上进一步思考了"元元理论"，即"以语言观为核心的语言哲学的思考"。对学科结构系统进行纵向划分，比如语言学分为：语言哲学（实为哲学语言学）、理论语言学、应用语言学和语言实践四个层次。他又把洪堡特以来中外60多种语言的定义分成四种类型的语言观：自足系统观（索绪尔为代表）、交际工具观（斯大林为代表）、天赋能力观（乔姆斯基为代表）、文化语言观（洪堡特为代表），并论证了这四种语言观和地球进化所经历的三个世界（自然、社会、人类）与人类三大知识领域（自然科学、社会科学、人文科学）的密切关系。他还归纳出《马氏文通》以来中国语言研究"借鉴的三个层次"：具体语言规律、普通语言学、语言哲学。就这样他在史论结合的基础上提出了一个新的语言的定义，用比较与辨析的方法对定义中四个关键范畴（认知、表述、方式、过程）作了多层面的界说，转述了叶斯柏森对索绪尔的批评，明确指出对比语言学研究的语言"是包含'言语'和'语言'在一起的语言、人们实实在在使用的语言"。阅读此书的这一部分使我想到：任何学科都应该建立以自己的研究对象为中心的范畴体系。范畴的提出、比较、辨析与界定是理论研究的最基础的工程，在此基础上才可能构建范畴的逻辑系统（即理论体系）。我国学术界常有人批评范畴研究是"脱离实际，空对空"，"在概念里兜圈子，毫无意义的争论"，这是我国许多学科没有自己理论体系的重要原因。如果只注重用归纳法进行微观分析，不注重范畴史与各范畴之间关系的研究，那何时才能建立起系统的理论？自主创新体系的建设最需要的就是自主创建各学科的理论体系。

While the Polish contrastivist Jacek Fisiak proposed a meta-theory, the authors went one step further to consider meta-metatheoretical issues that are language ideological conceptions with language perspective in the core (Chapter 4). On a horizontal plane, the discipline can be structured into four levels: philosophical linguistics, theoretical linguistics, applied linguistics and linguistic applications. Wenguo further singled out from over 60 definitions of language and four types of language views: the self-sufficient view (Saussure as representative); the instrumental view (Stalin as representative); the innate gift (Chomsky as representative); and the cultural view (Humboldt as representative). These four types of language views were first testified against the three worlds of nature, social and humanity, which were part of evolution on Earth, and then against the three major knowledge systems of humankind: namely natural sciences, social sciences and humanities, to show how closely these were knitted together. On this ground, three levels of borrowing from the West since *Mashi Wentong* were identified: specific language rules, general linguistics, and linguistic philosophy. The emphasis on conclusions drawn from historical development led to a new definition for language, and the four keys (cognitive, presentation, method and process) were analysed with contrastive methodology in multi-faceted details. In the process, Jespersen's critique of Saussure was quoted to support the opinion that the research target of contrastive linguistics is the language of real life, that which encompasses both *parole* and *langue*. This part of the book led me to think that the categorical systems in all disciplines ought to be centred round their particular research object. Fundamental theory research must be the comparison, analysis, definition and setting of categories. Without this basic engineering, no logical categorical system (theoretical system) is possible. In

China, categorical studies are not appreciated by most literati: They think that it is off-based and empty at both the starting and ending points; and that merely circling around concepts and related debates is pointless. We can now understand why most disciplines to be found in China do not own a theoretical system of their own. Should we focus only on micro-analysis using generalization and neglect the historical development of categories and relations between the various categories? How could the theoretical system for a discipline ever be set up? Any independent and innovative body of system would require a structuring of theory in full autonomy.

第二，在学科论层面上提出了一个新的学科体系。

A new framework for the discipline proposed strictly on disciplinary grounds

他围绕学科的目标、范围、性质、定位几个重要范畴，用史论结合的方法对洪堡特、叶斯柏森、沃尔夫、拉多（Robert Lado）、菲齐亚克、克尔采斯佐斯基（Krzeszowski）、切斯特曼（Chesterman）、黎锦熙、王宗炎、赵世开、许余龙、刘重德等中外学者关于对比语言学学科体系的思想和系统作了纵与横两个系统的比较，遵照7条原则（刘重德4条，潘文国3条）组建了一个新的学科体系，用三种属性和四个层级交叉结合，组成了8个研究领域（详见书中表格）。这个体系的建构一是扩大了学科研究的领域和层次，二是为其他学科理论体系的建设提供了方法论的借鉴。学科是否独立最主要的标志是看有没有自己的理论体系。理论体系主要靠范畴系统来体现，人文学科的范畴系统不易做到像欧几里得几何学那样严密，但至少应划分出几个不重叠不交叉的等级与层次，而且不应该缺少学科的哲学论、方法论和理论史三部分。我们的学术传统中虽然有义理的研究，但由于"没有创造出欧几里得几何学那样的完整体系，也没有创造出亚里斯多德的形式逻辑的严密体系"（张岱年），所以我们学术传统的价值系统中缺少理论体系研究的评价标准。这种影响至今依然存在。

Western and Chinese scholars have shared many thoughts on disciplinary frameworks, and various models were proposed. Considering the objective, scope, nature and positioning of the discipline, Wenguo surveyed the ideals of Humboldt, Jespersen, Whorf, Lado, Fisiak, Krzeszowki, Chesterman, Li Jinxi, Wang Zongyan, Zhao Shikai, Xu Yulong and Liu Zhongde both horizontally and vertically. On this basis, seven principles (by Liu Zhongde, and by Pan Wenguo) were used to guide a proposed framework sitting on three attributes and four interlinking levels and branching out to eight sub-fields (refer to in-text table). The proposed framework, while expanding on the scope and depth of contrastive linguistics, also serves as a reference to other discipline-building in terms of methodology. A discipline can claim to be independent only if it owns a set of theories that will run the system. That body of theory owes its existence to a set of categories defining the boundaries. Although categories in humanities can never be as stringent as those of Euclidean geometry, this approach should set up some non-overlapping, non-crossing hierarchies and levels in the least with three key elements of philosophy, methodology and theoretical history. In the Chinese scholastic tradition, there is exploration into philosophical issues; nevertheless, we "did not create anything close to Aristorian formal logic since we have no system like Euclidean geometry (Zhang Dainian 张岱年). Such being the case, to this date, assessment criteria for theoretical frameworks do not yet exist within our traditional scholastic value system.

第三，在学科本质论层面上提出了一个新的对比语言学定义。

A new definition for contrastive linguistics grounded on the nature of the discipline

他先研究了和对比语言学关系最密切的两对范畴"比较"与"对比"以及"同"与"异"，既分析了它们之间的关系和发展的过程，又分析了它们的方法论和本体论意义，从而得出结论："对比"和"异"皆有方法论和本体论意义；异同不可分离，异为世界的本质，求同求异皆从求异开始，强调异或同体现理论研究的不同终极目标。这是新定义的第一个基础。第二个基础是研究了洪堡特、拉多、菲齐亚克、詹姆斯（Carl James）、许余龙、王宗炎、杨自俭等人的关于对比语言学定义的研究成果。在这两类成果的基础上提出了这个新的定义。这个定义修正和增加了不少内容：哲学基础、和普通语言学的关系、异同的侧重性、理论与应用的不同层面、方言、语言与精神活动的关系、促进交流理解与和谐。他在分析定义中特别强调了洪堡特、高本汉、沃尔夫的崇高境界和远见卓识，求异不是相互争斗，制约发展，而是二者互补，共同进步，让人类的语言生活和精神世界更加丰富多彩、和谐美好。

The new definition is set on a few grounds. To begin with, the two pairs of categories of "similarity vs. difference" and "compare vs. contrast", most essential in contrastive linguistics, and their relation and evolution, were discussed with regards to methodology and ontology. Here, the conclusion sheds light on the sense that "contrast" and "difference" hold in methodology and ontology. Similarities and differences are inseparable concepts. In differences lie the nature of this world, and it follows that the quest for similarities or differences begins with seeking differences. The emphasis on similarities and differences serves only to distinguish the separate concerns of diverging theoretical studies. Second, it draws from the definitions and findings variously attributed to Humboldt, Lado, Fisiak, James, Xu Yulong (许余龙), Wang Zongyan (王宗炎) and Yang Zijian (杨自俭) among others. The proposed definition adds and re-addresses many issues such as those of philosophical basis, relations with general linguistics, preferences about differences and similarities, theoretical and applied aspects, role of dialect, relations between language and ethnic spirit, functions in facilitating exchanges, understanding and harmony. The analysis holds in high regard the exceptional magnanimity and vision of Humboldt, Bernhard Karlgren and Whorf in their understanding that seeking differences has nothing to do with competition or imposing restriction: Rather, their aim is to complement each other for total progress so that the linguistic and spiritual worlds of humankind would flourish beautifully in their own ways and in accord.

　　下定义是一种很重要的研究方法，但这是我们的短处，我们的学术传统中用比喻说明概念的多，下定义的少，改革开放以来这方面有了不少进步。我在《语言和语言学》（2002）一文中讲过形式逻辑定义的公式与规则以及辩证逻辑对定义的要求，但还有两个与定义法密切相关的重要问题需要讨论。第一是形式逻辑概念和辩证逻辑概念的差别。前者是从思维形式结构研究概念，它是思维的基本单位，反映事物抽象的同一性，不包含差异和矛盾，概念稳定，不关注其发展变化，关注个体概念，为人类思维发展初级阶段的抽象概念；后者是结合认识的具体内容研究概念，它是认识的总结，反映事物具体的同一性，包含差异和矛盾，概念流动，关注其发展变化，关注概念系统，为人类思维发展高级阶段的具体概念。第二是具体1——抽象——具体2的认识过程与方法。具体1是指人在社会实践中从客观事物的丰富材料中获得生动具体的知觉表象，即低级的感性的具体认识。这是认识的最初出发点。在此基础上用比较分析的方法区分具体1认识中的偶然现象与必然本质，用概念、判断、推理等形式表示事物的本质与规律，这时认识就从具体1进入到了抽象。它虽比具体1更深刻，但还不能达到全面具体的认识。然后以这种本质抽象为出发点，用综合的方法，把事物各方面的本质认识联系起来，进而获得事物内在的各种本质属性的统一全面具体的认识，到达具体2认识阶段。认识始于具体1，通过抽象完成形式逻辑的任务，最后到达理性中具体对象的具体真理。从具体1到抽象的方法是形式逻辑的形式论证，从抽象到具体2的方法是辩证逻辑的辩证否定论证，前者是后者的辅助手段，只有通过后者才能揭示事物的内在本质及其发展的必然规律，到达逻辑终点具体2，这是辩证思维的一个周期。客体运动无限，人的认识运动无限，所以辩证思维运动也无限。一个逻辑终点对范围更广与层次更高的认识来说，它又是一个逻辑的起点，认识深化，概念发展，过程无穷无尽。运用这个辩证逻辑的方法有利于建立学科的范畴系统，因为它的结果是经过一步步辩证推演和转化产生一系列逻辑范畴，进而形成比较完整的相互联系与制约的范畴系统。比如马克思在《资本论》中从"商品"开始，经过价值——货币——资本——剩余价值——工资等，一直推演到"分配关系与生产关系"，最后推演到"阶级"的范畴。如果把"人"定义为"能制造工具并使用工具进行劳动的、有语言和思维能力的高等动物"，反映的是区分人和动物的外在共性，这是人的"抽象概念"，属于形式逻辑概念。若把"人"定义为"一切社会关系的总和"，反映的是人的内在本质——社会性，这是人的"具体2概念"，属于辩证逻辑概念。我们的学术研究需要形式逻辑，更需要辩证逻辑，你读完潘著，回头再思考学术研究和逻辑学的关系问题，我想你一定会跟我有同感：该书一系列概念的比较辨析、推演转化、分类界定都显示了逻辑学的力量，也体现了文国同志的逻辑学水平。

  The importance of definition as a research method cannot be overemphasized. However, this is exactly where the Chinese lack experience. Our scholarship has traditionally explained concepts using analogy, not definition. This has changed for the better since China opened its door. In "Language and Linguistics" (Preface to the *Multidisciplinary Research and Application of Linguistics*) I have deliberated on the equation and rules using formal logic for definition as well as the requirement of dialectical logic on defining. Two other concerns in methodology for definition need discussion here. At the outset, it is necessary to differentiate the concepts of formal logic and dialectical logic. Formal logic examines ideas and concepts about the formal structure of thought. It is the basic unit of thought, reflecting how things are similar in their abstract forms, disregarding disparities and contradictions. Ideas and concepts are deemed to be stable and, instead of giving attention to developmental changes, individual ideals and concepts that represent the abstract conception of the human mind at its initial stage of evolution are the focus. Dialectical logic examines concepts in specific details resulting from experiences to put forth a summary of experiences and understanding reflecting specific consistencies in things, giving due consideration to differences and contradictions. Ideas and concepts are deemed to be fluid and therefore developmental variations are of concern, particularly the system of concepts that reflects the specific conceptions of the human mind at its matured stage of evolution. The next refers to the experience process and method, moving from Specific 1 to Abstract to Specific 2. During social practices, vivid concrete perceptive representations—termed Specific 1—are derived from a realm of resources of the objective world. It is the lower form of concrete perception that forms our preliminary understanding of things. It is upon this foundation that Specific 1 may be differentiated from any accidental phenomenon or the essential nature by way of comparative analysis. In this way we may appreciate the nature, pattern and rudiments of things through their various faces such as notions, judgments and inferences. When this happens, we will have progressed from the preliminary understanding (Specific 1) to the abstract stage, which is understanding in a deeper sense but is far from arriving at comprehensive understanding. Proceeding from such abstractness in formal logic, we can then piece together the various aspects of the natures of things and the synthesis would give rise to a complete awareness of the inner attributes of any subject. This is the stage of Specific 2, representing the concrete truth of a specific object in rationality. In moving from Specific1 to abstractness, we use formal argument in formal logic. To advance from abstractness to Specific 2, we use negative dialectic argument in dialectic reasoning. The former method complements the latter, which is necessary for revealing the intrinsic nature and the consequential developmental law leading to a logical ending in Specific 2. This is a complete dialectical cycle. While the movement of objects is infinite, there is no limit to human understanding. Therefore, we expect the dialectic thought-cycle to be infinite. We move from cycle to cycle as we gain understanding in deeper, higher and wider scopes. Intensification of awareness and notional development are everlasting processes. We could take advantage of the dialectic reasoning method to design a category system for the discipline. Since such logical categories would be the results of some step-by-step deduction and transformation processes, the resultant system could be expected to be relatively comprehensive, and the linkage between as well as constraints on each other would be clear. To illustrate, we shall look at Karl Marx's *Das Kapital*. Beginning with "commodity", the reasoning process goes through "value—currency—capital—surplus value—wages", and so on, to arrive at the "distributive relations and production relations" and finally the "social class" category. In another instance, by defining "human" as a type of "higher animal capable of making tools and use them in labour, possessing language and thinking ability", reflecting the discriminating exogenous characteristics of human and animal, we are referring to the "abstractness" of "human", a notion in formal logic. If, on the other hand, "human" is defined as "the summation of all social relations" to reflect the intrinsic social nature of human beings, that is Specific 2, belonging to dialectic logic. Scholarly research requires the use of formal logic and, even more, the use of dialectic logic. You may agree with me, after reading this book, that we should redefine the relations of academic research and logic: The book truly demonstrates a higher level of logical reasoning in aspects such as notional comparison, deduction and transformation, definition and classification.

3. 方法和方法论研究的批判继承性与多元性
Research in method and methodology: Critical inheritance and plurality

本书方法论这一章重点讲了5个方面的问题：方法论研究的回顾、研究的原则、研究的出发点、对比的方向性以及求同求异的方法论。文国在这一章告诉我们如何研究和建设一个学科的方法论问题。我们的学术传统轻视理论，当然也轻视方法论。改革开放以来有了进步，但对于一个学科的方法论进行系统研究的还很少，涉及语言学的，国人写的我只读过桂诗春、宁春岩的《语言学方法论》（1997）、陈保亚的《20世纪中国语言学方法论》（1999）、徐通锵的《汉语研究方法论初探》（2004）。翻译的读过陈小荷等人译的A. Woods、P. Fletcher、A. Hughes合编的《语言研究中的统计方法》。桂著讲的理论方法、描写方法、实验方法主要来自西方，书的重点是介绍这些方法的理论基础、内容和用法。陈著是理论语言学专著，他说"一种方法论就是一种理论，语言学方法论就是语言学理论。"实际此书更像一部"20世纪中国语言学理论史"，但他研究的路线是揭示语料背后隐藏的方法，追求方法对语言现象的解释力。徐先生的大作是他20多年研究成果的结集，他用这17篇文章回答了中国语言学研究的道路问题：以汉语研究为"结合"的立足点，坚持走中与西、古与今、方言与标准语三种结合的路线。统计学的方法实际就是数学的方法，用数学的方法研究语言学是一种特殊的方法，主要是适应语言形式化的要求，以求用机器代替人的一部分复杂的脑力劳动，由于语言是一个元素多、联接方式多、层次多、变化多的开放的复杂巨系统，所以机器永远只能替代人的一部分复杂的脑力劳动。文国对方法论的研究和上述著作相比有以下特点：

The work highlights five aspects in methodology research: retrospection of research methodology, research principles, research starting point, contrastive direction, and methodology in similarity/difference seeking. Chapter 5 is about the "hows in the research and building of a discipline. If theory has a lesser place in the Chinese linguistic tradition, we do not imagine that methodology would be any better. While things have been better since China opened up, systematic research in methodology remains rare. Only a few local works on linguistic methodology come to mind: *Linguistic Methodology* by Gui Shichun (桂诗春) and Ning Chunyan (宁春岩) (1997); *Chinese Linguistic Methodology of the Twentieth Century* by Chen Baoya (陈保亚) (1999); *Research Methodology for Chinese: A Preliminary Study* by Xu Tongqiang (2004); and a translated work led by Chen Xiaohe (陈小荷) on *Statistical Methods for Linguistic Studies* by A. Wood, P. Fletcher and A. Hughes. Gui and Ning (1997) introduce the basis, substance and application of Western methods for theory, description and quantitative survey. Chen (1999) is essentially a work on theoretical linguistics. He proclaims that: "In itself, a methodology is a theory. Linguistic methodology is really linguistic theory. In this light, we could describe the work as a theoretical history on Chinese linguistics of the twentieth century in that Chen unveils the methods underlying linguistic data analysis and examines the respective power of these methods in explaining language phenomena. Xu (2004) exhibits his findings, after 20 years of research, in 17 essays addressing the approaches to Chinese linguistics. He insists on a research line of three "conjoins: Western theories with Chinese linguistic facts, the historical research tradition with that of modern ones, and the linguistic facts in both dialects and standard form, with the study of Chinese itself as the firmest foothold. The statistical method is really mathematical in its application in linguistics for its ability to formalize language patterns so that they may be programmed into computers. Given the many elements in language, many ways of connecting and layering the structure of expressions and the variations expressions are susceptible to, machines will never be able to take over from humans in resolving language complexities. In comparison with the above-mentioned works, this book offers more in terms of the following aspects.

(1) 把方法论作为一个系统来研究，用范畴辨析的方法构建本学科方法论体系

Examining methodology as a system and differentiating the categories to establish a schema for the discipline

他首先区分了方法和方法论，然后区分宜和不宜看作本学科方法论的方法，然后又区分兼具和不兼具本体论与方法论意义的方法，在此基础上论证了方法论原则、出发点、方向性等问题。西方语言学19世纪以历史为中心，20世纪以结构实体为中心，21世纪将转向以关系为中心，比如元素之间、单位之间、内部系统之间、内部大小系统（即整体与部分）之间、内外大小系统之间、复杂巨系统（如社会、人体、大脑、语言之间等）之间等各层次、各系统之间的关系研究将成为学术研究的主要价值取向。文国的方法论研究在对比语言学领域应该说是这种复杂关系研究的开端。

The concepts of method and methodology are first distinguished to establish what should and should not be considered as a means in methodology for the contrastive discipline. The book then identifies the processes of method and methodology in both disciplines. The ground is then ready for discussions on the principles, starting points and directions concerning methodological studies. Development in Western linguistics reveals that while history was at the core of linguistics in the nineteenth century, it was a structural entity in the twentieth century and will be related in the twenty-first century. Relations between the constituents, the units, the internal systems, the whole and parts of the internal systems, the whole and parts of the external and internal systems, the various levels and sub-systems of the complex macro system (such as between society, human body, brain and language) will dominate future research in linguistics. The path charted for contrastive linguistics in the present work signifies an initial attempt to explore these intricacies.

（2）只有批判的继承才能创新
Innovation through critical inheritance

我在《中国传统译论的现代转化问题》（王宏印著《中国传统译论经典诠释》序）中讨论过继承与创新的关系，主要简析了章太炎与贺麟主张的"守旧出新"和胡适与汤一介主张的"破旧立新"。当时只说到"对传统的东西进行现代的阐释，在找到古今通约性的基础上，通过现代转化使传统的东西进入现代文化传统。"这个问题还需要进一步讨论。研究传统的东西要找到古今通约的内容，使其转化为现代的东西。但首先要搞清楚何谓古今通约性？比如洪堡特方法论思想哪一部分和今天对比语言学方法论有通约性？判断有无通约性的标准是什么？然后要探讨如何才能找到古今通约性，比如意念与语言的关系问题是沿着历史发展的顺序（从叶斯柏森（1924）——林语堂（1933）——吕叔湘（1942））去找还是反方向去寻？这是研究如何继承传统中的优秀成分，仅是一个方面。另一方面，传统中除了有优秀成分之外还有过时的甚至错误的成分，创新常常是从批判这些成分开始的，但这些成分并不是明摆着的，而是和优秀成分杂陈一起的，所以如何找到这些成分就成了既重要又困难的问题。这就是爱因斯坦说的："提出一个问题往往比解决一个问题更重要。因为解决问题也许仅仅是一个数学上或实验上的技能而已，而提出新的问题、新的可能性，从新的角度去看待旧的问题，却需要有创造性的想象力，而且标志着科学的真正进步。"（刘元亮等《科学认识论与方法论》第129页）找到这些成分之后怎么办？那就要下批判功夫，汤一介说："如果不把它不适应现代生活要求的那些东西批判透了，反而无法发现它的真精神在哪里。"进一步问批判透与不透的标准是什么？首先要分类，可分出过时的、有片面性的、有局限性的、肤浅的、不系统的、证据不足的、观点与方法不当或错误的等。其次就是通过对这些缺点或错误的分析批判找到解决这些问题的目标、途径与方法。最后把这个解决问题的方案付诸实施，变成现实。创新都是针对前人成果的，对其优缺点都需要批判，只是批判的对象、方式方法不同，但目标一样，一是好中选优，留下培养；一是差坏改好，培植发展，二者皆为创新，其过程就是批判的继承，所以无此过程创新都是不可信的。若问在无人研究的新领域创新如何批判继承？一是要搞清楚是否真的从来无人涉足，这要花很大的工夫，也需要很高的水平，因为时空大、资料多；二是会有与其类似的或者相关的事物，你的研究应该从这里开始，批判继承也从这里开始，而后才能走向创新的道路。本书不论对历史还是对理论的研究都充满了批判的精神和方法，而且在中西、古今、方言与标准语三方打通上做了多项有益的尝试，结论都是通过对前人研究批判继承的创新结果，如语言的定义、对比语言学的定义和学科体系就是其中突出的代表。

In the essay "On the modern transformation of translation thoughts in Chinese tradition, Preface to *Critique of Translation Theories in Chinese Tradition* by Wang Hongyin (王宏印), I touched on the connections between carrying on with tradition and being innovative, quoting the renowned Chinese scholars Zhang Taiyan (章太炎) and He Lin (贺麟), who suggested keeping to and broadening out from traditions, on the one hand, and on the other hand, Hu Shi (胡适) and Tang Yijie (汤一介), who suggested breaking through traditions in order that something new may be cultured. Then, I stopped short at the comment that "[We shall] seek to explain traditions in modern terms and where we can grip the commensurability between the past and present, and go for modernizing traditions as it blended into modern cultural traditions." This deserves further discussion. But first, it is necessary to understand about commensurability between the past and present. For instance, which part of Wilhelm von Humboldt's thought is commensurable with the methodology presently applicable to contrastive linguistics? What criteria can be used to assess the presence of this "commensurability? How can we establish this commensurability? For example, regarding the relations between notion and linguistic expression, do we proceed forward along sequential development (starting with Jespersen (1924); Lin Yutang (1933); Lü Shuxiang (1942)), or do we backtrack from where we are? Looking at how to carry on the thoughts and finer points of the scholarly tradition is but one aspect. Finer points apart, there are obsolete and even fallacious compositions that could lead to discoveries. However, these are not labelled: more often than not, they coalesce into finer elements. Knotty as it is to uncouple and to tell them apart, the end result would prove to be all the more significant. As Albert Einstein wrote, "The mere formulation of a problem is far more essential than its solution, which may be merely a matter of mathematical or experimental skills. To raise new questions, new possibilities, or to regard old problems from a new angle requires creative imagination and marks real advances in science." (*qtn* Liu Yuanliang et. al *Scientific Epistemology and Methodology*: 129/Alice Calaprice ed.) So what do we do next? Assess them. I quote Tang Yijie, "Unless we critically scrutinize all that seems irrelevant to modern living right down to the core, the true spirit is nowhere to be found." Further, how do we know we have achieved this aim? First, we will have to classify the ideas to see whether they are outmoded, or that the reasoning is one-sided, limited, superficial, unsystematic or not fully substantiated or inappropriate, and even that wrong representations and methods are used. A critical analysis of these shortfalls should then enable us to determine aims, approaches and methods of reaching possible solutions, finishing by putting to the test and realizing the planned solution. All innovations challenge the achievements and shortcomings of our predecessors, and have a different object and method each time. However, the objectives are all the same. We should analyse and screen out the inadequacies and imperfections. Both actions are means of innovation through a diagnostic process of inheriting past legacy that lends weight to the innovation. Critical inheritance and therefore innovation must be analysed, and this requires great effort and outstanding scholarship to discern mountains of materials spanning through history and across boundaries. And there must be something closely related or similar enough where one may begin the critical inheritance process and embark on the journey of innovation. In its handling of history and theory, the present work is a critical piece, of spirit and of method. Reasonable attempts and efforts are also made to tear down barriers between Chinese and Western linguistic traditions, classical and modern linguistic resources, dialect and standard form. This diagnostic inheriting process gives rise to many novel conclusions, including the definition of language and of contrastive linguistics and the proposal of a framework for the discipline.

（3）**方法的多元性**

Pluralistic in method

本书首先把方法分成两大类，宜和不宜纳入本学科方法论的方法，然后又把前者分成本体论和方法论相兼的和只有方法论意义的方法，这就把本学科的专用、非专用和常用、非常用几类方法区分开来，理论上有利于体系的建设，应用上便于选择与操作。把"对比和比较"、"求异和求同"、"共时和历时"确定为既有本体论意义又有方法论意义的方法，这是文国在理论研究上的创见，它会有力地促进学科自身的理论建设，摆脱对其他语言理论的依赖。另外对背景原则、选择原则、同一原则以及6种"出发点"的论证都是开拓性的研究，在方法论系统中都给它们找到了比较合适的位置。总之，本书的方法论研究对本学科方法论系统的建设作出了奠基性的贡献。说到一个学科方法论建设的多元性问题，我一直感到应包含哲学的（包括逻辑学的）、系统科学的、相关学科的和本学科的至少四个层次的方法论。因为现代的科学研究对方法论不但需求种类多而且依赖程度深。当然为一个学科建成这样一个多层次的方法论系统那不是很短时间就能完成的。

In terms of method, the current work distinguishes between methods that should be employed for the discipline and those that should not. Methods belonging to the discipline are then further classified into those that are significant only in terms of methodology and those that are central to both ontology and methodology. In this way, methods are differentiated according to their applicability: specific to or very specific to the discipline; frequently or very frequently used in the discipline. Theory-wise, the grouping is useful for framework-building; application-wise, it is friendly for selection and usage. Here the aim is to establish the following research methods as serving ontology as well as methodology needs: "compare and contrast", "seeking similarities and differences", "synchronic and diachronic". This is the kind of understanding required for theory construction in the discipline, as it will help lift the dependence on other linguistic theories. In addition, the discussions initiated on the three principles of background, selection and homogeneity and the six types of "starting point" break new ground, with the subject matters fitted into the methodology framework as appropriate. In sum, the present work lays a foundation for establishing a methodological framework for contrastive linguistics. One word I would like to add is about pluralism in the setting up of methodological framework for any discipline. I believe that in terms of methodology, modern scientific research needs more kinds of methodology and is deeply dependent on methodology and that, therefore, at least four levels of methodology should be considered: of philosophy (including logic), of systems science, of related disciplines and of the discipline. No doubt it would take time to establish a multi-level methodology framework.

4. 为对比语言学理论史建设奠定了良好的基础
A firm grounding for theoretical history construction in contrastive linguistics

文国在这本书中为学科的理论史研究做了三项基础性的工作，一是确立了理论史分期的标准：用国际的眼光，站在普通语言学的高度，围绕学科理论建设和发展审视中西对比语言学及其研究所走过的路程。二是比较有说服力地完成了中西对比语言学分期问题。西方从洪堡特开始至今，划分为三个时期；中国从《马氏文通》开始至今划分为五个时期，其中每个时期开始的标志都选择得比较合适。这对深入研究理论史来说是一个很好的基础。三是从普通语言学的高度比较了中西语言研究的传统，这是一种有特别意义的对比，不但容易找到中西理论史各自的特点，而且有利于准确理解与把握理论范畴的发展过程与内涵。

Three fundamental methods vital to the progressive work on theoretical history in contrastive linguistics are established in this volume. First, it sets down the conditions that demarcating the phases of development needs to satisfy, such as having a global vision, being in tune with general linguistics, taking into account theory construction for the discipline and capturing the full picture of development and research in China and the West. Second, It proposes a convincing scheme of demarcation for both China and the West. Lines for three phases are drawn, for the West, beginning with Wilhelm von Humboldt, while for China there are five stages, since *Mashi Wentong* and the landmark events starting off each stage are appropriate for the purpose. Advanced research into theoretical history may take off from this solid ground. Last, but not least, a special attempt is made to contrast the scholarly traditions of China and the West on the higher ground of general linguistics. The significance of this attempt lies in setting out the characteristics of Western and Chinese theories so that development in theoretical categories and what it means may be better understood in perspective.

5. 关于学科理论史建设问题
On theoretical history construction

这方面我过去发表过一些意见，现在想再做些补充。

Further to my previous discourse on the subject, here are some progressive elaborations.

（1）关于学科理论史的研究和分期的标准问题

On research and demarcation criteria

我认为重点是要紧紧抓住理论观念（研究对象、性质与定位、范畴系统，以及相关学科的关系、功能与价值等）的转变和研究方法的更新。如我们确定了这样的标准，就容易找到写学科理论史的基本模式：

I think it most important to track notional changes in theory (research target, nature and positioning, category schemes, relations with other disciplines, functions and values, and so on) as well as updates in methodology. On this basis, it will be less laborious to lay down a basic discourse model on theoretical history in the following directions:

1）开创前阶段（或萌芽阶段、前科学阶段）

Evolving stage (the embryonic stage before the founding of the discipline)

这个阶段一般都比较长，从业者大都没有理论意识，少数有思想的从业者会写出一些体会与感想，有时也有闪光点，大都很零散而不系统。要超越这个阶段最主要的工作是要发动大家研究、讨论理论和实践的关系，并认真寻找理论研究和应用研究的界限。

In this stage, researchers are vague in theoretical notions and while the more outstanding among them would share some illuminating thoughts here and there, nothing systematic could be expected. Advancing from this stage requires some facilitation to gather resources and momentum to follow up on the relations between theory and practice and to explore the boundaries governing theoretical studies and applied studies.

2）开创阶段（或称初期阶段）

Founding stage (or initiating stage)

这个阶段的主要任务是确定学科建设的方针和评价标准，在此基础上制订学科发展规划，规划的重点是研究队伍建设、学科规范建设、管理制度建设等。

The main task for this stage is to determine and set down direction and strategy for development as well as the assessment criteria and to build upon this basis a growth plan focusing on building up of research capacity, standards for the discipline as well as a management system.

3）建设与发展阶段

Moulding and development stage

这个阶段一般也比较长，其主要工作是一面修订前一个阶段的发展规划，一面实施规划，精心建设，推动发展。这个阶段的结束应是这个学科的真正完全独立，基本达到了学科建设的标准。

This will be a longer stage looking into carefully refining as well as executing the plans of the previous stage. The conclusion of this stage marks the full autonomy gained by the discipline in meeting all requirements set for discipline-building.

4）逐步成熟的阶段

Maturing stage

这个阶段一般会很长，长到无法预见它的衰败与消亡。但可以预见它会按照自身的发展规律和社会的需求产生不同的流派和成熟程度不同的发展阶段。

This is an exceptionally long stage whose future course is anybody's guess. While we may not be able to tell if it is under way, we could project some of its course of development such as various schools of thought within the discipline and the differing stages of maturity according to its developmental pattern and societal demands.

(2) 学科理论史的内容问题

Content issue

为了找到发展规律促进学科发展，应该首先研究学科产生的依据，包括学理的积累、接续或借鉴以及社会的需求问题，把学科产生的背景和过程搞清楚。其次要研究分期的标准和分期问题，其中不但要写名家名著、学术团体、学派、重要会议等大事要事，而且要写每个发展阶段的转折与衔接。再次要写学科的研究对象、性质、理论系统、研究方法和相关学科的关系等理论问题的演变与发展。写演变与发展既要有纵向的比较，抓住连续性写好继承问题，也要有横向的比较，抓住相关性写好学科内外相互影响问题。当然还有中外哲学对该学科的影响问题也不可忽视。

The purpose of writing theoretical history is to seek a developmental trend that can be utilized in turn to promote the discipline. For this purpose, material on the emergence, including background and processes of the discipline, the validation, the accumulation, succession and borrowing of theoretical thoughts and the needs of the society, is imperative. Next, any such writing should deliberate on issues concerning demarcation and the relevant criteria. In this relation, important works and authors, associations and societies, schools of thought and key conferences are among the landmarks to be included. It is also essential that crucial turning points and successive stages are detailed. Another focal aspect is the evolution and development of a series of theoretical issues such as research object, nature, theoretical framework, methodology and relations with close disciplines. Description must necessarily cover horizontal and vertical comparisons so as to reveal continuity and consecutivity as well as influences from internal and external sources. The philosophical tenets of China and the West likely to have impact on the discipline are also worthy of consideration.

（3）学科理论史编写的困难问题

Challenges

1）学科理论范畴继承性的准确把握和阶段转折点的准确定位

Precise reading of the continuum of theoretical categories as well as the precise positioning of turning points throughout the development

在学科发展史中最重要的是研究学科理论范畴发展变化问题。比如"比较"（comparative）和"对比"（contrastive）这两个范畴是如何产生的，从纵横两个系统来看哪些学术思想对它们产生了影响，从产生到现在它们的内涵与外延发生了哪些变化，什么时间发生的变化，为什么这个时间发生变化等。发展中的阶段转折必有重要范畴产生，因此要抓住这些重要范畴研究它们的来龙去脉。范畴史是学科理论史的核心，所以要写好学科理论史必须研究好范畴史。

Studying categorical changes during the progression of the discipline is one area no work on disciplinary history should miss. Take the emergence of the comparative category and contrastive category for example. We may analyse both horizontally and vertically to examine the factors contributing to its consolidation and expansion, to observe what, when and why at that time changes have occurred to the intension and extension. With all critical turnings, categories of significance emerge. Everything about these categories, from the point of initiation, are of interest to us. Central to the history of any discipline is the historical development of such categories. It follows that if we do well in categorical history, half the job is done.

2）学科理论史上代表人物的学术思想来源问题

Tracing the scholastic thoughts of key scholars

写学科理论史必然要写代表人物，写代表人物最主要的要写其学术思想的来源和发展变化。其中来源问题最困难，因为他们受的影响可能是多方面的，比如来自国内还是国外，来自前辈（包括古代的）学者还是同辈学者，来自本学科还是来自相关学科等等。

In such discourses, we cannot avoid mentioning key figures, and nothing is more important than tracing the origins and transformation of their scholastic thought. Where the origin is complex, having influences from internal and external sources, predecessors (including archaic figures) and peers and even receiving ideas from other disciplines, it presents the greatest challenge.

3）代表人物的著作和当时社会思潮的关系

Relations between the works of key scholars and ideological trend of the time

我们研究学科理论史过去一般都集中在名家文本上，但现在看来至少有以下问题：名家文本中的思想在社会思潮中是主流还是支流，与社会思潮是一致还是不一致。名家文本在当时起了什么作用，官方如何评价，大众如何评价。今天官方如何评价，大众如何评价，其局限性有哪些等等。

To date, research in historical development of most disciplines focuses on the texts by key scholars. We may now question this approach on the following considerations: Do the thoughts presented in those texts represent the mainstream ideological trend or otherwise? Are they consistent with mainstream ideology? What impact do those texts have on the society? What are the official assessments? How about in the eyes of the public? What are the limitations?

4）学科的先驱与开创者的准确定位问题

Precise positioning of pioneers and founding members

一个范畴、一个思想、一个命题、一个方法等谁是第一个提出者，这是写学科理论史的人无法回避的。要解决这种问题需要研究者认真下考据工夫。当证据不准确的时候，要留有余地，不应轻易在时空跨度很大的范围内用"第一"或"最早"的说法。不然很容易造成被动和误导。

A category, a thought, a proposition, and a method must first belong to someone. This is a question authors handling historical development in any discipline must research meticulously for textual proof and evidence. Giving credit to "the first" or "the earliest" does not come easily, particularly because of the vast spatial and temporal span, and where such evidence is suspected to be incomplete we have to exercise care and control not to mislead or be misled.

6. 关于范畴研究的几个问题

On the study of logical categories

范畴研究最主要的有三项工作，一是范畴的源头与发展变化的考据；二是范畴的界定；三是范畴间的关系与系统研究。前两者的目标是建设范畴史，为后者提供研究基础，后者的目标是建设理论体系，为前者提供观照与指导。每个学科都不应该轻视这三项研究，因为这两个目标是学科独立的标志，对比语言学和翻译学当然也不能例外。读了文国的书稿我联想最多的是范畴之间的关系问题，现在提出来和大家一起讨论。

Category study involves three main tasks: first, to research the textual evidence of the origin and evolution of categories; next, to define the categories; third, to examine inter-categorical relations and categorical systems. The first two tasks align with the objectives of categorical history and provide the basis for research into the third. The third task undertakes the construction of theoretical system, which will in turn guide the continued study of the first two tasks. No independent discipline, marked by the existence of categorical history and theoretical system, should take these three tasks lightly, and of course not contrastive linguistics and translatology. In reading the present volume, most of the thoughts invoked relate to inter-categorical relations, about which I invite discussion as follows.

（1）哲学中本体论、认识论、价值论、方法论四者的关系如何？这些范畴应不应该和能不能移植到其他学科中去？为什么？如果应该与能够，那如何去做？"同"和"异"属于主客体统一的逻辑范畴，哲学上一般叫做"共性"和"个性"，在客体中二者孰轻孰重？还是一轻一重？在主体中如何？在研究策略上应不应和能不能分主次？还是二者并重？事物的本质是同还是异？为什么？本质和异同各是什么关系？有个说法"本质乃是具体揭示客体的整体联系的范畴"，这个命题对吗？为什么？黑格尔说："方法并不是外在的形式，而是内容的灵魂和概念。"（《小逻辑》第427页）这个论断的深刻含义是什么？它和本体论、认识论有什么联系？

(1) In philosophy, in what ways are ontology, epistemology, axiology and methodology related? Should and may these categories be transplanted to other disciplines? Why should they and why may they? If so, how? "Similarity and "difference belong to logical categories touching on subject-object unity, commonly known in philosophy as "generality and "individuality. How important is each of their roles in the object? Are they weighted with bias? How about in the subject? Going by strategy, should we and can we separate primary and secondary research targets accordingly? Or should we treat both equally? Is "similarity" the nature of

things or is it "difference"? Why is it so? What have "similarity and "difference" to do with the nature of things? There is a saying that "nature is that category revealing specifically how things are linked as a whole in the object". Can we accept this proposition and, if so, why?

（2）人类的知识有三大系统，也就是自然科学、社会科学与人文科学。这三类科学在本质上的异同是什么？三者的关系与相互影响如何？其价值标准的不同是如何形成的？三者的方法论之间有什么样的关系？目前自然科学方法论如何向人文、社会科学领域渗透与移植？该提倡还是该限制？人类的语言具有自然、社会、人文三种属性，这三种属性中哪种为本质属性？为什么？如何理解语音学和句法学、音位学和语篇学、韵律学和修辞学分别体现了上述三种属性？语音、词汇、语法也能分别体现这三种属性吗？

(2) The body of human knowledge is classified into three broad systems: natural sciences, social sciences and humanities. What are the essential similarities and differences among them? In what ways are the three systems related and mutually influential? How is it that they each adopt a different system of value judgment? How are they related in terms of methodology? Currently, methodologies in natural sciences are infiltrating, and adapting to, humanities and social sciences. How is this possible? Should we allow it to continue or should we contain the movement? It seems that human languages are at the same time attributed with the qualities of natural sciences, social sciences and humanities. Which of these functions is the primary attribute, and why? When we pair phonetics and syntax, phonemics and text linguistics, prosody and rhetoric and say they represent respectively the attributes of the above three knowledge systems, what do we really understand from this representation? Can the same be said of phonology, lexicology and grammar?

（3）人文、社会科学中除了形式逻辑、语言学和考古学等学科的某些问题的研究之外，一般说都属于一定的意识形态范畴，因此在这两大领域中时时处处都存在意识形态性和科学性的矛盾。如何处理好二者的关系？如何解决意识形态"中心化"和其方法的泛化问题？如何发挥科学性对上述两化的的抵制与制约作用？语言学与对比语言学研究领域过去与现在在处理科学性和意识形态性的关系问题上存在什么问题？如何解决？

(3) The studies of humanities and social sciences are generally recognized as belonging to the category of ideology, except for aspects formal logic, linguistics

and archaeology. As such the contradictions of ideology and science are everywhere in these two systems. How can we best address the paradox? How can we best address the issue of "centralizing" ideology and the overgeneralization of other methodologies? How do we make use of scientific validity to counter and contain the above conflict? With regard to linguistics and contrastive linguistics, what are the issues in the ways the paradox has been and is being handled? Any solution?

（4）人文、社会科学具有较强的传统性与古典色彩，在研究领域有崇尚历史、轻视现实问题的倾向。如何处理好历史和现实的关系问题？语言学和对比语言学研究领域有这种倾向吗？具体表现在哪些方面？如何解决这种问题？

(4) Traditional and classical approaches in humanities and social sciences are strong and the inclination is for the fields of study to place weight on historical studies more than on practical problems. How do we balance practicality with history? Are there such preferences in linguistics and contrastive linguistics? Specifically, where is this bias and how should we deal with it?

（5）语言是个开放的复杂巨系统，其中"开放"、"复杂"、"巨大"三者是什么关系？思维和语言如何发生联系？二者有无相对独立性？如何表现？思维如何帮助语言发展？语言如何帮助思维发展？语言和文字是什么关系？文字有无独立性？仅是语言的辅助工具吗？语音和语义的关系除了任意性还有象形性，这两性是什么关系？在研究中如何处理好母语和外语、古语和现代语、口语和书面语、方言和标准语等两者之间的关系？哲学语言学和理论语言学的关系如何？语言和语言学的定义属于前者还是属于后者？还是二者的结合之物？语言学研究中的"应用"、"技术"、"实践"三者是什么关系？三者和理论研究各有什么关系？语境有多少层次？它是如何影响人在交际中选择语言的？语言研究的方法有描写法、解释法、数学法（形式化方法）等，这三种方法有什么样的关系？

(5) Language is a huge, complex, open system. What sense does it make to associate "huge", "complex" and "open"? How is thought related to language? Are thought and language relatively independent from each other, and in what ways? What is the role of thought in language development? What is the role of language in thought development? Are language and script related? Can script be independent? Must it only play the supplementary role to language? Besides arbitrariness, sound and meaning are also related in terms of iconicity. Is there anything behind

arbitrariness and iconicity? In our research, there are many pairs of relation awaiting our attention: mother tongue and foreign language, archaic and modern language, spoken and written language, dialect and standard form. What about the relations between philosophical linguistics and theoretical linguistics? Is the definition of language part of philosophical linguistics or theoretical linguistics or both? What do we understand by the "applied", "technical" and "practical" aspects of language research? How are they related to theoretical study? How many levels can we find in a context? How does each of these levels act on the choice of language in human communication? In language research, there are the methods of descriptive, interpretive, mathematical (formal methods) among others. How are these methods related? When Georg Wilhelm Friedrich Hegel says: "It thus appears that the method is not an extraneous form, but the soul and notion of the content. (*The Logic of Hegel*) What underlines this profound statement? How can we relate this statement in terms of ontology and epistemology?

　　读了这本书稿想说的话很多，总之希望有更多的学人关注这本新著，虽然书中还有一些问题没有说充分、说系统，但从深度与广度上来看明显超过了国内外同类著作，在史和论两方面对许多问题都展开了讨论，这些问题会给语言学和对比语言学领域的研究带来有力的推动和许多启迪。

Thoughts are rampant in my mind reading this volume and the sharing above just do not seem enough. All I wish now is for the book to catch the attention of more scholars. There are issues inviting further discussion for greater adequacy and systematic presentation. All in all, the present work obviously rises above books of the same category within and outside China in terms of depth and breadth. The deliberations on various issues concerning history and theory are thought-provoking and will serve to advance research in linguistics and contrastive linguistics.

　　潘文国是个有崇高学术追求的学者，我很赞赏他为本书选的两句名言：（1）"究天人之际，通古今之变，成一家之言。"（司马迁）（2）"历史的方法将来仍须伴之以哲学的方法，对纯粹思维的任何忽视，定会损害人们的科学研究。"（威廉·冯·洪堡特）最后我愿用文国在《语言哲学与哲学语言学》一文中的话结束我的序文。他说："人类认识世界、社会和自身是无止境的，因而哲学的探索也永远不会有止境。对一个研究者来说，重要的不是他已经发现了什么，而是他还能发现什么，这是科学研究永远的动力。"

The high pursuit of Wenguo can be read from two of his favourite quotes, which I also enjoyed: "Inquiring into the relationship between Heaven and man and probing into the changes from ancient to present to build up a doctrine of my own." (Han historian Sima Qian) and "(The Philosophical) course will still have to be followed in future alongside the historical approach, for any neglect of pure thought will always perceptibly take its toll throughout man's scientific endeavours." (Wilhelm Von Humboldt) As a closing note, it is perhaps appropriate to quote from Pan Wenguos *Language Philosophy and Philosophical Linguistics*: "There is no limit to man's inquiry of the world, the society and of oneself as there is never ever an ending to the exploration in philosophy. To the scholar, it is not what he discovered that speaks loud; rather it is that which he is able to further discover that will ultimately drive scientific research to eternity."

第一章
西方对比语言学研究

Chapter 1
Contrastive Linguistic Studies in the West

学科史研究意义重大。《大学》云:"物有本末,事有终始,知所先后,则近道矣。"清代学者叶燮(1627—1703)谈研究学问时也指出,要"先辨其源流本末,而徐以察其异轨殊途,固不可执一而论"(《已畦集卷十一·与友人论文书》)。从史的角度研究对比学问,要探讨的不仅是特定语言现象的历时发展,也包括学科的演变脉络、理论的兴替本末以及方法与方法论的精粗杂细。对于特定语言现象的历时发展,西方的历时语言研究甚为重视、成果颇丰。对于学科的演变脉络、理论以及方法的兴替本末,则有意义的成果凤毛麟爪,而且往往因材料芜杂,同一课题材料散见于各民族语言,整合和整理殊为艰辛,且问题是否已经谈得周全或者是否发前人所未见,也难以论断。然而,学科的演变脉络是任何学科建设和更新理论的基础,是学科往前发展所必需的积淀,也是疏通学科间关系的锁钥,这个工作尽管艰辛,还是得有承担者去一步一步踏踏实实地做。以对比语言学来说,其源头就像是个谜,众说纷纭,莫衷一是,且往往语焉不详(谭慧敏,2012:57—59)。尽管如此,我们还是愿意作出探索。

The significance of researching into the historical development of any discipline cannot be overemphasized. "Things have roots and ends; Events have starting and concluding points; Learn that inherent ordering and we are near the Dao or the Way," so advised in Confucian classic *The Great Learning*. Qing scholar Ye Xie (1627—1703) was succinct when he noted that in academic study, it is important to "discern first and foremost, the headspring from the branches, the commencement from the ending before gradually tracing the various paths of development. It's undesirable to look at only a part of the whole cause of event." (Letter to a Friend on Essay Writing, in *Collected Works of Ye Xie*, Vol 11.) For our purpose, the historical viewpoint goes beyond the diachronic development of specific linguistic phenomena, the development pathways of the discipline, the rise and fall of theories, as well as the progression in methods and methodology. The diachronic developments of specific linguistic phenomenon widely prevail in Western scholarship, and contributions were in abundance. In comparison, far fewer material works shed light on the development of discipline, theories, methods and methodology. The imbalance was compounded by the scale of linguistic data and barriers in accessing research published in various ethnic languages. Such circumstances warrant a prudent man in believing that claims of comprehensive study or discovery have to be taken with a pinch of salt. Huge as the odds may seem sorting out the whole course of development, with concerted effort and a down-to-earth approach, perseverance will take us through in re-establishing the theoretical grounds much needed for both identifying the niche the discipline stands for and differentiates itself with and advancement going forward. So, let's deal with the first task for contrastive linguistics in tracking down the headspring which remains an unresolved puzzle with multiple suggestions that are largely vague (Tham, 2012: 57—59).

1.1 越过拉多和沃尔夫
1.1 Beyond Lado and Whorf

事对比研究的人都知道，"对比语言学"这一名称最早是美国人类学语言学家沃尔夫（Benjamin Lee Whorf，1897—1941）提出来的，但令人费解的是，西方许多谈论对比研究的论著却有意无意地略去了沃尔夫的名字。例如对比语言学必读名著——詹姆斯（Carl James）的《对比分析》（*Contrastive Analysis* 1980），就根本没有提及沃尔夫的名字；乌拉•孔纳（Ulla Connor）的《对比修辞学》（*Contrastive Rhetoric*，1996）里专辟了一章——"对比修辞学的历史演进"，强调沃尔夫的语言相对论是"对比修辞学的基石"（the cornerstone of contrastive rhetoric）（Connor，1996：28），却对沃尔夫给对比语言学下的定义视若无睹。沙亚伐拉回顾对比语言学发展的文章中也只是一语带过地说，对比语言学有两个起点：19世纪末至20世纪初；20世纪30年代，早期的理论宗旨在薇茵莱希（Uriel Weinreich, 1953）和拉多（Robert Lado, 1957）的对比分析兴起后就完全被忽视了，然后文章就集中讨论1940年代萌发的现代对比研究。（Sajavaara, 1977：9—10）。中国一些介绍国外对比研究的文章也往往沿袭了这一说法。言之凿凿的是戚雨村（1992），他认为对比源头有三：欧洲、俄国苏联以及美国，上溯到最早的是波兰学者博杜恩•德•库尔德内（Jan Nieclslaw Baudouin de Courtenay, 1845—1929）的对比分类，并突出布拉格学派领袖马泰休斯（Vilém Mathesius, 1882—1945）的贡献。杨自俭（1999；2004）则提到马泰休斯和沃尔夫，并把他们的论述视为现代对比语言学的两个起点：欧洲和美国。许余龙（2001：18）也倾向欧、美两个源头的说法，认为欧洲传统也包括俄国学者的贡献。不过，杨、许所指的美国源头并不相同。20世纪以前的发展情况，往往一笔带过，谈不上述，更谈不上论。这反映了学界对"对比语言学"在20世纪以前的发展重视不够，只关注20世纪中期以来的状况，这同时也反映了"对比研究/分析"作为应用语言学一种方法广受承认的程度。

The term "contrastive linguistics" was first suggested by American anthropologist Benjamin Lee Whorf. Since this is a fact well known to all in the field, it remains puzzling that most publications on contrastive studies in the West should have passed over Whorf in silence. Carl James, for example, entirely missed mentioning Whorf in his critically acclaimed Contrastive Analysis (1980), a must-read for students of contrastive linguistics. In a closer analysis, Ulla Connor's *Contrastive Rhetoric* (1996) described Whorf's linguistic relativity as "the cornerstone of contrastive rhetoric" (1996: 28) when dwelling on the historical development of contrastive rhetoric, but chose to let go of Whorf's definition of contrastive linguistics. In presenting the past and present of contrastive linguistics, Kari Sajavaara (1977: 9—10) skimmed through with a passing remark that "CA has a twin starting point, although this has not always been recognized". This concerns both the contrastive type of linguistic analysis at the turn of the century and in the thirties. The theoretical objectives were almost entirely forgotten in the wake of Weinreic's (1953) and Lado's (1957) work." The paper then turned to the development since 1940. The twin starting-point was often cited by Chinese scholars introducing Western studies in the discipline. Qi Yucun (1992) was most positive when he suggested that triple roots could be traced in Europe, Russia or former Soviet Union and the US, with Polish scholar Jan Niecislaw Baudouin de Courtenay (1845—1929) being the forerunner while highlighting the contributions by Vilém Mathesius (1882—1945), leader of the Prague School. Yang Zijian (1999; 2004) offered no ambiguity as he took Mathesius and Whorf to be the twin groundbreakers, the former working from Europe while the latter the US, laying foundations for modern contrastive linguistics with their works. Xu Yulong (2001: 18) bought into the twin starting-points in Europe and the US too, but begged to differ from Yang in their descriptions of the development in the US. What came before the twentieth century in contrastive linguistics was a mention of date and at most a name as the only detail. There was little description, much less discussion on the subject, which is a genuine reflection of the general disregard. On the other hand, the attention given to the development since the mid-twentieth century underlined contrastive analysis as a popular method in applied linguistics.

略去了沃尔夫等人，对比研究就只能从拉多谈起，詹姆斯就是这么做的，他说：

Whorfs aside, it seems that the beginning of contrastive studies can be traced to Robert Lado, as Carl James did:

> 我无意重建对比分析的历史：迪·皮德娄（Di Pietro, 1971: 9）找到了格朗根特（C. H. Grandgent）1892年出版的一本书，其中对比了英语和德语的语音系统。对我来说，我认为现代的对比分析始于拉多的《跨文化语言学》。（詹姆斯, 1980: 8）
>
> I shall not attempt to reconstruct the history of CA: Di Pietro (1971: 9) finds an early example of CA in C. H. Grandgent's book on the German and English sound systems, published in 1892. For me, modern CA starts with Lado's *Linguistics Across Cultures* (1957). (James, 1980: 8)

詹姆斯的兴趣显然只在"现代对比分析"。从拉多讲起，把现代对比语言学等同于应用对比分析，给西方的对比语言学研究带来了不利的结果：第一是造成了对西方对比语言学史的片面理解：似乎对比语言学于上世纪五十年代产生，六十年代昙花一现，七十年代就开始走下坡路，直到八十年代才开始重振；其次，抹杀了拉多之前的学者在这一领域的重要、甚至是后人难以替代和企及的杰出贡献，对比分析就始终同第二语言教学或应用语言学联系在一起，缺乏更为宽广的视野和对更深层理论的追求，而对比分析作为方法附属于应用语言学，对比语言学作为独立学科的学术地位就难以确立。这带出第四个不利，即无法厘清对比语言学与其他学科，如语言类型学、应用语言学之间的关系；而跳过了沃尔夫乃至更前面的洪堡特（Wilhelm Von Humboldt, 1767—1835），就使得当代西方对比语言学缺少了高瞻远瞩的理论建构。

Apparently, it interests Carl James only to focus on "modern CA". The "modern bias" to start with Lado confuses modern contrastive linguistics with practical CA and brings necessarily undesirable results. First, it has led to a partial reading of the development of contrastive linguistics by the West, with the view that contrastive linguistics arose only in the 1950s, flourishing during the 1960s just to be brought down in the 1970s for a revival in the 1980s: a complete distortion. And in under-emphasizing the almost unsurpassable significant scholarships before Lado, contrastive analysis has been found to be lacking in research vision, something vital to the quest for more profound theoretical search, and therefore stuck with second-language learning or applied linguistics and unable to soar high in theoretical linguistics, to say nothing of posing itself as an independent academic discipline. Acknowledging neither Benjamin Lee Whorf and, above and before him, Wilhelm Von Humboldt, contrastive linguistics in the contemporary West appears pale in the absence of a high theoretical framework that could well be inspired by Whorf and Humboldt.

1.2 对比语言学起源与西方对比语言学史
1.2 Origin of contrastive linguistics and reconstruction of its history in the West

1.2.1 从沃尔夫的定义看对比语言学的起源
1.2.1 Origin of contrastive linguistics by Whorf's definition

那么，沃尔夫究竟是怎么给对比语言学下定义的呢？对比语言学是从比较语言学中生发出来的。在《语言与逻辑》一文中，沃尔夫区别了对比语言学和比较语言学，说：

So, what is it that is important in contrastive linguistics for Benjamin Lee Whorf? Essentially, it is out of comparative linguistics that light was shed on contrastive linguistics, and in order to establish contrastive linguistics as a discipline in its own right, there must be a sharp distinction between the two concepts. Whorf explains that,

> 植物学家和动物学家为了研究世上的物种，开始是觉得有必要描述全球每个角落现存的物种，考虑到历史的因素，又加上了化石；接着他们觉得有必要对这些物种进行比较和对比，以分门别类，理清进化过程，了解其形态和类型。语言科学也正在做同样的工作，而我们现在从事的对距离遥远的事件的研究是研究语言与思维的一种新方法。把地球上的语言分成来自单一祖先的一个个语系，描写其在历史进程中的一步步足迹，其结果称之为"比较语言学"，在这方面已经取得了很大成果。而更重要的是将要产生的新的思想方法，我们可以称之为"对比语言学"，它旨在研究不同语言在语法、逻辑和对经验的一般分析上的重大区别。（沃尔夫，1941a: 240）

> Botanists and zoologists, in order to understand the world of living species, found it necessary to describe the species in every part of the globe and to add a time perspective by including the fossils. Then they found it necessary to compare and contrast the species, to work out families and classes, evolutionary descent, morphology, and taxonomy. In linguistic science a similar attempt is under way. The far-off event toward which this attempt moves is a new technology of language and thought. Much progress has been made in classifying the languages of earth into genetic families, each having descent from a single precursor, and in tracing such developments through time. The result is called "comparative linguistics". Of even greater importance for the future technology of thought is what might be called "contrastive linguistics". This plots the outstanding differences among tongues—in grammar, logic, and general analysis of experience. (Whorf, 1941a: 240)

事实上，区别"比较"与"对比"是对比语言学得以建立的最重要的原则之一，詹姆斯本人也是这样认为的，他说：

Plotting the outstanding differences among tongues is the premise. Carl Jamesp concurred with:

> 比较语言学家就如其名称所暗示的，认为尽管各种语言均有其个性，但所有语言之间有足够的共同点使人们可以对它们进行比较并分成各种类型……对比分析不关心分类，而且如同其名称所暗示的，更关心语言间的异而不是同。（詹姆斯，1980: 2—3）

> The comparativist, as the name implies, proceeds from the assumption that, while every language may have its individuality, all languages have enough in common for them to be compared and classified into types… (CA) is not concerned with classification, and, as the term contrastive implies, more interested in differences between languages than in their likenesses. (James, 1980: 2—3)

因此他之忽视沃尔夫实在是不应该的。也许是沃尔夫给对比语言学规定的任务，即"采取一个新的语言和思维相结合的方法去研究距离较远的语言事实，研究不同语言在语法、逻辑和对经验的一般分析上的重大区别"并没有真正进入他的视野？

It is therefore rather disturbing that James should disassociate from Whorf. Perhaps the departing point lies with scope. While Whorf considered that the objective of contrastive linguistics is to adopt a new technology of language and thought in plotting the outstanding differences among tongues that are remotely connected—in grammar, logic and general analysis of experience—this was not something James cared for.

如果我们接受沃尔夫给对比语言学下的定义，再往上追溯，就可以发现他还不是提出这一原则的第一个人，早在詹姆斯提及的格朗根特（1892）之前半个多世纪，德国语言哲学家洪堡特（Wilhelm von Humboldt, 1767—1835）就已经意识到要区分"比较"和"对比"：

Granted, Whorf's view is far from being the first to have harboured the idea of contrast. Nor was C. H. Grandgent's above-mentioned work, published in 1892. It is Wilhelm von Humboldt (1767—1835), the German philosopher and linguist, who initiated the line to be drawn between *compare* and *contrast* some half a century before Grandgent did.

只有当人们看到语言这一观念有这么多种体现，并能对不同民族的语言特点从个别和一般两方面进行比较和对比（compare and contrast）之后，才能更清楚地理解一个民族的语言及其语言特点。（洪堡特，1820：8）

Both the language and the linguistic character of a nation appear in a clearer light when one sees the idea of language realized in so many individual ways and when one can compare and contrast the linguistic character of one nation with that of others, both in general and individually. (Humboldt, 1820: 8)

并倡议进行"比较语言研究"，而他的"比较语言研究"与"只具历史性质的"和"比较语言研究"之间是不同的：

With this in mind, Humboldt encouraged research into what he called "comparative study of languages" that was in no way similar to what we now term historical comparative linguistics.

不计其数的民族作为人，以各种不同的途径担负着创造语言的任务，而比较语言研究的目的就在于详尽地探索这些不同的途径；倘若忽略了语言与民族精神力量的形成之间的联系，比较语言研究便会丧失所有重大的意义……要是我们不以民族精神力量为出发点，就根本无法彻底解答那些跟最富有内在生命力的语言构造有关的问题，以及最重大的语言差异缘何而生的问题。根据这一出发点，虽然不能为本质上只具历史性质的比较语言研究找到材料，但唯有如此，才能弄清事实的初始联系，达到对语言这一内在联系的有机体的认识，从而再促进对个别部分的理解。（Humboldt, 1836: 21/16—17）[1]

The comparative studies of languages, the exact establishment of the manifold ways in which innumerable peoples resolve the same task of language formation that is laid upon them as men, loses all higher interest if it does not cleave to the point at which language is connected with shaping

---

[1] 本书所引言论大部分由笔者翻译成中文。洪堡特与沃尔夫的言论，如有中译本，则在原著页码之后以斜杠区分注明中译版的页码。洪堡特言论之中译大多出自姚小平《论人类语言结构的差异及其对人类精神发展的影响》（1997）；而有关沃尔夫的言论之中译皆出自高一虹等译《论语言、思维和现实》（2001）。

of the nation's mental power…There can be no basic answer to those very questions which refer to the formation of languages in their inmost life, and from which at the same time their most important differences arise, if we do not ascend to this point of view. We cannot, indeed, seek there the material for a comparative linguistics, which by nature must be dealt with in merely historical fashion; but we can only obtain there that insight into the original connection of the facts, and that apprehension of language as an internally connected organism, which then promotes in its turn the correct evaluation of the individual. (Humboldt, 1836: 21)

但由于他对二者都使用了"比较语言研究"这个术语——尽管他在1820年就使用了"对比"这个概念——后人几乎都没有注意到其间的根本差别，也就是说，洪堡特的"比较研究"不是为历史比较语言学服务的，也不是它的组成部分。
Although the concept of contrast was formulated in 1820, Humboldt failed to set apart the differing notions encompassed by his definition of "comparative linguistics". This explains why few noticed the divergence Humboldt was pointing at. Indeed, the "comparative studies" as referred to by Humboldt was not meant to serve the purpose of historical comparative linguistics, much less to serve as its component.

而继洪堡特之后，法裔波兰籍的历史比较语言学家、结构语言学先驱库尔德内在1902年讨论斯拉夫语言比较文法的文章中明确而具体地指出，比较的方法包括三种[1]：第一，比较没有任何历史和亲属关系的语言。第二，比较在历史上有亲属关系的语言。第三，比较在地理位置、社会和文学方面临近的语

---

1 库尔德内（1901）列举两种比较方法，1902发表的文章将两种细分为三种。1901年的文章以波兰语写成，题为"Linguistics in the 19th Century"发表于 *Prawda*（1：1—23）。1902年的文章题为"The Comparative Grammar of Slavic Languages"，在圣彼德堡出版，其他出版资料不详，英译摘要见于Edward Stankiewicz编译（1972）*A Bauduoin de Courtenay Anthology: The Beginnings of Structural Linguistics*，布鲁明顿：印第安纳大学出版社，319—322。
In his 1901 paper written in Polish "Linguistics in the 19th Century" (*Prawda*, 1:1—23), Bauduoin raised two types of comparative surveys and subsequently expanded to three when he delivered "The Comparative Grammar of Slavic Languages" in 1902. The latter paper was known to be published in St. Petersburg without further details. A translated version can be found in *A Bauduoin de Courtenay Anthology: The Beginnings of Structural Linguistics*. (1972) Ed. & Tr. by Edward Stankiewicz, Bloomington: Indiana University Press, pp.319—322.

言。为从历史角度比较两种或者更多的语言打下了坚实的基础。（见Fisiak，1984：139；杨衍春，2009：25；Grucza，2001：71）

Following Humboldt, Polish comparative linguist of French descent and one of the chief precursors of structuralist linguistics, Jan Baudouin de Courtenay (1902) identified three types of comparative surveys:

"Comparative surveys, and comparison in general, of linguistic phenomena can be of three types:

I) Linguistic processes can be examined without regard to linguistic kinship, in order to establish the degree of similarity or differences between the structures of two languages.

II) Two or more linguistic areas may be compared without regard to their historical origin, if they show similar linguistic phenomena as a result of their territorial proximity.

III) Finally, there is the comparative study of linguistic areas which are assumed to stem from a common historical source and which can, therefore, be viewed as variants of one originally common state that has subsequently broken up into the very same variants that are being compared. This kind of comparison constitutes so-called comparative grammar in the strict sense of the word." (Edward Stankiewicz, 1972: 319—322; cf Fisiak, 1984: 139; Yang Yanchun, 2009: 25; Grucza, 2001: 71)

横跨多个语言学次领域，著述丰厚的库尔德内大力提倡比较没有亲属关系的语言，目的原是为了找出语言发展过程的共性，及其静态（不变）与动态（变化）因素，这在当时进一步区分了语言的历史比较研究和语言的演变研究，同时又与纯粹静态语言研究大不相同（见Adamska-Salaciak，2001：186；Kroner，1972b：265），为今天的对比语言学垒下更为坚实的基石。

As a linguist with an impressive scholarly output in several linguistic fields including what are now known as psycholinguistics and sociolinguistics, Bauduoin understood the complications in the language-society nexus in championing the survey of linguistic processes without regard to linguistic kinship in alignment with his notion of history, looking into both the change (Courtenay's dynamics; Saussure's diachrony) and unchanging (Courtenay's statics, Saussure's synchrony) which are complementary, allowing us "to arrive at universal linguistics phenomena" (Stankiewiez, 1972: 320). If the study of language is for Saussure essentially static, that for Courtenay was essentially the opposite and the dynamic emphasis demarcated historic comparative study of language and developmental changes in linguistic processes. (cf Adamska-Salaciak, 2001: 186; Koerner, 1972b: 265) That laid the corner stone for contrastive linguistics today.

可以这么说，比较是任何研究都用得上的科学方法，语言学以比较为方法也含有试图建立语言学的科学地位之意。而在历史比较语言学正式用上比较方法后，洪堡特立足于总体语言和民族心理，尝试突破语言研究追溯共同源头的局限，而库尔德内则立足于社会语言变化与心理联系，解放了比较方法在各个语言研究层面和领域中的使用。这么一来，历史比较语言学的研究不再垄断19世纪的语言研究，语言研究传统也慢慢发生了变化，从生物谱系和逻辑，转而向其社会和心理属性扩宽。人们都承认洪堡特是普通语言学的创始人，但普通语言学意味着什么，普通语言学与历史比较语言学的关系如何？普通语言学与今天我们所说的对比语言学的关系又如何？却很少有人进行寻根问底的探讨。

It could well be said that any discipline or research may use the contrastive tool as a scientific means of investigation, and turning around, the use of contrastive methodology in linguistics could well be seen as an attempt to raise the scientific status of the discipline. Insofar as the formal employment of comparative survey in historical linguistics was an innovation, it had also provided the impetus for further breakthrough as Humboldt endeavoured to break the monotony in identifying cognates and called for the survey of language as a whole with a focus on ethnic forces whereas Courtenay relaxed the usage of the contrastive tool and extended it to all kinds of linguistic studies on the basis of social and psychological changes. The efforts of Humboldt and Courtenay had certainly induced changes to the linguistic scene as the 19th century was no longer dominated by historical linguistics which gradually bowed out. Most obviously was the change in the tradition of linguistic study which evolved from being subordinated to biology and logic to focusing on the social and psychological attributes. It has been generally professed that Humboldt was the founder of general linguistics, but little has been asked about the discipline he advocated, not to mention inquisition into the relations between general linguistics and historical comparative linguistics as well as the relations between general linguistics and contrastive linguistics in today's sense.

而在沃尔夫提出对比语言学的名称之前，丹麦语言学家叶斯柏森（Otto

Jespersen,1860—1943）也提出了一种"新的比较语法"，此说似有两重含义。其一，在此之前，语言研究着重于重构历史源头，关注从语音和词汇切入，相对而言，句法研究滞后了。而在语言学家逐渐舍弃唯理传统之际，大家对于如何重新定义"句法"莫衷一是，叶斯柏森的比较语法突出语法意义上的句法，此乃一新（见Graffi, 2001: 74—96）。其二，这个"新的比较语法"通过比较多种语言，区分特有与普世的语言法则，实际上同样也就是对比语言学，只是没有使用这一名称而已。叶氏在其名著《语法哲学》一书结尾时说：

Well before Whorf commits to the terminology contrastive linguistics, Danish linguist Otto Jespersen (1860—1943) also shared aloud his thoughts on "a new comparative grammar". There were two implications by what he meant by "new comparative grammar". As we all know, in its pursuit of internal reconstruction of phonology and morphology, the historical comparative method literally neglected syntactic study. But as linguists started moving away from the traditional Port-Royal model, they inevitably occupied themselves debating "What is Syntax?" Jespersen's idea gave prominence to grammatical subject and predicate befitting the emergence of a new paradigm shift (cf Graffi, 2001: 74—96). And by comparing grammars of multiple languages, Jespersen's comparative grammar was able to differentiate exceptions from general linguistic principles. That is contrastive linguistics in substance short of giving it its proper name. At the close of his illustrious publication *Philosophy of Grammar*, Jespersen so remarked:

> 比较语法和历史语法生气勃勃的巨大影响已经得到普遍的承认，但是请允许我在结束本书之前指出，这本书观察语法事实的方法可能会为比较语法创造一种新方法，或者创造一种新的比较语法……这种比较不必局限于属于同一语系、同一起源而通过不同道路发展起来的语言，对差异最大、起源迥然不同的语言也可以加以比较。我在这里所做的可以当作一种意念性比较语法的简单雏形，我希望那些眼界比我开阔、语言知识比我更丰富的人能接过这项工作并加以进一步的发展，以便帮助我们比本书更深刻地理解人类语言和人类思维的最内在的本质。（叶斯伯森，1924/1951: 346—347）

> The great vivifying influence of comparative and historical grammar is universally recognized, but I may be allowed to point out here before I

close that the way in which the facts of grammar are viewed in this volume may open out a new method in comparative grammar, or a new kind of comparative grammar…This comparison need not be restricted to languages belonging to the same family and representing various developments of one original common tongue, but may take into consideration languages of the most diverse ancestry. The specimens of this treatment which I have given here may serve as a preliminary sketch of a notional comparative grammar, which it is my hope that others with a wider outlook than mine and a greater knowledge of languages may take up and develop further, so as to assist us in gaining a deeper insight into the innermost nature of human language and of human thought than has been possible in this volume. (Jespersen, 1924/1951: 346–347)

由此可见，西方的对比语言学不但不是从拉多开始的，甚至也不是从沃尔夫开始的。西方的对比语言学史必须重建，必须寻找一个更早的源头（未必是一个单一的）、更清晰的宗旨。

There is no mistake that contrastive linguistics in the West does not begin with Lado, or with Whorf. The history of contrastive linguistics in the West has to be reconstructed for a complete and multifaceted understanding of the object of inquiry, and it must date even further back than it does presently.

1.2.2 西方对比语言学史的重建
1.2.2 Reconstructing history of contrastive linguistics in the West

　　原则上，只要有不同语言的接触，特别是有了外语教学和语际翻译，就必然会有自觉不自觉的语言对比活动。这在中国以及全世界都是共同的。撇开关于三代和秦汉的零星记载，中国的这一阶段至少可追溯到公元2世纪开始的佛经翻译[1]，不单是词汇、语音，在句法上也有所得。在西方，撇开《圣经》翻

1　3世纪支谦的《法句经·序》第一次提到"天竺言语，与汉异音。云其书为天书，语为天语。名物不同，传实不易"；4世纪道安的《摩诃钵罗若波罗蜜经钞·序》提到"译胡为秦"（或译梵为秦）的"五失本，三不易"，更是对中西（主要是当时的西域诸语言，如梵文、巴利文、吐火罗语等）语言对比的最简要概述。二文均见罗新璋（1984）编的《翻译论集》。

译等不谈，对比语言学家克尔采斯佐斯基（Tomasz P. Krzeszowski，1990：1）也追溯到了1000多年前，提到了公元10世纪前后修道院改革运动（Benedictine Reform）中伊弗利克神父（Aelfric）所著的《语法》（*Grammatica*），因书中简略涉及了英语和拉丁语语法的一些异同[1]。16—18世纪期间，欧洲各国出于文化、贸易、政治、外交等原因，重视外语的学习，包括亲属与非亲属语言：古典拉丁语、古典希腊语；欧洲各国语言；欧洲以外的语言（如阿拉伯语、耶稣会教士传回来的汉语），这时也流行通过与母语比较来帮助学习外语。（谭慧敏，2011）德国作家、评论家兼学者施莱格尔（Friedrich Von Schlegel，1772—1829）因为对印度宗教产生了兴趣，进而研究梵文，1808年著书比较梵文和印欧语言，包括词汇和语法，并在书中创出"比较文法"（Comparative Grammar）一词，但是施氏更关心的是通过对比的手段来追寻共同的历史源头，不是今天语言对比的意义。

Theoretically speaking, whenever and wherever languages come into contact, particularly where foreign language teaching and interlingual translation are required, somehow, in one way or another, contrastive analysis must have set in. Early accounts of contrastive activities are not easy to trace. With respect to China, scattered accounts of the pre-Qin apart, contrastive analysis may well have begun with the rendering of Buddhist texts since the second century. On the other hand, Bible translation aside, earlier traces of contrastive analysis in the West, as descried

---

For instance, Zhi Qian of the third century mentioned for the first time in his *Preface to the Sutra of Dhammapada* that Indian differs from Chinese in the pronunciation and the Sutra is written in Indian language and uses Indian words to describe Indian things, which are really difficult to translate. Dao An of the fourth century, in his *Introduction to the Sutra of Mahāprajñāpāramitā*, discusses the "five instances of losing the source and three difficulties" in translating from Indian to Chinese, which may be regarded as a basic description of the differences between the two languages. Both articles can be found in Luo Xinzhang 1984.

1 Aelfric的书原名*Excerptiones de Arte Grammatica Anglice*或*Excerpts from a Grammar Textbook Rendered into English*，以英语撰写拉丁文法，供以拉丁文为二语的传教士学习拉丁文法。当中没有系统的对比，只有术语的翻译和解释。
Aelfric's book, entitled *Excerptiones de Arte Grammatica Anglice*, or *Excerpts from a Grammar Textbook Rendered into English*, is a book of Latin grammar written in English, to help the friars to study Latin. The book lacks a systematic comparison, and contains only a translation of terms and some explanations.

in Tomasz P. Krzeszowski (1990: 1), go back in time some 1,000 years to the age of Benedictine reform in the tenth century AD, when Father Aelfric brought out his book *Grammatica* mentioning some similiarities and disparities between English and Latin syntax. That needs grew in the period during 16th—18th centuries where foreign language learning took center stage in the interest of exchanges in culture, trade, politics, diplomacy and the likes. Foreign languages that may or may not be in the same language family flourished alike, including classical Latin, ancient Greek, various European languages, languages outside of the Europe continent (such as Arabic and Chinese language shared by the Jesuits) and they were learned most commonly through comparison with the mother tongues (Tham, 2011). A more serious scholastic study was perhaps that by German writer and critic Friedrich von Schlegel (1772—1829) whose interest on religions in India boosted his study of Sankrit and subsequently authoring a book in 1808 comparing the morphology and syntax of Sankrit with Indo-European languages. Schlegel coined the term "Comparative Grammar" in his book as a means of constructing cognates, shedding little light on what was later known as contrastive linguistics.

从更现实的角度看，我们可以说西方对比语言学有两条主干发展路线：一是语言学习，或者说应用语言学的路径。至少从16世纪以来，就有不少文献记录对比在语言学习上的作用，早期称之为"对立比较法"（syncrisis），除了寻找共性，也注意研究母语在外语学习中的迁移作用，如Elisha Coles（1677）、John Hewes（1624）、Mark Lewis（1670）等。（见Salmon，1985：52—62；Krzeszowski，1990：2—3）。19世纪，历史比较语言学兴起后，外语教学策略转向文法翻译法，注重书面语言。与此同时，由于语言研究传统也在逐渐改变，洪堡特、库尔德内等均倾向于研究活生生的语言，结构和功能的观点开始萌芽，如F. Strohmeyer和P. Aronstein开始从功能角度提出外语学习的策略，20世纪上半叶布拉格学派的马泰休斯即受此启发良多。（见Vachek，1984：9）而后又有弗理斯（Charles Fries，1887—1967）、拉多等的说法，而其实他们的观点，多与前人无异。至此可见，对比在语言教学上的应用先于对比语言学的出现，然后在对比语言学作为独立学科发展后，对比在语言教学上的应用该如何纳入学科的指导里成为讨论重点之一，对比分析属于应用语言学抑或是对比理论的应用也成了关键。这也是对比语言学理论和应用问题的背景。

To paint a more realistic picture, contrastive linguistics in the West may have journeyed on two pathways. The first path started with language learning, or it could be put as the applied linguistics path. Records showed that at least since the 16th century, the use of contrastive method in language learning was a commonplace and it was described as Syncrisis in literatures. Besides looking at similarities, what is presently known as shifts and transfers of mother tongue were also noticed. Notable papers include Elisha Coles (1677), John Hewes (1624), and Mark Lewis (1670), to name a few. (Salmon, 1985: 52—62; Krzeszowski, 1990: 2—3). In 19th century, with the rise of historical comparative linguistics, strategy for foreign language teaching took a turn towards Grammar Translation Method with a focus on written language. By which time, the philosophy behind linguistic study took a subtle turn with Wilhem von Humboldt and Baudouin de Courtenay both championing the study of living language data in the midst of structural and functional theories taking shape. Taking bearing from the emerging trend, scholars such as F. Strohmeyer and P. Aronstein advocated functional strategies in foreign language acquisition, which influenced Vilé Mathesius and the Prague School in a big way (Vachek, 1984: 9). It was against this backdrop that the claims of Charles Fries (1887—1967) and Robert Lado surfaced. Putting Fries and Lado in perspective, their views were not new. The above brief account at least attests the fact that the contrastive method in applied linguistic set earlier footprint than contrastive linguistics. And as contrastive linguistics moved to become a branch in its own right, one major discussion centered around the incorporation of constrastive method as a subdivision so as to formalise contrastive linguistic approaches in applied linguistics. The contention on contrastive analysis being part of applied linguistics or part of theoretical contrastive linguistics is thus clear. That accounts for the application and theoretical issues revolving contrastive linguistics.

二是从历史比较语言学拓展出来的语言对比。广义的比较方法中世纪就已经出现了。欧洲扩张时期，民族语言增加了，翻译事业大兴，早在文艺复兴萌芽时期，史学家兼大主祭威尔士的杰拉德（Giraldus Cambrensis，1146—1223）、意大利大诗人但丁（Dante Alighieri，1265—1321）就尝试给当时的欧洲语言分类，主要的目的是为了探讨词义和词源。16—17世纪名学者如作家兼博物学家格斯纳（Konrad Gesner，1516—1565）、语言学家斯卡利杰（Joseph Justus Scaliger，1540—1609）、思想家莱布尼兹（Gottfried W. Leibniz，1646—1716）、语言学家阿德隆（Johan Christoph Adelung，1732—

1806）等都曾注意探讨人类多元论以及语言的亲属关系，研究目的慢慢移向构拟语言原型和亲属语言分类。19世纪更进一步开创了全面比较的时代，凡语言学、社会学、人类学、历史等无不希望从比较中往上推导历史的演化。（见Campbell，2007；Robins，1990：164；Matasovic，（年份不详）；Hoenigswald，1963；Pyenson，2002：5）语言学的比较时代也是从这里全面展开的。从亲属语言之间的比较到非亲属语言之间的对比；从历史比较进而到语法、文化层面的语言对比；语言研究思维由博而约，从历史比较到专注于语言内部的结构主义，20世纪20年代在马泰休斯的带领下，透过语言结构研究提取普遍描写单位来做类型研究，从而发展出另一支流，如此延续发展，整个过程绝非偶然，亦不断受到新兴语言理论的冲击。

  Contrastive Linguistics may also be viewed to have branched out from historical comparative linguistics. Broadly speaking, we have seen that by the middle age, some form of contrastive method had evolved. Following the expansion of Europe into other continents as well as inland developments, more national languages in contact supported the prosperity enjoyed by the translation industry. As early as the budding stage of the Renaissance, attempts to classify language family were pioneered by great figures as Gerald of Wales (Giraldus Cambrensis, 1146—1223) and Italian poet Dante Alighieri (1265—1321) with an aim to seek out the senses and etymology of words. the Into 16th—17th centuries, the variety issue on language and cultural diversity attracted attentions from big guns including Swiss naturalist, bibliographer and classical linguist Konrad Gesner (1516—1565), the most learned man of his time, philologist Joseph Justus Scaliger (1540—1609), German polymath and philosopher Gottfried W. Leibniz (1646—1716) and not the least, grammarian and philologist Johan Christoph Adelung (1732—1806). Their various endeavours on the relations between languages gradually move the study of linguistics into building language prototype and classification of language families. That endeavour go full steam ahead in the 19th century to become a historical comparison trend across disciplines where even sociology, anthropology, history to name a few jump on the bandwagon and started backtracking along development paths in search of prototypes by way of comparative methodology. (cf Campbell 2007; Robins 1990:164; Matasovic (n.d.); Hoenigswald 1963, Pyenson 2002:5) The comparative era in linguistics unfolded in full swing. It is not by chance that the scenes proceeded from comparing between languages of the same family to that between languages of distant family; from historical comparison to synchronic comparison in syntactic structures and cultural imprints. Linguistic research vision began eyeing on specific themes after going after the broad picture at large for some time. So, historical comparison gave way to structuralism to focus on the internal structure of language. The story went on with Vilém Mathesius leading the Prague School in 1920s to exam linguistic typology surveying the structures and extracting the universal units for description. Mathesius successfully blazed a trail. And things are at where they are now—by no means accidental—following these threads of developments and continually refreshed with emerging theories.

从学科建设和发展的角度看，我们认为近代以来的西方对比语言学至少可以分为三个时期。第一期从19世纪20年代至20世纪40年代对比哲学思想的奠基时期；第二期是20世纪40—70年代，那是在主流语言学理论转向中寻求立足点的开拓时期；第三期是1980年至今，走向宏观和注重理论建构，要求整合对比理论与应用。

From the angles of discipline building and development, we suggest three phases of development of contrastive linguistics in the West since the nineteenth century. To begin with, the period from the 1820s to the 1940s was groundbreaking, scaling a height in the philosophy of contrast. There followed a rough time for contrastive linguistics, striving to carve out a niche in the massive transitions of mainstream theoretical linguistic thoughts in the period from the 1940s to the 1970s. Ever since 1980, focus in contrastive linguistics has shifted to the macro perspective with a view to establish the study as a discipline with sound theories and due applications.

1.3 第一期（19世纪20年代至20世纪40年代）：对比哲学思想的奠基
1.3 Phase 1 (1820s—1940s) Evolving period of philosophy on contrast

第一个时期从十九世纪的洪堡特开始，到二十世纪初欧洲的叶斯柏森和美国的沃尔夫。这一时期最重要的文献有：洪堡特的《语言比较研究与语言发展不同阶段的关系》（1820）和《人类语言结构的多样性及其对人类精神发展的影响》（1836）、叶斯柏森的《语法哲学》（1924）和《语言学家眼中的人类、民族和个人》（1946），以及后人为沃尔夫编的论文集《语言、思想与现实》（1956）等，后人为库尔德内编译的《库尔德内文选——结构语言学的开端》(1972)[1]。

This phase began with Wilhelm von Humboldt in the nineteenth century and was rounded off with otto Jespersen and Benjamin Lee Whorf in the first half of the twentieth. Important works of this phase include Humboldt's *On the Comparative Study of Language and Its Relation to the Different Periods of Language Development* (1820) and *On Language: The Diversity of Human Language-Structure and its Influence on the Mental Development of Mankind* (1836); Jespersen's *The Philosophy of Grammar* (1924) and *Mankind, Nation and Individual: From a Linguistic Point of View* (1946), a compilation of essays by Whorf, *Language, Thought and Reality: Selected Writings of Benjamin Lee Whorf* (1956), as well as an edition of Baudouin de Courtenay's theoretical works, *A Baudouin de Courtenay Anthology——The Beginnings of Structural Linguistics* (1972), among others.

这一时期是对比语言学的形成期，对比研究的许多理论问题在这一时期实际都已提出来了，只是没有引起后人的足够重视与研究而已。

This evolving period encompassed a whole range of theoretical issues and research questions that regrettably were not taken seriously by the later generations and generated insufficient attention among linguistic researchers.

1　这是英语翻译文选。另有将库尔德内的俄文、德文论文编辑成集者。这些文集各收集库尔德内的一部分著作。库尔德内和索绪尔一样，没有把自己的想法综合成书，而比索绪尔不幸的是，库尔德内没门生把他的观点辑录起来。他对同一个课题的观点，散见各篇，而他生前写的文章数以百计，又因其兴趣广泛，文章种类繁多，以致其思想精华不容易把握，就连西欧学界对他也不甚了解。
This English translation of Baudouin de Courtenay's work with an introduction by Edward Stankiewicz was published by Indiana University Press. Also available are the Russian two-volume edition of Courtenay's work (1963) and an incomplete Polish edition (begun in 1974) and a German edition (1984). Each of these collections was vested in their own interest and only represented part of Courtenay's work. Like De Saussure, Baudouin de Courtenay did not write books to record his viewpoints, but unlike De Saussure, Courtenay was more unfortunate not having any student to help compile his thoughts which were all over the places for the same subject matter. Given that Courtenay was highly productive and talented in many areas, it is quite a challenge to summarise his thoughts and that accounts for the little understanding we have in the man even the West was guilty of.

1.3.1 对比语言学的诞生——洪堡特的《语言比较研究与语言发展不同阶段的关系》

1.3.1 Birth of contrastive linguistics: Humboldt's "On the Comparative Study of Language and Its relation to the Different Periods of Language Development"

对比语言学最早、最卓越的文献是德国学者洪堡特的《语言比较研究与语言发展不同阶段的关系》（1920）。在这篇文献中，洪堡特就对比研究的一系列基本理论问题进行了阐述，他是当之无愧的对比语言学奠基人。

The first and most significant work on contrastive linguistics was written in 1820. Humboldt expounded on the fundamentals of contrastive analysis in this work, and we cannot overemphasize his contributions in laying the ground for future development in contrastive linguistics.

1.3.1.1 对比语言学的定义
1.3.1.1 Defining contrastive linguistics

《语言比较研究与语言发展不同阶段的关系》的第一句话就为对比语言学下了第一个定义：

The very first sentence in Humboldt's "On the Comparative Study of Language and its Relation to the Different Periods of Language Development" defined the scope of Contrastive Linguistics for the first time:

> 语言比较研究如果要成为独立的学科，提出自己的目标和宗旨，那么，它只能是用来深入持久地探讨语言，探讨民族的发展和人类的进步。（洪堡特，1820: 1）

> The comparative study of languages can only be used to acquire lasting and significant insights into language, the development of nations, and the progress of mankind, when it has been made into an independent branch of study with its own goals and purposes. (Humboldt, 1820: 1)

这个定义有两个特点：第一，洪堡特的"比较语言研究"是广义的，重视语言的多样性与变化，而所谓多样性与变化立足于世界观之相异。（Gipper，1986：124）在本质上，与"普通语言学"追求的目标是一致的，而这个目标也是现今所谓对比语言学所不应该偏离的。洪氏的眼光始终是关注着作为整体的人类语言（单数的"语言"），为着这个终极关怀，不仅要了解语言的历史源头，更要求比较具体的、活生生的语言（复数的"语言"）。可见，在洪堡特的心目中，对比语言学乃是普通语言学的格物方法。从这一角度看，洪氏的对比语言学视野比今天一些学者自以为在从事的"对比语言学"（只是语言教学上的"对比分析"）要宽广得多，比近一个世纪来一些埋头株守于"发掘汉语特点"的中国语言学者也要深邃得多。第二，它特别强调语言与民族发展、人类进步的关系。这是洪堡特的一贯主张，人们早已耳熟能详。问题是，现在研究"普通语言学"或"对比语言学"的人，有多少还记得"普通语言学"创始人（依我们看也是对比语言学创始人）这一终身坚持的主张？有多少人认真关注这一关系并愿意同洪堡特一样，把它作为语言研究的基本出发点？索绪尔以后，20世纪的普通语言学离开这条道路越来越远，20世纪50年代以后，参与对比语言学研究的多数人也将这条原则置之脑后，社会不断发展，语言研究的目标不断改变，我们很难对这是福还是祸，是前进还是倒退加以评断。

The definition by Humboldt above stood out in two ways. "Comparative study of language" was in a broad sense in Humboldt's term, paying overriding attention on language diversities and transformations in the context of differing world views and cultures (Gipper, 1986: 124) That is consistent with the aims and objectives of general linguistics, from which contrastive linguistics today shall not deviate. Humboldt's main contention rests in human language as a whole ("language" in singular) and for this matter, historical comparison in search of a cognate origin was far from being sufficient and therefore the call for more specific comparison into living languages ("languages" in plural). It can safely be said that for Humboldt, this "comparison study of language" is a way to study the nature of language serving the purpose of general linguistics. In this light, Humboldt's horizon was definitely much wider than those who took contrastive linguistics as contrastive analysis for pedagogical needs and certainly more insightful than those who confined themselves to using contrastive study for the mere exploration of the uniqueness of the Chinese Language in the past century. Second, he emphasizes the relations language has with national development and human progress, the familiar advocacy of Humboldt. Lamentably, few who work on general linguistics or contrastive linguistics bear the lifelong campaign of Humboldt in mind, and we doubt if they remember or acknowledge Humboldt as the founder of general linguistics——and of contrastive linguistics too, in our view. There is scarcely anyone currently taking after Humboldt in upholding the above second emphasis as the ultimate aim of linguistics research. General linguistics since Saussure has gradually departed from the path lit by Humboldt, and his ideas remain obscure to most scholars committed to contrastive analysis from the 1950s. Is this a blessing, or shall we describe this as "progress"?...

1.3.1.2 对比语言学的对象和目标
1.3.1.2 Contrastive linguistics: object and objective

洪堡特还提出了语言对比研究的两个领域：
Humboldt also identified two areas of research in contrastive linguistics:

> 为简便起见，我将语言比较研究的两个领域表述如下：考察各语言的有机体组织；考察各语言的进一步发展状态。（洪堡特，1820: 6）
>
> For the sake of brevity, I will denote the two aspects of the comparative study of languages as follows: examination of the organism of languages, and examination of languages in their state of further development. (Humboldt, 1820: 6)

洪堡特认为语言是一种活动（energeia），而不是成品（ergon）。（见Humboldt，1836/1999：49；Gipper，1986：125）考察各语言作为一种有机体组织倾向于共时研究，而其进一步发展状态则属于历时研究。今天有些人很容易把这两个方面作机械两分，把一个看作是静态的、共时的，一个看作是动态的、历时的。洪堡特生怕别人作这样简单的两分，因此特别指出，语言作为"有机体组织"并不是语言"发展"的毫无变化的结果，而"发展"在到达最后状态之前也可能对"人机体组织"产生影响。（Humboldt，1820/1997：6）洪堡特的观点可以说是开创了对比的共时研究，为了要探讨语言的变化，他认为必须从言语中去观察。后来，索绪尔提出从言语系统中抽出语言系统的观点。其静中带动，动中带静的看法与后来库尔德内、马泰休斯着重语言系统的共时而动态性质不谋而合。

Humboldt opined that language "in itself is no product (ergon) but an activity (energeia)" (see Humboldt, 1836/1999: 49; Gipper, 1986: 125) and angling language as an organism leads to synchronic study of language where its developmental study would then be classified as diachronic study. There is a tendency at present day to conveniently equate synchronic and diachronic study mechanically as static or dynamic respectively. Humboldt took pain to highlight that "the organism" is not left completely unaltered by the further development of language, and the "development" may have had some influence on the "organism" before it reached its final state. (Humboldt, 1820/1997: 6) Synchronic study in language was really a further enhancement of Humboldt's viewpoint that the examination of parole was necessary in order to investigate changes in language, which was to be taken up by de Saussure who suggested extracting language system from parole. That observation of dynamism is within a static structure inseparable from a dynamic system inspired Bauduoin de Courtenay as well as Vilém Mathesius, emphasising that language system shall be studied synchronically without negligence on its dynamism.

对前一个任务，洪堡特强调必须经常进行比较，比较的范围越广越好；而对后者，则需要研究者对个别语言进行深入细致的考察；亦即前者需要广度而后者需要深度。在此基础上洪堡特提出了从事这种研究需要的条件：一是懂得的语言越多越好，二是必须对一两种语言有非常精细的研究。由于前者永远无法充分做到，因而后者更重要（Humboldt, 1820（1997）: 7）。在这一认识基础上，洪堡特提出了经验性对比研究的目标：

For the first area of research, Humboldt advised concentration on as wide a scope as possible. For the second area, more detailed analysis of one single language is required. In brief, while the former requires breadth of research, the later requires depth. Hence his prerequisites for contrastive research: investigate a large number of different languages—indeed, if possible, all languages—but always start from a detailed knowledge of one single language, or of very few. Since the first requirement can never be achieved in full, the second requirement seems all the more crucial (*ibid*.: 7). With this, Humboldt brought forth the objective of experimental contrastive analysis:

> 依上法进行对比研究，要能指出人类发明语言的各种方式，其中传输了人类知性世界的哪一部分。还要能指出语言如何受到各民族个性的影响，又反过来如何影响各民族的个性。（同上: 7）
>
> The empirical study of comparisons between languages, if undertaken in this manner, can indicate the various ways in which the human race produced language and can show what part of its intellectual world it has succeeded in transferring to it. It can also show how language has been affected by the individual character of the nations and how, in its turn, language has had an effect on them. (*Ibid.*: 7)

在16年后发表的《人类语言结构的多样性及其对人类精神发展的影响》（1836）里，洪堡特进一步阐述了他的"民族的语言即民族的精神，民族的精神即民族的语言"（1836：46/姚小平，1997：50）的思想，并且提出了对比研究的最高的、终极的目标，以及达到这一目标的方法：

Sixteen years later, Humboldt took a closer look at language and contended that "Language is, as it were, the outer appearance of the spirit of a people; the language is their spirit and the spirit their language" (1836: 46), which points to the ultimate concern of contrastive studies and hints at the method to go about achieving this objective:

> 如果我们把语言看作解释精神发展过程的依据，那当然就必须把语言的发生归因于民族的智能特性，而这种智能特性则需要到每一种语言的结构中去发现。为能比较成功地完成这里提出的研究，我们必须更详细地考察语言的本质和语言差异对精神发展可能产生的反作用。通过这样做，我们就可以使比较语言研究达到最终、最高层次的目的。（洪堡特，1836：47/52）

> If we look upon languages, therefore, as a basis for explaining successive mental development, we must indeed regard them as having arisen through intellectual individuality, but must seek the nature of this individuality in every case in its structure; so that if the considerations here introduced are to be carried to completion, it is now incumbent on us to enter more closely into the nature of languages and the possibility of their retroactive differences, in order thereby to couple the comparative study of languages to its last and highest reference-point. (Humboldt, 1836: 47)

后来他又把这个意思归结成一句话：

He summed it up in one sentence:

> 语言如何从精神出发，再反作用于精神，这是我要考察的全部过程。（同上：54/63）

> We are to consider the whole route whereby, proceeding from the mind, it (the language) reacts back upon the mind. (*ibid.*: 54)

这就是他给普通语言学亦即对比语言学规定的根本任务。

This is the primary object he assigned to general linguistics as well as contrastive linguistics.

1.3.1.3 对比语言学的方法
1.3.1.3 Methodology of contrastive linguistics

洪堡特还提出了语言对比研究的方法，认为语言与精神的联系在概念上主要表现在两个方面："其一是具体概念的构造，其二是语言所拥有的一定类型概念的相对丰富程度"（1836: 85/106）；而在"词语结合"上表现为"独特性"（同上：86/107）。这两者他总称为"内在语言形式"，是对比研究的重点：

Humboldt regarded the influence of national individuality in language in two ways: "in the *formation* of particular *concepts*, and in the relatively different *abundance* of the language in *concepts* of a certain kind" (1836: 85); and "the ordering of speech" revealed much "national uniqueness" (*ibid.*: 86). Such "inner forms of language" are what he felt ought to be the locus of contrastive studies, and he suggested handling it in the following ways:

> 为了实现上面提到的目标，我们在研究中就必须首先将注意力集中在语言结构的差异上，而这种差异并不能追溯到一个语系最初的统一性。事实上，这样的差异首先要到语言方法与语言有限的努力之间最紧密的联系之中去找。于是，我们便以另一种方式回到了概念的指称及思想在句子中的联系这个问题上。（洪堡特，1836: 90/114）

> If the above-mentioned goal is to be reached, it is precisely here that the inquiry must especially keep in view a diversity of language structure which cannot be traced to the uniform character of one linguistics family. Now this diversity will primarily have to be sought where the practice of language is most closely tied to its finite endeavors. This leads us back, though in another connection, to the designation of concepts and the linkage of thought in a sentence. (*ibid.*: 90)

1.3.2 库尔德内的贡献
1.3.2 Contributions of Baudouin de Courtenay

菲齐亚克（Fisiak, 1984: 139—140）论对比源头时把其中一个源头指向库尔德内和索绪尔，并指出库尔德内（1902）奠定了对比语言学的基础。这么说固非偶然。库尔德内和索绪尔都是结构语言学的先驱，从历史比较语言学发展到结构语言学,可谓语言学科学化的一个进程,比较和对比扮演了重要的角色。洪堡特倡议的语言比较研究,说法比较抽象和宏观。库尔德内首先确定比较或对比之法为普遍应用的科学方法,论述中肯而客观。如前文所述,他也确切点出语言比较的三大类别。戚雨村(1992:2)指出用库尔德内的话来看,历史比较语言学是真正的"比较文法";不管历史渊源,比较两种或多种邻近地区的语言如何相互影响而出现类似语言现象,属于"地域语言学";而不考虑亲属关系来研究语言过程,从而确定两种语言结构的异同,属于"对比语言学"。他大力推动没有亲属关系的语言之间的比较。一些语言之间既没有亲属关系,也没有任何的历史渊源和地理位置上的相邻,但在这些语言中却总能找到同样的特征、同样的历史过程和变化。通过比较,可以对这些语言的共同特征进行分类和对比,他指出"在语音领域和形态领域,甚至在语义学领域,或者在词语和短语意义领域,类似的对比语言的方法成为最广泛的语言学的概括基础。"(杨衍春,2009:25)

In tracing the origin(s) of contrastive study, Jacek Fisiak (1984: 139—140) attributed one of the sources to Baudouin de Courtenay and De Saussure, and hailed Courtenay (1902) as laying the cornerstone for contrastive linguistics. Fisiak certainly has his points. The inroad from comparative linguistics to structural linguistics with the use of comparative and contrastive tools marked an important milestone in the scientific study of language and linguistics for which the roles of Baudouin de Courtenay and Ferdinand de Saussure, both pioneers in structural linguistics were crucial. While Humboldt championed the "comparative study of language", he may have been a little abstract and too general. Courtenay seemed more objective and hit to the point when, at the outset, he ascertained the methods of both comparative and contrastive to be general tools in scientific research and moved on, as mentioned earlier, to establish three types of language comparison. Paraphrasing De Courtenay's three classifications, Qi Yuchun (1992: 2) understood Baudouin as follow: Historical comparative linguistics is "comparative grammar" in genuine sense; attempts to compare two or more languages in the same neighbourhood to survey how they have influenced each other as well as the resultant similarities regardless of historical closeness may be known as "arena linguistics"; attempts to study the similarities and disparities between languages regardless of their family distance shall be known as "contrastive linguistics". Baudouin's main thrust was in the comparison of non-related languages, i.e. languages that are remote in relations and have no historical linkages or geographical relations, and yet demonstrated similar structures, and/or underwent similar development paths and adjustments. The use of contrastive tools in such cases to single out the comparable features for classification and comparison in the fields of phonology and morphology or even semantics, or the study of structural senses of phrases or constructions offers the most universal generalisation for linguistics. (Yang Yanchun, 2009: 25)

然而，我们更应该认识到，库尔德内生活的时间段正处于历史比较语言学与结构语言学之间，也就是现代语言学正在发展之际，之所以提出这一系列看法，其实是在塑造一种科学的语言观。库尔德内的老师施莱赫尔（A. Schleicher, 1821—1868）抱持语言为生物的观点，将语言学附属于自然科学。洪堡特视语言为有机体组织而非"生物"，是"活动"而非"成品"。库尔德内再往前走一步。当时，虽然语言学列入自然科学之中，人们却又普遍认为语言学非科学。库尔德内希望改变人们的看法，要证明语言学尽管不是自然科学，甚至不是物理一类的科学，却是科学的，不仅能像历史语言学般的收集语言事实，而是能进行描写、解释和预测。因此，如果说歌德在为生物分类时致力于发现自然界隐藏的定律，洪堡特愿意把分类应用到文化世界特别是人类言语中去发现规律，而库尔德内则要把特定的规则都摆在桌面上。虽然不是为了特定的学科或方法建言，库尔德内努力塑造语言观而提出的一系列看法，无意中推动了对比语言学的发展。但是也正因为库尔德内其实并非为了"对比"本身而建言，我们必须从他的诸多论述中自行整理他的思想中有益于对比语言学发展的观点。这样的讨论，至今非常少。

What is even more noteworthy is the fact that De Courtenay lived in the transition window between historical comparative linguistics and structural linguistics, or more exactly, witnessed the taking off of modern linguistics. The main contribution of Baudouin was to give linguistics a genuine scientific perspective. De Courtenay was a student of A. Schleicher (1821—1868) who subscribed to a tradition that viewed language to be an organism or a specie in the biological world, subordinating linguistic study to natural science. Whilem von Humboldt differentiates between "organism" and "organic", declaring that language is an "energia" or an activity, but not an "ergon" or product. Language, to Humboldt, is a very specific human activity that forms an organic unity (a system). De Courtenay, begging to differ from Schleicher, moved a step further than Humboldt. At a time where linguistics, being part of natural science, was generally disregarded as a science, De Courtenay served to be a game changer in his effort to prove that linguistics, although not exactly part of natural science nor even of physics, is in fact scientific, not merely fact gathering, but able to describe, explain and predict. So while Goethe, in developing his theory for organic types, sought for some hidden law in the natural world; Humboldt applied it to the cultural world, specifically to the world of human speech; and Baudouin liked to bring all linguistic rules and laws into the open. Although De Courtenay did not mean to serve specific sub-linguistic field or methodology, his viewpoints on language and linguistics quietly turned things inside out and advanced the cause for contrastive linguistics. Precisely for the fact that Baudouin did not serve the interest of contrastive linguistics in particular, we have to collate relevant viewpoints in support of contrastive linguistics from his voluminous writings. Effort in that direction is, regrettably, sparingly scarce.

在方法上，他建议采用对比，因为对比的归纳和演绎有科学基础。为此，他必须确立比较方法的动因。身处历史比较语言学兴盛之期，身为历史比较语言学教授，库尔德内一方面批评语文学派走向"极端实证"，结果只能导出"描写语法、文本校对和字典"；一方面则批评历史比较语言学走向另一个极端，倾于"先验"，虽然认识到解释现象的重要性，结果却"把语言事实强行套在理论中"，最终得到的是扭曲的解释。库尔德内认为语言学可以借助于归纳法，做到描写（充分的语言数据）与解释（按数据的充分性加以演绎）并重，如此方能确立语言规则，亦能对语言的走向作出预测。（见 R. Williams，1993：32）

To Baudouin de Courtenay, contrastive method was recommended for its duality in deductive-inductive approaches giving it scientific basis. For that matter, motivation for contrastive study has to be established to consolidate the science of linguistics. Born into the era of historical comparative studies and being a professor in the field, Bauduoin did not mince his words when he criticised the "extreme empirical" approach of philologists for fact gathering resulting only in "descriptive grammars, text editions, and dictionaries" on the one hand; while taking the "aprioristic" approach adopted in historical comparative studies to task for it "forces the facts to fit the theory" even though it "recognises the need to explain phenomena", and consequently producing a "distorted explanation".

The truly scientific approach, according to Courtenay, is to make use of inductive science to achieve a goal that is both descriptive (adequate data) and explanatory (generalisation from the data) in order that linguistics laws can be discovered and behaviour of the phenomena can be predicted or deduced from the theory. (R. Williams, 1993: 32)

实际上，只追究历史源头的比较法令语言学研究犹如栽进了死胡同，要理解任何一种语言现象，追溯亲属源头并非唯一的方法。德国数学、理论物理学家兼哲学家外尔（Hermann Weyl）指出：

In fact, the use of comparative method to identify cognates and divergence of a proto-language sends linguistics research into a no through road. Obviously, the relationship between languages is not the only way to explain linguistic phenomena. As German mathematician, theoretical physicist and philosopher Hermann Weyl pointed out:

> 认识世界的基本原则根本就不在于了解其演变；就性质的分析而言，了解演变乃是最后得出的结果，不是分析的第一步。任何现象的解释不应该从根源处着手，而应该着眼于该语言的内在规则。换言之，要真正了解各语言的初始，我们需要更充分的语言知识。因迫切缺乏这样的语言知识，19世纪这数十年来语言学界盲从达尔文主义而对谱系以及语言系统所做的揣测，只能说是不成熟的看法。"（转引自E. Stankiewicz，1966：497）

Fundamentally, our understanding of the physical world is never through atomistic understanding of development in material forms. In terms of explaining the nature of things, developmental study only serves the interest of the final outcome instead of being the starting point of analysis. No explanation of phenomena should begin from genetic reconstruction, and as far as linguistic phenomena is concerned, the only thing that matters is the inherent laws of languages. In other words, genealogical investigation requires a broader framework, i.e., a full description on synchronic states and stages and understanding of the functions of linguistic forms within a system. The lack of such sufficiency saw decades of linguistic study of the 19th century blind-folded by Darwinism and led by presumptions on language families and systems of languages. Those are at most, pre-matured views. (cf E. Stankiewicz, 1966: 497)

因此，好比历史比较法只在语言内部使用对比方法，那还是不足以得出语言的内在规则，库尔德内转而循几个方向来推进这方面的研究，从而也促进了语言学的发展。首先，反对谱系理论，从社会功能和地缘联系来探寻语言发展演变的其他因素，指出表层的相似未必指向亲属关系，可能是各种共时接触所造成的。库尔德内也因此被誉为社会语言学先驱，而很多讨论也止于此。我们认为，库尔德内提出社会与地缘因素的大前提不能忽略，那是为厘清语言演变的面貌，从而了解语言内在规则而服务的，这个启示对于对比语言学来说，即无论是求同还是求异，最终必须落实到语言之间内在规律来讨论，凸显"语言现象和内在的力量或本质分类和概念的因果联系"，否则就只是隔靴骚痒。而所谓的语言内在规则指的是：

As such, comparative method used to study the internal structures of language itself cannot yield understanding of the inherent language rules. That essentially was where Courtenay worked to advance the course of linguistics. To begin with, Courtenay strongly opposes the language family theory and turned instead to social and geographical linkages to seek out factors contributing to linguistic change. He brought to the obvious that surface similarities in language constructions need not point towards a common origin since it may be consequential of diachronic contacts. For his champion on social and geographical factors, Courtenay was hailed as the pioneer of social linguistics. That most discussions tend to stop short at this point is most understating. To de Courtenay, the fronting of social and geographical factors has a premise in clarifying linguistics changes so as to outline the laws in languages. With this at the core, discussions in contrastive linguistics on similarities and differences without referencing or highlighting "the forces and laws or the fundamental categories and concepts that connect the phenomena and present them as a chain of cause and effect" totally miss the point. Courtenay gave the following definition of his conception of linguistic laws:

这里所谓规则就是一种公式表达，一种通则，用以说明在某种条件下，随a或b出现的是x和y，抑或说属于某个范围的现象（比如，某种语言、某个词类或某个语言的形式）a和b，与另一个范围的x和y相

对应。"（转引自威廉姆斯，1993:32）

Law here means a formulation, a generalization that states that under certain conditions, after a or b, there appears x and y, or that a and b in one domain of phenomena (for example, in one language or in one category of words or forms of a given language) corresponds to x and y in another domain. (cf. R. Williams, 1993: 32)

威廉姆斯解释说，普遍规则可以是"时间上的发展规律"或者是在"存在过程中任何时候"可以界定语言者。（同上）由此可见库尔德内主张的普通语言学的高度。值得注意的是，库尔德内区分语言的一般范畴（语言单位）与语言学的一般范畴（对语言现象具说明意义的抽象通则）。20世纪的类型学，无论是从词法或句法上来探讨语言的分类，都未能在语言规则上深入。而今的对比研究大多按语言的一般范畴立论，没能就语言学的一般范畴进行对比探索，也就无法深入普遍规则，对比语言学的理论也因而一直停滞不前。

Radwanska Williams (ibid.) explains: "The generalisations as defined above may state either the 'laws of development in time' or laws that define language 'at any given moment of its existence'." The above thus shows the depth of general linguistics in Courtenay. It is noteworthy that Courtenay distinguishes general categories of language (language unit) and general categories of linguistics (abstract rules that explain language phenomena). Typological studies in both syntax and morphology of the 20th century, however, narrowly missed that goal set by de Coutenay to pursue the inner law of languages. Contrastive linguistic studies in present day confine themselves to comparison between general categories in language, rather than within the scope of linguistic categories.

除了外部的因素，库尔德内也十分重视语言的心理属性，指出语言是"一种工具也是一种活动"。内外结合方能体现语言的系统性，了解语言系统在共时和历时交互作用下的面貌，看到语言如何受内外因素的影响。在当时，这一切推动了语言学研究的前进，而所赖以达标的方法就是语言现象的比较或对比（comparison of phenomena）。在他看来，"比较或者对比"作为一切科学的方法，要成就一种语法是合于语言科学的，但是要分出一种"比较语法"却嫌多余。

And de Courtenay also thought that a science of language cannot be psychologically naive. Language is both "a tool and an activity". The assimilation of both inner and outer factors would then present language in its systemic totality so that it is neither too synchronic nor too diachronic, but an integrated outcome of time and space bearing marks of inner and outer adjustments. Through the comparison of phenomena, Baudouin de Courtenay quietly moved linguistic studies of his time forward with his views. He opined that a science of language has to be done through comparison of phenomena which is the basis of scientific methods, but it would be unnecessary to have a subdivision called comparative grammar.

语言学的心理基础,语言心理的问题在整个语言学发展史上,起起落落,就对比语言学论,洪堡特、库尔德内、沃尔夫三大巨头,尽管具体观点迥异,都一致确定心理因素在语言学研究中的位置。由是,无论是语法或文化对比研究,最后必以语言心理因素为依归。库尔德内对于语言学的心理基础(1903),看法自成一格,笔者以为还要比洪堡特和沃尔夫的观点更为适合指导当前的对比语言学的前进,希望这方面今后能有更多的研究。

One particular common factor that stood out in the developmental survey of contrastive linguistics is the central role psycholinguistic basis placed by Whilem Von Humboldt, Jan Baudouin de Courtenay and Benjamin Lee Whorf. While their specific viewpoints may differ, they have all made it a point to underline the importance of psychological factors in linguistic studies as well as cultural study in language. The path of psycholinguistics in the history of linguistics is tumultuous. It is hopeful, nonetheless, that more can be achieved as we uncover more of De Courtenay's proposal on the socio-psycho basis for linguistic studies, which, in our humble view, could provide more impetus for the advancement of contrastive linguistics than those of Humboldt or Whorf.

库尔德内于1912年以俄文著书切实地以对比方法比较了波兰语、俄语以及古教会斯拉夫语的文法。进而在1927年著书说明语言的计量作用,透过计量来看语言的发展,甚而考察"语言思维"(linguistic thought),不过他所谓的计量方法与今天的统计频率的方法大相径庭。[1] 中西方对于库尔德内的研究委实不足,而东欧和俄国对于库尔德内的研究资料又需要跨越语言障碍,对于他的认识以及他对于当前对比语言学发展所可能起的推动作用上我们只能期盼更上一层楼。

Courtenay put into practice his comparison of phenomena in his Russian work

---

1　Wincenty Lotoslawski: http://www.glottopedia.de/index.php/Wincenty_Lutos%C5%82awski (assessed in Dec 2011).

Polish in Comparison with Russian and Old Church Slavonic (1912). In another work published in 1927, *Quantity as a Dimension of Thought about Language*, he further explained the use of statistical method in linguistic studies as a tool for developmental study and to survey linguistic thought. However, Courtenay's statistical model for linguistics is quite different from what we are familiar with today. It was hoped that there could be greater interest in Baudouin de Courtenay by our Western counterparts to help transcend the language barriers in reading Courtenay, and in the course of so doing, break through the current limits faced by the discipline.

1.3.3 马泰休斯的贡献
1.3.3 Contributions of Vilém Mathesius

说到布拉格学派领袖马泰休斯,一般联想到功能语言学、语用学、语篇学、语言类型学等,很少把他和对比语言学联系起来,即便提到,也语焉不详,甚至认为马泰休斯的学术研究与对比无关。伐切克(Vachek,1980)充分肯定马赛休斯为语言对比所作的贡献,称他为对比语言学的先驱;匈牙利对比语言学者德塞(Laszlo Dezsö,1991:117)视马泰休斯的两部作品(Mathesius,1928,1936)为对比语言学代表作,认为比之现代语言类型学,马泰休斯的研究更为成功地为两种或多种语言提炼出基本特征。但正如德塞所指出,马泰休斯的论文以捷克语发表,世人多不理解,而斯拉夫语学者虽然少了语言障碍,却又对马泰休斯所讨论的英语没多大兴趣。实则,对比语言学史欠马泰休斯应有的交待,少了这一部分的研究,对比语言学与语言类型学的关系变得隐晦,20世纪以来西方主流语言学界何以把对比语言学划入应用语言学的对比分析也就难以看得透。初步看来,马泰休斯的对比贡献在于语言特征学和语言类型学。他的语言特征研究真正贯通了对比语言学与语言类型学,对于语言描写以及普通语言学的建立有莫大的示范作用,忽视他的研究在对比史上的意义甚为不该。

At the mention of Vilém Mathesius, lead scholar of the Prague School, what comes to mind includes functional linguistics, pragmatics, text linguistics, linguistic typology—all but contrastive linguistics. The few who linked Mathesius with contrastive linguistics gave little details; some may even think his scholastic achievements are unrelated to contrastive linguistics. Vachek (1980) stood out prominently in acknowledging in full the credits of Vilém Mathesius in contrastive linguistics, honouring him as a forerunner of the discipline. A more unique insight was offered by Hungarian scholar Laszlo Dezsö. Dezsö (1991: 117—118) holds that Mathesius (1928) and (1936) made exemplary works in contrastive linguistics, particularly illustrative in theoretical significance. In his paper, Dezsö opines that Mathesius, with his trailblazing scheme of comparison, drew out more characteristics for 2 or more languages than modern linguistic typological studies did. Why did the contrastive linguistic world miss Vilém Mathesius? It is probably language barrier again since Mathesius published in Czech that few could understoan and while Slavic scholars could, they are not as interested in the English language that Mathesius discussed, Dezsö suggests. In any case, the history of contrastive linguistics owes it to Vilém Mathesius, for passing him blurs and breaks the link between contrastive linguistics and linguistic typology and left obscured the reason mainstream linguistics in the West should group contrastive analysis under applied linguistics. Mathesius's conception of linguistic characterology, a true marriage between contrastive linguistics (or what Mathesius termed as analytical comparison of languages) and linguistic typology, is exemplary of linguistic description and carries a torch to the completion of general linguistics. It is totally unjustified and unfortunate to have left him out in the contrastive linguistic discourse.

  语言特征学（linguistiká charakteristika, linguistic characterology）可以说是马泰休斯提出的语言类型的雏形。语言特征是特定语言的结构—类型特点，是相互制约或相互兼容的功能总集，体现出该语言的个性面貌，对该语言结构上的相对稳定程度提前做了规定。[1]马泰休斯承认受洪堡特的影响，这个具体的提法和洪堡特要求研究语言自身发展的规律遥相呼应。为了做到这一点，"语言特征学只与某种语言在特定时间内重要的本质特征打交道，要在普通语言学的基础上对这些特征进行分析，努力弄清楚它们之间的关系"（转引自戚雨村，1993：53）。这无疑奠定了重要的对比基础。 换言之，了解了甲语言的特征，比之于乙语言、丙语言等等，就能说明其中可以预测（同）和不可预测（异）之处。语言的预测性质必然要立足于有特征意义的语言规则，与库尔

---

1 www.thefreedictionary.com

德内要求考虑语言规则（语言学的一般范畴）的立场如出一辙。智者如库尔德内和马泰休斯显然太超前了，直至今日的主流语言学思想和方法都无法撑起他们的理念。20世纪50至60年代，拉多从预测角度把对比分析纳入外语教学中，对比分析后来却遭遇严苛的批评，他只知其一，不知其二。20世纪70年代乔姆斯基（Noam Chomsky）引发了语言学界的地震，就在于提出要把语言视为规则系统来研究，然而，我们至今仍然深陷"有限规则，无限运用"的围困，惑于现象，即便是最简方案（Minimalist Program）也还在纷繁的表层语言现象中打转。我们必须再说明，马泰休斯所谓特征，属于很高的层次，需要深刻的洞察力方能提炼出来，不是今天一般研究文章所探讨的表面语言单位的差异。综合这些年来的研究，语音的特征研究相对清晰和明确，不比词法和句法，受多种不确定因素干扰。可是这本身可能就是个问题，充分地把语音、词法和句法割裂后，要找最深层的特征规则是否已经不可能？然而，要把语音、词法和句法当成一个整体，还需解决"拨乱反正"的难题，"乱"来自于地理语言和社会语言接触和联盟，从马泰休斯的功能观点来说，这就要在一个个有限的范畴中去提炼特征规则。

Linguistic characterology could well be seen as Mathesius's initial attempt to linguistic typology. Characterology in linguistics refers to potential structural-typological features, or characteristics, of a given language, essentially only those that may be regarded as mutually conditioned or mutually compatible. The sum of all such mutaully conditioned characteristics constitutes the general type or character of a language and predetermines the relative stability of its structure. Admittedly influenced by Wilhem von Humboldt, specifications in Mathesius's description of characterology echoed Humboldt's call to examine the pattern-system of language development. As a footnote, Qi Yuchun (1993: 53) added that linguistic characterology deals with the critical nature of a language in a specific time period, analysing these characteristics on the basis of general linguistics to seek out their relations in a language. Characterology in linguistics is really the key to contrastive studies. The characterology of language A, when compared against that of language B, C and the rest, would made possible prediction (due to convergence) and tell apart the unpredictables (due to divergence). For the necessity that linguistic predictability must fall back on the inherent laws of language (linguistics categories) governing the characteristics, Mathesius is agreeable with Courtenay. Nonetheless, the keen insights of both de Courtenay and Mathesius were too avant-garde for their times, and perhaps even the present mainstream linguistics, may not be able to support well. Robert Lado was severely criticised in the 1950s-60s as he tried introducing predictability into contrastive analysis for foreign language teaching. The criticism contrastive analysis attracted only served to show that while we understood the conception of characterology, inherent language laws or pattern-system, we are far from executing them. In the 1970s, Norm Chomsky turned the whole linguistic world upside down when he "revolutionalised" research in linguistics in favour of rule-based study. Despite all the herculean effort, we remained deeply trapped in the awkward deadlock of infinite generations from finite rules as we kept whirling around surface phenomena. Even the Minimalist Program gets itself entangled on the complexities of surface structures. For this matter, we cannot over emphasized that Mathesius's linguistic characterology is nothing present research on surface comparison of linguistic units has ever come close to. Characterology depiction requires much more insight into the depth beneath surface structures. Over the years, research findings on phonetic characteristics stood out relatively well, whereas researches into morphology and syntax were perturbed by many uncertainties. Indeed, it may be asked if it is even possible to draw out characterology when we see phonology, morphology and syntax in segregation. After all, the three have been treated so independently for years. And even if we are able to assemble the three separated units as an organic whole for study, there is one last issue to be resolved, that of "irregularities" or "convergence" due to geolinguistic and sociolinguistic factors. In the functional view of Mathesius, that would require law discovery from each and every specific category.

1.3.4 叶斯柏森的贡献
1.3.4 Contributions of Otto Jespersen

继洪堡特与库尔德内之后，在欧洲提出对比语言学构想的是丹麦语言学家叶斯柏森，叶氏是英语研究的大家，在英语学界名声显赫；他的《语法哲学》更奠定了他作为理论语言学家的地位；然而同样，他的对比语言学倡议却没有受到人们的重视，也许是因为放在该书的最后一节，有"顺便提及"的味道，因而人们容易看走眼？

Succeeding Humboldt and Courtenay in Europe was Otto Jespersen, and suffering the same fate of attracting no attention to his call on contrastive analysis, probably because the remark was "casual" enough to be made just before he closed his masterpiece *The Philosophy of Grammar* (1924) that landed him a place in theoretical linguistics.

实际上，在提倡新学科的同时，叶斯柏森还具体指出了进行对比研究的方法。他首先提出了要区别"句法范畴"和"意念范畴"，句法范畴以实际结构为基础，而意念范畴具有普遍性。"语法学家的任务是，研究各种情况下意念范畴与句法范畴之间的关系。"（Jespersen，1924：55）在这个基础上，他提出了对比研究的方法：

In fact, Jespersen was more than suggestive in his push for contrastive analysis. He made plain the specific research method throughout his book, differentiating between "syntactic category" and "notional category" at the outset. Syntactic category was based on real constructions whereas inner meaning category has universality. Accordingly, "It will be the grammarian's task in each case to investigate the relation between the notional and the syntactic categories." (Jespersen, 1924/1958: 55) On this ground, contrastive method would encompass:

> 如果我们采用本书使用的方法，即从C（意义或内在意义）出发，探讨全人类共有的每一个基本概念在各种语言里是如何表达的，由此通过B（功能）到A（形式），我们就会获得一种新的更有效的研究方法，并能在事实上创立一种新的比较句法学。（叶斯伯森，1924/1951：346—347）

> But we can obtain new and fruitful points of view, and in fact arrive at a new kind of Comparative Syntax by following the method of this volume, i.e. starting from C (notion or inner meaning) and examining how each of the fundamental ideas common to all mankind is expressed in various languages, thus proceeding through B (function) to A (form). (Jespersen, 1924: 346—347)

叶斯柏森主张的是一种多语言的对比。所以，我们在《语法哲学》一书中可以看到丹麦语、古丹麦语、英语、古英语、法语、古法语、德语、古高地德语、希腊语、意大利语、西班牙语、挪威语等不下二十种语言的用例。正是通过这种多种语言之间的对比、分析，许多语法现象与问题在叶斯柏森笔下得到了清晰的展示与阐述。如果说，洪堡特的文章在理论方面讨论得更多的话，那么，叶斯柏森的这本书，也许不妨看作是对比研究的第一次重要实践。

In Jesperson's work as many as twenty languages are quoted. It is precisely through this contrastive exercise that he was able to reveal and exhibit the many linguistic phenomena. If Humboldt was the theorist, Jespersen was the practitioner, and *The Philosophy of Grammar* may be regarded as the epitome of contrastive methodology.

叶斯柏森的另一个重要观点是强调语言比较研究中本民族的"语感"：

Another key concept raised by Jespersen is the speech instinct of the native speaker in contrastive analysis:

> 在比较词汇学中，我们常常可以看到词所表示的事物由于不同语言的不同习性而以不同的方式分类，在一种语言中融为一体的东西在另一种语言中却被区别开来……语法上也是如此，任何两种语言之间的分类及区别都是不同的。因此，在研究一种具体语言的语法时，重要的是尽可能仔细地了解该语言中实际存在的区别，而不是建立一个未经该集团或该民族的语感认可的、实际语言事实不能表现的范畴。
> （叶斯伯森，1924/1951: 49）

> In comparative lexicology we constantly see how the things to be represented by words are grouped differently according to the whims of different languages, what is fused together in one being separated in another…It is the same in grammar, where no two languages have the same groupings and make the same distinctions. In dealing with the grammar of a particular language it is therefore important to inquire as carefully as possible into the distinctions actually made by that language, without establishing any single category that is not shown by actual linguistic facts to be recognized by the speech-instinct of that community or nation.
> (Jespersen, 1924: 49)

在语言和民族性格的联系方面，叶斯柏森可能是走得颇远的一个，他不仅继承了洪堡特的"民族的语言即民族的精神,民族的精神即民族的语言"的思想,而且进行了实践,通过他对英语的深入而持久的研究,他提出了语言与民族性直接相通的观点。1938年,他出版了《英语的发展与结构》,得出了这样的结论:

It was also Jespersen who has ventured the most into the relations between language and nationality on Humboldt's premise of "the language is their spirit and the spirit their language". As an expert in the English language, Jespersen, a Dane, held that language corresponds exactly with nationality, so commented in *Growth and Structure of the English Language* (1938):

> 总体来说,英语是种有条有理的、有力的、讲究实际而头脑清醒的语言,它不太追求华丽和优雅,但追求逻辑上的一贯性,在语法及词汇上都反对过于严格的规则以致使生命变得狭窄。英语是如此,英语民族也是如此。(叶斯伯森,1938/1978:16)

> To sum up, the English language is a methodical, energetic, businesslike and sober language that does not care much for finery and elegance, but does care for logical consistency and is opposed to any attempt to narrow-in life by police regulations and strict rules either of grammar or of lexicon. As the language is, so also is the nation. (Jespersen, 1938: 16)

这可说是将洪堡特思想用到一个具有悠久历史和文化的民族语言的第一次大胆实践,这是叶斯柏森将英语与欧洲及其他地方许多语言(包括汉语)作比较后得出的结论。这本书对中国的林语堂有很大影响,林在看了这本书后,于同年出版了他的《吾国与吾民》的第二版,其中加进了论语言和民族性的一节。就像叶斯柏森将英语特点归结为"男性气质"(Jesperson,1938:2—16)一样,林语堂将汉语的特征归结为"女性气质"(Lin,1938:77—80)。潘文国(1997a/2002:110—113)曾对此进行过评论,

This was the conclusion Jespersen drew from contrasting the English language with many other languages from within and outside Europe, including the Chinese language. The Chinese scholar Lin Yutang was inspired by Jespersen's writing. Upon reading Jespersen (1938), Lin brought out a second edition of his book *My Country and my People* in the same year, with a new chapter on language and nationality in which he described the characteristics of the Chinese language as "feminine" after Jespersen's description of the English language as masculine (see Pan Wenguo, 1997a/2002: 110—13 for comment).

1.3.5 沃尔夫的杰出贡献
1.3.5 Contributions of Benjamin Lee Whorf

到今天为止，在对比语言研究中提及沃尔夫的，基本上没有超出我们在前面所引的一段话的范围，似乎沃尔夫对对比研究的贡献只是凑巧提出了一个对比语言学的术语而已。这是有失公允的，实际上这也是西方的对比语言学最终没有沿着沃尔夫所设想的方向前进的一个重要原因。在重新梳理西方的对比语言学史的同时，我们有必要对沃尔夫设想的对比研究作进一步考察。

To date, any mentioning of Whorf, if ever, in present contrastive linguistic literature has been strictly confined to the quote mentioned above as if it was mere by accident that Whorf coined the term "contrastive linguistics" and that it is all that he contributed to the study. This has done Whorf great injustice inasmuch that contrastive linguistics in the West finally chose to tread a path away from Whorf. We feel compelled to revisit Whorf's recommendation for contrastive analysis to gain a better perspective of the historical development of contrastive linguistics in the West.

沃尔夫在定义中提到，对比语言学"旨在研究不同语言在语法、逻辑和对经验的一般分析上的重大区别"，这句话到底是什么意思？他又是在什么基础上提出这句话的？综合考察沃氏的现存著作，我们认为这至少有以下几种含义：

Whorf repeatedly mentioned that it is the aim of contrastive linguistics to "plot the outstanding differences among tongues that are remotely connected—in grammar, logic and general analysis of experience." What exactly does he mean? What is the underlying base? Our attempt to answer these questions is as follows.

1.3.5.1 沃尔夫假说
1.3.5.1 Whorf's hypothesis

沃尔夫在语言学史上之出名，主要不是因为他提出了对比语言学的名称，而是因为以他名字命名的"沃尔夫假说"（或加上他老师名字的"沃尔夫—萨丕尔假说")。这一假说包括语言相对论和语言决定论两个内容,如果只谈论前者,就是一种"弱式"(weak form)的沃尔夫假说;如果兼包括后者,就是一种"强式"(strong form)的沃尔夫假说。沃尔夫假说提出以后,引起了轩然大波,遭到了来自各方面的批评。赞成者也多数停留在"弱式"上。据我们看来,很多批评者并未深入去理解沃氏的原意,而是从字面出发作了想当然的引申。本书不打算卷入这一争论,只想厘清沃氏的原意以及这一思想与他提出的对比语言学的关系。沃氏的"语言相对论"体现在下面一段话中:

Whorf got his name in the history of linguistics not for naming contrastive linguistics but for a hypothesis that has invited strong opinions. Named after him and his professor, Edward Safire, the Safire–Whorf hypothesis puts forward two assumptions: linguistic relativism and linguistic determinism. The former alone is a weak form of the hypothesis and to include the latter would result in a strong form. Those who supported support mostly the weak form. While it is not our intent to participate in the debate, it is our opinion that Whorf was not thoroughly understood and that most commentators dealt with the hypothesis only at face value. Going along the line of thought that led to his proposal of contrastive linguistics, we think the following quote best illustrates his original ideas of "linguistic relativity":

> 语言现象属于背景现象,说话的人对此浑然不觉,至多有一点十分模糊的意识。这就好比人们极少意识到屋里空气中尘埃微粒的存在,尽管语言对说话者的制约作用更类似于万有引力而非尘埃。这些必然的、无意识的语言型式并非为所有人所共有,每种语言都有自己特有的模式或型式。这些型式构成了语言形式化的一面,即"语法"。此处"语法"这一术语的意义远远超过我们在学校课本上所学语法的内容。由此即引出了我所说的"语言相对论原则"。用通俗的语言来讲,就是使用明显不同的语法的人,会因其使用的语法不同而有不同的观察行为,对相似的外在观察行为也会有不同的评价;因此,作为观察者他们是不对等的,也势必会产生在某种程度上不同的世界观。(沃尔夫,1940b/2001: 221/20—221)

> The phenomena of language are background phenomena, of which the talkers are unaware or, at the most, very dimly aware—as they are of the motes of dust in the air of a room, though the linguistic

phenomena govern the talkers more as gravitation than as dust would. These automatic, involuntary patterns of language are not the same for all men but are specific for each language and constitute the formalized side of the language, or its "grammar"—a term that includes much more than the grammar we learned in the textbooks of our school days. From this fact proceeds what I have called the "linguistic relativity principle", which means, in informal terms, that users of markedly different grammars are pointed by their grammars toward different types of observations and different evaluations of externally similar acts of observation, and hence are not equivalent as observers but must arrive at somewhat different views of the world. (Whorf, 1940b: 221)

而沃氏的"语言决定论"体现在下面一段原话中：
His original ideas on "linguistic determinism" are contained in the following:

> 我们已经发现，背景性的语言系统（或者说语法）不仅是一种用来表达思想的再生工具，而且它本身也在塑造我们的思想，规划和引导个人的心理活动，对头脑中的印象进行分析并对其储存的信息进行综合。想法的形成不是一个独立的、像过去被认为的那样非常理性的过程，而是特定语法的一部分，在不同的语法中或多或少有所不同。我们用自己的本族语所划的线切分自然。我们从现象世界中分离出范畴和种类，并不是因为它们客观地呈现于每一个观察者面前；相反，呈现在我们面前的世界是千变万化的印象流，它们是通过我们的大脑组织起来的——在很大程度上是用我们大脑中的语言体系组织起来的。我们将自然进行切分，用各种概念将它组织起来，并赋予这些概念不同的意义。这种切分和组织在很大程度上取决于一个契约，即我们所在的整个语言共同体约定以这种方式组织自然、并将它编码固定于我们的语言型式之中。当然，这一契约是隐性的，并无明文规定，但它的条款却有着绝对的约束力；如果我们不遵守它所规定的语料的编排和分类方式，就根本无法开口讲话。（沃尔夫，1940a/2001：212—214/211。着重号是原有的。）
>
> It was found that the background linguistic system (in other words, the grammar) of each language is not merely a reproducing instrument

for voicing ideas but rather is itself the shaper of ideas, the program and guide for the individual's mental activity, for his analysis of impressions, for his synthesis of his mental stock in trade. Formulation of ideas is not an independent process, strictly rational in the old sense, but is part of a particular grammar, and differs, from slightly to kalei-doscopic flux of impressions which has to be organised by our minds—and this means largely by the linguistic systems in our minds. We cut nature up, organize it into concepts, and ascribe significances as we do, largely because we are parties to an agreement to organize it in this way—an agreement that holds throughout our speech community and is codified in the patterns of our language. The agreement is, of course, an implicit and unstated one, BUT ITS TERMS ARE ABSOLUTELY OBLIGATORY; we cannot talk at all except by subscribing to the organization and classification of data which the agreement decrees. (Whorf, 1940a: 212—214)

沃尔夫通过自己对美洲印第安人的一些语言，特别是霍皮语（Hopi）等的研究论证了他的看法，这里不引。更重要的是沃尔夫由人类语言的不同引发了对人类文化和思维方式的深入思考，下面一段话体现出了他远远超出一般语言学家的博大胸怀，从而足以使他进入20世纪重要的思想家和哲学家的行列：

We do not intend to discuss the evidence Whorf drew from his research into the Hopi language and other Indian languages. What we want to highlight are the reflections Whorf had on the relations between human culture and its thought patterns sparked off by the differences in languages. In his own words,

> 语言学对科学的一大重要贡献可能是视角意识的进一步发展。我们不会再把印欧语系的几种同源语以及以之为基础发展出来的理性化方法看作人类心智的顶峰，也不会把它们目前的广泛传播看作是适者生存的结果，而只会把它看作是某些历史事件的结果——只有从受益方的狭隘观点来看，这些事件才可能被称为好事。我们不会再认为这些语言以及与之相伴的我们的思维过程囊括了全部理念和知识，而会认为它们只是广袤星系中的一个星座。当我们充分地认识了全球语言系统惊人的多元性，我们就会不可避免地感到，人类的精神令人难以置信地古老；我们以文字记录的几千年历史，在衡量我们在这个星球以往经验的尺度

上，不过是细细的一道铅笔痕。（沃尔夫，1940a/2001: 218）

One significant contribution to science from the linguistic point of view may be the greater development of our sense of perspective. We shall no longer be able to see a few recent dialects of the Indo-European family, and the rationalizing techniques elaborated from their patterns, as the apex of the evolution of the human mind, nor their present wide spread as due to any survival from fitness or to anything but a few events of history—events that could be called fortunate only from the parochial point of view of the favored parties. They, and our own thought processes with them, can no longer be envisioned as spanning the gamut of reason and knowledge but only as one constellation in a galactic expanse. A fair realization of the incredible degree of diversity of linguistic system that ranges over the globe leaves one with an inescapable feeling that the human spirit is inconceivably old; that the thickness of a pencil mark on the scale measures our past experience on this planet; that the events of these recent millenniums spell nothing in any evolutionary wise, that the race has taken no sudden spurt, achieved no commanding synthesis during recent millenniums, but has only played a little with a few of the linguistic formulations and views of nature bequeathed from an inexpressibly longer past. (Whorf, 1940a: 218)

因此，为他的论文集作序的蔡斯（Stuart Chase, 1955：x）将他与爱因斯坦并提，并非完全没有道理。

In the above, Whorf demonstrates a breadth of mind sufficient to rank him among the most prominent thinkers and philosophers of the twentieth century. It is not without reason that Stuart Chase (1955: x) put him on par with Einstein.

对沃尔夫假说如何评价，这里暂不讨论。但沃尔夫假说是沃尔夫提出对比语言学的根本出发点，这里却不能不提及。下面我们来看看这一假说如何导致他的对比语言学思想以及他的对比研究方法论。

While we reserve our comments on Whorf's hypothesis, we have to state that it is the underlying premise for the formulation of contrastive linguistics. How is that so? What was in Whorf's mind when he proposed contrastive linguistics, and how did he propose to apply it? We shall see below.

1.3.5.2 从沃尔夫假说到对比语言学
1.3.5.2 From Whorf's hypothesis to contrastive linguistics

从沃尔夫假说出发，沃尔夫自然而然地得出了三个结论。第一，既然语言和思维方式的差异是多种多样的，因而要了解人类的全部智慧，就必须研究和比较各种各样的语言，特别是差别很大的语言。他说：

It is natural for Whorf to deduce from his hypothesis three conclusions. Given that there exist a variety of languages and thought patterns, to have a grasp of human wisdom necessarily means studying and contrasting the languages, particularly those that are remotely connected. Whorf explained his first belief as follows:

> 如果一条规律没有例外的话，它就不会被当成规律或其他什么，就成了我们无意识当中经验背景的一部分。如果我们从来没有经历过与之形成对比的东西，我们就不可能将它分离出来，概括成规律；只有随着经验的丰富和参照系的扩大，当我们体验了规律性的打破之后，才能将它分离、概括出来。（沃尔夫，1940a/2001: 209/206—207）

> What it might well suggest to us today is that, if a rule has absolutely no exceptions, it is not recognized as a rule or as anything else; it is then part of the background of experience of which we tend to remain unconscious. Never having experienced anything in contrast to it, we cannot isolate it and formulate it as a rule until we so enlarge our experience and expand our base of reference that we encounter an interruption of its regularity. (Whorf, 1940a: 209)

> 当语言学家能够用一种批评的、科学的态度去检验许多模式差别很大的语言的时候，他们的参照基础便得到了扩展；在此以前被认为具有普遍性的现象，其普遍性已被打破；一种全新的意义秩序进入了他们的视野。（沃尔夫，1940a/2001: 212/211）

> When linguists became able to examine critically and scientifically a large number of languages of widely different patterns, their base of reference was expanded; they experienced an interruption of phenomena hitherto held universal, and a whole new order of significances came into their ken. (Whorf, 1940a: 212)

第二，由于以上认识，因此他对当时以印欧语为中心的比较语言学以及在此基础上形成的一元语言观特别担忧：

It was in this regard that Whorf was particularly fearful of the intensification of linguistic monism as a likely consequence of the European-centric contrastive view:

  假如我们只比较现代欧洲语言，或者再加上拉丁语和希腊语，这一令人惊讶的结论（笔者按：指语言相对论）并不明显。这些语言的基本模式带有一致性，而这种一致性初看起来似乎证明了自然逻辑。但这种一致性的存在仅仅是出于以下原因：这些语言是同属印欧语系的同源语，其基本轮廓大致相同，从历史角度看是从很久以前的同一个言语共同体传承而来；这些同源语长期以来分担了形成一种共同文化的任务；这种共同文化中较为理性的许多成分，源于拉丁语和希腊语的语言背景。所以，这组语言是满足了上一段末尾"除非"从句的条件（笔者按：指"除非它们的语言背景相近，或是可以通过某种方式得到校准"），是语言相对论原则中的一个特例。（沃尔夫，1940a/2001: 214/212）

  The rather startling conclusion (referring to linguistic relativity) is not so apparent if we compare only our modern European languages, with perhaps Latin and Greek thrown in for good measure. Among these tongues there is a unanimity of major pattern which at first seems to bear out natural logic. But this unanimity exists only because these tongues are all Indo-European dialects cut to the same basic plan, being historically transmitted from what was long ago one speech community; because the modern dialects have long shared in building up a common culture; and because much of this culture, on the more intellectual side, is derived from the linguistic backgrounds of Latin and Greek. Thus this group of languages satisfies the special case of the clause beginning with "unless" in the statement of the linguistic relativity principle at the end of the preceding paragraph (i.e. "all observers are not led by the same physical evidence to the same picture of the universe, unless their linguistic backgrounds are similar, or can in some way be calibrated"). (Whorf, 1940a: 214)

他甚至说："现代中国或土耳其的科学家们在对世界进行描述时，使用了和西方科学家们一样的术语。这一事实只说明他们全盘套用了西方的理性体系，而不意味着他们立足于本族语观察角度证实了这一体系。"（同上）他批评有人设想将来的世界是一个只讲一种语言的世界，认为这是一种错误的理想。他进一步说：

He was sharp to point out "that modern Chinese or Turkish scientists describe the world in the same terms as Western scientists means, of course, only that they have taken over bodily the entire Western system of rationalizations, not that they have corroborated that system from their native posts of observation." (*ibid*.: 214) Disapproving of and denouncing thoughts that envision a future world speaking only one language, Whorf contended that it would:

> 一元语言世界会对人类思维能力的进化造成极大损害。西方语言已经通过自己的语言对现实做了某种暂时性、试探性的分析，如果没有更正，这一分析就会被当成是最终的、绝对的。要更正它，唯一的出路在于其他语言。（沃尔夫，1941/2001: 244/247）

> …hold a misguided ideal and would do the evolution of the human mind the greatest disservice. Western culture has made, through language, a provisional analysis of reality and, without correctives lie in all those other tongues which by aeons of independent evolution have arrived at different, but equally logical, provisional analyses. (Whorf, 1941: 244)

第三，因此在对比研究中，必须寻找与母语非常不同的语言来进行对比。沃尔夫说：

From the above came his third point of view, that is, meaningful contrastive analysis must be grounded on comparison with languages that are distant from the native tongue. Whorf explained:

> 要评价语法范畴如此广泛深远的影响是非常困难的。一方面它涉及语言运用时的背景特征，一方面也因为我们很难站在作为我们的习惯和文化的语言之外来客观地审视我们自己的语言。而如果我们选择一种非常不同的语言，这种语言于我们而言就成了自然的一部分，我们甚至有可能像对待自然那样来对待它……在研究它的过程中，无论我们愿意不愿意，我们都不得不脱离母语常规的束缚。而后我

们会发现，外来语言是观察我们自己语言的一面镜子。（沃尔夫，1939a/2001: 137—138/123）

But the difficulty of appraising such a far-reaching influence (of grammatical categories) is great because of its background character, because of the difficulty of standing aside from our own language, which is a habit and a cultural *non est disputandum*, and scrutinizing it objectively. And if we take a very dissimilar language, this language becomes a part of nature, and we even do to it what we have already done to nature…and the best approach is through an exotic language, for in its study we are at long last pushed willy-nilly out of our ruts. Then we find that the exotic language is a mirror held up to our own. (Whorf, 1939a: 137—8)

以上三方面可说是沃尔夫对比语言学观的根本内容。理解这一点，对理解对比语言学在西方和中国的不同发展历史是有意义的。我们就会知道，为什么西方后来的对比研究会在相当程度上偏离沃尔夫的路线，因为他们从事的往往是与他们的母语相差不远的语言的"对比"研究，而汉语学者在面对面貌迥异的西方语言同时执着地寻找"汉语特点"的过程中，却自觉不自觉地、而且随着时间推移越来越强烈地接受了沃尔夫的对比语言学观。

These three standpoints represent Whorf's underlying position in contrastive linguistics. Without this understanding nothing significant could be said about the separate paths contrastive analysis has taken in the West and in China. Without this understanding, it will not be obvious that unless Western analysts start contrasting the native tongues with languages in distant families, it will be necessary for contrastive studies in the West to move away from the Whorfian ideology. In contrast, Chinese scholars in their tenacious quest for things unique to the Chinese language unknowingly and increasingly buy strongly into the Whorfian contrastive notions.

1.3.5.3 范畴研究——沃尔夫的对比研究方法论
1.3.5.3 Categorical research: the Whorfian contrastive methodology

沃尔夫短短的一生（1897—1941）为现代语言学留下了三个带有他个人印记的术语：沃尔夫假说、对比语言学和隐性范畴。三个术语都分别为人所经常引用，但迄今为止还从未有人将这三者联系起来进行过论述，仿佛这三者都是各自独立、互不相关似的。其实据我们看来，这三者是密切相关、互不可分的，缺少了其中之一，就不是对沃尔夫学说的全面理解。沃尔夫假说或语言相对论是沃尔夫语言学的哲学基础；对比语言学是他实际从事（并不只是"提出"一个术语）并期望后人能够继续的整个语言学或普通语言学的研究，从这一点看，他和洪堡特的"普通语言学即对比语言学"的精神是一脉相承的；而包括隐性范畴在内的范畴研究则是他所提出的对比研究的方法论。

In modern linguistics, the Whorf hypothesis, contrastive linguistics and covert category are three common terminologies bearing the mark of Benjamin Lee Whorf, a gift from his stay with us in the years 1897 to 1941. However, as if the three are separate entities altogether, no one has ever attempted to link up the three concepts. In our view, not only are they closely related, but they form an organic whole. Whorf's hypothesis or linguistic relativity is the cornerstone of his philosophy, whereas contrastive linguistics is what he actually put into practice—not merely a shallow jargon—with the expectation that this particular business of general linguistics would be carried on by later generations using such contrastive methodologies as those proposed by him, including covert category in categorization research. In this light, Whorf and Humboldt are on the same side, taking general linguistics to be contrastive linguistics in essence.

沃尔夫非常不满将印欧语研究得出的一些结果简单地推向世界其他语言，他说：

Europe-centric researchers often extrapolate the conclusions drawn from contrasting Indo-European languages to other languages of the world. Whorf was particularly critical of this:

> 语言学家们已经将印欧语系诸语言研究了很长时间，他们能将这些语言句法结构上的典型序列及产生的语义效果归纳为某些一般形式，例如主语和襄助语、施事、动作、目的、定语和中心语、外向

结构和内向结构。对于那些与印欧语非常不同的语言，他们也能对其中与印欧语有表面相似性的关系进行命名和分析。但是后面这种能力在很多情况下实际上不过是一个幸运的巧合，有时则可能是不幸的巧合。（沃尔夫，1939b/2001: 160—161/149—150）

> Linguists have studied the Indo-European languages so long that they have been able to generalize their most typical sequences and resultant semantic effects into such general formulas as subject and predicate, actor, action, and goal, attribute and head, and exocentric versus endocentric; also to tag and handle relations that have a superficial similarity in languages that may otherwise differ greatly from Indo-European. But this last ability must turn out in many cases to be only a happy, or at times perhaps an unhappy accident. (Whorf, 1939b: 160—161)

正是在这一认识的基础上，沃尔夫提出了研究语法范畴的思想。从某种角度看，语法范畴的研究正是为了避免具体语言、特别是"均质印欧语"（Standard Average European）的先入之见，这有点类似于后来的对比学者提出的寻找"对比中立项"的立场。沃尔夫说：

This very perception is exactly where Whorf grounded his call to study grammatical categorization. To a certain extent, the purpose of examining grammatical categorization is really to prevent dominance of the subjectivity of specific languages, especially standard average European languages. A similar concept in present-day analysis would be *tertium comparationis*. Explaining his proposal, Whorf said:

> 人们似乎有一种自然倾向，喜欢使用传统语法的术语，如动词、名词、形容词、被动语态等，来描述印欧语系以外的语言。这种倾向极有可能引起误解。我们十分需要采用某种方法来定义这些术语，以便我们能够利用它们带来的便利，并在可能的情况下，将它们以科学的、一致的方式应用于外语。为做到这一点，我们必须采用全球视角来观察语言现象，重新审视在语言中发现的各类语法范畴，在某种新的意义上建构和修订概念，增加必要的术语。（沃尔夫，1937/2001: 87/62）

> The very natural tendency to use terms derived from traditional grammar, like verb, noun, adjective, passive voice, in describing

languages outside of Indo-European is fraught with grave possibilities of misunderstanding. At the same time it is desirable to define these terms in such a way that we can avail ourselves of their great convenience and, where possible, apply them to exotic languages in a scientific and consistent way. To do this, we must re-examine the types of grammatical category that are found in languages, using a worldwide view of linguistic phenomena, frame concepts more or less new, and make needed additions to terminology. (Whorf, 1937: 87)

为此他提出了显性范畴和隐性范畴、选择范畴和系数范畴、具体范畴和一般范畴等一些概念，其中最重要、也最为后人称道的是隐性范畴的概念。沃尔夫指出：
The categories raised by Whorf include overt categories and covert categories, selective categories and modulus categories, specific categories and generic categories. Of these, the covert category is the single most important concept:

> 一个隐性范畴也可称为"隐型"（cryptotype），这一名称引起人们去注意这类词组具有相当隐秘的性质，特别是当它们在意义上没有强烈的差异，也没有被经常出现的反应特征（如代词）标记出来的时候。它们很容易被忽略，也很难定义，然而会对语言行为有深远的影响。（沃尔夫，1937/2001：68）
>
> A covert category may also be termed a *cryptotype*, a name which calls attention to the rather hidden, cryptic nature of such word-groups, especially when they are not strongly contrasted in idea, nor marked by frequently occurring reactances such as pronouns. They easily escape notice and may be hard to define, and yet may have profound influence on linguistic behavior. (Whorf, 1937: 92)

从这一点看，它与洪堡特提出的"内蕴语言形式"十分相似。
From the above elucidation, a cryptotype is equivalent to Humboldt's "inner forms of language".

从上面的论述可以看到，沃尔夫对对比语言的贡献不仅仅是提出了一个名称，而是提出了一个相当完整并且具有实际可操作性的研究体系。但是这一设想后来居然会在它的发源地美国以及其他地方被忘得干干净净，这是很值得对比语言学界重新检讨的。芬兰学者沙亚伐拉（Kari Sajavaara）后来指出：
In sum, Whorf went way beyond a mere terminology to provide a relatively

complete and workable research framework. It is extraordinary that this whole idea is being forgotten for the most part in its birthplace. It is indeed food for thought. Finnish scholar Kari Sajavaara remarked:

> 尽管人们们没有意识到，对比分析其实有两个出发点。一个是世纪之交和三十年代的语言类型的对比研究（参见Fisiak，1975: 341），一个是四十年代后的现代对比研究（Fries，1945; Trager，1949）。在怀恩来赫（Weinreich，1953）和拉多（Lado, 1957）的著作发表以后，对比研究的理论目标几乎被忘得干干净净了。在很长一段时间里，他们的观点，即学习中的困难等于所对比的两种语言间系统的差异，对于对比分析有着极大的影响。（沙亚伐拉，1981: 34）

> Contrastive analysis had a twin starting-point, although this has not always been recognized. This concerns both the contrastive type of linguistic analysis at the turn of the century and in the thirties (see Fisiak, 1975: 341), and the beginnings of modern contrastive analysis in the forties (Fries, 1945; Trager, 1949). The theoretical objectives were almost entirely forgotten in the wake of Weinreich's (1953) and Lado's (1957) work. For a long time, their idea that learning difficulties are equal to the difference between the systems of the two languages contrasted remained highly influential in contrastive analysis. (Sajavaara, 1981: 34)

不过他所说的"世纪之交"和三十年代的对比研究并不是我们所说的叶斯柏森、沃尔夫等人，而是前面提到的格朗根特等人和布拉格学派的马泰修斯（V. Mathesius）等人。可见在这些回顾者的心目中，沃尔夫也早已被忘却了，而他所谈到的对比语言学的"理论目标"，也同沃尔夫等人的设想有了不小的差距。

However, Sajavaara was really referring to C. H. Grandgent, V. Mathesius of the Prague school and others when speaking of contrastive linguistics at the turn of the century as well as in the 1930s. In other words, Whorf was still missing from the picture in all these historical reviews. Therefore we do not expect his lament on disoriented "theoretical aims" to be arguing on the same grounds, as these were probably a different set of aims from those suggested by Whorf and the rest.

1.4 第二期（20世纪40—70年代）：在主流语言学理论转向中寻求立足点的开拓

1.4 Phase 2 (1940s—1970s): Riding the waves of transition in theoretical linguistics

第二个时期从弗里斯（Charles Fries, 1945）和拉多开始，主要活跃在五、六十年代，其特点是以美国结构主义语言学和行为主义心理学作为其哲学和方法论基础，并且以第二语言教学为唯一指归。弗里斯和拉多的下面两段名言是整个这段时期对比研究的南针：

The two notable figures in this phase were Charles Fries and Robert Lado, both active in the 1950s—1960s. In their hands, contrastive linguistics draws theoretical and methodological inspirations from the structuralists and behaviourists. Servicing the needs of second language pedagogy was the single most important aim. As Fries and Lado put it:

> 建立在将学习者母语与目的语进行细致描写并比较基础上的教材，是最有效的教材。（弗里斯，1945: 9）
>
> The most effective materials are those that are based upon a scientific description of the language to be learned, carefully compared with a parallel description of the native language of the learner. (Fries, 1945: 9)
>
> 本书的基本假设是，通过系统地比较母语和目的语的语言文化，我们能够预测并描写哪些型式在学习时会造成困难而哪些不会。（拉多，1957: vii）
>
> The plan of the book rests on the assumption that we can predict and describe the patterns that will cause difficulty in learning, and those that will not cause difficulty, by comparing systematically the language and culture to be learned with the native language and culture of the student. (Lado, 1957: Preface)

从文献来看，我们调查了芬兰学者沙亚伐拉和雷托能（Jaakko Lehtonen）编的《应用对比研究文献1965—1980》（Sajavaara, Jakko, 1981）中的60年代部分，这部分文献共92篇，其中一半（46篇）是一般性讨论，其余的几乎全涉及其他语言的英语学习者将母语与英语对比，其中德语10篇，法语4篇，芬兰语4篇，波兰语3篇，塞尔维亚—克罗地亚语3篇，伊朗语2篇，瑞典语2篇，荷兰语、意大利语、西班牙语、丹麦语、汉语、斯瓦希利语（Swahili）、日语、锡兰语（Ceylon）、匈牙利语、泰语、菲律宾的塔加拉语（Tagalog）、塔米尔语（Tamil）、印第安人的Navajo语各1篇，牙买加的克利奥耳语（Jamaican Creole）1篇，德语、法语、拉丁语合在一起与英语比较1篇，西班牙语、匈牙利语与泰语合在一起与英语作比较1篇，印第安人的Navajo语、Chotaw语和Papago语合在一起与英语比较1篇，合计45篇。英语之外的只有1篇，是教说英语的人学习塔米尔语的。可见这一时期的对比分析主要是为在全世界推广英语服务的。这一阶段的文献，除拉多的名作之外，主要有1962年至1965年出版的一套结构对比研究系列和1968年乔治顿圆桌会议的论文集（Alatis, 1968）。乔治顿会议是这一时期对比研究的最高潮，同时也标志着对比分析走向衰落，因为就在这次会议上，人们对对比分析提出了严厉批评，并提出以偏误分析（EA, Error Analysis, 由于"error"的通常意义"错误"是个负面概念，而在第二语言学习中产生"error"又是正常现象，因此中国学术界译成了一个中性词"偏误"）来与之竞争，此后对比分析随即淡出美国语言学界。美国应用语言学中心（Center for Applied Linguistics, Arlington, Virginia）所计划的英语与五大主要语言的对比研究系列最后只出版了三种[1]。欧洲从1960年代中期起，也开始了一系列与英语比较的项目，如德语—英语、波兰语—英语、塞尔维亚—克罗拉亚语与英语、罗马尼亚语—英语、匈牙利语—英语，20世纪70年代后又增加了芬兰语—英语、丹麦语—英语、法语—英语等。虽然都有些阶段性成果，但真正完成的对比语法只有《英波对比语法导论》（Fisiak et al. 1978）和《德英对比语言学》（Burgschmidt et al. 1974）两部，而且其重点都不是语法而是对比一般理论。美国学者迪·皮德娄（Robert Di Pietro）的《语言结构对比》（1971），完全从乔姆斯基开创的转换生成语法的角度进行对比研究，体现了这一阶段后期的研究趋势。这也是继拉多之

---

[1] 英德比较：Moulton（1962）的《英德语音比较》、Kufner（1962）的《英德语法比较》；英西比较：Stockwell与Bowen（1965）的《英西语音比较》、Stockwell、Bowen与Martin（1965）的《英西语法比较》；英意比较：Agard与Di Pietro（1965）的《英意语音比较》和《英意语法比较》。

English vs. German: Moulton (1962), *The Sounds of English and German*; Kufner (1962), *The Grammatical Structures of English and German*; English vs. Spanish: Stockwell and Bowen (1965), *The Sounds of English and Spanish*, Stockwell, Bowen and Martin (1965), *The Grammatical Structures of English and Spanish*; English vs. Italian: Agard and Di Pietro (1965), *The Sounds of English and Italian* and *The Grammatical Structures of English and Italian*.

后，第一部完整意义上的对比语言学理论著作。

  From the bibliography in the applied contrastive analysis edited by Sajavaara and Jaakko Lehtonen (1981) for the period 1965 to 1980, in the 1960s alone, out of the 92 papers collected, 46 (50 percent) were general discussion, while the other half analysed various native tongues against the English language from the English learners' point of view: ten on German, four on French, four on Finnish, three on Polish, three on Serbian-Croatian, two on Persian, two on Swedish and one each on Dutch, Italian, Spanish, Danish, Chinese, Swahili, Japanese, Ceylon, Hungarian, Thai, Tagalog, Tamil, Navajo and Jamaican Creole; one comparing German, French and Latin with English, one comparing Spanish, Hungarian and Thai with English and one comparing Choctaw and Papago with English. The only paper targeted at English-speakers was teaching them how to speak Tamil. As can be seen, contrastive analysis in the period worked almost singlemindedly to promote use of the English language worldwide. In terms of publication, besides the anchor work of Lado, we cannot fail to mention the series of structural contrastive analysis published in 1962—1965 and the essay collection of the Georgetown roundtable conference of 1968 (Alatis, 1968). The Georgetown conference marked both the height and the fall of contrastive linguistics in this period. It was at this conference that contrastive analysis was most critically scrutinized. It was also here that error analysis (EA) was suggested as the challenge. The rise of EA was the end of CA, at least in America. The plan by the Center for Applied Linguistics, Arlington, VA, to contrast English with five other major languages halted at only three. Turning to Europe in 1960s—1970s, there was a very prosperous business of comparing and contrasting the native tongues with English. That includes German, Polish, Serbian-Croatian, Romanian, Hungarian, Finnish, Danish and French, among others. Although there were some findings from these researches, something more complete can be found in only two of them. Fisiak et al., *The Poznan' Polish-English Contrastive Project* (1978) and Burgschmidt et al., *Kontrastive Linguistik Deutsch/English* (1974) both touch on the general contrastive principles rather than concentrating on syntax. With the rise of Chomsky and transformation grammar, scholars made every attempt to apply the theory to CA. Representing the research trend of the later part of this phase was Robert Di Pietro, whose *Language Structures in Contrast* (1971) is, in a theoretical sense, the next abstract book on CA after Lado.

1.4.1 拉多的划时代之作《跨文化语言学》
1.4.1 Lado's *Linguistics Across Culture*

1957年，拉多（Robert Lado）出版了《跨文化语言学：语言教师的应用语言学》一书，顿时声名鹊起，在语言教学界产生了重要影响，后来的对比语言学史家更把这一年和这一部书当作是对比语言学诞生的标志。对于这样一部书，站在今天的立场上，我们有必要来作一番认真的回顾和探索，特别是对其历史地位，要作出恰如其分的评价。

Linguistics Across Culture (Lado, 1957)—a landmark work that represents the birth of contrastive linguistics—has had great repercussions in language teaching and has won Robert Lado fame. A book of such significance deserves careful reading and review to give it a justifiable place in history.

《跨文化语言学》一书篇幅不大，全书共分6章，第1章谈比较语言文化的必要性，第2—5章分别讨论如何比较语音系统、语法结构、词汇系统、文字系统及文化。这是一部实用性远大于其理论性的著作。而且全书唯一提到"理论对比分析"之处，是说"将外语与本族语比较得出的问题分门别类，对于教学、测试、研究及理解特别有用。但这样列出的一个目录只是假设性的，要最终产生效果，必须放到学生实际使用的言语中去检验。"（Lado, 1957: 72）显然这样的"理论"，与此前沃尔夫等人谈的理论没有什么共同之处。那它的历史价值体现在哪里呢？我们必须联系整个对比语言学的发展史来看这个问题。

Linguistics Across Culture comprises six chapters and opens with the necessity for comparing languages and cultures. Chapters 2—5 examine the methodology of comparing sound systems, syntactic systems, lexicographical systems, writing systems and cultures. It is a practically oriented book, and the only "theoretical" part is the mention of the use of theoretical comparative analysis: "The list of problem resulting from the comparison of the foreign language with the native language will be a most significant list for teaching, testing, research and understanding. Yet it must be considered a list of hypothetical problems until final validation is achieved by checking it against the actual speech of students" (Lado, 1957: 72). Obviously, the "theory" Lado referred to was nothing similar to what Whorf and the rest were talking about as mentioned above. The question is, then, what historical significance is there in Lado's point? To answer that, we will have to begin with the development of contrastive linguistics.

1.4.1.1 对比研究的重大转向
1.4.1.1 Major trend shift in contrastive linguistics

老实说，在拉多之前，对比语言学虽已提出了十多年，但根本不为人所知，拉多的书也没有提及"对比"一词，自始至终用的都是"比较"。只是拉多的书在第二语言教学界产生影响之后，"对比分析"变得广为人知，追根溯源，人们才将创始人的桂冠戴到了拉多头上。因而从对比语言学发展史的角度看，拉多的书确实有着重要意义。这个意义可以从两个方面去理解：如果我们撇开沃尔夫等人，我们可说拉多引发了语言比较研究的一个新时代，开创了一个新的研究传统，并从目标和方法上奠定了一套新的基础和操作规则；但如果沿着历史的长河、将他与以前的对比语言学研究联系起来看，我们可以给他另一个历史定位，那就是标志着对比研究的重大转向。这个转向表现为：

We note that for more than a decade before Lado, contrastive linguistics as a new terminology and as a specific research vision was already in existence, but rather quietly. The low awareness is also evident in Lado's work, in that "compare" was used throughout and the term "contrast" was nowhere to be found. Ironically, it was the popularity of Lado's work in the second language acquisition field that contrastive analysis was all of a sudden made common. Now we understand why Lado was traced to be the source. His work is indeed significant from the historical development point of view. But we could interpret further. Others aside, Lado really opens up a new era, a new research tradition in the contrastive analysis of languages, setting new goals on new grounds and new rules of games in terms of methodology. Historically speaking, alongside all previous developments, we could perhaps view his contribution as earmarking a major shift in research trend. The shift is demonstrated in the following ways.

（1）从理论转向应用
(1) From theory to application

无论在洪堡特、叶斯柏森还是沃尔夫的眼里，对比研究都是为语言研究的根本目标服务的，是理论语言学的一部分，或者说，对比语言学就是普通语言学。在拉多的书里，我们看不到洪堡特和沃尔夫那样的博大胸怀，而是非常现实的外语教学的需要。弗里斯在为该书写的"前言"（见Lado，1957）中说，结构主义语言学的兴起使外语教学的关注点从教学法转向了教材编写，而教材编写的前提就是对两种语言文化进行系统的比较。拉多更在其"序言"的开头开宗明义地说：

Be it Humboldt, Jespersen or Whorf, contrastive analysis is a means to an end; it is for the ultimate concern of language research that is essentially part of theoretical linguistics. Or we could say contrastive linguistics, taken to be providing the framework about describing languages and the universal aspects of languages, is, in their eyes, general linguistics. Such were high aims not seen in Lado's work, which was directed at the needs of foreign language teaching. In the foreword, Fries (1957) begins by saying that the rise of "structural" analysis has served to shift the focus of first attention from methods and techniques of teaching to the basis upon which to build these materials. And building the materials will involve the preliminary work of systematic linguistic-cultural comparisons to find the special problems arising out of any effort to develop a new set of language habits against a background of different native language habits. Lado phrased it even more plainly in the beginning of his book:

> 本书探索的是应用语言学及文化研究的一个崭新的领域，即通过比较任何两种语言和文化，来发现和描写一种语言的使用者在学习另一种语言时会碰到的问题。这一比较的结果对于教材编写、教学测试及学习实验具有十分重要的意义。外语教师懂得了这些知识，就会具有明锐的眼光，掌握一种工具，用来评估教材和试卷中的语言文化内容、在使用中补充新材料或编写新教材，以及精确地诊断学生在学习中的困难。（拉多，1957: vii）

> This book presents a fairly new field of applied linguistics and the analysis of culture, namely the comparison of any two languages and cultures to discover and describe the problems that the speakers of one of the languages will have in learning the other. The results of such comparisons have proved fundamental value for the preparation of teaching materials,

tests, and language learning experiments. Foreign language teachers who understand this field will acquire insights and tools for evaluating the language and culture content of textbooks and test, supplementing the materials in use, preparing new materials and tests, and diagnosing student difficulties accurately. (Lado, 1957: Preface)

在洪堡特等人构想的"比较语言研究"或"对比语言学"里，对比语言学就是语言学或普通语言学或理论语言学；而到了拉多这里，比较研究（即后人称的"对比分析"）却成了应用语言学的一部分，更确切地说，只是为外语教学服务的实用工具。这是一个重大的、根本性的转向。我们甚至可以说，从此以后，"对比语言学"有了两种版本，一种是洪堡特等人开创的，一种是弗里斯和拉多开创的，两者虽然有联系，也有共同之处，但在根本的旨趣和目标上多有所不同。每个有志于从事对比研究的人，在开始前实在应该好好想一想，你想从事的是定位于"语言学"的对比研究呢？还是定位于"应用语言学"的对比研究？

The comparative study of languages or contrastive linguistics conceived by Humboldt and the like is general or theoretical linguistics in itself. In the hands of Lado, comparative study (or later referred to as contrastive analysis) is really part of applied linguistics and specifically services foreign language acquisition. This is a shift at the root. We could even say that from then on there have been two branches of contrastive linguistics; one goes on the Humboldt tradition and the other goes along with Fries and Lado. The two fall on different grounds having a different object of inquiry. Anyone interested in contrastive analysis should distinguish between the two and find their place in either "linguistics" or "applied linguistics".

（2）从意义转向形式

(2) From meaning to form

洪堡特和沃尔夫等人的对比研究注重语言与民族精神的关系，其背后隐然有着"语言世界观"的理论的影子，意义在其中的重要性毋庸赘言。而纵观拉多的书，尽管从第2到第6的各章具体对比中，他处处强调要比较三个方面，形式、意义，以及形式和意义的分布，但可以看得出，他的重点始终在形式上。表现在他在谈到与形式密切的语音、语法对比时头头是道（第2、3章），谈到与意义密切的词汇时左支右绌（第4章），而谈到形式难以描述的文化对比时简直有些不知所云（第6章）。不过反过来，对只具"形式"的文字进行对比（第5章）也有些勉为其难，实际上像各说各的。大约由于这些原因，因而拉多之后，在西方搞对比研究的，大多注重语音语法，很少人搞文字文化，词汇对比也鲜见出色之作。

Contrastive study in the Humboldt tradition undertakes to uncover the relations between language and the spirit of the people believing that, in every language spoken, there exists a peculiar view of the world and that this necessarily lends weight to meaning of utterance. On a separate ground, Lado stresses comparison on three fronts: forms, meanings—however, and the distribution of forms and meanings, but forms remained the centre of attention in his illustrations. His comparison of sound and syntactic systems (Chapters 2 and 3) demonstrates the most strength. It seems a little short on the comparison of vocabulary systems (Chapter 4) that is closely linked to meanings; as for the chapter on cultural comparison (Chapter 6) which is loose on forms, he seems quite lost. But even on the comparison of writing systems that are "form-governed", his descriptions seem fragmented (Chapter 5). The above apparently accounts for the convergence on comparison of sound and syntactic systems in the West. Few can work when analyzing writing systems or culture, and those on vocabulary shed little light.

这里以拉多提出的词汇对比的方法为例：
The methodology proposed by Lado for comparing vocabulary should explain why:

比较母语和外语的词汇，会发现这些情况：（1）形义均相同；（2）形同义不同；（3）义同形不同；（4）形义均不同；（5）结构类型不同；（6）基本义相同内涵不同；（7）意义相同但地理分布受限制……"同"指在两种语言里的一般功能"相同"，由于语言行为中没有什么绝对相同的，因而这个"同"指的只是翻译中的对等物。"形"指的则是读音，而非字形。（拉多，1957: 82）

Comparing the foreign language vocabulary with that of the native language we will find words that are (1) similar in form and meaning, (2) similar in form but different in meaning, (3) similar in meaning but different in form, (4) different in form and meaning, (5) different in their types of construction, (6) similar in their primary meaning but different in connation, and (7) similar in meaning but with restrictions in geographical distribution…The term similar is restricted here to items that would function as "same" in both languages in ordinary use. We know that complete sameness is not to be expected in language behavior. The actual behavioral boundaries of similarity depend on the items that persons of one language "identify" or "translate" as same from and into the other language. References to form are to the sounds of the words, not to the spelling, even though spelling rather than phonetic representation is often used in this chapter. (Lado, 1957: 82)

"形义均同"、"形同义不同"……看起来滴水不漏，但由于他的"形"指的是读音，因而在绝大多数语言之间失去了可比性，除非是同一语系内部诸语言间的同源词，以及不同语言之间的借词。该书后面举例分析的正是日语中的英文借词。这样一来，拉多式的"词汇对比"，其应用范围和作用就非常有限。The listing (1) to (7) seems complete. However, when "form" was taken to mean sound, as was the case in Lado, it lost comparability in most languages, except for cognate words found in languages of the same family or loan words between different families. This was exactly what was illustrated in *Languages Across Culture*—comparison of English loan words in Japanese. In this sense, lexicological comparison by Lado has very limited application and effect.

（3）从"遥远"转向邻近

(3) From distant to close family

　　值得注意的是，拉多在谈到语法意义时也提到了"性"、"数"在各种语言中的不同表现（1957：63—64），甚至提到了沃尔夫对霍皮语（Hopi）语的研究，说："无疑这种宇宙观的不同造成了巨大的障碍，使说霍皮语的印第安人很难学另一种语言，也使说其他语言的人很难学霍皮语。"（Lado, 1957: 65）这与沃尔夫的研究颇有接近之处，可惜他未能进行任何有效的对比，更没能提出任何解决办法。这就使他的"比较研究"无可奈何地只能局限于差异不大的语言，更确切地说，局限于沃尔夫所说的"均质印欧语"。事实上，在拉多榜样性的影响下，五、六十年代的对比研究，确实更多地在印欧语内部进行，而在别的语言间乏善可陈。因为他的方法确实很难用到"相距遥远"的语言中去。

It is noteworthy that Lado discussed the different performances of categories such as "gender" and "number" in different languages when he dealt with linguistic meaning. (1957: 63–64) He mentioned Whorf's research on Hopi language: "needless to say that this difference in viewing the universe would constitute a serious obstacle for the Hopi Indian learning another language and for other speakers learning Hopi." (1957: 65) Coming this close to the Whorfian view, it is regrettable that Lado did not propose any effective comparison, thereby confining his comparison study to what Whorf referred to as "Average Standard European", which has little difference. In fact, under the influence of Lado, contrastive analysis in the 1950s and 1960s was largely conducted between Indo-European languages. But, of course, the methodology proposed by Lado is not appropriate for comparison between distant languages.

1.4.1.2 在应用性对比上的贡献
1.4.1.2 Contributions to applied contrastive study

但拉多的研究，对于以教学为服务对象的对比研究是有贡献的，主要表现在：
In any case, Lado has done great in language teaching, mainly in the following areas.

（1）第一次提出了外语学习中的"迁移"理论
(1) Initiated "Transfer" theory in foreign language learning

拉多说：
Lado holds that:

> ……本书的基本假设是：人们在外语学习中倾向于将本族语言文化的形式、意义，及形式和意义的分布迁移（transfer）到外语语言文化中去。在用外语语言文化进行表达时是这样，在接受外语语言文化时也是这样。（拉多，1957: 2）
>
> Implied in Fries' assumption for effective teaching materials, and as observed in bilingual studies and in testing research, is the fundamental assumption of this book: that individuals tend to transfer the forms and meanings, and the distribution of forms and meanings of their native language and culture to the foreign language and culture—both productively when attempting to speak the language and to act in the culture, and receptively when attempting to grasp and understand the language and the

culture as practiced by natives. (Lado, 1957: 2)

1964年，他更给迁移下了这样的定义：

> 有意无意地将本族语的习惯引申到外语中去，要是这种习惯可以接受，就可促进外语学习；如果不能接受，则会干扰外语学习。（拉多，1964: 222）

> In 1964, he defines and explains transfer as "the extension of a native-language habit to the target language, with or without awareness. When the transferred habit is acceptable in the target language we have facilitation; when it is unacceptable we have interference" (Lado, 1964: 222).

这一理论作为拉氏"对比研究"的基石，后来对外语教学产生了很大的影响。
This is the cornerstone of Lado's comparison study, and has great bearing on foreign language teaching and learning.

（2）将语言间的"异同"作为学习语言"难易"的决定性因素。
(2) Degrees of similarity as determiners of degree of ease in language learning

从迁移理论出发，拉氏提出了学习外语的难易问题，说：
It is common for language learners to comment on the ease or difficulty of learning a foreign language. Lado approached the topic on the basis of transfer theory:

> 异同决定难易。由于像德语与英语这样接近的语言间在形式、意义及形式意义的分布方面也有重大的区别，更由于学习者总爱将母语结构的习惯迁移到外语中去，我们就找到了学习外语难易的主要原因：相似的结构学起来容易，因为它们迁移到外语中后会起积极的作用；相异的结构学起来难，因为迁移到外语中去后无法起好作用而必须作出修正。（拉多，1957: 59）

> Similarity and difference are determiners of ease and difficulty. Since even languages as closely related as German and English differ significantly in the form, meaning, and distribution of their grammatical structures, and since the learner tends to transfer the habits of his native language structure to the foreign language, we have here the major source of difficulty or ease in learning the structure of a foreign language. Those structures that are similar will be easy to learn because they will be transferred and may function

satisfactorily in the foreign language, those structures that are different will be difficult because when transferred they will not function satisfactorily in the foreign language and will therefore have to be changed. (Lado, 1957: 59)

这就必然会将"比较"的重点确定在语言间的"异"上，从而造成这种"比较研究"不同于历史比较语言学的"比较研究"。拉多没有用"对比"这个字眼，但却直接导致了"对比"概念的产生。

The comparative emphasis of this approach necessarily falls on differences, distinguishing itself from the comparative study of historical linguistics. By not using the term "contrast", Lado sends forth the precipitation of the concept on contrast.

（3）提出了对比研究的操作性程序

(3) Proposed contrast mechanism

不论是洪堡特、叶斯柏森还是沃尔夫，虽然他们都提出了关于对比研究目标、方法等很好的设想，但却都没能提出一个具体进行操作的工作程序，这使他们的研究缺乏直接的继承者。作为一个重视实用过于重视理论的人，拉多提出了第一个可操作的对比研究程序，这使他的书出版以后，很快地推广了开来，其在对比语言学领域产生的影响足以使此前的大家们变得默默无闻。以语法对比为例，拉多提出了一般程序与具体程序。一般程序指对每种结构都要了解其形式、意义及形式意义的分布。具体程序是：

While there was much discussion of the research vision and methodology of contrastive analysis by Humboldt, Jespersen and Whorf, specific and workable contrasting processes were never touched upon. This probably accounts for the lack of a direct successor to their ideas. As a practitioner, Lado proposed the first workable contrasting process, which was spread far and wide following the distribution of his volume. The impact was great enough to seal off memories of his well-known predecessors. For example, in syntactic comparison Lado proposed a generic mechanism as well as a specific process. Being generic, it emphasizes the forms, meanings and distribution of forms and meanings for every construction. He describes the specific procedure as follows:

第一步：找出有关语言最好的结构描写，对两种语言的描写都应包括形式、意义及结构分布。如果一种型式没有经过形式、意义及结构分布的描写，或者描写得不充分，那就必须先进行精确的描写，然

后才能进入下一步。（拉多，1957: 67）

First step: Locate the best structural description of the languages involved. Both descriptions should contain the form, meaning, and distribution of the structures. If the form, meaning, or the distribution of a pattern is not described, or not adequately described, an attempt must be made to describe it accurately before proceeding any further. (Lado, 1957: 67)

第二步：把所有的结构概括为简约的纲要形式。比方说，如果所比的语言中有英语，我们就可把句型分为疑问、陈述、祈请、呼喊等。而在疑问句下，我们又可分出若干型式：带动词be的疑问句，带do, does, did的疑问句，带can, may, will等的疑问句，带when, where, why等加上词序颠倒的疑问句，带who, what作为主语的疑问句，带中升调而不管词序的疑问句，以及其他次要的疑问句型。（同上：67—68）

Second step: Summarize in compact outline form all the structures. If English is one of the languages involved, we would describe the sentence types in it as questions, statements, requests and calls. Under questions would be several patterns: questions with the verb *be*; questions with *do, does, did*; questions with *can, may, will*, etc.; questions with *when, where, why*, etc., plus reversal of word order; questions with *who, what*, etc., as subject; questions with a mid-high intonation sequence regardless of word order; and other minor types of questions. (*ibid.*: 67—68)

第三步：一个型式、一个型式地进行两种语言结构的比较。（同上：69）

Third step: Actual comparison of the two language structures, pattern by pattern. (*ibid.*: 69)

第四步：把小的难点型式归并为大的难点型式。经过上面的比较，我们可以发现学习中的所有问题，但一种型式学习过程中的问题与另一种往往是平行的。（同上：70）

Regroup single problem patterns into larger patterns of difficulty. By comparing each pattern in the two language systems we can discover all the learning problems, but often the problem involved in learning one pattern is parallel to or actually the same as the problem in learning another pattern. (*ibid.*: 70)

请注意第一个程序，它要求在比较前对所比语言的结构有个精确的描写。换言之，没有经过精确描写的语言，就不能随便拿来进行对比研究。可惜将这一理论用到印欧语以外的语言中去的人往往忘了这一条。

Attention is drawn to the first step, where a detail description of a particular language structure is required before any comparison take place. In other words, contrastive analysis may not proceed without grounds on descriptive linguistics. Regrettably, this is a much forsaken rule in the contrastive studies of languages outside the Indo-European languages.

1.4.2 迪·皮德娄的《语言结构对比》
1.4.2 Di Pietro's *Language Structure in Contrast*

迪·皮德娄（Robert Di Pietro）的《语言结构对比》出版于1971年，其时已是1968年乔治顿圆桌会议之后，对比分析方法遭到了严重批评；而1965年乔姆斯基《句法理论面面观》出版，确立了转换生成语法的"标准理论"。对比语言学可说已经淡出了美国语言学界，迪·皮德娄的书于此时出版，实在有点像这一阶段对比研究的"天鹅之歌"。尽管如此，这本书在对比语言学史上还是有其价值。

When Robert Di Pietro brought out *Language Structures in Contrast* in 1971, contrastive methodology had just been censured at the 1968 Georgetown roundtable conference. In fact, even earlier, in 1965 when Chomsky's *Aspects of the Theory of Syntax* swept across the linguistics field with generative transformation grammar, contrastive linguistics had lost its foothold in American linguistics circles. *Language Structure in Contrast* did seem to be a swan song. Nevertheless, its value in history cannot be denied.

1.4.2.1 第一次对对比语言学的发展史进行了回顾
1.4.2.1 The first historical review

上面提到，是迪·皮德娄最早把对比研究的源头溯到了1892年的格朗根特（Charles H. Grandgent），其实他还提到了好些人，如法国语音学家帕西（Paul Passy, 1906）、布拉格学派的马泰修斯（Mathesius）等。特别是提到了赵元任

（1933）的《英汉语调浅探》一文，认为它是对比研究引起关注的第一个信号（Di Pietro，1971：10）。这是西方出版的有关对比研究的论著中第一个、恐怕也是唯一的一个提到中国语言学家名字、并且放在如此重要地位的。

Di Pietro made an attempt to trace early contrastive activities. As mentioned above, he cited the work of Charles H. Grandgent, Paul Passy and Mathesius of the Prague school. In particular, he cited the work of Chao Yuen-ren (1933) and considered this to be "the first sign that a momentum was building in the contrastive study of languages" (Di Pietro, 1971: 10). This is probably the first and only work on contrastive linguistics by a Western scholar to have attached such significance to a Chinese linguist.

迪·皮德娄也完整地引述了沃尔夫关于对比语言学的那段著名语录，可惜的是，他没有对之作任何展开或分析。究其原因，还是因为拉多等带来的对比研究的转向。正如鲍林杰在为他的书作的序中第一句话所说的：对比语言学产生于课堂实践。（皮德娄，1971：vii）

Di Pietro has also quoted Whorf in full on his idea of language comparison, though without further elaboration. It could be the result of the shift in contrasting direction lead by Lado. As Bolinger aptly summarized in his foreword, "contrastive linguistics was born of classroom experience". (Di Pietro, 1971: vii)

可以说，这是那个时代对比研究的基调，因此迪·皮德娄尽管对历史进行了认真的追溯，也难以有所作为。

Given this environment, it is not easy for Di Pietro to protest, even though he has seriously retrospected the historical development.

1.4.2.2 明确提出对比分析要有理论指导
1.4.2.2 Advocate theory-guided contrastive analysis

洪堡特、沃尔夫等人心目中的对比研究就是语言研究本身最重要的任务，可说对比语言学就是普通语言学、理论语言学，因此不存在再找一个更高层面的什么指导理论的问题。从拉多开始，对比分析成了"应用语言学"的组成部分，人们就觉得在其上面应该还有个指导性的语言学理论。拉多和弗里斯用的其实就是结构主义理论，只是没有明说，也不需要说，因为当时美国的主流语言学就是结构主义语言学。到了皮德娄的时代，以生成语言学为代表的新兴语言学兴起，对比分析就面临着一个要不要理论指导、要什么理论指导，以及如何指导的问题。迪•皮德娄正式回答了这个问题。

If contrastive analysis itself is the single most important endeavour of language research, as is the case with Humboldt, Whorf and others, contrastive linguistics, with its goals, methods and techniques, aligns neatly with general or theoretical linguistics, and we do not need a higher theoretical framework to point the direction. As contrastive analysis repositioned itself in the applied field since Lado, for Fries and Lado the need to have a higher guiding principle arose. This higher principle lay in structuralism, the mainstream linguistic theory at the time. By the time of Di Pietro when generative linguistics dominated, it was high time for contrastive analysis to resolve the questions of higher theory—is there a need? What would be good? How can it help? Di Pietro addressed them all.

首先，迪•皮德娄引用并赞成这一说法，即认为"对比研究首重理论的应用，其次才是教学上的价值"（皮德娄，1971：12）。

First, Di Pietro quoted and supported the idea that "CA should be initiated with primary regard to theoretical implications and secondarily for its pedagogical worth". (Di Pietro, 1971: 12)

其次，在比较了各种语言学理论之后，他毫不犹豫地采取了转换生成语法作为其研究的指南：

Next, upon a survey of various linguistics theories, Di Pietro was decisive in his choice of the generative transformation model as the guiding principle:

> 有好几种语言理论模式都能达到一般化的目标……不过从目前来看，只有转换生成语言学发展得最好，因而也最适合用于对比分析。（皮德娄，1971：17）

> There are several linguistic models in use today which are capable of becoming generalized…At the present time, however, only the generative and transformational model has been developed in this direction and, by the same token, is the most suitable to CA. (ibid.: 17)

强调指导理论，似乎是这一时期对比语言学的一个特色，是自居"应用"地位的心态的流露。

Obviously the attachment to theoretical guidance as an applied discipline marked this phase of development in contrastive linguistics.

1.4.2.3 全面运用了转换生成语法的理论
1.4.2.3 Complete adoption of generative transformation model

这包括：

The complete application of the generative transformation model manifests in the following ways:

（1）普遍语法观

(1) Perception of universal grammar

迪•皮德娄完全接受了乔姆斯基的普遍语法观，认为所有语言都共享一些基本特点，这是对比研究得以开展的基础，也是对比研究的出发点（同上：4）。从这一立场出发，他认为语言间的差异只是语言共性在具体语法中的不同体现。（同上：5）

Embracing in full Chomsky's universal grammar, Di Pietro believed that the supposition that human languages share a number of essential features is crucial to achieving a level of adequacy in CA. If there were no such sharing of both a general framework and a number of grammatical processes, there would be no point of departure for the contrastive statements to be made in shared linguistics features in languages that are contrastive (*ibid.*: 4). On this basis, "any differences are to be found in the ways these universals are realized in particular grammars." (*ibid.*: 5)

（2）"深层结构—表层结构"理论

其次，迪•皮德娄提出了一个对比层次理论，这个层次就是乔姆斯基的从深层结构到表层结构的转换理论，而以普遍语法为最底层。他说：

(2) Theory of "Deep—Surface Structure"

In his next move, Di Pietro proposed a model for contrastive analysis founded on Chomskyan transformation theory whereby the underlying level is universal grammar and analysis moves from deeper levels to the surface. He explained:

> 我们希望我们的对比模式是个分层的结构，从最底部的深层结构，经过一些过渡层次，到达表层结构。语言间的差异是在组织过渡层的过程中产生的，到了表层结构就达到了最大值。（皮德娄，1971: 29）

We shall also require that our model of contrast have a leveled structure, going from a deepest level through various intermediate levels to a surface level. Differences are found in the intermediate levels of structuring and increase as the surface structure is approached. (Di Pietro, 1971: 29)

（3）语法是一套"规则"
(3) Grammar as a set of "rules"

同乔姆斯基一样，迪·皮德娄把语法看作一套规则，因而语言就是规则取向的行为，说话者是运用规则来理解和生成语言。（同上：6）从这个立场出发，他把学习外语看作学习另一套规则的过程：

Chomsky saw grammar as a set of rules. Thus Di Pietro and the psychological interpretation of language is a rule-oriented behaviour, which is to say, speakers of a language produce and understand its sentences by way of utilizing the rules of that language (*ibid*.: 6). As for foreign language learning, there is yet another process of rule learning:

只要很好地学会了外语的一套规则，他就能很好地应用。碰到他没有学到的规则，他就会转到母语或他所知道的其他语言中去找这些规则。这种用某一语言的语法来解释别的语言的过程就叫做"迁移"，在这过程中犯的错误就是因为"干扰"。（皮德娄，1971: 6）

At any rate, if he has properly learned the rules of the other language, he will be able to apply them. Whenever he has not learned the rules, he will have to revert to those of his native language or to those of other languages he knows. The process of interpreting the particular grammar of one language in terms of another is called transfer. The mistakes that result from the process are said to be due to interference. (Di Pietro, 1971: 6)

（4）区分"语言能力"（competence）和"语言运用"（performance）
(4) Differentiating between "competence" and "performance"

迪·皮德娄还把乔姆斯基的"语言能力"和"语言运用"理论用到对比分析中，强调对比分析的任何结果都属于"语言能力"方面，而不属于"语言运用"方面。他并以此来批评人们对于"对比分析无用"的责难：

Applying the language competence and language performance theory of Chomsky to contrastive analysis, Di Pietro stressed that "whatever contrasts are found, they are to be considered strictly in terms of linguistic competence and not in terms of linguistic performance" (*ibid.*: 29), hence his rebuttal to criticism of CA as being "useless":

> 既然外语教师关心的是如何建立一种新的语言能力，他就应该将目的语的语法与学生母语的语法进行对比。批评对比分析无助于预见学习中发生的错误的人看来未能明确区分语言能力和语言应用。教师不应该假设所有语言学家对语言的描写都与事实纹丝不差，都真实地描述了理想的说话人的语言能力。而且即使我们能够对两种语言进行精确而完整的描写，比较的结果也未必能预见犯错误的情况。要确切地知道学生会犯什么错误，需要大量的关于语言运用方面的信息。（皮德娄，1971: 21）
>
> Since the foreign language teacher is concerned with the building of new competences, it is appropriate that he contrast the grammar of the language being taught with that of his students. Criticism about the usefulness of CA in predicting learning errors (Wardhaugh, 1970) does not seem to make a clear distinction between competence and performance. The teacher is well advised not to assume that every linguist's description of a language is, ipso facto, accurate and therefore a true portrayal of an ideal speaker's competence. Even if we could obtain accurate and complete descriptions of competences, comparing them would not lead to prediction of actual instances of error. To know exactly when a student will commit a given error would require a vast body of information about performance. (Di Pietro, 1971: 21)

这实在是个悖论。一方面强调对比的结果都属于"语言能力"，一方面又说学生产生的具体错误都在"语言运用"。那对比研究如何解决教学的实际应用问题呢？更大的悖论在于，乔姆斯基早就宣称，他的理论不是为教学服务的，而"对比分析"又以教学为主要服务对象，这两者方枘圆凿，如何接得上榫呢？难怪迪·皮德娄的书出来以后，在实际上根本没产生什么作用，也无法阻挡对比分析的衰落。

This is in fact an antinomy. While all resultant contrast was taken as part of language competence, the errors made by language learners were considered part of language performance, and there could be no practical pedagogical solutions. The greatest antithesis is perhaps the open declaration of Chomsky that his theory was never meant for applied linguistics. Obviously, transformation theory is a poor fit for applied CA. It speaks for itself then that though adopting the prevalent theory, Di Pietro's work made no real impact and could not turn the decline of CA around.

1.4.2.4 拒绝话语分析，排斥社会和文化因素
1.4.2.4 Rejecting discourse analysis and functional factors

这一条当然不是迪·皮德娄的优点，但通过他的表述我们更可看到这一时期对比研究的局限及后一时期变革的意义所在。

Less than a contribution from Di Pietro, the rejection of discourse analysis and functional factors served to illustrate the constraints binding the development in contrastive linguistics in this period and as a foil to the significant adjustment of the later period.

迪·皮德娄引用了国际语言教师协会（Fèdèration internationale de professeurs de langues vivantes）1968年南斯拉夫会议上对于对比研究提出的十项建议，自许已做到了其中至少六条（还有两条是非专业性的），但对其中第五条却明确表示他做不到或不想做。这一条是：

Referring to the ten recommendations made by the *Fédération Internationale de Professeurs de Langues Vivantes* at a meeting in Yugoslavia in 1968, Di Pietro was only willing to seriously consider six of them (he supported another two, which were not pertinent to the technical aspects of CA). The recommendation that Di Pietro was not prepared to tackle was that:

> 对比分析应该超越句子层面进入话语结构，还应在语义层面、社会文化层面和心理层面进行。（皮德娄，1971: 12）
>
> CA should be undertaken beyond the sentence level into discourse structure, in semantics, and on the sociocultural and psycholinguistic levels. (Di Pietro, 1971: 12)

迪·皮德娄的解释是：

And the reason is:

> 社会文化和心理方面的资料太复杂、太多样，在一本进行语言对比的书里无法充分处理。而要对比话语结构，现在的理论基础还远远不够。（皮德娄，1971: 13）
>
> Sociocultural and psycholinguistic data are too varied and complex to be treated adequately in a volume which is devoted to the treatment of linguistic contrasts. As for discourse structure, much more theoretical ground must be gained before a CA of language-specific patterns can profitably attempted. (ibid.: 13)

这样，他甚至落到了拉多的后面。而我们后面将看到，詹姆斯、切斯特曼等人的新突破正是从这一条开始的。
In so doing, he is taking an even more backward position than did Lado, as we shall show in the section on Phase 3.

1.4.3 本期研究小结
1.4.3 Summary

这一个时期的研究，由于其基础理论（结构主义）和研究目标（第二语言教学）的局限，从总体上来说并不很成功。其原因是什么呢？据前人的总结和我们的看法，主要有以下几个方面：

Confined as it was by structuralist theory and the narrow research aims taken at second-language teaching, the contrastive analysis of this period had little influence. The main reasons are as follows.

1.4.3.1 没有达到为教学服务的目的
1.4.3.1 Pedagogic implications for language teaching

对比分析是以预测第二语言教学中的难点为标榜的，但后来发现其预测能力相当有限，对比所得出的一些结论，要么是大实话，稍有一点经验的教师都知道；要么是故弄玄虚，抽象得无法在实践中应用。而所谓"相同就是容易点，相异就是困难点"，在实践中也根本经不起推敲。同时由于60年代后期起，教育理论从教师中心转向了学习者中心，于是以教师预测教学需要为主的CA（对比分析），就不得不让位给以对学习者实际错误分析为主的EA，如科德（Pit Corder, 1967; 1971）、理查兹（J. C. Richards, 1971a; 1971b），以后又转向更具理论意义的interlanguage（中介语）研究，如赛林格（L. Selinker, 1969; 1972）。加上当时教学法上直接法和听说法盛行，利用母语的对比分析法显然与之格格不入。因此到1973年科德出版《应用语言学导论》时，第二语言教学中的对比方法实际已经基本被否定了。

If the chief aim of applying contrastive analysis in language teaching is to predict the difficulties in foreign language learning, the supposed predictions were too weak. The findings have so far been either plain fact that all experienced teachers are well aware of or something abstract that can hardly be applied. Henceforth, similarities and differences that were deemed to be determining the ease and difficulties in learning carried little weight where application is concerned. Meanwhile, it should be noted that since the 1960s there has been a change in education paradigm from a teacher-centred approach to a learner-centred approach. That is to say, CA, a tool employed by teachers to predict teaching needs, has to give way to EA (error analysis), as can be seen in the works of Pit Corder (1967, 1971), J. C. Richards (1971a, 1971b) and L. Selinker (1969, 1972) and has since turned to interlanguage studies, which has greater theoretical significance. Certainly, by the time Corder published his *Introducing Applied Linguistics* in 1973, contrastive analysis for second-language teaching and learning has in fact been abandoned.

1.4.3.2 语言学理论的变化
1.4.3.2 Remodelling of linguistic theory

20世纪50年代后期乔姆斯基"革命"革掉了对比分析赖为基础的结构主义语言学的命，是导致对比分析失宠的另一个原因。有的理论例如普遍语法理论对对比研究来说简直是釜底抽薪。因为在普遍语法看来，语言间的差别并没有大到无法预见的程度，各种语言间存在着大量共性，因此学会了一种语言，实际上对别的语言也已懂得了很多。加上各种语言的深层结构是一样的，其差异只是非常表面的，学习第二语言只要学习从深层到表层的转换规则就行了。对比分析根本起不了什么作用。迪·皮德娄的研究实际上成了转换生成语法的图解，加上他自己承认他只能解决"语言能力"问题，不能解决"语言运用"问题，实际上对比分析离开了原本想为之服务的教学，更变得无人问津。

One of the reasons for the downturn of CA was the "revolution" of Chomsky in the 1950s, which saw the rejection of structuralism, which was instrumental to the development of CA. And linguistic theory such as universal grammar attacks the root of contrastive analysis, as it does not hold that languages are varied enough to be unpredictable. Precisely due to this "universality", knowing one language is as good as knowing a lot of another language. In particular, since the deep structure is essentially the same and differences are apparent only at the surface structure, it suffices for a second-language learner to master the transformation rules. For this matter, contrastive analysis seems redundant. In fact, Di Pietro's effort, targeted at "language competence", was really a guide to transformational grammar only in that he acknowledged his limitation in resolving issues on language usage. The departure in language teaching only served to send CA to its grave.

1.4.3.3 对比研究本身在方法论上存在一些问题
1.4.3.3 Methodology issues in contrastive research

对比的一些方法，如翻译对等（translation equivalence）、迁移理论（theory of transfer）、共时原则、抽象原则（脱离语境与应用），以及无视学习者的差异（成人和儿童，学习者自身的进步）等，也是对比分析失宠的重要原因。此外，对比研究方法的三步曲"描写、并列、比较"（description, juxtaposition, comparison。参见 Halliday et al. 1964: 113—114），由于第一步作为基础并非各种语言都具有（可说世界上大多数语言都还没有做到描写充分），第二步将什么与什么并列往往带有任意性，从而使第三步比较成了为比较而比较。

Yet another significant factor that brought CA down was the methodologies deployed, such as translation equivalence, theory of transfer, synchronic principles, conceptual principles (out of context and application) and disregarding the differences in learners (for instance, adult leaner and child learner; learner's self-improvement, etc.). Moreover, the three-step research methodology of "description, juxtaposition and comparison" (Halliday et al. 1964: 113—14) has serious shortcomings. Not all languages fit the bill of description (most languages are far from being well described) and it is highly random in terms of juxtaposing, which means that most of the time we contrast for the sake of contrasting.

据我们看来，第二时期对比研究的失败也标志着微观对比研究的失败，只把对比停留在应用层面，不考虑语言学理论的变化；只停留在语法、语音、词汇等"纯语言"的对比，不考虑社会和文化的因素（拉多的书里专门有一章"文化的比较"，但在整个五、六十年代几乎没有引起过重视；迪·皮德娄更是明确表示撇开了）；只停留在对静止语言现象的观察，不考虑语言使用的动态变化。

To us, the disappointment in the second phase is in fact a setback in contrastive analysis at the micro-level. Contrastive linguistics would never ever be able to advance should we disregard the changes in linguistic theories to standstill at the applied field; or disregard the social and cultural factors (there was mention of this aspect in Lado's book which failed to arouse interest in the 1950s—1960s and Di Pietro even declared his rejection of it) to standstill at "purely" linguistic comparison at the syntactical, phonological and lexical levels; and disregard dynamic changes to standstill at observing static phenomena.

对此，沙亚伐拉（1977）的总结深中肯綮："'将目的语的语言文化与学习者的语言文化作系统的对比'（后来称之为对比分析的强式）是导致六十年代争论的主要原因之一，二十年后的今天再来看，我们实在看不到拉多的盲目乐观有何依据，人们甚至可以怀疑拉多的意见并不像有些批评者说的那么斩钉截铁。要知道在五十年代后期，现代社会语言学和心理语言学还没产生呢。拉多对文化比较的强调几乎被人们忘却，而正是我们今天重新认识对比研究价值的线索，在强调文化对比的同时拉多还强调了语言学习的心理因素。"（Sajavaara, 1977: 10）该文最终提议对比要找到出路，必须重新看待各个方面的语言研究，但是不能纯粹做平行研究，必须同时把心理语言学和对比社会语言学纳入框架之内。（同上：25）

Sajavaara (1977) was right when he commented, "'by comparing systematically the language and culture to be learned with the native language and the culture of the student' (which was later to be called the Strong Hypothesis for CA) may be considered as one of the primary causes of the controversy which ensured in the 1960s. Today, twenty years later, it is rather difficult to see the point in Lado's blue-eyed optimism and one can even venture to express the doubt that Lado never intended his remark to be taken as categorically as some critics of CA have taken it. It is to be remembered, however, that, in the late fifties, modern sociolinguistics and psycholinguistics did not exist. Lado's emphasis on the comparison of cultures was mostly forgotten; yet it is there that we can find a clue for a modern revision of the contrastive hypothesis. Side by side with cultural contrasts Lado also stressed the importance of the psychological aspects of language learning." (Sajavaara, 1977: 10) The paper proposed in the end that to find a way out for CA, one must regard the linguistic study of various aspects in a new way, surely not just parallel comparison, and psycholinguistic and sociolinguistic considerations must be brought into the framework. (*ibid.*: 25)

因此西方对比语言学的走向第三个时期实在是必然的。

It is therefore expected that contrastive analysis should move into its third phase of development.

1.5 第三期（1980年至今）：走向宏观和注重理论建构
1.5 Phase 3 (since 1980): towards theory construction in macro perspective

第三个时期从1980年詹姆斯出版《对比分析》一书和菲齐亚克主编他的第一部对比语言学论文集《对比语言学的理论问题》开始，一直到现在。这段时期比较重要的著作除菲齐亚克主编的四部论文集和詹姆斯的书之外，还有哈特曼的《对比篇章学：应用语言学中的话语对比分析》（1980）、斯奈尔杭贝的《德英语描写性动词语义场对比研究》（1983）、克尔采斯佐斯基的《对比语言学的范围》（1990）、孔纳的《对比修辞学》（1996）、切斯特曼的《对比功能分析》（1998）等等。

A few important works marked the third phase of contrastive linguistics: Carl James (1980), Jacek Fisiak (1980b, 1981, 1984, 1990), R. K. Hartmann (1980), Mary Snell-Hornby (1983), Tomasz P. Krzeszowski (1990), Ulla Connor (1996) and Andrew Chesterman (1998) covered aspects including but not confined to discourse analysis, semantic and functional analysis.

之所以把詹姆斯的书作为第三期对比语言学的开端，是因为正是从詹姆斯开始，对比语言学开始拓宽了它的研究范围，从微观研究进入了宏观研究。在对比研究史上，詹姆斯大约是第一个提出要进行宏观对比研究的：

We regard James (1980) as the demarcation of the third phase simply because we owe it to him that an expansion in research scopes was realized. Contrastive analysis was able to venture from micro-analysis to macro-analysis, largely due to the effort of Carl James, who first advocated macro-contrastive analysis. He said:

> 现在有必要进一步区分出微观语言学与宏观语言学。除了弗斯（1951）等少数例外，20世纪的语言学的研究目标只是对语言符号的描写，而不关注这些符号的使用，也不关注这些符号所承担的信息如何受到语境的影响。对比分析采取的也是这样的研究方式。但是最近人们却越来越注意到语境对信息及其意义的决定作用，越来越关注宏观语言学。这里我不想对这一重点的转移作出解释，但不妨指出，这一转移与人们对语义学、对社会语言学、对话语分析、对言语行为理论与对民族学方法论的越来越浓厚的兴趣是同步的。(詹姆斯，1980: 27)

It is now necessary to draw a further distinction that between microlinguistics and macrolinguistics. With certain notable exceptions (Firth, 1951) modern 20th century linguistics has seen as its goal the description of the linguistic code, without making reference to the uses to which the code is put, or how messages carried by this code are modified by the contexts in which they occur: modern linguistics has taken the microlinguistics approach. Consequently, CA has also taken this approach. There has recently however been increasing attention to contextual determination of messages and their interpretation, a growing concern for macrolinguistics. This is not the place to explain this shift of emphasis, but we may point out that it coincides with a growing interest in semantics, sociolinguisitics, discourse analysis, speech-act theory and ethnomethodology. (James, 1980: 27)

当然，从现在的眼光来看，詹姆斯的"宏观"恐怕还不那么宏观，因为詹姆斯的宏观语言学所指的其实只是篇章研究和话语分析：

Of course, in retrospect, what Carl took as macro was not really macro in today's sense. Carl was specifically referring to text and discourse analysis when macro contrastive linguistics is concerned.

上节所述可以使我们看到宏观语言学的某些特点：

(1) 关注交际能力而不是乔姆斯基的"语言"能力；

(2) 试图从语言外部来描写语言行为；

(3) 寻找语言组织中比句子大的单位。

From the preceding section, certain points emerge to characterize microlinguistics:

(1) A concern for communicative competence rather than for "linguistic" competence in Chomsky's sense;

(2) An attempt to describe linguistic events within their extra-linguistic settings;

(3) The search for units of linguistic organization larger than the single sentence.

总而言之，范围的扩大从纵向来看是寻找大的单位，而从横向来看是将语言与社会文化背景相结合。这一扩大已在两个方面取得了成果，其一是在形式层面，讨论句子如何组成更大的、超句子单位亦即篇章的问题；其二是在功能层面，观察人们如何使用语言，这就是话语分析的领域。（詹姆斯，1980：101—102）

In general, a broadening of scope is aimed at, both "vertically" in terms of larger linguistic units and horizontally, to incorporate socio-cultural settings within linguistics. This broadening of scope has so far been achieved in two ways. The first is on the formal level and addresses the question of how sentences are organized into larger, suprasentential units or texts. The second direction is the functional one, and looks at the ways in which people put language to use: this is the field of discourse analysis. (James, 1980: 101—102)

但其革命性意义却是不容置疑的。

Nevertheless, there is little doubt that this perception was indeed revolutionary at this time.

克尔采斯佐斯基在他1990年的书里，花了整整一章的篇幅（第XII章）批评詹姆斯，主要是讲他没有自己的明确观点，只是罗列各家之说，间或提出自己不温不火的批评（Krzeszowski，1989：233），这是有失公允的。其实詹姆斯一书的长处正在于他"提出的问题比解决的问题多",这是理论研究的一种非常可贵的态度,特别在一门学科转型的时候更是如此。因此詹氏的书在西方对比研究史上具有划时代意义,其最大的功绩,首先就在于从对比语言学自身的角度,对第二时期的不切实际的对比分析进行了总清算,从而揭开了第三期的序幕;其次是提出了宏观对比的设想,从他(1980:140)坦承"宏观对比是个有待开发的崭新研究领域",以及20余年来西方对比研究发展的情况来看,他的书确实具有一定的预见性,或者说,在关键的时刻起到了关键的作用,使西方的对比研究重新焕发了生命。20余年来西方对比研究最活跃的领域,就是篇章对比研究与话语对比研究,这正是詹姆斯所竭力主张的。

Krzeszowski (1990) devoted a whole chapter (Chapter XII) to a critical review of Carl James (1980), and was not satisfied with the fact that instead of advancing an argument of his own, James merely put together the literature with minimum and mild comments (Krzeszowski, 1989: 233). However, Krzeszowski may have jumped the gun. Indeed, by bringing attention to more issues rather than trying to resolve as many as possible, James (1980) made a precious contribution to theoretical research, specifically where the discipline was at a transitional phase. There are more reasons for James to shine in history. Sticking closely to the basis of contrastive linguistics, the work set out to chart a new direction for CA, reckoning in all impracticalities of the second phase. It was also admirable that he pushed for contrastive analysis at the macro level, stating: "It must be clear to the reader that macro-linguistic CA is a new field of enquiry, awaiting exploration" (1980: 140). Retrospective of developments in contrastive studies in the West for the last 20 years, James (1980) served its purpose at a time it was most called for, rejuvenating contrastive linguistic studies in the West. For the last 20 years, it has been witnessed that contrastive analysis at text and discourse levels are most prosperous, a scene James would be most delighted to see.

1.5.1 理论研究
1.5.1 Theoretical research

第三时期对比研究的第一个特点是注重理论的研究,不再如上一时期那样刻意把自身局限在"应用语言学"的范围内,不敢"侵入"语言学的领域。其中波兰学者菲齐亚克(Jacek Fisiak)起了重要的作用。上世纪七十年代起对比语言学研究的重心从美国转到欧洲，波兰、芬兰等国更为重中之重，其中菲齐亚克先后担任系主任、院长、校长的波兰波兹南（Poznań）地区亚当·米基维奇大学（Adam Mickiewicz University）及其英文学院更为全球对比研究者所注目，他在那里成立了对比语言学研究所，建立了英波对比研究系（Department of English-Polish Contrastive Linguistics），从1973年起，与美国华盛顿应用语言学中心合作出版第一家以对比研究为宗旨的杂志——《对比语言学论丛》（PSiCL或*Papers and Studies in Contrastive Linguistics*），担任主编一直到1996年[1]。同时，他从1971年起主持了近30届对比语言学国际会议。特别是从1980年到1990年他主编了四本具有重要影响的对比研究论文集。说他是30年来对比研究在国际语言学界最有名的代表人物，可能并不为过。他特别关注学科的理论建设，最早提出（Fisiak，1971）并竭力主张要区分理论对比语言学与应用对比语言学，并将前者作为学科建设的重点。1980年他主编的第一部论文集书名就叫《对比语言学的理论问题》，收集了七十年代关于对比语言学理论探讨的所有重要文章，突显了他对这一问题的关注。这是我们把1980年作为第三时期开始的又一个原因。在为论文集写的《导言》里他甚至说，只有加强理论建设，才能"将对比语言学从被迫为应用语言学服务的境况中解救出来，成为比较语言学下的一个独立学科"（1980：3）。他在回顾了对比研究的历史（有意思的是，他也认为对比研究史受到误解，原因在于受五、六十年代美国模式对比分析的影响）以后，指出，有两种对比研究，一种是理论研究，一种是应用研究。要想学科得到发展，必须将两者区别开来。他还引用杰克逊（Jackson，1976：7）的话说，

The first noticeable difference in this phase of development is the attention that theoretical research received. Rather than deliberately keep within the scope of "applied linguistics" as in the last phase, it ventured into other territories of linguistics. In this respect, we should mention Polish linguist Jacek Fisiak. Starting from the 1970s, the centre of contrastive linguistics shifted from the US

1　1997年新主编接任后该杂志更名为《波兹南当代语言学研究》（*Poznań Studies in Contemporary Linguistics*），并于1999年第35期出版时正式启用，但考虑到历史影响，仍沿用了PSiCL这一简称。

The journal was renamed *Poznań Studies in Contemporary Linguistics* in 1997 under the new chief editor and the new title was officially launched in issue number 35, published in 1999. However, the abbreviation remained as PSiCL to align with historical development.

to Europe, with Poland and Finland taking an important lead. This was the period when all eyes were on Adam Mickiewicz University, Poznań, Poland, and its College of English, where Jacek Fisiak has served as department head, dean and chancellor. Fisiak established an Institute of Contrastive Linguistics as well as the Department of English-Polish Contrastive Linguistics. In 1973, in collaboration with the Washington Institute of Applied Linguistics, Fisiak headed the first journal dedicated to contrastive linguistics, *Papers and Studies in Contrastive Linguistics* (PSiCL), and served as its chief editor until 1996. Since 1971, Fisiak has also run some 30 international conferences on contrastive linguistics, and edited four volumes of essays on contrastive linguistics in the period 1980 to 1990. We could safely conclude that Fisiak is the most prominent figure in the discipline for the last 30 years. Paying special attention to theoretical issues, Fisiak (1971) was among the earliest to differentiate between theoretical contrastive linguistics and applied contrastive linguistics and using the former as the basis for establishing contrastive linguistics as an independent discipline. In an effort to advance his idea, Fisiak et al. (1980) collected almost all the significant papers on theoretical construction of the 1970s. This adds to the demarcation of Phase 3 in 1980. In the foreword of this volume, Fisiak (1980: 3) stressed that contrastive linguistics could develop independently only when it was free from serving the purposes of applied linguistics, and that to achieve this necessarily required strengthening theoretical research. Interestingly enough, Fisiak also held that the history of contrastive linguistics was somewhat twisted by the American version of contrastive analysis of the 1950s and 1960s. His account of history arrived at a conclusion distinguishing contrastive analysis under two heads: theoretical and applied. To give the discipline a distinctive identity of its own, it was necessary to divide the two. Quoting Jackson (1976: 7), he concurred that:

> 只有从为教学服务中解脱出来，对比语言学才能自由地发展自己的理论，为语言类型学和语言共性研究，为理解个别语言及其构造作出贡献。

> Released from the necessity of having pedagogical relevance, CL can be free to develop its own theoretical principles and make a distinctive

contribution to linguistics generally. The theoretical conclusion of CL will contribute to the areas of language typology and language universals. The contrastive descriptions of specific languages and language systems will contribute to an understanding of individual language and their structures.

这番话使我们联想起久违了的第一时期学者论及的对比研究的目标。
It is not difficult to link this back to scholars of Phase 1 and the initial aim of contrastive analysis.

1990年，在他编的第四部也是最后一部对比语言学论文集里，他对八十年代的对比研究作了总结，认为对比研究主要是在五个方面展开：（1）元理论与理论问题；（2）纯粹的对比描写；（3）通过对比或比较研究证实关于普通语言学或某一特定语言的假设；（4）超句范围的对比研究（包括对比篇章语言学、语用学、话语分析、社会语言学、心理语言学、跨文化语言研究等）；（5）对比研究在语言教学法、翻译、双语词汇学、双语教育等领域的应用（Fisiak，1990：4）。

In Fisiak (1990), the fourth of the collective volumes he edited, Fisiak summarized the major research areas of CA in the 1980s on five fronts:

(1) Metatheoretical and theoretical issues;

(2) Contrastive descriptions of languages;

(3) Cross-language studies with the aim of validating general linguistic hypotheses or hypotheses concerning a given language on the basis of a general linguistic theory with the help of comparative/contrastive data;

(4) Expansion of framework, i.e. contrastive work beyond the sentence (e.g. contrastive text linguistics, pragmatics, discourse analysis, sociolinguistics, psycholinguistics and linguistic cross-cultural studies);

(5) Applications to language pedagogy, translation, bilingual lexicography and bilingual education. (Fisiak, 1990: 4)

而他在导言中特别强调的仍是"元理论与理论"问题，并具体提出了四个方面：（1）区别理论对比分析与应用对比分析；（2）对等与"对比中立项"问题；（3）语言学理论与对比语言学；（4）对比语言学与语言类型学（同上：5—16）。从前三个方面来看，菲氏认为理论对比语言学主要研究对比研究的模式，认为"对比中立项"是最重要的概念，认为选择适当的语言学理论也是理论对比研究的任务之一，等等，显然反映了当时对比研究的一股潮流，即把理论研究的重点放在"对比中立项"上，他的同胞克尔采斯佐斯基（Tomasz. P. Krzeszowski）就是一个代表。而第四个方面，就对比语言学界而言，除个别文章讨论到"对比类型学"（contrastive typology）外（如Comrie, 1986; Birnbaum, 1986），恐怕是乏善可陈。

Among the five listed above, Fisiak focused on four theoretical and metatheoretical issues: (1) the distinction between theoretical and applied contrastive studies; (2) equivalence and *tertium comparationis*; (3) linguistic theory and contrastive linguistics; and finally (4) the relationship between contrastive linguistics and typology (*ibid*. 5—16). In addressing theoretical CA, research on providing an adequate model for language comparison was singled out to be the aim. It was also obvious that much importance has been attached to *tertium comparationis* as the fundamental concept for more concrete model-building. Fisiak was also mindful of the right choice of linguistic theory to serve as the basis for comparison. All these were evident of the trend in contrastive studies in that period in which the concept of *tertium comparationis* aroused much interest and where the study of Tomasz P. Krzeszowski could well be representative. As for contrastive typology, some scattered papers (Comrie, 1986; Birnbaum, 1986) aside, no distinct development catches the eye.

克氏是菲氏之外另一位特别关注对比语言学理论建设的学者，早在1967年他就开始发表对比语言学的文章《结构对比研究的根本原理》，1974年出版《生成对比语法的理论基础》，提出了自己的理论构想。1980年菲齐亚克的论文集里收了他写于1974年的《生成对比语法》一文（Krzeszowski, 1974b; 1980）。在读了詹姆斯的书之后，他向第四届国际对比语言学大会提交了一篇论文《对比中立项》（*Tertium Comparationis*），于1984年正式发表（Krzeszowski, 1984），文中提出"对比中立项"处在比较研究的核心位置（lies at the heart of any comparison），并提出七项"对比中立项"，作为对比研究的基础，包括统计对等（statistic equivalence）、翻译对等（translation equivalence）、系统对等（system equivalence）、句法语义对等（semanto-syntactic equivalence）、规则对等（rule equivalence）、语用或功能对等（pragmatic or functional equivalence），以及实体对等（substantial equivalence）。在此基础上他于1989年发表《论对比研究的分类》，完成了他的理论架构。1990年他将历年的研究成果汇总为一本专著——《对比语言学的范围》。这是当代西方对比语言学的又一本重要专著。

Krzeszowski is the other active scholar eager to define theoretical contrastive study. He wrote on the subject as early as 1967 ("Fundamental principles of structural contrastive studies"), and brought out his proposal in *Contrastive Generative Grammar: Theoretical Foundations* (1974a). Responding to Carl James, Krzeszowski begun expounding on *tertium comparationis* (henceforth TC) and in Krzeszowski 1984 claimed that the concept "lies at the heart of any comparison", identifying seven measurements of contrast, including statistic equivalence, translation equivalence, system equivalence, semanto-syntactic equivalence, rule equivalence, pragmatic or functional equivalence, as well as substantial equivalence. A refined model of his theory grounded on *tertium comparationis* was given in "Toward a Typology of Contrastive Studies" (1989), which finally led to a comprehensive presentation of his findings in *Contrasting Languages: The Scope of Contrastive Linguistics* (1990), a representative work in contrastive linguistics of the West.

这本著作体现了克氏20余年来一以贯之、孜孜不倦的追求。纵观克氏1990年的著作，我们发现他的体系有三个特点：第一，强调对比一定要有共同基础，这个基础，以前人们爱用"对等"（equivalence），克氏更爱用"对比中立项"，因为这突显对比基础的超然性，不属于所比的任一种具体语言。从1980年起，克氏花了10年时间，完善（或"坚持"）他的"对比中立项"分类，以此作为他的对比研究的横向分类体系；第二，他强调对比的共同基础其实就是语义，特别是句子语义，这是"普遍的、适用于任何语言的语义表达"（universal, language-neutral, semantic representation）（31—33），因而他认为"句法语义对等"（semanto-syntactic equivalence）是七项"对比中立项"的基础。他认为句法语义对等从抽象到具体有五个层级："语义、范畴、句法、词汇和后词汇"（semantic, categorical, syntactic, lexical, and post-lexical），并认为这一层级体系也适用于其他六个"对比中立项"。这就实现了他的对比研究体系的纵向分类，并且巧妙地把他的新体系纳入了自己10多年前（1974年）提出的"生成对比语法"体系里，保持了20多年思想的"一贯性"；第三，克氏在坚持自己的体系同时又能保持一种理论的宽容性，并且有一种"与时俱进"的气度，适时接纳进新的语言学理论和研究方法。在他理论建立发展的20多年里，新的语言理论层出不穷，转换生成语法之后，生成语义学、格语法、社会语言学、心理语言学、认知语言学、词汇语法研究、语义学、语用学、篇章分析、话语分析，等等，尽管他的理论的根本基础是生成语言学、特别是生成语义学，但他对这些新出的语言学理论似乎都并不反感，而且尽量纳入他自己的体系。例如他在传统的"语音、句法、词汇"层面的对比之外加入了"语用"对比（同上：90），第XI章又引进了认知语法，提出"原型对等理论"（prototype theory of equivalence），（同上：222）等。由于克氏的体系过于庞大，因此后来切斯特曼说，还不如把克尔采斯佐斯基的对等分类看作是了解对比语言学历史发展的一条线索：

Krzeszowski 1990 is really 20 years of unwavering research into contrastive linguistics. The work was different in three aspects. Firstly, it emphasized the common ground for comparison, which used to be recognized as "equivalence", although Krzeszowski preferred to adopt *tertium comparationis*. TC, not belonging to any of the languages in comparison, represents an independent platform for contrasting. Krzeszowski spent some ten years since 1980 perfecting (or maintain) his categorization of TC to serve his needs for a horizontal typological system. It is also noteworthy that for Krzeszowski, underscoring the common ground of comparison is semantic; in particular semantic at sentential level is deemed as "universal, language-neutral, semantic representation" (Krzeszowski, 1990: 31—33). All his other measurements of TC are to be based on semanto-syntactic equivalence and there are five levels of semanto-syntactic equivalence (as well as the other six equivalences), namely, semantic, categorical, syntactic, lexical and post-lexical, beginning with the most abstract of all. This formed the basic structure of Krzeszowski's vertical system of contrastive analysis and was merged neatly into his contrastive generative grammar framework raised more than a decade previously in 1974 to demonstrate the consistency in his thought process. Equally remarkable was Krzeszowski's magnanimous intent to accommodate new theories while holding on to his own. Keeping abreast with the numerous novel and further theories springing up over the 20 years of development after Krzeszowski's own formulation, such as generative semantic theory, case grammar, sociolinguistics, psycholinguistics, cognitive linguistics, lexico-grammatical model, semantics, pragmatics, text and discourse analysis among others, he had the breadth of mind to absorb them into his own scheme as far as possible. For instance, contrast in pragmatics was added on top of the traditional phonology, syntax and lexical levels (*ibid.*: 90) and proposed "prototype theory of equivalence" based on cognitive grammar (*ibid.*: 222). Apparently, Krzeszowski's systems were far too huge, and on this account, the classification by Krzeszowski may well be a good way to understanding the historical development of CA. As Chesterman succinctly put it:

> 最早是建立在结构主义基础上的系统对等以及某种结构对等，加上翻译对等，转换语法带来了规则对等，生成语义学和格语法则聚焦在实体对等加上各种语义共性，而最新研究则带来了语用学的问题。
> （切斯特曼，1998：37）

> Krzeszowski's set of equivalence types actually serves as a useful guide to the way Contrastive Analysis has developed over time. The early (non-phonological) studies were structural, based on system equivalence and a kind of construction equivalence, plus translation equivalence. The era of transformational grammar brought an interest in rule equivalence, while generative semantics and case grammar focused more on the substantial equivalence furnished by semantic universals of various kinds (see especially Di Pietro, 1971). And more recent research has then branched out into pragmatic issues. (Chesterman, 1998: 37)

克氏的不足在于他坚持认为对比研究属于一种应用研究，其背后一定要有一种理论语言学作为支撑，因而缺乏一种对比语言学的自主意识，在他企图把针锋相对的语言学理论（如生成语言学与认知语言学）综合起来时，有时显得捉襟见肘。同时尽管他对乔姆斯基的理论多批评，但他的对比语言学体系基本上还是建立在由乔氏理论发展而来的生成语义学（提出生成语义学的莱柯夫等人后来转了向，这里不论）基础之上的。因而始终坚持深层语义的不变性和普遍性，这也影响了他的理论的深入。此外，他坚持对比研究要为教学服务，也局限了他的理论的发展。在他的书的开头，他提出他的书要解决三个悖论：语法悖论（grammatical paradox）、语义悖论（semantic paradox）和教学悖论（pedagogical paradox）。语法悖论指语法上相似性大的可比值大而不值得比，相似性小的可比值小而难以对比。语义悖论指语言间的不同只在表层，在深层结构上有很多相似之处，到了语义表达层就完全是普遍相同的，因而随着普遍语法的发展对比语言学就越来越没有必要。教学悖论指理论语言学家最不感兴趣、认为微不足道的东西往往是教学上最重要的。但看完全书，我们的感觉是他一个悖论也没能很好解决。

Insisting on CA as an application, which therefore must be supported by a linguistic theory, is where Krzeszowski may have fallen short in establishing CA, in its way, as an autonomous discipline. It was particularly inadequate when he attempted to integrate rival theories such as generative theory and cognitive theory. Rooted in generative semantics first developed from Chomskyan theory (not mentioning George Lakoff's gradual shift away), which, although he was not entirely satisfied, believed firmly the constant and universal characteristics of the deep semantic structure, Krzeszowski's theory cannot venture beyond the scope. Insistence on serving the needs of applied linguistics was yet another factor limiting the development. It is interesting to note that Krzeszowski identified three theoretical issues bedevilling CA:

(1) The grammatical paradox: refers to a situation where the degree of similarity over grammatical structure is large but renders comparison unworthy, while, on the other hand, where the degree of similarity is small, comparison is made extremely difficult.

(2) The semantic paradox: states that differences between languages are found only on the surface structure; similarities take control at the deep structure and languages are universally the same when it comes to the semantic level. It follows that contrastive linguistics is becoming redundant with universal grammar's development.

(3) The pedagogical paradox: states that issues that least interest linguists or that appear least significant are, more often than not, the focal from a pedagogical point of view.

He aimed to resolve these issues with his book, but there is still a long way to go.

1.5.2 篇章与话语对比分析
1.5.2 Contrastive analysis in text and discourse

1.5.2.1 篇章对比
1.5.2.1 Contrastive study of text

詹姆斯提出了对比篇章学的设想，而对篇章对比研究作出较大贡献的一位学者是芬兰的恩克维斯特（Nils Erik Enkvist）。恩氏从1960年代初就开始从事对比研究，1977年提出对比篇章学的构想，1984年发表《对比语言学与篇章语言学》一文，可能是这一领域最重要的文章之一。文中他提出了篇章研究的四种模式，以及相应的四种对比语言研究模式：

While it was Carl James who formally proposed the setting up of contrastive text analysis, it was Finnish linguist Nils Erik Enkvist who contributed significantly to CA in text. Enkvist started researching in contrastive linguistics back in the 1960s, and first shed light on text comparison in 1977. His paper "Contrastive Linguistics and Text Linguistics" (1984) is probably one of the most important documents in this area. Four types of text research corresponding to four types of contrastive text analysis models were raised in that paper and are outlined below.

（1）基于句子的篇章研究模式

（1）Sentence-based text model

主要是在传统句子研究模式基础上增加篇章的特点，如句间互参（intersentential co-reference）现象，以描写句子间的衔接问题（intersentential cohesion）。其不足之处是不能改变篇章内原来对句子的划分，因此需要——

This chiefly entails adding text characteristics to the traditional sentence-based analysis model, noting such phenomena as intersentential co-reference and intersentential cohesion among others. To supplement the inadequacies of this model, which was hand-tied in varying the segmentation of sentences in text, it was necessary to introduce a further model, as follows.

（2）基于述说的篇章研究模式

（2）Predication-based text model

与（1）的不同是不以现成句子为出发，而是以一组述说以及述说间的语义联系（interpredictional semantic relations），如时间关系（temporal）、致使关系（causal）等为出发点，以一个个述说作为"篇章原子"（text atom）、研究篇章策略（text strategy）及篇章化（textualization）过程，即同一组篇章原子如何能组成不同的篇章。其不足之处是无法解释说话或写作者为什么把这一组述说篇章化而不是那一组，因此需要——

Departing from model (1) above, this model did not depend on ready sentences in text, but on a group of interpredictional semantic relations, such as temporal, causal relations, which acted as "text atoms". This model also focused on text strategy and textualization to understand how the same group of text atoms could make up different texts. However, it failed to explain why it was that a particular group of atoms was chosen over another group for a given textualization. This leads us to the third model below.

（3）认知篇章研究模式

(3) Cognitive text model

与（2）的不同是不以现成的述说为出发点，而是以述说得以产生的经验和知识为出发点。由于述说产生过程基于联想网络（association network），其中概念及其联系分别为网络中的节点（nodes）和途径（paths），篇章策略的研究就变成对节点的切入和途径的选择，这也就是认知模式。但认知模式仍然无法解释说话或写作者的动机和意图（motives and intentions），因此需要——

Instead of using predication, the cognitive model seeks to begin from experiences and knowledge leading to the generation of predication. The predication process is based on the association network formed by concepts and relations denoted by nodes and paths respectively. Text strategy looks into the nodes and choices of paths, essentials of the cognitive model. Yet there are still questions regarding speaker or author motives and intentions, to be answered by the fourth model.

（4）互动篇章研究模式

(4) Interactional text model

与（3）的不同是更关注人们在交际过程中的互动行为方式（interactional behaviour patterns），从说话或写作者的意图出发来辨认诸如直接言语行为和间接言语行为、本意与反讽等。（3）与（4）常常结合在一起。

The deviation from the previous model was that the present model put more weight on the interactional behaviour patterns in a given communication process. The model made use of the known speech intention to tell direct and indirect speech acts, the real meaning and irony, apart. Models (3) and (4) were often used in integration.

从四种篇章研究模式出发，恩克维斯特提出了四种相应的对比研究模式：

Deriving from the above four text analysis models, Enkvist proposed four corresponding contrastive models for text analysis.

（1）与基于句子的篇章研究模式相应的是句法结构与信息结构间的影响研究。由于宏观的篇章结构控制微观的句法结构并与之发生交互作用（textual macrostructures govern, and interact with, syntactic microstructures），而各语言间的宏观篇章结构和微观句法结构又很不相同，这就为对比研究提供了很好的课题。

(1) The corresponding contrastive model to the sentence-based model examines the influence syntactic structure and information structure have on each other. Given that textual macrostructures govern, and interact with, syntactic microstructures, there exists ample room for research as the textual macrostructures and syntactic microstructures vary greatly across languages.

（2）与基于述说的篇章研究模式相应的是篇章内句子的划界问题，翻译中常发生要打散原文的句子界限并在译文中进行重新组合的问题，这就是"篇章原子"的分解和重新篇章化的问题。对比研究与翻译的关系密切，主要表现在这里。

(2) The corresponding contrastive model to the predication-based text model studies sentence segmentation issues within texts, including the breaking and making of sentences in the translation process. The function of the text atom is particularly evident here in that a text is being dissected and re-textualized in another language, illustrative of the closeness between contrastive studies and translation.

（3）与认知篇章研究模式相应的是更深层的认知范畴与文化图式（cultural schemata or frames）对比。认知体现了对世界结构的范畴化，如果接受沃尔夫关于说不同语言的人生活在不同的认知世界里的说法，我们就不能若无其事地对认知单位进行对比，而必须对整个认知网络包括其中反映的文化图式进行对比。

(3) The corresponding contrastive model for the cognitive text model delves further into the cognitive categories and cultural schemata or frames across languages. Cognition put the world structure into categories and, if we acknowledge the view of Whorf that speakers of different languages live in differing cognitive worlds, it is not possible to satisfy at contrasting cognitive units, rather we will want to get into the whole cognitive web, of which cultural schemata forms a part for more thorough comparison.

（4）与互动篇章研究模式相应的是社会语言传统和文化传统的对比研究。由于文化传统越远的语言越应该考虑互动因素，因此这一对比不仅包括对话、话论转换（turn-taking）、言语行为、风格、礼貌语域（registers of politeness）、面子等，还包括社会传统、叙事传统、文学传统等，实际上，宏观篇章结构还应包括全部文学理论和文学历史。（参见Enkvist，1984：46—50）

(4) The corresponding contrastive model for the interactional text model takes on sociolinguistic traditions and cultural traditions across languages. The further apart the cultural traditions inherent in a given pair of languages, the more interaction to be expected. In this regard, it is not only dialogues, turn-taking, speech act, style, registers of politeness and faces that would serve the contrasting purposes, but social traditions, narrative tradition and literary tradition must also be taken into consideration. In fact, textual macrostructures include all literary theories and history. (Enkvist, 1984: 46—50)

恩克维斯特的这一大纲规模宏大，其第四种模式不但包括了话语分析或语用学的对比研究，似乎还进入了书面语领域，不像一般话语分析或语用学研究大多停留在口语交际上。

Magnificent indeed was Enkvist's contrastive text analysis. In particular, the corresponding contrastive model for the interactional text model involves contrastive discourse analysis, contrastive pragmatics and may well have crossed into written text while most discourse and pragmatics research would stop at verbal communication.

1.5.2.2 话语对比
1.5.2.2 Contrastive discourse analysis

詹姆斯提到的另一个宏观对比研究领域——话语对比研究，在很长一段时间里进展似乎不大。尽管法国的莱利（Philip Riley，1979/1981）、美国的菲尔墨（Charles J. Fillmore，1984）和波兰的奥列克赛（Wieslaw Oleksy，1984）等都提出了他们关于对比语用学的构想，奥列克赛还主编了一本对比语用学的论文集（1989），拓宽了对比研究的领域，但其论述的内容和方法基本上没有超出当时语言学界正在兴起的话语分析理论和语用学的内容。三篇中相对来说写得较好的莱利的文章，也只是强调结构与功能的非一对一关系：同一形式可以表示多种功能，同一功能可由多种形式表示，并认为这是语用学分析与语法分析的最大区别（1981：125）；他还把语用对比分析建立在三个层次的结构上：语言或形式结构（locutionary or formal structure）、非语言或交际结构（illocutionary or communicative structure），以及对话或漫谈结构（interactive or discursive structure），也体现出一定新意（1981：128—129）。但总的来说成就不大。其原因据我们看来，是因为没能跳出语言与语言教学的圈子。奥列克赛主编的《对比语用学》（1989）就是一个明显的例子，这本论文集分为两部分，标题分别为"语用学与跨语言研究"（Pragmatics in Cross-language Studies）以及"中介语、二语习得与语用学"（Pragmatics in Interlanguage and Second Language Acquisition Studies）。

Yet another macro aspect of contrastive studies advanced by Carl James is contrastive discourse analysis. For a while, things seemed to be very slow-moving, despite the fact that there were a number of papers expounding on the subject in various parts of the West, such as Philip Riley (1979/1981) in France, Charles J. Filmore (1984) in the US and Wieshaw Oleksy (1984) in Poland. In an effort to expand the scope of contrastive studies, Oleksy edited a volume on contrastive pragmatics studies in 1989; however, the ideas and methodology adopted were bound within the most heated discussion in linguistics at the time, i.e. the theory of discourse analysis and pragmatics. In comparison, Riley's paper was perhaps more noteworthy. Maintaining that the relation of formal structure and function is more than one-to-one, i.e. one particular construction may possess more than one function, while the same function may be expressed in more than one construction, Riley thought it to be the chief difference between pragmatic analysis and syntactic analysis (1981: 125). He built his pragmatic analysis on a three-levelled structure: locutionary or formal structure and illocutionary or communicative structure, and interactive or discursive structure, which was novel to a certain extent (1981: 128—129). The limitation in scaling greater heights could be attributed to the attachment to applied and pedagogical thought patterns, in general. Oleksy (1989) encapsulated this when he divided his collection into two parts, entitled: "Pragmatics in Cross-language Studies", and "Pragmatics in Interlanguage and Second Language Acquisition Studies".

1.5.2.3 哈特曼的《对比篇章学》
1.5.2.3 Hartmann's *Contrastive Textology*

其实真正体现詹姆斯这一宏观研究设想的是德籍英国学者哈特曼

（Reinhard R. K. Hartmann），他的《对比篇章学：应用语言学中的话语对比分析》一书与詹氏的书同年出版，而时间略晚。如果说詹氏只提出了一个宏观对比设想，在内容上还比较虚的话，则哈氏的书可说在相当程度上弥补了这一缺陷。哈氏的书是一部理论与应用并重的书，全书八章，前四章讲理论，后四章讲应用。尽管他的书名是《对比篇章学》，好像只是对比语言学中的一个领域，但其不少分析很有深度，在对比语言学史上的地位至少不应低于詹姆斯。

Putting Carl James's macro perception to work was Reinhard R. K. Hartmann. This German brought out his book *Contrastive Textology: Comparative Discourse Analysis in Applied Linguistics* later the same year as James. If what James proposed is simply an ideal, a perception, Hartmann filled in the substance. The book, comprising four chapters in theory and another four in application, was balanced in its approach with much in-depth analysis. Though the title might read like a sub-field in contrastive linguistics, we opine that Hartmann has earned a place in the history of contrastive linguistics no less than Carl James.

哈氏的书有几个特点。第一个也是给人印象最深的是他的理论的综合性。在序言中他就提到当时对比分析出现了一些新术语，诸如"对比风格学"（contrastive stylistics）、"比较修辞学"（comparative rhetoric）、"翻译中的篇章语法"（text grammar in translation）、"对比语用研究"（contrastive pragmatic studies）等，而他的目标是将所有这一些不同的方面全部综合进一个体系。而他实际上也做到了这一点。他前三章的标题分别是"话语分析"、"对比分析"和"对比篇章学"，事实上第一、二章是对"话语—篇章分析"和"对比分析"的相关的历史的叙述，第三章则是将这两个方面综合进一个学科。而他叙述历史的角度又非常奇特，是从理论或学科发展的角度谈的，因而非常富有启示意义。例如谈话语分析的历史，他从古老的修辞学谈起，提到"修辞学"（rhetoric）、"文学风格学"（literary stylistics）和"训诂学"（exegesis），认为这些都是篇章研究的传统，但其不足在于未能概括交际过程的复杂性，也未能提供分析的工具：

Hartmann's work impresses in a number of ways. The most impressive is the degree of theoretical integration achieved. In his foreword, he summed up the new terminologies in CA at his time, namely, contrastive stylistics, comparative rhetoric, text grammar in translation, contrastive pragmatic studies among others and aimed to fit them into one united system. He did just that. The first three chapters on "discourse analysis", "contrastive analysis" and "contrastive textology" should really read as a historical development on "discourse-text analysis" and "contrastive analysis" for Chapters 1 and 2 while Chapter 3 was an attempt to assimilate the two different aspects previously into a sub-discipline. Hartmann anchored his description of history from a unique and revealing angle of theoretical or disciplinary evolution. For instance, he traced discourse analysis all the way back to the rhetoric traditions of ancient Rome, covering traditions in literary stylistics as well as exegesis alongside foundations to modern discourse analysis, and at the same time lamenting on the incapability of past studies to address the complexities in communication processes and the lack of tools for analysis:

> 这些与修辞有关的学科本身界限不清，未能概括交际过程的复杂性，特别是作为信息载体的"文本"需要分析的工具，而风格学与训诂学都未能提供。（哈特曼，1980：13—14）

> None of the rhetorical categories was in themselves differentiated enough to characterize the intricacies of the communication process; in particular the "text" as the carrier of the message required analytical tools which stylistic and exegetical practice was unable to supply. (Hartmann, 1980: 13—14)

由此他引进了注重言语交际研究的各种理论，如莫里斯（Charles Morris, 1938）、罗兰·巴特（Roland Barthes, 1964/67）等的"符号学"（semiotics），拉斯维尔（Harold Lasswell, 1949）、埃德尔曼（Murray Edelman, 1964）等的"内容分析"，奥斯汀（John Austin, 1962）、甘柏兹（John Gumperz, 1968）等的"言语行为理论"，卡普兰的"新修辞学"（new rhetoric，即我们下面要介绍的"对比修辞学"）。这些理论都是对传统修辞学的继承和拓展（accommodation and extension）。六十年代末，把语言看作篇章话语进行研究的想法日趋成熟，更重要的是，语言学理论界乔姆斯基对普遍语法的极端鼓吹已进入绝境需要有一个新的动力，这两方面的结合便产生了两门新的学科领域：话语分析（discourse analysis）和篇章语法（text grammar）。但哈氏认为这两个学科有互补性，最好合并成一个，叫"篇章话语学"（text-discourse theory）。他说：

> From here, he introduced theories with a focus on language communication,

such as semiotics by Charles Morris (1938) and Roland Barthes (1964/67); "content analysis" by Harold Lasswell (1949) and Murray Edelman (1964); "language behaviour theory" of John Austin (1962) and John Gumperz (1968) as well as "new rhetoric" of Robert Kaplan, which will be introduced below as contrastive rhetoric. All these were "accommodation and extension" of and from traditional rhetoric. Before the end of 1960s, regarding language as text and discourse in analysis grew in maturity and, as Hartmann put it, "most importantly, linguistic theory had—after Noam Chomsky's radical reappraisal of some cherished notions of general grammar—reached an impasse which could only be overcome by a very powerful thrust". Such were the forces that jointly propelled the birth of two new disciplines: discourse analysis and text grammar. To Hartmann, who felt the two disciplines complemented each other, the term "text-discourse theory" was preferable. He explained:

> 尽管这话语分析与篇章语法起源不同，研究方法也有异，但两者最好还是同时考虑，因为两者实际上是对同一个事实的互补的观点，只是以前没有明说而已：信息可以编码（或翻译）成话语，话语以篇章形式实现，而篇章必须以可解码的型式来组织。（哈特曼，1980：18）
>
> In spite of their different ancestry and research methods, discourse analysis and text grammar are best considered together, because they give us two complementary views of the single, but previously not explicitly articulated fact that messages are encoded as (or translatable into) discourse, discourse is realized as text, and text must be organized into a pattern to be decodable. (Hartmann, 1980: 18)

第二章对于对比语言研究发展的分析也是如此。对传统的"比较语言学"（comparative linguistics）、"区域语言学"（areal linguistics）、"类型语言学"（typological linguistics）、"借语理论"（borrowing theory）、"双语理论"（bilingual theory）、"语言接触理论"（language contact theory）以及"预测性对比分析"（predictive CA）、"深层结构对比分析"（deep-structure CA）、"偏误分析"（error analysis）、"克里奥耳理论"（theory of Creolisation）、"翻译理论"（theory of translation）等均作了综合考察，考察它们对发展对比语言学的意义。他特别指出加拿大的瓦伊尼与达贝尔内（Jean-Paul Vinay & Jean Louis Darbelnet, 1958）的"比较风格学"

（comparative stylistics）其实是最早在语言比较中给话语以恰当地位的，可惜后来没有受到重视。我们未必完全同意哈特曼的分析，但他看问题的方法很有全局感和历史感，很能启发人的思路。

Hartmann's treatment of the development in contrastive linguistics took the same approach. He surveyed traditional theories, including comparative linguistics, areal linguistics, typological linguistics, borrowing theory, bilingual theory, and theory of language contact, predictive CA, deep-structure CA, error analysis, and theory of Creolization among others for a comprehensive picture on the significance of each of these ideas relative to contrastive linguistics. It was brought to light that the idea of "comparative stylistics" by Canadian scholars Jean-Paul Vinay and Jean Louis Darbelnet (1958) was in fact the first to offer due recognition to discourse from the contrastive point of view, but did not attract sufficient attention. We need not seek consensus with Hartmann's analysis, but should nevertheless draw inspiration from his method of analysis which respects the overall picture as well as being strong in the sense of history.

第二，哈特曼的视野开阔，不但表现在熟悉的领域广，而且每个领域的诸家学说都能兼顾。例如篇章研究，他就列举并评述了三家模式：辛克莱和库尔哈德（Sinclair & Coulhard，1975）、韩礼德与哈珊（Halliday and Hasan，1976），以及凡尔利希（Werlich，1976）。认为三者的分类和研究各有侧重，如果合起来可以成为一个更好的模式。这一点对不少中国的研究者特别有启示意义，因为他们习惯于接受某一家外国作者的理论，自此再也离不开，例如在语篇研究上，很多人离开了韩礼德模式就不知怎么从事研究，不但这里提到的另几家对他们来说闻所未闻，就是通常被认为是篇章语言学创始人的波格朗与德莱斯勒（如Beaugrande & Dressler，1981）也不见有人提到。这显然会影响研究的深入。

Hartmann also impresses with his breadth of knowledge and vision, not only in his own areas of interest but also various other schools of thought. For example, in text analysis, he cited and commented on three models: those of Sinclair and Coulhard (1975), Halliday and Hasan (1976) and Werlich (1976). He suggested that the three models, having their own biases and advantages, could well be combined to become a better model. This suggestion should be borne in mind by Chinese researchers who are often nailed to one specific school of thought. In this instance, most Chinese scholars would have felt handicapped outside of Halliday's model as most of them have not even heard of the other two models, not to mention de Beaugrande and Dressler (1981), generally regarded as the founder of text linguistics. We can imagine how this would have hampered further research.

第三，在此之前的对比分析一般只服务于外语教学，詹姆斯提到了翻译，但未怎么展开，也许跟其本人不擅长有关。哈氏是国际著名的词典学专家，对双语词典、词典翻译研究有素。他的"加盟"自然充实了对比语言学的应用范围，更可贵的是，他花了四章即全书一半的篇幅谈了篇章对比的三个应用层面：翻译与比较文学、语码转换与语言学习、双语词典的编纂。

Additionally, Hartmann has made some breakthrough in contrastive studies and translation. We know very well that contrastive studies have been utilized for a period of time as a tool for foreign language teaching and although James touched upon translation, it was not elaborated on, probably due to unfamiliarity in this field. It was different with Hartmann, as he was a renowned lexicologist specializing in bilingual dictionaries and translation of dictionaries. His presence added weight to the application aspect of contrastive linguistics, evident in his devoting half of his volume to the application of contrastive textology on three fronts: translation and comparative literature, code switching and language learning and compilation of bilingual dictionaries.

哈特曼提出的名称虽然是"对比篇章学"，其实内容也包罗了句子以下层面，因而建立了一个相当完整的对比研究体系。（参见Hartmann, 1980: 34）

Although Hartmann called it "contrastive textology", the substance included elements below sentential level and could well be considered as a relatively complete contrastive model. (Hartmann, 1980: 34)

在方法论上，从篇章出发，哈特曼提出了一个"平行文本法"（parallel texts），认为这个方法可以用于各个平面，结合各种方法：

In terms of methodology, bearing text in mind, Hartmann proposed the concept of "parallel texts" to cover different platforms and integrating different approaches:

> 平行文本法在语言比较中可用于各个平面，结合任何方法。常识就告诉我们应该在话语框架内将有关音系学、词汇学、语法学、篇章学的知识，与概念—逻辑、批评—考释、关联—社会学，及实验-

科学方法结合起来，折衷成一个整体的研究方法。（哈特曼，1980:
37）

  Parallel texts can be used to make interlingual comparisons at all levels and with any method. Common sense dictates that we should (a) incorporate what we know about phonology, lexicology, grammar and textology within a discourse framework, and (b) combine the conceptual logical, critical exegetical, and experimental scientific approaches into an eclectic whole. (Hartmann, 1980: 37)

作为英国埃克斯特大学的资深教授，哈特曼培养出了许多有成就的学生，其中就有现在颇负盛名的哈丁（Basil Hatim）。他的《跨文化交际——翻译理论与对比篇章语言学》（1997）现在也已成这一领域的一部重要文献。
As a long-serving professor at the University of Exeter, England, Hartmann groomed many brilliant students among whom, Basil Hatim, author of the prominent work *Communication Across Cultures: Translation Theory and Contrastive Text Linguistics* (1977), was but one of them.

1.5.2.4 维尔茨皮卡的贡献
1.5.2.4 Contributions of Wierzbicka

  在语用对比方面，真正具有突破意义的是波兰出生的著名澳大利亚语言学家维尔茨皮卡（Anna Wierzbicka）。维氏是当代最重要的语言学家之一，其成就是多方面的，也不以对比语言学出名，她把她的语用研究叫做"跨文化语用"学（cross-cultural pragmatics）。

  Anna Wierzbicka must be mentioned when it comes to contrastive pragmatics. In any sense, the Poland-born Australian linguist has broken new grounds in real terms. Wierzbicka, an important contemporary linguist in her own right, is noted for her contributions in many areas in which contrastive linguistics was really not on the list. Her findings in pragmatics were collected in *Cross-Cultural Pragmatics: The Semantics of Human Interaction* (1991).

  维氏有几个重要的观点。第一，她从根本上质疑语法、语义、语用三分的做法，批评符号学创始人莫里斯这样做是把符号与符号使用者区别开来，认为就自然语言来说,语言外的世界和语言使用者的社会和心理世界是不能分开的;语言是个统一的系统,其运用的一切手段都是为了传递意义,也许可以说有"词汇的语义学、语法的语义学、交际的语义学",但像莫里斯那样分为语义学、语形学和语用学,对某些人造语言可能有点意义,对自然语言却毫无意义(Wierzbicka, 1991: 16);

Wierzbicka highlighted a few notable arguments in pragmatics. She first challenged the attempt to break syntax, semantics and pragmatics into three separate roles, criticising Morris, founder of semiotics, for dividing signs from its user in the course. For one, "the very nature of natural language is such that it doesn't separate extralinguistic reality from the psychological and social world of language users". Secondly, "language is an integrated system, where everything 'conspires' to convey meaning: words, grammatical constructions and various 'illocutionary' devices" and "linguistics falls naturally into three parts, which could be called lexical semantics, grammatical semantics, and illocutionary semantics". "A Morrisian division of the study of signs into semantics, syntax, and pragmatics may make good sense with respect to some artificial sign systems, but it makes no sense with respect to natural language, whose syntactic and morphological devices (as well as illocutionary devices) are themselves carriers of meaning." (Wierzbicka, 1991: 16)

第二,不能进行纯语用学的研究,尤其是跨文化的语用研究,因为语用学没有一个严密的系统可用来进行描写和比较,也没有什么能牢牢把握住的术语,可用来对无穷无尽的语言用法进行有力的分析与解释(同上:17);

Next, Wierzbicka contested the conduct of pure pragmatic research, or "pragmaticism", saying that "pragmaticism" proves very hard to apply fruitfully when it comes to actual description of meanings, especially in a cross-cultural perspective, because it has no rigorous framework for description and comparison, no firm grid in terms of which the endless vagaries of language use can be rigorously analyzed and interpreted. (*ibid.*: 17)

第三,有两种语用学,一种是语言学的"语用学",一种是其他学科的"语言使用学"(笔者按:两者维氏用的都是"pragmatics"一词),前者是语言能力的一部分,后者是社会学、心理学、民族学、文学等研究的领域(同上:19)。这两者之间有着很大距离,而语言的语用学与语言的语义学之间却没有鸿沟,甚至可把语用学看作是语义学的一部分,所谓的"语用"研究必须以语义研究的方法来进行（同上）；

Wierzbicka then proceeded to suggest the recognition of "two pragmatics": "a linguistic pragmatics which can form a part of a coherent, integrated description of linguistic competence" and "another pragmatics, or other pragmatics (in the plural): a domain or domains of the sociologist, the psychologist, the ethnomethodologist, the literary scholar, and so on" (*ibid.*: 19). She stated that while there is a gulf between pragmatics, there is no gulf between linguistic pragmatics and linguistic semantics, and that linguistic pragmatics can even be fruitfully seen as part of linguistic semantics and be described in exactly the same framework.

第四，为了比较意义在不同语言和不同文化中是如何表达的，需要一种独立于具体语言或文化、又能在各种语言中进行解释的"元语义"（同上：6）。这就有点像对比学者提出的"对比中立项"。不同的是，主张"对比中立项"的克尔采斯佐斯基等人都同意或不反对乔姆斯基的普遍语法说，而维尔茨皮卡却是乔氏理论的坚定反对者。在《跨文化语用学：人类交际语义学》一书中，维尔茨皮卡从语义出发，比较了英语、波兰语、黑人英语、澳大利亚英语、伊迪语（Yiddish）、希伯来语、日语、Walmatjari（一种澳洲土著语）、意大利语、俄语、汉语等不同语言文化背景下的语用情况，提供了很丰富的资料。同时，在"自然元语义"（natural semantic metalanguage）理论的基础上，她提出了"普遍初义"（universal semantic primitives）假设，作为进行语言文化比较的基础。但这个"初义"的数量在不断增加，刚提出时只有13个（Wierzbicka, 1980），1991年增加到27个（Wierzbicka, 1991: 8），2001年发展到62个（Wierzbicka and Harkins, 2001: 12），看来这个理论还在成熟过程中。近年来，维氏致力于"情感"（emotion）的跨语言文化比较（如Wierzbicka, 1999），又进而提出了"文化原迹"（cultural scripts）的理论（如Wierzbicka, 1994；1996；forthcoming），在以语义学取代语用学的路上走得越来越远，当然，从另一种角度看，也可以说是越来越深刻。对认知语言学、人类学语言学和对比语言学都有借鉴意义。

Regarding a comparison of the expression of meaning across languages and cultures, Wierzbicka suggested using a "semantic metalanguage", independent of any particular language or culture and yet accessible and open to interpretation through any language (*ibid.*: 6). This may be akin to *tertium comparationis* save that scholars such as Krzeszowski, who is fully for *tertium comparationis*, either support or do not object to Chomsky's universal grammar; Wierzbicka on the other hand, is a strong opponent of Chomskian theory. In Wierzbicka (1991), language usage across some ten languages of differing cultural background was compared using semantics, arriving at a rich set of data. The languages under survey include English, Polish, Black English, Australian English, Yiddish, Hebrew, Japanese, Walmatjari (a native language in Australia), Italian, Russian and Chinese. Based on her natural semantic metalanguage theory, an assumption on universal semantic primitives was proposed on which comparison across languages and cultures could be carried out. Such semantic primitives grew from an initial 13 (Wierzbicka, 1980) to 27 in 1991 (Wierzbicka, 1991: 8) and then 62 in 2001 (Wierzbicka and Harkins, 2001: 12). The theory seems still to be at its maturing stage. In recent years, Wierzbicka channelled her energy towards cross-cultural comparison of "emotion" and proposed a theory on cultural scripts. It seems that she is moving further and further away from replacing pragmatics with semantics, or, if seen from another angle, she is digging even deeper and her discoveries should shed lights on cognitive linguistics, anthropological linguistics and contrastive linguistics.

1.5.3 对比修辞学
1.5.3 Contrastive rhetoric

20世纪60年代末以后，对比语言研究的重心从美国转到了欧洲，很多人认为此后美国的对比研究就乏善可陈，其实不然，只是东方不亮西方亮，从另一个地方冒了出来而已。这"另一个地方"就是对比修辞学，经过30多年的发展，成果也已蔚然可观。对比修辞学与对比分析其实同出一源，都是想为二语教学、特别是英语作为外语或第二语言的教学服务。所不同者，一重在口语，一重在书面语。对比分析声势大、口气大，来得凶猛，退潮也快；对比修辞学却在几乎默默无闻中逐渐成长壮大起来了。

By the close of the 1960s, the centre of contrastive linguistics had shifted from the United States to Europe. This is not to say that relevant development in the US was no longer exciting. At this time, contrastive rhetoric caught on and, as it is widely acknowledged, over the past 30 years, much has been achieved. Contrastive rhetoric and contrastive analysis really shared the same basis of servicing foreign or second language teaching, particularly with English as the target. If there is any difference between the two, it is that one focused on verbal language and the other on the written form. While contrastive analysis stormed in and retreated fast, contrastive rhetoric gained strength in silence.

对比修辞学的创始人和领袖是美国南加州大学教授卡普兰（Robert Kaplan），1966年他发表了一篇他后来称之为"游戏之作"（doodle）的文章《跨文化教育中所见的文化思维模式》，是对比修辞学的滥觞。文中他用了五种图形来表示五种不同语言文化的人组织文章段落的方式，如说英语的人是直线型（straight line），说阿拉伯语的人是平行线型（zigzag formation），说东方语言的人是螺旋型（spiraling line），说俄语和罗曼语的人都是曲折型（digressional）等：

It is widely recognized that the father of contrastive rhetoric is none other than Robert Kaplan, professor with South California University. His "doodle" essay, published in 1966, entitled "Cultural Thought Patterns in Intercultural Education" was demarcating. The paper represented in five diagrams the thought patterns of speakers of five different languages and cultures as demonstrated in paragraphing in essays. Speakers of English think in a straight line, Arabic in a zigzag fashion, oriental in a spiralling manner and Russian and Romance speakers' thoughts are digressional. (Figure 1.1)

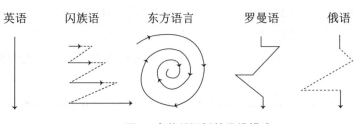

图1.1 卡普兰概括的思维模式

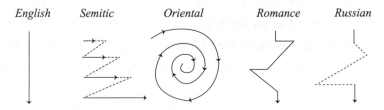

Figure1.1 Thought patterns by Robert Kaplan

此图曾被广泛引用，也引起了热烈的讨论。1972年卡普兰出版了《修辞解析：试论修辞学的一种功能理论》，一般认为标志着对比修辞学的正式诞生。其后从事对比修辞研究最重要的学者是出生于芬兰的美国印第安纳大学教授孔纳（Ulla Connor），1987年她与卡普兰一起主编了《跨语言写作：二语作文分析》，1996年又出版《对比修辞学：二语写作的跨文化视野》，成为这一领域的较新重要成果。

The diagram was widely quoted and enthusiastically discussed. In 1972, Kaplan authored another book, *The Anatomy of Rhetoric: Prolegomena to a Functional Theory of Rhetoric*, which was generally held to formally declare the birth of contrastive rhetoric. Taking after him was Ulla Conner who co-edited *Writing across Languages: Analysis of L2 Text* (1987) with Kaplan and released her more important findings in *Contrastive Rhetoric: Cross-cultural Aspects of Second-language Writing* (1996).

对比修辞学与对比分析都以二语教学为指归，但从一开始就表现出了侧重点的不同，从好几个方面看，两者可说是互补的：

Contrastive rhetoric serves second language teaching with a different focus from that of contrastive analysis. They complement each other nevertheless, in at least the following aspects.

（1）对比分析重口语，关心的是二语学习四大技能"听、说、读、写"中的"听、说"，对比修辞重书面语，关心的是其中的"读、写"尤其是"写"。重口语轻书面语是20世纪大部分时期语言研究与教学的偏差，直到最后20年才有所改进。对比修辞学可说是对这一偏差的弥补力量和改进的推动力量；

(1) Contrastive analysis, with its bias towards verbal form, pays more attention to listening and speaking skills, whereas contrastive rhetoric, keeping to written form, naturally concentrates on reading and especially writing skills. The bias towards verbal form in foreign language teaching was one serious shortcoming of language research and teaching in the twentieth century, but has been challenged in the past 20 years, in which process the development in contrastive rhetoric has been pivotal.

（2）对比分析受流行语言学说的影响，无论在CA阶段，还是EA和中介语阶段，均以句子为分析上限，对比修辞学从偏误分析（EA）着手，但没有经过中介语阶段,因此从一开始就没有把时间和精力放在句法问题上,它关心的是篇章的组织,可说是领了篇章语言学的风气之先。篇章语言学家恩克维斯特对之非常赞赏,1997年还专门写了一篇《我们为什么需要对比修辞学》的文章,说:

(2) Contrastive analysis was very much influenced by trends in linguistics and it has never gone beyond sentential level, be it at the developmental stages of CA, EA or interlanguage. Contrastive rhetoric began with EA but skipped interlanguage and zeroed in on essay organization from the outset, which may probably have been influenced by text linguistics. Explaining "Why We Need Contrastive Rhetoric" Enkvist said:

> 重要的是必须明白,篇章是句子之父,篇章组织先于个别句子的句子组织。让句子适合篇章,与篇章组织相一致,不是先有了句子之后,再作的表面上的美化加工;实际上,篇章的组织更加根本,是它决定了词语的选择以及句子的构造。对当代篇章与话语语言学家来说,这是个如此明显的事实,因此不禁觉得诧异,为什么几百年以来,语法学家和作文教师将这么多时间和精力放在单个句子的句法现象上,而对篇章组织和信息流畅的基本问题视而不见。(恩克维斯特,1997: 199)

> The important point is to realize that the text is the father of the sentence, and that the text strategies come before the syntactic formation of individual sentences. Giving a sentence its textual fit, its conformity with the text strategy, is not a cosmetic surface operation polishing the sentence after it is already there. Textual fit is a far more basic requirement, determining the choice of words as well as the syntactic structure of a sentence. To modern text and discourse linguists this is so obvious that it seems curious that grammarians and teachers of compositions have, through the centuries, spent so much time and effort on syntactic phenomena within individual sentences, while overlooking the fundamental questions of text strategy and information flow. (Enkvist, 1997: 199)

(3)对比分析只有在拉多的书里专门辟了一章谈文化比较,其后便一头钻进结构里,与此方向渐行渐远;而对比修辞学从一开始就以文化介入为基本研究手段，认为篇章、文体、风格等的差异都是由文化引起的。不仅承认各种语言间的差异，还对英语内部的各种变体，所谓的International Englishes感兴趣，这也是对比修辞学的原动力之一；

(3) Contrastive analysis only spared one chapter in Lado (1957) on cultural comparison and never once looked back in its journey in structural comparison. In contrast, cultural interference, being the single most important determinant of organization, style and genre, is the fundamental research method in contrastive rhetoric. Contrastive rhetoric not only recognizes differences across languages, it also recognizes variation internal to a specific language, for instance, the varieties of English. As such, interest in international Englishes was one driving force in its development.

（4）在指导思想上，对比分析先是结构主义，后是转换生成语法，七十年代后才加上了社会语言学和心理语言学；对比修辞学的指导思想从一开始起就是语言相对论，卡普兰曾被称为"新沃尔夫主义者"（New Whorfian），孔纳更强调沃尔夫的语言相对论是对比修辞学的基石（Connor，1996：28）。从这一方面看，对比修辞学的研究更符合沃尔夫倡导对比语言学的本意；

(4) Contrastive analysis first adopted structuralism as a guiding principle, then transformation grammar and from the 1970s sociolinguistics and psycholinguistics also played a role. As for contrastive rhetoric, it has been guided by linguistic relativity right from the outset—Kaplan was known as "new Whorfian" and Connor declared the Whorfian hypothesis to be the cornerstone of contrastive rhetoric (Connor, 1996: 28). We could then reason that contrastive rhetoric studies may be closer to Whorf's initiative of contrastive linguistics.

（5）与翻译理论的关系。对比分析与对比修辞学都注意到与翻译的关系，有趣的是两者关注的是不同的翻译理论（这与时代也有关系）。对比分析注意的是语言学派注重原文的翻译理论，特别是等值论，因而对比研究与翻译有共同的基础，即"对等"（equivalence），同时对比翻译有望对机器翻译作出贡献（参见Krzeszowski，1974b：185—186）；而对比修辞学注意的是文化学派注重译文和"迁移"（transfer）的翻译理论，特别是以色列翻译理论家图里（Gideon Toury，1980；1993）的"充分性"（adequacy）和"可接受性"（acceptability）的理论，认为这与对比修辞研究的目标有着共同性。

（孔纳，1996：123）

(5) Both contrastive analysis and contrastive rhetoric are aware of their relation with translation. Interestingly this probably has to do with their developmental backgrounds, each weighing up on a different translation theory. Contrastive analysis, favouring the linguistic school concentrating on the source text, established its connection with translation on the common concept of equivalence and has been helpful to the development of machine translation (Krzeszowski, 1974b: 185—186). Contrastive rhetoric, inclined towards the cultural school concentrating on the target text and theory of transfer, was particularly fond of Gideon Toury (1980, 1993) and found common language in such concepts as "adequacy" and "acceptability" as the object (Connor, 1996: 123).

由于重口语轻书面语的原因，对比修辞学所起的继承和弥补美国对比语言学的作用并不被许多人所认识，从而认为七十年代后美国对比语言学是一片空白。我们认为现在是给对比修辞学恰当地位的时候了。

The continued bias towards verbal data overshadowed the balance provided by contrastive rhetoric on written form, especially in the US where few really see it in this light in so far as to suggest that contrastive linguistics came to a halt in the US since the 1970s. It is high time to give contrastive rhetoric its proper place.

1.5.4 切斯特曼的杰出贡献
1.5.4 Chesterman's brilliant contributions

1998年芬兰赫尔辛基大学切斯特曼教授（Andrew Chesterman）的《对比功能分析》一书出版，使对比研究的局面有了很大改观。此书的书名 *Contrastive Functional Analysis* 别出心裁，既能作为一个词组，作为对比研究的新模式："功能对比语言学"；又可拆为"对比"、"功能"、"分析"三个词，分别讨论相关问题。作者正是兼用了这两个含义，在提出新的理论模式的同时，以"对比"、"功能"、"分析"三个词作为三章的标题，分别讨论对比研究的理论问题、方法论问题和应用问题，再加上第四章"修辞"，就组成了书的全部内容。

A true turning point came along with the release of Andrew Chesterman's *Contrastive Functional Analysis* in 1998. The professor with the University of

Helsinki brilliantly played with the construction of his book title. On the one hand, the book has a functionalist concern with its methodology and hence qualifying "analysis" with "functional". On the other hand, it can be presented as three separate headings of "Contrast", "Functional" and "Analysis" as adopted in the structuring of the book chapters to cover issues in theory, methodology and application. We did not forget of course that there is a fourth heading of "Rhetoric" to complete the picture.

也许是巧合，西方的对比语言学研究，大约每隔10年左右就要出一本有影响力的著作。即使不算1924年叶斯柏森的《语法哲学》和1940年代沃尔夫系列文章，从1950年代开始，就有拉多（1957）、迪·皮德娄（1971）、詹姆斯（1980）、克尔采斯佐斯基（1990）。克氏之后10年左右，重要的著作恐怕非切氏此书莫属。此书并不以理论为标榜，然而在理论研究的深刻性和全面性上超越了上述的任何一部著作（拉氏是草创之作，迪氏过于依赖早期生成语言学，詹氏采取"摆问题"主义，克氏的体系大而不精，而且20年间几乎只在原地踏步），可说是半个世纪来西方对比研究的集大成之作。该书的主要贡献是：

Looking at the publication dates of significant works in contrastive linguistics in the West, it may probably be mere coincidence, but there seems to be a kind of cycle of about ten years: Jespersen (1924) and Whorf's series of essays in the 1940s aside, we have Lado (1957), Di Pietro (1971), Carl James (1980) and Krzeszowski (1990). Close to ten years after Krzeszowski, Chesterman (1998) is arguably the next influential work, having a depth of theoretical perception surpassing any of the previous works. In the past 20 years, theoretical development in the field remained almost stagnant. Lado (1957) represented an initial attempt; Di Pietro (1971) relied too heavily on early transformational grammar; Carl James (1980) adopted a non-solution approach, whereas Krzeszowski (1990) proposed a complex yet less than sophisticated system. Chesterman (1998) did not start out to establish a theory but his lucid illustration of theoretical issues was convincingly the most comprehensive and mature, which succinctly wrapped up the development of CA for the last 50 years. The key contributions include:

（1）第一次对作为对比基础的一些基本概念如"相似性"（similarity）、"对等"（equivalence）、"意义"（meaning）等作了哲理性的探索。

(1) The first ever philosophical discussion on fundamental concepts in contrast, such as "similarity", "equivalence", "meaning", etc.

该书的开头部分可能是全书最精彩的章节之一。其中深刻地探讨了作为对比研究和翻译研究基础的"相似性"（similarity）问题。在此之前，我们还没有见过对比学者对相似性本身作过什么研究。切氏综合前人主要是心理学家（Sovran，1992；Tversky，1977；Goodman，1972；Medin & Goldstone，1995）的研究，得出了一些很深刻的结论。精彩之处不胜枚举，这里略举数例。如：

The book opens with an excellent and challenging deliberation of similarity as the basis for contrastive studies and translation. Similarity was an unclear concept that had been much taken for granted. Never before had there been any reasoning proposed to sort it out. Drawing on the findings chiefly of psychologists (such as Sovran, 1992; Tversky, 1977; Goodman, 1972; Medin and Goldstone, 1995, among others), Chesterman argues conclusively for the similarity concept to be established as the cognitive basis not only for the discipline, but also for his work. Breaking new ground on a seemingly old notion to place contrastive studies on a firm empirical footing, Chesterman succeeded in freshening readers up with inspiring thoughts. A glimpse of his interpretation and integration of the concept is as follows.

相似性既属于逻辑世界、社会世界，又属于认知世界（Chesterman，1998：6—7）；相似既有客观性，又有主观性，前者可称为"原发相似性"（similarity-as-trigger），后者可称作"附加相似性"（similarity-as-attribution）；对相似性的判断归根到底是人们心中对世界的认识的重新理解和整合（同上：9）；相似性不只涉及两方或三方，而是涉及多方，说A与B相似，实则是说，A与B在C的方面，根据D程序的比较，参照E标准的判断，根据F功能，为了G目的，两者是相似的；从类和例（type and token）的关系看，有两种相似性：由类到例是"分的相似"（divergent），由例到类是"合的相似"（convergent），翻译理论主要运用前一方法，而对比研究主要运用后一方法；看出某两件事物是否相似归根到底是想象力的问题，因而判断事物是否相似的能力是人类认知的核心，等等。这就为全书打下了一个非常坚实的认知理论的基础。正是因为有了对最基本概念的新的认识，就使全书新意层出不穷，新风扑面而来。

A problematic concept, similarity pertains not only to the world of logic or physical matter, or indeed the social world, but also to that of cognition (Chesterman, 1998: 6—7). There are two aspects of similarity that always present: similarity-as-trigger (objective, capturing perception from matter to mind) and similarity-as-attribution (subjective, capturing perception from mind to matter). However, any quantification, or assessments on similarity are ultimately ways of organizing and clarifying one's mental representations of the world (*ibid*,: 9). Concurring with Medin and Goldstone (1995) that similarity is a multi-place predicate, i.e. when we say that A is similar to B, what we really mean is that "A is similar to B in respects C according to comparison process D, relative to some standard E mapped onto judgments by some function F for some purpose G". (*ibid*.: 12) Chesterman draws important inferences of theoretical significance to contrastive linguistics and translation, making a relevant case on degrees of similarity much neglected previously. Adapting from the type-token relation analysis of Sovran, Chesterman proceeds to classify two types of similarity: divergent (moving from type to token) and convergent (moving from token to type). He explains that translation theories make use of the divergent concept whereas contrastive analysis use convergent. Similarity has its origins in imagination, it is closely bound up with perception and cognition and the ability to perceive similarities is limited only by the range of the human imagination (*ibid*.: 15). This is especially pertinent to translating.

（2）第一次将对比研究与翻译研究从理论基础上真正联系到了一起。

（2）Contrastive studies and translation studies are genuinely connected on theoretical fundamentals for the first time.

以往的对比研究虽然也提到翻译，但主要是借用翻译研究中的"对等"说，以之作为对比研究的出发点之一，或者悬想对比研究可能对机器翻译的贡献。哈特曼（1980）最早具体考察对比篇章语言学对翻译、文学翻译和比较文学具有的意义，而到了身兼翻译理论家与对比语言学家的切斯特曼的手上，我们又一次领略到了翻译理论与对比理论的完美结合。这种结合，不是将两者勉强凑在一起，而是首先为它们找到了共同的基础：两者都是在语言与语言行为的研究中专门处理异同问题的学科（同上：6）；两者在"类"和"例"关系的处理上正好处于互补的地位（见上条）；而且对比研究中的"相似性"本质上就是翻译研究中的"可译性"。把翻译与对比放在一起，改变了西方对比语言学始终只关注二语教学这一单一眼光，大大拓展了对比研究的理论视野和应用范围。

The mention of translation in past contrastive studies is mainly for the concept of equivalence to be used as a backbone to contrastive analysis or betting for CA to serve machine translation. Hartmann (1980) pioneered the testing of contrastive textology application against the intricacies in translation, literary translation and comparative literature. But it is through Chesterman, a translation theorist and contrastivist that we get to comprehend what a seamless theoretical fit neighbouring disciplines translation and contrastive linguistics could have. The fusion came naturally on common ground: both translation theory and contrastive analysis deal with the similarities and differences in the study of language and language behaviour (*ibid*.: 6). As aforementioned, approaches in translation theory focus on divergent similarity whereas those usually taken in contrastive analysis, on convergent similarity. This conceptual "sameness" in both disciplines could be paired with the various notions of "equivalence", leading to specification of the concept of contrastiveness (*ibid*.: 6). Pairing translation with contrastive analysis altered the one-way traffic from CA to second language teaching so that CA is now free to advance on a widened horizon and applicability.

（3）第一次提出以语言事实（instances）或语言现象（phenomenon）作为出发点的对比研究方法论。

（3）The first call for instances and phenomena of language behaviour as the starting point of contrastive research methodology

中国读者对此可能会感到惊讶，因为他们有幸生活在中国，从发出新时期第一声对比研究号角的吕叔湘先生开始，就一直强调要从语言事实出发进行对比研究；而在西方，尽管我们指出叶斯柏森（1924：346）很早就提出了"由内到外"的研究路线问题，沃尔夫（1937：87）也提出要"采用全球视角来观察语言现象，重新审视在语言中发现的各类语法范畴，在某种新的意义上建构和修订概念，增加必要的术语"的建议，但从五十年代起的对比研究传统却一直是从体系或者什么"第三方"出发的。我们看，詹姆斯（1980：169—178）讨论了三种出发点：表层结构、深层结构、翻译对等；克尔采斯佐斯基（1990：15—34）强调"对比中立项"（*tertia comparationis*），提出了令人眼花缭乱的七项"第三方"，但归根到底还是以"句法语义对等"为其核心；甚至维尔茨皮卡的"绝端语义主义"，也是以"普遍初义"（universal semantic primitives）作为共同的出发点。切斯特曼撇开了这一切，特别是在对比研究界颇有影响的"对比中立项"说，指出这种理论因其出发点与结论都是某种"对等",很可能会造成循环论证(同上:59)。在此基础上他提出要以语言事实(同上:54)作为对比研究的出发点,这在西方对比研究史上,真可说具有石破天惊的重要意义。在他之前,只有德国翻译兼对比语言学家斯奈尔杭贝(Mary Snell-Hornby)作过这样的尝试,斯氏在1982年出版了一本《德英语描写性动词语义场对比研究》,提出她的研究是"从观察语言的事实出发而不是从理论出发,不是运用某种现成理论而是从经验研究中提炼出理论概念"(Snell-Hornby,1982:13),但在对比研究的理论界并没引起足够的反响。

Chinese readers, used to a tradition that respects language phenomena, may be surprised at this call since they are most fortunate to have Lü Shuxiang as the anchorman for contrastive studies in China, who will not compromise on anything less than using linguistic facts as primary data sources. In the West however, although Jespersen has advocated the I-O research methodology (1924: 346) and Whorf also cried for "using a worldwide view of linguistic phenomena, [to] frame concepts more or less new" (Whorf, 1937: 87), the contrastive linguistic tradition since the 1950s has revolved around models or a *tertium comparationis*. To illustrate, the starting points for James were surface structure, deep structure and translation equivalence (1980: 169—178); those for Krzeszowski were seven types of *tertia comparationis* grounded on semanto-syntactic equivalence (1990: 15—34); while those for Wierzbicka, who is extremely pro-semantic, universal semantic primitives. Chesterman cast aside all these, including the concept of *tertia comparationis*, which has quite some influence in the field. He contends that the starting point and conclusion which were on the same form of equivalence of these models suggest meeting some form of circularity problem (Chesterman, 1998: 52, 59). He therefore proposes using utterances, or instances of language use as the primary data source (*ibid*.: 54). We can now see the weight the proposal carries in the history of contrastive studies in the West. Before Chesterman, perhaps, only Mary Snell-Hornby, German translator and linguist, ever adopted an empirical approach in her study. She defines her 1982 book *Verb-descriptivity in German and English* in the following words: "The study is based on direct observation of language and not on the theoretical considerations of other linguists; in other words, instead of applying already existing theories to the language, it proceeds from empirical research to a theoretical concept" (Snell-Hornby, 1982: 13). Regrettably, insufficient appreciation was accorded by theorists in the discipline.

与此相关的，是切斯特曼吸收了法国学者布鲁诺（Brunot，1922）、丹麦学者叶斯柏森（Jespersen，1924），特别是九十年代芬兰学者穆斯塔约基（Mustajoki，1993；1995）的观点，把"功能"理解为"意义的表达"，把他的研究角度称为"从意义到形式"（Chesterman，1998：1），并且明确宣布，这是一种"非生成"的语法，其关心的不是如何将意义"编码"为形式或编制出什么"运算程序"，而是跨越语言内各个平面如句法、词汇、构词法、韵律学之间的障碍，具体指出意思表达的各种可能（同上：71）。这一方法对于当代西方的对比研究有重要的意义，因为这有可能使之重回叶斯柏森和沃尔夫的传统；这个方法对于整个语言学研究，也具有革命性的改造意义，因为它将彻底告别乔姆斯基以来的演绎主义，重新走上脚踏实地的经验研究。

To support the empirical approach, Chesterman took from Brunot (1922), Jespersen (1924) and Mustajoki (1993, 1995) relevant ideas to interpret "function" as an expression of meanings and a functional approach is essentially one that is "from meaning to form" (Chesterman, 1998: 1). In a more specific manner, he indicates that "functional grammar is not generative, it is not interested in the process whereby meanings can be coded into forms, or in setting up algorithms to do this. Rather, it is interested in specifying the sets of options available, paradigms that may range freely across grammatical boundaries of all kinds, between syntax, lexis, word formation and prosody" (*ibid*.: 71). This contrastive methodology has contemporary significance in the way that it might lead the way back to the traditions of Jespersen and Whorf. To linguistic methodology at large, the proposal is also revolutionary with its empiricism that would possibly reform and change entirely the intellectual milieu governed by the deduction method of the Chomskian tradition.

（4）提出了一个更具可操作性的对比研究程序。

(4) CFA methodology: a workable contrastive procedure

对比研究究竟如何进行？实际操作步骤如何？这本来是每个从事对比研究的人都应考虑的问题，然而奇怪的是，多少年来对这个问题的解答总是语焉不详的。詹姆斯提出了一个四步法（1980：63）：①汇总资料；②进行描写；③根据需要补充资料；④进行对比。实际上对比到第四步才开始，而一开始就是结束。克尔采斯佐斯基依韩礼德的说法把传统的对比研究归结为一个三步曲

（1990：35）：①描写；②分类；③比较。"比较"也是在最后一步。而他自己提出的一个语用对比程序（1990：101），并不比上述方式更具操作性：

How should we proceed to contrast? What are the steps in reality? These sounds like rudiments all contrastivists should have first got right. This is not the case, however. James uses a four-step algorithm: ① assemble the data; ② formulate the description; ③ supplement the data as required, formulate the contrasts (1980: 63). Contrast begins and ends at step 4. Modeling after Halliday, Krzeszowski sets up three steps for "classical" contrastive studies: ① description, ② juxtaposition, ③ comparison (1990: 35). He proposed a procedure for directional contrastive pragmatic studies (1990: 101) that was no more realistic:

I. 已知语言i（CmLi）的一种社会文化背景m（C_m）。①在语言j里有没有一个对等的社会文化背景n（C_n）？如没有，②就进行社会文化对比；如有，③进入下一步；

II. 在语言j里有没有一种语言形式F_q。④与其社会文化背景CnLj在原型上的联系。⑤在某一方面类似于语言i里的语言形式FpLi与社会文化背景CmLi的联系？如没有，⑥注意语用对比；如有，⑦进入下一步；

III. FqLj与FpLi在句法语义上是否对等？如果不是，放弃对比；如果是，⑧进行句法语义对比直至找到在某一层面上的对比关系。

I. Given a socio-cultural setting in m(Cm) in a language i(CmLi), is there an equivalent socio-cultural setting n(Cn) in language j(CnLj)? If the answer is "no", note the socio-cultural contrast. If the the answer is "yes":

II. Is there a linguistic form (Fq) in L(FqLj) which is prototypically associated with CnLj in a way similar to the way in which FpLi is associated with CmLi? If the answer is "no", note the pragmatic contrast. If the answer is "yes":

III. Is FqLj a semanto-syntactic equivalent of FpLi? If the answer is "no", abandon the analysis. If the answer is "yes", proceed with semanto-syntatic contrastive studies until you find contrast at some level of analysis.

除了令人眼花缭乱的符号外，其实没有提供任何具体的对比程序，而且"对等"（equivalence）的发现和确定往往是下一个步骤的前提。难怪切斯特曼要指责"对等"说有循环论证的嫌疑。

Apart from being confusing in symbols, it does not offer specific procedures to find the contrast, but advancement to the next step requires an "equivalent" to be found and confirmed. It is no wonder that Chesterman has to challenge the circularity in the equivalent proposition.

切斯特曼提出的对比研究程序如下（Chesterman，1998：54）：

Chesterman outlined his proposal of a general contrastive functional analysis methodology as follows (Chesterman, 1998: 54):

① 原始资料：不同语言中语言行为的实例；

② 比较基础：感到语言A中的X现象与语言B中的Y现象之间有某种相似；

③ 提出问题：这一相似的本质是什么？

④ 初步假设：X与Y性质相同；

⑤ 进行验证：上述假设在什么基础上成立或不成立？需要什么条件？

⑥ 修正假设：如果相同的假设不成立,则X与Y应是如何如何的关系，或者运用X与Y应有如何如何的条件；

⑦ 验证修正后的假设。

如此一步步进行下去。

① Primary data: instances of language behaviour in different languages.

② Comparability criterion: A perceived similarity, of any kind, between a phenomenon X in language A and a phenomenon Y in language B. For a given contrastive analysis, this criterion is then defined operationally in terms of a constraint of relevant similarity.

③ Problem: What is the nature of this similarity?

④ Initial hypothesis: X and Y are identical.

⑤ Test: On what grounds can the initial hypothesis be supported or rejected? On what conditions (if ever) does it hold?

⑥ Revised hypothesis (if the initial hypothesis fails): that the relation between X and Y is such-and-such; or, that the use of X and Y depends on such-and-such conditions.

⑦ Testing of the revised hypothesis.

And so on.

切斯特曼（1998：60）特别强调，以往总认为一旦进行了对比，问题就一劳永逸地解决了，其实并非如此，"对比的结果只是有希望提出一个更好的假设，仅此而已。"

Chesterman stressed that "...the apparent belief in Contrastive Analysis that once an analysis has been done the problem is solved for good; not so, I think: the result of the analysis is no more than a (hopefully) better hypothesis" (1998: 60).

粗粗一看，切斯特曼提出的研究程序平淡无奇，但如果联想到整个对比研究的发展过程就会知道走到这一步并不容易。它必须要甩开从体系出发这一结构主义以来难以摆脱的情结；必须以"相似性"而不是以"对等物"或"对比中立项"作为研究的出发点。西方走到这一步花了整整40年。据我们看来，这一程序还有更深的意义，那就是，不把对比研究仅仅看作是某种理论的"应用"或验证，而是从语言事实出发作出新的假设和概括，在这过程中很可能有新的结果或理论被发现。这也就是沃尔夫说的"在某种新的意义上建构和修订概念，增加必要的术语"。这就为对比语言学的独立奠定了基础。

At first glance, it is a plain structure that Chesterman has proposed. That is simplistic thought. It is really not easy coming this long way after 40 years of entanglement with various systems since structuralism came into the picture. It is also a difficult process to reconsider setting off again with "similarity" rather than "equivalence" or *tertia comparationis*. Furthermore, the framework is neither an application nor a verification of a theory; it is new sets of assumptions and generalizations qualified from linguistic facts. It will be no surprise should there be new findings or theories arising as a result and must therefore, in Whorf's words "frame concepts more or less new, and make needed additions to terminology" (Whorf, 1937: 87). We see in it a new foundation for an independent discipline in contrastive linguistics.

（5）正面调解语言相对论与普世语言观。

(5) Reconciling linguistic relativity and linguistic universal

西方对比语言研究有个最大的悖论，甚至可以说是死结，就是语言相对论与普世语言观的矛盾。对比语言学的提出者沃尔夫也正是语言相对论的主张者，早期对比研究背后的美国结构主义，虽然其语言观未必如沃尔夫那样激烈，但所持的也是个别语言观，这正是对比之所以被需要的法理基础。然而令人难堪的是，就在第一部公认的对比语言学著作，拉多的《跨文化语言学》发表的同一年，乔姆斯基发表了他的《句法结构》（1957），从此美国乃至西方主流语言学进入了转换生成语言学的天下。这种理论竭力主张普世语言观，认为世上所有语言的深层结构都是同样的，了解一种外语，根本不需要对比，只要通过熟悉自己的母语就可以推导出来了（参见Krzeszowski，1990：7—8所引Preston，1975的话），实际上是取消了对比语言学。面临这样的局面，对比研究者的处境确实是很尴尬的：一方面要坚持自己的阵地，一方面又不想使自己的语言观"落伍"。于是他们就接过了普世观的"深层"说，作为对比的"对比中立项"（tertia comparationis），又接过"转换"和"生成"的口号，把对比的过程解释为从深层结构转化为表层结构的过程。从迪·皮德娄（1971）、詹姆斯（1980），到克尔采斯佐斯基（1990）无不如此。这种理论基础与实践操作过程的错位，正是西方对比语言学长期以来只是"语言学中的灰姑娘"（Cinderella in Linguistics）的根本原因。也正是因为这个原因，沃尔夫的名字被从对比语言学史上抹去了，对比研究也始终小心翼翼地自居"应用"的地位，不敢与其他各种语言学争一日之短长。

The biggest antinomy in contrastive studies, one that probably defies solution, is the contradiction of linguistic relativity and linguistic universal. The proponent of contrastive linguistics, Whorf, is also the proponent of linguistic relativity. Earlier supporting theory of CA, structuralism, though it does not hold its tenets as strongly as Whorf in relativity, actually helps legalize the need for CA, maintaining that languages and cultures differ from each other. The controversy really arose when Noam Chomsky's *Syntactic Structure,* published in the same year (1957) as Lado's *Cross-cultural Linguistics,* generally held to be the first formal work on contrastive linguistics, swept through the linguistics circle. Transformational grammar ruled the US and other mainstream linguistic theories of the West with its linguistic universal point of view. It hammers the point home that all languages are the same at deep structure and therefore knowledge of second language could be deduced from the familiar mother tongue, reducing completely the need for CA in foreign language learning (Krzeszowski, 1990: 7—8; Preston, 1975). Faced with the threat of a diminished discipline, contrastivists were extremely awkward: While they continued to hang in there, they did not like the idea of functioning with a "backward" linguistic view. This accounts for the acceptance of "deep structure" from a linguistic universal viewpoint as the *tertia comparationis*, and later the borrowing of "transformation" and "generative" concepts so that the process of contrast becomes the transformation process from deep to surface structures. A consistent inferiority runs through Di Pietro (1971) to James (1980), to Krzeszowski (1990). This mismatch in theory and practice in the West arose from the deeply rooted labelling of contrastive linguistics as the "Cinderella in Linguistics". This is the truth to denying Whorf his place in contrastive linguistics and it is now clear why CA restricts itself to the applied field and does not compete with other schools of thought for healthy development in linguistics.

切斯特曼此书的不平凡之处，就在于经过这么多年之后，他终于正面提到了这两种语言观的冲突，并且试图提出折衷调和的意见。他的观点一方面是主张"普世性"（universal base）有三个层次：形式层、语义层、认知层（formal, semantic, cognitive）（同上：48），从而比语义深层更前进了一步；其次，认为"语言相对论"本身也是"相对"的，而且不必用"（语言）决定（文化）"这样强的字眼，可以采用德国哲学家波普尔的说法，"弹性地控制"（plastic control）（同上：52）。同时，运用他自己的"相似性"理论，不把对比的基础建立在"相同点"（sameness or identity）上，而是通过比较"原型"（prototype）来观察其"重合"（overlap）程度。这确不失为一个解决问题的办法。

It is in this light that Chesterman (1998) has proved to be unusual: confronting the conflicting linguistic views head on and attempting to mediate an end to the controversy. Chesterman first sums up the different thoughts on the universal base hypothesis—that all human languages share a universal deep structure—on three levels, i.e. formal, semantic and cognitive (Chesterman, 1998: 48). This is a step further than merely looking at formal or semantic deep structure. Next, Chesterman holds that in so far as linguistic relativity hypothesis is itself "relative", using strong or dramatic assertion such as "determinism" to describe the effect of language on thought is not necessary. He likens the effect to what German philosopher Popper would call a "plastic control" (*ibid.*: 52). Finally, he dismisses the unduly binary debate between the two camps with the notion of similarity. Similarity, as innate formal universals underlying the grammars of all human languages, appeals to the universalists as a set of similarity constraints, at least from the cognitive psychological standpoint (*ibid*.: 50). These constraints determine which utterances will be construed as being "similar" to which other ones and serve as bases for generalization. However, where utterances are concerned, it would never be possible to arrive at exactness in meaning—it is neither all the same nor totally different—and therefore would be misleading to regard an "identical" universal base. That is to say, we are in fact looking at degree of overlapping. This is where relativity will set in. And the operation of CA is really not on the grounds of sameness or identity but a comparison of prototypes—which are culture-specific and thus not universally shared—and see to what extent they overlap. (*ibid*.: 50—52) Indeed Chesterman has taken a remarkable position with regard to linguistic relativity and universality.

　　如同詹姆斯用"纵向"（篇章）和"横向"（话语分析），来表述他对传统对比研究的超越那样，切斯特曼用"外向"（发展到语用学）和"内向"（探索语言使用者的心理）来描述对比研究的突破，并认为后者对他具有更重要的理论意义（Chesterman, 1998: 40）。如果说，早期对比分析的理论基础是结构主义语言学与行为主义心理学、迪·皮德娄的理论基础是转换生成语言学、詹姆斯的理论基础是社会语言学与心理语言学、克尔采斯佐斯基主要是生成语义学的话，切斯特曼则是在社会语言学之外，特别依赖认知语言学。在西方存在两家"认知语言学"（乔姆斯基也自称是认知语言学）的情况下，切氏运用了1972年诺贝尔医学奖获得者、神经生物学家埃德曼（Gerald Edelman, 1992）的研究成果，指出埃氏的理论支持莱柯夫（Lakoff）、兰格克（Langacker）等人的认知语法和罗斯（Rosch）等人的原型理论，不支持乔姆斯基的形式主义理论，大脑中也不存在什么"语言获得机制"（language acquisition device），意义是交互活动的产物，部分取决于环境，部分取决于特定的言语社团，部分取决于说话者本人（同上：47）。

On the breakthrough over traditional CA that he has achieved, James proposed it in two directions: horizontal (text) and vertical (discourse analysis). Chesterman epitomized his also in two directions: inward movement (towards cognition to probe into the language-user's mind) and outward movement (towards pragmatics), with more attention devoted to moving inwards, which he thought as having greater theoretical significance (*ibid*.: 40). We have seen how the theoretical basis for CA has evolved throughout the years: in the early period, structuralism; in Di Pietro's time, transformational generative linguistics; in Carl James' time, sociolinguistics and psycholinguistics; in Krzeszowski's time, generative semantics; and led by Chesterman, apart from sociolinguistics, cognitive linguistics played a heavy role. We note that with Chomsky claiming to be in the cognitive field, there are two schools of thought and Chesterman got his source of inspiration from renowned neurobiologist, Gerald Edelman (1992), the 1972 Nobel Prize winner in Medicine. He pointed out that Edelman is critical of formalist Chomskyan approach, not believing that there is some language acquisition device sitting ready in the head. Meaning itself is interactional, being determined partly by the environment and partly by a given speech community, and partly by the very body of the speaker. But Edelman sees his research supports the views of Lakoff, Langacker and others in cognitive grammar, and of Rosch et al. in prototype theory (*ibid.*: 47).

（6）打破条块分割，建立了也许是迄今为止最宏大又最细密的功能对比研究体系。

(6) Breaking barriers for a sophisticated contrastive functional analysis model to date

以往从事对比研究的往往各自为战，搞句法的不搞篇章，搞篇章的不搞语用；搞微观的不搞宏观，搞宏观的不搞微观。詹姆斯提出了对比研究的宏观转向，但没有提出什么具体的方案；恩克维斯特的篇章对比模式不够细化；奥列克赛等的语用对比缺乏新意；克尔采斯佐斯基的规模很大，但在篇章语用等方面显然力不从心；而孔纳等的对比修辞学似乎又游离在对比研究的主流之外。直到切斯特曼的这本书出来，才尝试将所有这一切研究都纳入他的"对比功能分析"或功能对比语言学的框架之内。切氏的第四章"修辞"实际上包括了篇章研究、语用研究，由于他把篇章定义为个人话语——主要是书面语、语用是交际话语——主要是口语（p. 151；186），因而把对比修辞学也吸收了进来。

The discipline has long been divided by the respective subfields, so much so that each concentrates on their own area, showing little or no interest in what others are doing. Those working on micro-perspective have no regard for macro-perspective and vice versa; those working on syntax know little about text and those specializing in text grammar do not cross over to discourse analysis. While James was instrumental in guiding development in the macro perspective, no specific proposal was tabled. Enkvist's contrastive model on text could have been further refined and Oleysky's contrastive pragmatics could have been more creative. Krzeszowski seems to have a magnificent model, but his handling of text and pragmatics is less than ideal. Connor has filled a gap, but contrastive rhetoric is apparently out of the CA research mainstream. Until Chesterman (1998), contrastive study is but scattered pieces. Chesterman put all of these pieces into his functional analysis framework and his last chapter on rhetoric is in fact inclusive of text linguistics and pragmatics, mainly because he defines text as written form and pragmatics as involving verbal form. (*ibid.*: 151, 186)

他的体系的特点,一是基础和目标统一,均以意义为出发点,寻找其在各个层面的表达方式及相关条件;二是范畴体系统一,句法、篇章和语用大体采用同一套范畴体系,或者用他自己的话来说,从句法到篇章是"纵向"的扩展,从篇章到语用是"横向"的拓展,分别称之为structure、macrostructure和interstructure;三是注意博采众长,如他的基本分析思路采用的是穆斯塔约基的观点,在篇章研究上吸取了恩克维斯特(1984)、凡尔利希(Egon Werlich,1976)、波格朗和德莱斯勒(Beaugrande and Dressler,1981)、韩礼德与哈珊(Halliday and Hasan,1976)、马丁(Martin,1992)、孔纳(1996)等的成果,在语用研究上则综合了梅伊(Mey,1993)、斯塔布斯(Stubbs,1983)、斯泊勃与威尔逊(Sperber and Wilson,1986)、布朗与莱文逊(Brown and Levinson,1988)、格特(Gutt,1991)等人的成果。令人惊异的是,这样大范围的"综合",却没有造成一个"大杂烩";相反,由于这个分类体系细腻而具体,具有很大的可操作性。

Chesterman's model makes distinctions in a number of ways. Starting with meaning, the model is consistent in theoretical basis and object, seeking to circumscribe the various ways meaning is being expressed at all levels and the respective criteria. The model is also consistent in its linguistic categorization at various levels including syntax, text and pragmatics or in his terms, structure, macrostructure and interstructure. Moving from syntax to text represents a vertical expansion, whereas from text to pragmatics, a horizontal expansion, to form macrostructure and interstructure. Chesterman is also exceptional in absorbing the best from existing research findings. His analytical framework was taken from Mustajoki; text linguistics was taken from Enkvist (1984), Egon Werlich (1976),

Beaugrande and Dressler (1981), Halliday and Hasan (1976), Martin (1992) and Connor (1996); pragmatics was taken from Mey (1993), Stubbs (1983), Sperber and Wilson (1986), Brown and Levinson (1988), as well as Gutt (1991). It is remarkable that Chesterman has cleverly fitted such a variety of thoughts into his framework. The result is of course a brilliant, refined and workable solution.

1.5.5 沃尔夫对比语言学思想的发展
1.5.5 The development of Whorf's contrastive linguistic standpoint

最后，我们不得不提及沃尔夫对比语言学思想在今天西方的发展。作为对比语言学的命名者和倡导人，沃尔夫的名字却在近半个世纪里、在大多数西方对比语言学的文献里不见踪影，像上面切斯特曼这样正面提到，是很难得一见的；以对比命名而又公开诉求于沃尔夫学说的对比修辞学一般又不算在对比语言学的研究范围里。这是什么原因呢？是不是沃尔夫的传统就此中断了呢？我们要从几个方面对这现象作出解释。

We should not close this chapter without considering how the contrastive linguistic standpoint first brought about by Whorf has evolved in modern research. Benjamin Lee Whorf not only gave contrastive linguistics a name, but also set a path for its growth, yet he has been denied due credit for almost half a century. Few acknowledge Whorf in their work like Chesterman did. When contrastive rhetoric does Whorf justice, even then he is not recognized as predominant in his field. Why not? Perhaps we could suggest some reasons:

第一是语言学思潮的兴衰。对比研究兴起之时也正好是"乔姆斯基革命"发生之时，新兴的语言学理论、特别是普遍语法的思想，与沃尔夫的语言相对论是完全针锋相对的。对比研究要追赶新的语言学潮流，使自己保留在"主流语言学"的体制范围里，就必须与这种"陈旧"的观点割断关系；

(1) Cycles in linguistic thoughts. Contrastive linguistics develops at a point where Chomsky is also staging a revolution with his theory. Novel linguistic theories, particularly universal grammar, are in deadlock rivalry with Whorf's linguistic relativity hypothesis. Contrastivists, for fear of being mocked and left behind new trends in linguistics, have to severe ties with "outmoded" viewpoints to stay within the mainstream linguistic system.

第二是对比语言学的自身定位。我们知道，对比语言学在英语里有几个说法：contrastive linguistics、contrastive analysis、contrastive studies等（参见许余龙，2002：17），还有comparative descriptive linguistics、linguistic confrontation（Fisiak，1980：1）及contrastive grammar等等。许多人包括詹姆斯、切斯特曼在内，都喜欢用"分析"这个名称。就是在对比修辞学里，其创始人卡普兰也倾向于用contrastive rhetoric，而不愿意用contrastive rhetoric theory（见Kaplan，2001：vii；Panetta，2001：xxii）。这是因为他们始终将对比研究定位在"应用语言学"的范围里，认为对比分析只是一门应用性学科，其任务只是为第二语言教学服务；尽管也有"理论对比语言学"，但其主要任务毋宁说只是为了寻找对比研究切入的方式或具体进行对比的模式，真正的"理论语言学"研究不是对比语言学的任务。因此一些对比语言学者都对理论语言学采取"仰视"的态度，"敬而远之"；而理论语言学也将对比研究看作是只管应用的"小儿科"，好像把自己归入对比语言学家会降低身份似的；

(2) The self-positioning of contrastive linguistics. As we know, there are various terms in use for contrastive linguistics: "contrastive linguistics", "contrastive analysis", contrastive studies (Xu Yulong, 2002: 17), and others like comparative descriptive linguistics, linguistic confrontation (Fisiak, 1980: 1), as well as contrastive grammar to name a few. Many like to use the term Contrastive Analysis, including James and Chesterman. As for Robert Kaplan, he is fonder of using contrastive rhetoric than contrastive rhetoric theory (Kaplan, 2001: vii; Panetta, 2001: xxii). This is evident of a positioning in applied linguistics, to think of it as an applied science serving the needs of second language teaching. Although there is so-called "theoretical contrastive linguistics", the aim of it is simply to search for a particular point of research or a particular model for specific analysis needs. In itself, research in theoretical linguistics is never the object of contrastive linguistics. For this reason, most scholars shy away from theoretical linguistics while theoretical linguistics does not take contrastive studies seriously.

第三是语言研究的分工。在西方那种讲究学科分类的学术传统里，学科之间壁垒森严，尽管新兴学科、交叉学科、跨学科不时冒出来，但一门学科一旦建立，马上就要划地为界，圈定自己的"势力范围"，努力不"侵入"他人的领域，也不容他人染指自己的领域，各人守住自己的一块。因此许多人宁可自己"独创"一门新的学科，也不愿在旧名称里拓展新的内容。例如沃尔夫的语言相对论已"约定俗成"是属于人类学语言学的"领地",对比语言学就不会再伸手。因此我们要了解沃尔夫观点的新进展,就不能在"纯"对比语言学的文献里找,而要稍微跳出对比语言学的圈子。

(3) Specialization in language research. In the Western scholastic tradition to have detailed classification of fields of study, each field is strictly confined to its own boundary. Although emergence of new fields, cross-disciplinary studies is common, once established as a discipline in its own right, trespassing of boundaries will be prohibited. As such most would rather "create" a discipline than renew the content under an old banner. For instance, when a consensus is formed to include Whorf's hypothesis in anthropology linguistics, contrastive linguistics will not try to expand into that boundary. For new development in Whorf's hypothesis, it will be more gainful to look beyond the "pure" land of contrastive linguistics.

事实上沃尔夫的语言相对论与他提出的对比语言学是不可分的,两者本来就是一回事,其背景都是当时正在美国蓬勃发展的人类学语言学。由于在实践中接触和了解了大量与英语乃至整个印欧系语言相距甚远的美洲印第安人等的语言,鲍阿斯(Franz Boas, 1911)、萨丕尔(Edward Sapir, 1949)、沃尔夫等人痛感19世纪以来以比较亲属语言为宗旨的历史比较方法在新的任务面前完全用不上。正是新的语言事实推动了新的语言理论的产生,萨丕尔沃尔夫假说(Sapir Whorf Hypothesis)的提出可说是顺理顺章的事,这正是对语言采取"对比"(比较非亲属语言)而不是"比较"(比较亲属语言)方法的结果;而语言相对论也只有在语言的对比中才有意义,不进行各种语言,特别是类型上相距遥远的语言的对比,只在一个语言内部进行研究,语言相对论也派不上用场。因此由沃尔夫提出"对比语言学"的名称和任务也同样是顺理顺章的事。沃尔夫等人希望的对比语言学是一种语言与文化结合的比较,以此来探索人类语言的本质。但历史的发展把"对比语言学"拉偏了它的轨道,经过了半个世纪,直到切斯特曼的"内向"转向,才在一定程度上又重新回到当初沃尔夫设定的轨道上来。这样看来,西方的对比语言学要发展,一定要注意从沃尔夫理论的思考中汲取营养。

In fact, Whorf's hypothesis on linguistic relativity cannot be separated from his idea of contrastive linguistics. The two are knitted together. To understand this, we have to go back in time. Whorf's hypothesis arose against the height of linguistic anthropology in the US when there were numerous empirical studies on a large number of languages belonging to completely different families, from English or the Indo-European family such as Indian languages. Involved in this wave of studies, Franz Boas (1911), Edward Sapir (1949) and Whorf realized the inadequacy of historical comparative linguistics applicable chiefly to languages of the same language family to meeting new aims in research. It is precisely being driven by new linguistic facts that a new theory finds its way to birth. The Sapir Whorf Hypothesis emerged rather naturally as a consequence of the need to contrast (unrelated languages) rather than compare (related languages). Linguistic relativity is only meaningful in the context of contrasting distant languages. Otherwise, it will be out of context. It is now obvious that Whorf has every reason to name contrastive linguistics and specify its task, which to Whorf and others would be a discipline that would seek contrast in terms of language and culture to reveal the nature of human languages. Historical development has seen a digression for about half a century. It is hopeful that with Chesterman's call for an inward moving approach, the discipline would have a chance to return to its original path set by Whorf. On this note, further advancement in the discipline in the West would have to draw inspiration from Whorfian theoretical thoughts.

自五十年代后期起普遍语法思想大行其道，形式主义甚嚣尘上，强调意义、语言与文化个性的沃尔夫假说被打入冷宫。七十年代起语言研究进入后乔姆斯基时期，语言的内在意义与心理、语言的社会文化因素重又得到强调，一些新的语言研究流派相继诞生。可以说，凡是侧重形式主义研究、相信普遍语法的，都对沃尔夫假说采取排斥态度；凡是重视语言的文化、社会、心理因素的，都或多或少有沃尔夫思想的影子。维尔茨皮卡（Wierzbicka，1991：282-283）曾说，这只是标签的不同而已：于洪堡特、浮士勒（Karl Vossler, 1904）等叫作"语言精神"（Sprachgeist），是"民族精神的表现"（language as an expression of Volksgeist），于萨丕尔（1921）、沃尔夫（1956）等叫作"语言是社会现实的向导"（language as a guide to social reality），于海姆斯等（Dell Hymes, 1961）称作"认知风格"（cognitive style），她自己倾向于叫作"跨文化语用学"，其实都是一回事。七十年代以后，沃尔夫的思想在以下这些领域都有强弱不同的表现，因有关文献太多，我们只各举一两本著作作为例子：

For a long time, since the end part of 1950, universal grammar has dominated in all senses. Formalism has its way, while the Whorfian hypothesis that stresses meaning, language character and cultural character has retreated. A shift was witnessed in the 1970s: Chomskyan ideas ruled. Themes resurfacing included implicit meaning of languages and psychology, and other sociocultural factors. Many subdivisions in linguistic study appeared. It is safe to conclude that formal approaches and those grounded on universal grammar tend to reject Whorf's hypothesis. On the other hand, any concerns on the cultural, social and psychological aspects of language would tend to have been influenced, more or less, by the Whorfian hypothesis. Wierzbicka put it as a different labelling: to Humboldt and Karl Vossler (1904), it is "the spirit of language" (Sprachgeist) and manifestation of ethnicity (language as an expression of Volksgeist); to Sapir (1921) and Whorf (1956), it is termed as "language as a guide to social reality"; to Dell Hymes (1961), "cognitive style" and Wierzbicka herself would address it as cross-cultural pragmatics (Wierzbicka, 1991: 282—283). It's all but the same. Since the 1970s, Whorf's ideas were configured in the following areas in different degrees. The list and related papers are too voluminous to be exhaustive and we shall list only one or two representative works.

人类学语言学：杜朗蒂（Alessandro Duranti, 1997）；福莱（William Foley, 1997）

认知人类学：但特雷特（Roy D'Andrade, 1995）

民族语言学：马索特（Madeleine Mathiot, 1979）

社会语言学：海姆斯（1964；1966）

认知语言学：莱考夫与约翰逊（George Lakoff & Mark Johson, 1980）

语用学：维尔茨皮卡（1991）

语义学：维尔茨皮卡（1992；1997）

民族句法学：维尔茨皮卡（1979）；恩菲尔德（N. J. Enfield, 2002）

对比修辞学：卡普兰（1966）；孔纳（1996）

心理语言学：布鲁姆（Alfred H. Bloom, 1981）

普通语言学：霍凯特（Charles Hocket, 1987）

跨文化交际学：斯坦法特（Thomas M. Steinfatt, 1989）

Linguistic anthropology: Alessandro Duranti (1997); William Foley (1997)

Cognitive anthropology: Roy D'Andrade (1995)

Ethnic linguistics: Madeleine Mathiot (1979)

Sociolinguistics: Dell Hymes (1964; 1966)

Cognitive linguistics: George Lakoff and Mark Johnson (1980)

Pragmatics: Wierzbicka (1991)

Semantics: Wierzbicka (1992; 1997)

Ethno-syntax: Wierzbicka (1979); N. J. Enfield (2002)

Contrastive rhetoric: Robert Kaplan (1966); Ulla Connor (1996)

Pyscholinguistics: Alfred H. Bloom (1981)

General linguistics: Charles Hocket (1987)

Cross-cultural communication: Thomas M. Steinfatt (1989)

更值得注意的是对沃尔夫理论本身的讨论，随着"沃尔夫热"的回升，近年来出版了好几本有关沃尔夫及其理论的专著，主要有：

It is also noted that as the discussion on Whorf's hypothesis has persisted, it has become more heated and more dedicated works are available in the market, such as:

卢西（John Lucy）的《思维与语言的多样性：语言相对论假说的重建》（1992a）和《语法范畴与认知：语言相对论假说例证》（1992b）

甘柏兹与莱文逊（John L. Gumperz & Stephen Levinson）的《语言相对论的重新思考》（1996）

朴兹与凡思普（Martin Pütz & Marjolijn Verspoor）的《语言相对论探讨集》（2000）

倪梅尔与迪文（S. Niemeier & R. Dirven）的《语言相对论举证》（2000）

John A. Lucy. (1992a) *Language Diversity and Thought: A Reformulation of the Linguistic Relativity Hypothesis*; and (1992b) *Grammatical Categories and Cognition: A Case Study of the Linguistic Relativity Hypothesis*

John L. Gumperz and Stephen Levinson. (1996) *Rethinking Linguistic Relativity*

Martin Pütz and Marjolijn Verspoor. (2000) *Explorations in Linguistic Relativity*

S. Niemeier and R. Dirven. (2000) *Evidence for Linguistic Relativity*

此外，李（Penny Lee）的《沃尔夫理论情结》（1996）一书搜集了沃尔夫大量未发表过的作品，是对沃尔夫思想的最全面和系统的梳理。

In addition, Penny Lee's *The Whorf Theory Complex*（1996）: *A Critical Reconstruction* collected a number of unpublished articles by Whorf and could be regarded as the most complete and systematic compilation of Whorf's thoughts to date.

这些都为对西方语言对比研究的深入探讨提供了丰富的资料。

All these are valuable additions for the advancement of contrastive linguistics in the West.

1.5.6 西方第三期对比研究小结
1.5.6 Summary for Phase 3

现在我们可以对西方第三期的对比研究作一个小结。1980年代初对比语言学开始复苏以后，对比语言学在世界不同地区有了不同的发展："主流"对比语言学在欧洲，其中波兰和芬兰的学者，包括在波兰和芬兰工作的学者（如菲齐亚克、克尔采斯佐斯基、詹姆斯、恩克维斯特、切斯特曼），以及从波兰和芬兰走向世界各地去的学者（如孔纳、维尔茨皮卡）在这一事业中起了很重要的作用，其发展的理论基础从生成语义学、社会语言学、心理语言学到认知语言学，而由切斯特曼集其大成；美国则是对比修辞学的阵地，其理论基础继承了沃尔夫的思想，在跨文化研究和书面语写作的对比研究上有着自己的特色；澳大利亚以维尔茨皮卡为代表的一批学者尽管没有以对比语言学为号召，实际上却是沿着沃尔夫的路子做得最好的一批人，他们的研究成果非常值得重视；对沃尔夫思想的研究从作者来看主要在澳洲和欧洲，而从出版社来看似以剑桥大学出版社为大本营。

We are now in a position to close the third phase of development in the West. The revival of contrastive linguistics in 1980 saw a few centres appear in different parts of the world, with the "mainstream" in Europe; particularly noteworthy are Poland and Finland, where local scholars (such as Fisiak, Krzeszowski, James, Enkvist and Chesterman) flourished together, with those venturing out to other parts of the world (such as Connor, Wierzbicka), driving the discipline in unparalleled influence. Contrastive linguistics in the European world has developed its base from generative semantics to sociolinguistics and then to cognitive linguistics. Chesterman served as the anchorman. In the US, contrastive rhetoric, rooted in Whorf's hypothesis, found a space in cross cultural studies and writing and they can now be proud of its growth. In Australia, researchers led by Wierzbicka, while they did not claim to be conducting contrastive linguistic work, are in fact guided most closely by Whorf's hypothesis. Their findings are weighty. By researcher, development of Whorf's thought is in Australia, whereas by publisher, Cambridge University Press has been the most supportive.

从对比研究的总的发展趋势来看，如果说詹姆斯的"纵向"（vertical，指超越句子层面进入篇章）和"横向"（horizontal，指结合语用和文化）代表了"高"和"宽"两个维度的话，切斯特曼的"内向"（inward，指语言使用者的心理）又增加了"深"这第三个维度，再加上对比修辞学从侧面、澳洲语言学从背面的推动，对比语言学不得不以一种立体的态势，向宏观更宏观的方向发展，这可以说是一种历史的趋势。

On the whole, if James has driven the discipline to develop both vertically (into text) and horizontally (into pragmatics and culture), taking the discipline in the height and breadth dimension, the inward movement of Chesterman (into language user's minds) has added the depth. With contrastive rhetoric pushing at the side and developments in Australia pushing from the back, contrastive linguistics is ready to grow in full dimensions as a magnificent discipline with high macro research vision. This is historical momentum.

实际上在这个时期开展对比研究的，除了欧美和澳洲之外，还有第四个地区，这就是中国。这是一个不容忽视的地区。根据芬兰Jyväskylä大学沙亚伐拉（Kari Sajavaara）和雷托能（Jaakko Lehtonen）编的"应用对比研究文献1965—1980"（1981）的不完全统计，这16年内西方总共发表的论著是678篇（部）（这是在他们作的1965—1975年的统计基础上加上他们后来作的1976—1980的统计，发表在菲齐亚克主编的第二部对比研究论文集《对比语言学与语言教师》（1981）上，数据不会有误。有的学者说光是前一个统计数字就有1000多篇，恐怕是据传闻），年均42篇（部）；而我们前几年作的不完全统计（Pan，2003），从1977年5月到2001年6月这24年的时间里，中国发表的光是涉及英语与汉语之间的对比语言学论文（中国的对比研究除了汉英之间，还有汉俄、汉日、汉朝（韩）、汉越以及汉语与境内外少数民族语言之间的对比，因为我们对之缺少研究，因此没有将这些数量不菲的成果统计在内）就是1447

篇，著作和论文集82部，合计1529篇（部），年均64篇（部）。当然，数字不能说明问题，而且沙氏等理解的对比语言学比我们范围要窄，但至少可以证明，世界范围的对比语言学研究，不能缺了中国这一块。中国与世界需要加强彼此的了解，从本章的情况来看，中国对世界的了解并不如人们自以为了解的多；而世界对中国的了解可能更少。中国的对比语言学要与国际对比语言学加强互动，先要从彼此了解开始。我们要以全球的研究为背景，来考察中国对比语言学研究的发展及其在全球对比研究中的地位。

Additionally, besides Europe, the US and Australia, there is a fourth region, China, where progress in contrastive linguistics amounts to something. According to the statistics (incomplete, to be sure) in Sajavaara and Lehtonen (1981), in the 16-year period 1965—1980, there are 678 articles/books on contrastive linguistics, averaging 42 articles/books per year. According to Pan (2003b), in the period from May 1977 to June 2001, spanning 24 years, papers involving English and Chinese as point of reference alone, there were 1,447 articles and 82 books, totalling 1,529 articles and books published in China, not to mention many other papers on other minority languages of the country as well as Russian, Japanese, Korean and Chinese. On average, there have been 64 articles and books published per year. While statistics are inconclusive and the definition of contrastive linguistics adopted in the two sets of statistics may be different (Sajavaara may have taken a narrower sense), it suffices to say that we cannot afford to miss out on the advancement in China in this area. We like to stress that Chinese scholars do not understand the world more than they claim to and the world has even less understanding of the development of contrastive linguistics in China. Before more interaction should be encouraged, we could begin with more understanding of each other's effort. It is the intention of this volume to survey contrastive linguistics in China with a world perspective.

第二章
中国对比研究简史（上）
Chapter 2　Contrastive Linguistics in China I

2.1 研究中国对比语言学史的意义
2.1 Significance of the study

　　上一章的结尾提到：从1965年到1980年，西方出版的对比语言学论著，年均42篇（部）；而从1977年5月到2001年6月，中国的对比语言学论著是年均64篇（部）；[1]据另一项统计，从1995年到2003年，中国的年均对比语言学论著更达到了247篇（部）。[2]当然数量多并不是人们需要关注中国的对比语言研究的理由，何况这些论著的水平参差不齐，内在实质不一致。事实上，中国的对比语言学研究之所以值得中国以外的学者和专家关注，还有着更重要的原因。

　　Before we rounded off the last chapter, a set of statistics was revealed. In the period 1965—1980, the average number of articles or books published in the West on the subject was 42. In the period May 1977 to June 2001, the average number of articles or books published in China on the subject was 64 (Sajavaara and Lehtonen, 1981; Pan 2003b). The latest figure spanning the period 1995—2003 showed

---

1　参见Sajavaara and Lehtonen（1981）；Pan Wenguo（2003）。

2　王菊泉、郑立信指出："据我们不完全统计，1995年到2003年国内这方面的论文就已超过2100篇，专著和论文集有124部之多"（王菊泉、郑立信，2004b：1）。两者合计2224篇（部），以9年平均，得247。
Wang Juquan and Zheng Lixin pointed out that: "Omission granted, essays on the subject in China during the period 1995—2003 amounts more than 2,100, while books and collections total up to 124" (Wang Juquan, Zheng Lixin, 2004b: 1). The figure 2,224 means an average of 247 articles/books per year over the nine-year period.

the average to be 247 in China. Volume is of course the least reason for taking the development of contrastive linguistics in China into consideration, as not all publications are up to the mark. There are far stronger and more pressing reasons. Before going into that, it is necessary to survey in general why it is that linguistic studies in China have attracted little attention.

2.1.1 为什么国外学者对中国的语言研究缺乏兴趣？
2.1.1 Why do linguistic studies in China appear uninteresting?

入题之前，我们先分析为什么总体而言，中国的语言研究引不起国外学者的兴趣。在中国境外从事汉语研究的，绝大多数是华人和华侨，汉语本来就是他们的母语或共同语。这些学者大部分只能蜗居在"东亚语言"或"汉藏语"研究的小圈子里，很少能跻身国外语言研究的主流，在理论语言学研究的国际会议上，几乎听不到他们的声音。就对比语言学来说，中国发表的论著其绝对数量占据了世界语言对比研究的半壁江山，但国外对此几乎是闻所未闻。这是什么原因呢？我们认为，有这么两个重要原因：

Outside China, researches into languages in China are conducted mainly by Chinese nationals or ethnic Chinese whose mother tongue is Chinese. Even when the studies are done overseas, they do not enter into the mainstream of research in other countries. Most of them are confined within the small circle of "East Asian languages" or "Sino-Tibetan languages". Furthermore, they are not heard of at international conferences on theoretical linguistics. Take contrastive linguistics for instance, in figure terms, Chinese publications number is more than double in comparison with their counterparts in the West, but little is known about these publications. Why is that so? For two possible reasons, we think.

（1）语言隔阂：中国国内的对比研究论文，几乎都是用中文发表，这就为国外绝大多数的语言学家带来了阅读上的困难。我们不能要求别人花费巨大的时间精力先学好了汉语再来研究我们的论文。在当今全球经济一体化的背景之下，通用语言、包括学术语言的国际化已经是个不可回避的事实。不管人们多么不愿意，英语作为主要的强势语言已经牢牢地占据了这个阵地，连昔日威风一时的法语也无法望其项背。在这形势下，如果一个学者的学术观点没有机会用英语表述，那等于就是不想为世人所知。在现在的世界学术界，不要说欧、亚、非、拉的一些小语种，就连法语、德语、俄语等在西方有着传统势力的语言，其学术成果要想为世界所知，就不得不译成英语。中国语言学家必须能用英语流畅地表达自己的观点，学界也必须提高学术翻译的能力，让中国学术进入世界学术之林；

  Firstly, the language barrier. Almost all findings on the subject by the Chinese are written in Chinese, creating a barrier for foreign scholars. There is no reason for them to spend huge amount of resources to pick up the language just to read an original paper in Chinese. Where globalization is the trend, internationalizing working languages, including academic languages, is almost a necessity. Like it or not, we have to acknowledge the sole dominance of the English language in this respect. Viewpoints that are not presented in or do not have a chance to be translated into English amounts to not wanting the world to know. This is the case even for languages such as French, German and Russian which are all well established in the West. Said to have the largest learning population, the standard of English is variable simply because most tried going on the fast track to get a quick result. As a consequence, few in China could really give fluent presentations in English, even among linguists, not to mention writing in English. Until such time as a turn-around of the current situation, it will remain arduous for Chinese scholars to make a presence in world map.

  （2）缺乏原创性：在少数能用英语表述观点的学者以及身处国外、主要以英语进行著述的汉语背景学者中，原创性的论著非常少，难以见到能在理论上令人瞩目的创见。笔者曾经与一些在境外工作的语言研究者，谈起国内外的研究风气的大不同：国内的学术会议上，发言者往往喜欢就大题目谈宏观的问题；但在国外（主要是美国）接受教育的一些中国留学生，老师教他们的却是一定要做小题目，做得越细越好，能用许多事实说明一个两个理论问题就是成果。他们以此反观，担心国内学者的研究思路、研究方法有问题。我当时回答他们说，国外语言学研究难道就没有宏观层面的问题、就没有大题目需要人们去思考？如果国外语言学研究也有大的理论问题需要解决，为什么就只能由外国人来做而不许中国人染指？事实上近二、三十年国外语言学理论的创新炫人眼目，但为什么这些新理论、新体系就只能由外国人来做，而轮到中国人，就只能在这些理论的框架下做一些阐释性的工作呢？为什么国外有些人鄙夷不屑地说，汉语研究的"材料在中国，理论在美国"，而甚至一些从中国出去的汉语学者也都鹦鹉学舌地跟着这样说？理论研究本来就贵在创新，如果理论上没有新意，完全是袭用别人的现成理论，那么即使你的材料再丰富，人家也不会看。这个只要从我们自己的阅读经验就可以知道。我们读菲齐亚克等人编的对比研究论文集，很少会对那些具体而细微的波兰语—英语、芬兰语—英语，或者丹麦语–英语的对比文章感兴趣，因为我们不懂那些语言；即使多少懂一点的，如德语—英语、法语—英语等，我们也不会太感兴趣，因为它们未必对我们学习英语、德语或法语有多大的用处。但我们还是愿意读那些论文集，为什么？因为其中有一些理论文章有闪光点，会对我们理解整个对比语言学这个学科有意义。由此可见，真正有普遍意义的学术研究是带有理论创新意义的研究，目前在世界上用英语写的关于汉语研究的论著绝大多数在理论上没有什么创意，只是西方理论的汉语例解，因而这些论著引不起理论语言学界的关注就是很自然的事情了。

The second reason is theoretical originality. Among the English papers produced, including those by ethnic Chinese scholars, few generated enough originality theorywise. In a way, courage could be an issue. Linguistics scholars working overseas often comment on the differences in research approaches inside and outside of China. In mainland China, big topics at macro-level are almost the norm in local conferences, whereas elsewhere (mainly in the US), most Chinese postgraduates are taught to and only allowed to work on small topics in minute detail and are encouraged to use large amounts of data to prove one or two theoretical issues. In terms of approach and methodology, they are concerned for scholars in mainland China. This issue is not of concern to us. Certainly there are macro perspectives to be considered in linguistic studies abroad; someone will have to take care of the bigger issues. And big issues are not proprietary to the West. Anyone can work on it. It is extraordinary that novel ideas in theory over the past 20 or 30 years all happened in the West and all the Chinese scholars could do was interpret them. Have we ever wondered why some, including mainland Chinese scholars who have ventured abroad, mockingly commented that in the research of the Chinese language, China has the data, but the US has the theory? The key to success in theoretical research is originality. One may have all the data, but so long as they are used to support an existing framework, there is nothing new to attract attention. It is easy to prove this point from our own reading experience. Fisiak's collection of essays includes many micro perspective papers contrasting languages that most Chinese scholars do not speak Finnish, Danish and Polish with English. These are deemed to be less interesting papers even if the languages were French or German which more people know about. However, often we would still read it, not for learning the languages, but for the light these papers shed on theoretical issues and for the value they add to the understanding of the discipline. It follows therefore that only research of theoretical originality may be regarded as possessing real universal scholarship. By this criterion, it saddens us to say that there are fewer works on the Chinese language to date worth mentioning in terms of theoretical originality. They are at most attesting Western theories with Chinese linguistic facts. That says it all on the attention they could attract.

这两个方面加起来，用中文写的，也许不乏有创意的观点，但人们无从知道；用英语写的，大多没有原创性，人们不感兴趣。这样，中外语言学界的隔阂就是难免的了。要解决这个问题当然要从两方面着手，一方面要鼓励汉语学者用英文（最好在国际上）发表原创性的成果；另外当然也要鼓励有更多的非汉语语言学家愿意学习中文、研究中文。当然在目前，前者是主要的。但为了"鼓励"（不如说"吸引"）后者，我们也要作些"宣传"，例如下面要论述的了解汉外对比研究对世界语言研究的意义等等。

All in all, papers written in Chinese might be original enough but have failed to impact nonetheless. Papers written in English overcame the language barrier, but with less to offer in terms of creativity failed to impact too. Such being the case, it is not going to help scholastic communication between the linguists of these two worlds of language. To resolve the issue, we should on the one hand encourage more Chinese to publish their original findings in English at international standard. On the other hand, generate sufficient awareness and relevance to sustain the interest of non-Chinese scholars in the Chinese language, which is one of the intentions of this book.

2.1.2 汉外对比研究对世界语言研究的意义
2.1.2 Significance of contrastive studies involving the Chinese language

2.1.2.1 汉语不可替代的类型学意义
2.1.2.1 Unique typological importance in the Chinese language

沃尔夫（Whorf，1941：240）在提出对比语言学的术语的同时，强调指出对比研究的对象是相距遥远的事实（far-off event），其目的是研究"语言与思维"的关系，研究"不同语言在语法、逻辑和对经验的一般分析上的重大区别"。他的语言相对论之所以引起广泛争议，涉及的正是"语言与思维"的关系、"不同语言在语法、逻辑和对经验的一般分析上的重大区别"。而沃尔夫之所以产生这样的想法，正是把英语跟与其"相距遥远"的一些美洲印第安人语言加以对比研究的结果。从理论上来说，语言之间的距离越大，沃尔夫倡导的这一研究就越有实际意义，提出的问题就会越尖锐、越富挑战性，得出的结论也就越会有理论和应用价值。因此应该说，对比研究更适合于非亲属语言、特别是类型相距遥远的语言。然而，自20世纪50年代对比分析因对英语教学的需要在美国开展以后，由于实用的需要，不以人类学和文化学作为对比语言研究的基础；取而代之的是英语与许多跟其相距并不遥远的语言的对比，尤其是印欧语大家族成员的语言如德语、法语、西班牙语、波兰语、俄语等，用沃尔夫的话（Whorf，1939：138）来说，都属于"均质欧洲语"（SAE，或Standard Average European）的大类。虽然也有和其他语系的语言如芬兰语对比，但芬兰语与英语一样亦属形态语言特别是屈折语言的大类，从类型上来说相距也未必很遥远。与英语在类型上相距遥远的语言如汉语、越南语、日语、韩语等，以及一些南亚语言、阿拉伯语言、美洲印第安人和澳洲土著人的语言的对比研究当然也不是没有，论数量、研究面都嫌少而窄，且多数采用的比较方法与印欧语之间的比较大致相同，所得出的结论，难免有所不足，甚至偏颇。

At the same time Whorf proposes the term contrastive linguistics, he stresses for contrasting activities to be applied on far-off events in order that "outstanding differences among tongues—in grammar, logic and general analysis of experience" could be observed (Whorf, 1941a: 240). This relation on language and thought is precisely what his debatable hypothesis on linguistic relativity rests upon. What gives rise to this proposition? It was exactly from his contrastive studies involving

English and the Amerindian languages. Theoretically speaking, the more remotely connected the pair of languages to be contrasted is, the more realistic sense we could make out of Whorf's proposal on the discipline, and the more challenging the issues to be confronted and, henceforth, more meaningful and practicable the conclusions to be arrived at. Seen in this light, contrastive linguistics means more to distantly related language pairs, particularly in terms of typology. However, things took a twist when contrastive studies in the US started servicing the needs of teaching English as a foreign language. As this practical need prevails, studies in anthropological linguistics give way to analysis of English with closely related languages, particularly those under the big umbrella of Indo-European family: German, French, Spanish, Polish and Russian to name a few. Even though languages such as Finnish belong to another family, in so far as it being morphological and inflexional, they could not be said to be far off in typology. As Whorf puts it, they are all Standard Average European (SAE) languages (Whorf, 1939: 138). What languages would constitute far-off events? In relation to the English language, these will include Chinese, Vietnamese, Japanese and other south Asian languages, Amerindian languages and aboriginal languages in Australia, among others. There are a few papers examining the differences of these languages with the English language using the same method as contrasting between related languages, rendering the findings insignificant.

沃尔夫所倡导的"对比语言学"与"(历史)比较语言学"本是两个学科，研究对象和研究宗旨大相径庭，但"对比语言学"提出以来，研究对象反而变得模糊了，在"任何两个语言之间都可以进行对比"的借口下，大量进行并作为理论建设基础的是亲属语言间的"对比"；而研究的宗旨也悄悄地变成了"比较"的方法之争，是"求同"还是"求异"？如何求异？方法之争也变相成为理论和应用之辨，如何才能对二语教学更加有用？结果"对比语言学"变得个性不清，往往成了其他语言学科的旁支，如"比较语言学"、"外语教学"。对比语言学研究"语言与思维"关系的任务被忘却了，"不同语言在语法、逻辑和对经验的一般分析上的重大区别"也不大有人关心了，"语言相对论"越来越成为谁也无法说服谁的口舌之争。

In Whorf's ideal, contrastive linguistics and comparative linguistics are two disciplines with completely different objects and targets. As contrastive linguistics established itself as a discipline, the target somehow turned fuzzy. Justified by the excuse that one may contrast any two languages, large amounts of resources and energy were channelled into analysing related languages, thereby gradually shifting the focus to a methodological debate within the premise of "comparative" studies. Should differences or similarities be sought? How to proceed? How would it help foreign language teaching? In consequence, "contrastive linguistics" has lost its character to become a subfield under "comparative linguistics". Also lost in the process was its mission of exploring the relations of language and thought by means of digging out the "outstanding differences among tongues—in grammar, logic, and general analysis of experience" (Wharf, 1941a: 240). Linguistic relativity thus becomes a superficial battle of words in which neither side is convincing.

问题出在哪里呢？就出在"相距遥远"上。如果语言之间相距不遥远，甚至只是同一个语支下的兄弟姐妹，那无论如何比，其在类型上的差异总不会太大，更不大可能会大到思维方式迥异的程度；在这样的框架下讨论"语言相对论"，无异于硬要辨清左手和右手的异同，其结论是可以下在争论开始之前的。

What could be the real issue? Far-off events. If the languages to be contrasted in pair are close enough or even relatives in the same family, they would not present outstanding differences in typology that would ultimately surface as differences in thought. No sensible discourse on linguistic relativity could be expected. As in trying to tell the differences of the right hand from the left, the conclusion has been reached even before exchanges in words could begin.

因此，要彻底地进行沃尔夫所提倡的对比语言学，最理想的是找两个在类型上，甚至在各个方面都"相距遥远"的语言。在这方面，可以说汉语是最合适的对象。拿汉语与英语或印欧语族的其他语言比，最容易实行沃尔夫提倡的目标，也最可以检验"语言相对论"等理论的得失。

To follow Whorf's idea on contrastive linguistics, the ideal target would be a pair of languages each belonging to a typological class in no way related with each other. On this note, the Chinese language could be the best partner to contrast with English or other Indo-European languages. Whorf's idea would then be within reach and the hypothesis on linguistic relativity could then be thoroughly tested and fairly justified.

我们想比沃尔夫更往前走一步，主张在对比研究中，选择汉语要优于选择美洲印第安人语言或澳大利亚土著人语言。[1]沃尔夫以及美国人类学语言学的先驱鲍阿斯、萨丕尔等人都是从研究美洲印第安人语言开始他们的学术生涯和理论构建的。美洲印第安人语言对于他们的学说的创建功不可没。但就世界语言学的研究而言,美洲印第安人语言(以及与之类似的澳大利亚土著人语言和南岛诸语言)并不是最理想的对比对象。为什么?因为这些语言没有文字,更没有自己的语言学家和语言研究传统,我们对这些语言的认识是通过西方语言学家的描述来了解的,有关描述一般由西方语言架构出发,从某种程度上说带有一定的"人为"性,未必就是这些语言的本来或自然面貌。在学习普通语言学著作的时候,我们常感到一种强烈的困惑:为什么我们熟悉的语言,其谱系就这么简单,而我们不熟悉的语言,其谱系就如此复杂?例如横跨欧亚大陆、涉及十几亿人、[2]几十个国家和民族的语言就只是一个"印欧语系";而仅几万、几十万人的美洲印第安人语言、澳洲土著人语言就有几千种,几百种,甚至"语系"也有几十种?[3]从人类学、人种学、语言发生学,乃至地理学、考古学等任何一种学科的逻辑上去推论,这种情况可能吗?唯一的解释是,因为

---

1 这里我们只从普通语言学角度讨论问题,不涉及民族问题。从民族角度看,当然印第安人语言和土著人语言对美国和澳大利亚的重要性大得多。

Let it be emphasized that it is an academic issue that we are concerned with, nothing ethnical. In fact, from an ethnic point of view, contrastive linguistics bears even greater significance in choosing Amerindian or Aboriginal languages in the respective contexts of the US and Australia.

2 肯尼思·卡兹纳在《世界的语言》(Katzner, 1975:11)上说:"操印欧语的总人数……占总人口的一半左右。"

Kenneth Katzner in *The Languages of the World* (Katzner, 1975: 11) said, "The total number of Indo-European speakers is about 1,875,000,000 people, approximately half the earth's total population."

3 肯尼思·卡兹纳在(Katzner, 1975:34)上说:"美洲印第安语的数目在千种以上,非洲的语言接近1000种,单单新几内亚的一个岛屿就有700多种语言。"(序言)"澳洲土人只有五万人,却操着好几百种语言。"(前言)"据信单单在北美洲一地,就有50多个不同的语系,这些语系分别构成几个大语系,但是这样的分类只是推测性的,有待于进一步修改。"

ibid.: "…we do know that the American Indian languages number more than a thousand, the languages of Africa are close to a thousand, and the single island of New Guinea contributes some 700 more" (Preface). "There are still several hundred languages spoken by only 50,000 surviving Australian aborigines…" (Foreword by Charles Berlitz). "In north America alone there believed to be some fifty different families. These in turn have been grouped into a few great superfamilies, but the designations are still tentative and subject to further revision" (p.34).

印欧系的语言都是人们熟悉的、有书面语历史的而且经过无数学者深入研究因而相对较为成熟的语言，因为熟悉，我们可以通过历史比较法对它们进行细致的比较和重建，一探分化以前的源头。而印第安人语言从来就没有过成熟的书面语言，甚至从来没有过书面形式（唯一留有记载的玛雅人文字由于西班牙殖民者的破坏已残缺而无法完全破译），更从来没有过本族人对其自身语言文化的研究或描述；现今所有关于这些语言的"面貌"全部都是使用英语的语言学者经过田野调查以后、用同英语一样的拉丁字母记录下来、并用英语给我们加以解释的。我们非常尊重这些语言垦荒者所做的工作，也非常愿意相信他们所提出的结论，但是这三个"从来没有过"加上一个"全部都是"告诉我们，其实我们现在对这些语言的"了解"，从科学的角度看，只能算是一种"假设"；在这过程中，不管语言记录者如何力图做得"客观"，其中难免掺杂了研究者自身的语言文化特点，甚至这就是"语言相对论"造成的悖论：说英语的语言调查者，其调查结果难免会给所调查的语言及相关描述记录留下英语文法的烙印！试设想，如果进行这些语言调查的不是20世纪说英语的美国人，而比方说是16世纪郑和下西洋时只会说汉语、写汉字的中国人，所调查出来的"印第安人语言"会是我们现在所看到的这个面貌吗？再进一步推论，假如在中国这片土地上由于种种原因从来就没有出现过汉语的书面形式及其相关语言研究，这一大片土地上的人们还是各自说着自己的方言，到了20世纪，使用英语的美国人类学家来调查、记录汉语，他们辛勤地四处奔波，先是用音标记下汉语各种方言的音，然后采用"发现程序"和"分布理论"等手段，建立起汉语的各级单位，然后描写其"形态"和"句法"。其结果，汉语会是现在我们所知道的这个样子吗？美国人类学家调查印第安人语言时所碰到的最棘手问题——词和句子界限不清——在汉语中同样要面对（这就是美国结构主义语言学家把语法单位从传统印欧语的词和句子两级扩大成语素、词、短语、小句、句子五级后，广受中国语言学家欢迎的原因）[1]。而在同样的假设条件下，汉语

---

[1] 吕叔湘（1979：14—15）说："讲西方语言的语法，词和句子是主要单位，语素、短语、小句是次要的。（这是就传统语法说，结构主义语法里边语素的地位比词重要。）讲汉语的语法，由于历史的原因，语素和短语的地位不亚于词，小句的重要性不亚于句子。"
Lü Shuxiang remarked that: "For Western grammar, word and sentence are the main units, morpheme, phrase and clause are secondary (traditionally speaking, Structuralism attaches more weight in morpheme than word). For Chinese grammar, historical reasons have it that morpheme and phrase are as important as word, whereas clause is as important as sentence." (Lü Shuxiang, 1979: 14—15)

各地方言的歧异由于失去了汉字这一工具的维系而将遭夸大无数倍,给语言调查者带来我们无法想象的巨大的困难。我们能保证那样调查出来的"汉语"不是数十、数百个"语系"吗?而汉语的"语法"也必然会比现在更繁杂不知多少!恐怕少不了会有许许多多的"形态"与"形态标志"!索绪尔说:

> We would like to go a step further than Whorf to suggest that preference be given to the Chinese language over Amerindian or aboriginal languages in Australia in contrastive linguistics. No doubt pioneering anthropological linguists, Boas, Sapir and Whorf got their inspiration, built their theories and advanced their academic careers from their research of the indigenous languages of the Americas. In that sense native American languages are important, but conceivably not to the extent as to contribute extra miles to global linguistics research. Objectively speaking, native American languages (as well as Australian Aboriginal languages and Austroasiatic languages) are not the best contrasting target we can have on the grounds that these languages do not come with a written form and do not have language researchers or a linguistic research tradition of their own. All that we know about these languages are essentially the descriptions of Western linguists; that is to say, there are certain degrees of "make-up" from the undisguised forms. More often than not, the study of general linguistics is clouded with strong skepticism: Why is the tree diagram of familiar languages simple and that for unfamiliar languages complex? For instance, languages of billions of people across Europe and Asia are grouped under one Indo-European language family. Why is it that the Amerindian languages and Australian Aboriginal languages governing a few ten or hundred thousands should be classified into hundreds and thousands of branches and isolated under a few tens of "language families"? From all plausible logical angles of anthropology, ethnology, language genetics and even geography and archeology, how does this deduction sound? The only possible explanation would be because we are most familiar with the Indo-European family—it has documented history in texts, numerous linguists have worked on it and meticulous reconstruction and comparison among the languages are possible by way of historical comparative linguistics. It is therefore regarded as a relatively matured language system. By contrast, *no* matured written form of the Amerindian languages has ever been developed, *not even* any written form in fact (texts left by the Maya were perhaps the only source but were unfortunately

mostly destroyed by Spanish colonists, which prevented plausible decoding). It is also important to note that *no* speaker of the language has ever made a description of or research into their own linguistic culture. The ideas we have on these languages are all fieldwork recordings in Latin alphabets by English speaking researchers. What a work indeed! We have due respect for the excellent effort and are more than willing to believe the explanations and conclusions on the languages. Nonetheless, we conclude that there are reasonable doubts as to how much we really understand those languages. The descriptions are at best some assumptions, scientifically. We can imagine that in the process, however objective the researchers care to be, the descriptions must have more or less been tinted with perspectives of researchers' own linguistic culture. In fact, the findings would have been paradoxical for research in linguistic relativity. If English-speaking researchers tend to impose the English language culture on these languages, how about if the fieldwork were conducted by researchers speaking another language, say the great navigator of the sixteenth century, Zheng He, who spoke and wrote only Chinese? Would it change the understanding we have of Amerindian languages? Assuming again that for some reasons, China has never had any written form or past research on the language and dialects prevailed in this vast land until this day of the twenty-first century. Say an English speaking American anthropological linguist came along to do fieldwork, running around to make recordings of the different dialect tongues with phonetic symbols and finally, with their systems of "discovery procedure" and "distribution theory", established a linguistic system for the Chinese language—language units at different levels, morphology, syntax, etc.—would the "Chinese language" be the Chinese language? What confronted anthropological linguists in describing the indigenous languages of the Americas was that there is no distinct marking for words and sentences. They would face the same problem for Chinese. Indo-European languages have only two levels: word and sentence level, and these are not good enough for Chinese and some other languages. This is exactly why structuralism's proposal of expanding into five levels, comprising morpheme, word, phrase, clause and sentence, was greatly welcomed by Chinese linguists. Everything remains constant, without Chinese characters serving as the link; the differences among Chinese dialects could be overly exaggerated and could prove to be too formidable for language survey. We are certain that if that should happen, language survey will yield a few tens or hundreds of "language families" from China. We could also imagine how complex the "grammar" of Chinese would then become with all the "morphological changes" and "markers" added out of good will! Saussure once remarked:

> 我们一般只通过文字来认识语言。研究母语也常要利用文献。如果那是一种远离我们的语言，还要求助于书写的证据，对于那些已经不存在的语言更是这样。（索绪尔，1916: 24）

> But we generally learn about languages only through writing. Even in studying our native language, we constantly make use of written texts. The necessity of using written evidence increases when dealing with remote idioms, and all the more when studying idioms that no longer exist. (Saussure, 1916/1986: 23)

因此我们有理由认为，像印第安语这样经过加工的"半人工"语言，诚然对于对比研究有一定的意义，而拿成熟的、有悠久书面语历史的、经过本族人描写和研究过的"相距遥远"的语言作为对比对象，其普通语言学上的意义要大得多。二十世纪五十年代，中国政府为了帮助没有文字的少数民族发展其语言，曾经派遣专家帮助他们创制文字。由于历史的原因，少数民族最初创制的文字是以汉字为模式的，五十年代以后创制的文字是以拼音文字为模式的。这样造成的两种文字乃至"书面语言"在面貌上就很不相同。但对原来的少数民族而言，这两种文字体系都未必反映他们语言的真正面貌，充其量也只是个语音模写而已。而如果就以这些文字记录下来的东西作为这些民族的"语言"去和别的语言进行"对比研究"，其"科学性"和结论就非常值得怀疑。这也可能是为什么人们总觉得"语言相对论"既无法证明也无法证伪的一个重要原因：因为材料本身无法验证。

We have all the reasons to believe that "semi-processed" languages such as Amerindian languages are meaningful to contrastive linguistics, but what could have contributed even more would be matured far-off languages backed by historical texts and studies of speakers of the languages. Inferences from the latter would have greater impact on general linguistics. In the 1950s, to help develop minority languages, the Chinese government tasked a team of experts to formulate suitable writing systems for the respective languages. For historical reasons, the minorities have at the initial stage used a writing system based on Chinese characters. The 1950s models were based on alphabets. That is to say, minority languages in China own two sets of entirely different writing systems each. To the ethnic speakers, perhaps none of the systems represent their language well enough. These systems only act as phonetics. We have to be very careful in using these "written records" as the basis for contrastive analysis. This inability to verify primary data constitutes one criticism of linguistic relativity: It can neither prove nor disprove.

而拿汉语同英语或其他印欧语言比就完全没有这样的问题。汉语的成熟性、历史性、文化性等，与英语等相比，可说有过之而无不及。而汉语与印欧语在类型学上的距离之远又是众所公认的，[1] 几乎没有一种普通语言学的语言分类法不把汉语和印欧语特别是其中的拉丁语作为遥远的两极。但是汉语和印欧语之间的类型学差别到底有多大？孤立语和屈折语背后究竟反映了什么样的人类思维的不同模式？语言相对论在汉语和印欧语这两大人群之间究竟有没有道理？这些问题在洪堡特之后可说很少得到认真的重视和研究。陈望道《文法简论》（1978：114）尖锐地指出："一般语言学的理论到目前为止还没能或者说很少能充分地、正确地概括世界上使用人口最多、历史极其悠久、既丰富又发达的汉语事实和规律。"一些西方语言学家尽管承认汉语在语言类型学上的重要性，但实际上却没下过大功夫对汉语进行认真研究，充斥在他们著作中的"汉语"状况几乎全是"二手货"，绝大多数是经过西方语言学的透镜过滤过的，谈不上反映汉语的本来面貌。而一些汉语学者为了急于"跟国际接轨"，也很少认真思索汉语自身的类型学特点，仅满足于在西方理论的框架下填补汉语的例子，其反映出来的同样不是汉语的真实面貌。因而，进行汉外对比研究，实际上是中外语言学家共同的当务之急和严峻的考验。世界语言学要发展，理论语言学要取得突破，不能依旧在印欧语的范围内兜圈子，或者再点缀一些非印欧语的例子，那是没有出路的。可以说，没能反映汉语特点的普通

---

[1] 例如洪堡特说："随便读一段中文，所得到的第一印象是其语法结构与几乎世界上所有语言都不同，与习惯称为'古典'的语言形成的对比更是强烈。"（Humboldt, 1826: 95）
For example, Humboldt (1826: 95) remarked: "The first impression created by reading a part of any Chinese book is that in its grammatical structure this language differs from more or less all other languages. It contrasts most with those normally called classical…"

语言学理论都是不完整的理论,不能解释汉语现象包括古汉语现象[1]的普通语言学理论都是片面的理论。著名汉学家高本汉(Benhard Karlgren)说:

The above issue will not be a concern at all if the Chinese language is used instead to contrast with other Indo-European languages. In terms of maturity, history and culture, the Chinese language is as good as Indo-European languages, if not better, and it is common knowledge that, typologically, Chinese and Indo-European languages definitely belong to two remote classes, by all standards of classification in general linguistics. The questions to ask are then to what extent are they typologically different? How different is the thought pattern behind isolated language type and inflexional language type? Can linguistic relativity stand between this pair of contrasts? These are questions not taken care of after Humboldt. Linguists in the West may recognize, in words, the typological importance presented by the Chinese language, but real actions and effort to establish the claim are yet to be taken up. Their understanding and description of the Chinese language was actually the "purification" result by Western linguistics, not the uncovered truth of the linguistic facts. Of course the onus is also on linguists who are speakers of the language. However, all of them cannot be said to have seriously thought through the valid typological characteristics of Chinese and some are even satisfied by filling in examples from the language to the framework constructed using Western theories just to show that they are "in line with international practice". The urgency and challenge are real in contrasting Chinese with matured foreign languages, and the responsibility shouldered by Chinese and non-Chinese linguists is equal. Continuing to look within Indo European languages will be of no help towards a breakthrough in global linguistics as well as in theoretical linguistic development. It will also be of no help to merely decorate the theories with examples from non-Indo European languages. Any general linguistic theory not reflecting the characteristics of the Chinese language is incomplete, and any general linguistic theory not able to explain

---

1 因为据一般看法,古汉语是更典型的孤立语。而近几十年来,连汉语学者自身也很少从类型学的角度去研究古汉语。

It is generally held that traditional Chinese serves a classical example of isolated language. Nevertheless not even Chinese scholars have paid much attention to the typology of traditional Chinese in the last few decades.

the phenomena in Chinese, including ancient Chinese, is one-sided. Renowned Swedish sinologist and eminent philologist Benhard Karlgren has this to remind:

> 这样看来，即使对语言学问题感兴趣的一般读者，能够了解一点关于汉语最主要特点的介绍也是有好处的。不过这种对汉语特点的描述，不能像我上面提到的大部分著作一样，只局限于当代口语，而必须考虑这种语言的早期情况及其历史。只有这样才能对汉语在我们迄今所了解的语言类型里占据什么地位有一个恰如其分的评价。（高本汉，1949: iii）

> Thus, even to the general reader who takes an interest in linguistic matters, it may be valuable to have available a brief sketch which gives the principal characteristics of Chinese. But such a description should not be limited to modern colloquial speech as is largely the case in the general surveys just mentioned. It must also take into account what we know about earlier stages of the Chinese language and its history. Only thus can a just estimate be formed of the proper place of Chinese among the language types known at present. (Karlgren, 1949: iii)

2.1.2.2 汉语独特的语言研究传统
2.1.2.2 The unique scholastic tradition of Chinese

汉外对比研究对普通语言学的另一个意义是对普通语言学理论本身的检验。迄今为止的普通语言学虽然号称是全人类的"普通"语言学，在其举例中有时也会涉及到多种多样甚至是罕为人知的语言，书后更常会列出一个"世界语言谱系表"，大有已把世上所有语言一网打尽的样子。但明眼人都知道，所谓的普通语言学是在对印欧系语言分析的基础上建立起来的，对印欧系语言的分析还差强人意，对其他语言的分析，例如前文所说对印第安人语言的分类，尽管言之凿凿，还是很难令人完全信服。介于两者之间的，譬如说对所谓汉藏语系的研究，也往往使人疑窦丛生。有时人们会怀疑，语言学家对印欧语系、对汉藏语系及其他语系、对印第安人诸语言的分类能否保证采用的是同一个标准？否则怎么会把历史上地理阻隔、类型上又很少有共同点的汉语和藏语起劲地归并在一个语系[1]，而把地域相对狭小又没有多少人在使用的印第安诸语言和澳洲土著诸语言却不嫌其烦地要分成数量众多的"语系"？难道那些语言的语法特点真是大到无法在一个"语系"内相容的地步？人类语言的分布怎么会是这个样子？有多少是人为的因素？说穿了，印欧语系比较语言学的成功，使语言学家尝到了谱系分类的甜头，其他语系的"建立"乃至整个语言学中的谱系分类法都是仿照印欧语系的方法进行类推的结果。如果说印欧语系的建立是经过几乎一个世纪的精细研究的产物（在这过程中也有争论和不同意见，此处不赘），则其他"语系"的建立就要粗疏得多，很少有别的语系的建立也经历过印欧语系那样长期扎实的积累过程；也许正好相反，语言学家是先根据有限的资料，假设某些语言属于同一语系，在此前提下再"证明"这些语言的某些词语确实有着语音上的"同源"关系。通常的做法似乎是：先从理论上列出某个"语系"在语法上的一些共同"特征"，亦即设立一些标准（例如汉藏语系的"单音节、有声调、量词丰富"等等），再拿相关的语言去对照，于是，一个个分类就搞好了。萨丕尔对此有个形象的批评："曾经提出过好多种分类法，每种都有可取之处，但是没有一种叫人满意。它们与其说是把所知的各种语言都包罗进去了，不如说是强迫各种语言坐在窄小的直背椅上。"（Sapir, 1921：122）

1　《世界的语言》（Katzner, 1975：81；102；185—187；237；83）一书中说到，语言学家区分佛兰芒语（Flemish）与荷兰语（Dutch）、塞尔维亚语（Serbian）与克罗地亚语（Croatian）、印地语（Hindi）与乌尔都语（Urdu）、印度尼西亚语（Indonesian）和马来语（Malay），以及卢森堡语（Luxembourgian）独立于德语，主要都是因为政治、宗教或文字的原因。依此，也许从"语言学"角度看，汉语成为一个大的语系恐怕已绰绰有余了。该书（1975：29）还说："目前，还远不能确定这四族（指上文说的汉、藏缅、傣侗、苗瑶四族语言）中的每族语言和其他三族语言是否有谱系上的联系。"既然如此，侈谈"汉藏语系"，会不会引起语言研究的误导呢？

It was mentioned in *The Languages of the World* (Katzner, 1975: 75; 95; 96; 177—179; 233; 276) that it is chiefly out of political, religious or writing system reasons that linguists divide Flemish and Dutch; Serbian and Croatian; Hindi and Urdu; Indonesian and Malay; and single out Luxembourgian from German. That is to say, purely from a linguistic point of view, it is probably good enough for the Chinese language to form a big language family of its own. It was also mentioned (1975: 24): "that the languages of each of the four branches (author's note: referring to Chinese, Tibeto-Burman, Tai, Miao & Yao) are genetically related to those of the other three is still far from certain." Such being the case, is it not misleading talking about the "Sino-Tibetan" family as it is?

From the perspective of general linguistics, conducting contrasting Chinese with a typologically different language offers yet another opportunity to attest the theory of general linguistics. General linguistics, as the name implies, should ideally be applicable to the whole human race and it does attempt to do so by including examples from a variety of unheard of languages, complete with a list of tree diagrams of world languages, as if no language is left behind. Nevertheless, we do know the trick. To date, general linguistics is built upon findings on Indo-European languages. With our analysis of the Indo-European languages accepted as complete and perfect, our analysis of other languages in other language families sounds too good to be true and unbiased. We sometimes cannot help but ask: Are linguists applying the same standard in their analysis of the Indo-European languages to Sino-Tibetan languages, Amerindian languages, and the others? Otherwise how could the Chinese languages and the Tibetan languages be banded as one language family when they are separated geographically and typologically do not have much in common? And how could languages of the Amerindians and Australian tribes be distinguished into hundreds of families when they are closer to each other geographically and have only limited users? Do the linguistic characteristics really differ too much to prevent the forming of phyla? Is this distribution right? How much human factor is at play? The answers are not too difficult to guess at. The success of Indo-European comparative linguistics aroused interest in developing tree diagrams for languages, linguists are eager to seek out the tree structure of other language families, and as a result, the success recipe was copied, deduced and imposed on to all possible language families in the human world. We know that the Indo-European tree diagram is the product of a whole century of detailed research, not to mention the arguments and divided opinions in the process. By comparison, the establishment of many other "tree diagrams" experienced a much shorter and sketchier process and few evolved out of careful research accumulation over a sufficiently long time span. Worse still, it could have been the product of hypothesis testing, i.e. an assumption on the language tree membership based on limited data was first made and on this premise, an attempt to prove that the lexes of the languages concerned are cognates. The normal procedure for this testing is as follows: first, list the shared "characteristics" of the pre-assumed "language family" with some criteria (for example, characteristics of the Sino-Tibetan family include "monosyllabic, tonal and rich in the use of classifiers", among others). Next, test the language concerned against these criteria. One by one, we have the languages neatly classified. Commenting on this, Sapir did not mince his words: "Various classifications have been suggested, and they all contain elements of value. Yet none proves satisfactory. They do not so much enfold the known languages in their brace as force them down into narrow, straight-backed seats" (Sapir, 1921: 122).

如果我们同意语言谱系学是建立在印欧语系模式的基础上，按照同样的思路、同样的原则、同样的方法，通过类推建立起来的，对此我们无法进行证明或者证伪，因为除了印欧语系之外，没有一个其他语系拥有这样丰富的历史语料（包括位居第二的"汉藏语系"，因为汉藏语系的构建使用的不是2000多年间活生生的汉语语料，而是将虚拟的3000年以前的"上古汉语"，与不足1000年历史的藏语以及历史更短的其他一些语言进行比较的结果，那个虚拟的语料的可靠性颇成问题）。那么，使我们马上联想到的是，普通语言学的其他分类法，不也是经过类似的顺序确立起来的吗？所有语言都有名词、动词或其他种种词类之分；所有的名词都可以有性、数、格之分；所有的动词都可以有时、态、数、体、人称等等的变化（只是数量多少和表现形式不同而已）；所有的句子都有主、谓之分，有主、动、宾的次序问题等等。整个普通语言学大厦就是这么建立起来的。对此很少有人表示过疑问，更多人想不到去表示疑问，因为2000多年来，人们就是一直在这么做的。语言理论此升彼降，但作为语言研究的这些基本概念却很少有人怀疑过。也许上一章引用过的沃尔夫是一个例外，他说过："人们似乎有一种自然倾向，喜欢使用传统语法的术语，如动词、名词、形容词、被动语态等，来描述印欧语系以外的语言。这种倾向极有可能引起误解。"（Whorf, 1937：87/62）英国语言学家帕麦尔（Frank Palmer）是另外一个，他说："许多传统语法书不假思索地认为所有语言的语法都是一样的，而那就是拉丁语法。"（Palmer, 1971：19—20）同沃尔夫一样，他认为印欧语言内部的相似性是一种"不幸"（unfortunate），而这种相似是"多少世纪的文化接触造成的，远非天然和普遍的"（同上：19）。但多数人并不这么想。沃尔夫所提出的语言相对论，还使他的整个理论处于不利的地位。

If we agree that the tree diagrams were built by adapting the base model of Indo-European model languages with some deduction on the way, we could neither verify nor prove it wrong, as there is not a second language family equipped with the same depth of historical data, —including the Sino-Tibetan family, which was founded on dubious data contrasting reconstructed data of early archaic Chinese some 3,000 years ago with Tibetan language of less than 1,000 years old, as well as other younger languages, leaving aside 2,000 years of living linguistic data. It then becomes clear that the same procedure applies in other classification requirements in general linguistics. All languages have nouns, verbs and other word classes. All nouns may have categories such as gender, number and case. All verbs may change, in various manners, with respect to one or more of the following categories: tense, voice, number, aspects, mood, etc. All sentences may be segmented into subject and predicate arranged in a certain word order, such as subject—verb—object. The adapting and fitting mechanism goes on. Finally, we have the whole general linguistics built up. Few ever doubted the process; most do not even bother to question it. What is wrong? Haven't we done it for 2,000 years? New theories come and go, yet the fundamentals have been left untouched. Benjamin Lee Whorf is such an exception. He commented: "The very natural tendency to use terms derived from traditional grammar, like verb, noun, adjective, passive voice, in describing languages outside of Indo-European is fraught with grave possibilities of misunderstanding" (Whorf, 1937: 87). British linguist Frank Palmer is yet another. He remarked: "Many traditional grammar books of foreign languages have taken it for granted that all languages have the same grammar, and usually it was assumed that this was identical with Latin grammar" (Palmer, 1984: 20). Like Whorf, he used the term "unfortunate" to describe the internal similarities present in Indo-European languages, and this similarity is in fact "a result of cultural contact over the centuries. But it is in no sense natural or universal" (*ibid*.). Notwithstanding the wisdom, most like to think otherwise. It is also unfor tunate that Whorf's theory was seriously suspected because people did not buy his idea of linguistics relativity.

　　但是，汉外对比研究很可能会对这个问题提出更令人信服的答案。人们常说人类有三大语言研究传统：印度语言学传统、希腊语言学传统和中国语言学传统，不过前两种传统后来合流了，共同成为印欧语的研究传统。如果此说成立，则世界上现存的只是印欧语与汉语两大研究传统。我们斗胆问一句，"现代语言学"建立的这一百年以来，有没有真正把汉语研究传统作为一种与印欧语传统不同的语言研究传统来对待呢？有没有在普通语言学的建立过程中真正纳入汉语研究传统的因素呢？建立普通语言学基础的那些概念都来自于印欧语研究传统，如果运用这些概念就能够轻而易举地解释汉语及其历史，那当然也就不必承认"汉语研究传统"了，而很多学者包括中国本身的学者一直朝这个方向所做的努力，也应该持续得到鼓励。可事实上，"汉语研究传统"之所以有存在的必要，而且能够同印欧语研究传统分庭抗礼，是因为2000多年来，汉语始终在走着一条独特的语言研究道路，直到19世纪末才有所变化。这一段历史并不会随着汉语研究的"现代化"而消失，相反，这一部分经验，正有待于包括汉语学者在内的全世界语言研究者去共同继承，而这正是汉外对比语言学研究的一项重要内容。

Yet, a solution may be found by contrasting with the Chinese language. Generally speaking, it is believed that there were three main linguistic traditions: the Indian, the Greek and the Chinese. The first two converged to become the Indo-European research tradition. If this premise is true, we are then left with two scholastic traditions in languages: Indo-European and Chinese. If this stands, has the traditional research in Chinese language, so vastly different from the Indo-European tradition, dare we ask, ever been taken seriously? Who in the process of instituting general linguistics truly factor in considerations from the Chinese scholastic tradition? All primary concepts of general linguistics mentioned above are given by the Indo-European research tradition. If these concepts could be easily applied to analyse and explain the Chinese language as well as its historical development, it would not be necessary, or meaningful, to try recovering a place for the scholarship in Chinese language, which many academics are fighting hard at, Chinese intellectuals included. In reality, for some 2,000 years in its unique research path, the Chinese linguistic tradition has strived in co-existence with the Indo-European tradition. Just before the close of the nineteenth century, probably influenced by the socio-political climate of China at the time when modernization and Westernization were taking place, things started changing and Western research was taken as standard. Yet, the linguistic scholarship remaining true to history will never diminish with the "modernization" process that induced novel but not always creative research on the Chinese language. In fact, the lessons accumulated all these years await inheritance by all linguists, not only ethnic Chinese linguists. This is one major target for contrasting the Chinese language with a foreign language.

因此，汉语所能提供给世界语言学的，就不仅仅是最独特、最悠久、文化最丰富、同时也是与印欧语"相距最远"的一个成熟语言样本，它还能提供世界上唯一的、与印欧语传统不相同的语言研究传统。人们现在对于印欧语的研究传统，几乎都是耳熟能详；但不知道有多少人能说清楚：汉语的研究传统是什么？汉语独特的语言类型、独特的文字形态对语言研究传统的建立有什么意义？汉语没有形态（或至少"缺少严格意义上的形态"），与世界绝大多数语言不同，因而不可能产生西方那种语法传统，那中国人是怎么对其语言进行研究的？这种不同于西方传统的研究能不能称为科学？算不算世界语言研究传统的一部分？在世界语言学史中的地位如何？对人类的语言研究有什么意义？我们觉得，世界语言学有这个责任，抓住这唯一的印欧语之外的发达典型，不但重视汉语和印欧语的语言之间的对比，还要重视汉语与印欧语的语言研究传统之间的对比，这样才有可能集中人类的智慧，建立起具有相对普遍意义的普通语言学，绝对意义的普通语言学是难以成就的，因为汉语和印欧语之外还有大量的语言，只可惜它们缺乏可资参考的语言研究传统，难以总结为普通语言学的一部分。

Enough said about the contribution the Chinese language can offer to global linguistics as a language most irreplaceable, the longest in history and richest in culture in the least, and as a linguistic sample most distinct from the Indo-European languages and the only language in the world with a research tradition differing from that of Indo-European. It is high time to ask how much we know about the research tradition of the Chinese language when the research tradition of the Indo European language is so well publicized. In what ways have the unique language typology as well as the special writing system played a role in building the research tradition? Being a language without morphological changes, at least not in the strict sense, Chinese language is separated from most other languages of the world and not likely to follow the Western grammar tradition. How did the Chinese go about studying their language? Can research tradition, different from that of the Western tradition, be considered as scientific? Can we count it as part of world linguistic tradition? How to account for its place in the history of world linguistics? How may it contribute to language research as a whole? Linguists of the world should take it upon themselves to make good use of this classic sample outside the Indo-European family for contrastive analysis in terms of both languages and scholastic traditions in language. We hope that with this concerted effort, a general linguistics with greater universal significance could be achieved. We may not be able to get any higher, as there are far more languages in the world than Chinese and Indo-European languages, but for the short of scholastic traditions, meaningful inclusion may be impossible.

2.1.2.3 中西语言学对话的窗口
2.1.2.3 Window for dialogue between Chinese and Western linguistics

应该说，在普通语言学的研究中，还是有不少语言学家给予汉语应有的关注，尤其是洪堡特、萨丕尔、高本汉、韩礼德（M. A. K. Halliday）、霍凯特（Charles Hocket）等，但他们的工作并没有引起当代更多的语言学家的注意，特别是，还没有西方的理论语言学家、对比语言学家甚至人类学语言学家，真正把汉语当作与印欧语"相距遥远"的最可靠、最有价值的语言和文化样品；把汉语的研究传统看作与印欧语研究传统并行、即使不是势均力敌也至少是戛戛独造的传统，有可能通过对它的研究来丰富、充实世界的普通语言学。我们所见到的是，在前一种情况下，人类学语言学家往往认为罕为人知的原始部落的语言才具有文化与思维研究的价值，已广为人们知晓的语言、特别是大语种的语言已经太熟悉、太平凡到失去了这种研究价值；在后一种情况下，许多人在理论上似乎也承认汉语研究有其独特的传统，但在实际上，不仅千方百计地将受了西方语言学影响的现代汉语的研究纳入西方语言研究的传统，甚至也不放过中国与西方接触之前的汉语研究。换句话说，是采取一种抽象承认、具体否认的虚无主义态度，有人甚至觉得只有把汉语的研究传统全部纳入了印欧语的研究传统，才是对汉语传统最大的尊重。连中国自己的许多语言学者都持这种意见。

We recognize that many linguists have given Chinese language sufficient attention in their research in general linguistics, particularly Humboldt, Sapir, Karlgren, M. A. K. Halliday and Charles Hocket, among others. However, their work did not get many contemporary linguists excited, especially Western theoretical linguists, contrastivists and even anthropological linguists, to actually treat Chinese language as the most reliable, most valuable language and most far-off event for contrast with Indo-European languages; and to consider the Chinese linguistics tradition as running parallel with that of the Indo-European language family in a distinctive way and tapping into it could possibly help to enrich general linguistics. In the first instance, anthropological linguists tend to think that languages of some rare uncivilized tribes offer higher value in understanding culture and thought, not those popular language types that are widely known and deemed to have lost characteristics. In the second instance, while many do admit the uniqueness of the linguistic tradition of Chinese language, that is plain theory. In reality, they try all ways and means to fit both modern Chinese language and Chinese in pre-modern days into the Western tradition to the extent that some, including linguists in China, would regard this as being respectful to the Chinese language tradition.

在对待汉语问题上,语言研究者可以划分为以下九类,其中前五类主要是西方语言学家或汉学家,后四类主要是汉语语言学家:

According to the treatment given to the Chinese language, we could single out nine types of linguists; the first five are mainly Western linguists or sinologists, the remaining Chinese linguists.

第一类语言学家不懂汉语,由于历史和现实的原因,不可能也未必有机会去学习汉语,他们的汉语知识都是间接的,不是来自语言学教科书上的那几句老生常谈,就是从研究论文中得来的只言片语。国际语言学家中的大多数划归此类。对此我们无法苛求,只是希望他们能更理性地对待汉语:第一,在为新的语言学理论立论时,如果是把这个理论推向概括全人类的语言,那就千万不要忽视使用者占全球五分之一的汉语;第二,要能独立求证,既不要满足于教科书上的先入之见,也不要轻易以他人的结论为结论;第三,如果必须对汉语的规律有所表述时,应当谨慎,不要用自己研究西方语言得出的结论想当然地去进行推理。事实上,我们发现,保持头脑清醒的语言学家在西方是越来越多;

The first group does not know Chinese and most probably has been denied the chance to learn the language due to historical reasons or other realities. They acquire knowledge of the language from secondary sources such as typical descriptions from textbooks or other articles on the language. The majority of foreign linguists belong to this group. We could not ask for more than a rational approach to the Chinese language in considering the following issues: firstly, with users chalking up one fifth of the world population, Chinese language should be given due consideration in the formulation of linguistic theory that is universal in nature; secondly, to demonstrate independent thinking and not rely solely on the subjective descriptions in textbooks or simply buy in the conclusions of other research papers; and finally, to be meticulous in presenting the linguistic patterns of the language to avoid presumptuous deductions based on Western language patterns. It is fortunate that more and more linguists in this group have a clear and unbiased mindset.

第二类语言学家懂汉语甚至做过深入研究，也倾向于把汉语当作一种独特的样品来研究，对汉语的类型学定性最初其实就是他们作出的。这批学者为数不多，真知灼见却不少，如洪堡特、萨丕尔等人。他们的精辟见解还有待于后人去理解、发挥和补充；

The second group knows the language and may even have done some indepth research on it and tend to study it as a unique sample. In fact, they are the first to have determined the typology of the language. There aren't many members in this group but we find the most constructive ideas from them. They are people like Humboldt and Sapir. Worthy views from these sharp minds await further exploration and development.

第三类语言学家也懂汉语或学习过汉语，但西方语言学的背景使他们无法真正做到把汉语当作汉语来研究，而多多少少把它当作西方语言的一种特殊的样品，他们的"汉语研究"是在西方语言学的框架内进行的，至多只是对西方语言学无法解说的部分进行解说；

The third group of linguists also knows the language, or may have learnt it, but their Western linguistics training prevents them from studying the language as it is; that is to say, most of the time, Chinese language is treated as a special specimen of Western languages. Their research on the language is conducted within Western theoretical framework and their role is to supplement an explanation to what could not be handled by the framework.

第四类是西方汉学家，特别是其中对语言学有研究者。有的汉语造诣很深，例如高本汉（Bernhard Karlgren）、马伯乐（Henri Maspero）等，他们对汉语的钻研之深甚至超过了中国自己的很多学者。对这类学者我们要进行个案研究。以高本汉为例，他对汉语的理解相当深刻，出版于1923年的《中国语与中国文》和1949年的《汉语的性质及历史》二书上的许多见解，比许多现代的中国语言学家还要透彻；而他本人对汉语的研究，以其代表作《中国音韵学研究》为例，却又无可避免地受到了他所接受的西方语言研究理论和方法的影响（对高本汉音韵研究的评价参见潘文国1997b"后记"，此处不赘述）；

The fourth group comprises sinologists, including linguists. Some of them, such as Bernhard Karlgren and Henri Maspéro, developed such deep understanding of the language that they could put many Chinese linguists to shame. The high standard of research conducted by them cannot be easily surpassed. For this group, we have to study each of the members. Taking Karlgren for example, it is not an overstatement to say that he knows the language inside out, as demonstrated by the numerous insights he shared in his two publications, *Sound and Symbols in Chinese* (1923) and *The Chinese Language: An Essay on Its Nature and History* (1949) at a depth that few contemporary Chinese linguists could equal. However, his Western linguistic training was evident in his representative work, *Études sur la phonologie chinoise* (1915—1926). In fact, Karlgren was often introduced as the first to use European-style principles of historical linguistics to study the Chinese language. (For comments on *Études sur la Phonologie Chinoise,* please refer to Pan Wenguo, 1997b: Epilogue.)

第五类也是西方汉学家，他们不是语言学家，只是在研究、传播汉学的时候对汉语发生了兴趣，还有人甚至编写过汉语教科书，甚至汉语语法、汉语词典之类，例如西方早年到中国去的那些西洋传教士。不过他们对汉语的认识尽管得自第一手资料，但解释却未必可靠。一个典型的例子是"世界上第一部正式刊行的汉语语法"——瓦罗（Francisco Varo，1703）的《华语官话语法》（姚小平，2003：F3）。此书共分15章，包括"名词和代词的格变"、"形容词的比较级和最高级"、"抽象动名词"、"指小词"、"动词及其变位"等，法国当代汉语学家贝罗贝（Alain Peyraube）批评说，"可以肯定地说，作者希望将汉语纳入印欧语言而并没有考虑汉语的特征。例如他在书中讲到性、数、格的变化，而这一现象在汉语中并不存在"。（贝罗贝，2000：151）此话说得颇为严厉，但恐怕不够通达，因为这些人本来就不是语言学家；按瓦罗自己的想法，他没有想过要编写合乎汉语的语法专书，他想做的只是"把中国人的语法翻译成我们的语法"（中译本：3），以便于传教士学习汉语而已。还是这本书英译本的《导论》的作者白珊（Sandra Breitenbach）博士说得好：

The fifth group also concerns sinologists who are not linguists. Members include Western missionaries in China. They became interested in the Chinese language during the process of researching and spreading sinology. Some compiled dictionaries or textbooks for Chinese learners and even wrote on Chinese grammar.

Although they have had first-hand contact of the language, their explanations may not hold that well. To illustrate, known as "the first published grammar of the Chinese language in the world" (Yao Xiaoping, 2003: F3), Francisco Varo's *Grammar of the Mandarin Language* (1703) comprises 15 chapters including "Case Variations in Noun and Pronoun", "Comparative and Superlative Adjectival Construction", "Abstract Noun", "Diminutive" and "Verb and Its Conjugation". Alain Peyraube, contemporary French linguist of Chinese, commented: "…This certainly explains why the author wants to mold the Chinese language after Indo-European languages, without accounting for its special features. He explains, for example, gender, number, and case are; terms which do not really apply to the Chinese language" (Peyraube, 2000: 151). This criticism could have been more understanding as these people are no linguists. Varo did not plan to write a well constructed grammar for the language; all he wanted was to "translate the Chinese grammar into ours" (Yao Xiaoping, 2003: 3) to help missionaries master the language for their specific purposes. In the introduction of the English version, Sandra Breitenbach is fair to say that:

> 首先，有一点我们必须清楚，当人们借助某种模式来描绘一个错综复杂的对象时，如何选择和应用这种模式始终是任意的决定，即，只是代表了一种观察对象的特殊途径；这一途径并非为对象语言本身所固有，而只不过是一种试图更好地了解对象之本质的描述方式。自然，对语言教学来说，使用这种方式的主要目的在于更有效地学习或教授语言。（白珊，2000: F42）

> At the outset, we must keep in mind that, when trying to represent complex subject matter by means of a model, the choice and application is always an arbitrary decision representing only one particular way of viewing the subject material, which is not inherent in the language per se, but merely a way to represent the material in question in an attempt to better understand its nature. Naturally, for language instruction, this would mainly have the goal of learning or teaching the language more effectively by structuring and categorizing it in such a way that it is familiar to the community confronted with the topic. (Breitenbach, 2000: xxxviii)

但由于在相当长的一段时期内，中西方的交流主要是通过这些传教士，这批人的权宜处理对西方真正的学者的汉语观影响很大，对后来汉语语法的建立影响也不小；

We should not forget that for a long period of time, missionaries were the main vehicle for China's communication with the West. Their makeshift attempts unknowingly shaped the concepts of Western linguists of the Chinese language and even the impact on the construction of a Chinese grammar at a later time.

第六类是20世纪上半叶以来一批学兼中外，既有深厚的中文功底、又了解世界语言研究发展大势的学者，许多人后来成了中国有影响力的语言学大师，如赵元任、王力、吕叔湘等。他们在接受现代西方语言学理论洗礼的同时能保持清醒的头脑，积极探索西方理论与汉语事实之间的关系，努力做到两者的完美结合；并从汉语事实中抽绎出规律，以弥补、充实世界语言学理论。他们的精辟见解和治学思想至今仍被许多中外汉语学者视为楷模；

The sixth group includes scholars of the twentieth century who are well versed in both Chinese and Western knowledge. Grounded on a solid foundation in the language, scholars such as Chao Yuen-ren, Wang Li, Lü Shuxiang and others can identify with major trends in language research of the world and they need no introduction as some of the most influential linguists in China. Trained in Western linguistics, they are sharp enough to see the differences between Western theories and linguistic facts in Chinese and actively attempt to marry the two in the most harmonious way. Drawing Chinese language patterns from empirical studies, they have supplemented and enriched theoretical development in world linguistics. Today, the methods used by them may have been outmoded, but their insights and meticulous scholarship are still very well respected by linguists within and outside China.

20世纪中叶以后，中国大陆与西方世界几乎有30年时间不相往来，学术交流几乎完全中断；七十年代末中国实行改革开放政策，国门重新打开，一部分年轻人面对着光怪陆离的西方世界，面对着经济全球化的汹涌浪潮，心态严重失衡，在政治、经济、文化等各个方面出现了"一面倒"的情绪。这半个世纪的特殊国情，造就了吕叔湘深深为之忧虑的"两张皮"现象，[1]第七、第八两类人就代表了这"两张皮"的两极：

---

1 "两张皮"指近几十年来中国大陆语言学者中一种相当普遍的现象：学中文的不懂外语，学外语的只管引进介绍西方语言学观点而不管与汉语实际的结合。
The "two-skin phenomenon" refers to a common phenomenon among Chinese scholars over the last few decades: those who study Chinese do not speak a foreign language, whereas those who learn a foreign language are not mindful of the linguistic facts in the Chinese language as they introduce Western linguistic theory.

The second half of the twentieth century saw China being cut off from the world for almost 30 years. Academic ties were severed. Reformation in China at the end of the 1970s was advanced by implementation of open-door policy. As the door re-opens, the flux of events from the West as well as waves of economic globalization prove to be overwhelming for some of the younger generation. These people were completely swept off their feet and were stubbornly biased in all aspects as politics, economics, culture, etc. This special state of affairs continued for half a century, giving rise to what Lü Shuxiang worryingly described as a "two-skin phenomenon". The two extremes of this phenomenon constitute the next two groups.

第七类人是五十年代以后中国闭关锁国政策的产物,他们不懂外语,或者所学的一丁点儿外语根本不敷应用,因而不了解世界上语言研究发展的潮流和动向,更谈不上如何结合新的理论来思考汉语的问题。当中比较理性的也想关心国外的研究动态,但苦于外语能力,只能求助于二手资料,在苦苦的摸索中求其"结合"。这批人的精神非常可佩,可惜为数不多。为数更多的只知埋头就汉语而研究汉语。如果当中治古汉语者因其对象的特殊性还情有可原的话,那些治现代汉语甚至"普通语言学"的,对自己的不谙外语处之泰然甚至对别人的批评振振有词,那就不仅可怜而且可悲了。目前中国"全民学英语"、把英语成绩与毕业、就业、职称晋升等挂钩,有些地方设卡或者可以商榷,不过对汉语和语言学界倒是好事,一个研究现代汉语或现代语言学的人必须通过外语考试,这样其学术水平可能更高;

Group seven represents products of the closed-door policy first implemented in the 1950s. They either speak no foreign languages or could not do very much with the limited foreign language knowledge gained. As such, they are not following the trends and developments in linguistic research in the world, and of course are not in a position to consider issues in Chinese language from new theoretical viewpoint. The sober ones, though seeking to make an effort to follow up on happenings outside China, are constrained by the language barrier and only gather scattered pieces of information from secondary sources for their efforts in connecting the two worlds of research. This small number of scholars deserve our mention because they maintained a higher research vision than the majority who covered only the Chinese language in their research. We can understand it if it is traditional Chinese they are talking about, but not when they claim to be exploring modern Chinese and general linguistics. We have to drive home the message that sufficient command of the English language is crucial to keep abreast with linguistic development elsewhere and only then do we expect to produce analyses of a higher standard on the Chinese language. Again, the emphasis on English is not targeted with a mechanical fitting of theories with data, but a widening of horizons in approaches as well as taking a part in real linguistic universality.

与第七类人相反的是第八类人,这包括一直在国外从事汉语研究的华裔学者,也有不少是大陆改革开放的受益者,他们在大学读的是热门专业——外语,许多人因之获得了出国留学的机会,甚至因种种机遇在国外找到了工作;回到国内的也往往成为"中外交流的使者",在中西学术交流中起着桥梁作用。这是一批中国非常需要的人才,但是也由于种种原因,其中不少人的中文功底不够,先天不足,过早地甚至全身心地浸润在外语之中使他们对自己的母语缺少感受,因而他们对母语的了解(特别是高本汉说的对古代汉语和汉语史的了解)远远不如他们对外语的知识。如果说第七类学者多半是"不知有汉,无论魏晋"的闭关自守者,则第八类学者中相当一部分便是"只知希腊,不知中国"的西化论者,他们提到"西方现代语言学"有着抑止不住的崇敬,但真正比较熟悉的也就是他所受到教育的某一家某一派,谈理论、引汉语例子,离开这一家一派就无法进行。300年前的西班牙传教士瓦罗还肯承认他的书只是努力把汉语语法"翻译"成西方人熟悉的语法,而现在有些"挟洋以自重"的学者却要人们相信他在某种西方理论框架下提供的汉语例证就是汉语自身的规律!

In direct contrast to group seven, group eight includes either ethnic Chinese who have all this time been working on Chinese language overseas or beneficiaries of the reformation and open-door policy who picked up a foreign language and get to study abroad, where they may either stay on or return to act as "ambassadors" for foreign exchanges. These are much needed talents. However, many of them may have become alienated from their native Chinese tongue after years of concentration in learning foreign languages. As such, their judgement in the Chinese language, particularly traditional Chinese and history of Chinese language that Karlgren has stressed, cannot hold up to their awareness of the foreign language. Fond of modern linguistic theories of the West, this group of scholars is in effect so attached to that specific school of thought they received education in while outside China, that theorizing with examples from the Chinese language would be tough. While Varo admits that he is only "translating" Chinese grammar according to the schema of Western grammar, some scholars in this group are presumptuous enough to think that what they have proven with Western theoretical frameworks described the natural language pattern of the Chinese language.

最后，第九类人，是近十多年来中国正在形成的一批新的学者群，其中相当一部分是新兴的汉外对比语言学的研究者。他们从总结汉语研究史上正反两个方面的经验出发，努力克服第七、第八两类学者的弊病，积极以第六类学者为榜样，一方面不断吸收国外的新知，另一方面刻苦加强汉语自身的修养，厚此而不薄彼，通过汉语与西方语言特别是英语的对比，[1]认真总结汉语自身的规律，并力求发展、丰富普通语言学的内容，使之真正成为全人类的财富。

Last but not least, a new group of scholars has gradually come together over the last decade, among them emerging contrastivists specializing in contrasting against the Chinese language. Drawing from both positive and negative lessons in the research history of the Chinese language, they strive to overcome the deficiencies and weaknesses of scholars in groups seven and eight and make scholars in group six their example. On the one hand, they continue to absorb new insights from abroad; on the other hand, they make every effort to strengthen their appreciation of the Chinese language. By contrasting Chinese language with Indo-European languages, particularly the English language, much is learnt about the linguistic rudiments in Chinese. It is on this ground that general linguistics could be further developed to live up to its aim to be universal.

对于国际上真正关心汉语的语言学家来说，在上述的九类语言学者中，第一类就是他们自己；第三类和第八类本质上没有什么大区别，这些人的意见对

1　当然也不缺乏汉俄、汉德、汉法、汉日等的比较。上述比较研究的综述文章包括许高渝《中国汉俄语言对比研究综述》、陈坤泉《中国汉德语言对比研究综述》、王宝平《中国汉日语言对比研究综述》、唐珍《中国汉法和英法语言对比综述》。（见俞约法，1992：1）

There are certainly researches of contrastive study between Chinese and other languages such as Russian, German, French or Janpanese. Papers can be found in Xu Gaoyu's *A Review of Contrastive Study between Chinese and Russian in China*, Chen Kunquan's *A Review of Contrastive Study between Chinese and German in China*, Wang Baoping's *A Review of Contrastive Study between Chinese and Japanese in China*, and Tang Zhen's *A Review of Contrastive Study between Chinese and French, and Chinese and English in China*. (See Yu Yuefa, 1992: 1)

于普通语言学没有什么价值，大可不听；第五类可以姑妄听之，作为参考和谈助，但不必太当真；第七类人提供的语料也许有点用，但对于主要关心理论的人来说，意义也未必大；真正要听的是第二、第四、第六和第九类人的意见，由于二、四、六三类人们已熟知，而第九类是正在形成的新兴力量，他们的声音尤其值得听取，这是当代中外语言学家对话的一个最合适的窗口。而这股力量的形成正与中国对比语言学的发展息息相关。因而我们有必要研究中国的汉外对比发展史，从中来观察汉语研究和中国普通语言学研究的真正进展。

Of the nine groups, group one being linguists sharing a genuine concern in the Chinese language have exemption rights to this discussion. Groups three and eight offer no help to general linguistics; opinions of group five may have some worth as a reference while the examples of group seven may have some use but no significance for theory formulation. The opinions of groups two, four and six are worthy of consideration and they are all well known. As the emerging forces, voices of group nine deserve the most attention and these scholars merit as the most appropriate window for dialogue between linguists in the two worlds of research tradition. This is also the power that development in contrastive linguistics in China has gathered for itself. Looking into the research history of contrasting Chinese with a foreign language, we get to realize the true development in Chinese language research as well as general linguistics research in China.

2.2 汉外对比研究发展史再探

2.2 Further exploration into Chinese-foreign language contrastive analysis

几年前，我们（潘文国，2002a）曾对中国的对比研究史作过一番粗线条的梳理，分析了其现状并预测了其发展趋势。那篇文章主要是从"内"，或者说，是从中国内地对比研究本身的发展情况立论的。这里我们想换一个角度，从"外"，也就是以国际的眼光，从普通语言学的角度来重新作一番观察，看看哪些现象和变化是值得国际语言学界了解和借鉴的。因此我们的叙述不仅同上次的文章不一样，同一般的"汉语语法学史"的叙述也不一样。我们想把重点放在这一过程中具有普通语言学意义的部分，对一些国内似有"定评"的东西也会从普通语言学的角度重新审视。希望这样的研究不仅对中国的读者有意义，也能引起国外普通语言学和理论语言学家的兴趣。

Pan Wenguo (2003b) surveyed the history of contrastive linguistics and predicted its trend from an inward-looking point of view, i.e. limited to situations internal to China. Here, we would like to adopt an outward-looking approach, i.e. to survey the history of contrastive linguistics in China from international standards as well as from general linguistics standpoints. This approach is also different from the normal practice in historical survey of Chinese grammar studies. We like to place emphasis on processes which are meaningful to general linguistics and like to review, from the general linguistic perspective, some of the judgement passed in China. It is hoped that in this way, the book will be of interest to Chinese readers as well as international colleagues in general linguistics or theoretical linguistics.

在这样的宏观背景之下，我们发现，中国的对比研究史可以分为五个时期，其中第一、第三期分别是第二、第四期的准备和铺垫；第二、四、五这三个时期则与西方对比研究的三个时期颇有相似之处，对照起来看是饶有兴味的。

Against the macro background, we propose to divide the research history in contrastive linguistics in China into five phases. It is interesting to highlight that phases one and three were preparatory periods for phases two and four respectively and phases two, four and five correspond to the three phases of the West.

2.3 第一期（1898—1921）：比较与对比之间：《马氏文通》及其意义

2.3 Phase 1 (1898—1921): Compare or contrast: the significance of *Mashi Wentong (Ma's Grammar)*

2.3.1 对比研究的前奏：马建忠的创始之功

2.3.1 Prelude to contrastive studies: Ma Jianzhong, the ice-breaker

我们以1898年《马氏文通》的出版作为对比研究第一期，也就是整个中国现代对比语言学的开端。这有什么理由呢？

The year 1898, when *Mashi Wentong* got published, also marked the beginning of contrastive studies in China, as well as the beginning of modern contrastive analysis in China. What grounds do we have for this?

对比研究以什么时候作为开端，这不是一个随随便便的问题。西方许多学者如詹姆斯（James，1980）把拉多的《跨文化的语言学》（1957）作为对比研究的开端，那是纯粹把对比研究看作应用语言学的一个分支、从语言教学的立场上去看问题的结果；菲齐亚克（1980：2）不但提到了对比语言学名称的倡始人沃尔夫（1941），更将对比语言学的开端时间上推到1892年，举到了格朗根特（1892）、维托尔（Wilhelm Viëtor，1894）、帕西（1912）、库尔德内（Baudouin de Courdenay，1912）、博戈尔迪奇（Vladimir Bogordickij，1915）等的著作，那是从对比实践的立场上去看的。我们对两家的做法都不赞成。詹姆斯的不妥不用说，菲齐亚克从实践出发也同样不妥，从他所举的例子来看，那些著作大部分围绕语音对比的例子，仿此，中国近代的第一篇论文似乎应是赵元任的《英汉语调浅探》（1933）。但其实还可上溯得更早，比方在瓦罗的书（1703）的"前言"里他就对汉语的发音进行了描述，并且将之与他家乡西班牙的卡斯蒂利亚语（Castilian）以及法语进行了对比，我们是否也要上溯到那个时候呢？如果这可以成立，我们还可进一步上溯，比瓦罗更早，还有西方"汉学之父"利玛窦（Matteo Ricci）的《西字奇迹》（1605）和金尼阁（Nicolas Trigault）的《西儒耳目资》（1626），这两部书也都是为帮助传教士学习汉语发音的，也就必然要对汉语的语音与西方的语音做一番比较。这是不是中国对比语言学的开端呢？这是讲语音，如果考虑到语言的另两个要素词汇和语法，我们还会有别的上溯的办法。因为双语词典的编纂就是两种语言词汇比较的结果，而翻译必然涉及到两种语言的句法比较问题。那么我们就可推理，什么时候有了翻译和双语词典编纂的实践，特别是有了相关的言论，对比研究就可上溯到什么时候。依此，早在魏晋以前，佛经翻译家就从翻译实践中感到了"胡语"与"中土文字"的不同，东晋道安（约314—385）更总结为"五失本"，论及译文语序问题及其处理（曹明伦，2006：52）。但没有人会同意中国的对比研究应该从道安讲起，那我们就必须确定一个标准，说明不能这样做的理由。我们的标准就是，对比研究的溯源不能仅仅从对比实践出发，而要从有没有对比的理论和观念出发。正是根据这一标准，我们把西方对比研究的"源"溯到了洪堡特，也同样把中国的"源"溯到了马建忠。

Determining the starting point is by no means a lighthearted issue. In the West, when Carl James (1980) chose to see it as initiated from Robert Lado's *Linguistics across Culture* (1957), it was a conclusion from the pedagogical viewpoint that saw contrastive analysis as a branch of applied linguistics. Fisiak (1980: 2) mentioned Whorf, founder of "contrastive linguistics", and dated the commencement to the year

1892, listing the works of Grandgent (1892), Viëtor (1894), Passy (1912), Baudouin de Courdenay (1912), and Bogordickij (1915) as support. This was a conclusion from the practicality. We agree with neither. We have in the previous chapter explained why James is at fault; we have to say Fisiak is not wiser in this respect. The works listed were all on contrastive phonology. If this is acceptable, it follows that the first article on the subject in modern China seems to be Chao Yuen-ren's "A Preliminary Study of English Intonation and Its Chinese Equivalents" (1933). But if we trace back further, there is the foreword in Francisco Varo (1703) which contained an earlier description of Chinese sound production and how it compared with his native Spanish tongue Castilian as well as French. And if this stands, we could go even further back in time to the father of sinology, Matteo ricci's *Miracle of Western Writing* (1605) and Nicolas Trigault's 1626 book *Le Chinois Romanisé*. Both works were written in aid of missionaries speaking Mandarin and therefore comparison with Western pronunciations was necessary. Could this be the beginning of contrastive linguistics in China? Considering that the above were merely works on phonology, it is quite certain that there were other works on lexis and grammar written at even earlier date. For example, bilingual dictionaries would involve comparing lexis in two languages, and where translation activities became active, there are bound to be comparisons of syntax. It would then be logical to deduce that we could trace back to those times where concrete activities of bilingual dictionary compilation and translation took place for relevant analysis in contrastive linguistics. We would then in this light pin down the period of time in the Northern and Southern dynasties where translators for Buddhist sutras experienced the differences between "languages of foreign tribes" and "the Chinese language in the mainland". For instance, Dao An talked about word order (Dao An, 1984). Nevertheless, no one would agree that contrastive linguistics in China originated from Dao An. For this matter, there must be a criterion to help determining the commencement as well as explaining how it is that tracing back to Dao An is not acceptable. We suggest that in tracking the source, specific activities are secondary to relevant theory and ideas. Accordingly, the history of contrastive linguistics in the West would have its source in Humboldt while in China, Ma Jianzhong (1845—1900).

马建忠的《马氏文通》只是中国学者写的第一部汉语语法书，并不是世界上的第一部汉语语法书。比他早的,瓦罗之外,仅姚小平(2003:F3)提到的传教士语法就还有:马若瑟(Joseph Henri de Prémare)的《汉语札记》(*Notitia Linguae Sinicae*,1728(1831))、马士曼(Joshua Marshman)的《中国言法》(1814)、马礼逊(Robert Morrison)的《汉语语法》(*Grammar of the Chinese Language*,1815)、艾约瑟(Joseph Edkins)的《官话口语语法》(1864)和《上海方言语法》(*A Grammar of Colloquial Chinese as Exhibited in the Shanghai* Dialect,1868)、高第丕(Tarlton Perry Crawford)与张儒珍合著《文学书官话》(*Mandarin Grammar*,1869)等。其中当然都含有对比的成分,但我们却不把它们算作对比语法学的著作,其原因就是上面提到的,这些都是为了帮助传教士学习汉语用的,白珊说:"我们应当记住,传教士们热衷于编写外语语法,主要不是出于科学兴趣,而是为了尽快学会外语,以便更有效地宣讲福音。"(2000:F22)"为此就要梳理语言结构,以一种为学习者所熟知的方法来分析其类别,归纳其范畴。"(F42)说得白一点,这是一种刻意地将汉语向西方语法拉拢甚至尽可能纳入西方语法框架的做法。在这情况下,如果把它们看作认真的汉语语法著作或严肃的对比语法著作,就可能会产生误导作用。因此我们的对比史不能从这些书讲起,尽管它们本身的存在有着巨大的历史作用和历史价值,对后来汉语语法的形成也有着巨大的影响。比较有特色的有19世纪名震一时的法国汉学家雷慕萨(Abel-Rémusat)的《汉文启蒙》(*Elements de La Grammaire Chinoise*,1822;1857)及其高足法国籍犹太汉学家儒莲(Stanislas Julien)所著的《汉文指南》(*Syntaxe Nouvelle de La Langue Chinoise*,1866),据了解,这两部著作比较尊重汉语本身的特色,有意识地避免以印欧语法来解释汉语。(Peyraube,2001:346)而被誉为19世纪写得最好的汉语文法书则是德国语言学家甲柏连孜(Georg van der Gabelentz,又译为加贝伦兹)运用19世纪普通语言学理论以德文完成的《汉文经纬》(*Chinesische Grammatik*,1881)。甲柏连孜的书至今深获(德国)学术界的好评,影响颇大,不过由于以德文写作,汉语界对它认识不多,研究论文也少,且不评论。

Mashi Wentong (1898) by Ma Jianzhong, is the first Chinese grammar written by a Chinese scholar but not the first ever on Chinese grammar. Prior to him and besides Varo, there are other early grammars of Chinese by missionaries. Here are some of the most notable ones: *Notitia Linguae Sinicae* (1728, 1831) by Joseph Henri de Prémare, *Clavis Sinica* (1814) by Joshua Marshman, *Grammar of the*

Chinese Language (1815) by Robert Morrison, *Elements de la Grammaire Chinoise* (1822) by Jean-Pierre Abel-rémusat, A *Grammar of the Chinese Colloquial Language, Commonly Called the Mandarin Dialect* (1864) and *A Grammar of Colloquial Chinese as Exhibited in the Shanghai Dialect* (1868) by Joseph Edkins and *Syntax Nouvelle de La Langue Chinoise* (1866) by Stanislas Julien, just to name a few (Yao Xiaoping, 2003: F3). All these works contained some extent of contrastive analysis, but could not be taken as real works on contrastive linguistics, just as Dr. Breitenbach has pointed out: "When examining the first Chinese grammars, we must bear in mind that it was not primarily scientific interest that prompted the missionaries to write grammars of foreign languages, but rather the goal of learning the respective languages as quickly as possible in order to preach the gospel more effectively" (Breitenbach, 2000: xxi—xxii). For this purpose, they would structure and categorize the language "in such a way that it is familiar to the community confronted with the topic" (*ibid.*: xxxviii). Put more plainly, the Chinese language was intentionally pushed into the Western syntactic framework. It would be misleading to take them as serious descriptions of the Chinese language, and worse still as momentous volumes on contrastive linguistics. For this reason, in no way should the history of contrastive linguistics begin with these publications, although one shall find in them considerable historical effects and values, including influencing the formulation of syntactic rules in the Chinese language.

《马氏文通》也一直被许多人指责为"模仿语法",但实际上,这本书的情况与上述传教士的书有很大的不同,表现在:

All along, *Mashi Wentong* was attacked for "aping Latin grammar". In reality, the book differs from those written by missionaries in many ways, as illustrated below.

第一,它是认真的汉语语法之作,而不只是帮助外国人学汉语的权宜之作。马建忠说,他"爰积十余年之勤求探讨以成此编,盖将探夫自有文字以来至今未宣之秘奥,启其缄縢,导后人以先路",(马建忠,1898:11,序)这个口气只有1500多年前沈约发现汉语的四声时可与之相比:"以为在昔词人,累千载而不悟;而独得胸衿,穷其妙旨,自谓入神之作"。(《南史》卷五十七《沈约传》)

1. It is a substantial piece on Chinese grammar, not a learner's guide for foreigners. Ma Jianzhong proudly declared in his preface that the treatise, a

consolidation of ten years of industrious explorations, serves to pioneer the way to unearth the mysteries and covert facts under wraps since people began writing (Ma Jianzhong, 1898: 11, Preface), in a tone only comparable to Shen Yue of some 1,500 years ago, who felt so dignified by his depiction of the four tones in the Chinese language unenlightened throughout thousands of years of poetry compositions (History of Southern Dynasties Vol. 57 on Bibliography of Shen Yue). Indeed it is with Mashi Wentong that the Chinese started conceptualizing a theory of grammar for the Chinese language and, more importantly, it is made known that a modern concept such as grammar could well be applied to traditional Chinese texts.

第二，它不是简单地将汉语语法"翻译"成西方语言的语法，而是认真地主张通过用比较或对比的方法来建立汉语的语法。"斯书也，因西文已有之规矩，于经籍中求其所同所不同者，曲证繁引，以确知华文义理之所在。"（1898：13，后序）这句话包含了三层意思：第一，借鉴西方（"因西文已有之规矩"）；第二，通过比较和对比（"于经籍中求其所同所不同者"）；第三，得出汉语规律（"以确知华文义理之所在"）。

2. Instead of "translating" Chinese grammar to suit the jacket of Western grammar, Ma took it to heart in adopting comparative or contrastive methodology to establish a system for Chinese grammar, stating explicitly in his "Introduction" that "This book seeks to find in our traditional texts those points which are similar or dissimilar to the preexistent rules of Western writing so as to elucidate and assert the principles governing the Chinese language" (Ma, 1898: 13, Introduction). Between the lines, the emphasis is on: (1) Drawing on the Western model; (2) Means of comparing and contrasting; (3) Asserting the rudiments in Chinese language.

第三，即使就其教学目标来说，它考虑的不是外国人学习汉语的便利，而是中国儿童学习本国语的效率："童蒙入塾能循是而学文焉，其成就之速必无逊于西人"。（同上：13，后序）它甚至要进一步达到中西文互通的目标：

3. Regarding pedagogical aims, Ma has in mind the learning efficacy of young native speakers, not the convenience of foreign learners. (ibid.: 13, Introduction) Furthermore, he wanted to achieve bilingual literacy at one easy go:

此书能抉前人作文之奥，开后人琢句之门，非洞悉中西文辞者不办。人苟能玩索而有得焉，不独读中书者可以引通西文，即读西书者

亦易于引通中文，而中西行文之道，不难豁然贯通矣。（马建忠，1898：245，自记）

This book illuminates the writing secrets of our elders and provides for later generations, ways to perfect their writings. This task could not be accomplished without good command of both the Chinese and Western languages. Chinese readers careing to explore would attain mastery of the Western language and vice versa. You would then see in clear lights the ways to good writings in both languages and be able to draw on them with ease. (Ma Jianzhong, 1898: 245, autobiographical note)

乃至世界大同的理想：
As well as world unity:

则是书也，不特可群吾古今同文之心思，将举夫宇下之凡以口舌点画以达其心中之意者，将大群焉。（马建忠，1898：13，后序）

And with books as such, not only unity among speakers, past and present, of the same language could be attained, all who communicate in speech and writing in this universe shall be united as one big family. (ibid. 1898: 13, Introduction)

第四，就其影响说，《马氏文通》建立了汉语研究史上第一个汉语语法体系，"在中国历史上，马建忠第一个把汉语研究纳入了世界语言研究的共同轨道，使汉语研究成了世界语言研究的一部分、全人类语言研究的一部分。"（潘文国，2002b：4）

4. In terms of influence, *Mashi Wentong* sets up the first ever grammatical system of the Chinese language. Pan Wenguo (2002b: 4) remarked: "Ma Jianzhong scored a first in the Chinese history to put Chinese scholarship in language research on the same track as other languages of the world. In so doing, researching in Chinese language becomes part of researching in languages in the world or even of the human race."

一部中国语法学史也就是一部中国对比语言学史，这在世界语言研究史上是罕见的。因此，将《马氏文通》作为中国对比语言学的开端，是有深刻的历史含义的。

As the history of Chinese grammar doubles up the history of contrastive linguistics, something rarely seen in the history of linguistic research in the world, we accord deep historical significance to mark the beginning of contrastive linguistics in China with *Mashi Wentong*.

2.3.2 中国对比语言学的特色
2.3.2 Characteristics of contrastive linguistics in China

"中国特色"本是政治领域中使用的一个术语,但许多人却将它移之于各个领域,以突显与世界各国之不同之处,为其各种"与众不同"的做法及理论观点辩护。因其运用过多过滥,有时更被人刻意庸俗化,引起反感,结果又走到了另一端,"中国特色"有时竟变成了一个调侃之词,弄得人们在该用时也觉得理不直气不壮了。我们觉得庸俗化和刻意回避两种态度都是不可取的。在全球化的背景下,有时诚然不能过于强调某种特殊性;而有时却不得不承认某种特殊性。而且往往只有从其特殊性入手,观察其与世上类似事物间的异同,才能对事物的根本性质有深刻的了解。对比语言学本来就是以讨论异同问题为其宗旨的,在这方面尤该通达。从理论上说,对比语言学作为普通语言学的一支,当然不容许有国别或语别的不同,遑论什么"中国特色"!但由于不同的历史、文化和语言背景,近百年来的中国对比语言学研究确实在与世界上其他地方的对比语言学有着共性的同时,也有着一些明显的不同之处,如能从其相异处入手,也许更便于寻找其相同处,发现其共同的规律。而这一相异,正是从《马氏文通》肇其端的。

"Chinese characteristics" was a phrase first used by Chinese politicians to describe the socialism in China to highlight the peculiarities of the system as implemented locally. Since then, it has been widely borrowed, infiltrating into many areas, covering the many practices and theoretical ideas that send China into the limelight as being against the world. The term is somewhat overused and gets even trickier when it was deliberately debased to the other extreme to mean sarcasm. Notwithstanding, it is clear that with globalization, while certain peculiarities must not be overly stressed, there are attributes we have to recognize and acknowledge. More often than not, it is from disparities that we realize the divergence and develop a better understanding of the essential nature of the subject matter. Contrastive linguistics concerns itself with discourse in similarities and differences and appreciates the need to emphasize differences. With backgrounds in history, culture and language that are one of a kind, contrastive linguistics in China does depart in some ways from the common practices in the discipline. *Mashi Wentong* is exactly where we begin to look for differences.

中国对比语言学的特色表现在三个方面。

The characteristics of contrastive linguistics in China are to be seen in the following three aspects.

2.3.2.1 "从比较走向对比"还是"从对比走向比较"
2.3.2.1 "From compare to contrast" vs. "from contrast to compare"

回顾世界上对比语言学发生的历史，我们发现，"对比语言学"是从"比较语言学"生发出来的，是对"比较语言学"局限于亲属语言研究的不满足，而希望拓展"比较"的范围，从亲属语言扩大到非亲属语言乃至世界上所有语言之间。叶斯柏森、沃尔夫乃至洪堡特都是在提到并强调"比较语言学"的重大贡献和成就之后，才谨慎地提出或建议他们的"另一种"比较语言学或"对比语言学"的。而正因为"比较语言学"是在"求同"的基础上建立起来的，"新的"比较语言学亦即对比语言学就往往以强调"求异"为特色，以突显其与旧的做法的不同。

Looking back, contrastive linguistics evolved out of comparative linguistics and expanded the scope of "comparison" to go beyond related languages. Humboldt, Jespersen and Whorf all acknowledged the brilliant contributions and achievements of comparative linguistics before their proposal on contrastive linguistics was carefully tabled as an "alternate" comparative linguistics or contrastive linguistics. For it is on similarities that comparative linguistics focuses; the "new" comparative linguistics or contrastive linguistics naturally focuses on differences instead.

中国的情况正好相反。汉语在历史上与西方文明长期隔绝，与西方任何语言之间都不存在发生学上的关系（与藏语的"亲属关系"在马建忠之时还没有人提出，而且至今也还只是个"假设"，只是相信的人较多而已），因而汉语研究历史上从来不存在"比较语言学"时期，也就不存在"对比语言学"从中生发的土壤。中西语言之交，一开始就发生在"相隔遥远"的语言之间，如果要研究其间的关系，那一开始就得走"对比语言学"的路，即强调两者之"异"。这显然不合马建忠当时竭力引进西方语言学的宗旨和本意。我们曾经分析过马建忠的心态。

The development in China is altogether different. Historically, the Chinese language was not in contact with Western civilization for ages. It has no ties whatsoever with any of the languages of the West. In fact, the assumption that Chinese language and Tibetan language form a family was not raised during Ma Jianzhong's time. To date, it remains an assumption to be attested though most people still choose to believe in it. Therefore, in the scholastic history of the Chinese language, there never existed a period ruled by comparative linguistics where contrastive linguistics had yet to evolve. At the outset, Chinese language and languages of the West made contact as distant languages. To see the two language families at work, contrastive linguistics has to be adopted from the very beginning and big differences to be sought. This apparently does not fit the object and intention of Ma Jianzhong in his effort to introduce Western linguistics.

> 马建忠生当清末，面对国势积弱、列强欺凌的现实，是一个有志于学习西方、振兴中华的维新自强之士。……他以拉丁语法为范本，写出了一本汉语语法，"证明"了汉语并不劣于欧洲诸语言，中华民族并不劣于西洋诸民族。这在当时，对于提高民族自信心、提高汉语乃至中华民族的国际地位，是有重要意义的。汉语既然可以与西方诸语言平起平坐，中国人也可以跟西方诸强平起平坐。这是马建忠当时的心态，是一种积极的、爱国主义的心态。（潘文国，2002b：14）

Born before the fall of the ailing Qing Dynasty, Ma, positive and patriotic, was determined to learn from the West with the aim to help the rise of China when the time was ripe. Modelled after Latin grammar, Ma's Chinese grammar serves to demonstrate the strength of the language as well as the character of the nation behind the language. This was meant to be very encouraging in boosting ethnic pride and raising the international status of the language and the nation at his time. If by contrasting with Western languages, Chinese language is put on level ground, the Chinese, as a nation, may play the powers of the West on level ground too. (Pan Wenguo, 2002b: 14)

在这样的背景下，马建忠便不能强调中西之异，而只能刻意强调两者之"同"，只在不得已时，才提出"华文之独"，就是可以理解的了。他的"同"是建立在全人类只有一个语言的基础上的：亘古今，塞宇宙，其种之或黄、或白、或紫、或黑之钧是人也，天皆赋之以此心之所以能意，此意之所以能达之理。（马建忠，1898：12，后序）

Given this mindset, it is not the differences Ma Jianzhong would like to stress, but rather, it is similarity that is the gem. Highlighting the uniqueness of the Chinese language is only a by-product in the higher quest for universal language. Ma has his ideas rooted in language universalism, as he explained that dissemblances are "man-made, artificial and in the known dimensions of space and time, innate to all human beings, regardless of the skin colors, is the truth where minds can connect and meanings get across." (Ma Jianzhong, 1898: 12, Introduction)

由于以"求同"为目标，"求异"就成了对事实不得已的承认，结果就使《马氏文通》走上了一条独特的对比语言学道路，就是前面所引的"斯书也，因西文已有之规矩，于经籍中求其所同所不同者，曲证繁引，以确知华文义理之所在"这句话。实行这句话的结果，一方面使中国的对比研究在开始时就既不同于西方的对比语言学又不同于西方的比较语言学，而是奇奇怪怪地介于两者之间；另一方面，使200年来西方传教士如瓦罗等人为解决西方人学习汉语而在拉丁语或其他西方语言语法基础上编写汉语语法的权宜之计，变成了汉语语法的正宗。白珊博士在研究了瓦罗的《华语官话语法》后评论说：

With seeking "similarity" as the object and "differences" becoming facts for admission where required, *Mashi Wentong* trod an extraordinary path in contrastive linguistics. Ma Jianzhong probably did not realize that his mission statement of "seeks to find in our traditional texts those points which are similar or dissimilar to the preexistent rules of Western writing" carried more weight than he could have imagined. Emphasizing similar points and discernible dissemblance at the same time, contrastive linguistics in China follows neither the comparative nor the contrastive linguistics traditions of the West, right from the start, taking an exclusive position in between the two disciplines. On the other hand, Ma's words kind of legitimized the stopgap Chinese grammar guidebooks based on Latin or other Western grammatical systems written by missionaries such as Varo and others over the previous 200 years. After her research in Varo's *Arte de Lengua Mandarina*, Breitenback pointed out that:

> 就当时占据主导地位的科学环境而言，采纳拉丁语结构是可以理解的，但这种做法并未因此就能逃脱批评，因为选择拉丁语的结果必然会影响到汉语语法概念以后的发展。也许，早期的传教士之所以这样做，只不过是想减轻学习汉语的困难，使新来的教士易于把握这种语言。这样形成了一种对后世的语言研究思路影响极大的态度，因为这种拉丁语模式一旦被接受，便无异于锲入某种思维定式（mind-set），以致在两个多世纪里妨碍了人们深入窥测汉语的真实结构。其结果是，拉丁语像是一道不幸的箍，限制了它的发展。
>
> （Breitenbach，2000：F36）

This adoption of a Latin structure, even though understandable within the prevailing scientific environment, cannot escape criticism in light of the effects of their choice on the further advancement of Chinese grammatical concepts. Presumably, the early missionaries only attempted to lighten the difficult task of learning the language in order to make it easier for the new friars entering the mission. By viewing Chinese through a "Latin lens", an attitude was created that was to have a most influential effect on the course of later language studies, as this Latin approach, once adopted, ingrained a certain approach and mind-set which detracted from a deeper understanding of the true structure of the Chinese for more than two centuries. As a consequence, Latin exerted an unfortunate constriction on the development of Chinese grammatical studies. (Breitenbach, 2000: xxxiii)

其实，真正使拉丁语起到了限制汉语的"箍"的作用的，不是瓦罗等人，而是马建忠。一种外来文化要在中国扎根不是那么容易的，外因只有通过内因才能起作用。我们只要看瓦罗的书出版近200年，除了在西方传教士中广为传播，并引发了前面提到过的一系列传教士汉语语法著作之外，对中国士林及汉语自身语言研究传统几乎没有发生什么影响。而马建忠出于不同的心态，却不期而然地运用了同样的方法，结果却造成了整整一个汉语研究新时代，即所谓"汉语研究的现代期"。这个时期到今天还没有结束。这就不仅是瓦罗等人，甚至连马建忠自己也始料不及的。马建忠之后，汉语研究的格局为之一变，一切传统的研究，文字、声韵、训诂，都退居次要地位；语法一跃成为语言研究之绝对中心。对此变化的得失，笔者曾有专文讨论（潘文国，2000），此处不赘述。这里希望强调的是，对比研究在现代汉语语言学形成和发展过程中所起到的巨大乃至决定性的作用，这是西方对比学者所难以想象、更难以奢望的。这一现象背后有很多值得思考的东西。

While Breitenbach sees the constraints Greco-Latin grammatical tradition effected on the Chinese language, she may not have been so precise as to blame this on Varo and others. If anyone has to shoulder this responsibility, it has to be Ma Jianzhong. Planting foreign culture in China is no small matter and unless internal factors act up, external factors could not hope to produce any effect. For instance, Varo's *Arte* may have influenced the series of early grammars of Chinese after him, but only within the missionary circle. Factual inaccuracies appear in Varo's grammar, forcing Chinese syntax into the straitjacket of Latin-based grammatical categories; in the absence of indigenous models, Varo had risen above the daunting task with his work in handling an "alien" tongue and we would not deny its place in the history of linguistic thought, especially from a cross-cultural perspective (Matthew Chen, 2003: 4—7). Nevertheless, for 200 years since, not a ripple has been cast in the Chinese scholarship. When it comes to Ma, things evolved differently. As explained earlier, Ma had a reason in adopting the Latin model and his application created an entirely new era of modern linguistic research in Chinese that lasts to this day. The strong influence of Western traditions penetrating as a result of this opening in grammar must be something outside of Varo or Ma's imaginations, particularly as Ma was shaped by traditional Chinese scholarship. Ever since Ma's grammar, traditional scholarship in Chinese graphics, phonology and exegesis has gradually given way to grammar studies that claim almost absolute dominance. (For comments, please refer to Pan Wenguo, 2000.) Modern Chinese linguistics, with its formation and the process heavily influenced by Western theories and methodology, has everything to do with the underlying idea of contrast and we cannot overemphasize its role—a role not often explicit in the description of the formation of modern Chinese linguistics. At a time when the idea of contrast is only budding and taking a long time to mature in the West, it has done far more in a shorter period in China. It leaves us many worthy questions to ponder over.

2.3.2.2 一部"对比"史伴随着"模仿"与反"模仿"之争
2.3.2.2 The debate on "imitation" and "anti-imitation"

《马氏文通》之后，语法研究登上了汉语研究的中心舞台。一批批有影响力的语法著作相继出版。有意思的是，在将近半个世纪里，几乎所有的语法书都是以这样那样地批判马建忠作为自己著作的开头、立论的起点。这究竟是怎么回事？这里我们想从对比语言学的角度对这一现象进行分析。

Research in Chinese after *Mashi Wentong* is essentially grammar centric. Influential grammars of Chinese were published one after another. Interestingly, for close to half a century since, almost all publications on grammar begin with criticizing Ma Jianzhong. We would like to offer an explanation from the contrastive linguistics point of view.

从前面的叙述可知，在西方，对比语言学与比较语言学的界线是清楚的，甚至可说井水不犯河水。对比语言学源自比较语言学，但两者的不同是显而易见的，在沃尔夫等人看来，比较语言学比较的是亲属语言，目标是建立语言谱系，而对比语言学比较的是距离遥远的语言，目标是探索语言与思维的关系；在第二期以后的对比语言学者看来，比较语言学比的是亲属语言，从事的是历时的研究，求的是同；而对比语言学不限亲属语言，从事的是共时的研究，更关注的是异。对比语言学不会致力去从事比较语言学的工作，相当多的人甚至对语言理论也不感兴趣，越来越把关心的焦点放在语言教学上。

Comparative and contrastive linguistics form two distinct disciplines in the West as we have seen. Branching out from comparative linguistics, contrastive linguistics works on a defined scope of a different object. Comparative linguistics analyses languages with relations in order to construct a tree diagram tracing to a common historical source. Contrastive linguistics analyses languages that are typologically different with an aim to establish the relations between thought and language. After the second phase, scholars in the West tend to think that comparative linguistics compares related languages diachronically for similarities whereas contrastive linguistics contrasts languages, related and unrelated, synchronically for differences. Most contrastivists are not interested in comparative linguistics, even less in theoretical linguistics and tend to focus on instructional needs.

而在中国，从马建忠通过编写《马氏文通》建立现代语言学起，对比和比较的双重任务就同时落在中国语言学家头上。一方面，汉语与印欧语言有着巨大的历史差异性和类型差异性，如要有所"比较"，就只能采用对比语言学的原则，探求其到底"异"在何方，及其对东西方民族思维的影响；而另一方面，《文通》编写的本意又是要在中西语言间建立联系，证明汉语不是无"法"，而是有"法"，而且此"法"与西方之文"法"也相去不远，以至熟读《文通》之后，古今中外均可贯通，所谓"不独读中书者可以引通西文，即读西书者亦易于引通中文"（马建忠，1898：自记），这样一个目标就不得不采取让中西语文互相靠拢的办法，舍弃其表面上的"异"，追逐其本原上的"同"，这就走上了"比较语言学"的路子。马建忠的办法是区别"音韵文字"与语法：音韵文字是表面的、"人为的"、各种语言都不相同的，而其背后"所以声其心而形其意"的规律即语法却是各种语言都相通的。马建忠为此进行过西方语言的历史源流比较研究。我们不妨把前文引过的一段话及其上下文稍微多引一点：

Unlike the West, following the rise of modern linguistics in China after Ma's grammar, Chinese linguists shoulder the tasks of both comparative and contrastive linguistics. In a sense, the wide historical as well as typological gaps call for contrastive principles even if there is anything to "compare" to first understand the differences and the influences it has on thought patterns in both the West and the orient. In another regard, the intention of *Mashi Wentong,* by way of establishing the links between Chinese and Western languages, is to show that there are guiding principles in Chinese writing, and such principles resemble closely those applied in Western writing. Henceforth, Ma believed that sedulous studying of his grammar would result in mastery of both Chinese and Western grammars, as cited before. This target setting itself encourages the use of methods that would seek similarity at the root and disregard surface disparities, thereby closing the gaps in the languages. In this regard, comparative linguistics serves the aim better. Ma's solution is to single out syntax from the rest, such as phonology and the study of Chinese graphics, for other than syntax, the rest are deemed to be superficial and designed by man to be specific to languages. To seek the underlying principle in syntax, there is a need to compare the historical development and he refers to the Western languages:

然而言语不达者，极九译而辞意相通矣。形声或异者，通训诂而经义孔昭矣。盖所见为不同者，惟此已形已声之字，皆人为之也。而亘古今，塞宇宙，其种之或黄、或白、或紫、或黑之钧是人也，天皆赋之以此心之所以能意，此意之所以能达之理。则常探讨画革旁行诸国语言之源流，若希腊、若辣丁之文词而属比之，见其字别种而句司字，所以声其心而形其意者，皆有一定不易之律，而因以律夫吾经籍子史诸书，其大纲盖无不同者，是则此编之所以成也。（马建忠，1898: 12, 后序）

In all efforts of translation, we could overcome the language barriers and communicate. We can uncover meanings hidden in changes in sound and form with exegesis. What appears to be different in existing sounds and forms are made up and constructed by man. Throughout history and filling this universe, we are all human beings regardless of the skin colors yellow, or white or violet or black. Nature blesses us with a set of principles where thoughts in our mind could be understood and communicated. If we study diligently the origin and development of languages recorded horizontally, such as Greek and Latin, and make a comparison between them, it would be obvious that there is a constant and unchanging principle behind their morphological and syntactical differences. This principle is also applicable to the language used in our classics in philosophy, history, literature and others. On this ground, this book shall stand. (Ma Jianzhong, 1898: 12, Introduction)

最后一句话是把他从西方语言历史比较得出的结论引申到了汉语。这样，汉语甚至可以纳入西方语言的大框架里去了，在这样的情况下，"华文所独"之处就不能不处在次要的地位。这是马建忠此书的真正本意。这样，我们就看到，马建忠从对比的立场出发，最终走向了比较语言学，而两者的界线在汉语中也就泯灭了。

In Ma's own words above, conclusions from his historical comparison of Western languages cover even the Chinese language; that is to say, Chinese language could be included in the Western linguistic framework and in this light, the unique points in Chinese are only secondary. This is the real aim of *Mashi Wentong*. We also see that starting off with a contrastive principle, Ma Jianzhong finally ends up in comparative linguistics, confusing the lines between the two disciplines in Chinese.

中国现代语言学的这样一个独特的开头就给后来的继承者带来了严重的问题：进入20世纪，汉语无法再走以前那样独立发展的道路，汉语研究尤其无法置身于世界语言理论发展的潮流之外，中西语言、语言理论、语法体系的碰撞是不可避免的。在这样一种形势面前，每个汉语研究者都必须回答一个问题，对待中西语言的接触，你是采取"比较"的态度呢，还是采取"对比"的态度？亦即，是舍异求同呢，还是力探其异？再或者，是强调共性呢，还是强调个性？这样一种论争，可说是贯串了《马氏文通》迄今一个多世纪汉语研究的始终。而《马氏文通》首当其冲，以其"因西文已有之规矩"而被指责为"模仿"，一些人则积极地反其道而行之，"从汉语特点出发"，另起炉灶，编写新的语法。而这些新的语法由于难免要依托新的西方语言学理论，又被更后起者指责为"模仿"。如此循环不已，黎锦熙曾借王船山《俟解》中的话来总结当时的情况："一脚踢开拉丁文法而欲另建中华文法者，是'迷其所同'也；一手把住拉丁文法而遂挪作中华文法者，是又'失其所以异也'"（黎锦熙，1933：13）朱德熙所谓"后之视今，亦犹今之视昔"（朱德熙，1985：iii）一部中国现代语言学史也就成了对比语言学史，更成了一部在"比较"与"对比"前不同取向的"模仿"与反"模仿"史。在西方现代语言学史里面，上世纪五十年代以后的对比语言学由于偏离了沃尔夫订立的宗旨、专注于语言应用，而成了语言学附属学科，甚至其研究者自嘲为"语言学中的灰姑娘"，而汉语的对比问题始终处在汉语语言研究的风口浪尖，几乎一个世纪来所有关于汉语语言学的理论问题都是由此而引起的。

Undoubtedly, this choice introduction to modern linguistics in China is the onset of a series of contradictions confronting generations down the line, presenting the dilemma of the twentieth century. Evidently, linguistic research in China can neither tread the independent path as before nor afford to be separated from global theoretical linguistic trends. Clashes in language use, theories and systems are much to be expected. Each and every student of the Chinese language must therefore be prepared to face the question central to the debate persisting for more than a century since *Mashi Wentong*: to "compare" or to "contrast" when it comes to contact with the West? Put another way: Are we to seek similarity or differences? Or rephrasing further, are we to underline universality or individuality? Bearing the brunt is *Mashi Wentong*, for "imitating" "preexistent rules of Western writing". Others, being more positive, attempted at grammars highlighting the "characteristics" of the Chinese language but still cannot escape from being labelled as imitation, since these grammars fail in their reliance on the Western linguistic framework. As Zhu Dexi commented, "we will be assessed the way we assess our forerunners." (Zhu Dexi, 1985: iii) Therefore, a history in modern linguistics in China offers more than the title; it could well be a history of contrastive linguistics and a history in the "imitation" debate before deciding on compare or contrast. In sharp contrast the diminishing status of contrastive linguistics as the Cinderella amongst linguistic sub-disciplines in the Western context in the 1950s took on a different route from the Whorfian tradition. The issue of contrast remains the crux in debates on Chinese linguistic research, particularly in theoretical research for Chinese linguistics, over the past century and into the future.

2.3.2.3 "对比"或"比较"的目的是为了建立汉语自身的语言学
2.3.2.3 Compare or contrast: aiming for a Chinese linguistics

中国对比语言学的另一个重任，也是西方对比语言学同行们恐怕要艳羡不已的，是中国对比语言学实际上承担着汉语语言学自身建设的任务。由于汉语汉字的特殊性，中国古代没有西方那样的语法研究传统，中国古人的语言研究走的是另外一条路子。本来这个不同是对比研究的好材料，但在19世纪末急于要使中国走上现代化、走上富国强兵之路的中国许多语言学者看来，没有西方式的语法是中国语言研究的一大缺陷，是中国文化教育落后的根子，因而付出了几代人的努力，孜孜于为汉语建立一个西方式的语法体系。马建忠是最强烈、最自觉地意识到这一点的，黎锦熙等也以此作为自己的使命。对比或比较研究，居然可以担负起国家和民族如此沉重的责任，这恐怕是他国的对比语言学家们所想象不到的。西方对比语言学的鼻祖们，即使是洪堡特、叶斯柏森和沃尔夫，大约也没有想到过对比语言学可以成为一个民族语言学建立的基础。他们的想法还只是探索语言背后的文化，至多是探求"民族精神"，以及"语言与思维"的关系，大约还没有具体到为一种语言建立一个语法体系或语言研究体系。他们当然也了解所谓的"传教士语法"，而且他们本身调查世界各地语言（如洪氏之于卡维语、沃氏之于霍皮语等）的结果如果归纳起来大约也不过是某种程度较高的"传教士语法"，但他们大约只是作为一种研究手段，还没有认真到就想把这样描写得出的结论看作卡维人或霍皮人自己使用的"语法"。然而在中国，由于马建忠作出的榜样，传教士们"为掌握汉语减轻烦恼"（Varo，1703：3）的小册子性质的著作，经过汉语学者的包装取得了合法地位，并被认为是"童蒙入塾能循是而学文焉，其成就之速必无逊于西人"（马建忠，1898：后序）的汉语文法典范，学习西方语言学，甚至以西律中被认为是汉语语法乃至汉语语言学得以建立的必由之路，对比语言学就成了汉语和汉语语言学研究的基础。马氏之后，从事中国语言学（不包括被贬为"语文学"的传统古汉语研究）研究无不需先通外语和外国语言学理论，而语言理论研究也好，比较或对比研究也好，其最终目的无一例外是为了建立中国自己的汉语语法体系，至少到20世纪50年代为止是如此。马建忠之后，中国语言学家和语言学大师辈出，各自透过所编写的汉语语法书体现"革新"的语言学思想。如刘复《中国文法通论》（1920）、陈承泽《国文法草创》（1922）、金兆梓《国文法之研究》（1922）、胡以鲁《国语学草创》（1923）、黎锦熙《新著国语文法》（1924）、《比较文法》（1933）、何容《中国文法论》（成书1937年，出版1942年）、王力《中国现代语法》（1943—1944）、《中国语法理论》（1944—1945）、吕叔湘《中国文法要略》（1942）、高名凯《汉语语法论》（1948）等。五十年代以后情况变化，"两张皮"现象逐渐形成，学外语的眼睛看着的是外面的世界，不屑于关注汉语；学汉语的死守"家法"，孜孜于繁琐的材料搜集和分类整理工作。直至九十年代起情况才再次改变，但这已是后话，这里先不提。

One important undertaking of contrastive linguistics in China, something more challenging than the Western counterparts, is to establish Chinese linguistics as a tradition. For the unique language and writing systems of the Chinese, there is nothing like syntactic research in the old days. Our ancestors took on language research in other ways. Supposedly, the difference in research traditions serves as excellent subject for contrastive studies. However, the urge to modernize in the late nineteenth century blinded many Chinese linguists to think that the lack of a Western grammatical model signified the weakness in Chinese language research, and was the root to backwardness in education and culture. So, a few generations of labour sunk into setting up a Western grammatical model for the Chinese language. Ma Jianzhong certainly felt the strong calling, so did scholars like Li Jingxi. It would never occur to any linguist in the world that a linguistic discipline in contrastive studies could be tied to the fate of the nation. Not even Humboldt or Jespersen or Whorf could ever imagine laying the foundation of ethnolinguistics in contrastive linguistics. All they could think of is the exploration of culture hidden within the languages and at most, about "ethnic spirit" and the relations between language and thought. They were also far from having specific thoughts about establishing a grammatical structure or linguistic research tradition for any particular language. Of course they knew what missionary grammars were and even with addition of conclusions from all their field works, the result is nothing better than missionary grammar of a higher standard. In any case, it did not cross their minds that their means of research could be seriously taken as the "grammar" of their native subjects. In China, however, with Ma Jianzhong taking the lead, instructional booklets written to "alleviate the troubles of missionary trying to pick up the Chinese language" (Varo, 1703: 3) gained acceptance after repackaging by Chinese scholars as classics on Chinese grammar as well as Western linguistics, that "if children could follow the model systematically in school, they could pick up the language as fast as the Westerners" (Ma Jianzhong, 1898: Afterword). To go a step further, applying Western grammatical structure to Chinese was also deemed as the only way to own a grammar of Chinese and even a linguistic system. In this way, contrastive linguistics became the foundation to research in Chinese language and linguistics. Starting from Ma, to engage in Chinese linguistic studies (not including those in "philology", i.e. traditional research on classical Chinese) requires background in foreign language and foreign linguistic theories. Regardless of the field of linguistic research, the ultimate aim, be it in theoretical linguistics, contrastive linguistics or comparative linguistics, was to set up a grammatical system the Chinese language could call its own, at least this was the case until the 1950s. After Ma Jianzhong, there emerged a galaxy of linguistic masters whose thoughts penetrated the grammars written by them. The notable ones include: Chen Chengze (1922), Hu Yilu (1923), Li Jinxi (1924, 1933), Wang Li (1943—1944, 1944—1945), Lü Shuxiang (1942), Gao Mingkai (1948). New development after the 1950s saw the "two-skin" phenomenon gradually prevail. Foreign language learners were only interested in anything foreign, paying no attention to Chinese language. Those studying the Chinese language, locked in their own rules, occupied themselves with tedious data collection and compilation work. It was not until the 1990s that things changed again. We shall come back to this in a later section.

这样一个明确的目的形成了中国对比语言学的第三个特点，同时也使中国的对比语言学（不管以前是否有这个名称）的地位与国外同行不同，因此我们希望关心中国语言学的西方学者要从关心中国的汉外对比史开始，就是有充分理由的。

With a clear and specific aim, contrastive linguistics in China, whatever it was called previously, formed its own characteristics and status as compared with its development elsewhere. As such, it is important for foreign scholars having an interest in Chinese linguistics to first have an understanding of the piece of history involving contrasting Chinese with a foreign language.

2.3.3 《马氏文通》提出的世界性问题：能否以比较语言学的方法从事对比语言学研究？

2.3.3 Question from *Mashi Wentong*: May contrastive studies adopt comparative methodology?

与西方对比语言学家不同，从马建忠开始的中国语言学家有一个最明显的观点，就是不区分比较语言学与对比语言学。马建忠是这样，其后的学者例如黎锦熙，甚至吕叔湘也是这样，黎锦熙说：

Unlike their Western counterparts, Chinese linguists from Ma Jianzhong have obviously no intention of differentiating between comparative linguistics and contrastive linguistics. Similar evidence could be found in Li Jingxi and Lü Shuxiang. We quote Li Jinxi:

> 比较文法者，一，以本族语之文法与世界其他族语相比较；二，以本族本支语（如汉语）之文法与同族异支之兄弟姊妹语（如藏、缅、泰、苗等语）相比较；三，以标准国语（如汉语之现代北京语）之文法与各地不同之方言相比较；此皆属于语言文字学（英名Philology）之范围。四，以汉语中今语之文法与古文相比较，此可作为"汉语发展变迁史"之一部分，固亦不在语言文字学范围之外，唯在语文教育上颇有偏重应用之意味。（黎锦熙，1933：19）
>
> There are four branches of comparative grammar: (1) comparison between Chinese and languages of other language families; (2) comparison between Chinese and languages in other branches of the same language family (such as Tibetan, Burmese, Tai, Miao, etc.); (3) comparison between standard Chinese (for example Mandarin) and various dialects; all three of them belong to the domain of philology; and (4) comparison between modern Chinese and traditional Chinese, as part of the evolution history of Chinese language and well within the domain of philology with emphasis on application in terms of language education. (Li Jinxi, 1933: 19)

而吕叔湘说：
And Lü Shuxiang:

> 要明白一种语言的文法，只有应用比较的方法。拿文言词句和文言词句比较，拿白话词句和白话词句比较，这是一种比较。文言里一句话，白话里怎么说；白话里一句话，文言里怎么说，这又是一种比较。一句中国话，翻成英语怎么说；一句英语，中国话里如何表达，这又是一种比较。只有比较才能看出各种语文表现法的共同之点和特殊之点。（吕叔湘，1942：上卷初版例言）
>
> The only way to understand the grammar of a language is to have it

compared. One way of comparison is comparing within traditional texts and within colloquial texts. Another way of comparison is to see how a sentence expressed in traditional texts is to be expressed colloquially and vice versa. Yet another form of comparison is to see how a sentence expressed in Chinese is to be expressed in English and vice versa. Only through comparison may we see through the points in common and points that are unique in each grammar. (Lü Shuxiang, 1942: Preface, first edition, Vol. 1)

语言的比较可以有语内（intra-linguistic）和语间（inter-linguistic）的不同，而语间又有亲属语言（related languages）间和非亲属语言（non-related languages）间的不同，这种种比较的性质是不同的，手段也未必相同，因而才有了各种语言学分支如比较语言学、对比语言学等。我们不知道上面几位学者是不知道呢，还是明知而故意混同，好为他们将拉丁语或英语与汉语直接相比较并借用这些语言的语法来构建汉语语法张目（吕氏的情况不同，他似乎只是就方法论方法）？不管怎样，马建忠及他之后许多中国语言学家的实践带来的是一个世界性的问题，即能不能将"比较语言学"与"对比语言学"的任务混在一起，让偏重历史、古代的比较语言学回到人间，使之现代化、共时化、世俗化，并扩大化，来完成本应由对比语言学完成的任务？同时，把对比语言学的任务由追求"语言与思维"的关系，缩小为在本来相距遥远，因而差别很大的语言间存异求同，同时构建一个可以彼此"相通"的语法体系，以便各民族间的交流？我们知道，在拉丁语语法的基础上创建一部现代语语言的语法，马建忠并不是第一个，所有欧洲近代语言的语法，包括意大利语、法语、英语等等都是这样建立起来的。但这都是在同系的语言范围之内，其间的异同属于比较语言学研究的领域。马建忠的创新在于他将这一做法延伸到了非亲属语言，延伸到了不论从历史、从地界、从谱系，到语言类型都相距极远（有人称之为poles-apart）的语言。也许在马建忠之前也有过别的非印欧系民族语言的语法体系是这样建立起来的，[1]但将这样的实验放到一个有几亿人口、几千年历史

1　日本大槻文彦的《日本文典》脱稿于1896年，刊行于1897年，比《马氏文通》早一两年，也是在印欧语语法的基础上建立起来的。在日本国内的命运与《马氏文通》差不多。One year earlier than Ma, in 1897, Otsuki Fumihiko published his *Kou Nihon Bunten* (*An Enlarged Japanese Grammar*), which is also written after the Indo-European model, and has met a similar fate in Japan to Ma's in China.

的人类最重要的一种语言中来,马建忠也是第一个。如果他的实验成功,这将具有世界语言学史的伟大意义。因为现在世界上的语言,除印欧语之外,有语法的少,无语法的多(我们指的是成文的语法体系,不是各种语言中客观蕴藏的语法),有多少语言等待着我们的语言学家去为之创制语法!这一经验绝对地具有推广和应用价值。但如果他的实验失败了,全世界的语言学家就将被迫去寻找新的途径来解决众多"嗷嗷待哺"的语言的语法体系问题。这个问题也可以换一句西方学者熟悉的话来说,也就是,几百年以来在世界上许多地方产生的"传教士语法",到底能走多远?因为西方真正的语言学家和汉学家是不赞成用这种方法去编写各种语言的语法的,1927年冬王力到巴黎大学留学,博士论文原想做中国语法,但巴黎中国学院院长格拉奈(Granet)先生就劝他不要做,尤其"不能像《马氏文通》那样做"。(见王力,1943/1985:18)那么,除了印欧语及少数有自己研究传统的非印欧语的语言之外,全世界这么多的语言的描写究竟应该如何进行?

There are two broad categories of language comparison: intra-linguistic and inter-linguistic. Inter-linguistic comparison can be between related languages or between non-related languages. The natures as well as the means of comparison are different for each type. This accounts for the sub-branches in linguistic studies, such as comparative linguistics and contrastive linguistics. It would be surprising not to distinguish between them. While we could understand that Lü Shuxiang seems to be coming from methodology discussion, it would not be helpful for other scholars to try to mix the two branches of linguistics. In any case the practice of Chinese linguists led by Ma Jianzhong raises a universal question: can the objects of comparative linguistics and contrastive linguistics come together? Is it possible for comparative linguistics, originally confined with historical data, to be modernized, synchronic and to expand to meet the objectives of contrastive linguistics? At the same time, is it possible to further limit the task of contrastive linguistics, which is to seek the relations between language and thought, to find ways of accommodating the great differences between far-off events so that "interlinkable" grammatical systems could be established for ease of communications between ethnic groups? Ma Jianzhong is certainly not the first to attempt to construct a grammar based on the Greco-Latin tradition. Almost all modern grammars of the Europeans, including

Italian, French and English among many others, are rooted in that tradition. They are within the same language family and their similarities and differences are within the domain of comparative linguistics. The creative proposal of Ma Jianzhong is to expand this method to non-related or, as some suggested, poles-apart languages in all senses of history, geographical boundaries, family tree and typology. Before Ma Jianzhong, there may have been other non Indo-European ethnic groups who attempted to build their own grammatical structure in this manner. But in running the experiment on one of the most significant languages of the world that has thousands of years of history and a user population of over a billion, Ma was second to none. Were he successful, it would be the most brilliant record ever in the history of world linguistics. Many languages would be waiting for their turn to have their natural grammar written down. That would be the most valuable experience to be popularized. In the opposite scenario, linguists in the world would have to stretch their limits to find new ways to resolve issues of grammatical structures for the many languages without an indigenous model. Western scholars could easily recall a familiar question they are often asked: how far could missionary grammars go? Truthful linguists and sinologists in the West do not approve of such grammars. The eminent Chinese linguist, Wang Li has this experience to share. He was at *Université de Paris* in the year 1927 for his doctoral study and he wanted to write a treatise on Chinese grammar. Professor Marcel granet, well known sinologist who was then dean of the *Institut des Hautes Etudes Chinoises*, advised Wang Li against the idea, particularly "not the approach of *Mashi Wentong*" (Wang Li, 1943/1985: 18). Outside the Indo-European family, there are only a few languages with their own traditions, the vast majority of which are without documentation. How then shall we go about describing these languages?

对于《马氏文通》功过的争论，在中国已经进行了一百年，客观地说，到现在还没有争出个子丑寅卯来。看来还要进行下去。我们认为这个问题值得全世界语言学家关注。

Discussion on the merits and demerits of *Mashi Wentong* has been on going in China for a century and it will persist. It's high time that we invite participation and opinions from the world.

与此相关的还有两个问题，一个是比较语言学领域的，一个是对比语言学领域的。

In relation to the issue, there are two other questions, one on comparative linguistics, the other concerning contrastive linguistics.

前一个问题是，根据我们的研究（潘文国，1996a），即使在同一个语系内，在一个历史较早的语言（如拉丁语）的语法体系的基础上，构建一个历史较晚的语言（如英语）的语法体系也未必成功，自17世纪在拉丁文语法基础上建立英语语法之后，两百年来，类似对《马氏文通》的"模仿"与反"模仿"之争在英语语法界也没有断绝过，直到1891年斯威特（Henry Sweet）的《新英语语法》及其后叶斯柏森等人的英语语法书相继出版，才以英语自身语法的最后胜利而告终。但时至今日还不时可听到英语语法学家的抱怨，说英语语法里有太多挥之不去的拉丁语法的影响。例如帕麦尔说：

On the first question on comparative linguistics, according to Pan Wenguo (1996a), even within the same language family, constructing a grammar for a historically new language (such as English) on a historically old model (such as Latin), may not yield satisfactory results. Debates on "limitation" persisted for 200 years after the seventeenth century when English grammar was constructed modelled on Latin grammar. It was not until Henry Sweet's *A New English Grammar* (in two parts 1892—1895), and later English grammars by Otto Jespersen and others, that the debate would be closed. That was a sweet victory for English grammar, having been freed from the Latin jacket. Nevertheless, time and again, we still hear complaints about the influence of Latin grammars in English. Palmer is one of them:

> 英语语法教学大多建立在拉丁文基础上，许多英国儿童对之十分茫然，他们看不出英语何以有虚拟语气或与格；直到学习了拉丁语之后一切才清楚。拉丁语能够帮助他们学习英语语法，其原因恰恰在于，英语语法一直以来本来就是拉丁语法！（帕麦尔，1971：16）
>
> Since most English grammar teaching was based upon Latin, the students were often at a loss. They could not see why English had subjunctive or a dative case, but when they learnt Latin it all became clear. Latin helped them with their English grammar, but only because English grammar was really Latin grammar all the time! (Palmer, 1971: 16)

如果同一语系内尚且如此,将一种语言的语法体系移植到另一种原本不相干的语言中去,其风险和成功几率又有多大?

Even within the same language family we expect incompatibilities, so how much risk would there be to transplant a grammar tradition to a completely unrelated language? What is the probability of success?

后一个问题是白珊博士提出来的,她在研究早期传教士编写的汉语语法书时除了我们前面引过的话之外,还说了两段忧心忡忡的话:

The next question pertaining to contrastive linguistics was raised by Sandra Breitenbach. Her research on the early grammars of Chinese written by missionaries prompted the following concerns:

> 正是这方面的细节,透露了这些先驱者在描述一种未知语言时必须克服的障碍。从概念上看,这样做成功传递了传教士们自身拥有的语言哲学或语言世界观,因为他们的语言观受到了拉丁语结构原理的束缚,而这类原理往往未经任何批判的思考就被用在汉语上面。(白珊,2000: F47)

> It is precisely these details that reveal the hurdles these pioneers had to overcome when describing an unknown language. Conceptually, it effectively conveys a certain philosophy of language or linguistic world view of the friars, since their language perception is fettered by Latin structural principles, which are, quite often without any critical reflection, applied to Chinese. (Breitenbach, 2000: xlii)

> 通过比较汉语和拉丁语,人们意识到汉语的结构原理不同于欧洲诸语言;但不幸,这类比较也限制了对汉语的内在结构的真实认知。总之我们可以说,希腊—拉丁语法概念经过瓦罗解释之后,对语法概念在东方世界的逐渐展开具有持续不断的作用力,其影响直到今天在一定程度上仍能为我们察觉。(白珊,2000: F451)

> The comparison of Chinese with Latin created an awareness of the distinctiveness of structural principles in Chinese as compared to European languages, but it also exerted an unfortunate restriction on genuine understanding of the inherent structure of Chinese. In conclusion, it can be

claimed that the Greco-Latin concept, as interpreted by Varo, had long-lasting consequences for the unfolding of grammatical ideas in the East, which are, to some extent, still felt even today. (Breitenbach, 2000: xlv)

这就使我们不得不考虑沃尔夫的语言相对论的问题。而对这个问题的探讨即使在西方也是一个经久不息的话题，加上了语法体系由一种语言向一种遥远的语言的"迁移"问题，讨论起来就更加有趣而富有实际意义了。

These worries bring to mind Whorf's linguistic relativity. Relativism would be an even more exciting and challenging discussion with the "transfer" of grammatical traditions to far-off events added on.

2.4 第二期（1922—1955）：旨在建立汉语自身语法体系的对比研究
2.4 Phase 2 (1922—1955): Contrastive studies mindful of a Chinese linguistic system

从严格的意义上说，中国的对比语言学不应该从《马氏文通》算起，因为那是一个"比较"、"对比"相混杂，而"比较"的诉求显然重于"对比"的诉求的著作，而应该从其后发出第一声"反模仿"呐喊的著作，尤其是第一部立足"汉语本位"的语言学著作谈起。这发出第一声"反模仿"呐喊的著作就是陈承泽的《国文法草创》（1922），而第一部立足"汉语本位"的普通语言学著作就是胡以鲁的《国语学草创》（1923）。我们可以说，从这两部书开始，我们才有了真正的中国对比语言学。反对"模仿"，通过中西对比，建立汉语自身的语法和语言研究体系，是这一时期的主旋律。从两部"草创"开始，到王力（1935；1943—1944；1944—1945）、陈望道等（1943）、吕叔湘（1942）、何容（1942）、高名凯（1948）等都是如此，甚至包括一般被指责为"模仿"的黎锦熙（1924），因为从出发点来说，他也是竭力反"模仿"的。

Strictly speaking, contrastive linguistics in China should perhaps not be seen as beginning from *Mashi Wentong* given that it confuses comparative and contrastive concepts and weighs more heavily in comparative than contrastive studies. The next probable starting point would be the first grammar to stand against "imitation" or the first to have the benchmark set on the Chinese language itself. Chen Chengze's *A Preliminary Grammar of Chinese* (1922) let out the first cry against imitation.

Hu Yilu's *A Preliminary Study of Chinese Language* (1923) set forth to analyse Chinese as it is. These two publications mark the real commencement of contrastive linguistics in China. Rejecting imitation, a grammatical system true to the Chinese language could then possibly emerge through genuine contrastive studies. This was the theme for this phase and it ran through from the two *Preliminary* titles until the works of Wang Li (1935; 1943—44; 1944—45), Chen Wangdao et al. (1938), Lü Shuxiang (1942), He Rong (1942), gao Mingkai (1948) and Li Jinxi (1924) who was often criticised for imitating, but in fact whose intention is really against imitation.

但在讨论中国语言学家的贡献之前，我们要先介绍外国学者对发掘汉语特点的贡献。从某种角度看，中国学者走上"比较"道路的动力固然来自西方，而发掘汉语特点的原动力竟然也是来自西方。

Before we go on to discuss the contributions of Chinese linguists, we shall pause and digress to introduce a few foreign linguists for their commendable effort in bringing to light the characteristics of the Chinese language. To a certain extent, we could say that the West provided the driving force for Chinese scholars to embark on comparative studies. Little did we expect that the motivation behind unearthing the characteristics of the Chinese language comes from the West too.

2.4.1 洪堡特和高本汉论汉语

2.4.1 Humboldt and Karlgren on the Chinese language

自从16世纪末中西交通开通之后，西方很多学者就对汉语这一古老特殊的语言表现出了深厚的兴趣，更有一些汉学家以汉语研究作为自己终身的事业。在洪堡特之前，对汉语发表过真知灼见的就有莱布尼兹（Gottfried Wilhelm Leibniz，1646—1716）等人，在高本汉前后也有萨丕尔、马伯乐、叶斯柏森等人，但我们特别要提出这两人，一是因为他们两人都有研究汉语的完整论著，二是因为洪氏对下面要说到的中国学者胡以鲁的影响最大，对今天的中国对比语言学者更有重要的影响；而高氏的观点更直接影响了中国包括王力在内的一代著名语言学家。

By the end of the sixteenth century, the opening of transportation opportunities facilitated greater exchange between the East and the West. Many Western scholars were fascinated by the history and peculiarities of the Chinese language and some sinologists made the study of Chinese language their lifetime career. Before Humboldt, Gottfried Wilhelm Leibniz (1646—1716) and others gave insightful views on the Chinese language. After Karlgren came scholars like Edward Sapir, Henri Maspéro (1883—1945), Otto Jespersen and more. We single out Humboldt and Karlgren for their complete works on Chinese language and their influence on prominent Chinese linguists; for instance, Humboldt has particularly influenced Hu Yilu, whereas Karlgren has inspired Wang Li and others.

2.4.1.1 洪堡特论汉语
2.4.1.1 Humboldt on Chinese language

洪堡特是对比语言学—普通语言学的创始人，凑巧的是，他也是西方语言学家中对汉语进行完整论述的最早的学者之一，他发表于1826年的《论汉语语法结构》迄今有着重要的启示意义。据英国学者约瑟夫（John Joseph，1999）考证，为了写这篇文章，并与当时法国著名汉学家阿贝尔·雷慕萨（Abel-Rémusat）辩论汉语问题，洪堡特还专门花了几个月时间认真学习了汉语。他在文中提出的见解，至今读来仍富有新鲜感。

Humboldt, father of contrastive linguistics and general linguistics, was one of the Western scholars who pioneered into the study of Chinese and one of the earliest to have published works on Chinese. His paper of 1826, "On the grammatical structure of the Chinese", is still enlightening. According to British scholar John Joseph (1999), Humboldt spent a few months learning the language to write the paper and to engage the eminent French sinologist Abel-Rémusat in the discussion of Chinese.

洪堡特首先指出，一般人研究汉语只注意到其文字的独特性，而实际上，汉语的语法更独特、更值得研究，因为它自成一类，与所有已知的其他语言都不同：

Humboldt first pointed out that most people are attracted to the Chinese characters and missed the more unique structure of the language, different from the rest of the other known languages.

> 研究汉语的人往往把注意力放在汉字与汉语的关系上，结果往往对语言的实际组织法注意不够。实际上汉语是所有已知语言中结构最独特的一种，它代表的远非只是一种语言，而是在语言多样性中的一类语言。（洪堡特，1826：95）

> In studies of Chinese, it is normally the script and its connection with the language which attracts interest, to such an extent that relatively little attention is paid to the actual grammatical structure of the language. And yet this is one of the most remarkable language structures known; far from simply constituting a sub-division of one single language, it in fact, constitutes a class of its own within the grammatical multiplicity of all languages. (Humboldt, 1826: 95)

接着他指出汉语的最大特点就是汉语只有句法而没有其他语言都有的词法，这可以说是100多年后王力的观点的先声：

More than 100 years in advance of Wang Li, Humboldt noted that the underlying difference of Chinese rests with the fact that it has only the syntactic part and not the morphological part of grammar:

> 如果要说汉语与其他语言有什么最大的不同的话，那就是：汉语的语词并不靠语法范畴来联系，汉语的语法也不建立在词类的区分上，汉语是靠其他手段来表明思想的联系的。其他语言的语法都有两个明显的组成部分：词法和句法，而在汉语中却只有句法。（洪堡特，1826：95）

> If I had to ascribe this difference to one factor underlying all others, then I would attribute it to the fact that Chinese words are not linked according to grammatical categories, its grammar is not based on the classification of words; instead, Chinese uses other means to indicate the way that thoughts are connected. The grammar of other languages has two distinct parts, an etymological part and a syntactical part, while in Chinese only the latter is found. (Humboldt, 1826: 95)

1997年，潘文国（1997a/2002：126）曾提出了一个后来颇为著名的观点：英语的语法分析过程是"结构—语义"，"结构弄清楚了，句子的意义才清楚"；而汉语语法的分析过程是"语义—结构"，"从语义着手，把句子拆成一个个片段，弄清其间的关系。句子结构是语义分析的结果。"不想这一观点洪堡特早就说过了：

Pan Wenguo (1997a/2002: 126) offered quite a well known observation that to understand a sentence in English, one has to start analysing the structure before the meaning is clear, so the process is from structure to meaning. The reverse is true for Chinese, one has to grasp the meaning before understanding how the units are pieced together to form the sentence which is to say, sentence structure is the result of semantic analysis. This is no new discovery, as Humboldt said:

> 其他语言分析句子是从词的语法特点开始，词的语法性搞清楚了，句子也就理解了。这在汉语中完全办不到。汉语的理解必须从字典开始，词的意义、词在句中的位置、句子要传达的意思等等，这些搞清楚了，句子的结构才清楚。（洪堡特，1826: 95）

> In other languages, if one wishes to understand a sentence, one must start by examining the grammatical nature of the words and must then construe these according to that nature. In Chinese this is impossible. One must turn directly to the dictionary, and the construction will follow simply from the meaning of the word, its position in the sentence, and the sense to be communicated. (Humboldt, 1826: 95)

他最早提出西方语言的句子清晰而汉语的句子界限不清：

He was also the earliest to have noticed that sentence demarcation in Chinese is not as distinct as Western languages:

> 在我们的语言里，句子的统一性可以从屈折动词看出来，有多少个屈折动词就有多少个句子……而汉语里常不易确定一个句子从哪里开始到哪里结束。看起来明明像一个句子，翻译时却不得不处理成两句甚至两句以上。（Humboldt, 1826: 99; 100）

> In our languages, the unity of a clause is recognized in the inflected verb; there are as many clauses as there are inflected verbs…It is not always

certain in Chinese where a sentence ends and a new one begins, and in translations I am certain that what is regarded as just one sentence will often actually consist of two or several sentences. (洪堡特, 1826: 99, 100)

现在人们常爱说汉语的主要语法手段是词序和虚词。这一思想也来自于洪堡特：
It is often said that the main grammatical devices in Chinese are word order and functional words. This conclusion actually came from Humboldt:

> 汉语中没有任何可称之为屈折的东西，它所具有的唯一句法手段是助词或语法词以及词序。但这两者看来也不像是表明语法形式，而只是以另一种手段来帮助理解。（洪堡特，1826：102）
>
> The Chinese language possesses nothing that could by any means be described as inflexion. The only syntactical auxiliaries it possesses are particles (grammatical words) and word order. But these two devices do not appear to help denote grammatical forms, being intended rather to guide understanding by other means. (Humboldt, 1826: 102)

上一段话的后一句，今天可能很多人想不到，也没有去想过，但这却是洪堡特研究汉语语法想要表达的一个重要思想。在下面两段话中，他进一步申述了汉语语法中助词和词序的局限性：
We would like to highlight the last sentence of the above quote. The real function of word order and functional words is something that has slipped the mind of most people; it does not occur to most people that they are not part of grammatical forms. But this is exactly one significant observation by Humboldt in his study of Chinese. He elaborated on the limitations of these two devices as follows:

> （在分析了"之"的用法之后）这类词并不指明什么语法形式，而只是表明思想从一个部分向另一部分的过渡。至于连这个作用也没有的词，例如所谓介词，最好的办法还是联系它们的本义，而不是将它当作语法标志。（洪堡特，1826：104）
>
> (After analysing the function of Tchi 之) …These words are not means of denoting grammatical forms but rather indicate the transition from one

part of a thought to the next. Of those which do not do this, as with the so-called prepositions, it is almost always the case that their use can be better understood by referring back to their original material meaning, rather than by taking them as grammatical indicators. (Humboldt, 1826: 104)

> 汉语的词序不管有多严格，单靠它自身是绝对不够的，必须时时回过头来看词义及上下文。它最无助于标明语法形式，因为，譬如说，可以做主语的有很多形式，而在动词前的也未必是主语，还有状语，等等。（洪堡特，1826：104—105）

> So, however strict the word order may be in Chinese, it is never sufficient on its own, and one must always refer back to the meaning of the words and the context. Least of all can it indicate grammatical forms, since, for example, more than one can form the subject, and not only the subject can precede the verb, but also adverbial phrases. (Humboldt, 1826: 104—5)

对于那些至今死奉汉语语法手段主要靠词序和虚词的人来说，这两段话不啻是一帖清醒剂。汉语的缺乏形式使洪堡特想到：

This sounds like an alarm from heaven, a wake-up call to those who are adamant about word order and functional words being the main grammatical devices in Chinese. From the absence of markings, Humboldt noted further that:

> 任何语言的语法都有两个部分，一个部分是清晰地标明的，另一部分却是蕴藏的。汉语中前一部分比后一部分小得多。（洪堡特，1826：105）

> In the grammar of every language there is one part which is expressly indicated and another part which has to be tacitly added. In Chinese the former is infinitely smaller than the latter. (Humboldt, 1826: 105)

这使他特别强调上下文的作用：

And this is where he underpins the function of context:

> 其他语言的上下文对理解语法起辅助作用，而汉语中上下文起的是基础作用，句子的结构只有从上下文推导出来，甚至动词本身也只有通过动词概念辨别出来。（洪堡特，1826：105）

> In every language, context must come to the assistance of grammar.

In Chinese it forms the basis for understanding, and the construction of the sentence can often only be deduced from it. The verb itself is recognizable only through its verbal concept. (Humboldt, 1826: 105)

通过将汉语与其他语言特别是欧洲古典语言的对比，洪堡特得出了一个颇具普通语言学意义的结论：
Contrasting Chinese with other languages, particularly classical European languages, Humboldt arrives at a conclusion in the light of general linguistics:

> 人类语言在不同民族中会沿着两条完全不同的路径发展。其一是沿着概念的联系，表达时只使用那些非使用不可的东西，以使意义清晰明白，尽量不去使用那些作为思想的媒介和工具的语言所特有的手段；另一条路则是尽量使语言成为这样一种工具，充分利用它表现思想的独特方式，尽可能使语言世界与外部世界完全相等。（洪堡特，1826: 98）

> Language therefore can develop with different nations along two very different paths. It can primarily follow the relations of the concepts as such and, in expression, limit itself soberly only to whoever is absolutely necessary for the clarity and precision of this expression, making as little use as possible of what pertains to be the particular nature of language as a medium and tool of thought; or it can choose to develop language as such a top, keep to the particular manner in which language presents thought, and develop language wherever feasible into an ideal world equal to the real one. (Humboldt, 1826: 98)

显然，他将汉语归到了第一类。他对汉语的赞扬以及批评均出于此。今天有人不满他对汉语的赞扬，也有人不满他对汉语的批评，其实都是缺乏对他的思想的全面的了解。洪堡特对汉语研究乃至对整个普通语言学的挑战直到近200年后的今天我们还能强烈地感受得到！

Obviously, Chinese has gone on the first path and it is with this view that Humboldt sings his praises and records his criticisms on the language. Unless one has a complete understanding of Humboldt's thought, it is not easy to agree or disagree with him on his remarks on Chinese, positive or negative. For the 200 years until this day, the challenge Humboldt made to Chinese and, if we may posit, general linguistics, is as reinforcing as ever.

2.4.1.2 高本汉论汉语
2.4.1.2 Karlgren on Chinese language

洪堡特的文章本世纪之前并没有译成汉语，中国也未必有很多人读到过。胡以鲁很可能是在日本时接触到的，他恐怕也是五十年代之前提到过洪堡特的唯一一位重要学者。因此洪氏在中国的影响要到九十年代后才更多地显示出来。高本汉就不同了。1923年他在《世界语言文化手册系列》上发表了一篇《汉语的读音与符号》，1930年张世禄即将之译成汉语在上海商务印书馆出版，取名《中国语与中国文》。几乎所有的中国语言学者都见到了这本书，对三、四十年代的汉语研究有着极大的影响。五十年代苏联专家对中国语言学的批评，其矛头主要就是针对他（以及叶斯柏森等人）的。

Most people did not have the chance to read Humboldt before the Chinese version was made available in the late 1990s. Before 1950, Humboldt was only mentioned by Hu Yilu, a notable Chinese scholar who may have read Humboldt while studying in Japan. While Humboldt had no influence in China until the late 1990s, Karlgren received attention much earlier. His treatise adapted in English as *Sound and Symbol in Chinese,* first published in *The World's Manuals Language and Literature Series* in 1923, was translated and published by Chinese phonologist Zhang Shilu in 1930 under the title *Zhongguo Yu and Zhongguo Wen*. No Chinese linguists could have missed the book, for its impact in the 1930s and 1940s was immense. In fact, the attack on Chinese linguistics launched by "experts" of the then Soviet Union in the 1950s was really targeted at Karlgren (as well as Jespersen and others).

同洪堡特一样，高氏强调"中国的情况常和我们在西洋看到的情况截然相反"（Karlgren，1923：6），例如：

Like Humboldt, Karlgren understands that "…in China things are very often diametrically opposite to all that we are accustomed to in the West" (Karlgren, 1923/1971: 6); for example:

> 研究别的古老语言，第一步是先确定古代文字的音值，音值一定，读音也可确定了；而在汉语中我们看到的只是代表整个词的许多符号，其古代读音却完全不知道，结果在中国古代，字形的研究就占

了很重要的位置。（同上：7—8）

> In the study of other languages the primary task consists in fixing the phonetic value of the ancient characters; once this is done, the pronunciation can be determined. In Chinese, on the contrary, we have to deal exclusively with characters which are symbols for whole words—symbols the old pronunciation of which is unknown, and which cannot therefore be transcribed as they were read at the time. Consequently in the study of ancient Chinese the study of the script occupies a prominent place. (*ibid.*: 7—8)

接着他引用德国学者芬克（F. N. Finck，1910）的观点，提出了汉语的两条最大特点——单音节和孤立性：
Quoting the German linguist F. N. Finck (1910), Karlgren singled out the two most important characteristics of Chinese language:

> 现在我们来看汉语，看看它贯穿所有历史时期的最大特点是什么。这些特点被归结为两条：第一，汉语是单音节的；第二，汉语是孤立性的，也就是说，词好像是各自独立的单位，不随其在句中的功能而改变其形式。（同上：10）

> On the one hand, Chinese is monosyllabic, on the other hand, it is isolating, i.e. it treats the words as if they were isolated unities, without modifying them according to their function in the sentence. (*ibid.*: 10)

为了不致被误解，他特意通过与英语等的比较解释了汉语的"单音节性"：[1]
Karlgren has purposefully explained what he meant by monosyllabic in Chinese by contrasting it with English and other languages to avoid misunderstanding, unfortunately it is still pretty much misconstrued and we would like to highlight his point once again:

> 如果与英语作比较，汉语的单音节性有两个意思。第一，汉语所有的单词都是词干，也就是说，汉语不用派生词缀方式构成新词……汉语的词都是词干，源于上面说的孤立性，因其不靠词缀来表达语法

---

[1] 只可惜这一点还是常常被后人误解和曲解，这是我们特意在这里引用这段话的缘故。

意义。第二，不像别的语言，汉语的词干很少超过一个音节。诚然，在英语中，如果我们把各种各样的派生词缀拿掉，也常留下单音节词干；但同样经常的是，英语中也有很多双音节和多音节词干。印欧语祖语的词干有单音节的，也有双音节的；芬兰—乌克兰语的词干按例是双音节的。与这两大语系相比，汉语词干单音节的性质就很明显的了。（同上：13—14）

In comparison with the English language, therefore, the monosyllabism of Chinese involves two things. Firstly, all Chinese simple words are stem-words, i.e. Chinese refuses to form new words by means of derivative affixes… That all Chinese simple words are stem-words is due to the same tendency which we have considered above when speaking of the isolating nature of the language: Chinese in general does not express categories by means of affixes. In the second place, Chinese has not, as other languages have, stem-words of more than one syllable. It is true that we in English, after cutting off the various affixes of derivatives, often arrive at monosyllabic stem-words, but quite often the stems are disyllabic or polysyllabic. The old Indo-European mother language possessed disyllabic as well as monosyllabic stem-words, and the Finno-Ugrian languages have as a rule disyllabic stem-words. Compared with these two great families of languages, Chinese stands in sharp contrast with its system of one-syllable stem-words. (*ibid.*:13—14)

高本汉强调"把汉语定性为单音节和孤立语，主要是通过与其他语言的比较，同时，单音的定性也考虑了汉语自身"（同上，14）。几乎所有谈论汉语特点的见解都是从这两条特点生发出来的，围绕这两条特点的论争至今尚未结束。Karlgren cannot stress enough that "The definition of Chinese as on the one hand isolating, and on the other hand monosyllabic, is based mainly on a comparison with other languages; but at the same time, its definition as monosyllabic necessitates the consideration of Chinese by itself" (*ibid.*: 14). Almost all the discussion on Chinese stems from these two characteristics and debates on these two points are still ongoing.

但高氏此书中最为"惊世骇俗"的大约是他提出的下面一个结论：
Perhaps the most audacious and mind-blowing of Karlgren's ideas is the following conclusion:

总而言之，早先的理论认为汉语是一种"原始"的语言，尚未进化到屈折和派生的阶段，这与事实恰恰相反。实际上，汉语的发展路线与印欧语完全相同，即综合性的语尾和词干的语音变化渐渐丢失，更强烈地诉诸读者或听者的逻辑分析能力。从这方面看，英语可能是印欧语中最高度发展的语言，而汉语比它走得还要远得多。（同上，15—16）

> In short, the old theory which classified Chinese as a "primitive" language, not yet raised to the inflexional and derivative status, is the opposite of the truth. Chinese, in fact has followed exactly the same line of evolution as the Indo-European languages in the gradual loss of synthetic terminations and phonetic stem variations, with all the stronger appeal to the listener's (or reader's) faculty of purely logical analysis. English is perhaps in this respect the most highly developed Indo-European language; but Chinese has progressed much further. (*ibid.*: 15—16)

同时，在当时弥漫于中国的文字"改革"呼声中，高氏是最鲜明地主张汉字与汉语相适应、最坚决地反对汉语拼音化的一位学者。下面的分析出自这位外国学者之口，其启迪意义是不言而喻的：[1]

At a time where China was zealous with script "reformation", Karlgren was unambiguous in his view that the Chinese character is the best suit for the language, and tenaciously objected romanization. As a foreign linguist, here is how Karlgren sees the Chinese character:

> 中国口语与传统书面语之间的特殊关系，尤其是传统文言是一种目治而非仅仅耳治的语言，使我们得以解释一个奇怪的事实：为什么汉字这种古怪的文字必不可少。欧洲人可能老在想，为什么中国人不放弃他们那古老怪异的文字，而采用我们那种又简单又实用的字母呢？他们也会一耸肩就自己回答：中国人不肯在文字方面提升到跟我们一样先进，只能说明他们是难以置信地保守和不切实际的民族。
> （同上，30）

---

1 当然，有人硬要解读为"资产阶级学者反对汉字改革，以使汉语永远处在'落后'状态"，那也没有办法。
Politicking interpretation of Karlgren's objection as "capitalist scholar rejecting reformation of the Chinese character so that the Chinese language will forever stay as a 'backward' language" is not accepted. Comment is free, though.

In the peculiar relation between the spoken and the traditional written language in China, and above all in the nature of the latter as being a language that can be understood by the eye but not by the ear alone, we have the explanation of the strange fact that the peculiar Chinese script is indispensable. It must often have occurred to Europeans to ask the question: Why do not the Chinese abandon their monstrous antediluvian script in favour of our simple and practical alphabetic writing? And with a shrug they will have answered themselves: They must be incredibly unpractical and conservative, if they refuse to raise themselves to our position of superiority in this respect. (*ibid.*: 30)

在分析了采用拼音文字的利（"中国的学童可以因此而减少一两年的苦工"）和弊（1."不得不废弃3000多年的文献，因而也是整个中国文化的支柱"；2."维系这一巨大国家各个地区的工具、'书面的世界语'势必被打破"）之后，高本汉得出结论说：

Karlgren could only think of one advantage in romanising: "the schoolboys of China would be spared the toil of a year or two", and more than one disadvantage: (1) "the Chinese would be compelled to discard his literature of some 3,000 years and with this the backbone of his entire civilization", (2) "This marvelous tie between all the parts of the great country which is formed by its script, its written Esperanto, would have to be broken." Summing up, Karlgren writes,

> 中国人之所以没有放弃他们的古怪文字而采用我们的字母，这不是由于他们的愚蠢或者顽固保守。汉字和汉语是如此巧妙地适应，因而是无法废弃的。[1]（同上，31）
>
> If China does not abandon its peculiar script in favour of our alphabetic

---

[1] 这里根据的是高本汉1962年的香港修订版。在张世禄的译本（我们用的是1977年台湾文史哲出版社版）里，这句话后面还有一句："中国人一旦把这种文字废弃了，就是把中国文化实在的基础降伏于他人了。"（50页）因不知是否是高氏1923年版原文所固有，故引用在此。

In the first edition of his book of 1923, Karlgren has a slightly different version: "If China does not abandon its peculiar script in favour of our alphabetic writing, this is not due to any stupid or obdurate conservation. The Chinese script is so wonderfully well adapted to the linguistic conditions of China that it is indispensable, the day the Chinese discard it they will surrender the very foundation of their culture." (p.41) writing, this is not due to any stupid or obdurate conservatism. The Chinese script is so wonderfully well adapted to the linguistic conditions of China that it is indispensable. (*ibid.*: 31)

事实上,早在一个世纪以前,洪堡特已经先于高本汉发现了这个问题:
In fact, Karlgren has a predecessor in Humboldt, who commented a century before him that:

> 至于中国人,他们之所以坚持排斥早已为他们熟悉的欧洲人的字母,我认为原因决不只是在于他们对传统的依恋以及他们对异族事物的厌恶,而是更多地在于这样一个事实:由于其语言禀赋和语言结构的关系,中国人还没有悟识到对一种拼音文字的内在需要。要不是这样,中国人以其特有的高度发达的发明才能,并借助其已有文字符号,想必自己就能构造出一种真正意义的、完整和纯粹的字母体系,而不是像现在这样只是把语音符号当作辅助手段。(洪堡特,1824: 68/79)

> The fact that the Chinese continue so tenaciously to reject the European alphabets they have known so long by no means has its origins solely in their devotion to their own traditions and their aversion to what is foreign. Rather it is due much more to the capacity of their language and its structure that no inner need for the alphabetic script arose. If this were not the case, then the inventiveness they exhibit so greatly, as well as their own written signs themselves, would have brought them to the point where they not only, as is now the case, use phonetic symbols merely as an auxiliary device, but also to the point where they would have created complete, true, and pure alphabet. (Humboldt, 1824: 68)

高本汉还提出,正是汉字的特殊性造成了汉语的言文分家:汉语语音的简化造成了同音词增多,表义不表音的汉字正好可起区别同音词的作用,结果在西文与拼音文字语言的口语和书面语里会搅得一团糟的同音词问题在汉语里不会发生。但却造成了言文分家,在书面上一个"意"字就可以表达的东西,在口语中却必须说成"意思"两个音节。其结果是造成了一种简明的文体。(同上,26)他进一步认为这并不一定是坏事:

Karlgren further comments that it is the peculiarity of Chinese script that has brought about the split into a literary form and a colloquial form. Because of sound-simplification and its result, the multiplication of homophones, Chinese script, which is symbolic and not phonetic, is perfect in distinguishing the homophones in writing. So, Chinese will never have to face the problem of alphabetic script where homophones are quite indistinguishable in writing as in speech. However, the Chinese will have to live with the fact that while in writing the simple "*yi*" (意) for "meaning" is sufficient, it came to be inadequate in speech and has to be amplified into "*yisi*" (意思). As a result, a new colloquial style of writing is formed (*ibid.*: 26). This is not necessarily bad, as Karlgren writes:

> 不管中国在口头上有多少种不同的方言，整个国家却只有一种共同的书面语、书面的世界语。了解这种语言有很大的实用价值，这不但可使说着不同方言的人能自由交际，还能跟历代的古人亲密接触，而这是我们难以办到的……几千年的文献，对中国人来说都是开放的，中国人无比热爱他们的传统文化，可能跟其书面语的特殊性有关。（同上，28）

> While there is any number of different colloquial idioms in China, the whole population possessed in its old literary style a common book language, a written Esperanto, a knowledge of which had great practical value. Not only were the Chinese able, thanks to this excellent medium, to keep in contact with each other in spite of all the various dialects…they were also capable of communicating intimately with the Chinese of past ages in a way that we can hardly realize…To the Chinese the literature of millenniums was open; his unrivalled love for and knowledge of the ancient culture of his country was largely due to the peculiar nature of his literary language. (*ibid.*: 28)

这一见解，对后来郭绍虞强烈主张区别文字语和声音语无疑有着启示意义。
This particular opinion has probably influenced Guo Shaoyu who was a strong advocate for differentiating written and verbal forms.

2.4.2 第二期对比研究的要点
2.4.2 Highlights of Phase 2

从对比语言学的角度看,这一时期在下面这些方面的探索值得注意。
From the contrastive point of view, the following explorations are noteworthy.

2.4.2.1 在对比研究中要不要有所侧重?——关注弱势语言的诉求
2.4.2.1 The issue of preference: discernible demand from less prestigious languages

这一期最值得注意的观点是对关注汉语特点的强烈呼吁。从普通语言学的角度看,我们可以把它解读为:在对比中要强调对弱势语言的个性的关注。

We mentioned earlier that the theme for this phase focuses on the characteristics of the Chinese language. From the general linguistics point of view, we could interpret this urge as a call for contrastive studies to pay greater attention to the individuality of languages that are less dominant.

理想的语言对比,被用来比较的两种语言之间应该是平行的关系。但实际上,由于政治、经济、军事、历史、文化等各种原因,语言间并不能做到真正的平等。在"传教士语法"中,宗主国的语言处于强势地位;在"引进"性质的语言研究中,理论被引进的语言处于强势地位。当前世界上英语相对于任何语言均处于强势地位。在以英语为一方、别的语言为另一方的语言对比中,两者地位不可能是完全平等的。在19世纪末以来的汉外对比研究中,西方语言特别是拉丁语和后来的英语对汉语拥有无可置疑的强势地位,西方语言的语法特点和规律常被不恰当地强调,而汉语的特点常被有意无意地漠视。在所谓的"模仿语法"里,这种情况就更为普遍。因此反"模仿"的一方强调要"注意汉语特点"的呼求,应该看作是对比语言学研究中体现的一种重要思想。这种思想不大可能在西方语言间的对比研究中产生,因为很多西方语言本身已有较成熟的语法体系,其"弱势"相对来说并不明显。只有在需要借鉴西方语法来"创建"自身语法的语言中才会对此有强烈感受。这一思想产生在汉语中,并在一个世纪中成为此起彼伏的声浪,不是偶然的。放在世界范围内考虑这样一种诉求,应该说具有普通语言学的意义。

Ideally, language contrast should be applied to languages that are parallel in status. Ironically, for reasons of politics, economics, military, history and culture among others, no two languages can be treated on level ground. In missionary grammars, language of the suzerain rules; in linguistic research of an "induction" nature, the language that exports theories rules. Today, the power and dominance of English is unrivalled. Any contrastive studies involving English and another language can not hope to treat the two as equal. Since the late nineteenth century, contrastive studies involving the Chinese language with a Western language, particularly Latin or English, have witnessed the Chinese language in a weakened position. The characteristics and rudiments of Western languages are overly emphasized while those of the Chinese language are intentionally and unintentionally ignored, as exemplified in "grammars by imitation". As such, objections to imitation cried for refocusing on the characteristics of Chinese and this should be taken seriously in contrastive linguistics. It is unlikely that we will take notice of such a bias in contrastive studies involving only Western languages, which are mostly relatively matured language systems and the relative weaknesses are not obvious. However, the feeling is strong when there is a need to adapt from the Western framework for a structure to be constructed. It is no accident that the Chinese struggled with this thought over the past century. We should think it a valid request in the context of world languages and alignment with perspectives in general linguistics.

《马氏文通》出版之后，对它的批评要远远多于对它的赞扬。赞扬者主要称其为中国建立了第一个语法体系；而批评者则指其强以西文之法律中国。陈承泽的《国文法草创》就是第一部观点鲜明的批评性著作。他在书中提出了语法编写的三原则，第二条便是"独立的非模仿的"，在举了"中国文字与世界各国之文字有绝异者数点"之后，他呼吁说：

Mashi Wentong invited more criticisms than praise. Supporters applauded it as the first ever Chinese grammar, while critics dressed it down as imposing Western grammar on Chinese. Chen Chengze's *A Preliminary Grammar of Chinese*, the first opponent to Ma's grammar, did not mince its words. Chen proposed three guidelines to writing grammar, the second point being "a grammar in its own right, not arising from imitating some others". Following his illustrations on the characteristics of Chinese which are completely different from other languages of the world, he urged:

> 今使不研究国文所特有，而第取西文所特有者，一一模仿之，则

削趾适屦，扞格难通，一也；比附不切，求易转难，二也；为无用之分析，徒劳记忆，三也；有许多无可说明者，势必任诸学者之自由解释，系统歧异，靡所适从，四也；举国文中有裨实用之变化而牺牲之，致国文不能尽其用，五也。是故治国文法者，当认定其所治者为国文，务于国文中求其固有之法则，而后国文法脾性有告成之一日。自有《马氏文通》以来，研究国文法者，往往不能脱模仿之窠臼，今欲矫其弊，惟有从独立的研究下手耳。（陈承泽，1922：11）

Grammars overlooking the characteristics of Chinese and simply taking after Western grammars their characteristics fault in the following ways: (1) Acts of a Procrustean will not work out; (2) No appropriate illustrations to suit the transfer in grammar structure; (3) Unpractical explanations serve only to tax the memory; (4) Arbitrary explanations on the numerous unexplainable points tend to be confusing; (5) Sacrificing the practical changes in Chinese is as good as disabling the language. As such, grammarians have to bear in mind that they are dealing with Chinese and should seek to reveal the governing principles as it is. Only then would we have a grammar of character. Since the release of *Mashi Wentong*, the hands of grammarians are very much tied to imitating. It can be corrected only by starting from an independent research. (Chen Chengze, 1922: 11)

陈承泽宣布要从汉语着手"独立地"来研究汉语，如果真的这样做了，他的研究与我们讨论的对比研究就要无关了，然而看他自己的语法体系，却大体上仍是西方语法的格局。由此可见自《马氏文通》之后，要完全撇开西方语法那一套，另起炉灶，已变得很难。

Had Chen Chengze realized his promise of carrying out an independent research, we would have nothing to say from the contrastive point of view. Regrettably, Chen too was not able to break free from the Western tradition. It has become extremely difficult to escape the mould of the Western tradition since *Mashi Wentong*.

对《马氏文通》的批判不遗余力的还有黎锦熙，他是从方法论角度进行批评的，说：

Li Jinxi, the other scholar who has critical comments on *Mashi Wentong*, approached it from the methodological point of view:

> 偶忆王船山《俟解》中有句话:"不迷其所同,而亦不失其所以异。"可借用为比较文法研究的原则。一脚踢开拉丁文法而欲另建中华文法者,是"迷其所同"也;一手把住拉丁文法而遂挪作中华文法者,是又"失其所以异"也,——《马氏文通》是已。(黎锦熙,1933: 13)

> I recalled that the Ming philosopher Wang Fuzhi (1619—1992) has this to say in his work *Si Jie* ("Awaiting Interpretation"): "not overwhelmed by the common points and not loosing sight of the differences". We could well adapt it to be the principle in comparing grammars. To completely shake off Latin grammar and construct another system for Chinese is akin to "overwhelmed by the common points"; whereas moving Latin grammar point by point onto Chinese is akin to "loosing sight of the differences"—precisely what *Mashi Wentong* did. (Li Jinxi, 1933: 13)

他还提出了对比研究的方法论原则:
Li also proposed a contrastive principle in terms of methodology:

> 所谓比较,重在异而不在同:同则因袭之,用不着一一比较;唯其异,才用得着比较,或大同而小异,或小同而大异,或同中有异,或异中有同。(黎锦熙,1933: 13)

> In comparison, the focus is on the differences and not the similarities: common points need no comparison; we could just take it in. The differences on the other hand, require comparison: it could be a little different within a largely common point; it could be largely different with something in common; there could be differences within the common points and vice versa. (*ibid.*)

这与西方对比语言学的思想也是吻合的。但他的著作后来也被批评为"模仿",甚至比马建忠有过之而无不及。这是什么原因呢?这是因为他抱定了一个"各种语言背后有共同的逻辑"这样一个主张,在根本的语言观、语法观上,他同马建忠没有很大的区别。他说:
We see his idea above matches perfectly those of the Western contrastive linguistics. Later criticisms on Li Jinxi found his work to be aping the Western model even

more than Ma's grammar. This does not come as a surprise since in terms of the fundamentals, both on linguistics and grammar; he sees eye to eye with Ma Jianzhong that "all languages work on the same logic". Said Li:

> 思想底规律,并不因为民族而区分,句子底逻辑的分析,也不因语言而别异,所以熟悉了国语底句法,无论学习何种外国语,翻译何种外国文,自然要觉得工作容易些。(黎锦熙,1924:1)
>
> Thought pattern does not vary with ethnicity; sentence logic does not change with language. As such mastering the grammar of Chinese would allow one to pick up foreign language(s) or translate into foreign language(s) at ease. (Li Jinxi, 1924: 1)

将上述思想贯彻到他的汉语语法研究中,就出现了以英语语法为"先存之理",来看待汉语的词类、句子等,并使它们尽可能地和英语语法保持一致。结果就是我们(潘文国,2002a)指出的,"尽管马建忠的研究方法是刻意求同,而黎锦熙的研究是有意求异……但从总体来说,《马氏文通》固不能逃脱'模仿'之诟病,《新著国语文法》也只落得'英文法面貌颇浓厚,颇狰狞'之自嘲"。黎锦熙求异的结果还是回到了原地。

Applying the above into his grammar study, it is easy to understand how the "preexistent" grammar of English is being imposed onto the word classes and sentence structures of Chinese to keep the consistency. Summing up, Pan Wenguo (2002a) said "Even though in terms of methodology, Ma Jianzhong deliberately looked for the similarities and Li Jinxi deliberately sought the differences…On the whole, *Mashi Wentong* was minimized as 'imitation' while *A New Grammar of Chinese* was as Li self-mocked, ferociously tinted with English grammar." Li was only making circles on the same spot with his attempt to seek differences—this is an important lesson for us that contrastive linguistics is very much guided by language perspective.

其实主张在普通语言学指导下,独立地进行汉语研究最坚决的是胡以鲁。通常人们都说胡以鲁的《国语学草创》是中国第一部"普通语言学"著作(邵敬敏、方经民,1991),但胡氏自命其书是"国语学",而不是他自己在日本帝国大学学习的"博言"学即普通语言学,可见他更强调的是汉语学的研究。将两者结合起来,我们可以说这部书是第一部"汉语本位的普通语言学著作"，这正是今天我们所要致力的研究目标。

The most determined scholar who has made a real attempt to tread a different path under the guidance of general linguistics is Hu Yilu. Hu's *A Preliminary Study of Chinese Language* was known as the first publication on general linguistics (Shao Jingmin and Fang Jingmin, 1991: 28). However, entitling his work as "a study of Chinese language" instead of "general linguistics" he studied in Japan Imperial University, Hu shows that his focus is on Chinese itself. Putting the two together, we could say that it is the first Chinese publication in general linguistics with Chinese as the base point. This is exactly the theme of this research as well.

这部书受到缪勒（Max Müller）和叶斯柏森（Otto Jespersen）的影响，而受洪堡特的影响最深，特别强调"语言者，精神活动之结果，而亦助精神活动之发达者也"（胡以鲁，1923：44—45），而各民族语言差异在于洪堡特所说的"内蕴形式"（胡称为"内范"）：

Hu Yilu's *A Preliminary Study of Chinese Language* was influenced by Max Müller and Otto Jerspersen and, most of all, Humboldt. He stressed that "language is both the result of mental activities and the catalyst to mental activities" (Hu Yilu, 1923: 44—45), and the differences in ethnic languages are, as Humboldt has explained, the "internal forms", which Hu translated as "innerform". Hu writes:

> 此点见地之差，即各民族心意作用之差。此种心意作用，即Humboldt所谓内范"inner form"者也。内范者，对于言语之外范"outer form"而言，各民族心意作用之范畴也。由是内范之不同，乃生各民族着眼中心点之差异。各国语皆各有其特有之内范。吾国语大抵一节，多亦不过二节，以有限之音声表丰富之思想，其间相应尤为微妙。而其文字由形音意三者而构成，言语内范，探究亦易。（胡以鲁，1923：9）

Difference in viewpoint is the difference in ethnic spirituality. This spirituality is what Humboldt called innerform. Innerform, with respect to outerform, has to do with the spirituality of each nation. Variations in innerform result in variations in focus of each nation. Each and every language has its own unique innerform. Our national language is mostly monosyllabic, at times bi-syllabic. Profound thoughts are expressed with these limited sounds and it is intriguing how the forms and thoughts correspond. Our writing symbol represents a cohesive whole of form, sound and meaning. It is not too difficult to get to the bottom of our innerform. (Hu Yilu, 1923: 9)

而"内范"的研究有赖于本民族自身:
It is the responsibility of each nation to study their innerform:

> 甚矣研究外国语而欲知其语言精神之难也。不知语言之精神，漫以他语族之法则作归纳之论断，无怪其不能知厥真相矣！不得吾国语之真相，语言分类亦殆无望。而其真相之解决，则支那语国民之责任，不能望于他族也。盖发达之途既异，研究之蹊径亦自宜独辟。借鉴他语族之法则作他山之石可也，欲据以为范律则蔽矣！（胡以鲁，1923：80）
>
> We may learn a foreign language but it would be daunting to get to know their language spirit. If we try to deduce and conclude from a foreign grammar without knowing the underlying language spirit, it is no wonder we fail getting to the truth! In not knowing the truth of our language, it is entirely impossible to conduct language classification. Getting to the truth of our language is the responsibility of the Chinese, not of the foreigners. Since we each came from a different development path, it is only appropriate that a different methodology be adopted for our language study. We could well draw from the experiences of foreign grammars, but to adopt it as our standard would blind us from the truth. (*ibid*.: 80)

但不知何故，胡以鲁的影响，不但远不如马建忠，也不如陈承泽之惹人注意。后来的学者中，在强调汉语特点上走得最远的是王力。他也是从普通语言学的角度来看待这个问题的。他强调:
For some reasons, the scholastic impact of Hu Yilu was in no way comparable to Ma Jianzhong or Chen Chengze. Among the linguists to come, Wang Li has gone the extra mile to put the characteristics of Chinese in the limelight. Wang, too, held a general linguistics perspective on this issue:

> 语法既是族语的结构方式，可见离开了族语结构的特征，就没有

语法。许多语法学上的术语，只是帮助族语特征的一种工具；如果只知道套取语法的术语，而不知道说明特征，就等于不曾谈到某族语的语法的本身。每一个族语自有它的个别的语法，和别的族语的语法决不能相同。民族和民族之间，血统关系越微，语法的相似点也越少。咱们想要为全世界创造一种普遍的语法固然是不可能；就是要想抄袭西洋语族的语法来做汉语的语法，也是极不自然、极不合理的事；许多琐碎的区分，对于汉语是多余的，而汉语结构中的许多主要的特征，却因为无从抄袭而没有表彰出来。因此，本书的目的在于表彰中国语法的特征，汉语和西洋语言相同之点固不强求其异，相异之点更不强求其同，甚至违反西洋语法书中的学说也在所不计。西洋语法书是为西洋语言而设的，它的学说不能适用于汉语，不足为它的缺点，正像我们的书是为汉语而设的，我们的学说不能适用于西洋语言，也不足为我们的缺点一般。（王力，1943/1985：23—24）

Grammar is the manner ethnic language organizes itself. Falling outside the characteristics of ethnic structure, there shall be no grammar. More often than not, grammatical terminologies are devices to help identify the characteristics of ethnic structure. Extracting the terminology without an accompanying statement of the characteristics it represents is as good as not getting at that particular grammar at all. All ethnic languages have their own grammars, each being different from another. Between the ethnic groups, the thinner the relations in bloodline, the further apart their grammars are. Not to say that it is impossible to create a universal grammar for the whole world, to think of duplicating grammars of the Western languages for Chinese is not only unnatural but unreasonable. On the one hand, grammars of Western languages comprise many trivial classes irrelevant to Chinese; on the other hand, most important structural characteristics of Chinese fail to be presented by way of copying. As such, it is the intention of this volume to illuminate the distinctive characteristics of Chinese grammar. We shall not force a difference upon the common points shared among Chinese and Western languages. Neither shall we force something common out of the differences to the extent of twisting the Western grammar. Western grammars are designed for Western languages; we find no fault in them for not suiting Chinese. Likewise, our grammar is meant for Chinese and we find no fault in it for not suiting the Western languages. (Wang Li, 1943/1985: 23—24)

在《中国语法理论》里,他更把矛头指向了各语言间共同的"词类划分法及术语",说:

In his *Theory of Chinese Grammar*, Wang Li criticizes standardizing of word class classification and grammar terminology among languages:

> 像这样的一部中国语法书,分类法及术语部分都和西洋语法书相差颇远,如果先学中国的,则将来再学西洋语言有些地方竟须另起炉灶。如果同时并存,也有混杂的危险。这是关于实用上的困难问题。本来做学问就只顾真理,不顾其他。中国语法如果需要这种分类法和术语,咱们决不因为它们和西洋语法不同而有所迁就。何况专就实用而论,我们也只看见利多而害少。中国学生说起西洋语言来,往往是"中国式"的,这就因为他太注意词汇上的不同,而忽略语法上的不同。如果咱们借分类法和术语的不同,令他们明白中西语法的差异实在很大,将来他们学西洋语言(或写文章)的时候,就会知道完全换上一套语言习惯了。这样,不是利多而害少吗?(王力,1944—1945/1984: 9)

> Grammar of Chinese like this particular one adopted a classification method and a set of terminology quite different from those in the Western grammars. If someone were to learn this first, they may have to start all over again when they get in touch with Western languages. However, putting two sets together would be at the peril of confusion. This is the problem in practice. Actually in academic, it's the truth we care about, nothing else should bother. If the case is determined that a different set of terminology and another classification method are necessary for the description of Chinese grammar, we shall not compromise simply because they are not used in Western grammars, in terms of practicality, there are more pros than cons. Very often, we hear Chinese students speaking Western language in "Chinese style" for the very reason that they have traded off grammatical structure with vocabulary. If by the used of a different classification and terminology, we help to highlight to them the great differences in between, they will get used

to switching to another set of language habit when they have to pick up a Western language (or writing for that matter). Isn't it more beneficial? (Wang Li, 1944—1945/1984: 9 Note)

而他的书中发掘出的"汉语特点",提出的新概念、新术语、新理论也确是超越了同辈和后来的很多人。他和吕叔湘(1942)、高名凯(1948)的著作同被誉为中国语法研究史上的高峰,这不是偶然的。

In this volume, Wang Li has unearthed many characteristics of Chinese, more so than his peers and many more others to come. His insight into new concepts, new terminologies and new theories scaled a height few can match. It is more than convincing that Wang Li's work, together with Lü Shuxiang (1942) and Gao Mingkai (1948), is regarded as representing the height in research on Chinese grammar.

王力是清华国学院的研究生。虽然他师从赵元任,但探究他思想的来源,却不得不提到清华国学院四大导师中的另一位,陈寅恪。陈寅恪于1933年写了一篇《与刘叔雅论国文试题书》,对比较语言学和汉语语法研究提出了很多尖锐的意见,其中有的与王力很近似,有的则比王力更激进。他可以说是个比较彻底的语法个性论者,他说:

Wang Li was a postgraduate at the Tsing Hua Institute for national Culture. Although he was understudying with renowned linguist Chao Yuen-ren, he was also greatly influenced by Chen Yinke, one of the four big masters at the Institute. Chen had written an article in 1933 ("On Setting Test Questions for the Chinese Language—A letter to Liu Wendian") where he raised many critical questions on comparative linguistics and research in Chinese grammar. We can still see traces of it in Wang Li, although some of the more extreme views of Chen have been dropped. Chen, being a complete supporter of "to each language, its own grammar", does not believe in a grammar that can govern all languages. He remarked:

> 夫所谓某种语言之文法者,其中一小部分,属于世界语言之公律,除此之外,其大部分皆由研究此种语言之特殊现象,归纳为若干通则,成立一有独立个性之统系学说,定为此特种语言之规律,并非根据某一特种语言之规律,即能推之以概括万族,放诸四海而皆准者也。(陈寅恪,1933/1998:243—244)

For the grammar of a particular language, only a small part of which shares something in common with world languages, the greater part is a law of itself summed up from a study of particular phenomena of that language. It is impossible to expand rules of one particular language to include all other languages. (Chen, 1933/1998: 243—224)

因此他对《马氏文通》采取了几乎全盘否定的态度:
He therefore rejects *Mashi Wentong* completely:

> 从事比较语言之学,必具一历史观念,而具有历史观念者,必不能认贼作父,自乱其宗统也。往日法人取吾国语文约略摹仿印欧系语之规律,编为汉文典,以便欧人习读。马眉叔效之,遂有文通之作,于是中国号称始有文法……今于印欧系之语言中,将其规则之属于世界语言公律者,除去不论。其他属于某种语言之特性者,若亦同视为天经地义,金科玉律,按条逐句,一一施诸不同系之汉文,有不合者,即指为不通。呜呼!文通,文通,何其不通如是耶!(同上:245)

> To work on comparative linguistics, it is crucial that one has a sense of history and all who has a sense of history shall never take the foe for father, messing up the ancestry. In the past, the French having only a vague idea of our language, model after Indo-European tradition to produce grammar books for the convenience of the Europeans. Ma Jianzhong followed their suit and here we have *Wentong* and China is happy that we finally have a grammar…It takes the principles from the Indo-European grammars for granted, not only those that apply to world languages, but also those that are peculiar to specific languages, and applies each of them, one by one, on the Chinese language which is of a different language family. And where the principle does not apply will be labeled as ungrammatical. It's so sorry: "wentong", literally means a through road to grammar, but we are seeing now all but through roads! (ibid.: 245)

从对比语言学的角度看,陈寅恪、王力的主张和做法提出了一个新问题:在当今全球化的背景下,语言对比的目的之一就是为了加强不同语言和文化间的交流,因而寻求某种可以交流的共同平台是至关重要的。如果刻意突出某种语言之"异",甚至不惜采用完全不同的术语系统和分类系统,会带来什么样的问题?其"利""害"关系究竟如何?作为对比语言学者,我们在这一似乎"两难"的问题前面,能够和不能够做什么?这恐怕是我们必须回答的问题。

From the contrastive point of view, the opinions and actions of Chen Yinke and Wang Li point to a new issue: in the current context of globalization, one of the objectives for contrasting languages is to promote exchanges between cultures and languages and, for this matter, it is crucial to have a common platform for exchange. If we were to deliberately highlight the "differences" to the extent of adopting a completely new set of terminology and classification system, the necessity condition granted, what would be the resultant impact? What are the positive and negative considerations? What could or could not be done? These are tricky questions all contrastivists must seek to answer.

2.4.2.2 对比研究应该从什么出发?
2.4.2.2 What should contrastive studies begin with?

把两种语言放在一起进行比较或对比,应该从什么共同的基点出发?这也是中国对比语言学家在考虑的问题。回顾起来看,他们提出了五种答案。

When we put two languages together for comparison or contrast, what could be a common base point to begin with? This is one question Chinese contrastivists attempt to answer. There are five opinions so far.

马建忠的答案是"所以形其形而声其声,以神其形声之用"的"一成之律",即语法。黎锦熙的答案是"思想的规律",亦即"句子的逻辑的分析"。可说他们都是停留在形式或结构的层面。王力曾提到过翻译法,但他对之是持否定态度的,说:

The answer from Ma Jianzhong is grammar, where the soul of form and sound lies. Li Jinxi thinks it is the "pattern of thoughts", which means the "logical structure of the sentence". They both stopped at formal or structural level. Wang Li even thought of translation but has it ruled out:

> 但是,我们这里所要指摘的,是有意识地或无意识地,把西洋某词"译"成中国话,再把这中国话认为和西洋那一个词同一性质……

所以语法只该就一时一地的语言作个别的观察，一切的对译都是不能帮助词性或用途的确定的。（王力，1944—1945/1984: 4—5）

However, what we would like to criticize here is the idea of "translating" some Western lexis into Chinese, consciously or subconsciously, and thinks of this Chinese term as having the same attributes as the Western lexis…As such, grammar is only good for a specific period of time at a specific place. No forms of translation equivalent could possibly help to determine the word class or the function of the word. (Wang Li, 1944—1945/1984: 4—5)

相反，从吕叔湘主张通过"一句中国话，翻成英语怎么说；一句英语，中国话里如何表达"的话里，我们却感到他是主张利用翻译造成的两种文本作为对比的基础的。1977年他发表的名文《通过对比研究语法》，其中的实例就是通过翻译来进行对比的。王、吕都是中国语言学史上已有定评的大师，他们在这上面的不同是很有意思的。也是一个值得进一步探讨的题目。

On the contrary, Lü Shuxiang suggested examining "how a sentence in Chinese could be expressed in English and vice versa". This seems to be using translated texts as the basis of contrast. His well known paper of 1977, "To Study Grammar by Way of Contrast", quoted examples from translation. Wang and Lü are both great masters in the history of Chinese linguistics. It is interesting to note their divided opinions and examine further.

而王力主张先"就一时一地的语言作个别的观察"，来建立语法体系是极有见地的。西方传统对比语言学的三部曲是"描写、分类、比较"，"描写"是前提亦即要求在对比前，对所对比的语言要有比较全面准确的描写。这个前提在印欧语语言中常不是难事，而在大多数非印欧语语言中简直是无法完成的高要求。汉语中这个问题同样存在，直到今天还没有一个公认的汉语描写语法。但王力没有知难而退，他采用了一个当时还从来没有人试过的可以说是讨巧、也可以说是扎实的办法：对《红楼梦》一书进行地毯式的穷尽分析。结果产生了两项成果。其一是在纯汉语（指在受到西方语言影响之前中国人使用的汉语）基础上写出了一部汉语描写语法。其二是以之为基础，将它与受西方语言影响后的汉语相比，写出了一篇前无古人，后少来者的"欧化的语法"（《中国现代语法》和《中国语法理论》的第六章），不论在汉语研究史上还是语言影响史上都是浓墨重彩的一章。

Reverting to the quote on Wang Li above, he makes great sense in saying that a grammatical system is "good for a specific period of time at a specific place". Western contrastive linguistics has a three-step procedure of "description, classification and contrast". Description being the proposition for contrast requires an accurate and complete record of the language under examination. Compliance to this condition is not normally an issue in the case of Indo-European languages, but is a real issue for outside the Indo-European family. Chinese faces the same problem. To date, we do not have an acceptable descriptive grammar. Wang Li was not daunted. He used an untested method: combing thoroughly all phenomena found in the novel *Dream of the Red Mansion*. There were two achievements. Firstly, he managed to describe a grammar of Chinese based on pure Chinese (which is not tainted by Western influence). Secondly, using this as the base, he contrasted it with the Chinese language under Western influence and produced the first ever treatise on "Westernised Chinese Grammar" (Chapter 6 of *Modern Grammar of China* and *Theory of Chinese Grammar*). This is a chapter no one could have failed to place in historical context for its significance in Chinese linguistic research or language influence.

第四个标准是意义。明确提出从意义出发进行对比的是林语堂。林语堂是个语言文学的全才，但他作为语言学家的名声后来却为他作为文学家的名声所掩盖，其实他在语言学许多领域都作出过杰出的贡献。在《汉英对比研究一百年》一文（潘文国，2002）中，我们曾把"以实践为主的时期"分为两段，第一段"普世语法观观照下的对比研究"始于马建忠；而第二段"普通语言学观照下的对比研究"实际上就始于林语堂。在作于1923年的《研究方言应有的几个语言学观察点》一文中，林语堂提出：

The fourth answer lies in meaning, proposed by Lin Yutang. Lin was truly well versed in both linguistics and literature but he was better known as a littérateur than as a linguist. However, he contributed no less as a linguist. He wrote in his article of 1923, "The Compulsory Linguistic Points in Dialect Studies":

> 对于文法关系应做独立的语言学上的研究——何谓独立？即不为西洋（特别是英文）文法的模范所拘，好像以为英文文法的分类，便可以当作我们文法的分类。我们应该取较平正的眼光，由普通语

言学方面观察文法现象。英文中有三个"位"cases，nominative，possessive，objective，但是德文有四个，腊丁有五个，梵文有八个，Finnish有十二个。又如英文文法分voice为主动与被动，然而我们不要误会以为主动被动便是一切语言必有的分别，梵文与希腊文却有所谓中动（middle voice）或自动，梵文还有causative，intensive，desiderative的分别。所最要的就是我们不应持偏狭的态度以治中国文法，因为中国语言与西欧语言差更远了。（林语堂，1923：247）

There ought to have independent research on grammatical relations. What do we mean by independent? Not being bound by Western (particularly English) grammar or to think that the classification in English could be adapted for our purpose. We should be fair in judging grammatical phenomena from the perspectives of general linguistics. There are three cases in English, nominative, possessive and objective; there are four in German, five in Latin, eight in Sanskrit, and twelve in Finnish. In another instance, the voices in English are classified as active and passive. However, it should never be mistaken that such classification applies to all other languages. In Sanskrit and Greek for example, there is something called middle voice. And in Sanskrit, there are further changes as causative, intensive and desiderative. Given that the gap is even wider between Chinese and Western languages, it is most important for us not to manage Chinese grammar with a narrow perspective. (Lin Yutang, 1923: 247)

他特别推荐布龙菲尔德《语言论》关于形态学（morphology）的部分和萨丕尔《语言论》关于语言形式（form in language）和语言类型（types of linguistic structure）的两部分。他的见解对于开拓中国语言研究者的眼光起了很大的作用。

In particular, he recommended references in morphology by Bloomfield's *Language*; about form in language as well as types of linguistic structure in Edward Sapir's *Language*. His words of advice have greatly broadened the horizons of Chinese scholars.

1933年，他出版了《开明英文文法》一书，一时风靡全国，洛阳纸贵。此书的特点就是以意念为纲，以对比为手段，详细论述在真实的环境下如何学习英语。林语堂的语言观是意大利哲学家、美学家克罗齐的，他认为，"语法是表现的科学，一切语法形式和结构只是表达意念的手段。"（林语堂，1933：序言）他毫不掩饰他的语法书的编纂受到了法国学者布鲁诺（Ferdinand Brunot）的《思维与语言》（1922）和叶斯柏森的《语法哲学》（1924）的影响（林语堂，1933：序言）。令人惊讶的是，直到过了65年之后，我们才又一次见到这两个名字为同一位作者在同一本书里所引用，而且是为了说明同一种观点，这就是切斯特曼的《功能对比分析》（1998）。[1]我们不得不佩服林氏的远见。

His *Kaiming English Grammar* published in 1933, was very well received. The arrangement of the book was guided by ideas and illustrated with contrastive examples, mimicking English learning in real scenarios. Lin's conception of linguistics was very much influenced by the Italian philosopher and aesthetician Benetto Croce who suggested "grammar is the science of expression. All grammatical forms and structures are but means to express ideas." (Lin Yutang, 1933: Preface) In the same preface, Lin also acknowledged the influences of French linguist Ferdinand Brunot's *Thought and Language* (1922) as well as Otto Jesperson's *The Philosophy of Grammar* (1924). Around 65 years later, these two big names have been again quoted in another great work, *Functional Contrastive Analysis* (1998), by Andres Chesterman, to illustrate yet the same linguistic perspective (see Chapter 1). We have to take our hats off to the insightful views of Lin Yutang.

当前在中国对比研究领域已被广泛接受的观点，是认为对比研究有三个层次，其一是结构层次，其二是表达法层次，其三是语言心理层次。林语堂早在上世纪三十年代初就已经到达了第二层次，并且已经关注到了语言心理的层次，比起第四期搞对比的某些人在几乎半个世纪后还是停留在表面结构层次，这简直是一个奇迹。难怪1982年吕叔湘在为重印《开明英文文法》写的序中说："此书不仅解释了英语在表达相同概念时与汉语有什么不同，还深入指出了说两种语言的人对概念的理解本身就不同，从而引导学生去了解自己不熟悉的英语的思维方式。人们早就感到有必要进行英汉语法的比较或对比实用研究，这本书可说是最早最认真的尝试之一。"（吕叔湘，1982：Editor's Note）

---

[1] 参见上一章。
Refer to the previous chapter.

Currently, most Chinese contrastivists would buy in the view that there are three levels of contrastive studies: The structural level, the expression level and the psycholinguistic level. As early as in the 1930s, Lin Yutang has already dealt into the expression level and touched upon the psycholinguistic level; he is certainly more advanced than some of the scholars some half a century later who are still stuck at the structural level. At the reprint of *Kaiming* in 1982, Lü Shuxiang commented: "not only has this book explained the differences in conceptualization between English and Chinese, it has gone deeper to demonstrate the fact that speakers of two languages often hold a different understanding of the same concept. In this way, students are guided to famil- iarise with the thought pattern of English. We have long felt the need to conduct practical contrastive studies in Chinese-English and this represents one of the best efforts of the early days." (Lin Yutang, 1982: Editor's note by Lü Shuxiang)

而吕叔湘本人也是这一理论的实践者之一。他的《中国文法要略》（1942）上卷为"词句论"，下卷为"表达论"，就是分别采取了叶斯柏森提出的"从外到内"（从形式到意义）与"从内到外"（从意义到形式）两种语法编写方法。无独有偶，在他1982年写的"修订本序"里，他也同时提到了布鲁诺和叶斯柏森这两个名字。

Lü Shuxiang was himself a practitioner of contrastive theory. His work of 1942, *Essentials of Chinese Grammar* comprises two volumes, one on "Morpho-Syntactic", and the next on "Expression". Taking after Jespersen, the first volume adopted the O—I (from form to meaning) method, while the second adopted the I—O (from meaning to form) method. In the preface to his edited version of 1982, Lü too acknowledged Brunot and Jespersen.

第五个标准是语言心理。前面说过，胡以鲁受缪勒等人的影响很深，他的主张，可说是法国社会心理语言学派的主张在中国的体现。章炳麟在为胡的《国语学草创》作的序中，称赞他"本之心术，比之调律，综之词例，证之常言，精微毕输，黄中通理，用心可谓周矣"（章炳麟，1923：1）。"心术"指的就是心理学（"调律"是韵律学，"词例"是语法学），胡之书共十编，第一、第三编为"说国语缘起"、"说国语后天发展"，而第二、第四编即为"国语缘起心理观"、"国语后天发展心理观"，这种安排，在我国后来的普通语言学著作中也还没有见过。从社会心理出发，他反对语法是由逻辑决定的：

The fifth base point is language psychology. Earlier, we mentioned the influence of Müllet and others on Hu Yilu who represented the French socio-psycholinguistics viewpoints in China. In his foreword to Hu's *Preliminary Course*, eminent scholar Zhang Binglin is full of praise for the comprehensive and thoughtful organization of the work to include psychology, phonology and grammar with careful illustrations and enlightening integration with nuances well taken care of (Zhang Binglin, 1923: 1). In the ten chapters of the book, Hu devoted a few chapters to discuss "The psycholinguistic view of the origin of the Chinese language" and "A psycholinguistic view of the post-cosmic development of the Chinese language". We rarely, if ever, see a similar arrangement in later works on general linguistics. From the socio-psycholinguistic perspective, Hu is against using logic as the determinant of grammar:

> 语法之成立本非名理制定，特以心传心之惯习规约耳。习用则心理上起分化，斯为定法。法有时而参差，盖社会心理之差；法有时而变迁，亦社会心理之变也。（胡以鲁，1923：67—68）

> Grammar did not arise out of systematic and logical creation; it is the compilation of the norms in expressions passing down in words. It becomes rules when we accepted the habits psychologically. Precisely because there are socio-psychological changes, rules vary and change. (Hu Yilu, 1923: 67—68)

而心理分类，各民族并不相同，西方学者习惯于从形式出发来解释汉语，一个方法用不上，就用另一个，如开始时的"形态论"，后来的"语词之结合配置"（即所谓语序）、"主说语关系"（主谓关系）均如此，"不知形式之外亦有特长矣"。从这一理解出发，他得出了对汉语特点的认识：

We know that psychological classification varies with ethnicity. Western scholarship used to start with formal analysis on Chinese. When one fails, they will move to another method, evident by the successive switches from "morphology" to "syntagmatic arrangement" (i.e. word order) to "subject-predicate relations", etc. as Hu commented "not knowing the existence of other characteristics apart from formal structure". From here, Hu shared his understanding of Chinese:

但就形式观吾国语者，正其不知吾国语之自白也。吾国语之所以为国语者，惟其形式简单耳。简其外而充实其内，实质的意义宿于各语词之中，形式的关系的意义则寄于语词结合之际，不借音韵多大之劳，发挥思想之真义。此吾国语精神Sprachsinn之所存，即简单而明瞭也……于一音节之中作大小长短调节，使其与概念相平行，而文字更确定其倾向。虽后天之发展或为复合，或加形式，仍得保其独立而不相同化，此支那语国民之特长也。此而不知，不足与语吾国语矣。
（胡以鲁，1923：78）

Those who know Chinese only from the structural point of view are in fact exposing their ignorance of the language. Our national language, Chinese, is simple in structure but deep in meaning. Each character carries substantial meaning and the ways characters combine tell the meaning of forms. The true meaning of expressions has very little to do with phonology. This is the spirit (sprachsinn) of our national language. It's simple and clear… within one syllabus, one may vary the length of the tone to complement the ideas and confirm the shades of meaning in the character. Later development may have seen trends in compounding or other forms being added, Chinese remains as independent as it can be showing little signs of assimilation. This is the uniqueness of the language and its people. Knowing nothing of this serves to say that one is not fit to join the discussion. (Hu Yilu, 1923: 78)

胡氏之后，只有王力提到了语言心理，他称作"语像"（image verbale），这是他从法国语言学家房德里耶斯（J. Vendryès）那里借来的术语。他认为，语像的结构，说得浅些，就是人们的心理，"我们首先该注意到中国语的'语像'的结构与西洋语的'语像'的异同，而且我们该直溯到'语像'未成立时的精神行为的两个步骤：（1）分析作用；（2）综合作用。……分析作用和综合作用都可与西洋语言不同。"（王力，1936/1985：97）他以此分析了"庖有肥肉，厩有肥马，民有饥色，野有饿莩"里的四个"有"字在中国人和西方人的心理，以及中西对"马跑、马壮"两种语像的不同。这本来是很有意思的一个题目，涉及到语言与民族心理和思维方式，但不知为何1936年以后再也没有出现过，连王力自己也绝口不提了。而作为中国语言学家中唯一学哲学出身的高名凯却坚决否认语法的结构能说明不同民族的哲学思想的观点（高名凯，1948/1990：14）。

After Hu, only Wang Li touched upon language psychology, which he termed as *image verbale*, an idea he adapted from prominent French linguist J. Vendryès. The structure of image verbale for Wang Li is, in layman's terms, the psychology of people. Wang Li explains: "We should first take notice of the differences and similarities underlying the image verbale structure in Chinese and that in Western languages. And we should trace the two spiritual behaviors that lead to the formation of such image verbale: analytical behaviour and generalization behaviour… Analytical and generalization behaviours may be different as compared with Western languages." (Wang Li, 1936/1985: 97) To demonstrate the difference in Chinese and Western psychology, Wang Li illustrated with an analysis of the verb "*you*" (有), as it appeared in the Mencius text "庖有肥肉，厩有肥马，民有饥色，野有饿莩" (*pao you fei rou, jiu you fei ma, min you ji se, ye you e piao*) (In the kitchen there is fat meat; in the stables there are well-fed horses; the people have a hungry look; in the outskirts there are bodies from starvation). He went further to discuss the difference in image verbale as contained in the constructions "马跑、马壮" (*ma pao; ma zhuang*) ("Horse-run, horse-fit"). Interesting as it is on the subject of language, ethnic psychology and thought pattern, we are puzzled by the abrupt termination of discussion after 1936. Not even Wang Li ever tried continuing with this discourse. And, as the only linguist in China well trained in philosophy at the time, Gao Mingkai rejected outright the argument that syntactic structure is illustrious of ethnic philoshophy (Gao Mingkai, 1948/1990: 14).

2.4.2.3 对比研究的目的是什么？
2.4.2.3 The object of contrastive studies

　　西方第一期和第二期的对比研究有着不同的目的。第一期的叶斯柏森、沃尔夫是希望对比语言学探索语言与思维、与民族精神的关系；而第二期的对比仅旨在二语教学。中国第一、二期的对比研究其目的何在呢？从上面提到的王力的尝试可说也曾涉及到语言与民族心理、思维方式的问题，但始终不强烈，只有林语堂比较明确地谈到了这个问题。对多数语言学家来说，更强烈的是表现在通过对比寻求汉语的民族特点上。可说这是中国对比语言学家心中最重要的目的。当然语言教学也曾是目的之一。

In the west, the object of contrastive linguistics changes for Phases 1 and 2. In Phase 1, Jespersen and Whorf were hoping to explore the relations between language and thought and language and ethnic spirit. In Phase 2, it was serving the needs of second language teaching. Back in China, although both Wang Li and Lin Yutang had some discussion on the relations between language and ethnic psychology as well as thought pattern, interest in this area did not grow. To most Chinese contrastivists, the single most important objective remains as the search on ethnic characteristics in Chinese. Of course, another aim is to support language teaching.

2.4.2.3.1 语言与思维
2.4.2.3.1 Language and thought

真正看到并强调语言特点对思维影响的是林语堂。林1935年在美国出版了一本《吾土与吾民》，向西方介绍中国文化的方方面面，产生了很大的影响。1938年，在看到叶斯柏森的《英语的发展与结构》之后，加进了关于汉语是"女性气质"的一节。而在同书的另一处，他专门有一节谈语言与思维的关系，非常鲜明地提出：

It was Lin Yutang who had strong feelings about thought being influenced by language peculiarity. He reinstated the feeling in his 1935 publication, *My Country, My people*. Published in the US, the book aims to introduce Chinese culture to the West. It was very well received. In 1938, Lin added a chapter on the "femininity" of the Chinese language after reading Jespersen's *Growth and Structure of English Language*. While this may be a contestable point, we would like to highlight something else in the same book. He offered a candid discussion on language and thought as follows:

> 中国文学的媒介，亦即汉语的使用，在很大程度上决定了中国文学的特殊发展。只要将汉语与欧洲语言作一比较，人们就能看出，中国人思维和中国文学的特殊性，其实就来源于他们的所谓单音节语言。中国人说的都是像*ching, chong, chang*那样的音节，这一事实导致了惊人的后果。这一单音节性决定了汉语书面语的特性，而汉语书面

语的特性又形成了中国不绝的文学传统，甚而影响到了中国人思维的保守性。（林语堂，1938: 205）

The accident of the Chinese literary medium, or the Chinese language, has largely determined the peculiar development of Chinese literature. By comparison with the European languages it is possible to trace how much of the peculiarities of Chinese thought and literature is due simply to their possession of a so-called monosyllabic language. The fact that the Chinese spoke in syllables like *ching, chong, chang* was appalling in consequences. This monosyllabism determined the character of the Chinese writing, and the character of the Chinese writing brought about the continuity of the literary heritage and therefore even influenced the conservatism of Chinese thought. (Lin Yutang, 1938: 205)

当时与林语堂观点比较接近的是郭绍虞（见后）。但由于西方式语言理论思维的定势，林与郭的"非语言学"观点没有引起足够的重视。几十年以后，语言学家赵元任也发表了类似的意见：

At that time, only Guo Shaoyu shared some similar viewpoints as Lin Yutang and we shall come to that later. However, the viewpoints of both Lin and Guo were taken as "non-linguistic" and therefore not taken seriously in a stereotypical environment bias towards Western linguistic theory. It was only a few decades later that eminent linguist Chao Yuen-ren echoed Lin and Guo:

音节词的单音节性好像会妨碍表达的伸缩性，但实际上在某些方面反倒提供了更多的伸缩余地。我甚至猜想，媒介的这种可伸缩性已经影响到了中国人的思维方式。……我还斗胆设想，如果汉语的词象英语的词那样节奏不一，如male跟female（阳/阴），heaven跟earth（天/地），rational跟surd（有理数无理数），汉语就不会有"阴阳"、"乾坤"之类影响深远的概念。（赵元任，1975，246—47）

It might seem that the monosyllablism in the word-syllable would tend to interfere with flexibility in the expression. But in some ways it gives more flexibility. I even suspect that this flexibility in the medium had its influence on the style of Chinese thinking. The brevity and regularity of meaningful units in the language tend to make structural words and phrases fall into convenient patterns of two, three, four, five, and sometimes larger numbers of syllables. I venture to think that if the Chinese language had the words of such incommensurable rhythm as male and female, heaven and earth, rational and absurd, there would never be such far-reaching conceptions as *yin-yang*, *ch'ien-k'un* (阴阳, 乾坤). (Chao Yuen-ren, 1976: 288)

语言哲学家褚孝泉则将这一观点引伸到了结构, 说:
And linguistic philosopher Chu Xiaoquan expanded on the above:

> 汉语的形式上的规整性对概念的形成的影响,并不只是在现代社会中才有的。从汉文化的创始时以来, 政治观也好, 哲学思想也好, 常常是以一种口号式的非常简洁的对称的文字形式出现的, 如"克己复礼"、"内圣外王"、"修身齐家治国平天下", 等等。这是由汉语的内在节律性所决定的, 也是因为汉语的句式特性造成的。……形式上的规整性, 并不只是个修辞的问题, 并不仅仅是个思想的终极产品的外观形象问题。因为人们是用语言来思想的, 这种对语言形式的规整的要求, 必然深刻地影响思想本身的面貌。可以说, 要懂得中国文化和中国哲学的特性, 我们不能不注意到汉语文字上的这种齐整对仗的要求所产生的思想模具作用。(褚孝泉, 1991, 152—153)

The matching prosodic or antithetic arrangement in the structure of Chinese writing has its influence in shaping concepts long since the existence of the Chinese culture. It does not only happen in modern society. At the very existence of Chinese culture, political views and philosophical thoughts are often expressed in neatly arranged slogans, such as 4-character phrases "克己复礼" (To restrain oneself to restore the ancient rites), "内圣外王" (Inner, to demand a Sage of oneself; Outward, to rule like a true King) or longer rhythmic phrases like "修身齐家治国平天下" (Cultivate oneself, regulate the family, govern the state, and successfully rule the whole kingdom) to list only a few. This is determined by the internal rhythmic structure of Chinese as well as the characteristics in sentence formation…This matching structure is more than a rhetoric issue and much more than merely an outer image of some ultimate product in thought. People think with language. The matching requirement in form necessarily reflects upon the outlook of thought in a profound manner. We could say that to understand the characteristic of Chinese culture and Chinese philosophy, we must note how thought is being mould by the structural match required in Chinese writing. (Chu Xiaoquan, 1991: 152–153)

这才引起了人们的重视。但那已是后话了。
Only then has sufficient interest been generated on the subject.

2.4.2.3.2 对比研究与语言教学
2.4.2.3.2 Contrastive studies and language teaching

《马氏文通》的教学目标比一般对比语言学者要大，他不但是针对二语教学（中国人学外语），更寄重望于一语教学（中国儿童学母语），而且以后者为主。但他这个目标是失败的。早在1918年，孙中山先生在他的《建国方略》之一"心理建设"的第三章"以作文为证"里就一针见血地指出：

Mashi Wentong has set a target in language teaching far greater than any other contrastive linguist would have proposed, covering both second language teaching (i.e. Chinese learning a foreign language) as well as first language teaching (i.e. Chinese children learning their mother tongue) which is the main focus. This is almost destined to fail. As early as 1918, Dr Sun Yat-sen, in Chapter 3 of his *Principles of Nation-Building: Preparation in Psychology*, hit the nail on the head to say that:

> 马氏自称积十余年勤求探讨之功，而后成此书。然审其为用，不过证明中国古人之文章，无不暗合于文法，而文法之学，为中国学者求速成图进步不可少而已；虽足为通文者之参考印证，而不能为初学者之津梁也。（孙中山，1918/1956: 129）
>
> Ma claimed that his work is backed by ten years of industrious study. However, on close examination, it only serves to demonstrate that rules are adhered to in traditional writings. The learning of grammar could only be said to be a must for Chinese scholars who wish to advance faster. While it is a good reference for matured learners, it has less use for beginners. (Sun Yat-sen, 1918/1956: 129)

刘复（1920/1924：116）更直截了当地说：（《马氏文通》）"可以引导已经通得些文义的人去看古书，但他不能教会一个不通文义的人写一张纸条"。马建忠兴致勃勃，说童蒙学了他的书如何如何，其实完全不切实际。个中原因后来王力指出来了：

Liu Fu (1920/1924: 116) is even more direct when he says that *Mashi Wentong* "may guide those who already know how to read to advance with traditional texts but it will not help someone who has no background in Chinese to write even a short note". Ma did not realize how impractical he was as he happily extended his scope of targeted readership to children. Wang Li helped to see the reason:

> 本来，把本国现代的语法教本国现代的人，目的并不在要他们说话，或做文章。一切语法上的规律，对于本国人，至多只是"习焉不察"的，并不是尚待学习的。（王力，1944—1945/1984：7）
>
> In fact, to teach modern grammar to modern nationals, the aim is not to teach them how to speak or compose an essay with it. To native speakers, grammatical rules are already known without them actually learning it. It is not something they have to learn. (Wang Li, 1944—1945/1984: 7)

吕叔湘也说：

Lü Shuxiang concurred,

> 学习文法只是在学习外国语的时候最为重要。汉语是我们从小学会了的，他的文法条理已经不知不觉的印在我们的脑筋里面，无须再学习了。（吕叔湘，1942：5）
>
> Learning grammar is important in the learning of a foreign language. We know Chinese as a child; the grammatical rules are existent in us unknowingly. It is not necessary for us to re-learn it. (Lü Shuxiang, 1942: 5)

因此除了学古文的时候有一点用，语法对本族语儿童学习母语可说完全无用。至于马建忠希望通过汉语语法帮助学外语，看来也是一厢情愿，好像至今学外语的人中没有谁是这么做的。只是这种想法却延伸到了中国对比研究的第四个时期，后面将会再谈到。对二语教学真正有用的并且成功的是林语堂的研究，但这方面却少见有人总结。其原因据我们看来，是因为中国对比语言学者关注的重点始终是放在"通过对比寻找汉语特点"上的，对理论的兴趣远远超过对教学实践的关心。

For the reasons mentioned above, children of native speakers do not find it useful learning the grammar of their own language unless for the study of traditional written text. As for Ma Jianzhong's wish of using Chinese grammar to aid learning of a foreign language, there is so far no practical evidence; nevertheless, as we shall see later, this particular thought finds its way into Phase 4. As for applying contrastive studies to second language teaching, only Lin Yutang has successfully attempted this at this time. We see little discussion in this area, with concern for language teaching always deemed secondary to the search for Chinese characteristics.

2.4.2.3.3 对比研究与寻找汉语特点
2.4.2.3.3 Contrastive studies and the quest for Chinese characteristics

从陈承泽（1922）起，寻找汉语特点的呼声一浪高过一浪。这是一百年来推动汉语研究发展的根本动力，也是对比研究不断发展的动力，因为"特点"的发现只能是跟外语比较的结果。[1]这么多年来，人们谈论的"汉语特点"已不知凡几，但圈内人谈得热闹的，未必会引起汉语以外的学者的关注。真正有价值的"汉语特点"应该是具有普通语言学意义的特点，尤其是那些对现行普通语言学一些基本原理会引起挑战的特点。我们想在这方面举几个例子，以引起国内外理论语言学界的关注。下面提到的一些观点，有的已广为承认，有的则还在争议之中：

The quest to look into the characteristics of Chinese cried louder and stronger since Chen Chengze (1922). It has motivated research in Chinese linguistics in the last century and keeps driving development in contrastive studies, as only by comparisons with foreign languages are "characteristics" observable, as shown in Karlgren's discussion above. Over the years, there have been numerous discussions on the topic, but those that would attract attention are of concern to

---

[1] 高本汉就说过，"把汉语定性为单音节和孤立语，主要是通过与其他语言的比较，同时，单音的定性也考虑了汉语自身。"（高本汉，1923：14）
Karlgren (1923: 14) pointed out: "The definition of Chinese as on the one hand isolating, and on the other hand monosyllabic, is based mainly on a comparison with other languages; but, at the same time, its definition as being monosyllabic necessitates the consideration of Chinese by itself."

general linguistics, especially characteristics that would challenge the fundamentals of general linguistics. We would like to highlight a few examples here as an introduction for feedback on more valuable opinions. Some of the contentions quoted are widely accepted; some are as yet inconclusive.

（1）汉语只有句法，没有词法。前面说过，最早有这一主张的是洪堡特，但人们更熟悉的是王力。王力说：

(1) Having syntax but not morphology. While we know from earlier quote that Humboldt pioneered the view, most people are more familiar with the stand of Wang Li. Wang explains,

> 西洋古代所谓语法，本包括三部分：（1）音韵学（phonology）；（2）形态学（morphology）；（3）造句法（syntax）。后来音韵学的部分渐渐扩大，现在已经独立成为一种科学，于是现代普通所谓语法，就只剩有形态学和造句法两部分。所谓形态的部分，是叙述各词的屈折形式，例如英语"饮"字，因人称和时间的不同而有drink, drinks, drank, drunk, drinking的分别。所谓造句的部分，是叙述各词的任务和句子的结构方式，如词在句中的次序，事物关系的表现等。汉语没有屈折作用，于是形态的部分也可取消。由此看来，中国语法所论，就只有造句的部分了。（王力，1944/1984：9）

> In the older days, Western grammar comprises three parts: phonology, morphology and syntax. Phonology gradually expands to become an independent discipline. Henceforth, it is commonly known in modern days that grammar refers to morphology and syntax. Morphology describes the inflexional changes in words, saying the English word "drink" may be written as drink, drinks, drank, drunk, drinking according to person and aspect. Syntax describes the functions of different classes of words and the structures of sentences, for example, the order of words in a sentence, relations in a sentence etc. The Chinese language does not make use of inflexions and morphology can be taken out. It follows that Chinese grammar is left with syntax only. (Wang Li, 1944/1984: 9)

从陈承泽起，汉语"没有形态"就是通过中外对比得出的一个普遍结论。中国的语法学家普遍重视句法，不重词法。甚至在《马氏文通》里，尽管全书用了十章里面九章的篇幅谈词类，但他还是要强调，"是书本旨，专论句读"（马建中，1898：15，例言），而前面九章讨论词类的时候也从不讲西方语法书中见惯的形态。

Chinese having "no morphology" is a conclusion accepted within and outside China since the time of Chen Chengze. Chinese linguists focus more on syntax than morphology. Even before in *Mashi Wentong*, although nine out of ten chapters are on word class, Ma stressed that "Syntax is the subject of this publication" (Ma, 1898: 15). And it may be curious that even in the nine chapters on word classes he seldom touches upon the common morphology in Western grammars.

胡以鲁（1923）最早提出了汉语研究中句法先于词法的设想：

The research preference on syntax over morphology was first proposed by Hu Yilu (1923):

> 语法职务，约言之，分语词形式"音声"、语词实质"词品"、词句范畴之三篇，然是不过便宜分法耳……在吾辈思之，论吾国之语法，或且不如混同之而自词句始。盖吾国语为立体质，词品迄无严格之分业，定词品不免先举句以为例，若然，则何如由句说起也？（胡以鲁，1923：104）
>
> Briefly speaking, the three functions of grammar are the form of word "phonology", the substance of word "parts of speech" and syntactic categories. This is but for convenience's sake...For our grammar, I should think we may consider putting everything together and begin from syntax. This is because our national language is a cohesive whole which means to say that there is no strict division in parts of speech, to determine the parts of speech would require looking at its position in the specific sentence. That being the case, why not start off with syntax? (Hu Yilu, 1923: 104)

黎锦熙（1924）高举"句本位"的大旗，以句法统率词法。到了王、吕、高"三大家"更以讲句法为主。但像王力这样直截了当地说汉语没有句法的还不多，想是多数人对完全"违背"普通语言学还有顾忌。但前面我们看到，这正是普通语言学创始人洪堡特的观点。我们没有见到王力与洪氏有什么渊源关系，很可能这是他自己独立思考的结果。王的直率使他就像安徒生童话《皇帝的新衣》里那个天真无邪的孩子，把实话兜底掏了出来。

Thereafter, syntax is used as the base point in, for example, Li Jinxi (1924) who formalized the idea of placing syntax over morphology. By the time of Wang Li, Lü Shuxiang and Gao Mingkai, syntax is all that matters in their master works. However few were as tenacious as Wang Li to declare outright that there is no morphology. Most felt uncomfortable going "against" general linguistics—though as we see the father of general linguistics Humboldt expressed exactly the same opinion as Wang Li before. There is no evidence that Wang is influenced by Humboldt. It is the independent thinking of Wang that leads him to the same conclusion and he is being honest to himself in speaking his mind.

问题既然提出来了，普通语言学就必须考虑这个问题。本来，词法和句法的关系，在各种语言里就并不相同。古代希腊和梵文的语法只有词法没有句法；拉丁文语法里慢慢有了句法，但并不占主要地位；到了形态简化的语言如英语里句法的地位日显重要，斯威特（Henry Sweet，1891）之后英语实际已进入了句本位时代；到了乔姆斯基的生成语言学，句法成了语法的主要内容，词法（morphology）实际上已等同于构词法（word-formation）。[1]但洪堡特之后好像没有哪个语言学家肯说某个语言只有句法没有词法的。汉外对比把这个问题尖锐地提出来了，语言学家恐怕非得认真对待不可。

The Pandora's Box is now opened for general linguistics to confront the issue head on. In reality, we see different relations of morphology and syntax in different languages. Archaic languages such as Greek and Sanskrit had only morphology and no syntax. Syntax gradually appeared in Latin grammar as something minor. For languages with simplified morphology such as English, syntax played a major role. English is in fact a syntaxled language as could be seen with the release of Henry Sweet's grammar of English in 1891. In Chomsky's theory of generative grammar, syntax is essential and morphology has diminished to become a synonym of word formation. And not many linguists after Humboldt are confident enough to make clear-cut claims about the existence of morphology and syntax. Anyhow, contrastive studies involving Chinese have drawn attention to the issue and there must now be a way to handle it.

---

[1] 关于本节讲到的内容，前一半请见潘文国（1996a）《比较汉英语语法研究史的启示》（上）；后一半请见潘文国、黄月圆、杨素英（1999）《当前的汉语构词法研究》。
Refer to Pan Wenguo (1996a) and Pan Wenguo et al. (1999).

（2）汉语的实词不能分类。这是高名凯提出来的。1953年，他发表了一篇论文《关于汉语的词类分别》，在批评了主张汉语实词有词类之分的四条理由之后，强调指出：

(2) Notional words in Chinese cannot be classified. This was the idea of Gao Mingkai. His paper of 1953 discussed the word classes in Chinese and contested all arguments for sub-grouping notional words in Chinese. He concluded firmly that:

> 经过上面的讨论之后，我们可以肯定的说，汉语的词并没有词类的分别，因此研究汉语语法，就不应当仿效西洋的语法，以词类为出发点。（高名凯，1953：272）
>
> From the above discussion, we are certain in saying that word class is irrelevant in Chinese. In this light, Chinese grammatical studies should not imitate Western grammar and use word class as a starting point. (Gao Mingkai, 1953: 272)

从而挑起了一场大论战。高名凯的观点对于他自己1948年的著作《汉语语法论》来说并不新鲜，当时他就指出：
With this, a heated debate was ignited. In fact, back in 1948, Gao has already stated something along the same line in his work *On Chinese Grammar*. Then, he wrote:

> 其实汉语的特点是在于实词的语法作用和虚词的补助表明句法，并不在于实词的词类，因为同一个实词在不同的地方有不同的词类功能。单独的实词只有词汇意义是明确的。在实际的语言之中，每一个实词和其他的实词都是有关联的，完全视其在句子中的地位如何而定，它的语法作用也由此关联而被确定。所以，研究汉语语法应当注重句法。（高名凯，1948：275）
>
> The truth is that Chinese is characterized by the grammatical functions of its notional words as well as the complementary role of empty words in syntax, not by the classification of notional words. The same notional word functions differently in different sentences. By itself, it is obvious that notional word has only lexical meaning. In real sense, notional words are connected among themselves according to their roles in the sentence. Only then could we say something about its grammatical role in the sentence. All in all, Chinese grammar should pay attention to syntax. (Gao Mingkai, 1948: 275)

只是这同马建忠（1898：24）的"字无定义，故无定类。而欲知其类，当先知上下之文义何如耳"，和黎锦熙（1924）"凡词，依句辨品，离句无品"差不多，没有形成很大冲击。而他公开提出的时间正值20世纪50年代上半叶中国语言学深受苏联语言学影响、大家都在拼命寻找汉语的形态的时候，[1]这种"离经叛道"的言论理所当然地引得群起而攻之。因此说是讨论，其实高名凯一方是绝对孤立的。[2]这场讨论的结果当然以多数人同意汉语有词类之分而结束，但高名凯并没有被说服，不仅在词类讨论中写了《再论》、《三论》，就是在讨论结束多年之后，1960、1963年还接连发表文章，坚持他的意见。而企图说服他的人包括吕叔湘、王力等也自知说服力不强，例如王力只是一味的自我检讨，[3]在勉强提出了个"划分词类的三个标准"说以后又说，"应该承认，汉语词类的划分，在实施上还是有不少困难的。"（1955：62）；吕叔湘在他长达3万字的长文《关于汉语词类的一些原则性问题》中，在讨论了"结构关系、'鉴定字'、重叠、兼类、活用"等各种情况后，说："这篇文章也许会使一部分读者感到失望，因为我在最后没有端出一整套划分定当的词类来。说实在的，现在谁都还拿不出无懈可击的一套。在这个问题上，我到现在为止还

1　关于这段历史的回顾可以参看潘文国等（1993，2004）《汉语的构词法研究》第三章："加缀法的研究"。

cf. Pan Wenguo et. al. (1993, 2004)

2　张志公几十年后回忆说，批评高名凯"一个重要的原因是高先生的观点直接冲撞了当时的一位苏联汉语专家的讲法"。（见张志公，1998：474，著者按。）

Years later, Zhang Zhigong recalled that one important reason behind the attack on Gao Mingkai was because "the view of Mr. Gao clashes head-on with the stand of a prominent Soviet Union specialist in Chinese". (See Zhang Zhigong, 1998: 474)

3　王力："说汉语语法中没有形态学是错误的。我本人过去曾犯过这个错误。我一方面发现了汉语有情貌等语法范畴的存在，另一方面又接受资产阶级语言学的传统说法硬说汉语没有形态学。这是应该批判的。"（1955：55）"过去我以为词类的划分只是为了语法说明上的便利，那种态度是反科学的。说为了便利，就等于承认汉语实际上没有词类的存在。"（同上：62）

Wang Li: "It's incorrect to say that there is no morphology in Chinese grammar. I made the mistake. On one hand, I recognised the existence of aspects categories in Chinese; on the other hand, I accepted the abrupt views of capitalist linguists that Chinese is not morphological. I should be criticized for this matter." (1955: 55) "I used to think that word classification is a convenient way out to explain grammar, this attitude is not being scientific. To say that is akin to saying that word class is irrelevant in Chinese." (*ibid.*: 62)

是个寻路的人。"（吕叔湘，1954：172）因为这个问题实际上是上一个问题的继续，就像赞同高名凯观点的刘正埮说的，"汉语和印欧语系语言不一样。汉语中没有分别词的特殊形式——形态，汉语的实词就不会有词类的分别。"（刘正埮，1955：23）更为意味深长的是，在经过了几十年之后，到了20世纪八十年代，不少人又重提昔日那场争论，甚至认为高氏的观点不无道理（如张志公，1986；申小龙，1989：139）。

But the view was not too exciting since it sounded familiar with the earlier suggestions of Ma Jianzhong and Li Jinxi. Ma's grammar concluded that "Words change in meaning and therefore cannot be grouped into fix classes. It must be in a context to know the class it belongs to" (Ma, 1898: 24). Li Jinxi's grammar in 1924 also arrived at "Words by themsewes show no attribute of class which is to be determined in the context of a sentence". However, the timing was wrong. At a time when Chinese linguists, under the dominating influence of the then Soviet Union, were deeply engrossed in finding all traces of morphology in the language in the 1950s (cf. Pan Wenguo, 1993, 2004), Gao's view was certainly going against popular beliefs and invited attacks from all. It was almost a one-sided "discussion" with Gao Mingkai completely isolated. The discussion ended with all, except gao Mingkai, agreeing to having word classes for Chinese. So insistent was Gao that he continued writing papers into the 1960s to try driving his point home. Linguists like Wang Li and Lü Shuxiang, among those who tried to convert Gao, understand that they do not have a strong case and the troubled Wang Li was almost forever reviewing his own thoughts. On one hand, Wang recommended the three criteria in determining class grouping; on the other hand, he acknowledged the difficulties in applying the criteria (1955: 62). Lü Shuxiang wrote a long treatise of 30,000 characters to discuss the principles in class grouping. Giving due consideration to issues including "structural relations, 'criteria determining characters', duplication constructions, double classification, contextual flexibilities", among others, Lü admitted: "This paper may have disappointed some readers because I did not dish out a set plan for word classification. In fact, as for now, no one is capable of drawing out a perfect word classification plan. At least, I am no more than a path-finder on the subject" (Lü Shuxiang, 1954: 172). The current issue is perhaps a continuation of the last problem mentioned above. As a supporter to Gao Mingkai, Liu Zhengtan was fair to say:

"Chinese is different from Indo-European languages. Words are not differentiated by way of morphology and therefore word classification would be irrelevant for substantive words" (Liu Zhengtan, 1955: 23). What is most intriguing is perhaps the fact that a few decades later, in the 1980s, many scholars revisited the great debate of the 1950s and began to side with Gao Mingkai (cf. Zhang Zhigong, 1986; Shen Xiaolong, 1989: 139).

高氏这一理论对普通语言学的挑战也是明显的，其理由跟上一条一样。而对汉语研究的挑战则更为直接。20世纪五十和六十年代，中国学者热衷于进行语法体系的"大讨论"，其中提出了不少有意义的问题，实词能否分类就是其中之一，可惜绝大多数讨论都没有结果，不了了之了。有的问题好像有了结论，如实词分类问题，但并没普遍接受，以后更有了反复。八十年代以后，中国学者的兴趣转向跟着国外的语言理论翻新。但他们没有想到，在西方语言学里，理论尽管可以不断翻新，诸如词类之分这些根本问题他们可是从来没有动摇过的。如果汉语不具备这个基础，在最基本的一些问题上也没有取得共识，对以往的争论（其实是认真探讨）又采取视而不见的办法，只管自己的理论跟着新潮流翻转，是否担心有朝一日会被人釜底抽薪呢？

Gao has challenged general linguistics with his viewpoint for reasons as mentioned above. In a sense, the challenge to Chinese linguistics is more direct. During the great debate of the 1950s and 60s, many meaningful issues were raised, including classification for notional words. Unfortunately, most discussions were not conclusive. Issues such as word classification seem to have reached consensus, but gained only partial acceptance and run the risk of being reversed. From 1980 onwards, the interest of Chinese linguists switches with new theories overseas. It does not occur to most Chinese that in Western linguistics, novel theories may be raised time and again; no one sways on fundamental issues such as word classification. Likewise for Chinese linguistics, unless agreement on fundamental issues is reached, any future contention would run the same escapist solution. How far can we run with new theories when the fundamentals cannot stand the trial?

（3）句型的三分

(3) Three sentence-types

王力说：

Wang Li said:

现代中国语里的句子，可以分为三类：（1）叙述句；（2）描写句；（3）判断句。这三类句子的界限是颇清楚的。大致说起来，叙述句是以动词为谓词的；描写句是以形容词为谓词的；判断句是在主语和谓语之间，加系词"是"字，为连系的工具的。（王力，1943/1985：72）

Sentences in Modern Chinese can be classified into three: Declarative, Descriptive, and Judgmental. Their boundaries are clear. In brief, declarative are sentences with verb-predicate; Descriptive are sentences with adjectival predicate; and Judgmental are sentences formed by joining the subject and predicate with a copula "*shi*". (Wang Li, 1943/1985: 72)

在《中国语法理论》里，王力更明确地说，句子分为三类，恰和实词的三类相当，判断句实际上是以名词为谓词，系词是主语和谓语间的媒介，以此与描写句相区别。并根据对比，认为英、法、德等语在逻辑上也该有名句、动句之分，但在语法上却没有这种需要；俄语和汉语一样需在语法上把名句和动句分开；汉语更进一步，在名句里还要把名词作谓词的判断句和形容词作谓词的描写句分开（王力，1944/1984：76—77）。

In his *Theory of Chinese Grammar*, Wang Li made it more explicit that the three sentence-types correspond to the three substantive word classes. Judgemental sentences are really noun-predicate sentences and the copula serves to join the subject with the predicate, thereby drawing the line with the descriptive sentence-type. Contrastive studies show that logically, there ought to be noun-predicate and verb-predicate sentence types in English, French and German, only they are grammatically not required. Russian and Chinese need to separate noun-predicate and verb-predicate grammatically. Chinese further requires the division in noun-predicate as expression of judgement and adjective-predicate as descriptive (Wang Li, 1944/1984: 76—77).

这个理论大概是现代汉语研究中最广为接受、最没有异议的理论。但是人们可能没有想到这个理论对普通语言学带来的冲击。因为在以英语为代表的印欧语语法中，谓语动词是核心的核心、灵魂的灵魂，几乎整个语法大厦是建立在动词中心上的，包括近几十年国外出现的形形色色的新理论，如格语法、配价语法等等。如果句子的核心成分可以不是动词，那对整个语法理论大厦影响可就大了。而那些积极引进西方语言理论的学者们可能也没有注意到，他们引进的几乎所有理论几乎都是建立在动词中心基础上的，即使这些理论在印欧语中被证明完全有用，而在汉语中却只能说明三分之一的句子（甚至只是四分之一，因为汉语中作谓语的除了动词、形容词、名词外，还有"主谓词组"，见下条），其价值怎么体现呢？

This theory on sentence type is probably the least contested in modern Chinese linguistic research. But will it be a challenge for general linguistics? In Indo-European languages represented by English, verb-predicate is seen as core of the core. Grammar of English is almost all centred on the verb, including new theories like case grammar, valence theory and the rest. If the verb is not the core, all theories in grammar founded on it would be shaken. Chinese scholars active in introducing Western theories may or may not have noticed this. Even if these theories have proven applicable for Indo- European languages, their explanatory power in Chinese is limited to at most one third of the sentence types (or maybe only a quarter, since besides predicates made up of verb, noun and adjective, there are so called "subject-predicate" predicates—see below).

事实上，区别名句和动句的理论已逐渐被普通语言学界注意到了。二十世纪六十年代后赵元任（1968：69），以及李讷和汤珊迪（Li and Thompson, 1976）等提出的以"话题—说明型"与"主语—谓语型"相对待的新的语言类型学理论，其根本基础就是汉语的非动谓句型。[1]

It is fortunate that the difference in theories concerning noun and verb have

---

[1] 国外最早提出可用"话题—说明"分析句子的是萨丕尔（1921：35）："句子是一个命题的语言表达。它把说话的主题和对这个主题的陈述二者结合起来。"（[A sentence] is the linguistic expression of a proposition. It combines a subject of discourse with a statement in regard to this subject.）；在中国是陈承泽（1922：14）："文法上发展之径路，与西文异。如标语，如说明语之不限于动字……"和王力（1927）提出的"纲目句"："先列纲领，如命题然，后乃或述或论，谓之纲目句。"（1927/1985：21）

Sapir (1921: 35) first suggested using "subject-statement" to analyse sentences. "[A sentence] is the linguistic expression of a proposition. It combines a subject of discourse with a statement in regard to this subject"; In China, Chen Chengze (1922: 14) has an early proposal: "Chinese grammar developed in a different manner from the Western languages. For example, attributes, and comments that are not limited to verb…" Also, In Wang Li (1927), he proposed "headrope-mesh sentence": "In a headrope-mesh sentence a headrope will be set up first just like a topic, then followed with a statement or a comment" (1927/1985: 21).

been noticed in general linguistics. Chao Yuen-ren (1968: 69) proposed the "topic-comment" theory, while Li and Thompson (1976) set it against "subject-predicate" typologically. These are attempts targeted at the fact that Chinese has predicates that are non-verbs.

（4）主谓谓语句

（4）Predicate made up of "subject-predicate construction"

王力的三分被汉语学界广为接受后直接被称为"名词谓语句"、"动词谓语句"和"形容词谓语句"，后来又加上"主谓谓语句"成为汉语的四种基本句型。据赵元任（1979：57）说，最早提出主谓结构可作谓语这一现象的是陈承泽。陈在发表于1921年的《学艺》第二期上说："得以句为说明语"。即是这一观点的滥觞。其后，吕叔湘在《中国文法要略》（1942：119）里谈到，"组合式词结"在文言里可以"作表态句和判断句的主语和谓语"，其中所谓"作谓语"谈的也是这个现象，只不过极其简略。赵元任在《国语入门》（1948：35）一书里正式提出了这一观点，后经中国科学院语法小组的宣扬（丁声树等1961），[1] 被汉语界正式接受。

Wang Li's classification of sentence-types was renamed as "noun-predicate", "verb-predicate" and "adjective-predicate" after gaining wide acceptance. It was later expanded to include "subject-predicate predicate" and together, they form the four basic sentence types in Chinese. According to Chao Yuen-ren (1979: 57), it was Chen Chengze who first noticed the phenomenon of using a "sentence-like construction as the predicate" in the journal *Xueyi* Vol. 2 (1921). Lü Shuxiang later

---

1 1952年到1953年，以中国科学院语言研究所语法小组的名义在《中国语文》上连续刊载"语法讲话"，其语法思想主要来源于李荣翻译的赵元任的《国语入门》（*Mandarin Primer*）的前言部分，出版时改名《北京口语语法》。《语法讲话》后来结集于1961年正式出版，改由丁声树、李荣等八人署名，书名《现代汉语语法讲话》。

Over the period from 1952 to 1953, a series of grammatical lectures in the name of the grammar group of the Academia Sinica was published in the journal *Zhongguo Yuwen*. The main source of reference was from the Chinese version of the Introduction of Chao Yuen-ren's *Mandarin Primer* translated by Li Rong as *A Grammar of Spoken Mandarin*. This series of notes was compiled and published in 1961 in the name of Ding Shengshu, Li Rong and six others. The book title is *Lectures on Modern Chinese Grammar*.

suggested that in traditional Chinese, a "nexus" (NB: Jespersen's term) may be used "either as the subject or the predicate in a declarative or judgmental sentence" (1942: 119). Chao Yuen-ren's *Mandarin Primer* formally adopted the term "S—P predicate" (1948: 35) and it finally gains acceptance through the publication of a grammar written by members of a research group of the Academia Sinica (Ding Shengshu et al. 1961).

主谓结构可以作谓语给普通语言学带来的冲击也是可想而知的。习惯于西洋语言思维的人可能根本无法想象这一语言现象。因此这也成了对外汉语教学中西方学生最感头痛的一个语法点，连名称都感到别扭："SS—P"，怎么看也不自然。分析起来尤其棘手。1979年，吕叔湘在《汉语语法分析问题》里举了一个五重套叠的主谓谓语的例子（吕叔湘，1979：82）：

We can easily imagine the impact such predicate structure has on general linguistics. This phenomenon may be difficult for people who are used to foreign thinking patterns and became a difficult learning point in Chinese as a foreign language. Even the naming sounds awkward: "SS-P" and analysis is particularly difficult. Lü Shuxiang (1979: 82) once gave an example of a SS-P sentence with 5 levels:

<u>这事儿我现在脑子里一点印象也没有了</u>。

[This- matter- I- now- mind-in-little-impression-also-nothing-modal particle]

全句的主语是"这事儿"；在剩下的谓语部分里，"我"又是主语；再剩下的谓语部分里，"现在"又是主语。接着，"脑子里"、"一点印象"都是主语。即使普通语言学能够接受这样的语法理论和分析方法,又放到什么位置去呢?[1]

"This matter" (这事儿) is the subject of the whole sentence. The remaining is an S-P predicate. In the remaining portion, "I" 我 serves as the subject and the remaining portion is again an S-P predicate. Then, "now" (现在), followed by "mind-in" (脑子里) and "little impression" (一点印象), one by one, serves as subject in the next three levels. Say this is acceptable in general linguistics, what would be the suitable context in which to position it?

关于汉语的主语谓语问题,还有王力提出的"递系式"(王力,1944/1984:133—140)、赵元任称之为"宾语兼主语"(Object-Subject,[2] 见Chao,1948:36;李荣,1952:19)、而后来的汉语语法学家干脆称之为"兼语式"的东西,和朱德熙(1982:101)一再强调是"汉语特色"的"谓词性主语"即动词、形容词作主语的问题,好像也对西方语法学理论引起了冲击,但实际上前者曾被解释为"宾语补足语",后者曾被解释为"名物化",虽然不少人反对,但至少西方语法对此还可以勉强对付。只有"主谓谓语"是西方语法对付不了的,西方语法学如要具有"普世"性,就必须正面对待这一现象。

With regard to issues on subject and predicate in Chinese, we would like to digress to two other interesting constructions in Chinese. First, it is what we now know as the pivotal sentence. Wang Li (1944/1984: 133—140) used to call it "linked structure" and Chao Yuen-ren termed it as object-subject (Chao, 1948: 36;

1　程雨民(2003:48)认为主谓结构中的"主语"根据所处的位置完全可以分析为状语,恐怕是没有看到这个现象的复杂性。像这里的例子就不见得能分析成五重(加上"也"应该是六重)状语套叠吧。

Cheng Yumin (2003: 48) holds that the "subject" in "subject-predicate" construction may well be analysed as adverbial according to its position in the sentence. This view may be oversimplified. For instance, the explanation is probably not good for the example given here.

2　赵氏的解释是:A substantive expression may be the object of a proceeding verb and the subject of a following predicate, thus serving as the overlapping part of two telescoped sentences is also called a *pivot*. (Chao, 1948: 36)

Chao explains: "A substantive expression may be the object of a proceeding verb and the subject of a following predicate, thus serving as the overlapping part of two telescoped sentences…The object-subject is also called a *pivot*." (Chao, 1948: 36)

Li Rong, 1952: 19). It is where two kernel sentences are knitted into one with the object of the first kernel sentence doubling up as the subject of the second kernel sentence, the first verb being causative. Next is what Zhu Dexi (1982: 101) stressed time and again as the characteristics of Chinese: predicative subject, meaning verb and adjective, are also functioning as a subject in a sentence. These challenges are handled by explanation such as "object complement" in the former case and "nominalization" for the latter. Although these explanations are less than ideal and may not be accepted, at least they could be accommodated in the Western framework. However, a predicate formed by a "subject-predicate" construction is really troubling for the Western framework. In terms of universalism, this is something to be addressed.

（5）文字语和声音语

（5）"Written language" and "spoken language"

20世纪初的新文化运动主张"言文一致"，反对文言文，提倡白话文。这一声势浩大的运动在语言学界也引起了持久不息的讨论，当然多数是为白话文提供理论上的依据。对这一问题思考比较深刻并从汉语汉字乃至中国文学特点来全面观察的是郭绍虞。我们不能肯定他的观点是否受到了高本汉（见前文）的启示，但两者显然有着相通之处。高氏是从分化的来源上进行分析，郭绍虞则是从分化后的功用上进行分析。他提出了汉语中存在着"文字语"和"声音语"两种语言的特殊现象，从而形成了很多特殊的使用规律，是汉语以外的语言所不曾见的。例如他说：

Cultural Movement in the early twentieth century advocating consistency in written and verbal forms, classical Chinese was being attacked and vernacular or colloquial Chinese was promoted. For this matter, the linguistic arena was not safe from the movement which triggered a round of heated debates, most of which were in support of vernacular Chinese. Among the people involved, Guo Shaoyu stood out with his comprehensive approach on the subject encompassing characteristics of Chinese language and literature. We are unable to determine if he was in any way being influenced by Karlgren mentioned above, but we certainly see the concurrence. While Karlgren approached the subject from the cause of cleavage, Guo considered the respective functions after the cleavage. He identified the fact that two languages coexisted in Chinese: a "written language" and a "spoken language", which he thought was the cause of many particulars in usage which was nowhere to be seen in other languages. He illustrates:

> 语言是声音语,文辞是文字语,按理说,这两种只是符号的分别,应当一致而不应歧异。可是,为了中国文字的特征,一点是单音,所以可以讲整齐,讲对偶,讲调平仄;又一点是孤立,所以又可以活用,为此两种关系,所以又可以利用声音语中方言的分歧,有转注方法以使同义之字而有不同之形,有假借方法以使异义之字具同一之形。于是,更增加了修辞上俪对或变化的诸种法门。把这些法门应用到文辞上,说得坏一些就成为文字的游戏,说得好一些,又成为创造的规律。(郭绍虞,1946:112—113)

Speech refers to the "spoken language" whereas text is the "written language". By right, the two should only be different in symbols, and others should remain consistent. However, the characteristic of Chinese script is such that it may be monosyllabic for neat, antithetic, prosodic arrangement on the one hand and isolating on the other hand which would then allow for flexibilities in grammatical functioning. For these two reasons, we could make good use of the variation in dialects, as part of spoken language, so that words of the same meaning could take on different forms and words of different meanings shared a same form, increasing thus the tricks that could be played in rhetoric and couplets. Such tricks, when used in written language, are in a way, playing with words in the negative sense, or rules for creation in a positive sense. (Guo Shaoyu, 1946: 112—113)

如果说高本汉的书面语指的主要还是文言,郭更进一步推广到语体文:
If Karlgren stopped at classical Chinese when he refers to written form, Guo moved one step further to include vernacular style:

> 中国的文字假使此后不改为拼音文字,则无论如何提倡语体文乃

> 至像现在一般人所主张的符合口语的语体文，我认为总不免受文字的牵制，不容易向这目标做去，达到完善的理想。（同上，112）
>
> Were Chinese scripts remain as it is and not romanised, then no matter how hard we promote vernacular style to read as if speaking as advocated currently, I should think that somehow there would be constraints from the characters to prevent us from meeting the perfect target. (*ibid.*: 112)

从三十年代到四十年代，郭绍虞接连发表了好几篇文章，对因语言文字特点而引起的文学修辞特点作了前无古人的论述。
Guo was published rather extensively in the period from the 1930s to the 1940s and was known for his niche in exploring into literary rhetoric from the characteristics of the Chinese language and scripts.

其实更早，西方的现代语言学"创始人"索绪尔也说过一段关于汉语的很重要的话，与这个论题有关。他说：
In fact, the father of modern linguistics Saussure touched on this topic. He said:

> 对汉人来说，表意字和口说的词都是观念的符号；在他们看来，文字就是第二语言。在谈话中，如果有两个口说的词发音相同，他们有时就求助于书写的词来说明他们的思想……汉语各方言表示同一概念的词都可以用相同的书写符号。（Saussure，1916：27）
>
> For a Chinese, the ideogram and the spoken word are of equal validity as signs for an idea. He treats writing as a second language, and when in conversation two words are identically pronounced, he sometimes refers to the written form in order to explain which he means…Chinese words from different dialects which correspond to the same idea are represented by the same written sign. (Saussure, 1916: 27)

但这段话几乎从没引起过中外语言学界的重视。人们更津津乐道的是他所说的"文字是符号的符号"之类的话，而且把他对西方拼音文字的这个看法不加区别地加到汉语和汉字头上。对于这种"有选择地引进"的做法和由此产生的"理论"，实在值得人们在汉外对比的过程中进行深思。

The above quote was almost transparent to linguists both in China and the West. People are more familiar with what he said about sound-image being sign and signifier and impose what he said about phonetic languages of the West on Chinese and Chinese characters indiscriminately. In the contrastive process, we should alert ourselves on such "induction by choice" and beware of any theory that may so arise.

中外语言文学学术文库

中西对比语言学
——历史与哲学思考(下)

Contrastive Linguistics in
China and the West
——Historical and Philosophical

潘文国 谭慧敏 著

华东师范大学出版社
East China Normal University Press

目录 CONTENTS

第三章　中国对比研究简史（下）　/ 281

3.1　第三期（1956-1976）：
　　"暂拟系统"——汉语语法"共同纲领"的确立　/ 281
3.2　第四期（1977-1989）：旨在为二语教学服务的对比研究　/ 298
3.3　第五期（1990- ）：瞄准普通语言学的汉外对比研究　/ 310

第四章　对比语言学的本体论　/ 389

4.1　从历史到哲学　/ 389
4.2　对比语言学的基础论——哲学语言观　/ 391
4.3　对比语言学的学科论——目标与范围　/ 430
4.4　对比语言学的本质论——对比观与异同观　/ 469
4.5　对比语言学的再定义　/ 487

第五章　对比语言学的方法论　/ 497

5.1　方法论研究的回顾　/ 497
5.2　方法论研究的原则　/ 502
5.3　对比研究的出发点　/ 570
5.4　对比的方向性　/ 592
5.5　求同求异的方法论　/ 604

参考文献　/ 612

第三章
中国对比研究简史（下）
Chapter 3 Contrastive Linguistics in China II

3.1 第三期（1956—1976）："暂拟系统"——汉语语法"共同纲领"[1]的确立
3.1 Phase 3 (1956—1976): The establishment of the "Provisional Schema", a "Common Programme" for Chinese grammar

3.1.1 为什么要在1955—1956年之间"切一刀"？
3.1.1 The need to divide 1955—1956

在几年前的文章（潘文国，2002a）中，我们把中国对比语言学的发展只分为两个时期，第一个时期从《马氏文通》起到1976年为止，第二个时期从1977年开始到现在。本书是在此基础上，对这两个时期再作进一步的细分。其中第一个时期细分为三期。第一期主要是《马氏文通》和马派著作如章士钊的《中等国文典》（1907）等，截止到1921年只是取其便利，因为我们把第二期的开始定在1922年；第二期以陈承泽《国文法草创》和胡以鲁《国语学草创》的出版为标志，理由未必很充分，因为同时或前后还有一些别的著作也发出了同样的呼唤，[2]只是陈的态度最鲜明，影响也较大，胡的著作从历史角度看更

---

1 汉语语法"共同纲领"一词，首见于吕叔湘、朱德熙《语法修辞讲话》序。
The phrase "Common Programme for Chinese grammar" was first adopted in the preface to *Lectures on Grammar and Rhetoric* (1952) by Lü Shuxiang and Zhu Dexi.
2 如刘复的《中国文法通论》（1920）和金兆梓的《国文法之研究》（1922）。
For example, Liu Fu's *A General Programme for Chinese Grammar* (1920) and Jin Zhaozi's *A Study on Chinese Grammar* (1922).

值得重视，因此我们以他们俩作为代表。这一期的对比主要是在反"模仿"声中努力建构汉语语法体系。区分一、二两期是为了区分"求同"和"求异"的不同追求目标，一期是求同，二期是求异，这在对比研究中有重要意义，最好不要加以混淆。第二期的下限和第三期的开始，我们分别定在1955和1956年，这种分期法在汉语语法发展史上是从来没有过的，可说是破天荒的，特别是将一贯并在一起提及的"建国后几次语法大讨论"也被分开了，[1]恐怕会引起许多人的诧异以至反对。因此需要重点作一些说明。

This portion of the book on the development in China is based on a previous paper by Pan Wenguo (2003b). In that paper, there were only two broad periods, with the first beginning from *Mashi Wentong* until 1976 and the next period since 1977. Here, we would like to put in more time pockets to allow filling in microscopic details to paint a better picture. Some of these demarcations may not have sufficient grounds although there are reasons to do so, out of convenience included. More specifically, the period from 1898 to 1977 is segmented further into three. The first, marked by *Mashi Wentong* and related works such as *Intermediate Grammar of Chinese* (1907) by Zhang Shizhao, ends in 1921 for Chen Chengze (1922) and Hu Yilu (1923) to be featured in the second phase starting from 1922. This is not at all fair as there are other publications before Chen and Hu working on the same theme or concerns, only that in the historical context, Chen's has a greater influence with the strongest stance in anti-imitation while Hu's offers greater significance from the historical perspective in his effort to construct a real grammar of Chinese. On top of this apparent favouritism, a good reason for division into the two periods is to distinguish the different objects in "seeking likenesses" for Phase 1 and "seeking differences" for Phase 2. These two objects are accorded with great importance in contrastive studies and will not be confused. But what could be most inconceivable, questionable and objectionable is the decision to assign 1955 as the ending of Phase 2 and 1956 the beginning of Phase 3. As we know in the periods before and after, there was a series of great debates on Chinese grammar as a continuous progression.

---

[1] 关于主语宾语问题的第二次"大讨论"发生在1955—1956年，关于单句复句的第三次"大讨论"发生在1957年。
The second debate of 1955—1956 concerns issues on subject and object while the third debate in 1957 centred on simple and complex sentences.

Such unprecedented and seemingly illogical historiography and demarcation of Chinese grammatical development warrants detailed explanation.

1953年的"建国后第一次语法大讨论"——关于汉语的实词能否分类的讨论，到1955年基本告一段落，讨论文章汇成《汉语的词类问题》（第一、二集）、《语法论集》（第一、二集），从1955年起先后出版；从1954年开始的"暂拟汉语教学语法系统"经过两年多的酝酿、试用，到1956年正式推行，首先在1956年秋季入学的中学新生中使用。[1]这两件事在汉语语法史上有重要意义，因为前一件事标志着一个时期的结束，后一件事标志着一个新的时期的开始。以此来划界是完全有道理的。

1953 witnessed the first great debate on Chinese grammar since the birth of the People's Republic of China. It was a debate on the need to classify notional words that concluded in 1955 with a series of publications in the few years that followed, *Issues in Word Classification in Chinese* Vols. 1 and 2 (1955/56); *Essays on Chinese Grammar* Vol. 1 and 2 (1955/56). Arising from the debate, A Provisional Schema of Grammar for Teaching Chinese at High School ("Provisional Schema") was designed in 1954 and formalized in 1956 after two years of pilot testing. Both are indicative events in the grammatical history of Chinese. The first signified the close of an episode while the latter the opening of a new chapter. This consideration is not entirely without grounds.

说前一件事标志着一个时期的结束，我们要从这场讨论与前一时期汉语研究的关系上去看。上一个时期，是以反"模仿"为标志，积极构建汉语语法体系的时期。从陈承泽（1922）到高名凯（1948）无不如此。从陈承泽、黎锦熙、王力、何容、吕叔湘到高名凯，所发现的汉语最大特点，无一不是汉语没有形态，因此汉语语法研究重点在句法。高名凯1953年挑起的这一场讨论其实是这样一条汉语研究主线的顺理顺章的继续和发展，"汉语实词不能分类"的思想在前引诸家的著作中虽然没有明说，但隐隐约约都可看出来，或者可按逻辑推断出来。高名凯只是说了一句大实话。但是他天真地估计了形势，没有想到学术讨论背后的政治背景，没有想到同样一句话在五年前也许可说，在五年后就不能说，他大约做梦也梦不到讨论的结果会是这样的"一面倒"，因此他

---

[1] 笔者之一有幸是这批新生之一，因此记忆犹新。
It was first applied to the autumn admission in 1956 where the author Pan Wenguo was among the first students and therefore keeps the memory is fresh.

之至死不服是有理由的。而更使半个世纪后的我们感到苦涩扼腕的是前一时期语法研究风云人物在这场讨论中的尴尬表现。黎锦熙、王力一而再、再而三地进行自我批判和检讨，吕叔湘在"这也可试试，那也有困难"背后实际上是在打太极拳，最后打起了哈哈："说句笑话，咱们现在都是拿着小本钱做大买卖，尽管议论纷纷，引证的事例左右离不了大路边儿上的那些个。而议论之所以纷纷，恐怕也正是由于本钱有限。"（吕叔湘，1954：173）。我们再看，1956年以后这些人在干什么：高名凯至死不悔，一有机会就要谈词类问题，但此后的工作重心却转向了普通语言学和外来词编纂；王力转向了汉语史、古代汉语、汉语音韵学、汉语词汇研究；[1]连主持"暂拟系统"的张志公，其个人的研究兴趣也转向了辞章学和传统语文教育。他们都不同程度地离开了语法学。惟一留在语法学界的吕叔湘一头扎进"发掘汉语事实"的无边无际的汪洋大海，并经常以钱串子和钱的比喻谆谆教导学生也这样做，[2]这成了相当一段时期汉语语法研究的指导方针。这些事实都清楚不过地表明了一个时期的结束。

When we say that 1955 puts an end to an episode, we are considering the

---

[1] 王力在1981年哈尔滨语法讨论会开幕式的发言中特别强调他没有参与"暂拟系统"的起草："1956年定的那个教学语法——《暂拟语法系统》，现在很多人误会，以为是我参与制定的。有位同志说王力先生参加编的。我否认，没有这个事。"（见王力，1982：23）。
Wang Li denied involvement in the drafting of the "Provisional Schema" speaking at the opening ceremony of the Harbin conference on Grammar in 1981. He said: "On the teaching grammar determined in 1956, the Provisional Schema, many misunderstood that I was involved in the process. One of our fellow comrades said that Mr. Wang Li is involved. I don't agree. No such thing." (Wang Li, 1982: 23)

[2] 这个比喻出自冯梦龙《古今谭概》："刘阁老尝议丘文庄著述，戏曰：'丘仲深有一屋散钱，只欠索子。'丘应曰：'刘希贤有一屋索子，只欠散钱。'"（刘阁老，刘健，字希贤。丘浚，字仲深，谥文庄）1980年在中国语言学会成立大会上，吕叔湘谈了这个比喻，然后说："你们说散钱和钱串子哪个重要呢？当然成串的钱最有用，可是如果二者不可得而兼，那末，散钱虽然不便携带，捡起一个钱来还有一个钱的用处，光有绳子没有钱可是毫无用处。"（见吕叔湘，1980b：10）
The Ming Dynasty publication *Tales of Past and Present* by Feng Menglong has a story about two literati mocking each other. Liu Jian says: "Qiu has a house full of loose coins, he needs strings." Qiu replies: "Liu has strings filling his house, he needs loose coins." Lü Shuxiang cited this story at the inauguration of the Chinese Linguistic Society in 1980 and advised: "Which do you think is more important, strings or coins? When bundled together, coins are most useful, when we cannot get the best of both, then, even though loose coins are inconvenient, they still serve as money. Having strings alone is useless." (Lü Shuxiang, 1980b: 10)

relations of the debate with that stage of research before. Before the debate, the Chinese were busy tearing down imitation labels and preoccupied with constructing a Chinese grammar, from Chen Chengze (1922) to Gao Mingkai (1948), without exception. With the efforts of big names at the time, including Chen Chengze, Li Jinxi, Wang Li, He Rong, Lü Shuxiang and Gao Mingkai, the biggest discovery in terms of Chinese characteristics is reaffirming the absence of morphology in Chinese and channelling all energy into syntactic research. The cogitation initiated by Gao Mingkai in 1953 was in reality a natural continuity of this research tenor. Tacit between the lines in the works of all the above-mentioned, was the logical deduction that "classification of notional words in Chinese is irrelevant". Honouring it explicitly was in fact Gao's ignorance of the political background acting behind academic discussions. Until his last breath, Gao did not understand why just five years previously something that could be freely uttered could create such a drastic and completely lopsided difference five years later. And half a century later, we could not help agonizing and feeling disappointed for these big names to have had to live through the awkward predicament. We see the numerous self-criticisms Li Jinxi and Wang Li made and we hear Lü Shuxiang saying: "we could try this", "that method is not without difficulties"—they were all trying to play tactics and to laugh it off at the end of the day, and we quote Lü Shuxiang: "Tell you a joke: we are doing big business with little start-off fund. With so much discussions on going, all that we could list as evidences are that few examples by the sidelines. And it's probably because we only have this much to say, we need to discuss even more" (Lü Shuxiang, 1954: 173). Let us turn to their development after 1956: Gao Mingkai, though insistent and taking every opportunity to reiterate, switched his focus to general linguistics and the compilation of loan words nevertheless; Wang Li directed his efforts to historical linguistics of Chinese, classical Chinese, Chinese phonology, Chinese lexicology; even Zhang Zhigong, presiding over the "Provisional Schema", dedicated himself to fields of text composition and rhetoric and traditional language education. They have all steered away from grammar to different extents. The only one who has persevered was Lü Shuxiang and he encouraged his students to join him with an analogy of coins and strings for coins. "Unearthing the facts of Chinese", the life devotion of Lü Shuxiang, is to some extent the guiding principle of this period.

All these point to the fact that it is over—an episode has been closed.

"暂拟系统"的推出是汉语语法研究史上的另一件大事。我们注意到，在第二期的对比研究中，中国学者已经做出了很大的成绩，但他们这些成绩一般都是作为学者的个人研究成就，除少数以外，很少用于课堂教学，特别是中小学课堂教学。马建忠期望的让"童蒙"从一开始就学习语法的想法在他之后的半个世纪里基本上是落空的。新中国成立后，1950年5月21日《人民日报》发表短评，号召大家"都来注意文法"；1951年6月6日，《人民日报》发表社论《正确地使用祖国的语言，为语言的纯洁和健康而斗争！》，指出："我们的学校无论小学、中学或大学都没有正式的内容完备的语法课程。"号召人们学习语法、修辞和逻辑。并且从同一天开始，连载吕叔湘、朱德熙的《语法修辞讲话》，此后不久，《中国语文》杂志开始连载中国科学院语言研究所语法小组的《语法讲话》，[1]《语文学习》杂志开始连载张志公的《汉语语法常识》，出现了全国范围的学习语法、教学语法、研究语法的热潮，短短几年里，出版了上百种语法著作。在这情况下，语法体系分歧的矛盾突出了。不同的体系，其实代表了不同作者的语言观、语法观，以及对于国外理论、汉语事实等不同的理解，本来可以通过争鸣的方式，使人们的认识不断深入。但在当时急于要把语法教学推广到中小学去的形势下，没有时间进行这一工作。1954年国家决定中学语文教学"汉语""文学"分科，必须为新设的"汉语"课编写教材。在这样的情况下，教育部委托《汉语》教材的主编张志公牵头，主持制定"暂拟汉语教学语法系统"（以下简称"暂拟系统"），经过两年多的艰苦工作，于1956年推出。首先在全国中学汉语教学中全面推行，接着也推广到了高校和社会上。

The big bang in the history of Chinese linguistics is putting in place the "provisional Schema". We noticed that the contrastive studies of Phase 2 flourished with results. But those are scholastic contributions of the individual not appropriate for classroom teaching, particularly not for primary and high schools. The ideal of Ma Jianzhong for grammar learning to begin with young children was still not realized 50 years after his departure. At the birth of new China, *Renmin Ribao* (*People's Daily*) posted a short commentary on 21 May 1950 to call for awareness in

---

[1] 1961年正式出版时改为《现代汉语语法讲话》，由丁声树、李荣等8人署名。
As mentioned in Chapter 2, these were compiled and published as *Notes on Modern Chinese Grammar* in 1961 in the names of Ding Shengshu, Li Rong and others.

grammar. The paper gave an editorial comment again on 6 June 1951 entitled "Use National Language Right, Strive for Pure and Healthy Language", pointing out that: "In our school system, be it primary, high school or university, there is not an official and complete course of grammar". The editorial called for the learning of grammar, rhetoric and logic. Starting on the same day, it ran a series of articles by Lü Shuxiang and Zhu Dexi on "Grammar and Rhetoric". Not long afterwards, the journal *Zhongguo Yuwen* began running a series of articles on "Grammar" by the Grammar Group of the Academia Sinica. Yet another journal, *Yuwen Xuexi* ran a series on "Common Knowledge in Chinese Grammar" by Zhang Zhigong. In just a short while, the whole nation was in a grammar-learning fervour, and over a hundred types of grammars were made available in just a few years. It is not difficult to imagine the divided opinions among the represented views carrying a variety of language perspectives, grammar perspectives and different applications of western theories on Chinese linguistic facts. Actually, given time, reconciliation could have been reached as discussions gained deeper ground. But in an urgency to spread grammar to schools, nothing can wait. In 1954, a national decree split language teaching into two subjects: "Chinese language" and "Literature". As a new curriculum, a new set of teaching material had to be made ready and Zhang Zhigong, who had edited a teaching series, *Chinese Language*, was commissioned by Ministry of Education to draft the "Provisional Schema". The Provisional Schema was officially adopted in 1956, first in high school, then in university and the community.

"暂拟系统"的出现恐怕是世界语言和语法教学史上的一个创新，这件事情的得失很值得好好总结。按照主持者当时的设想，"暂拟汉语教学语法系统"这个名称包含着以下三层意思："它是'暂拟'的，意思是说，它不是固定不移的，而是有待改进的；它只是适用于学校的'汉语教学'的，语法研究不受此限；它只是一个'系统'，就是教学中用的这么'一套'讲法，还说不上是个严密的、完善的'体系'。"（张志公，1980a：470—471）但实际上因为没有人预想到中学统编教材可能产生的威力，因此这三个方面可说全部"事与愿违"：第一，由于教材要求相对稳定，中学教育涉及全国几千万人，更不宜常变，因此一"暂拟"就"暂"了25年，尽管"汉语""文学"分科只试行了两年，尽管25年里批评的声音不断；第二，由于中学汉语师资是高校培养的，因而为了两者衔接，高校语法教学也纷纷采取与之相同或尽可能相似的体系，"语法研究"理论上说是不受限制，实际上不得不跟着它的路子走，至少必须以它为前提或出发点，客观上造成了极大限制；第三，尽管编者认为只是"一套"说法，但由于这"一套"为几千万人所用，为千万人所熟悉，对绝大多数非专业人士来说实际上成了"惟一"的说法，[1]别的"说法"此后都淡出了，连当初威震语法界的"三大家"著作，在有了暂拟系统之后，除了少数专业研究者外，也不大有人读了。在全国绝大多数人包括知识分子的心目中，"暂拟系统"就是汉语的语法系统，汉语的语法系统就是"暂拟系统"，两者之间是可以划等号的。

The "Provisional Schema" is by any standard, an innovation in the world in the history of language teaching and grammar teaching and deserves a fair assessment. As the name implied, the Provisional Schema of Grammar for Teaching Chinese at High School has at its initial intention to mean: (1) "Provisional", to be further improved; (2) appropriate for grammar teaching in schools only, not including grammatical research; and (3) it is only a schema for instructional needs and could not be taken as a rigorous "system" (Zhang Zhigong, 1980a: 470—471). However, no one has ever really expected the far-reaching influence of a high school curriculum. So, in fact, the three intentions become good. Despite the new curriculum on "Chinese" being halted two years later, the "Provisional Schema" was there to stay for another 25 years, never mind the continuous disparagement. In addition, considering the fact that high school teachers are groomed by higher institutions, higher institutions would have to adopt the same schema for consistency. Worse still, the non-binding clause on research turned restrictive and became guiding since the schema is often taken as the proposition or the base point to begin with. Consequentially, notwithstanding that its designers think it represents merely one possible explanation; with a user population in counts of millions, it became the *de facto* model, except in the eyes of the professionals in minority. Having forced out all other models, including the three masterpieces that were holding high at one time, most Chinese refer only to the "Provisional Schema" and gradually equate the "Provisional Schema" and the grammatical system for Chinese, intellectuals alike.

---

1 不妨比较一下中国高考和美国TOFEL考试的"指挥棒"作用。
It may be interesting to compare the "guiding" effect of the higher examination of China and TOFEL of the US.

因此"暂拟系统"出现以后，不管主持者原来的初衷如何，不管支持或反对者态度有多强烈，汉语语法研究很难回到1955年之前的状况中去了。说得通俗点，在此之前是"无法无天"，人人都可以写一本书，说这就是"法"；而在此之后，是"有法有天"，你要发表什么意见，得先看看这"法"上是怎么说的，然后再说。这也是第二、三次，特别是第三次所谓的"语法大讨论"后来进行不下去，只得不了了之的一个原因。

As we can see, with the "Provisional Schema" in place, regardless of its initial intentions, regardless of the objections, grammatical studies will never return to the days before 1955 where anyone could just call their publication a grammar. Now, there is the law to refer to before you could have your free comment. In this light, it is easy to see why the two following "great" debates could not reach far.

3.1.2 "暂拟系统"在理论上的特色及带来的问题
3.1.2 The "Provisional Schema": theoretical characteristics and issues

"暂拟系统"的建立，不仅在形式上开始了一个新时期，使汉语从"没有语法"到"有了语法"，从"诸侯混战"到"定于一统"；在内容上也改变了汉语语法研究的方向，结束了近半个世纪来汉语语法研究的基本方向，而开始了一个新的方向。关于这一点，很多汉语语法研究者是不愿承认的，但是如果我们能跳出汉语语法界的圈子，从"局外人"的眼光来看，会得到一个清晰的认识。

The "Provisional Schema" is more than symbolic in its marking of a new era. Its mere presence demonstrates that Chinese has progressed from an "absence of grammar" to "having a grammar", from "divided thoughts" to "benchmarking"; and more than that, grammatical studies take on a new direction, departing from the fundamentals of the past 50 years. Not many Chinese linguistic researchers have the heart to admit this, but unless we do that, we will not see a clear picture.

我们习惯上总以为，"暂拟系统"是个综合性的系统，是对此前各家语法体系采取"取长补短"、"折衷平衡"的结果，原先各家的基本面貌照理应该还在。但是如果我们仔细比较"暂拟系统"与前此各家的体系，就会发现实际上早已貌合神离。"暂拟系统"所综合的主要是五家体系：黎锦熙、王力、吕叔湘、张志公，以及中科院语法小组的《语法讲话》，但这五家无一例外都是采取"句法本位"的,即以句法领先词法,词法在各家书里都只是偶而一提,根本不占重要地位。这可以说是通过整整半个世纪的汉语和西方语言对比形成的汉语语法重要传统,是从马建忠到王力的一条汉语语法研究发展线索。[1]然而这个传统在"暂拟系统"里不见了,"暂拟系统"赫然有着词法、句法两大块,而且是词法在前,引领句法!可见这一系统并非简单地对各家系统的"整合",而是另有指导思想,这个指导思想就是以斯大林为代表的苏联语言学。

The "Provisional Schema" was founded on five models: Li Jinxi, Wang Li, Lü Shuxiang, Zhang Zhigong and the *Lectures on Modern Chinese Grammar* by the Grammar Group of the Academia Sinica. In turn, these five models trod along the same natural line of grammatical development from Ma Jianzhong to Wang Li. Fifty years of contrastive studies involving Chinese and the western languages have evolved a syntax-based tradition and the five were consistent as syntax-based models. Morphology was touched upon sparingly. We like to think of the "Provisional Schema" as a comprehensive system, adapting the strengths, complementing the shortcomings of the various models, compromised and balanced. A careful comparison will prove this to be a wishful thinking. The "Provisional Schema" has lost the syntax-based tradition: we find both morphology and syntax in it with morphology guiding syntax. This shows that the "Provisional Schema" is not a simple "integration". It has a guiding principle behind it—the Soviet linguistic tradition represented by Joseph V. Stalin (1878—1953).

1950年7月,斯大林的《马克思主义和语言学问题》在苏联《真理报》上发表,同月,文章中译文在《人民日报》上发表,10月出版了单行本。这篇文章就成为中国语言学研究的最高指导思想,凡与此不合的就都属于"资产阶级的"、"唯心主义的",受到批判和排斥。斯大林在书中指出:"语法(词法、句法)是词的变化规则和用词造句的规则的汇集。"(斯大林,1950:17)这就为汉语中必须有词法定下了基调。其后,苏联汉学家龙果夫、康拉德

---

[1] 从这个意义上说,20世纪50年代初高名凯引发的汉语词类问题讨论正是这一线索顺理顺章的发展,但高名凯可能没有想到,讨论过程会这样的"一面倒",而黎、王等居然会"倒戈",否定自己以前的观点。

In this sense, the discussion on word classification led by Gao Mingkai in the 1950s is a natural consequence. It never occurs to Gao Mingkai that Wang Li and others would give up their previous standpoints.

等人的著作相继在中国出版，他们的观点对中国语言学界来说简直是不容辩驳的，其观点的核心就在于要不要建立词法。例如龙果夫（A. A. Драгунов）说：

Stalin's essay on "Marxism and Problems in Linguistics" posted on *Pravda* on 20 June, 4 July and 2 August 1950 became the highest order for linguistic research in China. It was translated and published on *Renmin Ribao* (*People's Daily*) in July and later as a monograph in October 1950. Incongruent views were regarded as "capitalistic" or "idealistic" and must be criticized. In this essay, Stalin states: "Grammar (morphology, syntax) is the collection of rules governing the modification of words and their combination into sentences" (Stalin, 1950: 17). This is how there must be morphology in Chinese. Following this, China published the works of Soviet sinologists: A. A. Драгунов (Alexandr Dragunov, 1900—1955), H. И. Конрад (N. I. Konrad) and others. Their standpoints on morphology were not to be contested. Dragunov said:

> 词类是语法系统的中心，它反映在词组的结构和各种类型的句子中。离开词类就不能了解汉语的结构特点，也就不能说明汉语的语法。（龙果夫，1952：9）
>
> Word class is central to grammatical system. It is reflected in the combinations of words and the types of sentences. To understand the structural characteristics of Chinese and describe its grammar, there must be word classes. (Dragunov, 1952: 9)

康拉德（Н.И. Конрад）说：
And Konrad:

> 长期在汉学界里占优势的汉语单音节性和没有形态性的错误观念使汉语遭受到很大的损害，它引起汉语的"没有语法论"，同时长期地妨碍了这种语法的科学探讨。（康拉德，1952：48—49）
>
> Long in the field of sinology, there is this very wrong concept about Chinese being monosyllabic and having no morphology. It has done harm to the Chinese language for it leads to the conclusion that Chinese has no grammar and hampered any possible scientific discussion in Chinese grammar. (Konrad, 1952: 48—49)

如果我们要了解这些观点对中国学者的影响到底有多深,我们不妨看看一位有影响的学者在批评高名凯"实词不能分类"论时所说的一段话:"……按照这种'理论'只好取消汉语语法中的词法,取消了词法意味着进入句子的单词本身并无一定的语法特征,因此也就在实质上取消了句法,最后也就不得不否认汉语语法的客观存在。"(胡明扬,1955:79)按照这个逻辑,承认汉语有语法就必须承认汉语有词法,要研究汉语语法就必须先研究汉语词法,因而在汉语语法研究中突出词法成了当时的首要选择。正是在这个背景下,上世纪五十年代出现了寻找汉语形态的高潮,而作为"共同纲领"的"暂拟系统",首先体现的是中国的语法研究者并不"共同"的词法领先原则。

To gain an understanding of how these views have changed Chinese scholars, let's look at how a heavyweight scholar dressed down Gao Mingkai's claim that notional words cannot be classified: "…complying to this kind of 'theory' we could only abolish morphology in Chinese grammar, and this is as good as saying that word by itself has no determinable grammatical characteristics. Since words are the building blocks of sentence, abolishing morphology implies abolishing syntax, thereby denying the objective existence of Chinese grammar" (Hu Mingyang, 1955: 79). Going by this logic, to acknowledge Chinese grammar, it was necessary to admit that there is morphology in Chinese, and grammatical studies in Chinese have to start with morphology. Therefore it was important to give priority to morphology in grammatical studies at that time. It is against this background that we saw a height in morphological studies in the 1950s. As with the "Common Programme", the "Provisional Schema" was quick to present something not quite within the consensus among Chinese linguistic researchers.

如果承认这个事实,随之而来的就是一个难以回避的问题:这一转变对汉语语法研究史的影响究竟如何?因为事实上只有两种可能,一是这一改变是对的,那就意味着从黎锦熙到高名凯的这四分之一个世纪的方向是错的;一是原先的方向是对的,那么这一改变的指导思想就是错的。可惜这个问题从来没有被很好回答过。五十年代是没人敢提,后来则习惯成自然,甚至很多人以为汉语语法本来就是那样的。但我们想,到了今天,不应该再回避了。[1]

---

1 这首先是个理论问题,与这些年来词法研究本身取得的成绩无关。
This is a theoretical question to be separated from any findings in morphological studies throughout these years.

If we admit to this fact, the next question that confronts us would be: how has this shift impacted on the history of Chinese grammatical studies? Well, there can be only two possible answers: the shift is right, and that means for a quarter of a century from Li Jinxi to Gao Mingkai, we had been going on the wrong track. The other answer is the opposite. The shift is wrong, and what we had been doing before the shift is not wrong. For the past 50 years, the questions have not been raised nor answered. It has been taken for granted, so much so that many tend to think that this is the true Chinese grammar. It's high time we faced it honestly.

3.1.3 "暂拟系统"对汉外对比研究的影响
3.1.3 Effect of the "Provisional Schema" on Chinese-foreign-language contrastive studies

"暂拟系统"的建立，标志着在经过了50多年的纷争之后，中国终于有了一个至少"暂时"为各方接受的汉语语法的"共同纲领"。"共同纲领"在普及语法知识、推广语法教育上的功绩是不可限量的，但对学术研究的深入、理论视野的开拓，其负面影响也是不容小觑的。对于对比研究来说更是致命的。

As mentioned earlier, after 50 years of argument, at least there is a "Provisional Schema" signifying a "Common Programme" in Chinese grammar. Its impact in raising awareness in grammar and promoting grammar teaching is not to be overlooked. However, the discernible negative impact it has on research advancement and theoretical visioning is also alarming. In particular, it has harmed development in contrastive studies.

第一，实际上标志着汉外对比研究的结束或至少告一段落
1. Signifying the termination of Chinese-foreign-language contrastive studies

上半个世纪轰轰烈烈的中外对比，目标是建立"汉语自己的语法"。现在语法体系既已建立，目标已经完成，汉外对比实际上也就宣告结束。之后尽管还有人侈谈什么中西语言之别，实际上已成了"套话"；更有许多人鹦鹉学舌，根本不懂外语或对外语知之甚少，也能开口大谈西方语言如何如何，汉语特点如何如何，但实际上已没有多少人真正关心外语如何如何，而只是在汉语材料内部打圈圈，还自以为是在"发掘汉语特色"。主观上学术研究已经没有这种需要，客观上中国社会从五十年代以后又进入了闭关守国状态，这就使"两张皮"现象的出现成了可能。事实上，从"暂拟系统"诞生之后，到"文

化大革命"结束这20余年里,中国语言学界基本上没有什么语言对比研究可言。即使有对"暂拟系统"不满的,也早已失去上世纪四十年代及以前那种从根本上追究的勇气,而只是满足于方法之争、术语之争,自以为这就是"理论研究"。在这期间惟一可称为对比研究成就的是张培基发表于1960年前后的姊妹作:《习语汉译英研究》与《英汉声色词与翻译》,但也只是实践的总结,而没有理论的阐述。吕叔湘时而有一些精彩论述,如1963年关于汉语单双音节的问题,六十年代对汉语语法中"词"是否必要的怀疑(1980:40;46),都涉及到汉语的一些根本性的问题,也是对比研究的好题目。可惜孤掌难鸣,都没有得到很好的展开。最可惜的是王力,他的《中国语法理论》在内容和质量上都不亚于叶斯柏森的《语法哲学》,是中国对比语言学的一座高峰,如果继续这条路走下去,中国对比语言学早就可以在世界语言学上占有一席之地,但五十年代后不得不终止,他本人的研究重点也不得不另转方向。王力1981年反复强调他与"暂拟系统"毫无瓜葛,想来还是对此耿耿于怀吧?

In the first half of the twentieth century, contrastive studies involving Chinese and a foreign language was almost the way to constructing a grammar the Chinese could call its own. So much for the honour; now that there is a system in place, the target has been achieved and the case is closed for Chinese-foreign-language contrastive studies. The voices we continued to hear concerning the differences between Chinese and western languages were probably from people who scarcely know western languages. And in fact, most were self-indulged in their "Chinese characteristics" illusion; few really cared about what was happening to the foreign languages. As the need for contrastive studies diminishes, China, politically, began closing up since the 1950s (and hence the emergence of the "two-skin" phenomenon). Factually, for 20 years from the birth of the "Provisional Schema" until the close of the Cultural Revolution, there was little activity in contrastive studies. Those unhappy with the schema had lost the courage to pursue as in the 1940s and before. Most happily considered that their contention in methodology or terminology could be thought of as "theoretical studies". In this period, works that could be considered as contrastive studies were *How to Translate Chinese Idioms into English* and *Imitative and Colour Words in English and Their Translation* by Zhang Peiji in the 1960s, both being summaries of practical experiences. Theoretical discussion was rarely seen. At times, Lü Shuxiang would be kind enough to share some excellent insights on fundamental issues, such as on monosyllabic and disyllabic items in 1963 and suspect of the need of "word" in Chinese grammatical studies (Lü, 1980: 40, 46). Unfortunately, one cannot clap with a single hand. It was Wang Li we felt most sorry about. His masterpiece *Theories of Chinese Grammar* has no problem holding up as high as Jespersen's *Philosophy of Grammar*, in terms of content and quality. It could be seen as the peak of contrastive linguistics in China. Should we continue to pursue from there, we could have found a place in world linguistics. However, developments in the 1950s changed all of these.

第二，对于对比研究方法论的影响

2. Impact on contrastive methodology

西方对比语言学强调被对比的两种语言都应有比较成熟的语言描写。汉语的语音、词汇都不缺这样的描写，惟一的薄弱环节是语法。现在有了一个"公认"的语法体系，自然为对比研究"奠定"了一个良好基础。但由于"暂拟系统"本身的特殊性，以之作为对比基础，可说是把双刃剑，既有好处，又有害处，如果不能正确认识和处理，可能害处是主要的。一方面，在公众及外行眼里，这是一个普遍接受的"共同纲领"，是汉语语法的代表，当然也是进行对比研究的基础和出发点；另一方面，在真正的汉语专家包括这一系统的主持者眼里，这不过是一个折衷调和、临时用来应付教学需要的权宜之物，根本谈不上科学性，也基本上不符合汉语实际，如果认为它就代表了汉语的真实面貌，在对比研究中就会产生误导。上面最后一句话说得有些危言耸听。我们且来引述"暂拟系统"及其后身"试用提要"（中学教学语法系统提要[试用]）两项工作的主持人张志公的一段言论：

One important criterion for contrastive studies is the availability of a relatively matured description of the languages concerned. In the case of Chinese, except for grammar, detailed descriptions of the phonology and lexicology aspects were available. Now that a model "commonly" recognized is in place, it seems that a "good" foundation has been laid for further contrastive studies. However, as mentioned above, this schema is the standard for the masses but not in the eyes of real linguists, including the people behind the proposal, it is nothing more than a compromised stopgap product that is neither scientific nor representative of the Chinese linguistic facts. For its special reason, the "Provisional Schema" as the basis of contrastive studies acted as a double-edged sword. Unless managed with the right perspective, the disadvantages may override any advantages and lead to misleading conclusions. On this note, we quote Zhang Zhigong, the leader of the projects on "Provisional Schema" as well as the "Outline for High School Grammar Teaching System (Trial)" ("Trial Outline"):

> 这80年来，我们的语法研究，不管哪种体系，不管哪一家，共同的不足的地方就是始终没有摆脱西方语法学的羁绊……那些西方语言学家们有的对汉语并不十分了解。他们想象中汉语也得跟他们的语言一样，也得有形式。我们的语法研究工作就是始终在这种影响下进行的，说得过火一点，可以说形式的幽灵一直在我国的语法学家们的头上盘旋着，我们始终摆脱不了这个幽灵的控制。正因为如此，我们就没有能够抓住汉语的主要特点……所以始终没有建立起在具有我们自己的特点的基础上准备的描写语法，当然也不可能在描写语法的基础上建立起教学语法。（张志公，1980b：490—491）

> Over the last eighty years, the common inadequacies in our grammatical studies, whichever the school of thought or model, is that we have never been able to shrug off the restrictions western grammar has on us…All western linguists may not have a good understanding of Chinese. They imagine Chinese to be similar to their own languages, having morphology. Our labour in grammatical studies is ever under this kind of influence. To use a not quite appropriate analogy, they are like the spirit shadowing the Chinese linguists, swirling our mind, and we are so helpless in getting out of their control. Precisely for this reason, we have not been able to capture the key characteristics of Chinese…and therefore never been able to describe our grammar based on our characteristics. And of course, we could not construct any teaching grammar based on the descriptive grammar. (Zhang Zhigong, 1980b: 490—491)

甚至在受命主持修订暂拟系统的同时，他也表示出这样一种悲观的态度：
Zhang even demonstrated his pessimisms in undertaking the task to revise the provisional schema:

> 对于现在的语法体系修修补补，理理改改，我觉得是需要的，但

是要花太大的力气，在现在体系的基础上搞出点大名堂来，恐怕会是事倍功半，结果无非是在体系分歧之中再多生出几个新的分歧而已。（同上：499）

  All these work of corrections, amendments, patching, editing on the grammar schema that we have, I think there is a real need. But that is taking too great an effort. To have something more fruitful on the present schema, I am afraid it's going to be spending too much effort for too little achievement and the end result may be nothing more than producing a few more divided opinions. (*ibid*.: 499)

对于国内外迷信汉语语法暂拟系统的人来说，这些话是不啻一帖清醒剂，是发人深省的。
What a wake-up call for all those who are blinded by the provisional schema!

  由于对暂拟系统的理解不一，在有机会进行对比研究时，就会产生两种截然不同的态度。执迷于这一体系的，就会采取简单的办法，将其作为汉语语法的代表，与西方的语法体系进行系统对比；看清其不足恃的，就会撇开其束缚，在语言事实的基础上进行探索。实际上，第四期有相当一部分对比研究者采取的就是前一种态度，而第五期的大部分对比研究者就坚决采取了后一种态度。

The difference in understanding of the provisional schema may give rise to two extreme attitudes in contrasting Chinese with another language. Those on side with the schema would simply use it as the basis for comparison with the western systems. We shall see that this is exactly how some scholars would react in Phase 4. Those who know the inadequacies would prefer to leave it to one side and go on to explore with linguistic facts. We shall see that in Phase 5 most scholars are adamant about respecting the linguistic facts.

  这里有必要对分期情况再说几句：第一、第三期的分出是从对比语言学发展角度看的宏观分类，其实并没有进行实际上的对比，只是为紧随其后的时期（第二、第四期）创造了思想上的条件。从实质来看，中国的第二期与西方的第一期相当，而第四期则与西方的第二期相当。

  Before moving on, we would like to add one more note on the demarcation. Phases 1 and 3 are really macro-evolutionary stages, rather than actual development within contrastive linguistics, but each of these phases has an impact on the respective phase that follows, i.e. Phases 2 and 4, which involve actual activities in contrastive linguistics. Phase 4 is closely related to Phase 2 of the West in many ways, as we shall see.

3.2　第四期（1977—1989）：旨在为二语教学服务的对比研究
3.2　Phase 4 (1977—1989): Serving the needs of foreign language pedagogy

1977年5月5日吕叔湘在北京语言学院作了《通过对比研究语法》的演讲，揭开了中国对比研究新一期的序幕，本书称之为第四期。这一时期关注的焦点是对外汉语教学。

On 5 May 1977, Lü Shuxiang made a speech entitled "Study Grammar by Way of Contrasts" at the Beijing Institute of Languages that ushered in a new stage of contrastive studies in China. We mark it as Phase 4 for our purposes. This is a stage that concerns predominantly the pedagogy needs in teaching Chinese as a foreign language.

3.2.1 对比语言学的"开始"期
3.2.1 The "beginning" of contrastive linguistics

中外的语言学著作，在谈到对比语言学时，一般总将拉多（1957）看作西方这一研究的开端，而把吕叔湘（1977）看作中国这一研究的肇始。经过本书的研究，我们已知道实际上不是这么回事，对比研究在中外可说都是"所从来久矣"。但大家都这么看，也自有其一定的理由。我想最重要的理由有二：一是普及性，二是自我意识性。

It has commonly been taken as read that contrastive linguistics commenced with Lado (1957) in the West and with Lü Shuxiang (1977) in China. We have contested this from the historical perspective and, by now, it should be clear where the sources are. Nevertheless, there must also be a reason for the common perception formed. For one, it could be popularization, and for two, it could be self-awareness.

西方第一期的研究主要是从洪堡特到叶斯柏森、沃尔夫等人的个人著述，洪氏的论著很晚才译成英语，影响甚小；叶氏是在全书行将结束时"偶尔"提及，好像是个漫不经心的建议，不留心就不易发现；沃尔夫由于其本人的非

"专业"性,在语言学界也容易被人忽略。拉多的为人所注意到,语言教育大家弗里斯(Charles Fries)的影响起了重要作用,这是一方面。而另一方面,更由于拉氏的书适应了二次大战后急速发展的开展对外英语教学的需要,对比研究一下子成了一项重要事业的"基础",地位随之飙升,引人注目。同样,从《马氏文通》到高名凯的汉语研究,始终是书斋里学者的案头之物,人们建立新的汉语语法体系尚且顾之不及,哪还想得到无意中进入了另一个学科领域?而吕叔湘关于对比研究的言论在此之前发表过不少,从未引起过注意,直到这时,也因为适应了正在兴起的对外汉语教学的需要,被看作是这一教学的重要理论依据,这才一下推广了开来。

At the beginning stage in the West, the concept was mainly scattered in the works of Humboldt, Jespersen and Whorf. The English version of Humboldt came late and was therefore limited in influence. Jespersen's came at the close of his volume in a rather "casual" manner that slipped attention easily. As for Whorf, he was not seen as a linguist "by profession" and was largely ignored by the linguistic circle. How did Lado get his attention? Charles Fries the pioneer educator in TEFL played an important role. Following the rise of TEFL after World War II, contrastive analysis, as an important ground, gained sudden recognition and Lado's work fitted perfectly with the development. Likewise in China, from Ma Jianzhong to Gao Mingkai, their important works were only references in the studies. At a time where all attention focused on a new grammar for Chinese, no one realized that they had unknowingly stepped into another field of study. Lü Shuxiang shared much on contrastive studies previously but caught little attention. Only at a time where the need to teach Chinese as a foreign language has arisen and contrastive analysis looked upon as the theoretical basis has contrastive linguistics been popularized and made its true entrance. It is remarkable that both in the West and in China, contrastive linguistics gets to play on centre stage through its participation in foreign language teaching.

第二,由于得到了重视,人们开始将之当作一个"学科"来研究,从名称到定性、定位,一个个问题都开始引起了人们的兴趣。西方是围绕"对比分析"、"对比研究"、"对比语言学"等名称争个不休,对其原则、基础、出发点,"比较"还是"对比"这些问题逐一进行探讨;在中国则表现为大量介绍引进西方的对比语言学的理论,从1979年到1985年,数年里发表的这类启蒙性文章竟有10余篇之多，其中不乏名家之作，如赵世开（1979）、丁金国（1981）、胡壮麟（1982）、方梦之（1983）、王宗炎（1983）、徐烈炯（1983）、伍铁平（1984）、严学宭（1984）、张志公（1985）等，还不算直接翻译国外学者的多篇文章。这些普及性的文章对学科意识的确立起了巨大的推动作用。

With its growing importance, contrastive linguistics gradually gains recognition as a discipline in its own right and discussions on its naming, its nature and scope of study, its positioning and so on increases. In the West a conclusion has yet to be reached about calling it "contrastive analysis", "contrastive studies" or "contrastive linguistics", and there are still discussions on its principles, basis and intention, as well as issues on "compare" or "contrast". In China, the rush was to introduce theories in contrastive linguistics of the West. In the six-year period from 1979 to 1985, apart from numerous translations, there were more than ten introductory papers by big names like Zhao Shikai (1979), Ding Jinguo (1981), Hu Zhuanglin (1982), Fang Mengzhi (1983), Wang Zongyan (1983), Xu Liejiong (1983), Wu Tieping (1984), Yan Xuejiong (1984), Zhang Zhigong (1985) and others. These are great efforts in raising awareness on the discipline.

3.2.2 以二语教学特别是对外本族语教学为主要服务对象
3.2.2 Targets in teaching Chinese as a second language

西方对比语言学是洪堡特、叶斯柏森、沃尔夫等提出的，但真成气候却是在二战以后，伴随着开展对外英语教学的需要；同样，中国的对比研究，虽然实际上早已进行，但正式登上舞台，却也是随着国家实行改革开放以后，开展对外汉语教学的需要。吕叔湘的报告是在以对外汉语教学为主要任务的北京语言学院作的，在谈了一通比较研究的重要性之后，他特别说到：

As China opens up and globalizes, demand to learn and teach Chinese as a foreign/second language (TCFL/TCSL) rises sharply. The presentation by Lü Shuxiang mentioned above was made at an institution whose main function is to promote the teaching of Chinese as a foreign/second language. At the presentation, Lü Shuxiang made a special remark as follows:

> 语言学院的主要任务是教外国留学生学习汉语，就在中外比较上多讲点，主要是讲汉语和英语比较。……我们教外国学生如果懂得他的母语（或者他熟悉的媒介语），在教他汉语的时候，就能了解他的需要，提高教学的效率。（吕叔湘，1977：21）

> The main task to be undertaken by the Institute of Language is to teach foreign students Mandarin. I shall talk more about the comparison of Chinese with foreign languages, chiefly between Chinese and English…In teaching foreign students, if we speak or know about their mother tongues (or some other language medium familiar to the students) it will be easier to understand their needs in the process of learning Chinese, and we may then raise teaching efficacy. (Lü Shuxiang, 1977: 21)

在中国语言学会成立大会上他又说：
At the inauguration of the Chinese Linguistics Society, he again made the point that:

> 实际教学的研究在一定程度上也需要有两种语言对比的研究做基础，这方面的工作还有待开展。（吕叔湘，1981：21）

> To a certain extent, it is necessary that research for teaching practicality should be grounded on contrastive analysis of two languages. This is an area we have yet to start working on. (Lü Shuxiang, 1981: 21)

王力也说：
Wang Li echoed by saying：

> 对外汉语教学，我认为最有效的方法就是中外语言的比较教学。要突出难点。所谓难点，就是中国人看来容易，外国人学起来困难的地方。无论在语音、语法、词汇三方面，汉语都有自己的民族特点。这些特点往往就是难点。（王力，1985：395）

> In teaching foreigners Chinese, I think it most effective to teach by contrasting Chinese with foreign languages. We have to standout the difficult points. What we refer to as difficult points may seem easy enough for us, but painful for foreigners to master. In all aspects of phonology, grammar and lexicology, the Chinese language has its own ethnic characteristics. Such characteristics often make up the difficulties for foreigners. (Wang Li, 1985: 395)

对外汉语界最有影响的学者王还说得更明确：

And the clearest signal was perhaps from Wang Huan, one of the most eminent scholars in the field of TCFL/TCSL:

> 这里所说的对比即英语的contrastive analysis。这是一种共时研究法，只研究有关语言的现代形式，目的在于发现可用于语言教学翻译等实际问题的原理。我们作对比研究的目的就在于提高教学的预见性，从而解决学生母语的干扰问题。（王还，1986: 322）

> The *duibi* we are talking here is called contrastive analysis in English. This is a synchronic methodology focusing on the current forms in languages with an aim to seek out principles applicable for solving practical issues such as those in language teaching and translation. We conduct contrastive studies to help raising predictability of pedagogical problems so that we can help student to overcome interference from their mother tongues. (Wang Huan, 1986: 322)

其后相当长一个时期，汉外对比研究首先在对外汉语界开展，最活跃的一些研究者，除理论语言学界的赵世开、伍铁平外，王还、万惠洲、张孝忠、熊文华、赵永新等都来自对外汉语界。外语界只是在后来才慢慢跟上，而且胡文仲等人侧重的首先也是外语教学。

For a long period subsequently, Chinese-foreign-language contrastive studies were led by scholars in the field of TCFL/TCSL. Among the most active ones, only Zhao Shikai and Wu Tieping were from theoretical linguistics, others like Wang Huan, Wan Huizhou, Zhang Xiaozong, Xiong Wenhua and Zhao Yongxin were involved in TCFL/TCSL. It was much later that scholars such as Hu Wenzhong and others in the field of foreign language studies joined in and they were of course for foreign language teaching.

3.2.3 微观研究与对照研究
3.2.3 Microscopic studies and "side-by-side" referencing

这个时期的研究主要集中在微观上，有的更只是语法体系的对照研究。微观既是方法论问题，又是语言观问题，两方面都走到极端便造成了第二个特色，就是只进行语法体系的对照研究。前者可能跟吕叔湘的榜样有关。

Micro-perspective is both about methodology and linguistic perspective. When both are at an extreme, we are left with a second characteristic, which is side-by-side referencing in terms of grammatical systems. In this phase, microscopic studies predominate with some concentration in cross-referencing of grammatical systems.

前面说过，五十年代以后，吕叔湘改变了以前搞体系的做法，[1]提倡并身体力行一种注重发掘事实、不忙建立体系的审慎学风。在对比研究上也是如此，1977年的那次极有影响的讲话中，他谈了"汉语和外语"、"现代汉语和古代汉语"、"普通话和方言"、"普通话内部"四个方面的比较，都是一些具体的比较。而据我们（潘文国，2002a）的统计材料，1977—1989这13年里共发表汉英对比论文392篇，绝大多数都是语音、词汇、语法、修辞、教学、翻译上的微观问题，提到句子层面以上或者涉及语言心理的加在一起不超过10%，其中只有赵世开的一篇《英汉对比中微观和宏观的研究》（1985），和钱瑗用英文写的一篇《英汉衔接手段比较》（1983）影响较大。前文的观点与詹姆斯（1980）有异曲同工之妙，[2]后文是较早引进韩礼德的语篇理论并与汉语进行比较的。

The interest in micro-perspective studies may have a lot to do with Lü Shuxiang who, instead of preoccupying himself with grammatical system constructs, turned to promote studies targeted at unearthing linguistic facts after the episode in the 1950s. His personal involvement and meticulous scholarship have been inspiring. He sets an example in contrastive studies too. In his noteworthy speech of 1977, Lü Shuxiang illustrated with concrete examples four aspects of contrastive studies: "Chinese

---

1　有人认为吕叔湘一贯不主张搞体系，这种说法也不对。《中国文法要略》（1942）和他与朱德熙合作的《语法修辞讲话》（1952）都是有其体系的。但1950年以后他确实不主张搞体系，直到1979年发表《汉语语法分析问题》才重新谈体系问题。

Some maintained that Lü Shuxiang has never had the idea of constructing a grammatical system. We disagree. Both *Essentials of Chinese Grammar* of 1942 and his co-authored book with Zhu Dexi, *Lectures on Grammar and Rhetoric* (1952), are with a system. For a period after 1950, it is true that he does not suggest constructing grammatical system, not until his paper of 1979 on "Issues in Grammatical Analysis in Chinese" that touched on problems in system constructs.

2　赵文的文献目录引了迪·皮德娄但未引詹姆斯，显然尚未读到其书。

In his bibliography, Zhao listed Di Pietro but not Carl James; he probably had not had the chance to read James then.

and foreign languages", "modern Chinese and classical Chinese", "Mandarin and dialects" and "Mandarin internally". According to the statistics in Pan Wenguo (2002a), in the 13-year period of 1977—1989, there were 392 papers contrasting Chinese with English; most were on micro-issues in phonology, lexicology, grammar, rhetoric, pedagogy and translation. Less than 10 per cent discussed issues above sentence level or involving language psychology. Among them, we would like to highlight Zhao Shikai's "The Micro and Macro Perspectives in English-Chinese Contrastive Analysis" (1985) and Qian Yuan's "A Comparison of Some Cohesive Devices in English and Chinese' (1983). The former articles shared some similar viewpoints as James (1980) and the latter applied Halliday's text linguistics to Chinese for a contrastive study.

整个第四期汉外对比研究的专门著作不多，但以"对比"或"比较"命名、堪作为这一时期对比研究代表作的一些书，如张今、陈云清（1981）、任学良（1981）、吴洁敏（1981）、赵志毅（1981）、徐士珍（1985）、万惠洲（1988）等，除了第一本外，都是这样的作品。由于对一般读者来说，书的影响比论文要大得多，这就造成一种印象，似乎对比研究就应该是这个样子的。这就引起了反弹，一些学者忍不住撰文对这做法进行了批评，如王菊泉（1982）、刘新（1983）、王还（1986）等。王菊泉从英汉语法比较的宗旨、内容和方法等几个方面对任、吴、赵的几本书进行了比较全面的评述，特别指出这些书采取的方法，"很有点像两个球队从两个门入场，走到一起，对面立定一拉手，然后分别在自己那一半场地里玩起球来，有时候你扔一个球过来，我扔一个球过去，表示一下友好，可是始终不认真进行比赛"（王菊泉，1982：75），非常形象地切中了这类"对比"的弊病。王还则针对汉语语法体系的特殊情况，提出了进行对比研究要注意的三个原则：（1）"在议论语法问题时，首先一定要分清语法概念和一般的思维概念"（王还，1986：323）；（2）"同一语法术语在两种语言中所代表的内容不会完全相同"（同上：326）；（3）"同类词在不同的语言中功能不完全相同"（同上：327）。实际上王还说的情况正是由于暂拟系统本身的问题造成的，而她提出的主张也是在这种情况下最好的补救办法。

There were not many dedicated book publications in this phase though. However, if there were any, they were mainly side-by-side referencing works on grammatical systems. Among the book titles featuring "Contrastive" or

"Comparative" which are deemed to be representative of this phase, such as Zhang Jin and Chen Yunqing (1981), Ren Xueliang (1981), Wu Jiemin (1981), Zhao Zhiyi (1981), Xu Shizhen (1985) and Wan Huizhou (1988), only Zhang Jin and Chen Yunqing could be said to be real contrasting. Others were forced analogy. To the masses, the influence of books is much greater than journal papers. This ultimately created an impression on what contrastive linguistics is all about. Reacting to this situation, Wang Juquan (1982), Liu Xin (1983) and Wang Huan (1986) were full of critical comments. Wang Juquan (1982) surveyed the works of Ren, Wu and Zhao in terms of contrastive objectives, content and methodology and commented on the methodology employed: "It's like two teams of players entering from separate doors, coming together for a hand shake and then starting the game each playing with themselves on their side of the court. At times, they will throw a ball at each other as a friendly gesture but nothing more than a real match" (Wang Juquan, 1982: 75). This is a very pertinent comment pinpointing the common shortfall. In addition, Wang Huan (1986) proposed three principles in contrastive studies bearing the characteristics of Chinese in mind: (1) "In the discussion of grammatical issues, it is necessary to differentiate between grammatical concept and general concept" (p.323); (2) "The same grammatical terminology may represent things differently in two languages" (p.326); (3) "The same word class may function differently in different languages" (p.327). In fact, Wang Huan is driving at the problems caused by the "Provisional Schema" and her proposals are intended as remedies under such circumstances.

从对比研究发展史来看，正是对这种浮光掠影式比照的不满，才推动了对比研究向第五期发展。

In the context of history, the objection to such side-by-side forced analogy has moved development into Phase 5.

3.2.4 "对比分析"为"偏误分析"与中介语理论所取代
3.2.4 Replacement of contrastive analysis by error analysis and interlanguage theory

西方第二期的对比研究，以"预测"二语教学中的难点为目标，结果因成效不大而被偏误分析与中介语理论所取代；中国这一期的情况同样如此，也是以信心十足的"预测"开始，以效果不理想[1]而被黯然取代。早在1984年，还在人们热心地提倡用对比分析来解决外语学习中学生的难点问题时，对外汉语教学专家鲁健骥就已经根据国外的研究指出了对比分析的局限性：

> In Phase 2 of the development in the West, contrastive studies was given the aim to predict pedagogical difficulties in second language teaching. The less than ideal result has led to the replacement of contrastive analysis with interlanguage theory. A similar fate confronts contrastive studies in China. It began with all confidence in its predictability and ended up in disappointment and ultimately being replaced. As early as 1984 when everyone was so eagerly solving problems of foreign students with contrastive studies, Lu Jianji, an expert in TCFL, has warned of its limitation with reference to the fate of CA elsewhere:

> 语言的对比分析理论是建立在结构主义语言学的基础上的，而结构主义语言学又以行为主义心理学为基础。50年代末，由于乔姆斯基语言学理论的出现，特别是由于乔姆斯基对语言心理的研究，行为主义心理学受到巨大冲击，认知心理学随之重新抬头和发展。以结构主义语言学为基础的对比分析，同样受到人们的怀疑。人们发现，外语学习中的偏误并不能完全地、准确地用对比分析的方法预测、解释和分析，尤其在语法和词汇方面。后来的统计资料也证明了这种怀疑是不无道理的。（鲁健骥，1984：21）

> Contrastive analysis is founded on linguistic structuralism which in turn has its root in behavioral psychology. The late 1950s saw the emergence of the Chomskian theory of linguistics in which its research in language psychology in particular was a blow to behavioral psychology. Following which, cognitive psychology regained its place in linguistics and advanced ahead. Contrastive analysis with its root in structuralism must invite similar suspicion. It was realized that errors in foreign language teaching could not be perfectly and

---

1 当然这里的情况比较复杂，不能一概而论。其中既有汉语研究自身的问题，也有教材编写、教师知识结构的问题，还有运用方法的问题。

We have to qualify the disappointment in that there are other factors complicating the situation, such as the research status in Chinese, preparation of teaching materials, knowledge structure of instructors as well as application of methodology, etc.

completely predicted, explained and analysed by ways of contrastive analysis, especially in syntax and lexicology. Statistics has also proven that we have all the reasons to be suspicious. (Lu Jianji, 1984: 21)

同时，持同一观点的科德（Pit Corder）的《应用语言学引论》被译介到中国。此后，以鲁氏为代表的对外汉语教学专家逐渐将研究重点转向了偏误分析与中介语理论，到了八十年代末，对比研究实际上就已逐渐淡出了对外汉语教学界的主流，其命运犹如1968年乔治顿圆桌会议以后的美国英语教学界。这一极其类似的命运证明汉语的研究确实已很难离开外国理论的影响，对比分析在中国由盛到衰几乎是亦步亦趋地跟着西方的脚印走的。

At the same time, Pit Corder's *Introducing Applied Linguistics* (1973), which argued along the same line, was being translated for the Chinese readers. Since then, TCFL experts led by Lu gradually turned towards error analysis and interlanguage theory. CA was completely outmoded in TCFL/TCSL by the late 1980s, just as its fate in the US TEFL after the 1968 roundtable conference of Georgetown. The similar consequences of contrastive studies in China and the West are evidence of the difficulty in keeping out the influence of western theories on studies in Chinese language. The rise and fall of contrastive linguistics in China was almost always following in the footsteps of contrastive linguistics in the West.

3.2.5 本期对比研究小结
3.2.5 Summary for Phase 4

这一时期中国的对比研究给人一种"其兴也勃焉，其亡也忽焉"的感觉，从对外汉语界开始兴起，却在多数人还没弄清是怎么回事的时候，又从对外汉语界开始悄悄衰落。这一时期对比语言学的最大成就表现在三个方面。第一，经过八十年代初的"扫盲"，使人们懂得了什么叫对比语言学；第二，通过对任氏等几本书的批评，使人们弄清了"比较"与"对比"是不同的概念；第三，通过对比分析在对外汉语教学界的由盛至衰，使人们了解了这一研究在教学领域的局限性，从而引导人们把眼光扩大到别的方面。这三个方面加起来，为第五期对比语言学在中国全面深入展开创造了条件。

Contrastive studies in this phase was sharp in its rise and drastic in its fall. It was first mooted in TCFL/TCSL, and before long, and before everyone knew what was going on, it had quietly quitted from TCFL/TCSL. Still, something was achieved in this short period of time, particularly in three areas. First of all, awareness of contrastive linguistics was planted. Secondly, critics of the books mentioned above helped sort out the concepts of "compare" and "contrast". Last but not least, from the rise to its fall, its limitation in pedagogy was made known and that led to the expansion of its scope in other areas. All these are the thrust that paves the way for contrastive linguistics to develop into greater depth in Phase 5.

这三个方面中，第二条尤其值得一提，这可以说是吕叔湘对中国、也是对世界对比语言学的一个贡献。从四十年代到八十年代，吕叔湘三次谈到"比较"和"比附"的问题。在发表于1947年的《中国人学英文》里，吕叔湘强调区别比较与比附，求同与求异，说：

The second achievement above could be attributed to the good work of Lü Shuxiang. This is his contribution to contrastive linguistics of China as well as the world. During 1940—1980, Lü Shuxiang on three occasions spoke on "compare" and "adherence". In his paper of 1947 on "Chinese Learning English", he urged to differentiate between the two concepts, as well as between seeking likenesses and seeking differences. He writes:

> 比较是比较，比附是比附。要按主张纯粹直接教学法的人们的说法，简直不必比较。可是我们的意思，不但是不妨比较，有时候还不可不比较。比较是要注意英语和汉语不同之处，让学习者在这些地方特别小心，这是极应该的。而且，英语在咱们是外国语，汉语是咱们的本族语，要是我们不帮着学习者去比较，他自己会无意之中在那儿比较，而只见其同不见其异，那就是我们所说的比附了。（吕叔湘，1947：2）
>
> Comparison is comparison, and analogy is analogy. Going by the ideas of direct teaching method, there is no place for comparison. But we think otherwise, not only should we not mind comparison, sometimes, we cannot avoid it. To compare is to understand how English is different from Chinese so that learners could be warned. This is extremely necessary. Think about it, English is foreign to us while Chinese is our native tongue, if we do not

help the learners to compare, they will still make unconscious comparison—however they will see only the likelinesses and ignore the differences, this is what we meant by analogy. (Lü Shuxiang, 1947: 2)

1958年，吕叔湘又一次提到这两个术语：
And again in 1958:

> 不同的语言或方言可以互相比较，一切特点都是有了比较才更加明显，但是不能互相比附。必须实事求是，一切从事实出发，俄语还它一个俄语，英语还它一个英语，古汉语还它古汉语，现代汉语还它现代汉语。（吕叔湘，1958：60）
>
> Different languages or dialects may be compared with each other. All characteristics are illuminated by way of comparison. But we should not try to force an analogy. We have to respect the linguistic facts and begin from there. We have to keep to Russian Russian, keep to English English, and keep to classical Chinese classical Chinese, modern Chinese modern Chinese. (Lü Shuxiang, 1958: 60)

吕先生用的术语与我们今天用的有一点不同。他说的"比较"实际上就是我们说的"对比"，他说的"比附"就是我们说的"比较"。对比语言学是从比较语言学中生发出来的，经过长期的发展，现在"对比"和"比较"都有了专门的含义，前者指求异的研究，而后者则是求同的研究。吕先生强调在外语学习中一定要用对比的方法而不能用比较的方法，这是对对比语言学的一种正本清源的主张。

Lü Shuxiang has used a different term from that which is used now. What he meant by "comparison" is what we now called "contrast". What he termed as "analogy" is the present concept of "comparison". Contrastive linguistics branched out of comparative linguistics. At the initial stage, there were confusions in the terms both in the West and in China. After years of development, the two terms now have specific denotations. The former is a study to sort out the differences while the latter is to sort out the similarities with particular focus on the ancestry. Lü Shuxiang's affirmation on the use of contrastive studies but not comparative studies in foreign language learning helped clear obstacles for the development of contrastive linguistics at its root.

而八十年代王还、王菊泉等对任学良等著作的批评，实际上就是吕叔湘思想的体现，王菊泉文中所引的球赛比喻就是吕叔湘作出的。吕叔湘的这一思想来源于对从《马氏文通》起的中国对比研究的深刻反省，是中国对比语言学的宝贵财富。国外对比研究中其实也有这种类似的状况，但是好像还没有哪家说得比吕氏深刻。

The critical appraisal from Wang Huan and Wang Juquan on Ren Xueliang and the rest in the 1980s was exactly the manifestation of Lü Shuxiang's recommendation. The analogy quoted in Wang Juquan was in fact adapted from Lü Shuxiang, who was the teacher. Furthermore, this thought was Lü Shuxiang's deep reflections on contrastive studies in China since *Mashi Wentong*. It is the most valuable asset contrastive linguistics in China can own. While there may be similar situations elsewhere, we have not seen anything more insightful than that represented by Lü Shuxiang.

3.3 第五期（1990— ）：瞄准普通语言学的汉外对比研究
3.3 Phase 5 (1990—): Aligning with general linguistics

3.3.1 划分出第五期的理由
3.3.1 Reasons for demarcation

把1977年以后中国的对比语言学研究分为两期，要有充分的理由；特别是以哪一年或哪一个事件来划界，更要有一定的说服力。我们经过认真思考，把这一年定在1990年。在此之前是第四期，之后是第五期。这两期的根本区别在于对比研究的目标上，第四期主要是为了服务于第二语言教学，中外的实践都证明这实际上不是个非常成功的路子；第五期对比研究方向变了，变为重点通过对比研究，发现汉语特点，为普通语言学的建设作出贡献。也就是说，从原来的侧重于应用层面，变为更注重于理论的探讨和建设。这一改变不能说只是到1990年才发生，但1990年发生的事确实具有标志性意义。这就是杨自俭、李瑞华主编的《英汉对比研究论文集》的出版。这部书的出版至少有三个意义：

To chart China's development in contrastive studies after 1977 requires sufficient grounding, especially with regard to the watershed year and event.

We propose the watershed to be the year 1990. Before and after 1990 could be considered two phases because of the fundamental disparity in objectives. As explained earlier, Phase 4 was primarily committed to the needs in second language pedagogy which was proven to be not very successful both in the West and in China for its predictability, other usage apart. Thereafter, the direction changed. Contrastive studies should now be used to validate and enhance studies in general linguistics by unearthing the characteristics of Chinese with the methodology. We called this Phase 5 to mark the change from applied linguistics to theoretical linguistics. Of course, it did not just happen in 1990. But an epitome event in 1990 warrants the landmarking—the publication of *A Collection of Essays in English-Chinese Contrastive Studies* edited by Yang Zijian and Li Ruihua. This particular volume contains three significant points:

第一，这是对上一时期（1977—1989）的对比研究的集中检阅，使"英汉对比"作为一门新的研究领域深入人心；

1. This is a collective review of the last phase (1977—1989) in an effort to promote contrastive study between English and Chinese as a new field of study.

第二，吕叔湘为这本论文集题词：

2. Lü Shuxiang offered an unusual and unprecedented gesture to write a congratulatory note for the collection:

> 指明事物的异同所在不难，追究它们何以有此异同就不那么容易了。而这恰恰是对比研究的最终目的。（吕叔湘，1990）
>
> To point out similarities and differences is not as difficult as getting to the root of the cause to such similarities and differences. This is the ultimate concern of contrastive studies. (Lü Shuxiang, 1990)

据我们所知，吕叔湘从来没有为任何书或论文集题过词，这件事是破天荒的。从题词内容来看，这句话虽然简单，但可能是吕叔湘从自己半个世纪的对比研究中悟出来的道理。坦白地说，吕氏从1942年出版《中国文法要略》以来在对比方面做的工作一直是"指明事物的异同"，很少追究过"它们何以有此异同"，直到现在才体会到后者更重要，"恰恰是对比研究的最终目的"。可见透过题词，他对后来者寄托着深深的希望。而自那以后的对比研究，也确实是循着这一题词的精神在走的；

As far as we know, it is not his style to offer congratulatory notes to publications. This seemingly simple note contained the wisdom of Lü Shuxiang after 50 years of scholarship. Honestly, since the release of *Essentials of Chinese Grammar* in 1942, Lü Shuxiang's emphasis on contrastive studies has all along been "in search of the similarities and differences". Getting to the bottom of them was never raised. In this note, Lü Shuxiang may have felt the importance and maturity in scholarship of this endeavour to signify it as the ultimate concern. He demonstrates, through this note, the earnest expectations in future works of the discipline. Subsequent development to date has so far lived up to the guidance of his spirit.

第三，杨自俭、李瑞华在为论文集写的《英汉对比研究述评》一文中，劈头第一句就引了赵元任的一句话：

3. In their collection, Yang Zijian and Li Ruihua opened their commentary notes on English-Chinese contrastive analysis with a quote from Chao Yuen-ren:

> 所谓语言学理论，实际上就是语言的比较，就是世界各民族语言综合比较研究得出的科学结论。（引自杨自俭、李瑞华，1990b：1）[1]
>
> Theoretical linguistics is in reality the comparing [Authors' note: in the sense of contrast] of languages, i.e. the scientific conclusion arises out of the consolidated comparison of ethnic languages in the world. (Yang Zijian and Li Ruihua, 1990b: 1)

据我们所知，在洪堡特以后，中外语言学家中还没有一个人把语言对比提到这么高的地位的。这句话也成了1990年以后中国对比研究的主旋律，许多有成就的学者、有影响的著作都是本着这个精神来进行对比研究的。

---

1 按：这段话没有赵元任的原文，杨-李文引自《王力论学杂著》，我们查了收入《王力文集》的引文，与此稍有不同："几十年前，赵元任先生跟我说：'什么是普通语言学？普通语言学是拿世界上的各种语言加以比较研究得出来的结论。'"（王力，1984：544）
NB: We could not trace the original of Chao Yuen-ren. According to Yang and Li, this was quoted from Wang Li's *Wang Li's Miscellaneous Academic Papers* and what we found in *Wang Li Collection* was slightly different from the citation: "A few decades ago, Master Chao Yuen-ren told me this: 'what is general linguistics? It is the conclusion you have drawn after comparing all kinds of languages in the world.'" (Wang Li, 1984: 544)

In so far as we know, no one else in the world apart from Humboldt has ever accorded such high status to the contrastive study of languages. This remark of Chao's was taken as the principle for China's contrastive studies after 1990. And it is with this perspective that many discoveries in this phase were possible.

由于以上三个理由，我们认为，把1990年作为对比研究新时期的开端是合适的。另外，从数量上，我们也感到，1990年是个飞跃年。前面曾说到，根据我们2002年的统计资料，从1977到1989年，13年里发表的对比研究论文数量是392篇，年均30篇。而根据同一资料，1990年一年发表的论文数就是87篇，增加了将近两倍。

For the three reasons given above, 1990 was a valid watershed year that marked the beginning of a stage of development. In terms of papers contributed, there was also a quantum leap. As quoted earlier, in the 13-year period from 1977 to 1989, there were altogether 392 treatises, averaging 30 per annum, but in 1990 alone, there were 87, more than doubling the average.

1990年以后，还有三件事，对这一新时期的产生具有重要意义。

Three other issues after 1990 attached great significance to the new phase.

（1）1991年，刘宓庆的《汉英对比研究与翻译》出版。

(1) Liu Miqing's *CE-EC Contrastive Studies and Translation* was released in 1991.

国内将对比研究与翻译相结合的，最早见于香港出版的陈定安的著作《英汉比较与翻译》（1985）。陈定安指出：

In China, it was Chen Ding'an's *English-Chinese Comparison and Translation* (1985) that first paired contrastive studies with translation. Chen pointed out that:

> 英汉语言对比，是翻译理论的核心。因为英汉互译的理论、方法与技巧都是建立在英汉两种语言异同对比的基础上的。正因为有了"同"，才可以互译；正因为有了"异"，才产生了不同的方法与技巧。（陈定安，1985：序言）

> Contrast between English and Chinese is the core to translation theories. This is because the theory, methodology and technique in bi-directional translation between English and Chinese have their roots in contrasting the similarities and differences between English and Chinese. On grounds that there exist similarities, we therefore are able to translate. On

grounds that there exist differences we need the various methodologies and techniques. (Chen Ding'an, 1985: Preface)

但在英语界和翻译界真正产生影响的,还是始于刘宓庆的这本书。刘宓庆强调:

However, the work that has real influence over English studies and translation was Liu (1991). Liu highlighted that:

> 本书是一本以对比语言学为基本理论导向和基本理论依据来研究翻译、在研究中理论与实践并重的著作。(刘宓庆,1991:绪论)
>
> This is a book on translation based on the guiding principles and theoretical evidence of contrastive linguistics. It has theory and practise well balanced. (Liu Miqing, 1991: Introduction)

而且他最早构筑了一个完全不同于以往表层形式对比的汉英对比研究体系,产生了非常积极的影响,第二年就得以修订重版,在同类书中是罕见的。

He is the first to have constructed a Chinese-English contrastive framework that is completely different from the surface structure models of the past. The extremely positive effect of the book was evident in the need to edit for reprint by the following year, which was rare for books of that kind.

从今天的眼光来看,对比与翻译有天然的联系似乎是人所皆知的事实。但西方开始一直强调对比研究对教学的意义,在用于教学遭到挫折后隔了很长时间才认真考虑对比研究对翻译的意义和作用。而中国学者却早早就提出了这一问题,并把对比语言学作为"翻译理论的核心"或"基本理论导向"。是否是由于中西语言的不同导致了这一认识的先后,值得研究。但这一认识无疑为中国对比研究开拓了无限宽广的道路,却是不争的事实。这是1990年后中国对比研究重新振起而且势不可遏地繁荣起来的重要原因之一。

Looking back, it seems common sense that contrastive studies would have a natural tie with translation. However, the West was so focused on the application in applied linguistics at the outset that it waited long after the failure in pedagogical application before seriously considering studying the function and significance of contrastive analysis on translation. In comparison, Chinese scholars went a step ahead to use contrastive linguistics as "core to translation theories" or as "guiding principles and theoretical evidence". Is this lead by the Chinese advanced by the awareness of the great differences between Chinese and western languages? It would be interesting to delve further. In any case, the understanding has certainly widened the scope of contrastive linguistics in China. This is how the growth of the discipline after its revival in 1990 became incessant.

（2）1992年，许余龙出版了《对比语言学概论》一书，这不仅是中国也是世界上第一部关于对比语言学的教材，第一次对对比语言学的定义、分类、理论和方法进行了比较系统的叙述。我们说在世界上也是第一部，这是因为国际上对于对比语言学是否是一个独立的语言学部门始终存在着不同意见，甚至不愿堂而皇之地提出"对比语言学"这个名称。许余龙是在香港攻读博士学位的，深受西方语言学模式的熏陶，但这一创新突破了西方的藩篱，对中国对比语言学的发展成熟更起了重要的作用。

(2) In 1992, Xu Yulong brought out his work *Introduction to Contrastive Linguistics*, which is the first textbook in China and probably the world on the subject. For the first time, there was a systematic description on the definition, classification, theory and methodology. We say it is probably the first in the world because there is international division in recognizing contrastive linguistics as an independent discipline; some are even reluctant to adopt the term contrastive linguistics. Dr. Xu was conferred in Hong Kong and knows of the western linguistics models. However, instead of being bound by it, he broke through some barriers and contributed to the maturity of the discipline in China.

（3）同是在1990年，以刘重德为首的一批志同道合的学者在江西井冈山发起筹建"英汉比译学会"，从事英汉语言文化对比与翻译研究。此事得到了吕叔湘的支持，他欣然答应担任名誉会长，并建议学会名称改为"中国英汉语比较研究会"，经教育部和民政批准，于1994年在长沙正式成立，德高望重的老翻译家刘重德出任第一任会长。十多年来，这个学会以学会友，定期召开学术研讨会，出版学术论文集，已发展会员500多人，成为英汉对比研究的一股主力，在国内乃至国际上都有着越来越大的影响。

(3) Also in 1990, a group of like-minded scholars got together at Jingang Mountain, Jiangxi Province, in preparation for founding a national scholastic association. With the support of Lü Shuxiang, the China Association for Comparative

Study between English and Chinese (CACSEC) was inaugurated in 1994 at Changsha, Hunan Province. At the helm was the well respected senior translator, Liu Zhongde. Over the last decade, the association developed through scholastic activities such as conferences and publications and expanded in member strength to 500. It has become a vital thrust to English-Chinese contrastive study and is gaining in ensuing esteem within and outside of China.

由于以上这些原因，第五期的对比语言学在中国大陆发展非常迅速，势头已经超过了西方。由于目标瞄准的是普通语言学而不仅仅是应用语言学，因而在许多方面取得了突破。

We accounted for the rapid development in Phase 5 which saw the Chinese surging ahead of the West in some aspects. Aligning with general linguistics instead of applied linguistics is imperative for more breakthroughs.

3.3.2 对比研究的新突破
3.3.2 Breakthroughs in contrastive studies

九十年代中国对比研究进入第五期后，发展势头凶猛，已成为语言学研究一股不容小觑的力量。特别是这一研究，上接第二期研究关注汉语特点、反对盲目模仿的传统，中汲取第一、第三期过于依赖西方语法的教训，下又努力从第四期局限于"二语教学"的处境中摆脱出来，理论境界得到提升，学科发展也相应成熟。十多年来取得了有目共睹的成绩。这些成绩，不仅值得中国对比研究者认真总结，也值得国外的对比语言学和普通语言学界认真思考和借鉴。

The massive headways contrastive studies made in the 1990s propelled the discipline to emerge forcefully as a strong branch of linguistics in China. In particular, research in this phase, inheriting the tradition of Phase 2 and drawing on the lessons of over-reliance on western linguistics of Phases 1 and 3, continued to unearth the characteristics of Chinese and reject blind limitation in the process. It has also striven to set itself free from its predicament in applied linguistics. The rise in the theoretical level demonstrates the maturing of the discipline. The achievements over the last decade are worthy of serious consideration and experience drawing not only by China, but also by contrastive linguistics and general linguistics scholars elsewhere.

2002年，我们总结并提出了这一时期汉英对比研究的八大趋势，这就是：（1）学科的自觉意识越来越强；（2）学科的理论自觉意识越来越高；（3）从微观走向宏观；（4）微观研究的深入化；（5）积极引进和运用国外的理论和研究方法；（6）理论与方法的多元化；（7）对研究者的知识结构的关注；（8）汉语主体意识的觉醒（潘文国，2002a）。

Pan Wenguo (2002a) summed up the eight trends in Chinese-English contrastive study of this phase as follows:

1) heightened self-awareness in the discipline;
2) rise in theoretical awareness in the discipline;
3) moving from micro- to macro-perspectives;
4) greater depth in micro-perspective studies;
5) being active in introducing and applying western theories and methodologies;
6) diversity in theory and methodology;
7) paying greater attention to the knowledge structure of the researcher;
8) awakening to the subject consciousness of the Chinese language.

若干年多过去了，今天回过头来重新审视，我们发现在这八大趋势里，从微观走向宏观可以说是核心，是这一时期汉英对比研究的最大变化和发展。没有这样一种变化，汉英对比研究不可能有今天这样的局面，其他的七项变化也难以出现。正是宏观研究的兴起，推动了学科的自觉意识与理论意识，推动了国外语言学理论的引进与介绍，推动了研究方法的多元化和对研究者知识结构的关注，推动了汉语主体意识的觉醒，也才促进了微观研究的深化和细化。不妨设想，如果没有宏观研究，对比研究还停留在"对比分析"上，作为第二语言教学的一个手段，就只能作为应用语言学的一个分支，不会有独立学科的诉求；而如果没有学科独立意识，也就不可能有对学科理论建构的探索；而正是因为理论建设的需要，使人们越来越关注国外语言学乃至语言哲学理论的发展，致力于各种理论的引进、试用，并与自身的研究相结合，从而导致了研究方法的多元化；而这方方面面研究的深入，又促进了人们对研究者知识结构的关注；对比语言学上升到理论层面，引起关于语言哲学的思考，又促使了汉语主体意识的觉醒。甚至微观研究，也因为有了宏观研究作映衬、提示和指导，而出现了超越以往表层体系对照、不断向语法语义乃至语音深层进行探索的良好态势。这就是八大趋势的内在联系。

After a break of several years, we find that among these eight trends, the move from micro- to macro-perspectives is most crucial and represents the greatest change and development in Chinese-English contrastive study of this phase. Without this directional switch, Chinese-English contrastive study would not be at what it is today, and the other seven changes would probably not be in trend. The rise in macro-perspective studies is behind the increased awareness as well as theoretical awareness in the discipline. It further leads to the introduction of foreign linguistic theory that in turn helps diversification in methodologies and a check on the knowledge structure of the researcher and ultimately adds to the subject consciousness in Chinese, promoting deeper and more sophisticated research in micro-perspective. In the absence of macro-perspective studies, contrastive linguistics would stop at "contrastive analysis" and remain as a means to second language pedagogy and a branch in applied linguistics. It would be unthinkable to set it up as an independent discipline and have the ensuing exploration on theoretical construction for an independent field of study never follows. It is precisely out of the need to construct a theoretical framework that more and more attention is directed at foreign linguistic theories as well as development in language philosophy. As a consequence of the introduction, testing and integration of these theories with our own research purposes, a variety of research methodologies are being developed. The further investigation called for knowledge building on the part of the researcher. As theoretical research advances, it sparks off appreciation at the philosophical level that leads to consciousness in reckoning Chinese as a subject matter in its own right. Even for micro-perspective studies on the language, there must be guidance from macro-perspective studies to transcend above cross-referencing on grammatical systems and proceed to further details in grammar, semantics and phonology. The eight trends are interlinked as such.

  这个八条主要是针对国内的研究者谈的，有的如积极引进国外理论等对国外学者来说好像没有什么意义。下面我们换个角度，主要从普通语言学的角度出发，结合今天新的认识，对一些可能更具普遍意义的成果和体会作一番总结。

  The summary above is perhaps more meaningful to Chinese linguists. We shall proceed from another angle, the general linguistics viewpoint in modern days, to survey some of the achievements that could have universal significance.

3.3.2.1 强烈的学科自觉意识

3.3.2.1 Strong awareness towards the discipline

比较东西方的语言对比研究，我们发现，九十年代以后的中国对比语言学是学科意识最强烈的。在西方，对比语言学一直被看作语言学中的灰姑娘，至今地位仍然不高。而在中国，对比研究却越来越受重视。我们认为这与汉语在世界语言中的格局是有关系的。由于在西方基本上是印欧语言的一统天下，语言之间的差异并不十分严重，至少没有严重到要靠对比研究来解决各自的语法体系问题，因而对比研究被视作可有可无，至多可以在外语教学中发挥一点作用，或者用于满足对一些原始或准原始语言的猎奇研究；对待非印欧语系的一些有影响的语言如汉语、日语等，不客气地说，多数西方语言学家不习惯于从对比语言学的角度去看，而往往采用比较语言学的方法，正如王力在80年前指出的：

Putting the contrastive studies in languages in the West and in China together, it occurred that since the 1990s, there has been growing awareness in contrastive linguistics as a discipline in China. In the West, contrastive linguistics remained as the Cinderella. Its bubbling development in China has everything to do with the status of Chinese in the world map of languages. Languages in the West are largely from the Indo-European family with differences in their respective grammatical systems not great enough to warrant the application of contrastive linguistics for problem solving. As such, contrastive linguistics does not have a strong case to survive except for its use in foreign language teaching or for satisfying the curiosity about some aboriginal languages. In their treatment of non Indo-European languages such as Chinese and Japanese among others, we are sorry to say that most western linguists are not used to employing contrastive linguistic methodology. More often than not, comparative linguistic methodology is applied. As Wang Li observed some 80 years ago:

> 西洋人研究中国文法的时候，总想看看中国文法所无而西洋文法所有的东西究竟是否真正没有；如果现代的中国没有，还要问古代的中国是否也没有。这种精神原是好的，但其流弊就在乎先存成见，然后去找证据；遇着例外的时候，再去寻求解释。（王力，1936：94）

> When westerners study Chinese grammar, they very often like to see if that which is not found in Chinese but found in western grammar are really not in existence. And if it is not found in modern Chinese, is it also true for classical Chinese? While we appreciate the good intention, we are also aware of its shortfall as a proposition proving method where one would have to find an explanation to the exceptions. (Wang Li, 1936: 94)

这实际上是几百年之前的"传教士语法"的再版。不客气地说,如果西方语言学不改变这一态度,不把非印欧语言作为平等对比的对象,而看作是"解释"的对象,或者西方各种新语言理论的"实验田",普通语言学就很难在现有基础上再往前发展。

This is exactly what missionary grammars were all about a few centuries ago. We are surprised that the West is still trying to "explain" to this day. If western linguistics cannot treat non-Indo-European languages as fair contrastive targets and continue to try "explaining", or use them as a testing ground for novel theories, how could there be further advancement in general linguistics?

而中国现代语言学之诞生过程就是伴随着"模仿"与"反模仿"之争,亦即采用"比较"还是"对比"的方法之争。中国语言学每前进一步,都是在与西方语言和西方语言学对比之下取得的,可见对比研究实在是中国语言学的生命线,没有对比就没有中国语言学的发展。而在20世纪的头八十年中,中国有对比研究而没有对比语言学,有实践而缺乏理论的支撑。因之到了20世纪八、九十年代,一旦对比语言学的概念和理论得到了引进,就如火如荼地发展起来,其势头甚至压过了对比语言学的原产地。特别是王力所引用的赵元任关于"对比语言学就是普通语言学"的论断,更使中国对比研究者的思想得到了升华。就我们所知,赵元任的这番话,事实上最符合创建普通语言学的19世纪德国语言哲学家洪堡特的本意,但100多年来,真正领略到这一本意的却是中国学者赵元任。这恐怕是值得西方学者深思的。

Modern linguistics in China was born out of the debates in "imitation" and "anti-imitation"; or the use of "compare" and "contrast" methodologies. Every step of progress in linguistics in China is with reference to western languages and western linguistics. It is fair to say that contrastive linguistics charted the lifeline of Chinese linguistics. Without contrast, there could be no Chinese linguistics. In the first 80 years of the twentieth century, China had contrastive studies but not contrastive linguistics; which is to say, the practice was not sufficiently supported with theory. Therefore, in the 1980s and1990s, when concepts and theories of contrastive linguistics were introduced, it gained popularity in a short period of time, more heated than its development in its place of origin. The quotation by Wang Li on Chao Yuen-ren that "contrastive linguistics is general linguistics" is particularly enlightening to Chinese scholars, changing their vision. As for now, we understand Chao Yuen-ren to be the best interpretation of Humboldt's idea in establishing general linguistics in the nineteenth century. Interestingly, in the past century, it was a Chinese scholar that saw eye to eye with Humboldt.

由于不把"对比"仅仅看作是一种手段,而把"对比语言学"看作是语言学中的一个重要部门,因而中国学者对于对比语言学的定位有着同西方学者很不相同的看法。西方学者一般总摆脱不了把对比语言学看作一个具体的研究领域,纠缠于它应该属于应用语言学呢,还是属于比较语言学;虽然有人(如Fisiak,1980)也谈到了理论对比语言学与应用对比语言学的区别,但始终没有说清对比语言学与普通语言学的关系。中国学者的视野则要宽广得多。许余龙的观点可说是一个代表:

By not treating "contrast" merely as a means to an end, and taking "contrastive linguistics" to be an important branch in linguistics, the Chinese have positioned contrastive linguistics differently from their western counterparts. Western scholars are trapped in treating contrastive linguistics as a specific field of research and get themselves into trouble by classifying it into applied linguistics or comparative linguistics. Despite scholars like Fisiak (1980) who did suggest differentiation between theoretical contrastive linguistics and applied contrastive linguistics, few really clear up the relations between contrastive linguistics and general linguistics. On this note, Chinese scholars have a wider vision. The view of Xu Yulong is representative enough:

> 对比语言学作为语言学的一个分支,与语音学、词汇学、语法学等通常所说的语言学分支不同。这些语言学分支是一组相对独立、横向平行的语言学分支,而对比语言学则既是横向的又是纵向的一个语言学分支。从整体上来说,对比语言学是语言学的一个纵向分支,因

为其本身构成一个纵向的包孕等级系统，与语言学的分类平行。就构成对比语言学的各个分支之间的关系来说，同一层面上的分支又是横向平行的，各个分支构成同一层面上的语言学分支的一个组成部分。
（许余龙，1992：9—10）

As a branch in linguistics, contrastive linguistics is different from other common branches in linguistics such as phonology, lexicology and syntax. The common others are relatively independent, horizontally parallel linguistic branches whereas contrastive linguistics is a linguistic branch that is both horizontally parallel and vertical parallel. As a whole, it is a branch on the vertical axis as it encompasses structured systems that are vertically linked and it runs parallel with the classifications in linguistics. With regards to the relations of the sub-fields within contrastive linguistics, sub-fields at the same level are horizontally parallel and each sub-field is also a component of the respective linguistic branches at the same level. (Xu Yulong, 1992: 9–10)

这样一种定位是在西方对比语言学著作中没有看到过的。这样，对比语言学就成了整个语言学的分支而不仅仅是某个分支的分支。正是在此基础上许余龙提出了对比语言学的学科体系架构。

No such positioning accorded to contrastive linguistics has been seen in western linguistic works thus far. What Chinese linguists have done is to render the discipline a status parallel to other branches of linguistics, rather than as a sub-field within a branch. It is in this light that Xu Yulong has proposed a framework for the discipline.

3.3.2.2 对比研究分三个层面的思想
3.3.2.2 The three facets of contrastive studies

西方对比研究的三个时期各有侧重，第一期侧重通过语言对比探索不同民族的不同思维方式和民族精神，第二期侧重对比分析为语言教学服务；第三期在"外向"上拓展到语篇和语用，在"内向"上拓展到语言心理。但他们似乎还没找到贯穿这三个方面的一以贯之的理论。中国学者在第五期的对比研究中，提出了对比研究分三个层面的思想，比较好地解决了这个问题。

The three phases in the West have a different focus each. The first centred on thought patterns and ethnic spirit, the second on pedagogical needs and the third ventured concurrently in two directions: "outwards" to text linguistics and pragmatics and "inwards" to linguistic psychology. The three separate ways are in no sense connected with each other. In Phase 5 in China, scholars suggested structuring the discipline in three facets and approaching it in an integrated manner, providing the required internal linkage within the seemingly segmented sub-fields.

最早提出对比研究应该运用纵向透视法的是刘宓庆。刘氏在其《汉英对比研究与翻译》一书第一章，劈头就指出：

Liu Miqing took the lead in advocating a horizontal perceptivity in contrastive study. In the opening of his book *CE-EC Contrastive Studies and Translation*, he writes:

> 如果我们突破语言的表层结构（语音系统—词语系统），作纵向的透视分析，就可以发现语音—词语系统、表现法系统和思维方式（或风格）正是每一种语言的三个立面的结构层级：语言都具有音系规律和语法规律，语法规律通常受该语言的表现方法的制约，表现方法又通常受操这一语言的群体的思维方式的支配。因此语言对比不能"掐头去尾"，只在语言本身范围内作类比，摆脱不了类型学（typological system）的局限性。现代对比语言学应该坚持这种纵向透视法，以此作为我们的基本原则。（刘宓庆，1992: 5）[1]

> Breaking through levels at surface structure (phonology-lexicographical system) and examining language horizontally, we shall see how in every language, the phonology-lexicographical system, expression system and thought pattern represent themselves in a three dimensional structure. Every language is ruled in phonology and grammar. Grammatical rules are often bound by the expression system of the language which in turn is governed by the general thought pattern of the speakers of the language. As such, we cannot approach contrastive study with some parts in the head or tail being taken away. Looking only at the language itself, we are necessarily confined by

---

[1] 刘氏在1992年本书修订再版时对一些用语作了调整，为了更好地体现作者的思想，我们这里引用的是修订本的原文。

The original quote was different in terms of language in the two editions. The translation sticks closer to the second edition.

the typological system. Modern contrastive linguistics ought to stake out and vindicate such horizontal perceptivity and be impelled by it as the underlying principle. (Liu Miqing, 1992: 5)

潘文国在此基础上，提出汉英对比研究应分三个层次，这三个层次的研究分别适应不同的要求：
On this basis, Chinese-English contrastive studies should go on three fronts for different needs, as mooted by Pan Wenguo:

> 第一个层次是语音及语法表层上的对比，其目的是为初学外语者提供一个简便的拐杖。……第二个层次是语言表达法的对比。其对象是外语已有了一定水平而又经常需要在两种语言间进行转换（如第二语言教学或翻译）的人，帮助他们更地道地使用语言。……第三个层次是语言心理上的对比。这是更深层的对比，企图推导出隐藏在不同表达法后面的心理和文化背景，进行一种哲学式的思考，目的是为了最终建立中国的语言哲学。（潘文国，1997/2002：358）

> The first front is contrasting on the phonological and grammatical plane with a purpose of providing convenient walk-through for foreign elementary language learners…The second front is contrasting on language expression targeting at foreign language speakers of certain standard who need to switch between two languages (such as second language teaching or translation) with an object to raise standard closer to native-speaking…The third front is contrasting in terms of language psychology. This is touching on the deep structure and attempting to deduce the concealed psychological and cultural aura conditioning expressions. This form of philosophical exploration is good for the ultimate rooting of Chinese language philosophy. (Pan Wenguo, 1997/2002: 358)

2003年他进一步解释说：
And as these fronts are distinguished, they are at the same time contained within one contrastive linguistic framework, as Pan further expanded in 2003:

> 如果采用叶斯柏森的话，第一个层面相当于他说的"从O到I"的研究，第二个层面相当于他说的"从I到O"的研究，而第三个

层面则是他说的"更深刻地理解人类语言和人类思维的最内在的本质"。如果联系国外对比研究实践来说,第一个层面相当于国外第二个时期的研究,第二个层面相当于詹姆斯等人的研究,而第三个层面则是回归到了洪堡特和沃尔夫等人。(潘文国,2003:6)

In the words of Jespersen, we could akin the first front as moving from "O" to "I" and the second as moving from "I" to "O" whereas the third would be what he described as "gaining a deeper insight into the innermost nature of human language and of human thought." Looking at western practices, studies at the first level is the business of phase 1 in the west; those at second level is the business of Carl James and company while those at the third level returns to the traditions represented by Humboldt and Whorf. (Pan Wenguo, 2003: 6)

这就比较好地解决了对比语言学的不同服务对象及研究目的问题,同时也使西方三个时期的对比研究被纳入了一个统一的对比语言学系统里。后来,中国英汉语比较研究会的首任会长刘重德在为第二辑《英汉语比较与翻译》论文集撰写的序言中再次重申了这一思想,并把后两层概括为"宏观研究",以与第一层的"微观研究"相对待:

The same idea was reiterated by Liu Zhongde, the first president of CACSEC, as he penned the preface of the second essay collection published by the association where he further classified into micro and macro studies:

> 英汉对比研究应分三个层次:第一个层次是语言表层结构,第二个层次是语言表达方法,第三个层次是语言哲学。我这里说的宏观研究,就是这第二、三两个层次的研究。表达法表现一个民族认知世界的方法和规则。要考究这种语言的表达法是怎样形成的,那就要寻求其心理、文化和哲学上的根据。(刘重德,1998)

> English and Chinese contrastive analysis should go on three levels: The first level is at the surface structure, the second on the method of expression and the third is on language philosophy. What I meant by macro studies refers to the second and third levels. The method of expression concerns the way and rules by which a nation learnt about the world. To get to the bottom of how expressions are formed, we have to seek evidence from their mind,

culture and philosophy. (Liu Zhongde, 1998: Preface)

从而使这一说法成为中国对比语言学界的共识。
Consensus on the three facets is thus established among Chinese contrastivists.

在2009年召开的第一届英汉对比与翻译高层论坛上，潘文国进一步提出，
At the first Summit on EC-CE Contrastive and Translation Pan Wenguo further pointed out,

> 不仅在语言对比中存在着三个层面，在语言研究的对比中，也存在着三个层面，这就是语言理论层面、语言思想层面，和语言文化史层面。一定的语言观、语言理论，甚至语言研究方法论必然是特定时代、特定条件的产物。而不同的语言，由于其历史文化条件不同，其语言理论也必然表现出种种的差异。对比不同语言的社会和文化发展，对于解释其语言研究的不同发展道路有着重要的意义。（潘文国，2012：1）

> There are three escalating levels in contrasting different linguistic studies just as there are three levels in contrasting different languages, namely, the levels of linguistic theory, linguistic thought, and cultural histories of linguistics. All linguistic views, linguistic theories, and even linguistic methodologies are but products of certain historical periods and historical conditions. Languages and historical conditions differ, so does the studies of languages. The comparison of different social and cultural developments of different linguistic communities is of great importance in explaining the different roads that different linguistic studies take. (Pan Wenguo, 2012: 1)

他举例指出可以从语言研究的发生、语言研究的成熟、语言学各分支发展的不同步和语言研究的影响与传播这四个方面着手对比不同社会文化历史条件对语言研究的影响。
Such kind of comparison can be made, for example, by contrasting the emerging, the maturing, the unsynchronized developing of linguistic branches, and the spreading of linguistic studies, says Pan.

如果将东西方对比研究的发展作一个横向比较，我们可以发现一个有趣的现象，即都经历了相似的三个阶段：

表3.1 中西对比语言学发展的相似性

西方	中国	侧重	评论
1期	2期	研究语言背后的思维方式	西方学者说得更加明确
2期	4期	注重服务于二语教学的微观研究	理论和方法都受西方影响
3期	5期	都提出要区分宏观与微观研究	中西对"宏观"的理解不同

Comparing the development path in the West and in China horizontally, we find interesting convergence in three broad areas of experiences.

Table 3.1 Convergence in development

West	China	Experiences	Remarks
Phrase 1	Phrase 2	Concerned with the thought pattern conditioning language	Western scholarship demonstrated better appreciation.
Phrase 2	Phrase 4	Concerned with micro-perspective studies for second language pedagogy	There is a spread of focus between the East and the West in terms of linguistic themes and approaches.
Phrase 3	Phrase 5	Distinguishing between macro- and micro-perspectives	Different connotation of "macro" perspectives in China and West

在当前阶段，中西方都提出要区分宏观对比与微观对比，从詹姆斯（James，1980）到刘宓庆都是如此。可见这确是对比研究发展的全球性趋势。

At the stages the West and China are in currently, to mark out micro- and macro-studies seems a global trend in contrastive linguistics from James (1980) to Liu Miqing.

但仔细研究这似乎是"不约而同"的趋势，我们发现，尽管都主张宏观研究，但中外学者对"宏观语言学"的理解却并不完全相同。詹姆斯的宏观语言学所指的其实只是篇章研究和话语分析，是从纯粹的语言学角度去看的；而中国学者对宏观研究的理解却包括两层意思，其一是指表达法，其二是指思维方式，乃至语言心理、语言文化和语言哲学。这都是詹姆斯所不曾提及的。可见中国学者区分宏观和微观，不纯粹是从语言学着眼的，其中既有语言学上的问题，又有学术研究的方法论问题，乃至语言观的问题。从这个理解出发，在西方视作宏观研究的，如果不涉及到表达法和语言心理、思维方式，即使比较的是语篇问题或语用问题，中国学者仍倾向于看作微观研究。这样一种认识和处理，更便于把重点放在吕叔湘说的"对比研究的最终目的"上。

Closing up on the "coincidental convergence", it is necessary to discern the connotation of "macro" perspectives. The macro contrastive studies by James refer specifically to discourse analysis and text linguistics based purely on a linguistics approach. The Chinese beg to differ. Macro studies, in the Chinese sense, point in two directions: ways of expression and manner of thought including language psychology, language culture and language philosophy. All of which are not mentioned in James. Obviously, it is not by pure linguistic approach that the Chinese have chosen to weigh up and eyeball macro and micro. While there are certainly linguistics considerations, what could not be overlooked relates to scholastic traditions in methodology and linguistic conception. Viewed in this regard, contrastive text or pragmatic studies in the West that are considered as macro will tend to be taken as micro by the Chinese if it sheds no light on ways of expression, language psychology or thought patterns. It is exactly this understanding and approach that allows the Chinese to concentrate on the "ultimate concern of contrastive linguistics" defined by Lü Shuxiang.

从20世纪90年代到21世纪初，中国对比语言学在微观、中观和宏观三条线上都提供了比较有影响的著作。如：

Throughout the 1990s, output in all aspects of micro-, mezzo- and macro-perspectives are available. Listed below are the more notable publications:

    微观研究：　胡曙中《英汉修辞比较研究》（1993）
              邵志洪《英汉语研究与对比》（1997）
              刘英凯《英汉语音修辞》（1998）
              李国南《英汉修辞格对比研究》（1999）
              王逢鑫《英汉比较语义学》（2001）
              何善芬《英汉语言对比研究》（2002）

    Micro: Hu Shuzhong *Comparative Studies in English and Chinese Rhetoric* (1993)
        Shao Zhihong *Contrastive English-Chinese Studies* (1997)
        Liu Yingkai *Phonetic Rhetoric in English and Chinese* (1998)

Wang Fengxin *English-Chinese Comparative Semantics* (2001)

He Shanfen *Contrastive Studies of English and Chinese Languages* (2002)

中观研究：连淑能《英汉对比研究》（1993）

熊文华《汉英应用对比概论》（1997）

赵世开《汉英对比语法论集》（1999）

Mezzo: Lian Shuneng *A Contrastive Study between English and Chinese* (1993)

Xiong Wenhua *An Outline of Applied Comparative Studies of Chinese and English* (1997)

Zhao Shikai *Essays on the Contrastive Study of Chinese-English Syntax: A Cognitive-Functional Approach* (1999)

宏观研究：刘宓庆《汉英对比研究与翻译》（1991）

许余龙《对比语言学概论》（1992/2002）

潘文国《汉英语对比纲要》（1997a/2002）

周有光《比较文字学初探》（1998）

蔡勇飞、王之光《汉英文字比较研究》（2005）

Macro: Liu Miqing *CE-EC Contrastive Studies and Translation* (1991)

Xu Yulong *An Introduction to Contrastive Linguistics* (1992)

Pan Wenguo *An Outline of Chinese-English Contrastive Study* (1997a/2002)

Zhou Youguang *A Tentative Exploration of Comparative Graphics* (1998)

Cai Yongfei and Wang Zhiguang *A Comparative Study between Chinese and English Graphs* (2005)

一些理论语言学及其他领域学者的著作如申小龙（1993）、徐通锵（1997）、李葆嘉（2001）、辜正坤（2004）等也属于宏观层面的思考。

There were also works on the macro-perspective by some theoretical linguists such as Shen Xiaolong (1993), Xu Tongqiang (1997), Li Baojia (2001), Gu Zhengkun (2004).

至于西方看作宏观对比研究的语篇与话语分析对比研究，中国近几年也取得了显著的成绩，重要的著作有：

Recent years have also seen more research output on text linguistics and discourse analysis which are deemed as macro study by the West. The more noteworthy publications are:

张今、张克定《英汉语信息结构对比研究》（1998）

Scollon, Ron et al. *Contrastive Discourse in Chinese and English: A Critical Appraisal*《汉英篇章对比研究》（2000）

彭宣维《英汉语篇综合对比》（2000）

罗选民等《话语分析的英汉语比较研究》（2001）

朱永生等《英汉语篇衔接手段对比研究》（2001）

Zhang Jin and Zhang Keding *Information Structure—A Contrastive Study in English and Chinese* (1998)

Scollon, Ron et al. *Contrastive Discourse in Chinese and English: A Critical Appraisal* (2000)

Peng Xuanwei *A Comprehensive Comparison between English and Chinese Texts* (2000)

Luo Xuanmin et al. *Discourse Analysis: An English-Chinese Contrastive Study* (2001)

Zhu Yongsheng et al. *A Contrastive Study of Coherence in English and Chinese* (2001)

但中国学者所运用的语篇语言学的理论过多地依赖于韩礼德一家之说，缺乏更开阔的视野，这是美中不足之处。

As we see more contributions in new areas, there is also a need for Chinese scholars to expand their knowledge base and be open to more schools of thought; for instance, it would be so much better if we could venture out of Halliday's theory in text linguistics.

2006年本书初版问世后，又有不少新著问世，仅获得中国英汉语比较研究会2016年英华奖提名的著作就有：

After the publication of the first edition of present book more monographs have appeared, including following books which were nominated for 2016 Yinghua Prize for contrastive studies sponsored by CACSEC:

蔡基刚《英汉词汇对比研究》（2008）

陈虎《英汉语调音系对比研究》（2006）

何晓炜《英汉双及物结构的生成语法研究》（2011）

黄勤《英汉新闻语篇中的元话语对比研究》（2014）

赖彦《英汉新闻转述话语比较研究》（2016）

李晓红《双语语料库界面下英汉语义韵对比研究》（2015）

李雪《英汉移动动词词汇化模式的对比研究》（2011）
连淑能《英汉对比研究》（增订本）（2010）
刘礼进，徐真华《篇章视点回指语用论：一项以汉英长距离反身代词为中心的对比研究》（2012）
刘宓庆《新编汉英对比与翻译》（2006）
刘兴华《英汉语篇跨文化修辞研究》（2015）
陆国强《英汉概念结构对比》（2008）
苗兴伟，秦洪武《英汉语篇语用学研究》（2010）
南潮《被动义视角下英汉受事提升构句研究》（2016）
潘文国，谭慧敏《对比语言学：历史与哲学思考》（2006）
魏在江《英汉语篇连贯认知对比研究》（2007）
熊仲儒《英汉致使句论元结构的对比研究》（2015）
许余龙《对比语言学》（第2版）（2010）
赵宏《英汉词汇理据对比研究》（2013）

Cai Jigang *A Contrastive Study between English and Chinese Vocabularies* (2008)

Chen Hu *A Contrastive Study of English and Chinese Intonation and Phonology* (2006)

He Xiaowei *A GG Study of Bitransitive Structures in English and Chinese* (2011)

Huang Qin *A Contrastive Study of Meta-discourse in English and Chinese Journalist Texts* (2014)

Lai Yan *A Contrastive Study of Indirect Quotations in English and Chinese Journalism* (2016)

Li Xiaohong *A Contrastive Study between English and Chinese Semantic Prosodies in the Interface of a Bilingual Corpus* (2015)

Li Xue *A Contrastive Study of Lexicalization Models of English and Chinese Movable Verbs* (2011)

Lian Shuneng *A Contrastive Study between English and Chinese (Revised Edition)* (2010)

Liu Lijin and Xu Zhenhua *Discourse Anaphora Pragmatics: A Contrastive Study of English and Chinese Long-Distance Reflexives* (2012)

Liu Miqing *CE-EC Contrastive Studies and Translation: A New Edition* (2006)

Liu Xinghua *A Cross-Cultural Rhetoric Study of English and Chinese Texts* (2015)

Lu Guoqiang *A Contrastive Study between English and Chinese Conceptual Structures* (2008)

Miao Xingwei and Qin Hongwu *A Study of English and Chinese Discourse Pragmatics* (2010)

Nan Chao *A Study of English and Chinese Sentence Construction by Patient Ascension from the Angle of Passivity* (2016)

Pan Wenguo and Tham Wai Mun *Contrastive Linguistics: History, Philosophy and Methodology* (2006; 2007)

Wei Zaijiang *A Cognitive and Contrastive Study of English and Chinese Textual Coherence* (2007)

Xiong Zhongru *A Contrastive Study of Argument Structure in English and Chinese Causative Sentences* (2015)

Xu Yulong *An Introduction to Contrastive Linguistics* (Second Edition) (2010)

Zhao Hong *An English-Chinese Contrastive Study of Lexical Motivation* (2013)

如同菲齐亚克在波兰主持出版《对比语言学论丛》（PSiCL或*Papers and Studies in Contrastive Linguistics*）和主编对比语言学论文集一样，在中国，由刘重德和杨自俭先后担任会长的中国英汉语比较研究会在上海外语教育出版社等支持下，从1994年起先后出版了五本《英汉语比较与翻译》和一本《翻译与对比研究》论文集（刘重德，1994；1998；杨自俭，2000；2002；2004；潘文国，2005），还主编了三本《汉英对比研究》论文集（杨自俭、李瑞华，1990；李瑞华，1996；王菊泉、郑立信，2004），汇集了微观、中观、宏观各方面的文章，是中国对比研究力量的一个集中检阅。

In a similar way as Fisiak coordinating the publication of PSiCL (*Papers and Studies in Contrastive Linguistics*) in Poland and editing volumes of collections on contrastive linguistics, here in China, CACSEC, under the succeeding leaderships of Liu Chongde and Yang Zijian and with the support of Shanghai Foreign Language Education Press, brought out five collections of *English-Chinese Comparative Studies and Translation* and one collection of *Translation and Contrastive Studies* (in English) since 1994 (Liu Chongde, 1994, 1998; Yang Zijian, 2000, 2002, 2004; Pan Wenguo, 2005). Three other anthologies of *Language and Culture: Contrastive Studies between English and Chinese* were also published (Yang Zijian and Li Ruihua, 1990; Li Ruihua, 1996; Wang Juquan and Zheng Lixin, 2004), containing a fair selection of papers in micro, mezzo and macro standpoints. It is a concerted effort to consolidate contributions in the discipline.

2006年潘文国当选为中国英汉语比较研究会会长以后，组织并由杨自俭、王菊泉担任总主编，编写了一套八本的《英汉对比与翻译研究丛书》，于2008年起陆续出版。其中关于对比研究的有五本，分别是：

After Pan Wenguo was elected president of CACSEC in 2006, he organized and published a book series *English-Chinese Contrastive and Translation Studies* in eight volumes, with Yang Zijian and Wang Juquan as general editors. Five out of the eight were related to contrastive studies. They were:

潘文国，杨自俭主编《共性•个性•视角：英汉对比的理论与方法研究》（2008）

邵志洪主编《结构•语义•关系：英汉微观对比研究》（2008）

牛保义主编《认知•语用•功能：英汉宏观对比研究》（2009）

刘英凯，李静滢主编《比较•鉴别•应用：英汉对比应用研究》（2009）

左飙主编《冲突•互补•共存：中西文化对比研究》（2009）

Pan Wenguo and Yang Zijian (eds.). *Universality, Particularity, and Perspective: Theories and Methodologies for English-Chinese Contrastive Studies* (2008)

Shao Zhihong (ed.). *Structure, Meaning, and Relationship: Microlinguistic English-Chinese Contrastive Studies* (2008)

Niu Baoyi (ed.). *Cognition, Pragmatics and Function: Macrolinguistic English-Chinese Contrastive Studies* (2009)

Liu Yingkai and Li Jingying (eds.). *Comparison, Differentiation and Application: Implications of English-Chinese Contrastive Studies* (2009)

Zuo Biao (ed.). *Conflict, Complementality and Coexistence: Contrastive Study on Chinese and Western Cultures* (2009)

该系列文集是对中国30余年来的英汉对比研究（即本书所说的第五期）的一次集中检阅。其编辑也别出心裁，每卷均含总序、综述、编者札记、选文、重要论著索引和后记六个部分。其中总述是对整个学科发展的总结和指南，综述是对各分册领域的全面评价和趋势预估，札记是对每篇选文的评点，索引则是相关领域的一个相当完整的文献目录。这套书的编纂出版对推动对比研究在中国的发展起了重要的作用。

The series was a timely retrospect of the development of the discipline of contrastive studies over the previous thirty-odd years, co-incidentally the fifth phase of our classification. Each of the series contained six parts: preface, general survey, selections, editor's notes, bibliography and postscript. The preface, written by the general editors, was a summary of the development of the discipline and a prediction for its future development. The survey and the notes, prepared by compiler of each book, were respectively evaluation and comments of the particular sphere and the individual papers under selection. Bibliography offered a comparatively complete guide to the books and papers published in the past scores of years concerning respective subjects. The publication of this series in new arrangements played a positive role in promoting contrastive study in China.

2006年，潘文国、谭慧敏出版了《对比语言学：历史与哲学思考》，翌年，该书的英文版在英国学术出版社The Continuum出版。这是中国对比语言学著作第一次走出国门，并产生了世界范围的影响。如剑桥大学学者柯蒂斯（Svetlana Kurteš）评论说：

In 2006, Pan Wenguo and Singaporean scholar Tham Wai Mun cooperated and published their *Contrastive Linguistics: A Historical and Philosophical Survey* in China and its English version *Contrastive Linguistics: History, Philosophy, and Methodology* published in London and New York by the famous academic press The Continuum. This is the first time a Chinese Contrastivist's monograph was published abroad in the English language, and soon won high praise. Svetlana Kurteš, a contrastivist researcher in the University of Cambridge commented:

> 本书对对比语言学史的叙述是迄今为止最详尽的。作者对世界范围内对比语言学理论和方法的研究了若指掌，其深度和广度令人惊讶，令人赞叹。这样一部书可说人们期盼已久，它出现在2007年特别具有意义，因为这正好是对比语言学第一部重要著作、拉多的《跨文化语言学》发表50周年。在这一重要时刻，所有的对比研究者都应该认真回顾历史，总结以往各种范式的得失，从更宽广的背景对之进行观察和重新解释，从而更深刻、更全面地把握这一学科，以推动进一步的研究。（柯蒂斯，2008）

The present volume stands out as one of the most comprehensive surveys of the history of contrastive linguistics, quite possibly the most comprehensive one published to date. The width and depth of Pan and Tham's knowledge and understanding of the theoretical and methodological issues associated with contrastive linguistics scholarship on a global scale is nothing short of astonishing and truly praiseworthy. Such a volume was no doubt long overdue, but the fact that it appeared in 2007, the year in which contrastivists the world over celebrated the 50th anniversary of the publication of the charter of contrastive linguistics, Lado's Linguistics across Cultures, is eminently significant. It is a momentous occasion for all involved in contrastive linguistics research to reflect upon the results obtained through the implementation of various models of contrastive analysis, observe them and reinterpret them in a wider context, get a better, more profound grasp of the full potential of the discipline and reaffirm their commitment to carry on further research. (Kurteš, 2008)

3.3.2.3 对学科哲学基础的思考
3.3.2.3 Philosophical basis for the discipline

由于从学科层面来思考对比语言学，因此中国对比语言学者比他们的国外同行走得远了一步。正如潘文国后来（1997a：70—71）指出的："任何一门学科的建立都必须做好两项准备工作，一是确定理论基础，作为本学科研究的指导思想和出发点；二是整理本学科研究的历史，以明确本学科的发展过程、趋向和当前的使命。"他在1995年就发表文章，强调哲学基础的重要性：

Considering contrastive linguistics as a discipline, Chinese contrastivists are more progressive in a way. Pen Wenguo (1997a: 70—71) pointed out that in any disciplinary construct, two kinds of preparatory work must be in place: asserting theoretical grounds as guiding principles and compiling the scholastic history of the discipline to determine the progress, direction and current mission. This book is dedicated to these purposes in a way. As far as theoretical grounds are concerned, the reflection process began much earlier. Pan Wenguo (1995) states:

> 不研究哲学，不善于从哲学层面思考自己的研究对象和研究方法，就会使自己的研究陷入盲目性。几十年来，我国的语言研究缺少自己的理论，始终在洋框框里打转，跳出了一个框框，又进入另一个

框框，其根本原因之一，就是没有自己的语言哲学和语法哲学。（潘文国，1995：81）

At the peril of the soul of any research is the blind in philosophical considerations, i.e., not knowing how to consider the research target and research methodology on philosophical grounds. Episodes of the past decades really speak for it. We do not have a theory of our own and therefore have been circling within the western frameworks, hopping from one to another. We have not formulated our philosophy of language and of grammar. (Pan Wenguo, 1995: 81)

钱冠连是另一位对语言哲学特别关注的学者，他从比较国内外学者的理论研究中得到启示，提出：
Echoing this, Qian Guanlian has this to say out of his theoretical research on works by foreign and Chinese scholars:

中国的语言学家应该自觉地加强哲学修养，以哲学带动语言学，这是一条使语言学深刻起来的路子。（钱冠连，1998：44）

Linguists in China should take the initiative to strengthen their study of philosophy and use it to lead research in linguistics, only then would linguistic research turn profound. (Qian Guanlian, 1998: 44)

对于哲学在语言研究中的地位，钱冠连和潘文国都做了不少工作。从1999年起到2003年，钱冠连发表了《哲学轨道上的语言研究》（1999）等十篇"西方语言哲学系列研究"文章，产生了较大的影响。2005年，又出版了《语言：人类最后的家园》这一重要著作。从海德格尔"语言是存在的居所"（Die Sprache ist das Haus des Seins）这一命题出发，提出了"语言是人类最后的家园"这一崭新的命题（钱冠连，2005：24）潘文国（2004）则发表《语言哲学与哲学语言学》一文，对哲学在语言研究中的地位作了新的界定。
For the place of philosophy in language research, both Qian Guanlian and Pan Wenguo have done much. Starting with "Language research on the path of philosophy" (1999) Qian Guanlian has from 1999 to 2003 written some ten important papers about the language philosophy of the West, having quite an impact. In 2005, he put forward a new proposition that "Language is human's ultimate homeland",

inspired by Martin Heidegger's proposition of "Die Sprache ist das Haus des Seins" (Language is the house of Being. In its home man dwells.) (Qian Guanlian, 2005: 24). Pan Wenguo (2004) on "Language philosophy and philosophical linguistics" has also offered some new ideas.

对于对比语言学来说，只有解决语言观问题，才能正确处理对比研究中一些基本问题，例如对比的基础、可比性问题、从形式出发还是从意义出发等。潘文国具体建议以洪堡特的"语言世界观"作为对比研究的哲学基础，认为语言世界观有四个方面的意义：（1）给语言以本体论地位，是开展语言研究的强大动力；（2）是认识共性和个性的基础；（3）决定了语言对比必须联系文化和心理背景，以语言的"内蕴形式"为重点；（4）是正确认识语言影响、语言渗透、语际转换和语际翻译等问题的基础。

For contrastive linguistics, it is important to understand that unless we come to a conclusion on language perspective, fundamental issues in contrastive linguistics such as the basis for contrast, contrastability and contrasting in form or meaning would not be possibly handled in the right direction. Pan Wenguo specifically proposed adopting the "language as worldview" of Humboldt as the philosophical ground, explaining the four significances in guiding contrastive research: (1) accord language with a place in ontology which will give language research the thrust to move forward; (2) provide the basis to understand universality and particularity; (3) determine the fact that contrastive study must consider circumstances in culture and psychology, focusing on the "internal form" of language; (4) providing the basis to understand issues on language influence, language infiltration, language switch and interlanguage translation.

而从语言角度看，必须对"什么是语言"有个清晰的认识。2001年，潘文国发表《语言的定义》长文，比较了160多年来中外关于语言的68种定义，从哲学角度进行了分析，最后提出了自己的新定义，作为语言学包括对比语言学研究的基础："语言是人类认知世界及进行表述的方式和过程。"（潘文国，2001a：35）

However, from a language perspective, there must be a standpoint about what "language" is. Pan Wenguo in "The definition of language" analyses 68 definitions of language given over 160 years from the philosophical point of view to arrive at his own definition that would serve the purpose of linguistics including contrastive linguistics: "Language is the fashion and process in which man cognizes and states the world" (Pan Wenguo, 2001a: 35).

另一方面，钱冠连在中国国内第一次对"萨丕尔-沃尔夫假说"作了正面评述，用证伪法证明了"说语言框架决定了思维框架，应该是说得通的"（同上，253页），并重新进行了表述：

On the other hand, within China, Qian Guanlian (2005) offered the first positive comment on the Sapir-Whorf Hypothesis. Using falsification, he attests that "It is logical to say that the frame of language determines the frame of mind" (Qian Guanlian, 2005: 253). Qian paraphrased the hypothesis as follows:

> 每一种语言的自主运动形成了它独特的变异与选择途径，独特的变异与选择途径形成了各自合理的语言规则或框架，各自合理的语言规则或框架最终规定了操不同语言的人的思维框式。（钱冠连，2005：271）

> The self-movement of each language results in its idiosyncratic variation and path selected, which in turn, formulates its own rational linguistic rules or frameworks, and that ultimately determines the particular frame of mind of the speakers of the different languages. (Qian Guanlian, 2005: 271)

这是洪堡特语言世界观理论的最新叙述，也为对比研究奠定了语言哲学的基础。As the latest interpretation of Humboldt's language conception, the above quote also laid the philosophical ground for contrastive linguistics.

3.3.2.4 对研究者知识结构的关注
3.3.2.4 The knowledge structure of researchers

如果承认对比语言学是一个独立的学科，那么，除了对学科本身的定位、性质、学科体系要有明晰的说法之外，对于研究者的资质要求也应要有明确的标准。最早谈到对对比研究者资质要求的是王力，早在60年前他就提出了两个标准：

To say that contrastive linguistics is an independent discipline, not only must there be clearly defined positioning, nature and operational framework, researchers in the discipline must meet set criteria too. Wang Li suggested two such requirements back in the 1940s:

> 中国语法学者须有两种修养：第一是中国语史学（Chinese philology）；第二是普通语言学（General linguistics）。缺一不可。若只精于中国语史学（如所谓"小学"），而不精于普通语言学，就只知道从古书中大事搜罗，把若干单词按英语的词类区分，成为一部"新经传释词"。若只精于普通语言学，而不精于中国语史学，就只知道运用若干术语，把中国的语法事实硬凑上去，成为别开生面的"削足适屦"。即以现代语法而论，若没有历史的根据，也难免于穿凿傅会，所以叶斯泊生《现代英语法》的全题是《以历史为根据的现代英语法》（A Modern English Grammar on Historical Principles）（王力，1943：19—20）

> Chinese grammarians must satisfy two areas of cultivation: Chinese philology and general linguistics. Both are required, no bargain. If we know only Chinese philology and nothing of general linguistics, we will end up collecting large amount of data from classical texts and group the words according to the word classes in English and there goes a new dictionary on terms in classical texts. If we know only general linguistics and nothing about Chinese philology, we are only good at applying terminologies and end up forcing in Chinese linguistic data, that is the other way of "cutting the feet to suit the shoe". Even with regards to modern grammar, if it is not grounded on historical context, we may have been distorting facts and stretching senses. No wonder Jespersen's Modern English Grammar is in full, *A Modern English Grammar on Historical Principles* (Wang Li, 1943: 19–20).

王力在这里谈的是"中国语法学者"，没有说"对比研究者"，但这两者在当时可说是一回事，因为从《马氏文通》开始到20世纪40年代末，没有一位语法研究者是脱离了与外语的对比来谈汉语语法的，语法研究可以不懂外语关起门来搞，是五十年代以后中国独有的怪事。正因为出现了"两张皮"的不正常现象，因此潘文国在谈到从事对比研究的条件时就提出了四项：
Although it is grammarians that Wang Li was talking about, it applies to contrastivists all the same. It was not until the late 1940s beginning from *Mashi*

Wentong that grammarians would speak on Chinese grammar without referring to foreign languages. Studying grammar behind closed doors was a strange thing in China for a period after the 1950s. Referring to this unusual "two-skin" phenomenon, Pan Wenguo put forward four requirements in contrastive study:

（1）现代英语知识；（2）现代汉语知识；（3）普通语言学的知识；（4）汉、英语历史和文化有关知识。其中前三项是基本的，第三项尤其重要。二十世纪是语言学大发展的时期，语言和语言学的重要性已经提高到了哲学的高度。如果对此认识不足，或者没有明确的语言观和语言研究方法论的指导，对比研究就无法在一个高起点进行。（潘文国，1997a：19）

Knowledge on modern English; Knowledge on modern Chinese; Knowledge on general linguistics; Knowledge on the history and culture of Chinese and English. The first three requirements are fundamental, particularly knowledge on general linguistics. The 20th century saw great development in linguistics. The importance of language and linguistics has been raised to a philosophical height. If we do not understand this correctly, or are not guided by a clear perspective of language or methodology, it would be impossible to scale higher in contrastive study. (Pan Wenguo, 1997a: 19)

其中第一、第二条对于五十年代以前的研究者来说是不成问题的，但到了八、九十年代的中国就成了严重的问题。第三、第四条的精神与王力是一致的，而第三条的提出更是从八十年代初那些失败的对比研究著作中提炼出来的教训，因为那些著作有一个共同点，就是语言学理论素养很差。第四条中加进了"文化"知识，这是受到八十年代下半叶中国文化语言学研究的启发。

The first two requirements were not difficult to comply with for scholars before the 1950s, but in the 1980s, they became difficult requirements. The last two requirements are consistent with Wang Li's and the third is actually the lesson drawn from works that failed contrastive linguistics in the early 1980s—these were works deficient in terms of theoretical knowledge. The fourth is inspired by cultural linguistics that emerged in the 1980s.

在学科的概念深入人心以后，杨自俭更具体地论述了研究者的知识结构问题，提出：

As the concept of the discipline spreads, Yang Zijian felt the urge to be even more specific on the issue:

> 一个英汉语对比研究者的知识结构似应包括以下几个部分：一是比较丰富的自然、社会、思维三个领域的基础知识；二是英汉语言及其语言学的基础理论；三是英汉语言史及其语言学史；四是相关学科的基础理论（包括哲学、认知科学、心理学、文化学、人类学、社会学等）；五是方法论基础（包括哲学、逻辑学、系统科学、心理学、计算机科学与语言学的方法等）；六是对比语言学的基础理论和方法。（杨自俭，2001：XIV）
>
> The knowledge base of an English-Chinese contrastivist must include the following areas: (1) a relative rich bank of basic knowledge in natural science, social science and thoughts; (2) fundamental theories on English-Chinese languages and linguistics; (3) histories on English-Chinese languages and linguistics; (4) fundamental theories of related disciplines (including philosophy, cognitive science, psychology, cultural studies, anthropology, sociology among others); (5) fundamental methodologies (including philosophy, logic, systems science, psychology, computational science and linguistics and others); (6) fundamental theory and methodology of contrastive linguistics. (Yang Zijian, 2001: xiv)

他提出了优化知识结构的四条建议：（1）区分核心层次与辅助层次，核心层次为上述的二、三、五、六；（2）要明白整体系统大于各部分总和的道理，理清各知识系统的关系；（3）根据个人奋斗目标建立不同于任何人的独特的知识结构，才能有独创性；（4）要培养跨学科的人才。
More precisely, he states the four strategies to optimize the required knowledge structure from both the organization and individual points of view: (1) to differentiate between core and secondary knowledge, the core refers to points 2, 3, 5 and 6 of the above; (2) to understand that the whole is greater than its composing parts put together, i.e. the need to sort out the relations in the knowledge structure; (3) to build up a knowledge structure in accordance with the aim of the individual for unique contribution; (4) to groom cross-disciplinary talents.

与研究者知识结构最相关的是所谓"两张皮"的问题，这个问题最早是吕叔湘提出来的，他在1980年说了两段话，一段是针对研究者的：

The "two-skin" phenomenon is very much related to the knowledge structure of the researcher. Observing this, Lü Shuxiang has two pieces of advice. One is for researchers:

> 有两种偏向我想提一提。一种偏向是谨守中国语言学的旧传统埋头苦干，旧传统里没有的东西一概不闻不问。……另一种偏向是空讲语言学，不结合中国实际，有时候引些中国事例，也不怎么恰当。……如果从中国传统语言学入手的人能在吸收西语言学方面下点功夫，如果从西方语言学入手的人能在结合中国语言实际上下点功夫，那就最好了。（吕叔湘，1980b：7—8）

> I would like to talk about two preferences. One of them stick closely to the old scholarship in Chinese linguistics and work hard within that frame, rejecting anything out of the traditional frame…The other is kind of empty talking, speaking on linguistics without integrating the facts in Chinese or sometimes with inappropriate illustrations…Only if those who approach traditional Chinese linguistics could spare some time on western linguistics; and only if those who approach western linguistics could spare some effort to blend in the facts of Chinese, it would be just great. (Lü Shuxiang, 1980b: 7–8)

另一段是针对人才培养的：
The other piece of advice is on talent grooming:

> 语言研究的后备军主要是大学中文系和外语系的学生。现在的情况是中文系不管学生的外语，外语系不管学生的汉语。课程是有的，可是抓得不紧，结果是中文系的学生不能用外语做工具，不能阅读用外语写的参考书，外语系的学生对祖国语言的历史和现状相当隔膜。这样就很难培养出大量的适合做语言研究工作的青年学者。（吕叔湘，1980b：18—19）

> The main pool of reserves for language researcher comes out of graduates of the Department of Chinese and Department of Foreign Language Studies. The current situation is such that the Chinese department would not take care of the foreign language requirement while the Foreign Language

Studies department would not take care of the Chinese requirement of their students. Sure, there are courses available, but the requirement is not there. Consequently, graduates of the Chinese department can't make foreign language their tool to read foreign references while that of the Foreign Language Studies are distant from the history and current status of their native tongue. Under such circumstances, to generate a large pool of suitable young candidates for language research is quite a task. (Lü Shuxiang, 1980b: 18–19)

这两段话比较尖锐地指出了20世纪50年代以后中国语言教学和研究的现状，希望借助70年代"百废俱兴"的东风能够得以解决。但实际上直到九十年代末仍无大的变化，因此吕先生斥之为"两张皮"，为之深感忧虑（见沈家煊，1996）。许国璋、王宗炎等前辈学人也发出了同样的担扰，终于促成了以解决这个问题作为中心议题的两次全国性会议。[1]

Lü's critical advice is evident of the state of affairs in China's language education and research since the 1950s. He had hoped that things would turn to the better riding on the waves of reformation. Sadly, things remained pretty much the same at the close of the twentieth century. That had Lü desperately worried as he dressed it down as the "two-skin" phenomenon (Shen Jiaxuan, 1996). Other senior linguists such as Xu Guozhang and Wang Zongyan were equally worried and finally two national conferences were held to address the issue.

中国对比研究者越来越自觉地将消除"两张皮"作为对自身最基本的素质要求，正在努力追踪四十年代王力、吕叔湘等曾达到过的境界。一些学者如杨自俭（2001b）、潘文国（2001c）、王菊泉（2002）、钱冠连（2002）等专门就此进行了理论上的探索。钱冠连以赵元任、吕叔湘、张志公三位成功结合中外文的研究者为例，指出：

We see a more conscious effort on the part of Chinese contrastivists to shake off the label of "two-skin" as a self-demand and the standards of Wang Li and Lü

---

[1] 2000年在厦门召开的中国英汉语比较研究会第四次学术研讨会和2001年在大连召开的首届中国外语教授学术沙龙。
The first was The Fourth National Conference on English-Chinese Contrastive Studies in Xiamen in the year 2000; the next was the inauguration of the Scholastic Salon for Foreign Language Studies Professors in Dalian in the year 2001.

Shuxiang are their targets. To facilitate this, a group of scholars approached the issue theoretically: Yang Zijian (2001b), Pan Wenguo (2001c), Wang Juquan (2002) and, Qian Guanlian (2002) to list a few. Citing the successful integration examples of Chao Yuen-ren, Lü Shuxiang and Zhang Zhigong by their mastery in foreign languages, western theories and Chinese linguistics, Qian Guanlian points out that:

> 外语学者走上回归母语之路，不是汉语发展规律性、必然性的引导，而是一种学术自觉。……只掌握一种语言的人，使该种语言体系处于不可能被怀疑的地位。只有在不同的语言之间发生对比时才可能产生对语言价值观的质疑，因而掌握两种以上语言的人才能从不同语言的价值观的对比中由质疑开始探明真相。（钱冠连，2002: 68）

> The return to mother tongue by foreign language learners is neither part of the development pattern of Chinese language nor its necessary induction. It is a form of scholastic self-awareness…A monolingual would never have any suspicions on the language he/she speaks. Only when two languages are at contrast would suspicions be arouse on language values. As such, only bilinguals or multilinguals could get to the truth with the suspicions aroused by contrasting the values of different languages. (Qian Guanlian, 2002: 68)

他还提出两结合最好体现在一人身上：
He further suggests that the integration would be best achieved in single person rather than through cooperative effort:

> 由一人实现比较与吸收效应是理想状态。……由许多人（集体）完成两张皮合为一张皮的路子，虽然也是一条路子，但两类人难以合作得紧密、协调、同步，因而拖长了时间。（钱冠连，2002: 70）

> Ideally, to realize the conduct and effect of contrast in one single person would be best…If converging "two skins" onto "one-skin" requires cooperative effort involving many people, no doubt it is also a way out, but it would be more difficult to get two groups of people closely working together on the same frequency and at the same pace. It would drag the process. (Qian Guanlian, 2002: 70)

这个问题的最终解决，将使中国的对比研究从整体上更上一个台阶。不过至少就目前而言，虽然已有了一些先知先觉者，但总体形势还不容乐观。
If this problem gets finally resolved, the overall strength of the discipline in China would go up a notch. As it is now, though there may be higher awareness and some initiatives, it is still tough on the whole.

3.3.2.5 在对比研究中怎样对待西方理论？
3.3.2.5 Western theories in contrastive studies

由于整个中国"现代语言学"的大厦是从西方嫁接来的，而汉语又是如此不同于西方印欧语的语言，这就使在对比研究乃至整个汉语语言学的建设中，如何对待西方理论与如何对待"汉语特色"成了一个"永恒的主题"。所有的现代汉语和现代语言学研究者，尽管他实际上可能是个"知内不知外"的"两张皮"者，但在研究中都得装出个对比专家的样子，否则就无法谈什么"汉语特点"了；而那些一心一意引进西方理论、"知外不知内"的唯洋是从者，也爱在照搬照抄外语例子的同时，时不时举几个汉语例子（哪怕是将英语句子翻译过来），显得他们也是"结合汉语实际"者。20世纪这100年恐怕自始至终在"异"啊"同"啊这些问题上挣扎，只不过有时候"同"讲得多些，有时候"异"更强调些。由于人人都讲"结合"，这是每个在中国搞语言研究的人都逃不掉的一门课，因此吕叔湘要说：

The institution of modern linguistics in the whole of China is some form of "technology transfer" from the West. Given that Chinese is so vastly different from Indo-European languages, the positioning of western linguistic theories in contrastive studies as well as the whole construct of Chinese linguistics relative to maintaining "Chinese characteristics" becomes an eternal theme. As argued earlier, research in (modern) Chinese language and modern linguistics must necessarily involve some aspects of contrastive linguistics if not all. "Integration" is at the forefront of the minds of all language and linguistics researchers in China. Each and every student of modern Chinese and modern linguistics, despite being a "two-skin" who is not equipped with western knowledge, must act like an expert in contrastive studies in order to gain authority on the subject of "Chinese characteristics". And the ardent followers of western theories, who copy indiscriminately and are completely ignorant about their mother tongue, frequently throw in a few Chinese examples (even if those are examples translated from English) to show off their attempt at "integrating" the linguistic facts of Chinese. The last 100 years of the twentieth century has been overcast with struggles on "differences" and "similarities" in a range of shapes and tones at different periods of time. Lü Shuxiang therefore lamented:

> 过去,中国没有系统的语法论著,也就没有系统的语法理论,所有理论都是外来的。外国的理论在那儿翻新,咱们也就跟着转。这不是坏事,问题是不论什么理论都得结合汉语的实际,可是"结合"二字谈何容易,机械地搬用乃至削足适履的事情不是没有发生过。(吕叔湘,1986)

> In the past, there were no systematic grammars for Chinese and systematic grammatical theories were not found. All theories were imported. Whenever there is an update, we simply follow suit. This is not necessarily bad. The issue is whatever the theory, it has got to accommodate and incorporate Chinese as it is. And "integration", how easy said than done. It is not as if mechanical adaptation to the extent of distortion never had happened. (Lü Shuxiang, 1986, Preface)

前面我们已经看到了在之前的九十年里的情况,现在我们要着重来看看最近这十几年来对比研究在这个问题上的进展。为了看得清楚些,我们分成三节来谈。这一节(3.3.2.5.)谈如何对待外来理论,后面二节分别谈谈对"中国特色"的发现和对语言"异""同"问题的最新认识。

Building on earlier accounts of the situation before the 1980s, we now turn to the development on this issue over the last few decades. We shall organize the discussion as follows: management of induced theories (3.3.2.5); illuminating "Chinese characteristics" (3.3.2.6) and the latest opinions on "similarity and differences" (3.3.2.7).

在对待西方理论问题上,认为现有的西方语言学理论不符合汉语实际,恐怕是个越来越强烈的趋势。上面吕叔湘提出了个"跟着转"说,朱德熙则创造了个"印欧语的眼光"说:

On the management of western theories, it is generally reckoned that existing western theories fail to match with the facts in Chinese and are not appropriate for

Chinese. Increasingly, more and more Chinese are supporting the view. By what Lü Shuxiang described as "following" western theories, Zhu Dexi termed the phenomenon as using "Indo-European eyes" in his comment as follows:

> ……有一些语言学者企图摆脱印欧语的束缚，探索汉语身躯的语法规律。尽管他们做了不少有价值的工作，但仍然难以消除长期以来印欧语语法观念带来的消极影响。这种影响主要表现在用印欧语的眼光来看待汉语，把印欧语所有而汉语所无的东西强加给汉语。（朱德熙，1985：iii）

> …some linguists attempt to break out of the Indo-European frame to explore the self-contained grammatical rules within Chinese. They have no doubt, done a lot of valuable work. Nevertheless, it is not easy to get rid of the negative effect brought by Indo-European grammatical values all these years. One expression of such negative influence would be looking at Chinese with Indo-European eyes, imposing on Chinese what is found in Indo-European languages but that does not apply to Chinese. (Zhu Dexi, 1985: iii)

以上两位都是汉语学者，英语学者程雨民则提出了个"迁就说"：
These are not just the views of linguists on Chinese language, as this quote from English language scholar Cheng Yumin shows:

> 回过头来看汉语研究时，常觉得汉语学界太迁就欧美语言学理论。欧美理论中有许多不适用于汉语处，显然是由于欧美学者缺乏汉语知识而残留的，就像他们当年尚未认识欧洲现代语言时也曾带着拉丁语的成见看自己的语言一样。但中国语言学界都没有与他们较真。
> （程雨民，2003：1）

> Looking at research in Chinese language in retrospect, our counterparts in the discipline tend to give in too much to European and American linguistic theories. There are far too many mismatches when trying to apply these theories to Chinese. Obviously, this is because European and American scholars are ignorant of Chinese, in the way they treat their own languages with the prejudice of Latin eyes before they learnt of modern European languages. However, our fellow colleagues in the Chinese linguistics circle did

not bother to voice their objections. (Cheng Yumin, 2003: 1)

而钱冠连提出了个更激进的"死套"说：
Even more critical, Qian Guanlian described this as "dogmatic copying":

> 所谓"死套"，即用英语的语言文化概念或者语法模式套汉语，套不进也要套，套不全也要套，套不舒服也要套。（钱冠连，2000: 20）
>
> By "dogmatic copying", the language and cultural concepts of English or the grammatical model of English are modeled onto Chinese, even if they cannot be fitted in, even if the fit is partial, even if the fit is uncomfortable. (Qian Guanlian, 2000: 20)

就整个第五期的对比研究而言，对西方理论用于汉语的最激烈批评体现在两个问题上，一是"形态说"，二是"词"的概念。
To illustrate, two issues in Phase 5 have ignited the fiercest censure on the application of western theories on Chinese. One is on morphology; the other is on the concept of the "word".

3.3.2.5.1 对"形态说"从再次动摇到坚决否定
3.3.2.5.1 The morphology viewpoint: from again wavering to outright reject

马建忠引进西方"葛朗玛"，编出了中国第一本语法书《马氏文通》，同时也引发了长达一个多世纪的中西语法异同之争、特别是作为西方语法学核心的"形态"有无之争。大体上来说，20世纪50年代之前，在欧美语言学家和汉学家叶斯柏森、房德里耶斯、萨丕尔、高本汉、马伯乐等人的影响下，中国的主要语法学家几乎无例外地都主张汉语"无形态"，陈承泽、黎锦熙、王力、吕叔湘、何容、高名凯等对此都有精辟的论述。1950年斯大林著作《马克思主义与语言学问题》的发表与苏联汉学家关于汉语性质的论断的引进是一个转折点，自那以后，汉语有形态的呼声越来越高，寻找汉语形态的热情也越来越高涨，特别是高名凯关于汉语实词不能分类的观点遭到批判之后，一些老学者黎锦熙、王力、吕叔湘等或被迫检讨，或改变观点，或王顾左右而言他。六十年代以后，苏联语言学的影响式微了，拼命找汉语"形态"的势头有所遏制，但形态问题始终困扰着汉语学者。直到1979年吕叔湘发表《汉语语法分析问题》，提出"汉语缺少严格意义的形态变化"，"缺少发达的形态"（1979：11），才算对这番争论重新作了总结。此后吕叔湘的这两句话成了相当一段时期汉语研究的主旋律。但这句话实际上是含含糊糊、模棱两可的："缺少"，那就是还有；没有"严格意义的"、"发达的"，那就还有"非严格意义的"、"不那么发达的"，因此尽管支持了无形态论者，也给形态论者留下了口实。大约是因为吕叔湘还对五十年代的那场争论心有余悸，说得不很干脆。直到1990年，半个世纪来影响最大的另一位语法学家、两次汉语语法"共同纲领"的主持者张志公才鲜明地表达了对"形态论"的态度：

From the point Ma Jianzhong imported the concept of "grammar" and brought out the first ever Chinese grammar by Chinese, *Mashi Wentong*, he has also initiated a century long debate on the resemblanceness between Chinese and western grammars, especially on the subject of morphology at the core of western grammar. By and large, all eminent Chinese linguists under the influence of European and American linguists such as Otto Jespersen, J. Vendryès, Edward Sapir, Bernhard Karlgren, Henri Maspéro and others, do not buy in to the idea of morphology in Chinese. That was in the years before 1950. Their pertinent views were well documented in the works of Chen Chengze, Li Jinxi, Wang Li, Lü Shuxiang, He Rong and Gao Mingkai. The twist of events came about in year 1950 when Joseph Stalin released his essays on *Marxism and Problems in Linguistics* and the subsequent introduction of the judgment by Soviet sinologists. Since then, morphology is to be found in Chinese and, true enough, more efforts were directed at validating the existence of morphology. This was particularly the case after Gao Mingkai was criticized for advocating no word classification for notional words and senior linguists like Li Jinxi, Wang Li and Lü Shuxiang were impelled to review or change their minds or beat around the bush. The episode gradually died down following the diminishing influence of Soviet power after the 1960s, but the issue of morphology lingered and many could not ease their minds on the issue, not until Lü Shuxiang drew a conclusion in his paper of 1979 on *Issues in Grammatical Analysis in Chinese* where he declared "Chinese does not have morphological changes in the strict sense" and "there is a lack of matured morphological devices" (1979: 11). Thereafter, the conclusions by Lü Shuxiang dominated for quite a while. Clearly,

Lü Shuxiang was being vague. "Lack of" could mean positive; not "in the strict sense", lacking in morphological devices that are "matured" could be interpreted as having some morphological changes less strictly speaking, using less matured devices. So, his open support for the "no morphology" camp has in fact allowed breathing space for the morphology camp. With the debate of the 1950s still fresh in his mind, we could understand that Lü Shuxiang may have to choose to word it that way. It is Zhang Zhigong, the other most influential grammarian in the last 50 years, who presided over the projects on establishing a "common programme" in Chinese grammar with a bias towards morphology, who comes up with a clear stand on the morphology issue almost a decade after Lü spoke up. He wrote in 1990:

> 以印欧语系的语言为基础而产生的语法框架和语言学理论，从根本上同汉语不相适应。印欧语都是形态语，所以他们的语法框架照例包括形态学和造句法两大部分，尽管两部分内容有时相互交错。这个框架从根本上说是不适用于汉语的。汉语本身是"非形态语言"。形态语和非形态语是明显不同的两种语言体系，我们应当理直气壮、明白无误地确认汉语"非形态"这一事实，从而有勇气打破印欧语的语法框架探索和建立汉语自己的语法体系。（张志公，1990：415）

> Linguistic theories and grammatical frameworks having their roots in Indo-European languages are in essence unsuitable for Chinese. Indo-European languages being morphological are normal to have included morphology and syntax as the two components in their grammatical frameworks even though there may be overlapping content wise. Such framework is in essence unsuitable for Chinese. Chinese is a non-morphological language. Obviously, morphological and non-morphological languages are two language systems. We should stand fearlessly and confidently, plainly and unmistakably in acknowledging the fact that Chinese is non-morphological. Only then would we have the courage to break free from the Indo-European framework and explore on our own to establish a grammatical system truly Chinese. (Zhang Zhigong, 1990: 415)

一个不可忽视的事实是，在九十年代硕果仅存的老一辈汉语语法学家中，精通外语甚至是英语"科班出身"，完全不存在"两张皮"现象的只有吕叔湘、张志公两位。他们在晚年对形态问题乃至汉语研究根本问题的深刻反思，不能不说是他们从事对比研究一辈子做出的最后总结，他们的观点值得后来者认真咀嚼。

It should be noted that among the pioneers who are still around in the 1990s, only Lü Shuxiang and Zhang Zhigong are highly proficient in foreign languages, in fact they were both graduates of the English language, and do not exhibit the "two-skin" phenomenon. In the last lap of their life, both continued reflecting honestly on the issues of morphology and other fundamental issues in Chinese linguistic research. We ought to look at their conclusions drawn on a lifelong commitment on contrastive studies.

3.3.2.5.2 对汉语中"词"的概念的质疑
3.3.2.5.2 Questioning the concept of "word" in Chinese

《马氏文通》以来汉语在词类问题上的论争反反复复，汉语的实词能不能分类？该分哪些类？具体的词该如何一个个归类？经过多年论争，一位著名学者乐观地认为："现代汉语词类问题经过七十年的探索，通过多次讨论，应该说已经取得了重大进展。尽管目前还有一些不同意见，但是在不少主要问题上多数人的意见已逐步趋于一致。"（胡明扬，1996：44）但在同一本论文集里，另一位著名学者却不以为然："从《马氏文通》开始，一百年来词类成了汉语语言学的永恒主题，汉语学界年年谈，人人谈，但至今依然不如人意，依然是语法学中的一个'老大难'。"（史有为，1996：56）史有为还进一步指出了问题的症结：

Since *Mashi Wentong*, word class has long been an unsettled issue. May notional words in Chinese be classified? If so, what are the possible classes? How specifically may the words be classified? After years of deliberation, a well-known scholar became optimistic: "After 70 years of explorations and discussions, we could say that we have made great progress on the issue of word class despite some divided opinions. The majority are agreeing on most of the key issues" (Hu Mingyang, 1996: 44). In the same volume, another well-known scholar thinks otherwise: "For a hundred years from *Mashi Wentong*, word class remains as the eternal theme in Chinese linguistics. Year in year out, everyone in the Chinese linguistic circle speaks about it with no satisfactory outcome thus far. It is still a big old obstacle in grammar" (Shi Youwei, 1996: 56). Shi

Youwei proceeds to explain the reason behind this:

> 我们过于迷信词类：西方语言有词类，那么汉语也应该有词类，否则不成"落后"了吗？没有词类，我们又怎么讲语法呢？然而，当"词"这一单位的存在及其普遍性都有待证明的时候，我们又怎能迷信词类的存在是必然的和普遍的呢？说到底，对于汉语，现今的词类并非客观已有，它只是一种假说，是一种为了图解语言规则的工具，因此它也只是主观的产物。（史有为，1996: 57）

> We have overly believed in word class: There are word classes in western languages, so there must be word classes in Chinese, otherwise we would be deemed as "backward"! In the absence of word classes, how could we explain grammar? However, before we could attest the existence and universality of the grammatical unit "word" how could we believe blindly in its existence and universalism? To put it plainly, "word" for Chinese is no longer an objective existence, it is merely a hypothesis, a tool to illustrate grammatical rules, as such it is at most a product of subjectivity. (Shi Youwei, 1996: 57)

这里提到了"'词'这一单位的存在及其普遍性都有待证明"的问题，事实上，这正是八、九十年代以来汉语研究对普通语言学的最大挑战，其严重性更甚于词类问题。

Shi Youwei is absolutely right in saying that the grammatical unit "word" has its existence and its universality uncontested. In reality, this is the biggest challenge Chinese linguistics has had for general linguistics over the past 80 or 90 years. It is a tougher question than word classification.

在汉语研究史上，"字""词"之分，或者说，"词"的概念的提出是1907年（章士钊 1907）以后的事，以后黎锦熙、王力、吕叔湘、高名凯无不谈这个问题。高名凯主张汉语实词不能分类，但对"词"的概念的存在却没有什么怀疑。到了20世纪60年代，吕叔湘最早对此表示了怀疑，他在给《文字改革》杂志写的系列文章[1]中首次表露了出来：

In the research history of the Chinese language, the division of "character" and

---

[1] 这些文章到1980年集结成《语文常谈》一书。我们的引文出自该书。
These articles were compiled into a collection in 1980. We are quoting from the compilation.

"word" or the concept of "word" was after the year 1907 (Zhang Shizhao 1907). Since then, no Chinese scholars ever tried to avoid confronting the issue. Li Jinxi, Wang Li, Lü Shuxiang and Gao Mingkai have all deliberated. Gao Mingkai rejected the idea of word classification but he did not contest the concept of "word". It was Lü Shuxiang who first voiced his doubt about the concept of "word" in the 1960s. In one of his column articles for the journal *Wenzi Gaige* (《文字改革》), he writes:

> "词"在欧洲语言里是现成的……汉语恰好相反,现成的是"字"……汉语里的"词"之所以不容易归纳出一个令人满意的决定,就是因为本来没有这样一种现成的东西。其实啊,讲汉语语法也不定非有"词"不可。(吕叔湘,1980:45)
>
> "word" is ready made in European languages…the opposite is true for Chinese, "character" is on the shelf for us…It is not easy to reach a satisfactory conclusion on "word" in Chinese because we do not have it standing ready in our tongue. In reality, "word" is not necessary in our description of Chinese grammar. (Lü Shuxiang, 1980: 45)

但这一说法太"离经叛道",即使出自吕叔湘之口,也没有引起什么重视。1979年,在《汉语语法分析问题》里,吕叔湘引了赵元任的话:"我们为什么要在汉语里寻找那些存在于别的语言里的东西呢?进一步研究的更有成效的途径应该是,决定在那些单音字儿和句子之间有哪些类型的中间单位,而把管这些类型的单位叫什么这个问题放在次要地位去考虑。"(吕叔湘 1979:98)并特别注明这是从赵元任用英语写的一篇文章中翻译的,表明吕叔湘始终在考虑汉语到底有没有"词"的问题。1992年,吕叔湘所提到的赵元任的文章 *Rhythm and Structure in Chinese Word Conceptions*,连同赵氏的其他一些文章,被译成中文,收在《中国现代语言学的开拓和发展——赵元任语言学论文选》一书中出版,文中下面一段话特别引起人们关注:

Despite coming from Lü Shuxiang, the remark was too outrageous to be taken seriously. In Lü Shuxiang (1979), he translated a quote from Chao Yuen-ren as saying: "Why must we find in Chinese entities that exist in other languages? A more fruitful way of further study would be to determine just what types of intermediary units there are between the monosyllabic word and the sentence and then leave for secondary consideration on the question of what to call those types of units" (Lü Shuxiang, 1979: 98/Chao Yuen-ren, 1976: 282). In fact, Chao's paper "Rhythm and Structure in Chinese Word Conceptions" is very precise on the whole issue:

> 印欧系语言中word这一级单位就是这一类的概念,它在汉语里没有确切的对应物……如果我们观察用某一种语言说出的大量话语,例如英语,考虑一下这些话语中小片段的情况,并拿它们跟汉语中同样的小片段作个比较,我想,"字"这个名称(这样说是因为我希望先避免把word这个词用于汉语)将和word这个词在英语中的角色相当。也就是说,在说英语的人谈到word的场合,说汉语的人说到的是"字"。这样说绝不意味着"字"的结构特性与英语的word相同,甚至连近于相同也谈不上。(赵元任,1975: 233)

> The word unit in Indo-European languages is one of those conceptions that have no exact counterpart in Chinese. In the classical stage of the Chinese language, that is, in the language of the great classics and the early philosophers, there was perhaps a fair degree of resemblance between Chinese monosyllable and a word in the Western sense. But in modern Chinese this is far from being the case…If we observe a fairly large number of utterances in a language like English, for illustration, concerning small parts of utterances and compare them with similar utterances in Chinese, I think the name—for I want to avoid the use of the word "word" as applied to Chinese for the time being—the name Tzu¡ (字) would play a corresponding part that the word "word" plays in English; that is, on most occasions in which an English-speaking person speaks of words, a Chinese would speak of Tzǔ. But this is far from saying that the structural character of Tzu¡ is the same, or even nearly the same, as that of a word in English. (Chao Yuen-ren, 1976: 276—277)

这就是汉语语言学界近年来越来越令人瞩目的"字本位"说的滥觞。其后,徐通锵(1994a;1994b;1997;2001a)、潘文国(1996c;1997a;2002b)、陈保亚(1999)、王洪君(2000)、鲁川(2001)等发表了一系列有影响力的论文和著作,渐渐使"字本位"形成了一套比较完整的理论。
This could be the source that germinated the "Sinigram-based" theory of recent

years and which has been gaining greater grounds in Chinese linguistics. A series of important articles expounding on the theory helped shape and perfect the theory, including Xu Tongqiang (1994a; 1994b; 1997; 2001a), Pan Wenguo (1996c; 1997a; 2002b), Chen Baoya (1999), Wang Hongjun (2000) and Lu Chuan (2001).

英语界的学者程雨民经过深思熟虑之后，也彻底地否定了汉语中"词"的概念，他说：

From the English language field, Cheng Yumin also completely rejects the idea of "word" in the Chinese language after serious considerations:

> 汉语中历来没有欧洲语言中的"词"这一概念，过去用到"词"这字时，指的是"虚字"或"语辞"。直到近代，在西方语言学影响下，同时也由于看到汉语中双音化（包括多音化）的趋向，中国语言学家才想到建立"词"的概念，但一直未能找到一个满意的定义。（程雨民，2003：13）

> The concept of "word" in European languages is never found in the Chinese language. In the past, we use the character "word" (词) to refer to "empty words" (虚字) or "auxiliary" (语辞). Until recently, under the influence of western linguistics on top of the increasing disyllabicity (or even multi-syllabicity) of Chinese, have Chinese linguists gegun to consider establishing the concept of "word" but have to date, not been able to find a satisfactory definition. (Cheng Yumin, 2003: 13)

否定"形态说"和否定"词"的概念是语言对比研究带有全局性的大问题，牵一发而动全身，对普通语言学理论是个相当大的冲击。对多数持稳健态度的学者来说，这是个轻易触不得的"雷区"；但对有闯劲、有抱负的学者来说，这是一个重大的突破口。

The dismissal of morphology and the concept of word are two big issues in language contrast relating to the big picture, the slightest change would create great repercussions. These are great challenges to the validation of language universal. To many prudent scholars, this is a mine not to be swept easily. To the more aggressive and more idealistic scholars, this is the breakthrough point.

3.3.2.6 在对比中发现的"汉语特色"
3.3.2.6 Illuminating "Chinese characteristics" through contrastive studies

如果对比的结果拒绝了普通语言学的某些方面是属于"破",那么,发现普通语言学所没有论及到的"汉语特点"就属于"立"。王力在这方面是主张最积极的一个:

If the findings of contrastive studies found to be contradicting general linguistics could be looked upon as "destructive", then the discovery of "Chinese characteristics" which are not touched upon in general linguistics could be considered as "constructive". Wang Li is the most active proponent of being constructive:

> 中国所特有的方法规律,往往为马氏所忽略,因为马氏先看西洋方法里有什么,然后看中国有无类似的东西;至于西洋所不分别者,他就往往不能在中国文法里看出来了。此后我们最重要的工作在乎寻求中国方面的特点;比较语言学能帮助我们研究,但我们不能专恃比较语言学为分析中国文法的根据。(王力,1936/1985: 93)

> The unique methods and rules in Chinese are often neglected in Ma's grammar for Ma began by looking at what is found in western grammar, then he looked for them in Chinese. For things that are not distinguished in western grammar, Ma often missed the point in Chinese. From now on, it is most important for us to search for characteristics in Chinese. Contrastive linguistics may assist us in the process, but we may not rely solely on contrastive studies as the basis to analyse grammar in Chinese. (Wang Li, 1936/1985: 93)

他对"比较语言学"(实为对比语言学)似有所不屑,但对比不一定是由外到中,也可以由中到外;找到的"中国特点",也必须通过对比,确定在外国没有,那才是真正的"中国特点"。何况找的过程本身就必须通过对比来进行。可见王力这话有点过了头,这里面其实有个全面认识对比语言学的问题。

Here, Wang Li seems to be holding up on contrastive linguistics. Actually, contrastive study is not a unidirectional one beginning from foreign languages; it may begin from the Chinese language as well. To claim "characteristics" found, the processes must be by way of contrast to ensure that they are not found in other languages. Wang Li may have understated contrastive linguistics and that really involves a comprehensive understanding of contrastive linguistics.

3.3.2.6.1 "汉语特色"的三个层次
3.3.2.6.1 "Chinese characteristics" at three levels

一百多年来，人人都在讲"寻找汉语特点"，发现的"汉语特色"也可谓多矣。但据我们观察，就像对比研究可分三个层次一样，这些"汉语特点"也可以分三个层次。第一层，是借用西方的术语，但作出汉语的解释；第二层是在西方体系的框架内修修补补，增增减减；第三种是跳出西方体系，另辟蹊径。我们将会发现，第三种才真正符合对比研究的精神。

Over the past century, almost everyone has been talking about "Chinese characteristics" and we certainly have discovered many. However, these so-called "characteristics" may be grouped into three types. In the first level are those labelled with a western terminology but attached with a Chinese definition. Characteristics at the second level are generated by mending the western framework with some additions and subtractions. Characteristics at the third level jumped out of the western framework. Only those at the third level match the spirit of contrastive linguistics.

第一种比较典型的例子是主、谓、宾等这一套西方语法惯用的术语。事实上，按照现在流行的一些汉语语法体系，汉语和英语的主语、谓语、宾语已经很少共同点了。在汉语语法界影响极大的朱德熙的《语法讲义》里可以看得很清楚。表3.2 是朱书中"主语"、"谓语"、"宾语"的语义角色及其与英语的比较。

Typically belonging to type 1 is redefinition of the set of western terminologies such as subject, predicate, object, etc. In reality, according to popular grammatical systems for Chinese, there is little in common with English now in terms of subject, predicate and object. A survey of Zhu Dexi's *Notes on Grammar*—a little booklet that has far reaching impact on Chinese grammar analysis—demonstrates this. Table 3.2 is a summary of semantic roles of "subject", "predicate" and "object" explained in Zhu Dexi (1982) in comparison with English counterparts.

表3.2 汉语中使用的西方语法术语

	朱德熙分类（1982）	英语	特征说明
主语	施事 受事 与事 工具 时间 处所 周遍性主语 谓词性主语	√ √ √	汉语可以有谓词性主语，即动词、形容词可充当主语，形式上无须变化。表示"周遍性"也是主语的功能。
谓语	动词谓语 体词性谓语 形容词谓语 "是"谓语 主谓谓语 "的"字结构谓语	√ √	英语中的体词性谓语与汉语由"是"组成的谓语有相似之处。主谓结构谓语是汉语一大特色。
动宾关系	受事 施事 工具 结果 运动的终点 动作延续时间 处所宾语 时间宾语 存现宾语 准宾语 双宾语 虚指宾语 程度宾语 谓词性宾语 指称性宾语 陈述性宾语	√ √	英语中的动宾关系也很复杂，但情况不同。两种语言使用同样名称的结构情况很不相同，例如存在结构。计算语言学也显示两种语言中与"主语—动词"、"形名结构"、"副动结构"等相比，动宾结构最不相配。

Table 3.2 Use of western terminologies in Chinese grammar

	Classification in Zhu Dexi (1982)	English	Remarks in Characteristics
Subject	Agent Patient Dative Instrument Time Location	√ √ √	—Subject in Chinese may be "predicative" i.e. verb and adjective may serve as subject without changes in form. (p.101) —Indication of "all inclusive" is one of the functions of "subject". Therefore, patient, dative, instrument must occupy the subject position when referring to all the members. (p.99)
Predicate	Verbal Nominal Adjectival *Shi*-construction subject-predicate *de*-construction	√ √	—The predicate nominative in English is similar in part to predicate in Chinese constructed with the *shi*-construction. —Predicate formed by a subject-predicate construction in Chinese is a point of interest.
Verb-Object relations	Patient Agent Instrument Location Time Existential Degree Given-object Quasi-object Double-object etc.	√ √	Predicate-object relations in English can be as complex in a different way. Constructions by the same name may be represented in very different ways in the two languages——for example, existential construction. Research in computational linguistics also demonstrated that V-O mapping in the two languages is the lowest among other key relations such as subject-verb, adjective-noun, adverb-verb etc.

主语跟谓语合起来，英汉语可以对应的只有20%。而除了受事宾语和双宾语之外，80%以上在译成英语时是要处理成宾语以外的其他成分的。两种情况

下汉语和英语的差异都在80%，这个数字不可谓不小，完全可说体现了"汉语的特色"了。但是这样的"特色"从普通语言学来看有什么理论意义呢？人们会说，既然差别那么大，你干脆另外取一个名称好了，何必还要叫"主语"、"谓语"什么的呢？就好比英语"th"的发音，与其把它归到[t]或[s]里，然后再大讲其发音时如何不同于[t]或[s]的"特色"，不如另外用一个音标（[θ]）。前面讲到，王还（1986：326）强调对比研究要注意"同一语法术语在两种语言中所代表的内容不会完全相同"，其实这一不同完全是汉语语法学家自己造成的。随着这类"特色"发现得越来越多，对于对外汉语教学造成了越来越大的困难。60年前王力曾经说过一段颇为风趣的话：

> Equivalents of "subject" and "predicate" in English and Chinese in terms of semantic roles and syntactic forms account for only 20 per cent. As for the case of "object", in terms of translating into English, only patient and double objects remain as they are, while the rest have to be managed as other parts of speech. In sum, the difference could be as great as 80 per cent and there seems to be sufficient grounds to claim "characteristics". This then leads to the next question of what significance could be accorded to such characteristics from the perspective of general linguistics. The point is, why not give it a different name instead of adapting the same terminology? This is like the pronunciation of "th" in English; instead of grouping it under either [t] or [s] and explaining in pain the differences, dedicating a phonetic [θ] would save the trouble. Earlier on, we quoted Wang Huan (1986: 326) as a reminder of the disparity in connotation for the same terminology used in different languages; in fact, such disparity may be the creation of Chinese linguists. The more of such "characteristics" being "discovered", the greater will be the difficulty in TCFL/TCSL. Wang Li was being humorous in 1960 when he said:

> 假如有一个英国人跟您学习中国语法，您告诉他，"马"是名词，"白"是形容词，"跑"是动词，等等，又告诉他，在"狗咬吕洞宾"这句话里，"狗"是主语，"咬"是动词，"吕洞宾"是目的位，等等，那英国人一定大失所望，因为您只套取了英语语法的一些术语，并没有把中国语的结构方式告诉他。（王力，1943/1985：23）

> Say if a British tries to learn Chinese grammar with you and you tell

him ma "Horse" is a noun, bai "White" is an adjective, pao "Run" is a verb, etc, and you also tell him that in the sentence "dog bites Lü Dongbin", "dog" is the subject, "bites" the verb and "Lü Dongbing" is the object, etc, and he would definitely be disappointed because all that you have done is to abstract the terminology in English grammar without telling him how Chinese sentences are being structured. (Wang Li, 1943/1985: 23)

我们曾在课堂上多次引过这段话,学生们哈哈大笑,但实际上很少有人真正理解那英国人为什么失望,因为对于只是"就汉语而研究汉语"的人来说,能够知道"名动形、主动宾"不是够了吗?他们完全不能理解这些术语在以英语为母语的人心里引起的联想,决不只是贴上了几个标签那么简单。萨丕尔举过一个类似的例子,也许有助于我们体会这种心理:

Whenever we quote this example, students will break into laughter but few really understand why the British would be disappointed. For those who only research into the Chinese language, perhaps knowing a few terminologies like subject-verb-object, etc. would suffice; they could not understand what those terminologies really mean to native English speakers—more than just a label. Sapir has another example:

> 把The man kills the duckling译成汉语"人宰鸭",看来完全对等,但是中国人绝对不会意识到这一按字面直译的句子在我们说英语的人心里引起的那种幼稚、空洞、一顿一顿的感觉。三个具体概念,两个是物,一个是动作,都直接用一个单音节词表达,而每个音节还都表示一个基本成分;"主语"和"宾语"这两个相关概念就靠在动词前或后的位置来表示,仅此而已。指称的有定无定啦,动词所隐含的人称、数,以及时态啦,更不用说性了,在汉语句子中都不见了。(萨丕尔,1921: 92)

If we translate "The man kills the duckling" as "人宰鸭" in Chinese, it looks perfectly faithful but from this nominal translation, the Chinese will never ever share the same kind of naïve, emptiness, meals after meals feeling speakers of English will feel from the English sentence. Among the three specific concepts, two are objects, one is an action and all are monosyllabic with each syllabic representing a fundamental part in speech. The "subject" and "object" are just positions before or after the verb. Definiteness and indefiniteness case, numbers, aspects and tenses hidden in a verb, are gone in the Chinese sentences, not to mention about gender. (Sapir, 1921: 92)

这还是汉语与英语"相对应"的情况。如果像现在这样不相对应，那我们在教外国人时还得告诉他："喏，这是主语，但我们汉语的主语与你们英语是很不相同的，只有三种情况跟你们差不多，其余的在你们英语里要译成状语。还有，这个是主语谓语短语作主语，那个是主语谓语短语作谓语。"我想这个人一定比王力讲的那个英国人还要失望，而且会愤慨："这不是故意添乱吗！"看来汉语研究要跟西方接轨，先要从"不添乱"开始。这是我们通过对比得到的一点认识，也许可供国内的汉语研究者参考。

And Sapir was referring to an example where it is at least syntactically "equivalent". In cases where finding an equivalent is difficult, we will have to qualify further by telling our foreign students that "well, this is the subject, but 'subject' in Chinese is different from that in English except for three sub-categories. Others would have to be translated as adverbial constructions. And oh, a "subject-predicate" construction may occupy the position of subject or predicate." Perhaps the British in Wang Li's example would be even more disappointed if not angry at the confusion. If the Chinese really wanted an alignment with the West in scholarship, the first "don't" would be "not to be confusing". This is the lesson from contrastive studies.

　　第二种是在西方体系框架基础上增减调整。这一种的典型例子就是马建忠的"助字者，华文所独"。后来学者们谈得比较多的还有汉语的量词、汉语的重叠作为"形态"，等等。王力的"叙述句、描写句、判断句三分"，"处置式"，以及"连动"、"兼语"等也基本属于这一类。这些确实丰富了普通语言学的内容，但因为是在人家的体制内运作，等于是在人家现有的"势力范围"内硬挖出一块来，这就必须要妥善处理好与左邻右舍的关系；同时要考虑到我这个榫头打进去，会不会损伤人家的基本体系。在这方面，我们觉得就语法而言，"叙述句、描写句、判断句三分"可能是最成熟的，但至今也还只是在汉语学者中流行，还没有在以动词为句子绝对中心的普通语言学句法格局里找到自己的位置；西方出版的任一部普通语言学著作中也还没有收进过汉语的这一理论。"处置式"也是如此。"被字式"因为正好西方有"被动式"，很容易被接受了，而"处置式"（或"把字句"）因为西方没有，就始终难以成为普通语言学的课题。有哪位学者（不论中外）会想到去研究"处置"的概念在世界别的语言里是如何表达的吗？没有！"被动"现在已被列为"人类语言的普遍性"之一，但"处置"不是。这有西方语言学的责任，也有中国语言学的责任，因为你是在人家的体制内讨活，你没有能按别人的游戏规则来说清这个问题，它就进不了这个圈子。

Type 2 is mending the western framework to suit the needs of Chinese. A typical example would be Ma Jianzhong's *zhu-zi* or "words for mood", which he deemed to be unique in Chinese. Later scholars tend to name "classifier" and "duplication" as a form of morphology as the characteristics. Other examples such as Wang Li's "narrative, descriptive, judgmental" sentence types, "disposal" construction, "serial verbs" as well as "linked structure" all belong to the characteristics at this level. All these add up to enrich the content of general linguistics. However, with the data building on an external system, like an embassy in a foreign land, relationships with the sovereign have to be well taken care of, that their basic rules and customs are not hurt by our introduction. We have discussed earlier that the sentence type theory is by far the most matured characteristics but the theory has yet to find its place in general linguistics, so is the disposal construction (or *ba*-construction). Only the passive construction (or *bei*-construction), linked to a similar concept in the western framework is accepted. Why is the *ba*-construction being denied in general linguistics? While foreign scholars may not have sufficient interest, knowledge and awareness on Chinese data, Chinese scholars have not thought about exploring the "disposal" concept in other languages. While "passive" expression is determined as universal, we have to sort things out for disposal—and if we are doing this with an external system, we have to play by the rules.

按这种办法找"特点"，增加的比较好办，要减少就比较麻烦。因为减少的最方便说法便是"省略"，但省略用得多了，便有遁词的嫌疑。启功先生不无嘲讽地说，这就好像儿歌里唱的："两只老虎，两只老虎。跑得快，跑得快。一只没有尾巴，一只没有脑袋。真奇怪，真奇怪。"使人困惑不解的是为什么省略那么多之后的那些老虎，还那么欢蹦乱跳地活着。（启功，1991/1997：2-3）

Discovering "characteristics" in this way, it will not be as easy to try to cut something off the external system as to add on to it. To go round the problem, ellipsis is the easiest claim. The frequent use of ellipsis, however, does sound more like an excuse. Looking more closely at it, Qi Gong once commented: "We have a nursery singing: 'two tigers, two tigers, race rapidly, race rapidly. One is without tail, one is without brain. So strange! So strange!' It is really strange that tigers with so much omission are still alive and going vibrant!" (Qi Gong, 1991/1997: 2—3)

第三种是跳出西方语法框架，另辟蹊径。从对比研究的角度来看，上面两种都还属于第一层次，即表层结构上的对比。第三种则属于后两个层次。其共同特点是对现行汉语语法体系的基本否定。这个思想其实有国外的来源。60年前，何容（1942：28）第一次引用了英国《大英百科全书》十三版[1] "语法"条撰稿人塞斯（A. H. Sayce）说的一段话，后来张志公至少又引用了三次，[2] 其中一次说：

Type 3 is to break free from western framework and start afresh. From the contrastive point of view, the above two types are contrasting at structural level while the third belongs to the expression and psycholinguistic levels, challenging the existing Chinese grammar system. The go-independent thought in fact has a foreign origin—A. H. Sayce, who was responsible for the write-up on "Grammar" in the thirteenth edition. Sayce was first quoted in He Rong (1942: 28) some 60 years ago when anti-imitation was a common theme. Zhang Zhigong cited Sayce three times later, in one of these quotes, he says:

> 英国《大百科全书》第十一版《语法》条的起草人是一位东方学家，名叫塞斯（Archibald Henry Sayce），他说：Chinese grammar, for instance, can never be understood until we discard, not only the terminology of European grammar, but the very conceptions which underlie it. （要是我们不把欧洲语法的那些名称术语连同那些名称术语所表示的概念一起抛弃掉的话，我们就永远不会了解汉语语法。）这话说得也许有些过头，但是很值得注意。汉语是一种非形态语言，就是说，在这种语言里，怎样把词组织成句子，不依靠像印欧语言里所有的那种形态手段，即使它有某些同于或近于那种形态的东西的话。（张志公，

---

[1] 张志公引用时称"第十一版"，并注明出版于1910—1911年。
According to He Rong (1942: 280), Zhang Zhigong quotes it as eleventh.

[2] 分别见《关于汉语语法体系分歧问题》（1980a）、《语法研究与语法教学》（1980b）和《汉语辞章学与汉语语法》（1983：628—629）。
Refer to Zhang Zhigong (1980a；1980b；1983: 628—639).

1980a: 477)

The writer for "Grammar" in the 11th edition of Britannica encyclopedia Archibald Henry Sayce says that: "Chinese grammar, for instance, can never be understood until we discard, not only the terminology of European grammar, but the very conceptions which underlie it." He may be a little over the extreme, but his words are noteworthy. The Chinese language is non-morphological. That is to say, the construction of words into sentences is not by means of morphological devices as in Indo-European languages, even if there are forms so called close to or similar to morphology. (Zhang Zhigong, 1980a: 477)

张志公致力于汉语语法研究将近半个世纪，但念念不忘的是要打破现有体系，建立真正具有汉语特色的汉语语法体系。直到他去世的那一年，他还把用西方语法体系分析汉语比作"用吃西餐的餐具吃中餐"：

Devoted to Chinese grammar for half a century, Zhang Zhigong is committed to breaking the current system for a system the Chinese could really call its own. In the year he passed away, Zhang, not able to rest his case, described the current grammar based on western framework as "using silverware for a Chinese meal".

现在只有西餐餐具，没有中餐餐具，对付着吃饭照样也行。用现在这套语法，从教法上作一些改进，对付着教也是可以的，但这功夫要下得比较大。不过最后必须有真正符合汉语实际的具有汉语特色的汉语语法产生出来，才能从根本上解决问题。我觉得这是我们大家应该共同努力的目标。（张志公，1995：548）

Now we have only silverware, we do not have Chinese tableware. Yes, we may make do for meals. By the current grammar, we may also make do for teaching purposes with some adjustment; some effort would be required though. Ultimately, we need to design a system truly Chinese in characteristics reflecting the linguistic facts of Chinese in order to reach the roots of the problems. I think this is our common mission. (Zhang Zhigong, 1995: 548)

其实塞斯的思想还有更早的来源，那就是19世纪初的洪堡特。和20世纪的萨丕尔、高本汉、沃尔夫、帕麦尔等也是相通的。本书前面已有引用，读者不妨对照起来看。

We have seen that before Sayce, there were Humboldt, Sapir, Karlgren, Whorf and Palmer thinking along the same lines, right from early nineteenth century into the twentieth century.

3.3.2.6.2 音义关系的新探索
3.3.2.6.2 New explorations into the relation between sound and meaning

　　语言无非是"音、形、义"，西方语法是从"形"入手的，既然用它来讲汉语有困难，那就走"音、义"的路子好了。因此突破西方体系的语法研究无非是在义、音两方面动脑子。最早想到"义"的中国语言学家是王力。他提出汉语爱用"意合法"，是"人治"的语言。但他的意合主要还是指复句内的联接，并没有全面推开："中国语里多用意合法，联接成分并非必需；西文多用形合法，联接成分在大多数情况下是不可缺少的。"（1944/1984：472）以后的学者则是希望用意合来解决汉语语法的全面问题。

　　Language is all about sound, form and meaning. Western languages zero in on form and if it proves to be unworkable for Chinese, there are still ways round sound and meaning. That is to say, to break free from the western grammatical framework, Chinese linguists would have to turn their focus towards phonology and semantics. Wang Li led the way betting on semantics, bringing attention to the parataxis nature of Chinese not governed by form but by humans. However, by parataxis, Wang Li was somewhat confined to the relations between clauses in double- or multi-clause sentences: "Mandarin is mostly parataxis, connectives are not necessary; Western languages are mostly hypotaxis and connectives in most cases are indispensable" (1944/1984: 472). After Wang Li, the parataxis nature is seen as pointing the way to achieving a total solution for Chinese grammar.

　　李临定的《现代汉语句型》（1986），是最早跳出"主、谓、宾"等句子成分名称、纯从语义关系如施事受事等来分析汉语句型的第一部有影响力的汉语语法著作。他还著有《汉语比较变换语法》（1988），通过变换方法，来发现汉语的"隐性语法范畴"，与沃尔夫区分"隐性范畴"与"显性范畴"的主张有相合之处。但他仍保留了"名、动、形"等区分。后来徐通锵对来自西方语法的这一套概念提出了全面的质疑：

Li Linding' *Sentence Patterns in Modern Chinese* (1986) was one of the first publications of greater impact to have given up using parts of speech in analysing Chinese syntax, instead, semantic relations were used. His other work on *A Comparative and Transformational Chinese Grammar* (1988) employed transformational methodology to examine the "overt categories" in Chinese, responding to the overt and covert categories of Whorf, but keeping the differentiation between noun, verb and adjective. A complete oppugn came from Xu Tongqiang:

> 我们的祖先不讲主语、谓语、宾语和名词、动词、形容词这些词位句法概念，照样可以看书写文章，可以进行教学活动，而在印欧系语言的研究中这是不可想象的。（徐通锵，1991：321）
>
> More than ever without reference to syntactic concepts such as subject, predicate, object or noun, verb, and adjective or the like, our ancestors do well in writing and teaching, something unimaginable in Indo-European scholarship. (Xu Tongqiang, 1991: 321)

潘文国则继承了洪堡特的观点，明确指出印欧语与汉语在语言理解上的根本不同在于前者是"从结构到语义"，而后者是"从语义到结构"，这造成了两种语言不同的研究传统：
As Humboldt already mentioned, in Indo-European languages structure comes before meaning, whereas in the case of Chinese, meaning before structure; this difference is enough that they each represent a distinct tradition, as confirmed by Pan Wenguo:

> 而从语法分析的实际步骤来说，英语是根据形态（首先是动词、名词及主谓一致关系）先找出主语和定式动词，建立起句子的基本框架，然后将各种配件装上去。结构弄清楚了，句子的意义才清楚，其过程是"结构—语义"；而汉语看到的是一长串汉字，词跟词之间没有空隙（古汉语连句跟句之间也没有空隙），加上主语、谓语什么的都没有形式标志，要切分只有从语义着手，把句子拆成一个个片段，

弄清其间的关系。句子结构是语义分析的结果，其过程是"语义—结构"。这两个不同的过程告诉我们为什么在长期的历史中，语法对英语等西方语言是如此重要，因为非此不足以弄清语义；而汉语的语法始终不发达，因为并不是理解语义之必须。（潘文国，1997a/2002：126）

In the actual analysis procedure, first and foremost in English will be to single out the subject and finite verb according to the form (first verb and noun and the consistency between subject and predicate), with the basic structure installed, all other accessories may then be filled in. When the structure is clear, the meaning is obvious; therefore we proceed from structure to meaning. In Chinese, besides a chain of Chinese characters, there is no gap in between them (in classical Chinese, even sentences are not separated by gaps) or markings for subject, predicate and other. To dissect, we approach from meaning and break the sentences into chunks to see how they are dependable on each other. In this way, sentence structure is the result of semantic analysis and the process is from meaning to structure. These two distinct processes account for the long importance grammar is of to English and the negligible place grammar ever occupies in Chinese not being a necessary factor to reading meaning. (Pan Wenguo, 1997a/2002: 126)

从语义角度研究汉语的还有张黎、鲁川等。张黎著有《文化的深层选择——汉语意合语法论》（1994）、《汉语意合语法学纲要》（2001），鲁川著有《汉语语法的意合网络》（2001）。此外，李葆嘉的《理论语言学：人文和科学的双重精神》（2001）也花了很多篇幅谈他的"语义语法学理论"。[1] 但毫无疑问，这方面影响最大的是徐通锵的《语言论》（1997）。该书以"字"为出发点，以语义为核心，建立了汉语语义句法的新体系：

Works on the semantic approach include Zhang Li's *A Profound Cultural Choice: On Parataxis Grammar of Chinese* (1994) and *An Introduction to Parataxis*

---

1 马庆株（1998）、邵敬敏（2004）也提出了他们的语义语法。但与上面几家不同，他们的"语义"指的是"语法意义"。
Both Ma Qingzhu (1998) and Shao Jingmin (2004) proposed their ideas on "semantic grammar". However, they are actually referring to "grammatical meaning".

Grammar of Chinese (2001) and Lu Chuan's *The Parataxis Network of Chinese Grammar* (2001). Li Baojia's *Theoretical Linguistics: The Double Spirit of Humanities and Science* (2001) also deals at length with "the theory of semantic grammar". Undoubtedly, it is Xu Tongqiang's *On Language* (1997) that leaves the deepest imprint. Building his semantic theory with Chinese characters as the basis, Xu Tongqiang has established a new semantic grammar of Chinese:

> 印欧系语言以词为基本结构单位，它的研究重点始终是语法，从亚里斯多德到现在，这种重点从来没有发生过变化。汉语以字为基本结构单位，它的重点就不能是印欧语类型的那种语法，而是语义。
> （徐通锵，1997：自序4）

> Indo-European languages centered on word as the basic unit and grammar remains as the focus of research ever since Aristotle. The Chinese language has Sinigram as its basic unit and therefore grammar in the form of western languages cannot be its research focus, which has to be semantics.
> (Xu Tongqiang, 1997: Preface)

如果说王力的《中国语法理论》是吸收西方语法精华，强调汉语特色的第一部中国语法理论著作，则徐氏的《语言论》是《马氏文通》出版一百年以来第一部最有影响的立足汉语本体的普通语言学著作。两者都是中国对比语言学特别是宏观对比研究的重大成果。

If Wang Li's *Theory of Chinese Grammar* is the first Chinese grammar to have placed emphasis on Chinese characteristics with the gist of western grammars, Xu Tongqiang's *On Language* could be regarded as the first penetrating general linguistics volume based on the reality of Chinese in the 100 years since *Mashi Wentong*. Together, they make up the greatest contribution of contrastive linguistics in China, particularly on the macro-perspective.

从"音"或"节律"上出发的首先是一些对传统汉语或传统语文教育有较深造诣或研究的学者，如陈寅恪、郭绍虞、赵元任、吕叔湘、张志公、启功等，近年来持这一主张的较年轻一辈的学者如潘文国、冯胜利、申小龙等，也往往"出身"于汉语史专业，在古代汉语的教学与研究上浸润过相当一段时期。这个事实也许可从另一个侧面证明了高本汉（1949）说的熟悉传统汉语在研究现代汉语语言学时的重要意义。

Proceeding from "sound" or "prosody" are scholars trained in traditional scholarship, like Chen Yinke, Guo Shaoyu, Chao Yuen-ren, Lü Shuxiang, Zhang Zhigong and Qi Gong among others. Younger scholars in succession such as Pan Wenguo, Feng Shengli and Shen Xiaolong are also trained in historical linguistics in Chinese, having gained research and teaching experience of classical Chinese. Karlgren (1949) is absolutely right to observe the value traditional Chinese training adds to modern Chinese linguistic research.

从"音"上研究汉语组织规律主要表现在两个方面，一个是重视汉语语词的"弹性作用"及汉语单双音节在组词构语造句中的配合，另一个是强调骈偶在汉语组词构语造句中的超修辞意义。

Seen from this angle, the organization of Chinese is significant in two aspects. First, it is the "flexibility" of words in Chinese and interesting juxtaposition of monosyllabic and disyllabic words to form constructions and sentences. Secondly, it is the supra-rhetorical significance of parallelism in word and sentence construction.

前者发轫于战国时代荀子的两句话："单足以喻则单，单不足以喻则兼"。而在当代，是从郭绍虞发表于1938年的《中国语词的弹性作用》一文开始的，郭氏将汉语语词的弹性作用归纳为四类："语词伸缩"、"语词分合"、"语词变化"、"语词颠倒"（郭绍虞，1938：75—100）。但很长时间以来，在习惯于西方语法固定"程式"的人看来，这些都只是"修辞"现象，与语法无关。直到1963年吕叔湘发表《汉语单双音节问题初探》，明确地从语法角度来探索单双音节在汉语中的使用问题，才引起了语法学界的关注。1968年，赵元任指出"音节和节奏也就成为复合词的构词要素（赵元任，1979：223），这一观点随1979年吕叔湘该书中译本的出版而广为流传。郭绍虞于其晚年更指出："……汉语对于音节，看得比意义更重一些"（郭绍虞，1979：444）。之后才引起汉语研究者高度重视。申小龙（1988：471）提出的"弹性实体"说即来自于郭氏；潘文国等在《汉语的构词法研究》（1993；2004）一书中专门辟出一章，谈"音节、节律角度的构词法研究"，认为这是汉语中"独树一帜的构词法研究侧面"（潘文国等，2004：169），并指出，"构词法中可以包括用词法，恐怕是汉语的一个重要特色"（同上：10）；冯胜利（1997）则在西方韵律构词学（prosodic morphology）的理论框架下，研究了汉语的"韵律词"问题。

The first idea originated from Xun Zi of the Warring States: "keep to monosyllabic if it is sufficed to express, combine into a disyllable if otherwise." Expounding on this idea, Guo Shaoyu's 1938 paper on "the flexibility of Chinese words" listed four functions of the flexibility: the expansion and contraction of words, and the combination and separation of words, variation in words, reversal of words (Guo Shaoyu, 1938: 75—100). These were largely taken as rhetorical and not grammatical phenomena in the eyes of people used to the fixed format of western grammars. It was not until 1963, when Lü Shuxiang started exploring from the grammatical point of view how usage of monosyllables and disyllables are being conditioned in his paper "A Preliminary Discussion of the Issues in Mono- and Disyllables", that grammarians begin to show some interest. Chao (1968) also states that "syllabicity and rhythm play a very important part in *wenyan*, and since many compounds in the spoken language follow syntactical types in *wenyan*, the structure of compounds also depends upon these factors" (Chao, 1968: 483). This view was popularized with the Chinese translation of Chao (1968) by Lü Shuxiang (1979). Guo Shaoyu further pointed out that: "…Chinese language attaches even greater importance to syllables than meaning" (Guo Shaoyu, 1979: 444). It was only then that Chinese linguists began to take syllables and prosody seriously. The "flexible entity" theory of Shen Xiaolong (1988: 471) has its root in Guo Shaoyu; Pan Wenguo et al. (1993, 2004) dedicated a chapter to word formation from the syllabic and prosodic viewpoint and regarded it as a peculiar research angle, particularly unusual in Chinese in that word formation could include "word employment" (Pan Wenguo et al. 2004: 10). Guided by western prosodic morphology, Feng Shengli (1997) examined what he called prosodic word in Chinese language which is not grammatically determined and wrote other papers on prosodically constrained syntax in Chinese.

后者若要上溯，当然可溯到南北朝刘勰《文心雕龙·丽辞篇》的"造化赋形，支体必双"，但从《马氏文通》引进西方语法学之后，重新提出这一问题的则始于国学大师陈寅恪。陈氏激烈地反对《马氏文通》以来模仿西洋语法建立起来的中国文法学（参见第二章）。而他拿出来与《马氏文通》之类抗衡的居然是"对对子"。他说："对偶确为中国语文特性之所在，而欲研究此种特性者，不得不研究由此特性所产生之对子。"（陈寅恪，1933，227）他进而主张在"真正的中国文法"建立前，不妨以"对对子"作为代用品："无可奈何，不得已而求一过渡时代救济之方法，以为真正中国文法未成立前之暂时代用品，此方法即为对对子。所对不过十字，已能表现中国语文特性之多方面。其中有与高中毕业应备之国文常识相关者，亦有汉语汉文特殊优点之所在，可籍以测验高材及专攻吾国文学之人，即投考国文学系者。"（同上：224）因为这方法可以测试"分别虚实字及其应用"、"分别平仄声"、"读书之多少及语藏之丰富"以及"思想条理"。（同上：224—226）在当时乃至现代许多语法学家看来，陈先生的意见是有些近似于胡话的，[1]然而，搞了一辈子语法研究、又是汉语语法"暂拟体系"和"试用提要"主持人的张志公对本世纪以来的汉语语法体系也深感失望，在花了很大的力气认真研究了传统中国语文教育之后，他提出的替代西方式语法的居然也是"对对子"，这就不得不引起人们的重视了：

The effect of parallelism has its grounding in the classical work of literary criticism, *Wen Xin Diao Long* (Literary Mind and the Carving of Dragon) by Liu Xie of the Qi Dynasty (479—502). In the chapter on *li-ci*, or "Linguistic parallelism", Liu deliberated on parallelism, from which he formulated a writing theory. Calling attention to parallelism was none other than eminent scholar Chen Yinke who was opposed strongly to *Mashi Wentong* and all those grammars modelled after western frameworks (refer to Chapter 2). To illustrate the characteristics of Chinese, Chen cited the antithetic value in couplets and parallets (Chen Yinke, 1933: 227). He further proposed that before a real Chinese grammar is available, pairing couplets could be a substitute in the transition because many characteristics of Chinese would have shown in pairing a couplet of just ten characters (*ibid.*: 224—226). It can even be used to screen candidates who wish to read Chinese studies since the test could "tell empty words apart and check their usage; test the ability to tell even and uneven tones; test their knowledge and logical thoughts" (*Ibid*). To many grammarians,

---

[1] 陈先生当时就看到了这一点，但他仍充满自信，仿佛看到了今后的发展，说："此义当质证于他年中国语言文字特性的研究发展以后。今日言之，徒遭流俗之讥笑。"（同上：227）
Chen knew his view was not well taken but he was full of confidence, insightful enough to see through the development as he remarked: "Mark my words and compare it with the development in the research of Chinese characteristics down the road. The mediocre mocking at us today mocks for nothing" (*ibid.*: 227).

then and now, Chen sounded absurd. However, attention was aroused when Zhang Zhigong, a grammarian all his life who leads the design of the provisional schema and trial outline, in his despair with the grammar systems evolved since the early century raised the same idea after spending some effort studying traditional language education:

> 总体来看，属对练习是一种不讲语法理论而实际上相当严密的语法训练；经过多次训练之后，学生可以纯熟地掌握词类和造句的规律，并且用之于说话和写作，因为从一开始就是通过造句的实践训练的，而不是只从一些语法和抽象定义学习的。……属对练习能够通过实践，灵活地把语法、修辞、逻辑几种训练综合在一起，并且跟作文密切结合起来，这一点很值得作进一步研究。（张志公，1992，100；101）
>
> On the whole, pairing couplet is an exercise that does not dwell much into grammatical theories but is in reality a rather rigorous training in grammar. The fact is that the training begins with practical sentence construction exercises rather than abstract grammatical rules and definitions and, after many practices, students will be able to master skillfully the rudiments behind word class and sentence construction and use it for writing and speeches…Through practice, training in pairing couplet incorporates an all round training in grammar, rhetoric and logic, and knit the skills closely with writing. It is worthwhile doing further study in this respect. (Zhang Zhigong, 1992: 100—101)

而纵观郭绍虞几十年中关于语言文字的论述（见郭氏，1941；1948；1985），无论是关于音节问题，关于"文气"与"声律"问题，关于"骈文的语法"问题，都涉及到骈偶问题。无独有偶，1991年启功先生在香港出版《汉语现象论丛》，1997年在大陆增订再版，引起了极大的反响，中华书局还专门组织了一场《汉语现象论丛》学术讨论会。启功在书中提出的主要也是声律这一方面的东西，说：
Looking back, all of Guo Shaoyu's study of Chinese language and characters over a few decades (Guo Shaoyu, 1941, 1948, 1985), be it of syllables, writing style or prosody, or grammar of parallel essays, all concern "parallelism". And he

is not alone, when Qi Gong released the revised edition of his book, *Phenomena in Chinese Language* (1991, Hong Kong) in Mainland China in 1997, the response was overwhelming and the publisher had to organize a special forum to discuss ideas shared by Qi Gong, mainly on sound and prosody:

> 英语没有对偶、没有平仄、没有骈文、没有五七言等诗句,当然也不会有这些汉语文体中语言构造的接近例子。于是许多葛朗玛书中,关于这些方面的东西,都没列为研究对象。马氏说:"排偶声律说,等之自郐以下耳。"究竟是不值研究呢,还是因套不上而放弃呢?(启功,1991:前言)

> There is no antithesis writing, no even and uneven tones, no 5 or 7-character poems in English, and of course you will not find in English examples of similar constructions. These are not seen as research targets in many grammar books. Ma said: "couplets and prosody and the related are not worth discussing." Is it not worth studying or we have to give it up because there is nothing to model after? (Qi Gong, 1991: Preface)

接着就摆出了古代诗文中许多用现行汉语语法体系无法分析的现象。讨论会上人们集中攻讦的也是现行语法对汉语缺乏解释力的问题,呼吁语法研究要关注汉语的特殊"现象"。

He listed many examples from classical texts and poems that challenged the existing grammatical system. The forum was also unsatisfied with the explanatory power of existing grammars and called for more attention on "special phenomena" in grammatical studies.

在郭绍虞等前辈研究的基础上,将音节与骈偶两者结合起来,提出比较完整的理论体系的是冯胜利。冯先后出版《汉语的韵律、词法和句法》(1997)和《汉语韵律句法学》(2000)二书,建立了"汉语韵律句法学"这一新的理论体系。

Drawing on the experiences of the seniors such as Guo Shaoyu, an excellent attempt to integrate syllable and parallelism in a relatively complete theoretical system was carried out by Feng Shengli. Feng (1997, 2000) explored extensively the rhythm, morphology and syntax in Chinese to put forward his case for a new theory in "prosodic syntax in Chinese".

而将上述"义"、"音"两方面的努力结合起来,提出新的汉语观的是潘文国。他在1997年就提出:汉语是一种语义型语言,汉语又是一种节律型语言:

On the other hand, there were also attempts to integrate meaning and sound. Pan Wenguo (1997) offers a new standpoint that Chinese is a semantic language as well as a prosodic language:

> 在汉语中,起基本作用的规律是语义组织,或者说语序。但语序的背后是逻辑,纯粹按逻辑组织的语言在世界上可说是不存在的。……那么,汉语靠什么来打破逻辑的呆板次序,造成丰富多彩、有声有色的语言的呢?就是靠音节和节奏。大概没有一种语言像汉语这样依赖音节和节奏,从这个意义上,我们可以说汉语是一种节律型语言或者音足型语言。(潘文国,1997a/2002:116)

> In Chinese, the fundamental entity that produces effect is semantic construction or word order which is backed by logic. No language relies purely on logic...So, what do Chinese use to break the monotonous logical form to construct colorful and interesting language with audio and visual effect? It is syllable and rhythm. It is in this light that we say Chinese is a prosodic language. (Pan Wenguo, 1997a/2002: 116)

2002年他出版了《字本位与汉语研究》,在这一认识的基础上提出"音义互动律"是汉语语法组织的根本规律:

On this ground, Pan Wenguo (2002) further proposes the interaction of sound and meaning as the fundamental syntactic rudiment:

> 音义互动是汉语组织的最根本规律。这个规律从语用出发,实际上体现了汉语从音韵,到语形,到语义的所有规律,是所有这些方面规律的综合。……这一规律,正是汉语之所以为汉语的根本特点所在,一切外来的理论、外来的方法,最终必须经过这一规律的检验,才能确定是否真正适合于汉语。(潘文国,2002:246)

> The underlying rudiment in Chinese structure is the interaction of sound and meaning. Arising out of pragmatics, this rudiment displays and consolidates all Chinese characteristics in phonology, construction, and semantics...This

is the essential nature for which Chinese may be Chinese. All foreign theories, methodologies must ultimately pass the test of this rudiment for appropriate application in Chinese. (Pan Wenguo, 2002: 246)

3.3.2.6.3 对比研究与语言类型学
3.3.2.6.3 Contrastive study and linguistic typology

对比研究的深入必然导致对语言类型学的新认识。从句法角度最早对汉语和英语的语言类型进行定性的是美国学者李讷和汤珊迪（Li and Thompson），他们（1976）认为汉语（及日语、韩语等）是"话题突出性语言"，而英语是"主语突出性语言"。这个观点对国内的汉语研究产生了重要影响。另一方面，徐通锵（1991）最早对汉语和英语进行全面定性，认为汉语是"语义型语言"，与之对应的英语等是"语法型语言"。潘文国（1997a）修正和补充了这一观点，主张：

The furthering contrastive study naturally leads to new understanding of linguistic typology. The first attempt to distinguish Chinese and English from syntactic typology was Charles Li and Sandra Thompson who alleged that Chinese, as well as Japanese and Korean, was a "topic-prominent language" whereas English being a "subject-prominent language" (Li and Thompson, 1976). The hypothesis had much impact on later Chinese studies. In another respect, Xu Tongqiang (1991) was among the earliest scholars to define the nature of the Chinese and English languages, suggesting that the former was a "semantic-type language" and the latter was a "syntactic-type language". Pan Wenguo reviewed his arguments and complemented:

（1）汉语是语义型语言，而英语是形态型语言；
（2）汉语是音足型语言，而英语是形足型语言。（潘文国，1997a/2002：115）

(1) Chinese is a semantic-type language whereas English is a conjugation-type language;

(2) Chinese is a prosody-sufficient language whereas English is a declension-sufficient language. (Pan Wenguo, 1997a/2002: 115)

从词法角度对两种语言定性在对比语言学产生前就有了，最早是针锋相对的两种观点。林同济（1980：392）认为："汉语特点是动词优势，英语特点可说是关系词丰富。"而郭绍虞（1978：331）提出："西洋语法是重在动词，汉语语法则重在名词。"而从语言类型学角度深入探讨这一问题的则是沈家煊。

To compare Chinese and English from morphosyntactic point of view started even before contrastive linguistics came in force in China. Lin Tongji and Guo Shaoyu were two advanced scholars who made entirely different or even contradictory remarks on the question when Lin alleged that "the characteristics of Chinese is verb-prominent and that of English is rich in prepositions" (Lin Tongji, 1980：392), and Guo affirmed that "Western grammar lays emphasis on verbs while Chinese grammar on nouns" (Guo Shaoyu, 1978：331). However, the one who made special contribution in this respect was Shen Jiaxuan.

从2007年起，沈家煊在各种刊物上发表了数十篇文章，最后积集为《名词与动词》一书，于2016年出版。该书以吕叔湘的"一抛一捡"为理论动机,[1] 而起步于朱德熙对汉语中"名物化"的否定，从而形成了一个以名动关系为核心的汉语语法研究新格局，他称之为"名动包含说"。在他的新体系里，名词已不再是旧说的名词，而是"大名词"；语法也不再是旧说的语法，而是"大语法"。所谓"大名词"，就是名词为本，动词属于名词。沈家煊说：

Since 2007 Shen Jiaxuan has published scores of papers in different journals which he finally compiled into a book entitled *Nouns and Verbs* (2016). Motivated by Lü Shuxiang's idea about "abolition and picking up again", and started from Zhu Dexi's rejection of the concept of nominalization in Chinese, he developed a new framework for the study of Chinese grammar based on the relation between noun and verb, which he called "Super-noun Category" hypothesis. In his new system, nouns are no longer "nouns" of the old system, but "Super-nouns", and grammar is no longer "grammar" of the old system, but "big-grammar". The so-called "super-

---

[1] 吕叔湘（2002）提出："要大破特破。……要把'词'、'动词'、'形容词'、'主语'、'宾语'等等暂时抛弃。可能以后还是要捡起来，但这一抛一捡之间就有了变化，赋予这些名词术语的意义和价值就有所不同，对于原来不敢触动的一些条条框框就敢于动它一动了。"

Lü Shuxiang (2002) said: "Violent abolition seems necessary…We might temperately need to get rid of those terminologies like *word, noun, adjective, subject* and *object*, probably to be picked up later. But changes would certainly happen between abolition and picking up again, with new explanation and value added to the old terminology, and certain conventions or regulations would be broken up."

nouns" are nouns inclusive of verbs. Shen said:

> 英语noun和verb的对立好比"男人"和"女人"的关系,而汉语名词和动词"的区别好比"man"和"woman"的关系。英语的"man"有两个意思,一个意思包含woman,一个意思不包含woman;汉语的"名词"也有两个意思,一个意思包含动词,一个意思不包含动词。包含动词的名词可以叫做"大名词",不包含动词的名词可以叫做"小名词"。……这个格局就是名词和动词的包含模式,动词作为一个特殊的次类包含在名词这个大类里。(沈家煊,2011: 14)

> The noun-verb relation in English is of the male-female type, whereas in Chinese it is of the man-woman type. In English, "man" has two meanings, one including woman, the other not. Similarly in Chinese "nouns" has two meanings, one including verbs, the other not. The one inclusive of verbs can be called super-noun, while the one that does not can be named "minor-noun"....This is an inclusion model in which verb as a sub-category is included in the super-noun category. (Shen Jiaxuan, 2011: 14)

所谓"大语法",是相对于现在通常只包括"词法"和"句法"的小语法而言,有点像乔姆斯基"生成语法"的"语法",但内含不完全相同。沈家煊说:

The term "big-grammar" is used as against the traditional term "grammar" which consists exclusively of morphology and syntax. It is to certain extent similar to the "grammar" in Noam Chomsky's "generative grammar" yet with different connotations. Shen explained:

> 首先要确立汉语"大语法"的观念,大语法是语法、语义、语用甚至语音的综合,如果分开研究就破坏了它的完整性。讲结构类型必须联系重读轻读、音节的单双和单双组配来讲,还必须联系语义(包括语用意义)来讲。讲汉语语法,要用整体控制部分,从"自下而上"变而"从上至下"。(沈家煊,2016: 412)

> We must first establish a new concept of "big grammar" which is an integration of traditional syntax, semantics, pragmatics or even phonology.

All those must not be studied separately. Types of structure must be studied in relation to stressed and unstressed pronunciation, to mono- and bi-syllables and their arrangement, and, what's more, to semantic as well as pragmatic meaning. The study of Chinese must adopt a top-down instead of the habitual bottom-up method. (Shen Jiaxuan, 2016: 412)

在此基础上他提出转移汉语语法研究重点的建议,包括:
(1)把重点从讲语法转移到讲用法上来,从讲"句法"转移到讲"章法"上来;
(2)把重点从"整句"到"零句"和"流水句"上来;
(3)把重点从所谓"广义形态"转移到汉语自身的直观形态上来,即重叠和双音化。
(4)把重点从印欧语的"动词中心"转移到汉语的"名词为本"上来,从述谓语转移到指称语。
(5)把重点从词类转移到句类和结构类型上来。(同上:412—413)

He then put forward suggestions to shift the focus in studying Chinese grammar, including:

(1) To shift from grammar to usage and from syntax to textual study;

(2) To shift from "full sentences" to "minor sentences" and "run-on sentences";

(3) To shift from so-called "generalized morphology" to "intuitive morphology" in Chinese, i.e. reduplication and bi-syllabization;

(4) To shift from Western languages' "verb-focus" to Chinese "noun as base", or from predictability to refrentiality;

(5) To shift from word classes to sentence classes and structure patterns. (Shen Jiaxuan, 2016: 412—413)

关于汉语的词类,沈家煊特别强调:
As to Chinese word classes, Shen emphasized:

词类的区分,首先区分叠词和非叠词,即区分"状词"和"大名词"。"大名词"内部首先区分单音词和双音词,相对而言双音词述谓性强,单音词指称性强。形容词内部也首先区分单音和双音,单音

偏向定性，双音偏向摹状。突出形容词和名词动词的区别，饰词和被饰词的区别，相对淡化名词和动词的区别。（同上：413）

Words are first differentiated between reduplicates and non-reduplicates, or depictives and super-nouns. Super-nouns are further differentiated into mono-syllabic and di-syllabic words, with the former being more of predictability and the latter more of referentiality. Inside adjectives, the first division is also between mono- and bi-syllabic words, with the former inclined to qualitative and the latter to descriptive. Protrusion is made on the difference between adjectives and nouns/verbs, and between qualifiers and qualifiees, while relatively neglecting the difference between nouns and verbs. (Shen Jiaxuan, 2016: 412—413)

在句法上，他还主张取消宾语与补语的对立、定语与状语的对立。
And in syntax, he suggested canceling the opposition between objects and complements, and between attributes and adverbials.

如果说字本位理论植根中国传统，通过汉英对比，对主流汉语研究从外部发起了挑战的话，则名动包含说不啻在其内部爆裂了一颗原子弹，在"一抛一捡"之间，搅动了汉语语法研究的整个格局和体系，可说是继字本位理论之后，又一极具特色的中国语言学理论。

If sinigram-based theory, rooted in classical Chinese tradition and by way of English-Chinese contrasting, is challenging Western-influenced Chinese linguistics from outside, the Super-noun Category theory may be said to have burst an A-bomb inside the enterprise. Through abolition and picking up again, it stirred the entire system of contemporary Chinese grammatical study. It is notably a new linguistic theory with Chinese characteristics succeeding the former one.

3.3.2.7 对个性和共性的重新思考和实践
3.3.2.7 Revisiting particularity and universality

在对比研究中"引进西方理论"与"结合汉语实际"是一对永远的矛盾。不发掘汉语特点吧，"引进"成了"老谈隔壁人家的事情，而不联系自己家里的事情"（吕叔湘，1980b：8）；要发掘汉语特点吧，又担心离开世界语言的

"共性"。因此"共性"与"个性"这一矛盾在对比语言学的理论研究中是回避不了的。我们将在下两章讨论这一问题。这里先谈谈中国语言学家对待这问题的态度及最新的思考和实践。

In contrastive linguistics, "introducing western theories" and "integrating realities in Chinese" constitute an ongoing conflict. Without looking at the peculiarities of Chinese, introducing western theories is like "always talking about the businesses of the neighbour and forget about the businesses at home" (Lü Shuxiang, 1980: 8). While unearthing the peculiarities, we are worried about universality. Any theoretical study would have to meet head on the incongruity in particularity versus universality. Before we go into the theoretical aspects in the next two chapters, let us survey the thoughts and practices of Chinese linguists on the conflict.

20世纪的中国语言学家在对待"共性"问题上有两种态度。一种是不希望以"个性"掩盖"共性",这可以以黎锦熙和吕叔湘为代表;另一种是为了解决汉语的问题,不怕打破西方体系的坛坛罐罐,这可以以前期王力和后期张志公为代表。

Chinese linguists of the twentieth century are divided into two camps on the issue of universality. One camp does not wish for particularity to outshine universality, represented by Li Jinxi and Lü Shuxiang; the other is not shy to break free from the restrictions of western frameworks in order to get the house in order, as represented by Wang Li in the earlier stage and Zhang Zhigong in the later stage.

黎锦熙的观点前面已介绍过,他的立论基础是人类思维和"共性":

As mentioned earlier, Li Jinxi has his grounding on the universality of human thoughts:

> 过分地避免西方语法上相同的讲法,倒反要在语法理论上不时地"把西洋的问题搬到中国来";片面地强调本国语法上偶异的习惯,倒反使本国大众在使用祖国语言时看不到人类思维共同的抽象化的规律,到了需要文化交流和在语法认识上有了较高度的进展时,大众对于那些无端立异、刻意求"粗"的讲法也要感到不满足的。(黎锦熙,1951: 23)

> To overly avoid adopting from western frameworks the similarities, we

may end up "importing issues in western theories into Chinese" from time to time when dealing with grammatical theory. Emphasizing in biases the sometimes different norms in Chinese grammar would cover up the universal abstract patterns in human thought in the mass use of Chinese. At a higher level of grammatical development or when there is a need to exchange culturally, the masses will feel unsatisfied with theories that are unreasonably peculiar or intentionally "unsophisticated". (Li Jinxi, 1951: 23)

吕叔湘虽然对一些基本问题如"字"与"词"以及"词类划分"等等都有一点拿不定主意，但很担心反"模仿"反过了头：

Despite being vague on fundamental issues such as "Sinogram", "word" and "division of word classes", Lü Shuxiang is concerned about over "anti-imitation":

> 模仿过了头就成了削足适履，例如把一个以连接修饰语于被修饰语为其主要作用的"的"字分成语尾、介词、关系代词。模仿过头引起反作用又会走到另一极端，强调汉语的特殊性到不适当的程度，例如说汉语不能分词类，汉语一个字就是一个词，等等。再进一步就会说汉语没有语法，一切取决于字义，那就是因噎废食了。（吕叔湘，1978：335）

> Overly imitating is like sizing our feet to suit the shoe. For instance, classifying de (的) whose main function is to connect the modifier and the head, separately as suffix, preposition and relative pronoun. In opposing the overdoing, we may end up in the other extreme, underlining the peculiarities of Chinese to an extent inappropriate, for instance, insisting on words being unable to be classified into classes, or Sinograms representing words, etc. To move a step further would be to say that there is no grammar in Chinese and everything is dependent on the meaning of Sinograms. That is like refusing to eat in order to avoid getting choked. (Lü Shuxiang, 1978: 335)

王力前期是激进的反模仿论者，主张"相异之点更不强调求其同，甚至违反西洋语法书中的学说也在所不计"（王力，1943：23）。五十年代在苏联汉学家龙果夫等的"关照"下渐渐磨去了棱角，以后对语法也不甚关心。倒是主持汉语语法两个"共同纲领"的张志公越到晚年对百年来的汉语语法体系越是不满，他不止一次引用塞斯（Sayce）关于了解汉语语法要抛开印欧语语法术语的话，还不止一次地提出"往前看，往根本处看，需要逐步地建立一个新的确实切合汉语实际的语法体系。这个体系应当跟过去的很不相同。"（张志公，1980a：476）他还是第一个站出来为五十年代被批判的高名凯说话的人："如果真正考虑到汉语的特点，恐怕汉语词类的划分就应该重新考虑。"（张志公，1980b）这与上引的吕叔湘的话正好针锋相对。可惜的是，张先生晚年的认识曲高和寡，连他的学生和同事都未必理解。他去世后，有关人士举行了一个"张志公学术思想研讨会"，并出版了一本《张志公先生纪念文集》，遗憾的是《文集》中没有一篇文章谈到张志公晚期语法思想的变化。

Wang Li was an anti-imitation activist in the early period, maintaining that "we should not impose on the differences found in Chinese to be similar to western grammars, even if that means breaking rules in the western grammars" (Wang Li, 1943: 23). After the incidents of the 1950s where Soviet sinologists took the lead, Wang Li quieted down and turned away from grammatical studies. Instead, it was the man behind the two "common programmes", Zhang Zhigong, who was increasingly unhappy with the grammar systems developed over the past century as he grew wiser in age. More than once, he cited Sayce in calling for Chinese grammar to come out of Indo-European influence so as to "be forward looking, be grounded on the roots, and gradually develop a new grammar system—one that is quite different from what we have in the past—that would accommodate the realities in Chinese" (Zhang Zhigong, 1980a: 476). He was also the first to have stood up for Gao Mingkai who was being criticized in the 1950s, crashing head on with Lü Shuxiang saying that: "If we are really giving consideration to the characteristics of Chinese, we should revisit the word classification issue" (Zhang Zhigong, 1980b). It is rather unfortunate that Zhang was not well understood in his last years, even by his students and colleagues. After he passed away, a seminar was held to conclude his contributions and an essay collection was published in his memory; regrettably, it recorded nothing about the change in his grammatical thoughts in his later years.

20世纪80年代中国开始实行改革开放政策，国外的语言学理论如潮水般地涌了进来，常常一个理论还没捂热，新的理论又进来了。而有关方面和有关人士还在鼓吹要"不断引进"，认为中国语言学落后世界太多，只有不断引进才能赶上和超过世界先进水平。潘文国批评了这种"追赶论",认为从逻辑上讲这一"竞赛"就是不公正的:因为"一方是永远在前、永远在创新的;另一方是永远在后、永远在看样学样的"!(潘文国,2001b:4)

China's reformation and the opening of its doors in the 1980s saw western theories sweeping in. One theory zoomed past before another got warmed up. Apparently the thought was that Chinese linguistics had been lagging behind and the only way to keep abreast or even surpass advanced international standard would be to continue incessantly to introduce foreign theories. Logically speaking, such "matches" will never be fair and could never be tiled since one side is forever leading and creating and the other is forever following from behind. (Pan Wenguo, 2001b: 4)

因而,怎样处理"引进"和"独创"的关系,成了新时期中国语言学的一个迫在眉睫的问题。吕叔湘和徐通锵先后提出了"学习方法而非套用结果"、"学习立论根据"的主张:

Obviously, for Chinese linguistics in new China, the urgency is on the management of "importing" and "creating". Lü Shuxiang and Xu Tongqiang propose at different timing, that the focus should be "learning the methodology but not the end result", "learning the basis for reasoning". Lü Shuxiang says:

> 现在的问题已经不是要不要结合,而是如何结合的问题。我觉得,重要的是学习西方学者研究语言的方法,而不是套用他们的研究成果。(吕叔湘,1980b:7)

> Now, the question is not one of integration, instead it is about how to integrate. I think, learning the methodology of western researches is more important than adapting their research findings. (Lü Shuxiang, 1980b: 7)

"结合"并不是国外的理论加汉语的例子,也不是用国外的理论来解释汉语,而是要参照国外语言理论的立论根据,从中吸取精神,在汉语的研究中提炼出自己的理论和方法,以便能在宏观上把握汉语结构的特点;不能实现这样的要求,说明我们还没有摆脱用"印欧语的眼光"来观察汉语的窠臼。(徐通锵,1991:322—323)

Integration does not mean the sum of foreign theory and Chinese examples; it does not mean explaining Chinese using foreign theories. Integration means in the process of exploring Chinese, take reference from the basis of foreign theory, extract the spirit of it and refine our own theory and methodology. This would allow us to capture the structural characteristics of Chinese from the macro perspective. Failing to do so only serves to say that we are still trapped like in the past, reading Chinese with the eyes of Indo-European. (Xu Tongqiang, 1991: 322—323)

在具体实践上，徐通锵和潘文国不约而同地提出了一个"常数"论。徐氏的"常数"谈的是语言的结构：
In practice, both Xu Tongqiang and Pan Wenguo have spoken about a "constant". The constant for Xu Tongqiang refers to the structure of language:

> 不同语言的结构常数都是一个"1"，这是语言的共性；而这个控制语言结构网络的"1"处于哪一个结构层次上则决定语言的结构类型和结构特点。（徐通锵，1991：337）
>
> Structures of different languages have a constant of 1, which represents language universality. This constant takes control of the structural network of the language, the structural level at which it positions shall determine the typology and characteristics of the language. (Xu Tongqiang, 1991: 337)
>
> 英语等印欧系语言控制语言结构特点的"1"在句法层，一个句子要求由一个名词充当的主语和由一个动词充当的谓语组合构成。汉语的常数"1"集中在"字"上，由此产生一系列语义句法的结构特点。粘着语的结构常数"1"处于词的平面，可在一个词根的基础上加上若干个语素组成一个词，由元音和谐使不同的"1"内聚为一个整体——词。（徐通锵，1991：335—336）
>
> For English and other Indo-European languages, the structural characteristic control constant "1" is at the syntactic level, requiring a sentence be formed by 1 subject which is a noun or noun phrase and 1 predicate which is a verb or a verb phrase. For Chinese, the constant "1" rests at the Sinogram level and from there produces a series of structural characteristics akin to semantic syntax. For agglutinative languages, this constant "1" rests at the lexis level, so that a few morphemes could be affixed to 1 root stem, and

by achieving harmony in the vowel, the different "1s" congeal into a whole to form a word. (Xu Tongqiang, 1991: 335–336)

潘文国的"常数"谈的却是"语言组织的规律":
The constant referred to by Pan Wenguo is the "rudiment of language structure".

>语言组织的规律看来很像是一个常数,在某一方面欠缺了,就会在别的方面得到补偿。英语在走向分析性之后,形态上的损失不少,结果就从词序和虚词上得到了补偿,因此英语语法学家要自豪地宣称词序和虚词是英语的特点。汉语如果只有词序和虚词,语言组织手段似乎显得太贫乏,因而就从音节和节律上得到了补偿。(潘文国,1997a/2002:141)

> The rudiment of language structure is like a constant. Deficiency in one aspect is compensated by another. As English moves to analysis, it losses much of the morphological changes but gets compensated with word order and functional words. This is why English grammarians are proud to claim word order and functional words as its characteristics. If Chinese has only word order and functional words, the language is bare in terms of the construction devices and therefore it gets compensated in terms of syllablism and prosody. (Pan Wenguo, 1997a/2002: 141)

但有一点是两人共同的,即都从寻找汉语特色出发,最后都致力于寻找在更高层面上汉语和世界其他语言之间的共性,以便与国际语言学界对话。潘文国的《字本位与汉语研究》更是有意在这方面的追求。如果说他在写作《汉英语对比纲要》(1997)的时候基本立足于"个性",到了此时却主要是立足于"共性":
While their concepts of a constant may differ, they are joined in the search of the universality that Chinese has in common with languages of the world, and of a path where Chinese linguistics may dialogue with international linguistics, grounding firmly on the oncology of Chinese. Scholars like Pan Wenguo have moved from "individualism" in Pan Wenguo (1997) to "universality" in Pan Wenguo (2002b) in which the basis is on the sinogram, but the process has an international perspective:

"字本位"是一种非常具有汉语特色、汉语个性的理论，但人类语言还是一个整体，"字本位"再特殊，还是要想方设法纳入世界语言研究的潮流里去；从另一方面看，字本位理论如能取得成功，也将是汉语对人类的普通语言学做出的贡献。（潘文国，2002b：307）

The "Sinogram-based" theory is completely Chinese, exposing the particularity of the language. However, human languages ought to be considered as a whole. Whatever the extent of its peculiarity, the "Sinogram-based" theory has to find its way into the system of world language research. And when that is done, it will be the contribution Chinese has to offer to general linguistics. (Pan Wenguo, 2002b: 307)

该书从立论基础（字本位），到分支理论建立过程，无不考虑与国际语言学的接轨。徐通锵认为，这样"建立起来的理论体系虽然在表面上看起来与现在流行的理论有很大的差别，但实质上最接近接轨的精神，相互之间是形异神似"（徐通锵，2002：5）。在一定程度上，这也代表了当代中国对比语言学者所积极追求的目标。

As Xu Tongqiang puts it: "On the surface, such theory differs from those popular on the market but in essence, it is closer in the spirit of internationalization" (Xu Tongqiang, 2002: 5). In a way, this is an active pursuit of contemporary contrastivists in China.

沈家煊在通过汉英对比，建立"名动包含"新理论之后，也对语言共性问题提出了新看法：

Shen Jiaxuan has some new findings in linguistic universality after he successfully launched a new theory of Super-noun Category by contrasting Chinese with the English language:

语言的共性寓于语言的多样性之中，只有充分重视语言的多样性，语言共性的研究才会有真的收获。真正的语言共性也许不在语言的结构而在语言的使用，至少不能脱离后者。真正的语言共性也许不在语言之间有共同的内核，而在语言之间"相通"，"共性"应该叫"通性"。（沈家煊，2016：422）

Universality of language exists only in its diversities, and the study of linguistic universality can yield fruitful results only when linguistic diversities were fully acknowledged. True universality of language lies probably, not in its structure, but in its usage, or at least closely related to usage. And true universality does not mean certain "common core" within the languages, but the communicability between them. Hence "universality" is better renamed "generality". (Shen Jiaxuan, 2016: 422)

从语言的多样性看，语言的研究就是语言的比较研究。……比较无有止境，对语言的认识不断更新。（同上：422）

Judging from the diversities of languages, to study linguistics means to compare languages. As comparison has no end, the understanding of language is constantly refreshed as well. (*ibid*. 2016: 422)

从而使他的研究更有了哲学的厚度。
This finding and practice made his study more profound in terms of philosophy.

第四章
对比语言学的本体论
Chapter 4 Ontology in Contrastive Linguistics

4.1 从历史到哲学
4.1 From history to philosophy

在本书的前三章，我们回顾了对比语言学在西方和在中国发展的历史。回顾历史的目的不是为了发思古之幽情，而是要为当前的研究服务。因此我们对历史的回顾不应停留在昨天，而是要通过对昨天的追溯，了解当前的处境，明确今后的任务。西方和中国的语言对比史充满了起伏，可说波澜壮阔，在令人叹为观止的同时，也给我们提出了许多尖锐和发人深省的问题。研究这些问题、思考这些问题，讨论这些问题的解决方案，将使对比语言学学科得到更为深入的发展。因而从历史的回顾转至理论的思考，是学科建设和发展的必然。杨自俭（2000：14—15）在谈到如何建设英汉对比语言学的时候提出了三条意见，一是要认真研究英汉对比研究的发展史，他认为这是学科的发展的基础；二是要借鉴比自己先进的理论与方法，他认为这是学科发展必不可少的条件；三是要关注中外哲学的新发展，这是因为任何学术研究的发展必须以哲学思维的更新为先导。总起来说就是历史、交流、哲学。我们认为这是很有见地的，其中交流应该是双向的，中国应该学习西方、借鉴西方，西方也可从中国的发展中得到许多有益的启示。

The previous three chapters surveyed the exciting historical development of contrastive linguistics in the West and in China for an understanding of the missions expected of the discipline, current and still to come. The comparative development of the discipline in the two parts of the world ring many bells on issues requiring more profound thinking, and solutions to these issues will necessarily propel further advancement of the discipline. As part of the natural development process in constructing a discipline, it is necessary to take stock of history and consider the theoretical grounding. On establishing English-Chinese contrastive linguistics, Yang Zijian (2000: 14—15) listed three requirements: first, to lay a firm foundation for the discipline, undertake serious study of the history on English-Chinese contrastive study; secondly, as an indispensable condition in developing the discipline, take reference from advanced theory and methodology; thirdly, given that philosophy is directive in any disciplinary development, it is necessary to keep abreast with the latest development in foreign and local studies of philosophy. In sum, these are the conditions on history, knowledge transfer and philosophy. They are applicable to contrastive disciplines elsewhere in the world, for exchange is bidirectional; China should take strength from the West, and the West could also benefit from the development in China.

杨自俭在谈到学科发展史的研究时特别强调：

Yang Zijian especially highlighted the following points on disciplinary development with a view in history:

> 我国学科发展史的研究比较多的是文献史。文献史也有作用，但要推动学科进步，更重要的是研究学科的思想史，也就是重要观念和范畴发展变化的历史。要重点研究学科产生的原因以及发展的动力、规律与趋势，尤其要注意对各个转型期的研究，要抓住学科发展所遇到的难题，谁提出什么理论与方法，问题解决到什么程度等。这样一个阶段一个阶段从早期追踪到现在，就比较容易把形成的观念和认识升华成理论系统。（杨自俭，2000：15）

> Study on disciplinary development history in China mostly take the form of documentation history. No doubt, documentation history has its function; however, to push on, it is more important to survey evolvement of philosophical thoughts in the discipline to trace the development of important concepts and categories evolved through time. To center on the cause for disciplinary establishment and its development thrust, trend and pattern, particular attention must be paid to the various transitional periods to have a grasp on the developmental challenges, who proposed what theory and methodology, and to what extent are the issues being resolved. From the beginning to the present, by following through the various stages in this manner, it will be easier to consolidate the concepts and understanding for formulation of systematic theory. (Yang Zijian, 2000: 15)

本书的前三章特别注重学术思想的发展，可说是这种思路的一种实践。在这样的"思想史"的回顾过程中，自然而然地产生了一系列的问题，在"史"的叙述过程中当然可以有所涉及，但不宜展开；而有的由前人的理论或实践所触发的个人的思考更不宜凭空插在史的叙述中，因此将这些问题集中起来进行讨论，不但是自然的，而且也是必然的。这就是我们为什么要写接下来的两章的原因。这两章的主题我们定位在对语言对比研究的哲学思考，即由对比语言学史的回顾所引起的对这一学科的建设的理论思索。其中这一章主要讨论学科的本体论问题，诸如学科的哲学基础、语言观、学科地位、学科性质、学科目标与范围等，下一章则主要讨论对比研究的方法论问题，如对比的原则、对比出发点、对比方向、对比方法论等。两章的角度都是宏观的，侧重于理论探索，与一般对比语言学著作不同。即使在讨论"对比方法"时，本书一般也不会详细讨论语音、词汇、语法等具体项目的对比。

To keep presentation focused, certain details and elaborations, as a result, were deliberately saved till now. The next two chapters pinpoint those observations that would lead us to the philosophical thought behind contrastive linguistics on which the theoretical basis would be grounded. This chapter will answer ontology questions relating to metaphysical foundation, language perspective as well as the position, nature, aim and scope of the discipline. The next chapter will concentrate on methodology issues, such as contrastive principles, premises or starting points, direction and methods. Both chapters bearing a macro-perspective in mind are inclined towards theoretical discourse, unlike normal works on contrastivel linguistics, which tend to dwell on specific details of phonology, lexicology and grammar among others.

4.2 对比语言学的基础论——哲学语言观
4.2 Foundation of contrastive linguistics—Perspective from philosophical linguistics

4.2.1 语言观问题处在对比语言学学科建设的底座
4.2.1 Language perspective as the cornerstone in discipline building

首先要讨论的是语言观问题，或者说是，是"什么是语言"的问题。这个问题，在西方对比语言学史上，自第二期以来，除切斯特曼之外，几乎没有什么人提到过；在中国对比语言学史上，在第五期以前，也很少有人认真思考过。但很少有人提到，不等于说这个问题不重要，更不等于说这个问题早已解决、只是个"不成问题的问题"。事实上，这个问题对于对比语言学来说，是根本的问题、原则的问题，是第一个和具有决定性的问题。在这个问题上的不同认识，会导致对比语言学研究向完全不同的方向发展。对比语言学对比的是"语言"，但如果在什么是语言的问题上都不能取得共识，那怎能指望对比能在同一个基础上进行？许多对比语言学者正确地指出了对比研究要有一个共同的出发点，而且提出了各自不同的主张，但他们恰恰是疏忽了最基本、最要紧的出发点——语言观。西方第三期以来的语言对比研究，特别强调语言理论的指导，其中如菲齐亚克、如克尔采斯佐斯基等表现得更为自觉，菲氏（1990）甚至指出在"理论"背后有更重要的"元理论"问题。这已经接近了我们的观点，但可惜菲氏没有再往前走一步。菲氏的"元理论"指的只是相对于对比语言学理论的理论语言学的理论，但这些理论语言学的"理论"未必都认真谈到语言观的问题，因而尽管菲氏想到了"元理论"背后还有更值得思考的"元元理论"问题，这就是以语言观为核心的语言哲学的思考。因而，对于语言观在语言对比研究上的重要性，我们从两个方便去认识。

The first cardinal question has to be language perspective, or what is language. In the West, linguistics—not many besides Andrew Chesterman have considered this question since Phase 2 in history; while in China, few really took it up before Phase 5. That language perspective is not given the due attention does not diminish its importance nor make it an non-issue. As a fact, it concerns is the root and principle to contrastive linguistics. It is a question to ask first and foremost and is deterministic. Different takes on this question impact on the shape and direction the discipline will evolve. Consensus on what is language is necessary to establish a common platform on which contrastive study may be carried out. Most contrastivists converge on the need to have a common starting point; nevertheless, it is exactly this language perspective, the most essential starting point that was being neglected. Led by Fisiak and Krzeszowski, western contrastive linguistics studies since Phase 3 have put conscious weight on theoretical guidance. Fisiak (1990) was close when stressed that there are even "metatheoretical issues" on top of theoretical issues. That one step away from a metatheory for linguistics proves to be too far for Fisiak as he circled around theory for theoretical linguistics. And we suspect what Fisiak had in mind of metatheory remained a distant away from the edge of language perspective. We are suggesting that there are meta-metatheoretical issues to consider and those are language ideological conceptions with language perspective at the core. We may approach language perspective from two angles.

第一，哲学问题处于任一学科研究的底座，是学科理论研究的核心。First, philosophical issues, the backbones in any discipline, are at the core of all theoretical studies.

潘文国（2004）从总结人类学术发展史的角度出发，曾经提出过一个观点，认为学科研究除了可以横向分成自然科学、社会科学、人文科学等之外，还可以从纵向上进行分类。从纵向上，每个学科都可以分为四个层面。为了说明这一点，他举了一些学科的例子，其中包括语言学：

> Throughout history, scholastic development has always run on two axes. Horizontally, it may be divided as natural sciences, social sciences, humanities and others; vertically, it may be classified on four interrelated fronts, as Pan Wenguo (2004: 100) suggests:
>
> 每门学科都可以分成四个层面：学科哲学——学科理论——应用理论——应用实践。这四个层面不是彼此孤立的，其间有相承的关系：应用理论是应用实践的基础，对实践有着指导作用；学科理论是应用理论的基础，对应用理论的形成有着指导作用；而学科哲学是学科理论发展的原动力，是学科理论保持生气勃勃的关键。例如：
>
> 文学：文学哲学（或美学）——文学理论——写作理论——写作实践；
> 翻译学：翻译哲学——翻译理论——翻译技巧——翻译实践；
> 科学技术：自然哲学——具体学科理论——操作工艺——操作实践。
> 语言学：语言哲学（实为哲学语言学）——理论语言学——应用语言学——语言实践。（潘文国，2004：100）
>
> Each discipline may be classified on four fronts: philosophy of discipline, theories of discipline, applied theories, application proper, each building on one another in that application proper is founded on applied theories which in turn are grounded on theories of the discipline of which the root is at the philosophy of the discipline which is also the key to ensuring sustained development of the discipline. To illustrate,

Literature: literary philosophy (or aesthetics)——literary theories——composition theories——composition proper;

Translation: translation philosophy——translation theories——translation techniques——translation proper;

Science and technology: natural philosophy——theories of specific disciplines——technical mechanism——operation proper;

Linguistics: language philosophy (philosophical linguistics rather)——theoretical linguistics——applied linguistics——language practice. (Pan Wenguo, 2004: 100)

拿这个理论来检验中国和西方的对比语言学史，可以使我们看清和解释许多问题，也能启发我们从根本上理解为什么对比语言学的地位在中国和西方会如此不同，理解为什么西方的对比语言学迄今仍是个"灰姑娘"，以及摆脱这一困境的出路何在。

Upon this standpoint, many questions in the development histories of contrastive linguistics both in the West and in China are illuminated and well accounted for: that the discipline is positioned radically different in the West from in China, that contrastive linguistics purports to be the Cinderella of Western linguistic and the way to resolve this predicament.

在西方对比研究史上，许多人不敢或不肯承认对比研究是"语言学"，而只把自己的研究称为对比分析（CA），强调其对于二语教学的实践意义，这从表面上看来仿佛是谦虚，实际上是学科定位有问题，说明他们在认识上就已经将自己所从事的研究放在了学科纵向分类的最底层，即实践层面。自居最底层，还希望别人承认其学科地位，那无异于痴人说梦。还有些人胆子大了一点，亮出了"对比语言学"的名称，这比"对比分析"当然是高了一层，但我们发现他们在谈论"对比语言学"的时候总还是自觉底气不足，总还是以为对比语言学光凭其自身还不足与其他"语言学"分庭抗礼，因而要到处寻找某家某派"理论语言学"的支撑，仿佛没有某一家理论语言学的支撑，对比语言学就难以独立。这从他们的定位也可以看出来。这些主张"对比语言学"的学者，往往同时强调对比语言学属于"应用语言学"而必须接受"理论语言学"的指导。从上面的"四层次"理论来看，"应用语言学"属于第三层，比"实践"层面当然要高了一点，但比"理论语言学"层面还是要低。因而只要坚持对比语言学属于应用语言学,则比起西方特别是美国风起云涌的理论语言学流派来,"对比语言学"者当然自觉要矮人一截,它之不可能进入"理论语言学"者的视野,可说也是必然的。因而如果这个认识不改变,西方对比语言学要摆脱"灰姑娘"的命运可说永远不会有成功的一天。

Most western contrastive works do not acknowledge their studies to be a branch of linguistics as evident in their choice of the term "contrastive analysis" to emphasize its applied significance in second language pedagogy. Rather than doing it out of modesty, it serves to illustrate the positioning of the discipline, that western contrastivists put themselves at the lowest or applied rank of the vertical axis. That it is a self-conscious act, one could not expect others to accord the discipline its deserved right. Yet those who seemingly respect their works as contrastive linguistics give themselves away in clearly a vote of no confidence to the independent nature of the discipline, seek to dress up their works with some theories in theoretical linguistics. As if that is not good enough as a statement, this group of "contrastivists" often stress that contrastive linguistics came under "applied linguistics" and should be guided by "theoretical linguistics". While this seems to have elevated the discipline to the third rank of the axis under theoretical linguistics, the insistence of its belonging to applied linguistics will forever hinder the advancement of the discipline in the West, especially in the US where theoretical linguistics is so crowded, divided and challenging. It follows quite naturally then that contrastivists must feel inferior and contrastive linguisics fall out of the horizon of theoretical linguists. To resolve the situation, a change in paradigm is required.

中国对比语言学的发展在这个问题上经历了一番曲折。在第二期,学者们可说是不自觉地意识到了语言观问题的重要性,强调汉语的独特性、民族性,可说是其中最闪亮的表现。因而对比研究取得了不俗的成就。但正因为其认识是不自觉的,因而到了第三、第四期,在苏联和西方的语言学"理论"冲击之下,马上就一败涂地、落花流水,到了20世纪80年代后期,对比语言学甚至也已沦落到可有可无的境地,与西方的"灰姑娘"境地也相去不远。但从20世纪90年代以后,中国学者的认识明显有了升华。他们的最早动力来自于赵元任的启示,赵元任的"对比语言学就是普通语言学"论断,从时间上看应该出现得很早,但直到这时才真正变成了力量。在这一论断的鼓舞下,这一时期的对比语言学者更自觉地把对比语言学就当作普通语言学或理论语言学来研究,因而在实践中将这一学科提到了第二个层面。处于第二个层面，它就完全有资格与其他语言学理论并起并坐、分庭抗礼。处于第二个层面，中国的对比语言学也就有了西方对比语言学所缺少的两个特点。一是明确地主张语言对比研究有两个目标：理论目标和应用目标，不但不以追逐实际应用为惟一目标，而且从中国语言学的实际出发，更强调通过汉语和外语的对比对汉语特点的发掘，这就使中国当代的对比语言学研究成了语言学研究无法绕过和难以忽视的一股力量；二是由于处在第二个层面，中国的对比语言学就会更自觉地追求第一层面即语言哲学的指导而不仅仅是处于同一层面的其他现行的某家语言理论的指导。中国对比语言学实际上已经取得了"本体语言学"的地位，在中国语言学科建设中发挥着越来越大的作用。这一些，对于西方的同行来说，应该产生有益的启示。

Contrastive linguistics in China has been through an arduous path too in this respect. Phase 2 of the development saw some unwitting awareness of language perspective when emphasis on the uniqueness and ethnicity of the Chinese Language was at its height. The subtle effect of holding an ideology of language is evident by the achievements in contrastive linguistics of the period. Nevertheless, it would be a tall order to expect an unperceived awareness to hold out and even overcome the domineering influence of Soviet and western linguistic theories in Phases 3 and 4. Up until the late 1980s, contrastive linguistics in China mirrored its plight in the West as a Cinderella. Fortunately increasing realization on the part of Chinese linguists since the 1990s gradually turned the situation around. A timely revisit to an earlier comment by Chao Yuen-ren that "contrastive linguistics is really general linguistics" became the powerful agent sparked the watershed change. It spurred contrastivists to undertake research in contrastive linguistics as general linguistics or theoretical linguistics. The concerted effort saw contrastive linguistics, now at the second rank of the vertical axis, recognised as a branch in linguistics having its own rights, i.e. running parallel with other branches of linguistic studies. Contrastive linguistics in China is differentiated from its western counterpart in two ways. First of all, it is identified by two clear objectives: theoretical object and application object. On the one hand, it is released from the single objective in application, on the other hand, it is mindful of the realities of the Chinese language and accentuates contrastive studies aiming at revealing the peculiarities of the Chinese language. On this note, contrastive linguistics has become a powerful thrust that any contemporary linguistic research in China could not bypass or disregard. Secondly, at the second rank of the vertical axis, contrastivists tend to tune in to a higher level of guidance at the philosophical front instead of adhering to a particular linguistic school of thought of the same level. We could well say that contrastive linguistics in China has achieved full ontology rights in linguistics, which would allow the discipline to play a greater role in Chinese linguistics. This particular development should inspire counterparts across the globe.

第二，语言观问题是语言研究的最基本、最初始问题，决定了语言研究的方向。

Next, language perspective is fundamental to and directive on language studies.

坦率地说，在西方，就是理论语言学的众多学派，对语言观问题的重视也是不够的，更遑论划入应用层级的对比语言学。更进一步，甚至二十世纪初以来风靡西方哲学界的语言哲学，对"什么是语言"的问题也欠缺关注。西方语言哲学，特别是英美分析哲学，关心的是意义、意义的价值、语用、语言与现实，以及语境等问题，很少追问"语言是什么"；大陆派哲学虽然提出了"语言是存在的家园"（海德格尔）、"能被理解的'存在'就是语言"（伽德默尔）这样的命题，但从命题本身我们可以看出，他们真正关心的是"存在"（Being）这一西方哲学的本体问题，语言对他们来说，只是"器"而不是"道"，他们只是从语言的角度来思考哲学，不从哲学的角度来思考语言，没有认真思考和回答过"语言是什么"的问题。因而我们在上引的"四层"说里，对于语言学来说，处于最高一层的与其说是"语言哲学"问题，还不如更准确地说是"哲学语言学"问题，它要求用哲学的眼光来思索有关语言的各种问题。在这一思索中首当其冲的就是"语言是什么"这一最初始的问题。中国古代哲学家老子说："道生一，一生二，二生三，三生万物。"意思是说，天底下的事物千差万别，但归根结蒂是由"道"生成的。对于语言研究来说，语言观就是"道"，"道"的不同就会引起语言研究道路的千差万别。不同的语言观，决定不同的语言理论、目标、范围、途径、方法、重点、结果、政策、教学法等一系列根本问题。下面以人们熟悉的几种语言观为例，看看不同的语言观是如何影响到语言研究和应用的方方面面的：

To put it plainly, language perspective is not accorded with due recognition in the West, not even by the various schools in theoretical linguistics, much less by contrastive analysis in the applied field. Most regrettably, even in the area of language philosophy that excited western philosophy in early twentieth century, the question of what language is was not given sufficient discussion. Western language philosophy, particularly analytic philosophy of great Britain and the US, address themselves to meaning, value of meaning, pragmatics, language and realities, context and the like much more than what language all about. For continental philosophy, the limelight falls on Joseph Heidegger's idea that 'language is the house of Being' as well as Hans-Georg Gadamer's proposition on the linguisticality of understanding that "We are 'in' the world through being 'in' language." From these value propositions, it is the ontology question of "Being" that the European philosophers are after. Language to them is only a vehicle in aid of philosophical thinking; it is not the "logos". Essentially, philosophy drew heavily from linguistics more so than linguistics from philosophy. The question of what is language remains unanswered. At the helm of the vertical axis, it is philosophical linguistics rather than linguistic philosophy that should rule, i.e. to consider linguistic issues with a philosophical perspective. The primary question asks what language is all about. An ancient sage in China, Lao Tze proclaims that "Dao" (the way) is the genesis root of the myraids. And language perspective is akin to "Dao" in linguistics whereby splits in language perspective lead to diverse ways of investigating language. For every linguistic theory, its aim, scope, methodology, focus, consequence, policy and pedagogy are functional by the language perspective embraced. Listed below are some common language perspectives and how they have guided language study and areas of application:

表4.1 语言观种种

语言观	自足系统	交际工具	人的本能
理论	结构主义	交际理论	普遍语法
目标	建立语音语法体系	描写语言的使用	寻找先天语言机制
范围	语言内部；句以下	语言与社会、民族、文化	语言与心理学、生物学、脑科学
途径	语言调查、分析	语言调查、分析	假设、推理
方法	发现程序；分布理论（归纳法）	统计、归纳	解释；演绎法

（续表）

语言观	自足系统	交际工具	人的本能
重点	描写	功能	形式化
结果	越走越窄	被视作"语言"的边缘	越走越窄；自然科学化
语言政策	语言平等	多语多方言；规范化	无
教学	句型教学；替代法	功能法	无（但重视儿童语言习得研究）

Table 4.1 Language perspective at work

Language Perspective	Self-sufficient System	Tool of Communication	Human Instinct
Theory	Structuralism	Communication theory	Universal grammar
Aim	Establishing phonetic-grammatical systems	Describe language use	In search of inherited language acquisition devices
Scope	Language internal; below sentence level	Language and society, ethnicity and culture	Language and psychology, biology, neurology
Manner	Language survey and analysis	Language survey and analysis	Hypothesis, deduction
Methodology	Discovery procedure, distribution theory (induction)	Statistics, induction	Explanation; deduction
Focus	Descriptive	Functional	Formal
Consequence	narrowing	Regarded as at the borderline of language	Narrowing; inclined towards natural science
Language policy	Language equality	Multilingual, multi-dialectal; standardization	N. A.
Pedagogy	Sentence patterns; substitution drills	Functional and situational	N. A. (But emphasize child acquisition)

表中说的是一般的语言研究。语言对比研究也是如此，不同的语言观会导致对比研究在一系列根本问题上的不同面貌和表现。比方说，如果认为语言是人的先天本能、语法是全人类共有的一套机制，那对比研究简直就不必进行，或至多只需对枝节问题上的差异进行一些"解释"；再比如说，如果认为语言是一个自足的系统，而不同语言的系统不同，那对比时只要将两套系统排比起来对照就行了。如此等等。中西方的对比语言学研究都已有了一百多年的历史，其

中的观点也可以说是千差万别，但只要追溯到各自的语言观，我们就能理解分歧的由来。同时，也只有在比较中确定我们自己的语言观，我们也才能确定今天的对比研究应当如何进行。

The general cases above apply to contrastive linguistics just the same. For instance, for someone believing that language is an innate instinct and grammar is a universal mechanism shared by human beings, there will be no place for contrastive linguistics except to explain in details minor differences. On the other hand, someone of the view that language is a self sufficient system and varies across languages, then it suffices to put two systems side by side for analysis. Language perspective does have a bearing on the direction of research. Contrastive linguistics is a century-old discipline in both the West and China, and we expect varied and divided opinions in this process. Tracing this development path highlights the points of departure, and only through the comparison of this development are we able to shape and refine language perspective to guide the future direction of contrastive studies.

4.2.2 形形色色的语言观

4.2.2 Language perspectives

对比语言学的哲学基础即语言观，而学科的创始人的语言观当然值得关注。在本书第一章中，我们已经论证了对比语言学的创始人就是19世纪的洪堡特和20世纪的叶斯柏森、沃尔夫等人。因而这几位语言学家（同时也是语言哲学家）的语言观也应该成为对比语言学者的语言观。我们在最早论述对比语言学的哲学基础时（潘文国，1995）就是这么考虑的。但当时我们还只就对比语言学本身来立论。今天我们的认识又进了一步，认为对比语言学就是普通语言学，这就要进一步论证洪堡特等人的语言观不仅是对比语言学的哲学基础，也应该是整个理论语言学的哲学基础，这就需要比较各种语言观，从更宽广的角度来进行讨论。

It is curious enough what the founders and pioneers of contrastive linguistics hold as the philosophical basis or language perspective of the discipline. Chapter 1 associates the beginning of contrastive linguistics with von Humboldt in the nineteenth century, as well as Jespersen, Whorf and others in the twentieth century.

Their outlooks on language are important, since in their thinking we find contrastive linguistics and for the discipline to thrive, their perspectives should prevail amongst researchers in this area too. Pan Wenguo (1995) made an early attempt to map out the philosophical grounding for the discipline. With the proposition that contrastive linguistics is general linguistics, it is necessary to go further to establish that the ideologies of Humboldt and company are at the same time the philosophical basis of theoretical linguistics. For this, we have to start from the basic discussion of the various language perspectives.

在《语言的定义》（潘文国，2001a）一文中，潘文国搜集了自洪堡特以来160余年间中外学者关于语言的68种定义，发现对于"什么是语言"问题的歧异之大远远超出人们的想象。其中有的观点更是针尖对麦芒，可说是势不两立的。略举数例如下：

Pan Wenguo (2001a) compiled 68 definitions of language from the 160 years since Humboldt, only to be surprised at the heterogeneity in these definitions, some to the extent of being irreconcilable. The following illustrates this.

语言是本能还是非本能？生成语言学派的乔姆斯基（Noam Chomsky）[1]、品克（Steven Pinker）[2]等人强调语言是本能，强调语言能力的先天性；而人类学语言学家萨丕尔（Edward Sapir）[3]则强调语言不是人的本能，是人类后天习得的而非先天就有的能力；

Is language an instinct or otherwise? The generative school, represented by Noam Chomsky and Steven Pinker cannot emphasize enough the immanent

---

[1] "解决柏拉图难题的办法就是将人的语言能力归因于人身的组织，这是生物学上先天赋予的。"（乔姆斯基，1988：27）
"The solution to Plato's problem must be based on ascribing the fixed principles of the language faculty to the human organism as part of its biological endowment" (Chomsky, 1988: 27).

[2] "语言不是文化的产物，我们并不像学会看钟表或了解联邦政府如何运作那样学会语言。相反，语言是人类大脑的生理构成中的一个清晰的部分。"（品克，1994：18）
"Language is not a cultural artifact that we learn the way we learn to tell time or how the federal government works. Instead, it is a distinct piece of the biological makeup or our brains" (Pinker, 1994: 18).

[3] "语言是人类特有的、非本能的一种方式，借助于自身创造的一种符号体系，用来交流意见、感情和愿望。"（萨丕尔，1921：8）
"Language is a purely human and non-instinctive method of communicating ideas, emotions, and desires by means of a system of voluntarily produced symbols" (Sapir, 1921: 8).

property of language that is built into our biological development to be competent in language. At the other extreme are anthropological linguists, represented by Edward Sapir maintaining language as non-instinctive and largely acquired.

语言是工具还是方式？社会语言学或交际语言学派往往强调语言是工具，这一观点源自法国启蒙思想家卢梭（Jean-Jacques Rousseau，1772），在法国的影响特别大，其后苏联的列宁[1]和斯大林[2]均强调这一点，20世纪50年代以后在中国具有重大的甚至决定性的影响。文化学派的语言学家往往强调语言是人类活动的方式，如萨丕尔、马林诺斯基（Bronislaw Malinowsky）[3]、叶斯柏森[4]、克洛克洪（Clyde Kluckhohn）[5]、刘易斯（M. M Lewis）[6]等。

Is language an instrument or a mode of action? Sociolinguistics and the communication school saw language as an instrument which shaped the mainstream in France having its root in French thinker Jean-Jacques Rousseau (1772). Both

---

1　"语言是最重要的人类交际工具。"（列宁，1916：822）
"Language is the most important means of human intercourse" (Lenin, 1914).

2　"语言是工具、手段，人们利用它来互相交际，交流思想，达到相互了解。"（斯大林，1953：20）
"Language is a medium, an instrument with the help of which people communicate with one another, exchange thoughts and understand each other" (Stalin, 1950).

3　"语言的最原始功能是作为行为方式，而不是思想的对应记号。"（马林诺斯基，1923：296）
"Language, in its primitive function, is regarded as a mode of action, rather than as a countersign of thought" (Malinowsky, 1923: 296).

4　"在研究前人说法的过程中使我们明白了如下几点，这是要了解什么是语言所绝对不应该忘记的：个人的某种瞬间行为……"（叶斯伯森，1946：23）
"In the course of it, we have grasped the following points, which we must never be let go if one would hope to understand what language is: individual momentary actions of a particular kind" (Jespersen, 1946: 23).

5　"每一种语言都不仅仅是交流信息和观点的手段，都不仅仅是表达感情、泄发情绪，或者指令别人做事的工具。每种语言其实都是一种观察世界以及解释经验的特殊方式，在每种不同的语言里所包含的其实是一整套对世界和对人生的无意识的解释。"（Kluckhohn，1949，in Anderson & Stageberg，1962：53）
"Every language is also a special way of looking at the world and interpreting experience. Concealed in the structure of each different language are a whole set of unconscious assumptions about the world and life in it" (Kluckhohn 1949, in Anderson and Stageberg, 1962: 53).

6　"语言是一种活动形式，可能是人类最重要的一种行为模式。"（刘易斯，1936：5）
"Language is a form of activity, a mode of human behavior, perhaps the most important" (Lewis, 1936: 5).

Lenin and Stalin of the Soviet Union also bought into this thought and it has had a decisive impact on China since the 1950s. As Humboldt put it, "the most obvious but most limited view of language is to see it as a mere means of communication" (Humboldt, 1927: 128). The cultural school led by Edward Sapir, Bronislaw Malinowsky, Jespersen, Clyde Kluckhohn, and M. M. Lewis, among others, see language as being a mode of action.

语言是不是文化组成部分？品克强调语言不是文化的产物，这显然是为了便于将语言提炼出来进行"纯净"的研究；惠特尼（W. D. Whitney）[1]强调语言是文化的组成部分，这是人类学家的观点；而沃尔夫更强调语言的形式范畴都由其文化规定，更是为了人类学语言学的研究。

Is language a constituent part of culture? Pinker does not think that language is a cultural product, this would then fit his purpose of extracting language in a "pure" form. W. D. Whitney, as an anthropological linguist, holds that it is a component of culture. Whorf goes even further in suggesting that grammatical categories are determined by culture, as evident by the need in anthropological linguistic studies.

语言到底有哪些功能？各家定义中提到的有交际功能、思维功能、表情达意功能、信息功能、指示功能、认识功能等等，不一而足。那么，语言究竟是这些功能中的一个呢，还是这些功能中的某几项的排列组合？还有人说，一个交际功能就可以涵盖所有这些功能，是真的这样吗？

What are the functions of language? Mentioned in the various definitions are communicative function, thinking function, expressive function, informative function, referencing function and recognitive function, to name a few. So, is language one of these functions or a portfolio of these functions? Someone said that even the communicative function is all inclusive.

语言的范围，是只指口语（这是二十世纪初以来占压倒优势的看法），还是包含了书面语？还是进一步包括了手势语（David Crystal, 1997）？如果肢体语言也可以算"语言"，能不能进一步拓展到舞蹈语言，以至音乐语言、电影语言等；还有数学语言、计算机语言，动物语言、植物语言等等。这里面有的是外延问题，但也有内涵问题。问题还在于哪里是外延和内涵的界线：口语？书面语？手势语？

---

[1] "语言是获得的能力，文化的组成部分。"（惠特尼，1875：291）
"Language is an acquisition, a part of culture" (Whitney, 1875: 291).

Does the scope of language include only the verbal form (the mainstream opinion since the early twentieth century) or does it include the written form? Or even sign language (as in David Crystal, 1997)? If body language is to be included, should language be expanded to include dance language, music language, film language or, in another spectrum, mathematical language, computer language, animal language, plant language, etc…Besides issues of the extent, there are issues on the connotation as well as the boundary between the two: verbal form, written form or sign language?

语言是不是个自足"系统"？索绪尔（Ferdinand de Saussure，1916）之前很少有人谈语言是个系统，索绪尔之后几乎人人必称系统，这是为什么？对"系统说"有保留的，有功能派如马丁内（Martinet，1962）、文化派如申小龙（1990）、方式派如叶斯柏森、认知派如兰格克（Ronald Langacker），甚至包括生成语言学派如弗罗姆金（Fromkin et al. 1999）[1]，这是怎么回事？

Is language a self sufficient "system"? Few before Ferdinand de Saussure (1916) would call language a system and everyone calls language a system after Saussure. Why? Suspicious about the claim are functionalists such as Martinet (1962) and from the cultural school such as Shen Xiaolong (1990), Jespersen who thinks language is a mode of action, from the cognitive school, Ronald Langacker, and even some like Fromkin (Fromkin et al. 1991) from the generative school. This is interesting.

语言是动态还是静态的？索绪尔之前学者，无论是哲学语言学家洪堡特[2]，

---

[1] "如果只把语言看作交际系统，那么语言就不是人类所特有的，尽管人类语言有一些别的动物没有的特点。"（弗罗姆金等，1999：23）
"If language is defined merely as a system of communication, then language is not unique to humans. There are, however, certain characteristics of human language not found in communication systems of any other species" (Fromkin et al. 1999: 23).

[2] "从真正的本质上来看，语言是一件持久的事物，在每一个瞬间都稍纵即逝，即使通过文字保存下来的，也只是不完整的、木乃伊式的东西，只在描述当前话语时才重新需要。语言本身绝非产品（Ergon），而是一个活动过程（Energeia）。"（洪堡特，1836：49/54）
"Language, regarded in its real nature, is an enduring thing, and at every moment a transitory one. Even its maintenance by writing is always just an incomplete, mummy-like preservation, only needed again in attempting thereby to picture the living utterance. In itself it is no product (Ergon), but an activity (Energeia). Its true definition can therefore only be a genetic one" (Humboldt, 1836: 49/54).

还是进化论语言学家如施莱赫尔（Schleicher）[1]都主张动态，索绪尔之后的生成语言学派以"生成"为标榜，当然也主张动态，而索绪尔的"共时语言学"实质上却是主张静态的研究。问题在于语言究竟应该以动态的还是静态的方法去研究？

Is language dynamic or static? Before Saussure, everyone including philosophical linguist Humboldt and evolutionalist linguist Schleicher concurred on the dynamic nature of language. After Saussure, opinions are divided. The generative school, being "generative" supports the dynamicity in language whereas synchronic studies proposed by Saussure approach language from a static standpoint. So, should language study have a dynamic or static approach?

此外还有"约定俗成"、"音义结合的任意性"等，都充满着尖锐的矛盾与对立。读者如果熟悉当代西方的认知语言学，对此当有更清晰的了解。

Then, there are of course other views standing in contradiction, such as "accepted through common practice" and "arbitrary relation between sound and meaning".

这种种语言观把人看得眼花缭乱，这大概也是很少有人去进行认真梳理的原因。我们经过认真的爬梳和比较，认为从最本质的方面看，所有这些不同的对语言的定义都可以概括为下面四种语言观之一，即，自足系统观、交际工具观、天赋能力观，和文化语言观，即把语言看作是一种文化或一种民族的世界观。其代表人物分别是索绪尔[2]、斯大林、乔姆斯基和洪堡特[3]。其他的各种观

1　"语言是天然的有机体，它们完全不受人类意志的支配，它们根据一定的规律自发地产生和发展，它们会变老，也会死亡。它们会受到我们称之为'生命'的一系列现象的制约。"（施莱赫尔，1863：20—21）
"Languages are organisms of nature; they have never been directed by the will of man; they rose, and developed themselves according to definite laws; they grew old, and died out. They, too, are subject to that series of phenomena which we embrace under the name of 'life'" (Schleicher, 1863: 20—21).

2　"语言是一种自足的结构系统，同时又是一种分类的原则。"（索绪尔，1916：25）
"La langue, au contraire, est un tout en soi et un principe de classification." ("Language...is a self-contained whole and a principle of classification.") (Saussure, 1916: 25/1986: 10)

3　"任何客观的知觉都不可避免地混杂有主观成分，所以撇开语言不谈，我们也可以把每个有个性的人看作世界观的一个独特的方面。但个人更多地是通过语言形成世界观。而由于在同一个民族中，影响着语言的是同一类型的主观性，可见，每一语言都包含着一种独特的世界观。"（洪堡特，1836：59—60/70）
"Since all objective perception is inevitably tinged with *subjectivity*, we may consider every human individual, even apart from his language, as a unique aspect of the world-view. But he becomes still more of one through language...Since the subjectivity also affects language in the same nation; there resides in every language a characteristic *world-view*" (Humboldt, 1836: 59—60/70).

点都可以以这样那样的方式归纳进这四种最基本的观点之中。

Obviously the issues are more complex than the simple dichotomy presented above and probably for this reason, not many bother about resolving them. After serious consideration, with respect to the nature of the subject matter, the various definitions of language could be summarized and grouped into four perspectives, namely, self-sufficient system, communicative instrument, innate ability and cultural linguistics (which is a world view taking language as a culture or an ethnic world view). These perspectives are represented respectively by Saussure, J. Stalin, Noam Chomsky and Humboldt.

从更宏观的视角看,我们还把这四种观点与地球进化所经历的三个世界与人类所从事研究的三大学科门类相联系:

From the larger picture, these four perspectives may be put into the context of world evolution and the three large categories of human research:

> 人类迄今从事的所有科学研究都可以归纳进三个大门类:自然科学,关于自然或带有自然性质的科学;社会科学,关于社会或带有社会性质的科学;人文科学,关于人类自身的科学。这个分类是有其合理性的,因为它们分别是针对不同的对象。这三个门类研究的其实是前后相承的三个世界:天地之始,宇宙初辟,一直到第一种动物诞生之前,这个只有矿物和植物的相对静止的世界,就是自然世界;动物的出现带来了由自由活动的个体组成的群体,有了群体就必然有关系需要协调,有信息需要交流,这时就出现了第二世界——社会世界;动物进化到人,出现了人类世界,其与第二世界的区别在于人类有语言和思想。所有的学科都可以归纳进三大门类里,当然学科间可能会有交叉,有的还可能兼属于三个门类,但不管怎样,它首先有个基本的归属,而这个基本归属必然是所研究对象的本质之所在。给语言定性的关键就在于,对于语言这么一个复杂的现象,究竟应该从哪类学科的角度来给它作基本的定性,是关注于语言的自然属性呢,社会属性呢,还是人类本身的属性?这是必须解决的首要关键问题;也是在语言定义上各种分歧产生的根源。(潘文国,2001a: 31)

> To date, all scientific research by human beings could be classified into three: natural or belonging to natural sciences, social or societal by nature sciences, and humanities or the science about human beings. In fact, the

three categories of research correspond to three succeeding "worlds": at the beginning of heaven and earth, there exist only minerals and plants before the first animal came into being, this is the world of nature. With animal participating, groups or communities formed by free individuals begin to emerge. Coordination between relations become necessary, exchanges of information become a need. This constitutes a second world, a social world. As evolution advances, human beings came into existence, forming the human world, which distinguishes from the societal world on the use of language and thought. All disciplines could be grouped under these three categories, cross-linking in any two or even all three may be natural. In any case, there must be a base where things shall belong, and in this particular base the nature of the research target shall be found. The key to defining language, such a complex phenomenon, lies in answering the question, from which disciplinary perspective shall language be positioned? Are we to focus on its natural science attributes, societal attributes or humanity attributes? As the cause of divergence in definitions, this is the question to be resolved first and foremost. (Pan Wenguo, 2001a: 31)

由于语言既有自然属性，又有社会属性，还有人文属性，因而着眼于哪个属性就成为各种语言观的分野所在。自足系统观着眼于语言的自然属性，因而在语言最具自然科学属性的部门如语音学方面做得最有声有色，对结构性较强的语法特别是形态学方面也颇有建树，而对"系统"性不那么强的词汇、语义、语用等方面的成就就比较有限；交际系统说着眼于语言的社会属性，因而在语言的交际功能、语用功能、语境因素等领域做得最出色，语音研究也因为交际派提出的音位学而变得更富实用，但因对语言的结构本体关注不够而往往被前者"边缘化"；天赋能力观和语言世界观观都着眼于语言的人类属性，都是第三个世界的产物。但两者的侧重点不同，前者重视的是人类的自然属性，因而坚决主张用自然科学的方法去研究语言，认为这才是使语言研究科学化的惟一途径；而后者重视的是人类的文化属性，坚持语言学属于人文科学，必须用人文科学的方法，亦即联系民族的历史、文化等因素去研究语言。这两派的代表人物分别是乔姆斯基和洪堡特。许多人说乔姆斯基是洪堡特的重新发现者，但其实两人的语言观完全针锋相对。乔姆斯基强调语言研究中的自然科学方法，他说：

  Crossing the boundaries of natural sciences, social sciences and humanities, language perspectives could indeed be widely apart depending on the attachment in the three fields. To look upon language as a self-sufficient system is focusing on its qualities in natural sciences and would be strong on the aspects of language which have the greatest affinity to natural sciences, such as phonology or morphology, and weak in areas that are less systematic, such as lexicology, semantics and pragmatics. To look upon language as a communication means to put weight on the societal attributes in language and be therefore strong in areas that deal with the communicative, pragmatic and contextual functions of language. In a way, phonetic study also benefited from the study of phonemics put forward by the communicative school and became more practical. However, negligence in the structure of language has led to its being marginalized by the former school of thought. There are two perspectives coming from the humanities standpoint, one on innate ability and the other on linguistic world view, both products of the human world. However, the former, represented by Noam Chomsky, centred on the natural attributes of humans and therefore insistent on the use of natural science methodology, opined that this is the only way to ensure scientific research. The latter, exemplified by von Humboldt, concentrates on the cultural attributes of humans and stands firm on the use of humanities methodology in connection with ethnic history, culture and other factors. As Chomsky himself acknowledges the constant and unvarying mental process underlying all language posited by von Humboldt as the progenitor of his generative grammar, some tend to take Chomskian thought as the reconstruction of von Humboldt's scholarship. In fact, they are two conflicting perspectives. Chomsky has a heavy stamp of natural sciences in his approach as he indicates:

  这个世界有许许多多方面，有机械方面、化学方面、光学方面、电学方面等等，其中还有精神方面。我们的观点是，所有这些方面应该用同一种方法去研究。不管我们考虑的是行星的运动、力的场、高分子的结构公式，还是语言能力的计算性特征，都一样。我们可以称之为"精神研究的自然主义方法"，意思是我们希望用自然科学的理性探索特征来研究世界上所有精神方面的东西。（乔姆斯基，1996：31—32）

The world has many aspects: mechanical, chemical, optical, electrical, and so on. Among these are its mental aspects. The thesis is that all should be studied in the same way, whether we are considering the motion of the planets, fields of force, structural formulas for complex molecules, or computational properties of the language faculty. Let's call this a "naturalistic approach to mind", meaning that we seek to investigate the mental aspects of the world by the methods of rational inquiry characteristic of the natural sciences. Whether the results of a naturalistic approach merit the honorific term "science" depends on the results it achieves. One can sensibly ask how far a naturalistic approach might carry on towards topics of human concern and intellectual significance, but there is no question about its legitimacy, I will assume. (Chomsky, 1996: 31—32)

而洪堡特却强调语言中的民族精神，说：
But it is ethnic spirit in language that Humboldt underscored:

> 语言的所有最为纤细的根基生长在民族精神力量之中；民族精神力量对语言的影响越恰当，语言的发展就越合乎规律，越丰富多彩。由于语言就其内在联系而言只不过是民族语言意识的产物，所以，我们如果不以民族精神力量为出发点，就根本无法彻底解答那些跟富有内在生命力的语言构造的有关问题，以及语言的最重大差别由何产生的问题。（洪堡特，1836: 21）
>
> It therefore strikes with all the most delicate fibres of its roots into the national mentality; and the more aptly the latter reacts upon it, the more rich and regular its development. And since, in its integrated webwork, it is only an effect of the national feeling for language, there can be no basic answer to those very questions which refer to the formation of languages in their inmost life, and from which at the same time their most important differences arise, if we do not ascend to this point of view. (von Humboldt, 1836: 21)

对比语言学的学科建设，首先要解决的就是这样一个基础的哲学问题，我们必须在诸多的语言观中，或者至少在这四大语言观中作出选择。只有确定了语言观，才有可能真正建立起对比语言学研究的大厦。

Philosophical basis is constitutive to contrastive linguistics as a discipline; it is pertinent and preeminent that we make a decision among the four dominant perspectives in language. Only then can we erect an institution out of contrastive linguistics.

4.2.3 对比语言学的哲学基础——语言世界观
4.2.3 The philosophical basis of contrastive linguistics——Linguistic worldview

在这四种语言观中,九十年代以来的中国主流对比语言学选择了第四种,亦即洪堡特的语言世界观学说,作为自己建立对比语言学的理论基础。这是对四种语言观进行了反复比较和思考的结果。这一思考主要基于以下几个方面。

Among the four perspectives, Chinese mainstream contrastivists of the 1990s decided on Humboldt's idea of a linguistic worldview as their theoretical grounding. The considerations were as follows.

4.2.3.1 基于"三个世界"的理论
4.2.3.1 Rooted in the "three worlds" theory

自然科学、社会科学、人文科学,分别相应于自然世界、社会世界、人文世界,这并不只是偶然的巧合,而可能含有某种必然的因素;三个世界在历史发展过程中的前后相承关系,尤其是我们必须考虑的。就好像电脑的软硬件,后出的往往能"兼容"先出的那样,人类的身上,兼具自然世界与社会世界的特性,因而人类的语言,就既具有自然属性,又具有社会属性和人文属性。问题在于确定哪一种属性是语言的本质属性。"三个世界"理论的关键就在于:(1)肯定语言为人所特有,语言现象属于人文现象,而不是或不仅仅是自然现象或社会现象。把语言只当作自然现象或社会现象来分析,是一种简单化;(2)语言学是跟人密切相关的学科或者说是"人学",在语言所拥有的三种属性中,人文性是其本质属性,自然性与社会性尽管也存在,但不是本质的属性,因而语言学只能首先属于人文学科。从人文学科的立场来看,我们只能接受洪堡特的观点而无法接受另外三种观点;(3)自然—社会—人是历史发展的三个阶段,后面的可涵盖前面的,而前面的不能代替后面的;也正因为如此,后起的事物必然比先起的事物更复杂,因而需要更复杂的理论。简单地用适合于先起的事物的方法来研究后起的事物，就会有流于简单化的弊病。这是我们不能接受乔姆斯基所说的"精神研究的自然主义方法"的原因。因为用自然科学的方法去研究语言，表面上看来似乎搞得很复杂，其实是把复杂的语言现象简单化了。

It is not by coincidence that natural sciences, social sciences and humanities belong respectively to the natural world, social world and human world. There must be some inevitability particularly with regard to the successive development of these three worlds in history. Like hardware and software being compatible, we must find in human language attributes of the natural world and social world. The question is which of the attributes are essential? The theory of "three worlds" serves to: (1) Assert the unique language ability of man. Language phenomena belong to the human world, and do not merely manifest as natural phenomena or social phenomena. It would be simplistic to analyse language as natural phenomena or social phenomena. (2) Linguistics is closely related to man; it may be called a "human study" and among the attributes it owns, humanistic attributes are most essential since linguistics is predominantly a humanistic discipline. For this reason, we could only accept Humboldt's idea but not the other three perspectives. (3) The developmental sequence of natural—social—human is such that the later development stages encompass those before it but not the reverse. It so follows that later developments are necessarily more complex and require more sophisticated theories. Were we to adapt methodologies applicable to earlier stages to subsequent developments, we may be faulted as oversimplifying. We therefore have to reject Chomsky's reasoning of "naturalistic approach to mind". Apparently, applying the methodology of natural science on language seems complicated; closer examination would show that it is a blanket solution to language complexities.

4.2.3.2 基于对四种语言观的客观分析
4.2.3.2 Founded on objective analysis of the four perspectives

仔细地分析这四种语言观，我们发现前三种都有难以解决的问题。

Apart from Humboldt's opinions, there are tough nuts to crack in the other three perspectives.

"系统"说的要害在于它没有抓住语言的本质。我们前面说"系统说"适应于第一世界——自然世界，是因为世上万事万物，大至宇宙天体，小至细胞微生物，乃至原子中子质子，无一不在系统之中，无一不本身又构成一"系统"。既然任何事物都可以通过"系统"来研究，可见系统性并非是只有语言才有的特性，更不是语言的本质属性。至于把语言这个系统说成是"自足的"、"封闭的"，带来的问题就更多，当前学术界可以说已普遍否定了这一观点。语言系统既不是自足的，又不是封闭的，把语言当作自足的封闭的系统来研究，也许有一时的便利，但却使语言研究远离语言使用的母体——人，及语言使用的环境——社会，结果成为实验室里供解剖用的标本。这是20世纪相当长一段时期的语言研究留给我们的教训。

The vulnerability of the "system" theory lies in its inability to capture the nature of language. We mentioned that the "system" theory is a fit for the natural world in that of the myriad of things, vast as the universe, microscopic as microbiological cells or even the atom, neutron or proton, none fall out of the system and each makes up a system of its own. Since the "system" theory applies to anything and everything, it is not pertaining to language alone and could not be its essential nature. Even worse is to say that the system of language is "self-sufficient" and "closed". This view has largely been dismissed by academics. To treat language as a self-sufficient and closed system may have some convenience in research but the alienation from the breeding body—man, as well as the context—the society, only lands it as a specimen for the laboratory. This is a painful lesson we have drawn from the experiences of a long period of time in the twentieth century.

"交际性"同样不是语言的本质属性。这是因为"交际"同样不是人类所特有的，这是第二世界——"社会世界"的特征。凡是"社会性"的动物（social animals）都有这种需求，实际上也各有其进行交际的手段，如蜜蜂用舞蹈、猿猴用叫声、蝙蝠能发出超声波等。因而，这个定义没有能反映人类的本质特点。用"交际工具"来定义语言，即使加上"符号体系"，仍然为"语言"范围的不断扩大开了方便之门：计算机语言、数学语言、逻辑语言、音乐语言、舞蹈语言、动物语言，等等，尽管凭人们的直觉，这些与我们心目中真正的"语言"不同，但在"交际工具+符号系统"的定义下，却没有办法将它们拒之门外，这真可说是作法自毙，是其主张者所始想不到的。如果将这些"交际"手段一律当作"语言"来研究，就必然冲淡对人的语言的深入研究。

至于这一语言观中的"工具"说,所带来的问题就更严重,我们后面还要分析。

Similarly the "communicative" theory, not unique to mankind, is not essential for language. Characterizing the social world, communication is necessary for all social animals, man included, with the aid of some means: bees dance, apes cry, bats produce ultrasound and the list goes on. Therefore defining language as a communicative tool, despite the qualification of a "symbol" system, the scope of "language" is still large enough to take account of computer language, mathematical language, logic language, music language, dance language, animal language, etc. That is not recognized in our common senses as the language of man. It may be the oversight of the proponent that treating all the above means of "communication" as "language" would dilute efforts to look more closely into the human languages. We shall return to the more serious consequences of regarding language as a tool suggested by this perspective.

另外两种语言观都是考虑到人的,但为什么我们不赞成"本能说"呢?因为本能说强调人的语言的先天性,强调人类的生理和物理的构造,一句话,强调的是人身上的自然属性,这与强调人的历史文化属性的"世界观"说不同,后者才是人类世界所不同于前两个世界的本质属性。因而,本能说的要害在于:(1)自然属性并非人的本质属性,人之所以区别于动物并不是因为人在生理构造上与动物有什么本质的不同,而在于人有历史、文化和语言,文化和历史属性才是人的本质属性,也是语言的本质属性;(2)人拥有语言,既有先天因素也有后天因素,从语言的学习、运用、传承来说,后天因素可能更加重要。"本能说"将人的语言能力一切归于先天,必然会导致忽视人的后天因素,也就是忽视语言研究的更重要的方面;(3)强调自然属性必然会强调语言在生物学、脑生理学等方面的全人类共性,从而忽视各具体语言间的个性。关于共性和个性的问题,后面还要讨论,这里暂且不提。

The theory of "instinct" has consideration for man, notwithstanding; it is flawed fundamentally in standing out the *a priori* nature of language as well as the biological and physical constructs of human beings. In sum, it plays up the natural attributes of the physical build, entirely different from the worldview theory that places emphasis on history and culture which account for the essentials of the human world so different from the other two worlds. The "instinct" theory is susceptible in the following ways. (1) Natural attributes are not at the core of man's nature. Man is differentiated from animals not in terms of the biological build, but in that man owns a history, culture and language. Culture and history are at the core of man's nature, and of language's. (2) Man possesses language for pre-cosmic reasons as well as post-cosmic reasons. In terms of the acquisition, usage and inheritance of languages, post-cosmic reasons may carry more weight. However, under the theory implying that language ability is a gift from God, there may be an oversight on post-cosmic factors thereby passing over some more important aspects of language research. (3) Accentuating the natural attributes necessarily draws attention to the universality language shared in terms of biology and neurobiology, disregarding the particularity between specific languages. We will leave this to a later section.

谈到语言观问题，势必要涉及语言起源问题。这也是语言哲学研究所不能回避的问题。尽管对于语言的起源，人们现在所做的只能是假设，但假设也要看哪一种更合乎情理，更接近可能的事实。"系统"说和"本能"说其实都隐含了一个前提，即语言是一个在人类产生之前或人类诞生之时就已完成的东西。如果语言是个"完美的"、"自足的"、"先天的"系统，那只能是什么人（或"上帝"？）预先设计好的，然后一股脑儿、一齐"安装"到人的大脑里。所谓"一齐"，是指无一例外地、同时地安装到所有人的大脑里；所谓"一股脑儿"，是指无所缺陷地、完整地安装到每个人的大脑里。人类语言产生时是不是这样的情况，确实需要充分的想象力，特别是，我们很难想象在人类远古史上有那么一天，本来都不会说话的人们突然一下子都具有了这种能力，而且一开口就能说出彼此能懂的、"合乎语法"的语言。但即使是这样的情况，那怎样解释语言的后天变化和发展呢？比方说，为什么人类共同的语言会演变成不同的语系、语族、民族语言和方言？怎样解释语言的个人风格、人们在实际使用语言时所犯的各种不合语法或诸如此类的错误？难道真是上帝在人类建造巴比塔时对他们施了手脚？我们假设这也是真的，那人类语言的发展是不是只有分化一条途径，我们所看到的历史和现实中语言的融合只是假象？而一个完整的机制、自足的系统居然会不断分化，是不是意味着语言的发展也就意味着语言的退化？人类使用语言的过程就是一个语言不断退化的过程？

Discourse on language perspective must involve issues on language origin, which is also unavoidable in the deliberation of language philosophy. While we could only hypothesize about the origin of language, the hypothesis must be reasonable. The theories of "system" and "instinct" have a hidden proposition, i.e. language is something perfect and complete before mankind comes into existence, by production or by birth. To say that it is a system that is "perfect", "self-sufficient" and "pre-cosmic" is to say that someone (God?) had pre-designed it and installed it *all in one go and at the same time* into the human brain. By "at the same time", that means there is no exception and the installation is concurrent to all human brains. "In one go" refers to perfect and complete installation. It would require some imagination to understand how human brains could produce language in this way especially when it is difficult to imagine one of those days in ancient times when people who could not speak were all in a sudden equipped with an ability to utter something mutually understandable and grammatical. Even in this case, just how should we explain the post-cosmic development and changes in language? Say, the different language families, language branches, ethnic languages and dialects? Or the idiosyncrasies, bad language and errors? Perhaps God has set a trap at the time of building Babel? Suppose that was the case, is division the only path in development and what about the integration we see in languages? If we see continuous division in a complete and self-sufficient mechanism, does that mean regression characterised the process of development?

比较起来，我们还更愿意相信对比语言学另一位创始人叶斯柏森对语言起源的解释。在其《人类、民族与个人的语言学视角》一书中，叶斯柏森不同意语言是集体的创造，而认为语言是从个人开始的。一个人发出了某些声音，表达某种意思，对他个人的"方言"来说，这就是一个"词"。当然开始谁也不懂，但此人一再使用，形成了其个人的"习惯"。慢慢地他周围的人从他使用的场景中悟出了他的意思，而且也通过模仿，学会了用同样的声音来表达同样的意思。这样，由于交际的需要，这个"词"就会在他家庭和周围人的小圈子里流行开来，成为这一地域"方言"的组成部分。圈子越来越大，从村庄、乡镇、地区，一直到整个民族乃至全人类。语言就是这样产生的：

In comparison, it is easier to accept the explanation of Jespersen. In *Mankind, Nation and Individual* (1946), Jespersen suggested language originated from the individual as opposed to the theory of group creation. One produces some sound to express some emotion and to that person, it is his "dialect", a "word". It may not appear meaningful to the rest but when it is used repeatedly and becomes habitual, others will gradually pick it up and even imitate it to represent the same. Arising out of communicative needs, such "words" will spread outward from his inner circle of contact to become part of a regional "dialect". Or it may expand further to reach a wider scope of a nation or the whole human world. Jespersen describes:

> 通过反复与模仿，我们发现，个别行为转化成了习惯与习俗。因而语言世界有三个重要阶段：行为、习惯与习俗。一个民族的语言就是其成员习惯用来彼此交际的一套习俗。（叶斯伯森，1946：23）
>
> By way of repetition and imitation we have therefore got the single action converted into custom and habit. And so in the world of language there are the important stages: action, custom, habit. The language of a nation is the set of habits by which the members of the nation are accustomed to communicating with one another. (Jespersen, 1946: 23)

叶斯伯森的看法当然只是一家之说，人们也许未必都同意。但我们应当承认，这种假设比上面一种假设较有解释力。比方说，它能解释语言的多样性，解释语言的个人风格、地域和社会方言、语言的民族性、语言的文化性、语言的变异、语言的习得和学习、语言的传播、流行语等等"本能说"无法解释的难题，解释语言中不"规范"、不"合理"现象存在的合理性。例如"不要太……"句式表示"非常"的意义（"不要太潇洒"="非常潇洒"，"不要太好"="非常好"），于语义、语法上都无法找到理据，但就是能迅速地流行开来。又如"OK"一词，其语源至今未确定，但就是能不胫而走，从美国式英语走向整个英语，又走向几乎所有语言，成为最典型的地球人"共同词"。由于对比语言学（以及普通语言学）的研究目标与语言的多样性、民族性、语言接触和语言类型等等有关，因而，基于这一假设的语言观当然更适合作为对比研究的基础。

You may not agree with Jespersen's explanation, however you may have to agree that it is a more likely scenario than the above and offers greater explanatory power on the diversity of languages, idiosyncrasies, regional or societal dialect, language ethnicity, language culture, language variation, language acquisition, language communication and popular usage and more, all of which the theory of "instinct" would not provide explanation for, rationalizing non-"standardized", "unreasonable" phenomena in language. For example, in Chinese the construction "Don't be too…"

means "very" and we could say "don't be too good" meaning "very good" or "don't be too generous" meaning "very generous". Semantically and grammatically speaking, we could not understand why it could stand but it spreads wide and fast to become a unique expression. Take the example of "OK"; to date, we do not know its origin but that does not affect its popularity or its universality. Given the connection contrastive linguistics has with language diversity, ethnicity, language contact and typology, language perspective on this basis serves a better ground for contrastive studies.

4.2.3.3 基于二十世纪中国语言学研究的经验和教训
4.2.3.3 Drawing lessons and successful experiences from Chinese linguistics studies of the twentieth century

前文说过,一部20世纪中国语言学史,说到底就是一部对比语言学史,模仿与反模仿(后来徐通锵称之为"仿效论与对比论",见下文所引)之争表面上看来是对西方语言学、语法学理论的取舍问题,实质上反映的是在共性和个性问题上的不同取向,在比较和对比研究中的不同目标。这一情况在西方语言研究史上其实也发生过,[1]但20世纪的语言学家们对此恐怕已经淡漠了。而在主要从事印欧语内部研究的西方语言学家来说,发生在汉语研究与西方语言研究之间的尖锐冲突也是他们很难意识甚至想象到的。因而中国语言学发展的经验和教训也值得世界语言学界重视,对之进行研究和总结也是世界语言学的一份宝贵财富。

As mentioned before, the history of Chinese linguistics of the twentieth century is in fact a history of contrastive linguistics. On the surface, debates on imitation and anti-imitation (or imitation and contrastive theory, as Xu Tongqiang would put it) were about the adoption and rejection of western linguistics and grammatical

---

1 一部英语语法发展史从某种程度上来说也是一部模仿与反模仿史。这一段历史大约经历了200多年,直至斯威特(1891)的语法革新之后,反模仿派才取得了最后的胜利。(潘文国,1996a;1996b)

To certain extent, the grammatical development history of English is also a history on imitation and anti-imitation. This part of the history lasted for about 200 years drawing the curtain with Henry Sweet's grammatical reform of 1891, declaring victory for the anti-imitation camp (Pan Wenguo, 1996a; 1996b).

theories, while in spirit it is about the different inclination towards universality and individualism and the different objectives in comparative and contrastive linguistics. This seems to be a common stage of development, as we have witnessed this happen in the West too. However, Chinese linguists of the twentieth century feel rather distant from these series of events. To western linguists concentrating on Indo-European languages, the sharp conflict experienced within the discipline in both the West and in China was something they cannot feel or imagine. As such the developmental experiences and lessons of Chinese linguistics are assets upon which world linguistics should draw.

20世纪的中国语言学研究或对比语言学研究，在90年代之前，分成了四个时期。其中第一、第三、第四这三个时期从总体上看可说都是不成功的，只是第二时期取得了引人注目的成就。撇开其他因素，单就语言学角度来看，我们觉得以下几个方面的经验和教训是值得总结的。

We have divided into four periods the advancement of Chinese linguistics or contrastive linguistics in the twentieth century before the 1990s, of which only the second period has achieved significant results. Other factors aside, there are a few lessons for us look at purely from the linguistics standpoint.

第一，在"仿效"与"对比"之间，坚持"对比论"。

1. Between "imitation" and "contrast", insist on "contrast"

在《马氏文通》之后的汉语语法思想论争中，通常的概括是"模仿"与"反模仿"之争。吕叔湘（1947；1958）用的术语是"比附"与"比较"。潘文国（1997a）等用的术语是"比较"与"对比"。2001年，徐通锵提出了一对新的术语："仿效"与"对比"，并分别下了定义。"仿效"即是"用印欧语的语法框架、理论、方法来建立汉语的语法体系"（2001：82）；"对比"是"比较不同语言的结构差异，弄清楚每种语言的特点，进而对特点的成因作出理论的解释"（2001：81）。他进而指出：

Debates on grammatical thoughts after *Mashi Wentong* were often described as argument between imitation and anti-imitation. Lü Shuxiang (1947, 1958) used the terms "compare" and "force analogy". Others, like Pan Wenguo (1997a), expressed the ideas as "compare" and "contrast", while Xu Tongqiang (2001) redefined the discussions as "imitation" and "contrast". In Xu, "imitation" refers to building the Chinese grammatical system with the Indo-European grammatical framework, theories and methodologies (2001: 82), while "contrast" refers to "comparing the differences between structures of languages to understand the peculiarities of each language so as to offer theoretical explanation to the characteristics" (2001: 81). He further pointed out that:

> 从洪堡特开始，汉语语法研究的方法论，就其大的趋向而言，就是对比和仿效两种。这两种方法论的语言观基础，如前所述，是有差异的，对比论着眼于语言的特点，想通过对比重点研究语言的特性，并以此为基础建立相应的理论；仿效论着眼于语言的共性，自觉或不自觉地认为西方语言学的某一种理论是语言共性的反映，同样适用于汉语的研究。两种方法论从两个不同的立脚点出发处理语言的共性和特性的关系。从汉语语法研究的发展来看，对比的方法论成效比较好，因为它立足于语言特点的研究，能从对比中揭示出汉语的特点，使总结出来的规律具有比较深厚的语言基础。共性存在于特性之中，语言特点的发现和研究才能有助于语言共性的研究，因此科学研究的任务就是要设法解决矛盾的特殊性问题。四十年代的汉语语法研究和八十年代开始出现的汉语特点的研究以及其所取得的成果可以为这一论断提供有说服力的佐证。（徐通锵，2001：88）

In terms of general trend, two methodologies are employed in Chinese grammatical studies since Humboldt, contrast and imitation. As mentioned, the inherent language perspective in each of the method differs. The contrastive method spots on characteristics of languages on which all related theories would be based. Imitation method centered on language universal. Consciously or unconsciously, a particular theory of western linguistics is thought to be a reflection of language universal and therefore applicable to Chinese. The two methods handle from different standpoints, the relations between universalism and individualism. Development in Chinese grammar sides the effectiveness of the contrastive method which has language characteristics as the object and illuminates in the process, characteristics of Chinese and therefore the rudiments so concluded are more firmly grounded linguistically. Universalism is within individualism, and only with the discovery and study of characteristics that studies in language universal could advance. Hence, it is the mission of scientific research to try to resolve peculiarities that run in contradiction. Chinese grammatical studies of the 1940s as well as the successful research into Chinese characteristics since the 1980s are strong evidence. (Xu Tongqiang, 2001: 88)

可以说，这是对百年汉语语法研究方法论史的一个正确的总结。
This could be looked upon as a summary on the history of methodological development in Chinese linguistics over the last century.

第二，借鉴的三个层次。
2. Three levels of referencing

由于汉语没有西方意义上的语法学传统，汉语现代语言学尤其语法学几乎是凭空建立起来的，因而借鉴西方理论可说是必由之路。在这一过程中，汉语语言学家也建立了与西方语言学对话的途径。但在借鉴或引进过程中的不同态度，特别是盲目的模仿，也使我们付出了很大的代价。通过对历史的回顾，汉语语言学家认识到，引进或借鉴也有不同的层次，我们需要借鉴的是最高层次的理论。潘文国（1997a/2002）对此作了较好的概括：

The western sense of grammatical scholarship is not found in Chinese. Modern Chinese linguistics, particularly grammar, is almost plucked from the air. Referencing western theories is inevitable and dialogue is established in the process. However, attitudes varied in the referencing process, and particularly when it was pure imitation, high prices were paid. Looking back, Chinese linguists realize the different levels of referencing and what is required is theory at the highest level. Pan Wenguo (1997a/2002) summarizes as follows.

就语言研究来看，理论研究有三个层面：一是具体语言规律的层面，具体语言的语法、具体语言的音韵构造规律等等；二是普通语言学的层面，归纳各种语言的具体规律，抽象出较为一般和普遍适用的规律；三是语言哲学的层面，从更深一层探讨人类语言的本质，研究客观世界、主观意识和语言三者之间的关系。这三个层面一层深似一层，一层高于一层，后一层是指导前一层研究的基础。具体语言规律的研究要有普通语言学的理论指导；而普通语言学的研究要以语言哲学的研究作为前提。我们前面提到的汉语语法研究的两个阶段正是分别在第一、第二两个层面的引进：所谓"模仿语法"阶段是直接引进西方具体语言研究的规律,如马建忠之引进拉丁文法,黎锦熙之引进英文文法等;而文法革新讨论以后建立起来的几家汉语语法体系则是引进西方普通语言学的一般理论,并结合汉语的实际来进行研究,因此这几家都比较注意"发掘汉语特点",也取得了比前一阶段大得多的成绩。但是西方迄今为止的普通语言学理论还是以印欧语言为中心建立起来的,它所总结的规律对印欧语言适应性较大而对印欧语以外的语言不一定有很大的解释力,因而在这些理论指导下的研究始终摆脱不了西方语言研究的格局,原因就在这里。八十年代中期以来的反思使我们看到了这两个层面引进的不足之处,从而引发了第三个层面上的思考。这是语言研究深入和成熟的表现。(潘文国,1997a/2002:357)

  Within language studies, theoretical research has three levels. First it is on specific language rudiments, specific grammar, specific phonetic structures and more. Secondly, it is on general linguistics, generalizing on the specific rudiments of languages so that abstract rules universally applicable could be formulated. Third is on language philosophy that dwells deeper into the essence of human languages, the triangle relations between the objective world, subjective ideas and language. These three levels are progressive in nature, one being the foundation of the upper level. Specific language rules depend on the guidance of general linguistic theories whereas general linguistic study has to be guided by language philosophy…Studies of Chinese grammar at the "imitation" stage directly import specific western grammar rules, for instance, Ma Jianzhong brought in Latin grammar and Li Jinxi, English grammar. After the discussion on grammar reformation, a few Chinese grammars are built upon general linguistics transported from the West by incorporating the realities of the Chinese language. These few schools are mindful of unearthing the characteristics of Chinese and have achieved more than previous attempts. However, general linguistic theory to date is based on Indo-European languages and therefore the rudiments expressed, skewed towards Indo-European languages may fare badly explaining phenomena outside of the Indo-European family. As such, under the guidance of these theories, Chinese linguistics finds it difficult to get western scholarship off the back. That is the reason. Reflections since mid-1980s help to highlight the deficiencies of referencing at the first two levels and lead to thoughts at the third level. This demonstrates the deepening and maturing of language research. (Pan Wenguo, 1997a/2002: 357)

这三个层面，也就是前面提到的每个学科的学科建设所具有的四个纵向层面中的上面三层。语言哲学层面作为最高层，在这个层面上也最容易实现中西语言学的对接。而在哲学层面上，我们特别推崇洪堡特的语言世界观，持平而具有超越性，摆脱现有的以印欧语为中心的普通语言学理论的束缚，这样的语言观是为理想。

In fact the three levels are not really successive progressions built on each other; they are different but related points of reference. It is not as if there is no underlying basis in the first two levels of referencing. Awareness on the limitations and appreciation on language philosophy is rather weak. In terms of language philosophy, we could not say that Chinese is quiet in this respect; we could only say that in terms of referencing and relevance to contrastive linguistics, the humanistic worldview of von Humboldt would be preferred. To think that it could help lift Chinese grammars from the restrictions of the western framework is only the surface motivation. If the aim of contrastive linguistics is truly for a language universal, Humboldt's standpoint is regarded as a balanced and above-board approach to general linguistics. Respectable ethnic grammars are only hopeful when research is being guided by a philosophical principle closest to the essence of language, like that of von Humboldt's.

4.2.4 基于语言世界观的语言新定义
4.2.4 New definition of language under the language worldview perspective

洪堡特提出了语言世界观的学说，但他的论述散见在各处。洪堡特以后，一些语言学家如辉特尼、赛斯（Sayce 1880）、鲍阿斯（1911）、萨丕尔、马林诺斯基、刘易斯、沃尔夫、叶斯柏森、克洛克洪、戈第纳夫等人坚持和丰富了这一学说。在经过比较，选中了语言世界观作为普通语言学也是对比语言学的哲学基础之后，我们觉得有必要综合前人在语言本质方面的研究成果，给这一思想以更明确、更凝练、更简洁的概括，因而在2001年给语言下了一个新定义：

The worldview perspective of Humboldt was presented in a rather scattered manner. Later linguists, such as William Dwight Whitney, A. H. Sayce (1880), F. Boas (1911), Edward Sapir, B. Malinowski, W. W. Lewis, B. L. Whorf, Otto Jespersen, Clyde Kluckhohn, W. H. Goodenough and others, insisted and developed along this perspective. Deciding on the worldview perspective as the philosophical basis for general linguistics, including contrastive linguistics, it is necessary to consolidate findings on the essence of language in order that this idea is more clearly presented. Pan Wenguo (2001a) suggests:

> 语言是人类认知世界及进行表述的方式和过程。（潘文国，2001a：35）
>
> Language is the cognitive and presentation manner and processes of humankind. (Pan Wenguo, 2001a: 35)

这一定义有四个关键词："认知"、"表述"、"方式"和"过程"。使用"认知"一词，而不是一般用的"认识"，是为了强调人类语言的理性意义。"认识"的意义过于宽泛，除了可有"认知"（cognition）、"理解"（understanding）等意义外，还可以有"知道"（know）、"认出"（recognize）等一般含义，后者在动物身上也能出现（如"认出"其主人，"认识"其同伴，"知道"什么是食物、哪里有危险等），只有前者为人类所特有。同时，"认出"等不必诉诸语言，而"认知"必须诉诸语言。

There are four key words in this definition: cognition, representation, manner and process. Knowing is generic, besides cognition and understanding, it also comprises abilities to recognise and to know, for which animals are also capable of doing, as in recognizing their masters, knowing dangers and what to feed on etc.. Cognition is more than just knowing, it points to the rationality of human languages and is a unique faculty of man.

同样，用"表述"一词而不用"表达"，也是因为"表达"不一定诉诸语言（动物也有种种情绪的表达，人类也有非语言的种种表达如面部表情、眼神、及在惊恐悲喜等情绪下发出的各种声音等），而表述必须诉诸语言。

Similarly, "presentation" is used instead of "expression" because expression need not be conveyed through verbal language; even animals have different manners of emotional expression of sadness, happiness and panic through facial, eyes and other bodily signals and sound. Presentation necessarily involves the usage of speech language.

"方式"和"工具",有的语言学家并没有注意加以区分,其实两者是不同的,而且可以认为有本质的不同。方式是主体的一种行为,是主观能力的表现。这个能力可以是先天的(如走路),也可能是习得的(如说话,更不用说写作)。而"工具"从字面上容易理解为人的身外之物,更像一种现成的产品而不是一个创造过程。"工具"既然是外物,那就是可有可无的,而语言,按照洪堡特的观点,却与人的精神合而为一。一个人即使失去了言语能力和书写能力,但只要他能思考,他必然还在使用着语言。

"Manner", sometimes not differentiated from "instrument" by some linguists, is in fact poles apart in essence. Manner is an action performed by a subject, a demonstration of subjective capabilities which may be inborn or acquired. Literally, "instrument" is often associated with some external ready tools instead of a creative process. And being an external tool, it is dispensable. However, language, by Humboldt's definition, is united with the spirit of human. Even if an individual were to lose the ability to speak or write, if thought occurs, language is used.

"过程"是洪堡特思想中另一个重要方面,他说:

"Process" is the other important aspect in Humboldt's thought. He explains:

> 从真正的本质上来看,语言是一件持久的事物,在每一个瞬间都稍纵即逝,即使通过文字保存下来的,也只是不完整的、木乃伊式的东西,只在描述当前话语时才重新需要。语言本身绝非产品(Ergon),而是一个活动过程(Energeia)。……把语言表述为"精神作品",这个术语完全正确,非常充分,因为这里所说的精神只是指而且只能理解为一个活动过程。(洪堡特,1836: 49/54)

> Language, regarded in its real nature, is an enduring thing, and at every moment a transitory one. Even its maintenance by writing is always just an incomplete, mummy-like preservation, only needed again in attempting thereby to picture the living utterance. In itself it is no product (Ergon), but an activity (Energeia)…as a work of the spirit is a perfectly correct and adequate terminology to describe languages, because the existence of spirit as such can be thought of only in and as activity. (Humboldt, 1836: 49/54)

这与后来有些语言学家提出的"生成性"或"创造性"不同,因为后者只强调语言的"使用"（performance）方面，而"过程"显然还包括"习得"（acquisition）和"学习"（learning）方面。洪堡特的意见显然是一贯的并且经过了深思熟虑：

Obviously this is not the same concept as "generative" or "creative" raised by later linguists which stresses on performance. The "processes" we refer to include both acquisition and learning. von Humboldt has been consistent and considerable in his opinion when he says:

>"语言无论如何不应看作像什么死去的植物，语言和生命两个概念互不可分，在这个领域，学习往往就意味着创新。"（洪堡特，1836：93）
>
>Under no circumstances can a language be examined like a dead plant. Language and life are inseparable concepts, and to learn in this area is always merely to regenerate. (Humboldt, 1836: 93)

比起以往的语言定义来，这个定义最为简约。从上面所说的四个关键词来看，这个定义主要反映的是语言世界观派的观点。但由于我们前面指出的"后起理论可以兼容先起理论"的原因，它其实也可包容其他几派观点中的合理成分。但不一定反映在定义中，定义的原则应该是：说出必须说出的内容，不说可有可无的内容，尤其不能包括会引起歧见的内容。

The definition proposed here must be one of the most minimal. The four keywords align with the language worldview perspective. Some reasonable aspects of other perspectives may have been incorporated but not necessarily spelled out in the definition.

>例如"交际"。这是现在所能看到的语言定义中出现最频繁的字眼，而在最基本的四种语言观中，交际工具观与语言世界观说相对来说也是最接近的。但我们既否定了这一观点中的"工具说"，又不愿采用"交际"说，为什么呢？原因在于，尽管几乎没有人会否认语言具有交际功能，但第一，"交际"要后于"认知"，如徐通锵指出的，所谓"交际"，其实质是交流对现实的认知。（徐通锵，1997：21）
>
>For instance, "communication" is one of the most frequently used words found in the definitions of language. In all four fundamental perspectives, the communicative device perspective is closest to the language worldview

perspective. However, we have rejected viewing language as an instrument and are reluctant to adopt the "communicative" theory on the grounds that no one will ever deny the function of language in daily intercourse and, more importantly, "cognitive" must come before "communication". Communication is the realization of cognition (Xu Tongqiang, 1997: 21).

"表述"可以包括"交际"，但"交际"却无法包括"表述"。把一个人独自思考硬说成是自己跟自己"交际"，想法很聪明，但却是偷换概念。第三，"交际"不是人类语言的本质属性，"表述"非要用语言不可，而"交际"却未必。"满堂兮美人，忽独与予兮目成"，"身无彩凤双飞翼，心有灵犀一点通"，在这些例子里人与人"交际"的完成根本不需要语言。

On the other hand, "representation" may also include "communication", but not the other way round. Define self-thought as an exchange within oneself may be smart, but that was disguised displacment of the proposition. We have argued earlier that "communication" is not confined to human languages and in fact it may go beyond words or the necessity to maintain any communication channels when hearts are beating together and there is collaboration of minds. Whereas representation must be represented in speech language.

又如"符号"和"语音+词汇+语法"，特别是前者，也是语言定义中频繁出现的。但是我们也没有采用。诚然，语言由符号组成，语言中包括了语音、词汇、语法……，这些都是事实。但对一件事物下定义要解决的是它的外延问题，把它与别的事物区别开来，不是为了解决其内涵或者内部组成问题。例如对于人的定义，不论以前说的"人是会使用工具的动物"或是现在说的"人是使用语言的动物"，都是从这个角度着眼的。完全没有必要在这两句话之后再加上"通常由头、双手、双脚和躯干组成"之类的蛇足。给语言下定义也是如此，说语言是符号及由语音、词汇、语法组成等，也是无益的蛇足。

Other frequently used keywords in the definition of language, such as "symbol" and "sound, lexis and grammar" are also dropped. It is a fact that languages are formed with symbols and structured with sound, lexis and grammar and the like. However, in definition, it is more important to take care of the extent and differentiate it from other matters, connotation and composition belonging to another story. As in the definition of "Human", when we define it to be "an animal who is capable of handling tools" or "an animal who uses language", we are talking about its extent; it is entirely not required to state that man "normally comprises of head, two hands, two legs and a body" or the like. So symbol, grammar, phonetics and lexis are all understood.

为什么不讲许多语言学家爱用的"音义结合",不讲"任意性",不讲"系统性"?"音义结合"其实已经包含在"认知和表述方式"里了,而"方式"的范围比"音义结合"要广,它不但包括了"音义结合",还包括了"形义结合"如汉字,因为这是汉人"认知世界和表述"的方式。甚至还可包括聋哑人的手势语,因为这也可看作是人们"认知和表述的方式"。"任意性"是个有争议的问题,已经受到当代西方认知语言学中与之针锋相对的"理据性"说的挑战。而且不管怎样,"任意性"不是人类语言的本质属性,只是符号的一般属性而已,比方说,蜜蜂传递信息的舞蹈动作,同样具有"任意性"和"约定俗成"的特点。"系统性"现在引起的争议也不小,[1]而且如前所说,它也不是语言的本质属性,尽管在研究语言的时候,我们有时也不反对从"系统"着手。

Other frequently used words and phrases, such as "association of sound and meaning", "arbitrariness" and "system" were also not repeated in the definition because the manner of cognition and presentation would necessarily include "association of sound and meaning", and more, as in the case of Chinese, where the association of form and meaning since the use of sinograms is the manner in which the Chinese would present their cognitive knowledge of the world; so is the sign language of the hearing and speech impaired. The concept of "arbitrariness" is debatable and being challenged by motivation theory in contemporary cognitive linguistics. In any case, "arbitrariness" is not the essential nature of language but a general attribute of symbol. We could say that the dance by the bees to communicate messages is also "arbitrary" and "accepted as habitual". The concept of "system", as mentioned is also arguable. We do not object to approaching language research systematically though.

---

1 一种比较普遍的意见认为,语言即使是一个系统,也是一个不完全的、开放的系统。既然如此,讲"语言是个'系统'"就更没有什么积极的意义。
More commonly, even language is taken as a system; it is an incomplete and open system. In this sense, to speak of language as a system is less than meaningful.

这样看来，新定义是个综合性的定义，它以语言世界观说为基础，同时兼容了其他关于语言性质研究的合理部分，是适宜于作为新世纪人类语言研究的基础的。

The new definition proposed is consolidated with language worldview as the base incorporating other rational aspects of language nature. We could reasonably accept it to be the basis for human language research in the new century.

这个定义，除了跟自足观、工具观、本能观等对立之外，与二十世纪诸多语言的定义还有一个重要的区别，即它不强调，甚至可说不承认被二十世纪"现代语言学"视作基础的"语言"与"言语"之分。"语言"和"言语"之分是索绪尔学说的核心，也是二十世纪西方所谓"主流语言学"最重要的基石，在大半个世纪中，在语言研究中占了统治地位。但从七十年代起，这一主流地位受到了挑战。社会语言学、功能语言学、认知语言学、文化语言学、心理语言学等等的兴起几乎都是对索绪尔所设的樊篱的突破，研究的重点几乎都转到了前半个世纪中不被看重的"言语"方面。

This definition also distinguishes itself from other definitions of language of the twentieth century besides standing in opposition to the viewpoints of self-sufficiency, instrumental and instinctive in that it does not underline or even accept the division between "langue" and "parole" at the core of modern linguistics. Central to Saussure's theory that has ruled western linguistics for more than half a century, the division of "langue" and "parole" has been the cornerstone in mainstream linguistic theories. It has been challenged since the 1970s by the emergence of sociolinguistics, functional linguistics, cognitive linguistics and cultural linguistics, and psychological linguistics, which has "parole" that has been neglected for half a century as the locus of research.

在这里我们要着重指出，这也是对比语言学家的主张。对比语言学创始人洪堡特生当索绪尔之前很多年，当然没法对这一说法提出意见，但从他对语言是"过程"不是"产品"的强调，我们已能感知他对这一观点的态度。对"语言"和"言语"之分作出正面批评的，是对比语言学另一位大师和先驱者叶斯柏森。叶斯柏森在《人类、民族与个人的语言学视角》一书中花了10多页的篇幅点名批评了索绪尔等人在这问题上的观点，指出其在理论上的谬误之处。他的意见可以概括为：

It is to be highlighted that contrastive linguistics runs side by side with other branches of linguistics. Humboldt, who of course does not have the chance of rebutting Saussure, being born so much earlier, asserted that language is a "process" not a "product"; by this he could never agree with Saussure. Jespersen took the opportunity of committing ten pages of his book to dispute with Saussure and his followers. The gist of his opinion is as follows.

索绪尔说个人只拥有"言语"，既不能创造也不能改变"语言"，这不合事实。事实是个人能够创造一些东西来影响语言，无数的新说法和新用法都是这样产生的。它们首先在个人的"言语"里使用，然后扩展到同一语言社团许多人的"言语"里。另一方面，没有不受社会调节的个人"言语"，再个性化的"言语"也都含有社会性成分。所有人的"言语"都受到规约，这规约来自对周围他人"言语"的观察。因而"语言"实际上可看作是"言语"的复数，就好像英语中horses是horse的复数那样，复数的马是不同的个别的马加在一起的结果，民族语言也是将所有不同的个人言语加在一起的结果。这在词汇上表现得最明显。在语法和语音上，民族语言则可看作是个人言语的均约成分。（叶斯柏森，1946：11—22）

According to Saussure, language (langue) is something which the individual must take as he finds it, which he can neither make nor alter. This is a monstrous exaggeration. The individual, as a matter of fact, *can* make something new which has influence on the language of the whole community. This is of course the way in which the countless new formations and transformations which actually show themselves in the language come about. They appear first with the individual, in his "parole", but they become generally received and recognized when all, or at least many, people in the same linguistic community have adopted them; that is to say, when they use them in their own "parole". On the other hand, in every utterance of "la parole" there is a social element and even the most individual speech is socially conditioned. Every individual therefore has a norm for his "parole" given to him from without: it is given to him in fact by his observation of the individual "paroles" of others. We can say then in a sense that language ("la langue") is a sort of plural to speech ("la parole")—a plural in the sense that "many horses" is a plural of "one horse". At any rate we get this sort of addition sum so far as the vocabulary is concerned. With regard to other sides we may rather say that the national language is a sort of average of individual tongues, for example with regard to grammar, including "pronunciation" (Jespersen, 1946: 11—22).

对比语言学不强调"语言"和"言语"之分，不只是个理论问题，也是个实践问题。对比语言学作为一个理论和应用并重的学科，它所要对比的不仅仅是索绪尔式的抽象的"语言"，也不是乔姆斯基式的无从捉摸的"完全同质的语言社团中的理想的说话人和听话人"（Chomsky, 1965: 3），而是包含"言语"和"语言"在一起的语言、人们实实在在使用的语言。

The division of "langue" and "parole" is not cardinal to contrastive linguistics in both theory and practice. Contrastive linguistics places equal importance on theory and application and the languages to be contrasted are far from being abstract concepts in de Saussure nor faintly perceptible as Chomsky's "ideal speaker-listener in a completely homogeneous speech-community" (Chomsky, 1965: 3). It has to be real language, both "langue" and "parole", used by people.

4.3 对比语言学的学科论——目标与范围
4.3 Contrastive linguistics as a discipline: Aim and scope

人们常说，需要是发明之母。这一说法对学科的建立和发展也同样适用。任何学科的发展都是随客观需要而诞生、随客观需要而成熟的，不是任何个人脑袋一拍的结果。因而客观需要，或者说研究目标，对学科的产生和发展有着重要的意义，从某种程度上来说，它决定了学科的性质；从另一个角度看，目标的确定又为学科发展圈定了自身的研究范围，促成了学科体系的成熟。因而，对目标与范围，或者说对学科体系的探讨，就成为对比语言学理论建设需要研究的第二个重大问题。

The common saying that necessity is the mother of invention is equally applicable to the building of any discipline. Out of increasing necessity grow all kinds of disciplinary studies. Such needs or research aims are significant to the formation and development of a discipline and, to an extent, determine its nature. Aims on the other hand, set the scope of research and enhance the maturity of the discipline. Aim and scope are the next imperatives on the list.

在回顾对比语言学史的时候，我们将中外的发展史都划分成了若干个时期。从本质上来看，划分时期的依据就是不同时期对研究目标的不同追求。因而，总结历史，也就是总结不同时期不同追求背后反映的学术思想，看看它们对今天和未来的学科发展能起到什么作用。

We have seen that the various developmental stages can be divided by the research aims. In reviewing the history, we are really looking at the scholastic pursuit behind the different aims and how those pursuits could have an impact on current and future development in the discipline.

4.3.1 对比语言学目标、范围问题上的种种说法
4.3.1 Opinions on aims and scope

为深入讨论这一问题，我们想先就前人在这些方面有过的各种意见作一番梳理，以从中得到有益的启示。

We shall begin with a survey of the opinions on the subject to build the case for further discussion.

4.3.1.1 对比语言学追求的种种目标
4.3.1.1 Aims of contrastive linguistics

洪堡特是对比语言学的创始人，他为对比语言学所下的第一个"定义"，实际上就是为对比研究设立了第一个任务和目标：

Von Humboldt, the founder of contrastive linguistics, set out the first mission and aims for the discipline in an attempt to set apart the emerging practice:

> 语言比较研究如果要成为独立的学科，提出自己的目标和宗旨，那么，它只能是用来深入持久地探讨语言，探讨民族的发展和人类的进步。（洪堡特，1820：1）

> The comparative study of languages can only be used to acquire lasting and significant insights into language, the development of nations, and the progress of mankind, when it has been made into an independent branch of study with its own goals and purposes. (Von Humboldt, 1820: 1)

他特别强调要研究语言与民族个性间的相互关系：
Emphasizing research into the relations between language and ethnicity, he states:

> 依上法进行对比研究，要能指出人类发明语言的各种方式，其中

传输了人类知性世界的哪一部分。还要能指出语言如何受到各民族个性的影响，又如何反过来影响各民族的个性。（洪堡特，1820：7）

> The empirical study of comparisons between languages, if undertaken in this manner, can indicate the various ways in which the human race produced language and can show what parts of its intellectual world it has succeeded in transferring to it. It can also show how language has been affected by the individual character of the nations and how, in its turn, language has had an effect on them. (von Humboldt, 1820: 7)

对比语言学的另两位先驱叶斯柏森和沃尔夫同样是以提出任务的方法来提出他们对这一新兴学科的设想的：

Jespersen and Whorf have also drawn boundaries by way of defining the missions of the discipline at its emergence:

> 这种比较不必局限于属于同一语系、同一起源而通过不同道路发展起来的语言，对差异最大、起源迥然不同的语言也可以加以比较……以便帮助我们比本书更深刻地理解人类语言和人类思维的最内在的本质。（叶斯伯森，1924/1951：346—347）

> This comparison need not be restricted to languages belonging to the same family and representing various developments of one original common tongue, but may take into consideration languages of the most diverse type and ancestry…so as to assist us in gaining a deeper insight into the innermost nature of human language and of human thought that has been possible in this volume. (Jespersen, 1924/1951: 346—347)

> （对比语言学）旨在研究不同语言在语法、逻辑和对经验的一般分析上的重大区别。（沃尔夫，1941a：240）

> (Contrastive linguistics) plots the outstanding differences among tongues—in grammar, logic, and general analysis of experience. (Whorf, 1941a: 240)

这三位学者的追求目标可说是一致的，即都致力于通过语言对比研究，研究语言本质以及语言与民族、与人类精神的关系。因此我们将之作为西方对比研究第一时期的共同特征。

All three scholars are after the same pursuit of exploring the nature of language and its relations with ethnicity and the spirit of humans through language contrast. That highlights Phase 1 of contrastive linguistics of the West.

西方第二时期对比研究的追求目标可以用拉多的话来代表：

Phase 2 in the West, at the service of second language teaching, has its aims represented by Lado as follows:

> 本书探索的是应用语言学及文化研究的一个崭新的领域，即通过比较任何两种语言和文化，来发现和描写一种语言的使用者在学习另一种语言时会碰到的问题。这一比较的结果对于教材编写、教学测试及学习实验具有十分重要的意义。（拉多，1957：序）
>
> This book presents a fairly new field of applied linguistics and the analysis of culture, namely the comparison of any two languages and cultures to discover and describe the problems that the speakers of one of the languages will have in learning the other. The results of such comparisons have proved of fundamental value for the preparation of teaching materials, tests, and language learning experiments. (Lado, 1957: Preface)

西方第三时期的追求目标是在对第二时期目标的不满基础上的扩大，为詹姆斯的书作序的坎德林（Christopher N. Candlin）比较清楚地说明了他们追求的目标：

Unsatisfied with the practice in Phase 2, Phase 3 aspires to expand the scope, rather succinctly stated in the preface to Carl James's book by Christopher N. Candlin:

> 对比分析所能提供的不仅仅是语言学习者的困难。从上面提到的研究计划和詹姆斯经常投稿的期刊上的文章来看，对比分析可对以下领域有很大贡献：翻译理论、描写特定语言、语言类型学，以及语言共性研究。（砍德林，1980: iv）
>
> There was always more to contrastive analysis than making claims about learner difficulty. Through the major contrastive projects referred above, and through journals to which the present author has been a major contributor, contrastive analysis has had much to offer to translation theory, the description of particular languages, language typology and the study of

language universals. (Candlin, 1980: iv)

切斯特曼（Chesterman，1998：198—199）则从另一个侧面谈了对比语言学特别是他的功能对比分析所能服务的四个方面：（1）跨文化行为范式研究（cross-cultural behavior patterns）；（2）翻译；（3）外语和二语教学；（4）培养对某种单语的语言意识（language awareness in a single language）。

Approaching from another angle, Chesterman (1998: 198–199) opined that contrastive linguistics, particularly his contrastive functional analysis, could serve four areas: (1) cross-cultural behaviour patterns; (2) translation; (3) foreign and second language teaching; (4) cultivation of language awareness in a single language.

这些既是在第二时期基础上的新的拓展，又是向西方第一时期研究目标的回归。

That was considerable expansion of the aims and scope of Phase 2 to reinstate the objects of Phase 1.

中国对比语言学走过的道路与此相类似。除第一、第三两个时期可看作过渡时期以外，第二、第四和第五这三个时期可分别对应于西方的三个时期，其追求目标也与之相似。即第二个时期重对语言本质的探索（只不过在中国更具体化为对"汉语特点"的发掘），可以用胡以鲁的话为代表：

In terms of aims, contrastive linguistics in China has trodden a similar path. Phases 1 and 3 aside, Phases 2, 4 and 5 correspond to the three phases of the West as far as research aims are concerned. In Phase 2, the Chinese pay more attention to the essence of language, specifically referring to highlighting Chinese characteristics. Hu Yilu sums it up:

> 甚矣研究外国语而欲知其语言精神之难也。不知语言之精神，漫以他语族之法则作归纳之论断，无怪其不能知厥真相矣！不得吾国语之真相，语言分类亦殆无望。而其真相之解决，则支那语国民之责任，不能望于他族也。盖发达之途既异，研究之蹊径亦自宜独辟。借鉴他语族之法则作他山之石可也，欲据以为范律则蔽矣！（胡以鲁，1923：80）
>
> We may learn a foreign language but it would be daunting to get to know its language spirit. If we try to deduce and conclude from a foreign grammar without knowing the underlying language spirit, it is no wonder we missed

all the truth in our language! In not knowing the truth of our language, it is entirely impossible to apply language classification. Getting to the truth of our language is the responsibility of the Chinese, not of the foreigners. Since we each came from a different development path, it is only appropriate that a different methodology be adopted for our language study. We could well draw from the experiences of foreign grammars, but to adopt it as our standard would blind us from the truth. (Hu Yilu, 1923: 80)

第四个时期重在二语教学上的应用,可以用王还的话作代表:
Phase 4 directed all efforts to second language teaching, and we quote Wang Huan:

> 这里所说的对比即英语的contrastive analysis。这是一种共时研究法,只研究有关语言的现代形式,目的在于寻求可用于语言教学翻译等实际问题的原理。我们作对比研究的目的就在于提高教学的预见性,从而解决学生母语的干扰问题。(王还,1986:322)

> Here, we speak of *duibi* as contrastive analysis in English. This is a synchronic method focusing on the current language forms with an aim to seek out principles applicable for solving practical issues such as those in language teaching and translation. We conduct contrastive studies to help raise predictability of pedagogical problems so that we can help students to overcome interference from their mother tongues. (Wang Huan, 1986: 322)

在人们都沉浸于为教学服务的时候,只有赵世开(1979:35—37)清醒地提到了对比研究的理论价值和实用价值,前者是"通过两种语言结构的对比可以更好地认识语言的结构,进一步认识语言的本质",后者包括"外语教学"、"翻译工作"、"类型学研究"和"社会历史和文化的研究"四个方面。实际上为第五期的普遍认识起了"一鸟知春"的作用。

Just when everyone immersed themselves in pedagogical research with contrastive linguistics, Zhao Shikai was sober enough to remind us that there are practical values in examining the theoretical aspects. While pedagogical research will allow us to "better understand language structures through structural comparison so as to gain insight into the nature of language", Zhao spelt out that theoretical research would enable works to be carried out on "foreign language teaching", "translation", "language typology" and "social historical and cultural studies" (Zhao Shikai, 1979: 35—37). The revealing words of Zhao in fact prepared for the arrival of Phase 5.

第五个时期是以吕叔湘题词、刘宓庆著作的出版等开始的，从中可看出其目标已有了很大的转变。吕叔湘提出，"指明事物的异同所在不难，追究它们何以有此异同就不那么容易了，而这恰恰是对比研究的最终目的"。可见他的目光已透过表现上的异同直指背后的根源上去了。刘宓庆则说：

Turning the tide, Lü Shuxiang paved the way for Phase 5 with a congratulatory note indicating that "To point out similarities and differences is certainly easier than getting to the root of the causes which is the ultimate concern of contrastive studies" (Lü Shuxiang, 1990). Lü has a general linguistics undertone in his call to shift focus to uncover the radix to similarities and divergence in languages. Picking on Phase 2, Liu Miqing joined in:

> 对比语言学的任务就是在语言共性的总体观照下，探索研究和阐明对比中的双语特征或特点，以此作为参照性依据，提高语言接触的深度、广度以及语际转换的效率和质量。（刘宓庆，1991：IV）

> The mission of contrastive linguistics is to explore and explain the respective characteristics of the languages in contrast under the higher guidance of language universalism. With these characteristics as points of reference, we could have more profound contact in languages in terms of depth, extend, efficiency and quality of code transferring. (Liu Miqing, 1991: iv)

这一观点强调通过对比发掘所比语言的特点，对汉语研究有强烈的针对性。比较周密的论述则见之于潘文国的三个层次和三个目标说：

Liu sees contrastive linguistics as the way to standout linguistic features of the languages under, scrutiny. This is especially well-directed in terms of the Chinese language. Yet Pan Wenguo offers a more comprehensive elucidation differentiating three levels of research under three objectives. :

> 第一个层次是语音及语法表层上的对比，其目的是为初学外语者提供一个简便的拐杖。第二个层次是语言表达法的对比。其对象是外语已有了一定水平而又经常需要在两种语言间进行转换（如第二语言教学或翻译）的人，帮助他们更地道地使用语言。第三个层次是语言

心理上的对比。这是更深层的对比，企图推导出隐藏在不同表达法后面的心理和文化背景，进行一种哲学式的思考，目的是为了最终建立中国的语言哲学。（潘文国，1997/2002：358）

The first front is contrasting on the phonological and grammatical plane with a purpose of providing walk-through guide for elementary foreign language learners…The second front is contrasting on language expression targeting at foreign language speakers of some degree of proficiency who need to switch between two languages (such as second language teaching or translation) with an object to raise standard closer to native-speaking… The third front is contrasting in terms of language psychology. This is touching on the deep structure and attempting to deduce the concealed psychological and cultural factors conditioning expressions. This form of philosophical exploration is good for the ultimate rooting of Chinese language philosophy. (Pan Wenguo, 1997/2002: 358)

有趣的是，西方和中国的对比语言学的最新发展（西方之三期、中国之五期）都体现了两个特色，一是要继续前一个时期（西方之二期、中国之四期）的道路，不希望对之全盘否定；二是对早期（西方之一期、中国之二期）传统的回归。问题是，怎样将这些目标统一在一个更合理而且更具说服力的理论体系里？

Interestingly, the latest development both in the West (Phase 3) and in China (Phase 5) again showed some common characteristics. On one hand, neither rejects completely the pursuit of the previous stage (Phase 2 for the West and Phase 4 for China) and they actually like sustaining it. On the other hand, both try to fall back on the early traditions (Phase 1 for the West and Phase 2 for China). The challenge is how to put together all these targets in a more reasonable and more convincing theoretical framework?

4.3.1.2 对比语言学的范围与体系
4.3.1.2 Contrastive linguistics: scope and system

随着研究目标的明确和扩大，研究范围的问题也提上了议事日程，有的学者更在此基础上提出了对比语言学的整个研究体系。

Following the identification and broadening of the research aim, the issue of scope of research comes into play and on this basis some research systems of contrastive linguistics are tabled.

由于学科不成熟,早期学者对研究范围的问题谈得不多。洪堡特只谈到比较语言研究的两个方面:对语言本身组织的研究和语言与民族关系的研究,用我们现在的话来说,也许可以叫做语言组织学和语言民族学。叶斯柏森强调的是从内到外和从外到内的两种研究方法,分别相当于现在说的结构语法和意念语法。沃尔夫的范畴论也是一种意念语法。

As the concept of discipline did not crystallize until a later stage, there were few contributions from early scholars. von Humboldt only spoke on two aspects of contrastive linguistics: research on the organization of language and research on the relations between language and ethnicity. Jespersen's key points centred on methodology: "form to meaning" or in today's term structural grammar, and "meaning to form" or in today's term conceptual grammar. The category theory of Whorf is also some sort of conceptual grammar.

对比语言学的第一个体系应该说始于拉多。他的"如何比较语音、语法、词汇、文字、文化"五个章节可说提出了第一个体系,即对比语言学应包括对比语音学、对比语法学、对比词汇学、对比文字学、对比文化学。尽管从总体来这些都属于结构对比或从形式到意义的对比,与沃尔夫等正好反其道而行之。

Contrastive linguistics owes its first representational system to Lado. Lado (1957) comprises five chapters on the contrastive studies of sound systems, grammatical structures, writing systems, vocabulary systems and cultures. Whatever we may call it in modern terminology, the whole system is contrasting at structural level or adopting the form to meaning method, in opposite direction to Whorf and the rest.

其后,菲齐亚克最早(1971)提出要区分理论对比语言学与应用对比语言学。詹姆斯(1980)提出要区分宏观对比语言学与微观对比语言学,他的宏观语言学主要指篇章语言学和话语分析。1990年,在《当前的对比语言学元理论和理论研究》一文(Fisiak,1990)中,菲齐亚克提出了一个相当庞大的对比体系。对文中所提到的问题加以概括,并用现在的术语加以表示,可以归结为下面一个图:

Fisiak (1971) took the lead to suggest differentiating between theoretical contrastive linguistics and applied contrastive linguistics. James (1980) proposed drawing lines between macro and micro contrastive linguistics, where macro refers to text linguistics and discourse analysis. Fisiak (1990) proposed a gigantic system of contrastive linguistics as follows.

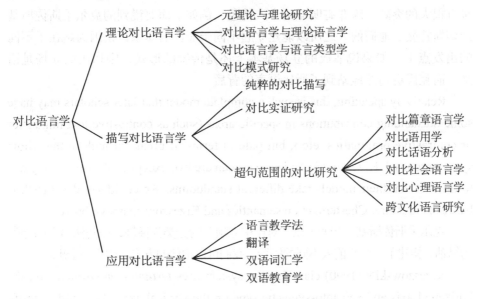

图4.1 菲齐亚克的体系

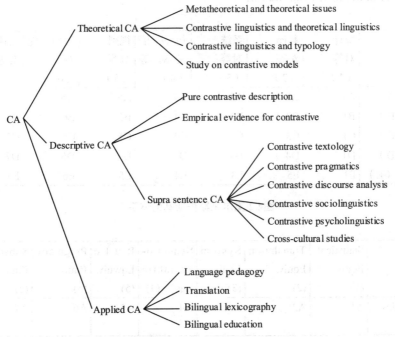

Figure 4.1 Fisiak's system

这是一个相对来说比较完整的体系。其后的研究者也许在某一领域作出比较多的贡献（如在对比篇章语言学、对比语用学等方面），但在整个体系上很难有很大的突破。除非有明显的个人特色，例如下面要说到的克尔采斯佐斯基及切斯特曼。他们两人之所以能建立起不同于菲氏的体系，是因为站在了不同的出发点上。如果说菲氏的立场基本上还是传统的形式，则切氏的立场是语义，而克氏更超然地站到了所比语言的背后。

Relatively speaking, this is such a complete model that later scholars may have some outstanding contributions in specific areas (such as contrastive text linguistics or contrastive pragmatics, etc.), but pale in terms of break through in the whole system proposal. Krzeszowski and Chesterman are two exceptional cases largely due to the fact that their models take different standpoints. We could say that Fisiak is based on structure, Chesterman on semantics and Krzeszowski above-board.

克尔采斯佐斯基（1990）以"对比中立项"的分类为横轴，以句法语义的分类为纵轴，构建了一个与前人不同的体系。我们可以把他的方案简化成一个矩阵：

Krzeszowski's (1990) classification system uses *tertium comparationis* on the horizontal axis and semanto-syntactic type on the vertical axis. We could simplify his model in the following matrix:

	统计对等（1）	翻译对等（2）	系统对等（3）	句法语义对等（4）	规则对等（5）	语用功能对等（6）	实体对等（7）
语义（A）	A1	A2	A3	A4	A5	A6	A7
范畴（B）	B1	B2	B3	B4	B5	B6	B7
句法（C）	C1	C3	C3	C4	C5	C6	C7
词汇（D）	D1	D4	D3	D4	D5	D6	D7
后词汇（E）	E1	E5	E3	E4	E5	E6	E7

图4.2 克尔采斯佐斯基的体系

	Statistical Equiv. (1)	Translation Equiv. (2)	System Equiv. (3)	Semanto-syntactic Equiv. (4)	R u l e Eqwuiv. (5)	Pragmatic Equiv. (6)	Substantial Equiv. (7)
Semantics (A)	A1	A2	A3	A4	A5	A6	A7

（续表）

	Statistical Equiv. (1)	Translation Equiv. (2)	System Equiv. (3)	Semanto-syntactic Equiv. (4)	Rule Eqwuiv. (5)	Pragmatic Equiv. (6)	Substantial Equiv. (7)
Category (B)	B1	B2	B3	B4	B5	B6	B7
Syntax (C)	C1	C3	C3	C4	C5	C6	C7
Lexis (D)	D1	D4	D3	D4	D5	D6	D7
Post Lexis (E)	E1	E5	E3	E4	E5	E6	E7

Figure 4.2 Krzeszowski's system

其中"A1"可解读为"语义的统计对等"、"C3"可解读为"句法的系统对等"、"D6"可解读为"词汇的语用对等",其余可以类推。可以看出,这是一个相当庞大的体系。

Where in the matrix, "A1" reads as "statistical equivalence of semantics", "C3", "system equivalence of syntax" and "D6", as "pragmatic equivalence of lexis", and so on. It is indeed quite an enormous system.

切斯特曼（1998）体系的最大特点是从意义出发建立他的对比语言学,并分成三个层级：句子语义结构对比、宏观语义结构对比和交互语义结构对比（Semantic Structure, Semantic Macrostructure, Semantic Interstructure）,后两者分别对应于前人的对比篇章语言学和对比话语分析,但切氏将篇章严格限于书面语,因而又吸收了此前从来未被主流对比语言学注意到的、由卡普兰和孔纳等开创的"对比修辞学"。

Chesterman's (1998) system is distinctive in his ground on semantics designed upon three levels: semantic structure, semantic macrostructure and semantic interstructure. The last two levels correspond to contrastive textology and contrastive discourse analysis proposed by scholars before him. However, Chesterman adheres strictly to written form and adds to his system contrastive rhetoric which was little noticed in mainstream contrastive linguistics.

中国早期的学者因为关注点在通过与外语对比寻找汉语的特点,因而没有致力于对比语言学学科本身的建设,更不要说建立什么体系。他们的成就主要体现在他们所建立的一个个不同汉语语法体系上。也许人们会奇怪为什么汉语的语法体系会歧异得这么厉害，原因就在于各家都借鉴了不同的西方语言理论，结合了对汉语的不同理解和解释。黎锦熙倒是在中国对比研究史上第一个提出了学科的范围问题，但对其性质却没有加以说明：

Back in China, scholars in the early stage concentrated on highlighting Chinese characteristics through contrastive studies without the intention of establishing a discipline out of contrastive linguistics, much less building a system for the discipline. The consequence is the formation of a few schools of Chinese grammars in loggerheads. The reason for disparity is none other than the fact that they were based on different western linguistics theories offering different explanations for phenomena in Chinese. In terms of scope, Li Jinxi was the first in China to have considered the issue without elaboration on the nature of the discipline. Li says:

> 比较文法者，一，以本族语之文法与世界其他族语相比较；二，以本族本支语（如汉语）之文法与同族异支之兄弟姊妹语（如藏、缅、泰、苗等语）相比较；三，以标准国语（如汉语之现代北京语）之文法与各地不同之方言相比较；此皆属于语言文字学（英名Philology）之范围；四，以汉语中今语之文法与古文相比较，此可作为"汉语发展变迁史"之一部分，固亦不在语言文字学范围之外，唯在语文教育上颇有偏重应用之意味。（黎锦熙，1933：19）

> There are four branches of comparative grammar: (1) comparison between the grammar of one's native tongue and those of other language families; (2) comparison between one branch (say Chinese) of a language family and languages in other branches of the same language family (such as Tibetan, Burmese, Tai, Miao, etc.); (3) comparison between standard Chinese (for example modern Peking Mandarin) and various dialects; all three of which belonging to the domain of philology; and (4) comparison between modern Chinese and archaic Chinese, as part of the historical development of the Chinese language and though fall out of the domain of philology, tend to emphasie on application in terms of language teaching. (Li Jinxi, 1933: 19)

第四期开始，多数研究者在从事的是句法范围内的比较，这与当时国内的语言学氛围有关。1980年前后，几乎所有语法学者都沉浸在析句方法的全国性大讨论中，论战的一方传统语法派主张句子成分分析法，另一方结构主义派主张短语基础上的直接成分分析法，两派都还没有精力关注到句子以上的单位。第一个提出要拓宽对比语言学范围的是王宗炎，他说：

Affected by the linguistic environment at the time, researchers in Phase 4 were mostly concerned about contrasts within syntax. The years around 1980 saw a few national debates in syntactic analysis that involved almost all grammarians. The traditional camp argued for sentence element analysis, while the other camp made a case for direct constituent analysis based on phrasal structures. Both camps were so engrossed that anything beyond sentence level was out of their horizon. It was Wang Zongyan who called for a broadening of research scope in contrastive studies:

> 现代语言学的发展道路，是从普通语言学到心理语言学和社会语言学。对比分析如果也走这条道路，视野就会越来越宽广，发现的问题就会越来越多。我们似乎不应该局限于多年以来占统治地位的句本位主义。以句子为限的东西（词汇、语音、句法）自然可以对比，比句子大的东西（句群、语段）也可以对比，句子以外的东西（语言环境）也可以对比。（王宗炎，1983/1996：20）

> The development of modern linguistics advances from general linguistics to psycholinguistics and sociolinguistics. If contrastive linguistics would follow the same path, the vision would expand wider and wider, and more and more questions would surface. We should not confine ourselves to the syntax-based theory that has ruled for years. Within the scope of syntax, there are of course elements for contrast (such as lexis, phonetics and syntax), but there are also supra-syntactic elements (such as multi-sentences and paragraphs) as well as elements outside of syntax (such as language environment) that warrant contrastive study. (Wang Zongyan, 1983/1996: 20)

其后，得西方语言学风气之先的赵世开最早（1985）提出了要区分宏观对比语言学与微观对比语言学，也是他最早（1990）提出了要区别理论对比语言学与应用对比语言学。第一个对比语言学体系是许余龙（1992）提出的，这也成了中国对比语言学走向成熟的标志之一。许氏体系可以概述如下：

Thereafter, Zhao Shikai who was a pioneer in western linguistics recommended differentiating between macro- and micro-perspectives in 1985, and in 1990 suggested differentiating between theoretical and applied contrastive linguistics. On these bases, Xu Yulong (1992) proposed the first contrastive linguistics model in China, symbolic of the maturing of the discipline. Xu's model is presented as follows.

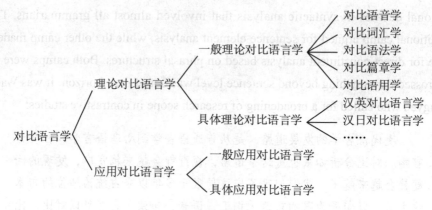

图4.3 许余龙的对比语言学体系

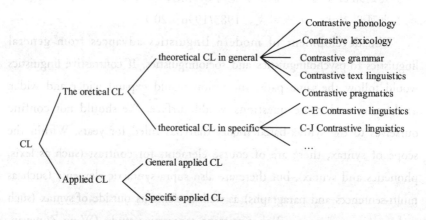

Figure 4.3 Xu Yulong's CL system

许氏体系有几个特点：第一，与一般将对比语言学看作语言学或应用语言学某个分支不同，许氏将对比语言学看作"既是横向的又是纵向的一个语言学分支"，"从整体上来说，对比语言学是语言学的一个纵向分支，因为其本身构成一个纵向的包孕等级系统，与语言学的分类平行"。（许余龙，1992：9）因而，上面的图中如果去掉每一项中的"对比"二字，就等于是个语言学的系统图。这样的认识和构架在中国和西方都是前无古人的，可说是延续了洪堡特和赵元任的思想。第二，许氏的体系中其实还存在着一个交叉，即语言学各分支学科与上述体系的交叉。如"语音学、词汇学、语法学……"既属于一般理论对比语言学，又属于具体理论对比语言学，还属于一般应用对比语言学和具体应用对比语言学。将这个意思一一表示出来会使上面的图示非常繁复，因而我们只在"一般理论对比语言学"下作了举例性的表示。第三，许氏赞同科特（1973）等的看法，认为"理论与应用是相对的"，因而主张采用第一序列的应用与第二序列的应用（first-order and second-order application）的说法。例如：

The above system by Xu Yulong stands out in a few ways. First, Xu treated contrastive linguistics as an independent discipline, not subordinated to applied linguistics. He took it as "a linguistic branch that has both horizontally and vertically dimensions. On the whole, it is a branch on the vertical axis as it encompasses structured systems that are vertically linked and it runs parallel with the classifications in linguistics" (Xu Yulong, 1992: 9). If we were to take away "contrastive" in the above system, it is actually a linguistic map. We have not seen similar ideas on scope and system being championed before Xu's. One could also sense the influence of von Humboldt and Chao Yuen-ren. Secondly, Xu's system intersects with other linguistic branches, for instance, phonology, lexicology and grammar, belonging at the same time to general and specific theoretical contrastive linguistics. We have not attempted to represent this in the diagram as it could be quite messy. Thirdly, Xu agreed with Pit Corder (1973) that "theory and application are relative to each other", and for this matter, he is the proponent of "first-order and second-order applications". For instance,

> 我们可以运用对比语言学的一般理论对英汉两种语言进行具体的对比研究，这是第一序列的应用。然后在此基础上写出一部为外语教学服务的英汉对比语法，这是第二序列的应用。如果再将英汉对比语法应用于某一具体的英语教学中去，这恐怕可说是第三序列的应用了。（许余龙，1992：12）

> We may apply general theory in contrastive linguistics for specific contrastive studies between English and Chinese. This is the first-order application. On this basis, we could produce a title on English-Chinese contrastive linguistics for the teaching of foreign language. That is the second-

order application. In the event that we apply the contrastive grammar of English and Chinese on some specific English language teaching programme, that may be the third-order application. (Xu Yulong, 1992: 12)

许余龙之后，刘重德（1998）为英汉对比语言学设计了一个最宏大的体系。这个体系可以图示如下：

Drawing on the experiences of pioneers, Liu Zhongde (1998) came up with a huge system as follows:

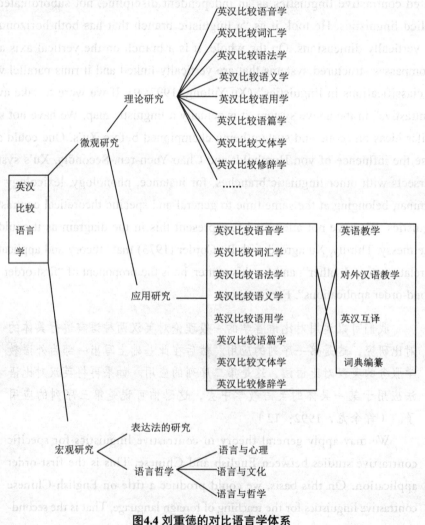

图4.4 刘重德的对比语言学体系

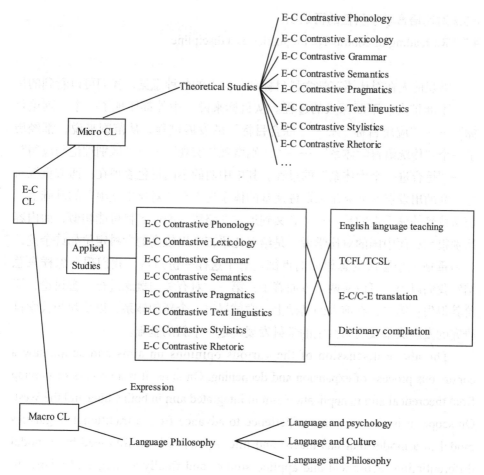

Figure 4.4 Liu Zhongde's CL system

这一体系的最大特点，当然是三个层次的思想，这体现了中国对比语言学的特色和优势。其次，同许余龙的体系相似，"语音学、词汇学、语法学"等既在理论和应用层面上交叉，又在具体应用的对象（教学、翻译、词典编纂等）上交叉。

The greatest feature of this model is the three-level manifestation of the characteristics and strength of contrastive linguistics in China. Secondly, it concurred with Xu's model that theory and application do cross with each other, and that there are also cross-overs within the specific application aspects (such as teaching, translation and dictionary compilation).

4.3.2 对比语言学学科性的再认识
4.3.2 Re-reading of contrastive linguistics as a discipline

纵观前人在对比语言学学科目标和范围上的各种意见，我们可以看到的是一个不断扩大、不断深入的过程。从目标来说，中外都体现了一个"理论目标"——"应用目标"——"综合目标"的发展过程；从范围来说，都经历了一个"传统语言学体系"——"区别微观与宏观"——"区别理论与应用"——"综合进一个大体系"的过程。其中中西的不同特色表现在：西方重视对比研究的出发点，如克尔采斯佐斯基的体系建立在"对比中立项"的基础上，切斯特曼的体系走的是一条从意义到形式的路线，因而名目可能相似，而内容区别很大；而中国的对比学者一是给对比语言学以较高的学科定位如许余龙，二是重视三个层次的思想如刘重德。对于这样一份财富，我们现在怎样来总结？我们以为，可以从两个方面着手：第一，对有关的概念进行一番讨论，评价其得失；第二，在前人的基础上，尝试提出一个新的体系，以反映当代学科研究的发展成果及为新世纪的学科发展奠定一个新的基础。

The above discussion of the various opinions on aims and scope saw a continuous process of expansion and deepening. On aims, it is a process of moving from theoretical aim to application aim to integrated aim in both China and the West. On scope, it is also common experience to advance from a traditional linguistics model to a model that has macro-and micro-perspectives, followed by a model differentiating theoretical and applied studies and finally a integrated whole. In this process, the symbolic part for the West is the emphasis on the starting point, for instance the use of *tertium comparationis* in Krzeszowski and the "meaning to structure" approach in Chesterman. Therefore it will be dangerous to look on superficial likenesses and disregard the disparities in content. Meanwhile in China, contrastivists are more concerned with the positioning and the organization of the discipline. For example, Xu Yulong attempted to accord the discipline a higher status and Liu Zhongde structured the discipline on three levels. The complementary diversity posed a challenge to our summary. We could critically survey the concepts involved for the respective strengths and weaknesses and, on that foundation, raise a new model to reflect the latest findings and lay the ground for disciplinary development in the new century.

4.3.2.1 对两个基本问题的讨论
4.3.2.1 Two basic questions

我们想着重讨论以下两个问题：微观与宏观；理论与应用。以及相关的学科定位问题。所谓"讨论"，主要是摆问题，解决方案我们放到后面去谈。

On the positioning of the discipline, the two pertinent issues would be micro and macro; theory and application. In this section, we are going to merely raise questions and leave the solutions until later.

4.3.2.1.1 微观与宏观
4.3.2.1.1 Micro and macro

中西的学者在拓宽对比语言学研究范围时都提出了宏观与微观问题，其实两者对此的理解很不一样。我们曾经指出，语言学研究中对宏观和微观这一对术语存在着三种理解：

As mentioned in Chapter 3, the connotations of micro and macro refer to one thing to the western contrastivists, and another to their Chinese counterparts. At least three understandings may be discernible.

（1）宏观指索绪尔所谓的外部语言学，微观指他所说的内部语言学。内部语言学也叫纯语言学，把语言看作一个封闭的、自足的系统，不考虑语言藉以存在的社会和人的因素，单纯地研究其内部的语音、词汇、语法等问题。索绪尔开创的现代语言学，一直到乔姆斯基为止，研究的本质上都是微观语言学。与此相对的是宏观语言学，即外部语言学，认为语言的存在和使用离不开社会、文化、特别是人的心理等等语言外的因素，只有综合考虑种种背景因素，语言研究才能真正做到切实有用。六七十年代以后，西方的种种带连字符的语言学，如社会语言学、心理语言学、人类学语言学、文化语言学等等，都属于宏观语言学。

（2）在内部语言学本身，也有宏观和微观的提法，这时的宏观微观以句子为标准，宏观指大于句子的研究，如句群研究、话语研究、篇章研究等等；微观则指小于句子的研究，这是传统研究最集中的领域。

（3）宏观微观还指一种研究方法或角度。宏观指高屋建瓴，对全局性问题的研究；微观指对细小和具体问题的研究。（潘文国，1997a/2002：225—226）

(1) Macro points to what Saussure would refer to as the external linguistics; micro points to what Saussure would refer to as the internal linguistics. Internal linguistics or pure linguistics looks upon language as a closed and self-sufficient system, disregarding social and human factors in the study of phonology, lexicology and syntax. From Saussure to Chomsky, the nature of research is primarily micro. Opposing is macro or external linguistics. External linguistics does not think language may exist free of the contexts of society, culture and particularly human psychology and only when these factors are taken into consideration, will language research be helpful in practical terms. Macro linguistics branches have grown in popularity since the 1960s—1970s, including sociolinguistics, psycholinguistics, anthropological linguistics and cultural linguistics.

(2) Within internal linguistics, it may be further divided into macro and micro. Macro in this sense refers to supra-sentence levels such as paragraphs, discourse and text analysis. Micro refers to levels below the sentence levels, which is the forte of traditional scholarship.

(3) Macro perspective may refer to a methodology or point of view, looking at the larger picture. Micro refers to specific issues. (Pan Wenguo, 1997a/2002: 225—226)

其中第三种理解涉及到研究方法问题，我们放到下一章去谈。在前两种理解里，西方学者如詹姆斯等主要取第二种理解，即把宏观研究看作对大于句子的单位的研究，而中国学者如刘重德等主要取第一种理解，即把宏观研究看作是语言结合社会、思想、文化等因素的研究，更具体表现为对语言表达法和不同民族语言心理的研究。这两种理解中可能有重叠的地方，如篇章和话语研究，可以只注重其形式和意义的一般方面，也可以注重其反映特定文化的特殊方面。这样,从西方学者的观点看,两者都是宏观研究,而从中国学者的观点看,只有后者才属于宏观研究,前者还是一种微观研究。又如光从表达法着眼,从意义到形式的研究在中国学者看来都认为是宏观研究,这样,切斯特曼的体系就完全是宏观研究体系。但在西方学者包括切氏自己看来,也许第一层"句子意义结构"的研究仍属于微观研究,只是到了macrostructure和interstructure才进入宏观领域。这一矛盾如何解决?这里面实际上体现了两个划界问题:

We shall leave point 3 above to the next chapter and concentrate on the other two types of understandings here. Western scholars such as James are looking at 2, i.e. that macro-perspective refers to research at supra-sentence levels, while Chinese scholars led by Liu Zhongde prefer to study macro issues in regards of social, thought and cultural considerations so as to be able to study more specifically the expressions of language in relation to the spirit of the nations. There are overlaps between the two camps in textology and discourse analysis where specific cultural elements have to be taken into account. From this angle, western scholars tend to regard both as macro studies, whereas Chinese scholars think otherwise. Take the research on expression alone, any study employing the "meaning to structure" method is considered macro to the Chinese, so Chesterman's model is entirely macro. However, in the eyes of western scholars, including Chesterman himself, his semantic structure is at micro level and only semantic macrostructure and semantic interstructure belong to the macro level. The point of contention is where to draw the line.

第一个是句子层面与句子以上层面的划界。把篇章与句子分开当然是有意义的,许余龙说:"篇章的组织结构形式与句子的组织结构形式有着本质上的不同……严格来说,篇章并不是一连串句子的组合,而是一个语义上的统一体。任何一个语言段,不论是口头的还是书面的,不论是一句话(或甚至是一个词)还是一部巨著,只要构成一个语义上的整体,便可称为篇章。"(许余龙,1992:226)因而在西方,句法研究与篇章(及话语)研究几乎是两个互不相涉的两个领域。搞句子研究的如乔姆斯基等人从不搞篇章研究,搞篇章研究的如波格朗(Robert de Beaugrande)和德莱斯勒(Wolfgang Dressler)等人(Beaugrande & Dressler 1981)也很少研究句子。西方学者将两者分别称为微观和宏观,无可非议。但在汉语中,由于汉语没有形态,句子的界限不清,因而很难将句子研究与篇章研究划分为两个不同的领域。在中国最早的语言层级体系里（刘勰 公元五世纪），"字、句、章、篇"是一个体系。直到整个二十世纪的中小学语文教学，只要不是刻意模仿西方来讲所谓的"语法"，课堂上教师讲解的还是"字、词、句、篇"。西方语言可分，汉语难分，这本身是个矛盾，体现在对比理论上，也无法采用同样的标准。

  Should it be between syntax and supra-syntax? The division is of course meaningful, since the structure of text and that of syntax are essentially different. Text structure is more than a group of sentences, it is more like a semantic whole, any semantically sufficient utterance, be it a word or a volume, verbal or written, may constitute a text (Xu Yulong, 1992: 226). As such, text analysis and syntax are two separate fields in the West that almost do not cross boundaries. The Chomskian camp would never go into textology, whereas text specialists such as Robert de Beaugrande, Wolfgang Dressler and others seldom research on syntax (Beaugrande and Dressler, 1981). It is understandable why the line between macro and micro is drawn here in the West. However, as a non-morphological language, it is difficult to define the sentence in Chinese and it is therefore unlikely to have meaningful division between text and syntax studies. In early accounts of units of language in Chinese, as defined by Liu Xie in the fifth century, there are the sinogram, phrase, sentence and text. In primary and secondary language teaching across the whole of twentieth century, what applies most is "sinogram, word, sentence and text". The root of the problem lies in the realities of Chinese and Indo-European languages and, for this matter, we shall not force consistency in the measurement of language units and apply a blanket standard in theory.

  第二个是"语言心理"的问题放在哪个层次？西方半个多世纪来的对比语言学者由于是从为二语教学服务起家的，因而所谓的心理主要是指语言学习者的学习心理，在对比语言研究中产生的理论主要是"迁移"理论。显然，在整个对比语言学体系里这只能算"理论对比语言学"的一个较小的组成部分。另一些学者如切斯特曼的解决方法是立足于句子语义结构，把向篇章与语用的拓展称作是"外向"，把向心理学的拓展称作是"内向"。但从他实际建立的体系里，我们却看不到"内向"的位置。心理因素在他的体系里真正起作用的地方是他对相似性（similarity）的分析。这实际上就是对整个对比体系起作用，而不仅仅是在某个层次。

And at which level should "language psychology" be considered? In the context of language teaching which contrastive studies in the West served over the last 50 years, psychology has to mean learner's psychology and that gives rise to the "transfer" theory. Obviously this may only be considered as a small part of theoretical contrastive linguistics. Chesterman's solution to begin from semantic structure and move towards textology and pragmatics would be exogenous and endogenic when towards psychology. Nevertheless it is not obvious in his model where this endogenic movement is positioned. Psychological factors really matter in his similarity analysis, that is to say, it acts on the whole, not at a particular level.

中国学者的想法不一样。他们把语言心理同时放在表达法和语言哲学层次，认为语言的表达法和表达形式体现了不同的民族心理。两个层次的区别在于前者研究的是"其然"（how）的问题，后者研究的是"所以然"（why）的问题。从这一点来看，中国学者的想法更接近对比语言学创始人洪堡特、叶斯柏森和沃尔夫的设想。中西学者的这一区别与研究对象的不同有很大关系。多数西方学者是在"均质印欧语"内部进行对比，其差距之大难以上升到语言心理的深层；而中国学者对比的是汉语和与其差别甚大的印欧语，语言心理距离之大是难以回避的。从建立普遍的对比语言学的角度来看，中国学者的观点是值得西方学者借鉴的。

Chinese scholars offer a different approach. Psychology acts in the expression level as well as the language philosophy level in order that ethnicity is demonstrated. The psychological factor at the expression level accounts for the question of "how", while at the philosophy level it answers the question of "why". In this sense, the approach has a heavy stamp of Humboldt, Jespersen and Whorf. We should say that the difference is also due to the nature of the research target. Most western contrastive studies are conducted within standard European languages; it will be difficult to imagine vast gaps at the psychological level. On the other hand, looking at data between two language families, it is quite natural to believe that language psychology plays up at the core. Were we to consider validating universals with contrastive linguistics, the findings of Chinese contrastive studies are worth taking into consideration.

4.3.2.1.2 理论与应用
4.3.2.1.2 Theory and application

菲齐亚克强调区分理论对比语言学与应用对比语言学，后来的学者包括中国的学者大多因循其说，把区分理论与应用作为建立对比语言学体系的必要之义。但这一观点也遭到了一些质疑。例如切斯特曼说：

Fisiak's call to differentiate between theoretical contrastive linguistics and applied contrastive linguistics is well taken even by counterparts in China and as can be seen in the models introduced above, and the division is taken as most necessary. However, not all buy into the idea. Chesterman challenges:

> 一些对比学者如菲齐亚克（1980）严格区分理论对比研究与应用对比研究，他们说理论对比是一种双向性的研究，从一种共同的或普遍的性质出发，观察其在两种语言中如何表现。这样看来理论对比有点像语言类型学研究，与普遍语法的概念有关。另一方面，应用研究是一种单向性的研究，从一种语言的某一特性或表达法出发，考察其在另一种语言中的表现。在这个意义上，应用研究总与语言教学有关。还有一些对比学者如克尔采斯佐斯基（1990），对这种区别教学法对比与纯理论对比的做法表示质疑，理由是我也同意的，即无论单向或双向的研究，与教学法或纯理论都有关。本书正想证明这一点。
>
> （切斯特曼，1998：40—41）

> Some contrastivists, such as Fisiak, draw a distinction between theoretical and applied contrastive studies. Theoretical studies are said to be non-directional, starting from some shared or presumably universal property and looking at its manifestations in two languages. Theoretical studies are thus akin to work in language typology and are relevant to the concept of universal grammar. Applied studies, on the other hand, are directional: they start from a property or expression in one language and investigate its manifestation in another. Applied studies in this sense have been assumed to be relevant to language learning and teaching. Other scholars, such as Krzeszowski, have queried this way of drawing a distinction between pedagogical and pure contrastive studies: In this view, which I share, both directional and

adirectional studies may be of both pedagogical and theoretical relevance, as this book indeed seeks to demonstrate. (Chesterman, 1998: 40—41)

如前面提到的，中国学者许余龙也认为理论与应用的区分是相对的，因而提出了第一序列应用和第二序列应用的概念。但他承认这样也会带来一些问题：

As we quoted of Xu Yulong above, he too thinks that the distinction between theoretical and applied contrastive linguistics is relative. This is why he proposes having first and second-order applications. Nevertheless, he admits that his proposal is not without flaws:

> 不过，这样一来也会给我们在理论上带来一个问题，即第二序列的应用是否必须在第一序列的基础上进行？如果我们比较一下这两个不同序列的应用，我们可以发现它们之间的目的是不同的，因而性质也是不同的。第一序列的应用（即具体理论对比）的目的是深入探讨两种或两种以上语言的异同，使我们对两种语言有更深刻的认识，从而也使我们对语言本身有更深刻的认识，所以它仍然是理论语言学的一个组成部分。而第二序列的应用（即具体应用对比）的目的是为外语教学和其他活动服务的，因而可说是真正的应用语言学的一部分。（许余龙，1992：12—13）

> [The first and second order sequencing] leads to a theoretical problem: is it necessary that second order application be conducted on the basis of first order application? Comparing the two orders, we find their aims different and therefore their nature. First order application (contrasting specific theories) serves to explore the similarities and differences between two or more languages to gain insights into the languages concerned; it remains as part of theoretical contrastive linguistics or pure linguistics. Second order application (specific contrastive application) serves pedagogical needs in foreign language teaching and other relevant activities, it could be said to be truly belonging to applied linguistics. (Xu Yulong, 1992: 12—13)

许氏所没有提到的是，这样的第一序列、第二序列……在对比语言学的总的体系中如何表现？是"应用对比语言学一"、"应用对比语言学二"……呢？还是将前者与理论对比语言学合并再分为"理论对比语言学一"（原理论对比语言学)、"理论对比语言学二"(原"第一序列"),再接"应用对比语言学"(原"第二序列")?如果是后一种处理法,则马上又会带来另一个问题:理论对比语言学有没有或需要不需要有第一序列、第二序列……之分?在对比语言学研究史上,这个问题转化为,对比语言学理论本身要不要语言学理论的指导?第一个对这问题提出答案的人是迪·皮德娄,他的答案是:要。并且具体提出了要以转换生成语言学作为对比语言学的指导:

It is therefore not clear in Xu's model, how would such first, second or more orders of application be positioned. Should it all come under applied contrastive linguistics to be labelled 1, 2, 3…or should it be grouped with the respective sub-fields as Xu himself stated? The immediate problem is of course is there and should there be ordering in theoretical studies? In the historical context, this question could be paraphrased as: must theory of contrastive linguistics be guided by theory of linguistics? Di Pietro has made a first attempt at answering the question positively and proposed generative transformational grammar as the guiding principle:

> 有好几种语言理论模式都能达到一般化的目标……不过从目前来看,只有转换生成语言学发展得最好,因而也最适合用于对比分析。(皮德娄,1971: 17)
>
> There are several linguistic models in use today which are capable of becoming generalized models…At the present time, however, only the generative and transformational model has been developed in this direction and, by the same token, is the most suitable to CA. (Di Pietro, 1971: 17)

第二个对这问题提出答案的人是凡·布伦(Paul Van Buren)。他认为对比分析不能预测错误所在,对外语教学没有用,其价值在于加深对所比语言异同的了解,增强解释力。而要这样做,对比语言学本身就需要理论的指导。他说:

Paul van Buren concurred with the need of theoretical guidance. Coming from second language acquisition and believing in linguistics to be totally explicit and explanatory, he opined that contrastive analysis is not predictive enough and not useful to foreign language teaching, but that the value of it lies in providing a basis to understand and better account for the disparities and resemblances of languages. To this end, theoretical direction is necessary:

> 我们坚持认为,所有对比语言学的根本目标是为了达到对语言的

解释能力，尽管这一洞察能力并不易达到。如果这一目标可以肯定，那么接下来的关键问题就是选择一个语言学理论作为对比的基础。（布伦，1974/1980: 83）

We do claim, however, that explanatory power should be the ultimate goal of all contrastive linguistics, even if the circumstances are such that explanatory insights are difficult to attain. Given this aim, a crucial question concerns the choice of a linguistic theory to serve as the basis for contrastive statements. (Van Buren, 1974/1980: 83)

而他的选择同样是转换生成语言学。这两人的共同选择使我们依稀看到七十年代初转换生成语言学如日中天时的无限风光。

And he too preferred generative transformational linguistics. In their choices, we see the prosperity generative transformational linguistics enjoyed in the 1970s.

但这种需要理论的"理论"确实也使对比语言学的定位发生了困难：如果别的语言学理论都不需要其他语言理论的支撑就能独立存在，甚至还可作为对比研究的基础，而对比研究没有别的语言理论作基础就无法独立存活，那对比语言学究竟是一种什么语言学呢？

In reality, such "theoretical requirement" leads to problems in the positioning of contrastive linguistics. If theories of other branches of linguistics need no guidance from the theory of another field of linguistics to stay independent and well and even to serve as contrastive basis, what kind of linguistics is contrastive to have to perish without the theoretical support from other branches of linguistics?

中国国内个别学者的观点还要离奇，他们认为对比语言学存在的价值就是为了为西方语言理论进行证实或证伪。如伍雅清说：

Even more outrageous is that some scholars in China tend to think that contrastive linguistics existed to validate or falsify western linguistics theories, as Wu Yaqing argues:

> 其一，我们的研究不应该是为比较而比较，满足于找出对立面，而应该突出共性，致力于对语言事实的解释和对普遍语法的探索。其二，既然我们的研究以普遍语法为中心，而英语是现代语言理论研究得比较深入和透彻的语言，那么，我们的比较研究就应该用汉语的语料对建立在英语和其他欧洲语言基础上的理论原则加以验证或证伪。

……我们的英汉比较,实际上就是用汉语的事实来检验以英语为蓝本的当代西方语言理论。(伍雅清,2000/2004:35)

First, we should not compare for the sake of comparison and be satisfied at arriving at some conflicting points. We should highlight the universality, work hard to explain linguistic facts and contribute to universal grammar. Secondly, given that universal grammar stands at the core and English being a more thoroughly analysed language by modern linguistics, our comparative studies should then validate or falsify theories based on English or other European languages with the data obtained from Chinese…English-Chinese comparative studies is in real terms the use of Chinese realities to inspect contemporary linguistic theories based on English. (Wu Yaqing, 2000: 35)

这种说法,第一,使对比语言学作为独立学科存在的合理性发生了问题;第二,对比研究并不必然"以普遍语法为中心",普遍语法理论在"当代西方语言理论"里也只是一家之说;第三,英语诚然是研究得比较深入和透彻的语言,但并不必然导致别的语言的研究就只能"对建立在英语和其他欧洲语言基础上的理论原则加以验证或证伪";第四,把英汉对比研究或者"英汉比较"的目标降格为"用汉语的事实来检验以英语为蓝本的当代西方语言理论",甘心充当别人的附庸,这比"老谈隔壁人家的事情"(吕叔湘语)的态度更不符合当代中国语言学发展的需要。

The argument has the following faults. First, by this reasoning, contrastive linguistics will always be secondary and subordinate. Secondly, it is not necessary for universal grammar to be set at the core of contrastive linguistics and universal grammar is but one theory in "contemporary western linguistics". Thirdly, there is no doubt that English is more thoroughly analysed, but that does not make "validate or falsify theories based on English or other European languages" the single most important target in the research of other languages. Fourthly, to think of "English-Chinese comparative studies is in real terms the use of Chinese realities to inspect contemporary linguistics theories based on English" is degrading E-C contrastive studies and it is a much worse attitude than what Lü Shuxiang described as "only talks about the business of others" that could hamper the developmental needs of contemporary Chinese linguistics.

而出现这种以验证现有理论作为对比研究目标的思潮的出现,其原因之一也是在学科的定位上有问题。由此可见学科的正确定位实在是学科建设的最根本的任务之一。

The validating or falsifying claim came about partly because contrastive linguistics is not properly positioned as a discipline. This is evidence of the imminent task of asserting the rights of contrastive linguistics as a discipline.

4.3.2.2 对比语言学学科体系的新建议
4.3.2.2 Recommendation for a new model

由于到目前为止的对比语言学体系都存在着这样那样令人不能满意的地方,因而考虑一个新的、更能反映目前认识水平的新方案就是摆在新世纪对比语言学者面前的一个重要任务。我们不揣冒昧,想在这里提出我们的一个初步构想。

To date, the models we have are not completely satisfactory and many of them are of some age. It would be a challenge to design a new model that would reflect the latest understanding and advancement in the discipline for working in the new century. Here, we would like to propose some preliminary thoughts.

我们认为,根据前人的经验,构建新方案要考虑到四个基本原则,这就是英汉比较研究会首任会长刘重德在几年前提出的:

Drawing from historical experiences, there are four principles underlying the design of any new model, as suggested by Liu Zhongde.

> 我们在开展学术研究和学科建设中要紧紧把握以下几个原则:理论和实践相结合的原则,国内的与国外的相结合的原则,宏观研究与微观研究相结合的原则,理论研究与应用研究相结合的原则,因为学术的健康发展仰仗于摆好上述两者之间的关系,切忌走绝端。只有两者兼顾,密切结合,才是正确而有效的治学之道。(刘重德,1998:4)
>
> We should bear in mind the following principles in our research or in the building of a discipline. The principle of integrating theory and practice; the principle of integrating foreign and local efforts; the principle of integrating macro and micro perspectives; the principle of integrating theoretical studies and applied studies. Healthy academic

development depends on the balancing of the above pairs and extremists is not welcomed. Only by proper incorporation of two ends, giving due considerations in both ways may we survive as effective in academic studies. (Liu Chongde, 1998: 4)

这四个原则实际上包容了上面讨论到的问题。要实现这些原则，必须努力体现我们对学科体系自身的新认识（如四个层级思想），同时尽量反映前人在学科建设上的已有成果，努力将各种丰富的思想综合进新的体系里。例如洪堡特等先驱提出的语言对比研究的最终目标，菲齐亚克提出的区分理论和应用、理论中又区分出"元理论"的观点，詹姆斯和切斯特曼提出的"横向、纵向"拓展和"外向、内向"拓展，刘宓庆提出的三个层次，许余龙提出的语言学纵向分支思想和应用的分序列思想。为了做到这一些，我们建议在四项原则之上再加上一条，即新体系必须建立在对比语言学的哲学基础，也就是根本的语言观上。我们既然确定语言的基本属性是人文性，而同时又具有自然属性和社会属性，我们就有可能从三个属性出发来建立对比研究体系，而把重点落在人文性上。

These four principles actually cover most of the issues discussed above. To be more explicit on these incorporation principles, it is necessary to place stress on latest findings (such as the four-level structure in any discipline) as well as capitalizing on the inspirational ideas of our forerunners, such as the ultimate object of contrastive linguistics by von Humboldt; the metatheoretical viewpoint of Fisiak and his proposal to distinguish theoretical and applied contrastive linguistics; the directions of advancement in James (1980) as well as in Chesterman (1998); the three-level structure by Liu Miqing and the vertical branching in linguistics and the application ordering by Xu Yulong. To address additional needs, we would like to add one further principle. The new model must be founded on the philosophical basis of contrastive linguistics, i.e. the ultimate language perspective. Given that language by nature exhibits attributes in all three boundaries of humanities, social and natural sciences, we could have built three models of contrastive linguistics based on the different slants. Following our earlier argument, it is preeminent to focus on the humanities aspects.

综合这些考虑，我们提出的新方案有两个要点：

In this light, the new model comprises two main features:

第一，根据所有学科从理论到实践都可以分四个层级的观点建立对比语言学的四层级体系："语言哲学——理论对比语言学——应用对比语言学——语言对比实践"。其中应用对比语言学和语言对比实践分别相当于许余龙的第一序列应用和第二序列应用。而理论对比语言学放在第二个层级也解决了它的学科定位问题，即与理论语言学处于同一层级。我们可以与语言学的学科层级相比较：

First, it is in accordance with the four-level structure any discipline would have developed in terms of theory and practice. In our case, it will be: language philosophy-theoretical contrastive linguistics—applied contrastive linguistics—application of contrastive studies. The last two levels would correspond respectively with Xu Yulong's first and second-order applications. And at second level, theoretical contrastive linguistics actually runs parallel to theoretical linguistics thereby resolving the positioning issue.

语言哲学——理论语言学——应用语言学——语言实践

Language philosophy—theoretical linguistics—applied linguistics—linguistics in practice

这样的定位解决了两个问题。第一，同理论语言学一样，理论对比语言学要受语言哲学指导，而且只受语言哲学指导。第二，理论对比语言学既然同理论语言学处于同一层级，它就不存在接受其他语言学理论指导的问题。对比语言学可以参照、借鉴其他语言学理论的研究成果，其他语言学理论也可以参照、借鉴对比语言学的研究成果。两者共同受指导的只是语言哲学（或确切地说，哲学语言学）。因此，菲齐亚克的"元理论"应该是语言哲学，他的想法很好，但是对象没有找对。还有一些西方学者总想找一家理论语言学安身托命，也是高估了其他语言学的地位，低估了自身的地位。

Two issues are taken care of with this positioning. As with theoretical linguistics, theoretical contrastive linguistics would and would only be guided by language philosophy or, more accurately, philosophical linguistics. Running parallel to theoretical linguistics, contrastive linguistics is not governed by theories of other branches of linguistics. Mutual referencing between the various branches is of course possible. In philosophical linguistics rest Fisiak's metatheory and contrastive linguistics, no longer needing to be guided by other branches of linguistics.

至于为什么对比语言学和普通语言学的上一层都是语言哲学，原因很简单，因为哲学管得宽。不仅对比语言学与普通语言学要受语言哲学指导，翻译学如果真要建立独立的学科体系，其最上层的"翻译哲学"从某种程度上看也属于语言哲学，因为翻译毕竟是语言间的交流："语言哲学（翻译哲学）——翻译理论——翻译技巧——翻译实践"。这也解释了为什么翻译学与对比语言学有相通性；同时也可看出对比语言学对翻译的指导作用并不是全方位的，它只能在第三、第四层级，不能直接指导翻译学理论的建设。如果想对之有所作为的话，也必须通过影响语言哲学来曲折地实现。

All branches of linguistics, including general linguistics, come under the guidance of language philosophy, which has a broad base. And not only linguistics, to a certain extent, translation as well if taken as a discipline has its philosophical grounding in part to be founded on philosophical linguistics. Language philosophy (translation philosophy) —theoretical translation—translation techniques—translating practice. Given that translation is a communication between languages, it shares something in common with contrastive linguistics, but is not completely guided by contrastive linguistics. Contrastive linguistics works most at the translation techniques and translation practice levels and indirectly, if at all, on the theories of translation. Unless contrastive linguistics is able to affect language philosophy at the highest level, its role in translation is otherwise limited.

第二，根据语言的本质属性，重新考虑语言对比三个层面的思想，定名为"从自然科学角度的研究"、"从社会科学角度的研究"、"从人文科学角度的研究"。从刘宓庆1991年首次提出语言对比研究分三个层次的思想并为中国大多数对比研究者接受以来，人们对这三个层面的理解一直是"语言表层结构"——"语言表达法"——"语言心理或语言哲学"。直到2003年，潘文国在他的《对比研究与对外汉语教学——兼论对比研究的三个时期、三个目标和三个层面》一文中才深入讨论了这三个层面，提出了一个新的想法："如果我们换一个角度去看这三个层面，我们还会发现，第一个层面的背景是结构语言学，第二个层面的背景是社会语言学，而第三个层面的背景是认知语言学。这也正是七十年代以后世界语言学发展走过的历程。对比语言研究要跟上世界语言学发展的步伐，这也是一条必由的途径"；"如果我们再换一个角度去看这个问题，我们还会发现，第一层面的对比是用自然科学的方法去研究语言，第二个层面是用社会科学的方法去研究语言，而第三个层面是用人文科学的方法去研究语言。这也体现了语言研究发展的大趋势。"（潘文国，2003：7；52）

Next, we reconsider the three aspects of contrastive linguistics based on the essential nature of language. We could term it as the natural science, the social science and the humanities aspects. Ever since the proponent Liu Miqing brought out the idea in 1991, most contrastivists in China regard the three aspects as "structural", "expression" and "language psychology or language philosophy". Pan Wenguo (2003) proposed the "three-world" theory on these three aspects. He suggested that the structural level, considering issues related to the natural attributes of language, was based on structuralism and mostly applied methodology in natural science. The expression level, considering issues on appropriateness in utterances, was based on sociolinguistics and mostly applied methodology in social sciences and the third level, considering humanities attributes of language in terms of psychology and philosophy, was based on cognitive linguistics and approached language research with humanities approaches (Pan Wenguo, 2003: 7, 52).

上引最后一段话其实是他在研究了语言的种种定义之后所悟出来的思想。事实上，"语言结构"考虑得更多的是语言的自然属性；"表达法"考虑得更多的是语言的社会属性，即如何表达更得体、更符合相关社会文化的要求；而"语言心理、语言哲学"更多地考虑的是语言的人文属性。这三者之间不应该是我们以前所说的"表层、中层、深层"的关系，而只是着眼点的不同。三种研究都可以做到"表层、中层、深层"，关键在于用的功夫如何。不再提"表层、中层、深层"，可以不致得罪人（同时也不十分符合事实）；而正面地提出对比研究可以以自然科学方法、社会科学方法、人文科学方法去进行，也有利于拓宽对比研究的范围和队伍。

Relations between the three are not hierarchical; they just have different focal points. Within each level, there may be different extent of progression, depending on the research effort. By associating with the methodologies of natural sciences, social sciences and humanities, there could follow the positive effects of expanding the scope and research team.

所谓自然科学的方法主要是从语言的自然属性出发，将两种语言分别当作一个静态的、稳定的系统去进行对比，甚至暂时不顾及其社会变异、文化背景及使用中的种种复杂情况。这一方法比较适合语音系统及教学语法系统，其对比结果主要用于二语教学。这里需要强调区分教学语法与实际语言的语法，因为前者强调规定性、规范性、有效性，与后者强调科学性、描写性、文化性不同，前者属于自然科学层面，后者属于人文科学层面。上世纪七十年代以后，质疑对比分析对二语教学的有效性似乎成了惯例，其实这里既有方法本身的问题，也有使用者的问题。进一步看，即使对比分析不能解决所有问题，无法预测学习者所有的困难；但不能反过来就认为它所有问题都不能解决，所有困难都无法预见。即使能解决部分问题、预测部分困难，对于学习者来说也是有益的。何况如果我们能将对比研究与偏误分析、中介语分析相结合，可以预见和解决的比例有可能更大。

Methodology in natural sciences assumes that language is static and stable and temporarily disregards variations, cultural and pragmatics complications. It is used more often in contrastive phonology and grammar for pedagogy. Findings are normally applied to second language instruction. We stress grammar for instructional pedagogy needs to be prescriptive, standard and effective in application. This is quite different from the description of real data which could take different forms. Since the 1970s, contrastive analysis has often been blamed for not being effective as a means to second language teaching. This involves methodological issues as well as user issues. While it is true that contrastive analysis cannot resolve all the problems and predict all the difficulties in learning, it is not true that it has solved nothing at all or it does not predict. Learners will appreciate the benefits even if the aid is partial. If we could blend contrastive analysis with error analysis or inter-language analysis, solving more problems and making more predictions may be possible.

所谓社会科学的方法主要是从语言的社会属性出发，将两种语言分别当作一个动态的、变化的系统去进行对比，考虑到社会、文化及使用者的种种情况。由于人们在交际过程中的情况非常复杂，要准确地把握，必须有一个抓手，这个抓手不可能是形式，而只能是意义。以意义为出发点，看同样的意义在不同的场合、不同的背景中，不同的语言是如何进行表达的。因而表达法对比就自然而然地成了这一对比方法的核心内容。人们进行交际主要是通过话语，广义地说也通过语篇，因而这一方法更多地适用于话语对比、篇章对比也是非常自然的，尽管不能排除语言的其他平面（语音、语法、词汇、修辞等）在交际过程中发生的变异。这一方法最适用的领域是翻译，因为翻译作为跨文化的语际交流，其本质就是（理解原文后利用译文的）表达，这与本方法的侧重点是一致的。其实翻译也可分为三种：教学翻译、实用翻译和文化翻译。教学翻译是机械的词句对换，适用于上一层面；实用翻译讲究得体的表达，属于这一层面；而文化翻译涉及到民族精神，属于下一个层面。

Methodology in social sciences, on the other hand, assumes the dynamic system in which language is situated and takes into consideration the social, cultural and user factors. Given the complexities in human exchanges, there must be a latch to hinge upon and this latch has to be meaning and not form. To see how meaning works for different languages in various settings naturally becomes the centre of contrastive studies using this methodology. Since the centre to communication is discourse and even text, the social sciences method is popular with contrastive discourse analysis and textology, although variations do occur in other language elements. Hinging on meaning, the method is also appropriate for use in translation as a cross-cultural communication platform in first grasping the meaning of the source language and then how it is expressed in the target language. In fact, mechanical word-for-word translation aside, practical translation and cultural translation would involve appropriate expression of meaning to the extent of giving due consideration to the spirit of the language concerned and naturally may be approached using methods in social sciences and humanities.

所谓人文科学的方法主要是从语言的人文属性出发,将两种语言分别当作各自民族文化的体现去进行对比,这是洪堡特、叶斯柏森、沃尔夫等创立这门学科的本意,是对比语言学最重要的任务、"最终、最高层次的目的"(last and highest reference-point)(Humboldt,1836:47)。如果说第一个层面是对规定性的结构的对比,第二个层面是对描写性的表述的对比,则这一层面可说是对所有这些异同背后的解释性的对比。这种解释,不是搬用术语、光在句子结构里移来移去的"解释",而是联系文化、历史、民族心理的人文性的解释。这一方法,适用于语言的各个平面,词汇是最容易切入的突破口,但核心是语法(真正的语言组织法,不是课堂上用的教学语法)。此外,修辞、文体、风格、韵律等也是可以大有作为的领域。对于汉语与任何外语,不可忽视的还有文字的对比。其实这对非汉语来说也是如此,洪堡特曾专门写过一篇《论字母文字及其与语言结构的关系》,论述过文字的重要性:

The humanities method contrasts languages with a view that each represents an ethnic culture. This is taken as the "last and highest reference point" (Humboldt, 1836: 47) by Humboldt, Jespersen and Whorf. If structural contrast is prescriptive, and expression contrast descriptive, contrast at this level would be explanatory, not by slotting in terminologies but through the understanding of culture, history, ethnic psychology and so on. This method may apply to all planes in language, including rhetoric, stylistics, prosody and vocabulary. But grammar is really the essence; we are not referring to grammar for pedagogy but real grammar on the organization of language. For Chinese and other languages, the contrast of writing systems could not be neglected. In Humboldt's words:

> 然而,文字是对语言更精妙的修饰,只是从有了书写以后才开始。这一件事极其重要,无论就其本身还是就其对民族文化发展的影响来说,都导致了语言间最特殊之点的差异,这比由原先粗糙的口语结构造成的差异要大得多。(洪堡特,1824:71)
>
> It is, however, the more delicate shaping of language, a phase which really only begins with the use of writing, which is of greatest importance, and which, both in its own right and in its effect on the cultural development of the nation, leads to differences in the peculiar characteristics of languages which are far greater than those resulting from their coarser original structure. (Humboldt, 1824: 71)

对于汉语之没有采用字母形式他也有非常富有哲理性的分析:中国人其实早就知道了欧洲的字母文字,但他们一直顽固地抵制使用,绝非因为他们如何忠于自己的传统或对外来事物的反感。而主要是由于汉语及其结构本身的能力,在内部没有产生对字母文字的需要。否则的话,就中国人所表现出的巨大的创造能力,以及他们所使用的书写符号本身,就会使他们不仅将声符作为一种辅助手段,还会创造一种完整的、真正的、纯粹的字母文字。(洪堡特,1824:68)

We recall in Chapter 2, Humboldt and Karlgren's insightful comment on the Chinese scripts, where Humboldt posited that the Chinese did not Romanize not merely because of devotion to tradition but "rather it is due much more to the capacity of their language and its structure that no inner need for the alphabetic script arose" (Humboldt, 1824: 68). Otherwise, with their inventiveness, they would have "created complete, true, and pure alphabet" (*ibid.*).

联系到二十世纪中国的语文政策走过的曲折道路,人们会有许多感慨。因此这一层面的对比不仅有精微的解释意义,帮助我们更深刻地理解民族语言和人类语言,也具有潜在的巨大实践意义。

Relating this to the twists and turns in language policies in China in the twentieth century, we cannot help but sigh at the intricacies contrastive studies at this level would reveal, not only in terms of explanatory power, but a more profound and practical understanding of ethnic languages and human languages as well.

这一层面的对比，按照沃尔夫的意见，当然是距离越远的语言越好，因此以汉语与外语作对比天生地比在印欧语之间作对比要有利得多，这也是为什么洪堡特等的思想在中国容易得到共鸣的原因。但对比语言学并不限制所比语言间关系的亲疏，由于人类文化的多元性，只要有心，就是有近亲关系的语言甚至方言间也可进行这一层面的对比研究。

By Whorf, contrastive studies at this level should involve languages that are as remote as possible due to the diversities of human culture, even though by itself contrastive linguistics does not limit the distance between the languages under consideration. On this note, Chinese has the natural advantage for pairing and more issues would surface than contrasting between Indo-European language pairs. It is not without reason that Humboldt's idea is so well received in China. Then again, if conducted well, even between related languages, contrastive linguistics we believe would be equally revealing.

这样，将四个层级和三个层面相配合，我们可以得到8个分支领域（语言哲学与理论对比语言学不存在三个层面），这就是我们所建议的对比语言学的完整体系。可以用表格简单表示如下：

So, we are now ready to put together the four-level structure in three facets. With language philosophy standing at the head, there could be eight broad domains in our model as follows.

表4.2 潘–谭体系

层级 属性	第一层级	第二层级	第三层级	第四层级	最适宜领域
自然属性	语言哲学（1）	理论对比语言学（2）	自然角度应用对比语言学（3）	自然角度应用对比实践（6）	语音、教学语法、教学翻译
社会属性			社会角度应用对比语言学（4）	社会角度应用对比实践（7）	话语、篇章、实用翻译
人文属性			人文角度应用对比语言学（5）	人文角度应用对比实践（8）	词汇、实际语法、修辞、文体、风格、韵律、文字、文化翻译

Table 4.2 Pan and Tham's model

Level \ Attribute	First Level	Second Level	Third Level	Fourth Level	Suitable Fields for Application
Natural Attribute	Language philosophy (1)	Theoretical CL (2)	Applied CL from natural sciences (3)	Application related to natural sciences (6)	Phonology, grammar for pedagogy, translation for pedagogy
Social Attribute			Applied CL from social sciences (4)	Application related to social sciences (7)	Discourse, textology, practical translation
Humanistic Attributes			Applied CL from humanities (5)	Application related to humanities (8)	Lexicology, real grammar, rhetoric, stylistics, prosody, writing systems, cultural translation

其中，"最适宜的领域"是举例性质的，实际进行对比时，当然可能有重叠、有交叉。如果觉得名称太长不便称呼，在行文时可以把三个层面简称为"结构层"、"交际层"和"认知层"，把四个层级简称为"哲学"、"理论"、"应用"和"实践"。如"结构层的应用对比"、"交际层的应用对比"、"认知层的实践对比"等。

The suitable specialized subfields for application are illustrative and in actual contrastive studies, there could be overlaps. For ease of reference, the three aspects could be abbreviated as "structure", "communication" and "cognition", whereas the four levels could be abbreviated as "philosophy", "theoretical", "applied" and "practical", such as theoretical contrastive linguistics at structure; applied contrastive linguistics at communication and practical contrastive linguistics at cognition.

4.4 对比语言学的本质论——对比观与异同观

4.4 Nature of contrastive linguistics: Contrastive perspective and similarity-difference perspective

哲学基础和学科体系之后，下一步需要讨论的是对比语言学的核心概念，也是本质属性，即"对比"还是"比较"的问题。与之相关的是"求同"还是"求异"的问题。

The next questions to ask are: What is the core concept at the centre of contrastive linguistics? Is it to compare or contrast? Do we seek similarities or differences?

4.4.1 对比与比较

4.4.1 Compare and contrast

从西方对比语言学发展史上，我们发现，对比语言学是从比较语言学中生发出来的。洪堡特、叶斯柏森和沃尔夫三人正好完成了这一过程的三步曲：洪氏（1820）在其文中仍是使用"语言比较研究"这一术语，但我们从他对这一研究的内容和任务的分析中明显地看到了这就是现代的语言对比研究；叶氏（1924）明确地说出了他主张"为比较语法创造一种新的方法，或者创造一种新的比较语法"；而沃尔夫则更直截了当地声称他所从事的是"研究语言与思维的一种新方法"，提出了对比语言学的名称，并且将对比语言学与比较语言学作了毫不含糊的对比：

We have noted from history that in the West, contrastive linguistics arises out of comparative linguistics. From von Humboldt to Jespersen to Whorf, this line of development is rather clear cut. von Humboldt (1820) was using the phrase "comparative study of languages" with a mission and objective pointing to contrastive linguistics of modern days. Jespersen (1924) clearly advocated "a new kind of Comparative Syntax by following the method of this volume". As for Whorf, he was resolute in his claim of the use of a new method to study language and thought and gave it the name "contrastive linguistics", with which he drew distinct comparison with comparative linguistics. He expresses:

把地球上的语言分成来自单一祖先的一个个语系，描写其在历史进程中的一步步足迹，其结果称之为"比较语言学"，在这方面已经取得了很大成果。而更重要的是将要产生的新的思想方法，我们可以称之为"对比语言学"，它旨在研究不同语言在语法、逻辑和对经验的一般分析上的重大区别。（沃尔夫，1941a：240）

Much progress has been made in classifying the languages of earth into genetic families, each having descent from a single precursor, and in tracing such developments through time. The result is called "comparative linguistics". Of even greater importance for the future technology of thought is what might be called "contrastive linguistics". This plots the outstanding differences among tongues—in grammar, logic, and general analysis of experience. (Whorf, 1941a: 240)

沃尔夫之后，由于第二期的对比语言学家不认同沃尔夫等的创始人地位，不但拉多的书中只用"比较"而不用"对比"，在别的学者中，"比较"、"对比"两个词一度也出现混淆，甚至还产生了一个新术语："confrontative"，菲齐亚克（1980）说，有些德国语言学家就把对比研究叫作"linguistic confrontation"，尽管主流意见还是称"contrastive linguistics"。直到詹姆斯（1980），才再一次确定了"对比"这一术语，并以之与"比较"相对立。

Regrettably, western contrastivists were not appreciative of the pioneering efforts of Whorf and the others; not only did they not acknowledge their due position in history, but they avoided even using the same terminology. Lado (1957) used "comparison" instead of "contrast"; in other publications, there was confusion in the use of "compare" and "contrast" to the extent that new terminology was coined: "confrontative". Fisiak (1980) recalled that some German linguists used the term like "linguistic confrontation" to denote contrastive linguistics which existed as a proper title. Not until James (1980) did the term "contrast" reaffirm its place in linguistics and stand opposed to "compare".

在中国，尽管早期的学者，如黎锦熙（1933）、赵元任，乃至吕叔湘（1942；1947）都曾有过以"比较"来指"对比"研究的情况，但从吕叔湘（1977）起，这两个名称的专用性和学科类别性得到了确立。赵世开在将对比语言学介绍进中国的时候把"现代的对比研究"与十九世纪的"比较语文学"作了比较,从四个方面论述了两者各自的特点(赵世开,1979/1990:35):

	19世纪	20世纪
研究的目的	系属关系	结构关系
研究的重点	历时现象	共时现象
研究的范围	词汇和语音	结构系统
研究的方法	传统的(偏重意义)	结构主义(偏重形式,注意结构单位和分布)
		转换-生成方法(区别深层结构和表层结构)
		层次的方法(区分不同的层级)

Up until 1977, early descriptions in China also lacked uniformity in denoting "compare" and "contrast" (Li Jinxi, 1933; Chao Yuen-ren; Lü Shuxiang, 1942, 1947). Since the watershed year of 1977, the two terms have finally had a specific domain of reference. And Zhao Shikai (1979: 35) made a distinct comparison between the two terms.

许余龙(1992:1—4)更从理论上对此进行了阐发。他根据语言比较对象的不同,设定了纵横两条轴线,横轴是共时或历时角度,纵轴是语内或语际角度,从而造成了四个象限:

In a further effort to separate the two, Xu Yulong (1992: 1—4) attempted a theoretical explanation. With respect to the targets of contrastive studies, he set two axes so that four quadrants were divided by the vertical axis representing intra-language or inter-language and the horizontal axis representing synchronic or diachronic directions.

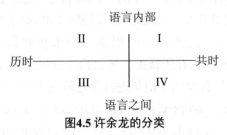

图4.5 许余龙的分类

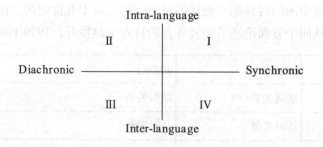

Figure 4.5 Xu Yulong's classification

象限I代表同一语言内部的共时比较,即索绪尔的共时语言学;象限II代表同一语言内部的历时比较,这是某一语言的语言史及其分科;象限III代表不同语言之间的历时比较,即比较语言学或历史比较语言学;象限IV代表了不同语言之间的共时比较,其中又根据"比较的目的和涉及的语言范围的不同",大致分为三类。一类是语言普遍现象研究,一类是语言类型学研究,而第三类就是对比语言学,它通常局限在两种语言间进行。

Quadrant I signifies synchronic comparison within the same language, such as that advocated by Saussure; quadrant II represents diachronic comparison within the same language, such as the history of a specific language and its subfields; quadrant III suggests the diachronic comparison between languages which is comparative linguistics or historical comparative linguistics; quadrant IV implies the synchronic comparison between languages which according to the "aims and language scope of comparison" can be divided into three types. Type 1 concerns language universals; type 2 concerns language typology; and type 3 concerns contrastive linguistics between two languages.

许余龙的分析眉目清楚,在一个时期内对确定对比语言学的性质起了很好的普及作用。不足之处是把对比语言研究局限于共时研究。王宗炎(1983)已提到对比分析有时不能不提历时因素,后来杨自俭(1992)和潘文国(1996d)都对许氏的说法有所修正。杨自俭(2000)强调:"共时与历时两种研究并重,因为要解释异同恐怕非进行历时研究不可。"

Xu's model is clear and precise, at one time contributing to the popularization of the nature of contrastive linguistics. However, the model limits contrastive studies to synchronic research. Wang Zongyan (1983) explains the need to refer to diachronic factors in contrastive linguistics. Yang Zijian (1992, 2000) and Pan

Wenguo (1996d) propose amendments to the model in which Yang stresses that: "Both synchronic and diachronic studies are equally important since to explain the causes of similarities and differences, it is necessary to probe into diachronic studies."

根据赵世开（1979）与潘文国（1997a）的意见，这里再将这两个学科的异同点列表如下。

The similarities and differences between the two disciplines are detailed below, expanding from Zhao Shikai (1979) and Pan Wenguo (1997a).

表4.3 比较语言学与对比语言学的异同

	比较语言学	对比语言学
相同点	比较或对比两种或多种语言以显示其特点。	
相异点		
对象	亲属语言	亲属或非亲属语言乃至方言
目标	建立语言谱系	沟通两种语言文化，为教学与翻译服务
方法与重点	历时方法。重点是寻找相似点，对不同点则居高临下从历史长河中寻找它们曾经相似过的证据，并对其嬗变成不相似的过程作出解释。	共时方法。注意相似点，但更注意不似点，包括此有彼无、此多彼少，尤其是貌同实异的地方。
历史与发展趋势	主要在学科内部方法论上的调整，以及调整分支学科的不平衡性。从语用学、话语分析等语言学其他学科汲取营养。	中西在大趋势上有所不同；发展成独立学科；强调理论研究；研究范围的扩大；等等。

Table 4.3 Comparative linguistics and contrastive linguistics compared

	Comparative Linguistics	**Contrastive Linguistics**
Similarities	Compare/Contrast two or more languages to exhibit the characteristics by comparison or contrastive studies.	
Differences		
Targets	related languages	language pairs which are related or not related and even dialects
Aims	construct language ancestry	a means to language teaching and translation with a purpose to bridge two cultures

(Continued)

	Comparative Linguistics	**Contrastive Linguistics**
Method and focus	diachronic; gathering historical data as evidence to attest any similarity in any two or more languages once shared despite their current faces are apparently different as well as to explain the development process that leads to disparity	mainly synchronic; emphasis on similarities but even more weight put on differences which include peculiar features and phenomena specific to either languages or apparent similarity that spells differences in reality
Historical and developmental trend	mainly adjustment within the discipline in terms of methodology and correcting imbalances between subfields; drawing from other branches of linguistics such as pragmatics and discourse	interesting convergence in larger trends between China and the West; gaining in autonomy; growing in theoretical studies; expansion in scopes

区别"比较"和"对比",在对比语言学的学科建设上有重要的意义。"对比"对于对比语言学来说,不仅仅具有方法论的意义,更具有学科本体论的意义,可说是对比语言学这一学科的灵魂和核心。当然,由于"比较"一词的宽泛意义,在具体写文章时,对比语言学家也不时会用到这个词,但对于"对比"一词的学科性意义,对比语言学家是十分清楚,也坚持不渝的,中外皆是如此。只有极少数学者,偶而还会坚持使用"比较"一词来代替"对比",任学良(1981)、伍雅清(2000/2004)、魏志成(2004:5)就坚持使用"比较"一词。恐怕除了对于对比语言学产生发展的历史不甚清楚外,也反映了人们在对学科性质的认定上还存在着一些不同意见。

This differentiation has a significant bearing on building a discipline out of contrastive linguistics. The concept "contrast", the soul and core of contrastive linguistics, is meaningful not only in the methodological sense; it has ontological substance too. Notwithstanding, the word "compare", wider in denotation, is also used time and again, both in China and in the West, in descriptions but in no way reducing the disciplinary implication of "contrast" well accepted by contrastivists. Only a handful of scholars have insisted on using "compare" in place of "contrast", for instance, Ren Xueliang (1981), Wu Yaqing (2000/2004) and Wei Zhicheng (2004: 5). This shows that apart from being ignorant of the history, scholars are disagreeing with the nature of the discipline.

4.4.2 重"异"与重"同"
4.4.2 Pinpointing "differences" or "similarities"

"对比"与"比较",在方法论上的表现就是重"异"还是重"同"。然而同"对比"一样,在对比语言学中,重"异"也具有本体论的意义。詹姆斯对此说得最为清楚:

In terms of methodology, the difference between "compare" and "contrast" is also a debate on pinpointing "differences" or pinpointing "similarities". James is expressive on this issue:

> 比较语言学家就如其名称所暗示的,认为尽管各种语言均有其个性,但所有语言之间有足够的共同点使人们可以对他们进行比较并分成各种类型……对比分析不关心分类,而且如同其名称所暗示的,更关心语言间的异而不是同。(詹姆斯,1980:2—3)

> The comparativist (Ellis, 1966), as the name implies, proceeds from the assumption that, while every language may have its particularity, all languages have enough in common for them to be compared and classified into types… Yet it is not concerned with classification, and as the term contrastive implies, more interested in differences between languages than in their likenesses. (James, 1980: 2—3)

甚至有的语言学家干脆就把对比语言学称为"差异分析"(differential analysis)。[1]

Some linguists would just call it "differential analysis".

在中国,对重"异"说得最明确的是刘宓庆,表现为对语言中异质的特别关注:

In China, Liu Miqing is not shy about his slant towards "differences", particularly the heterogeneity of languages:

> 就对比语言学而言,最基本的问题在于抓住对比中的双语(或多语)的不同素质,或曰异质(heterology),语言的许多形式问题其

---

[1] 参见哈特曼(1980:22)。
Hartmann (1980: 22).

实只是基于其特定素质而发之于外在的表现现象，是一种外在言语行为表现。我们无疑必须更加关注内在的、支配言语行为表现的各种内在机制（intrinsic mechanism），考察它们以何种形式作用于语言结构，而使一种语言有别于另一种语言。（刘宓庆，1991/1996：23）

For contrastive linguistics, the fundamental issue is to latch on the heterogeneity or heterology of the pair (or group) of languages in contrast. Most formal issues are phenomena of the peculiarity; an external manifestation. No doubt, we have to focus on the inner factors or those intrinsic mechanisms that take control of the forms of language, to observe the ways they affect language structures and lead to distinction from other languages. (Liu Miqing, 1991/1996: 23)

丁金国说得还要斩钉截铁：

Ding Jinguo also stands firm:

> 具体语言对比的最终目的与其说在于觅"同"，不如说在于寻"异"，即寻找两种语言间的殊异性（heterology）。……不管英语与汉语之间如何从两个不同的方向朝着同一个方向发展，但绝不会"殊途同归"。英语所具有的殊异性永远不会被汉语所取代，反之亦然。因而，考察与探索汉英两种语言的殊异性就很自然地成为研究汉英对比理论的出发点和归宿。（丁金国，1996/2004：3）

> The ultimate aim in contrasting specific languages is to sort out the differences rather than seeking out similarities. It is about the heterology of two languages…The English and Chinese languages may have been developing along the same direction but no matter how, it will never converge or come together. The peculiarities in English will never get replaced by those of Chinese and vice versa. As such attention on the heterology of Chinese and English naturally becomes the starting point as well as the destination of the study of Chinese-English contrastive theory. (Ding Jinguo, 1996: 3)

以刘氏等为代表的思潮对九十年代中国对比语言学研究影响很大，但近年来也出现了一些不同的声音，伍雅清就批评说：

These were the leading voices in the 1990s directing development in contrastive linguistics in China. Until recently, there have been some disagreements. Wu Yaqing criticizes:

> 这样的对比无疑是有一定意义的，但也存在着一些不可忽视的问题，如缺乏宏观的理论基础；罗列描写多，分析解释少；在研究中存在着实用主义的指导思想，过分突出两种语言的差异以及这些差异的实用价值；把作为科学的研究对象的语言和语言学科学和语言教学、翻译以及文化拴在一起，从而使科学通俗化，甚至庸俗化。对这些问题不深入思考，不加以厘清，就可能使我们的研究在指导思想上一开始就会出现偏差，甚至误入歧途。（伍雅清，2000/2004：30）

> There are of course reasons to believe in this kind of contrastive studies; the problems though, cannot be neglected. For instance, the lack of macro theoretical groundings; more descriptive than analytic; biased towards pragmatism philosophy to overly stress on the differences and the values of the dissemblance; to mix up the scientific target of language and linguistics with language teaching, translation and culture in such a way as to debase the discipline. If we do not take these problems seriously and have them sorted out, we will risk starting out with a biased outlook and be misled to the wrong track. (Wu Yaqing, 2000/2004: 30)

因而他回过头来主张重"同"，说："我们的研究不应该是为比较而比较，满足于找出对立面，而应该突出共性，致力于对语言事实的解释和对普遍语法的探索。"（伍雅清，2000/2004：35）

As such, he argued for similarities: "we should not compare for the sake of comparison and be satisfied at arriving at some conflicting points. We should highlight the universality, work hard to explain linguistics facts and contribute to universal grammar" (*ibid*.: 35).

第三种看法则是主张"异同并重"。杨自俭（1994：16）就主张，"客观实际应是两种研究同时进行，互相影响互相促进"，以后又作了多次强调。

Yang Zijian (1994: 16) offered a third viewpoint that both differences and similarities should be balanced in practical research so that they could promote each other.

由于伍雅清的论文中始终坚持用"比较"而不用"对比"一词，我们可以认为这代表了一种不同的语言观和语言研究方法论。他所主张的研究可以称作

"英汉比较语言学"而非"英汉对比语言学",这样分隶于两个不同学科,就不会有重"同"、重"异"的争执。然而他的批评和希望纠正的对象却又明白无误是当代中国的英汉对比研究,这就使我们感到有必要从理论上加以厘清了。

From the fact that Wu insisted on using the terminology "compare" throughout his paper, it is clear that he represented a different language outlook and methodology. His studies could be termed as "English-Chinese comparative linguistics" instead of "English-Chinese contrastive linguistics". In this way, the ruffled feathers can be smoothed. Nevertheless, his critical comments on the problems confronting contrastive linguistics in contemporary China are real. We therefore feel the need for clarification from the theoretical perspective.

从哲学的角度看,"同"和"异"是一对矛盾,可说处处不在:

Philosophically speaking, similarity is always at variance with difference.

从世上万事万物存在的形态来说,"同"是"一"或"统一",而"异"是"多"或"多样"。同是叶子,但"世上没有相同的两片叶子";同是家庭,但幸福的家庭处处相同,不幸的家庭各有不幸。

By the manner in which the myriad of things in the world exist, similarity signifies unity and difference signifies diversities. No two leaves are the same, and this is also true of families. Happy families are all alike; every unhappy family is unhappy in its own way.

从事物分类的层级看,"异"在下层,是具象;"同"在上层,是抽象。而且越往上层越抽象。如个体各不相同的马抽象为"马",所有不同类的动物(马、牛、羊等)抽象为"动物",所有不同类的生物(动物、植物、微生物等)抽象为"生物"等。

In terms of hierarchical classification, differences are concretization at the substrate while similarities are abstracts at the upper tier. So under "animal" there could be "cow, horse, sheep…"

从事物运动的角度看,"同"是静态、"共时"的,"异"是动态、"历时"的。运动员在运动场上的姿态千变万化,但一旦"定格",就成了一张照片、一具雕塑。

From the movement standpoint, similarities are static and synchronic, while differences are dynamic and diachronic. Change is the only constant. When we speak of similarity, it must be within a time frame, after which things will continue to develop and evolve, and only the pace matters.

从事物发展的形态看，不变是"同"，变化是"异"。苏东坡所谓"逝者如斯，而未尝往也；盈虚者如彼，而卒莫消长也。盖将自其变者而观之，则天地曾不能以一瞬；自其不变者而观之，则物与我皆无尽也。"

From the development outlook, constant means "similarity", whereas change means "difference". As the classical Chinese author Su Shi put it, "if you look at the aspect which changes, heaven and earth cannot last for one blink; but if you look at the aspect which is changeless, the worlds within and outside you are both inexhaustible."

从主客观的关系看，客观存在是"同"，而主观理解是"异"。同一件事物，由于观察的角度不同，可以有许多不同的解释。"一千个读者就有一千个哈姆莱特。"

In the light of subjectivity and objectivity, similarities are objective existence while differences are the subjective understanding. Chesterman (1998: 1) opens his volume with a question cited from *Alice in Wonderland*: "Why is a raven like a writing-desk?" Could it be because they both contain the letter "r"? Or "because it slopes with a flap (flap of a wing, flap (lid) of a desk)"? Depending on viewpoint, there could be one thousand Hamlets in one thousand readers.

从事物的本原看，"同"是相对的、暂时的、有条件的，"异"是绝对的、永恒的、无条件的。

……

At the source of all things, "similarity" is relative, temporal, conditioned, simple, abstract, static and objective; "difference" is absolute, eternal, unconditioned, complex, dynamic and subjective. While "similarity" shows strength in "unity, guiding, connecting and the metaphysical", "difference" may seem negative as "departing, discrete, isolating and physical".

…

可见"异""同"并存是宇宙的根本属性之一。见"异"不见"同"，与见"同"不见"异"，同样是偏执的、错误的。

As the two sides to a coin, this pair of antonyms is at the root of the universe. Preferences on either one are equally erroneous.

在对待语言的态度问题上,大概没有人比洪堡特对"同"、"异"的问题说得更透彻了:

Probably no one is as perceptible as Humboldt in their language attitude towards "similarity" and "differences":

在语言中,个别化和普遍性协调得如此美妙,以至我们可以认为下面两种说法同样正确:一方面,整个人类只有一种语言;另一方面,每个人都拥有一种特殊的语言。(洪堡特,1836: 53/60)

For in language the individualization within a general conformity is so wonderful, that we may say with equal correctness that the whole of mankind has but one language, and that every man has one of his own. (Humboldt, 1836: 53)

在另一个场合,洪堡特说得还要明确:
Or put more explicitly,

这样看来,差异便是同一,分离即是共有。事实上,如果把语言视为完整的精神个性,那么真正具有共性的东西就是绝为独特的。但惟有通过语言的表现自身,惟有在其个性非常惹人注目的地方,我们才会察觉到共性的存在。(洪堡特,1827—1829/2001: 237)

Viewed in this light, differences mean unity, departing means sharing. In fact, when language is taken as a spiritual character in completeness, it follows that truly universal elements are absolutely unique. But for self manifestation in language, and only in the very captivating, distinctive characters of the language could we realize the existence of universality. (Author's note: back translation from the Chinese version. Humboldt, 1827—1829/2001: 237)

可惜能真正全面理解这一睿智也是真正"科学"的论断,并毫不迟疑地将之作为语言研究基石的人不多,不少人囿于理论上、学识上、思维方式上的局限,或是只见树木,不见森林,只关注具体、个别的语言;或是偏执于对"一种语言"的追求,甚或把"一种语言"与语言研究的某"一种理论"挂起钩来。以"共性"为宗旨的当代普遍语法论、强调"异"的对比语言学,乃至强调发掘某种语言特色的个别语言学(如胡以鲁),都宣称洪堡特是其理论的源头,就透露出个中消息。似乎没有人想过,当代这些彼此矛盾,甚至争得不可开交的观点，当时是怎么统一在洪堡特一个人身上的？为什么洪堡特能将这些观点完美地结合起来，而今天的人却只能执其一端？洪堡特身上比今天的学者身上多了什么？这样一想，也许会打开我们新的思路。

We see in today's academic studies that there are far too many tenacious pursuits of "a universal language", even to the extent of bundling a particular linguistic theory to the one language in pursuit. Many others are also limited in a narrow focus of specific languages, missing out on the larger picture. Interestingly, Humboldt is looked upon as the founder of two seemingly contradictory thoughts: of general linguistics having an interest in universalism and of contrastive linguistics having an interest in the "differences" between languages. He is also being sought after by scholars like Hu Yilu who advocates unearthing peculiarities of a specific language. Has anyone ever realized that all these contradictions actually come from one man and how could it be and why? We are all too busy arguing to fully comprehend the wisdom in Humboldt. We are too adamant on the partial points to see the perfect integration in Humboldt. That is why we are hesitant about Humboldt, but it is precisely through his insights that we see the way out.

　　我们可以从这样的思考开始：既然"同""异"的问题无所不在，语言研究对二者就都是绕不过的，因而实际上不存在纯粹求异或纯粹求同的研究。对比语言学固然不应以求"异"为惟一目标，那种以求"同"为惟一目标的理论也并非就是最"科学"的语言学理论。关键是看如何结合本学科的研究目标，认识"同""异"的性质并予以恰当处置。

　　Given that we are surrounded by the antonyms, it is really a non-issue to seek purely "similarities" or "differences". Indeed, exhibiting "differences" will not be the single objective of contrastive linguistics; otherwise it is no more scientific than theories focusing solely on "similarities". The key is to fall back on the mission of the discipline to give "similarity" and "difference" their due positions.

　　切斯特曼的分析最为透彻。在第一章中我们曾指出切氏对"similarities"的剖析是他全书最精彩的部分之一。他在文中所引梅丁（Douglas L. Medin）与戈德斯通（Robert L. Goldstone）的一段话（Medin & Goldstone，1995：106）堪称认识"同"或相似性的经典：

Chesterman (1998) has the most interesting discussion on similarity. He has a splendid quote from Douglas L. Medin and Robert L. Goldstone (Medin and Goldstone, 1995: 106) that is classic:

> 对相似性的判断在比较者的头脑里是个创造性和建设性的过程，要受到方向性（A与B相似而不是B与A相似）、相关性、特征性、背景性、目的性等的影响。从逻辑上来说，相似性涉及的不只是两方（A与B相似）或三方（A与B在C方面相似），而是多方：说A与B相似，实际上是说，A与B在C的方面，根据D程序的比较，参照E标准的判断，根据F功能，为了G目的，两者是相似的。（切斯特曼，1998: 12）

> Similarity judgments are creative, constructive processes in the mind of the comparison-maker, affected by directionality (A is like B vs. B is like A), relevance or salience, context, purpose, and so on. Logically, similarity is a multi-placed predicate, not a two-place one (A is like B) nor even a three-placed one (A is like B in respect C): when we say that A is similar to B, what we really mean is that "A is similar to B in respect C according to comparison process D, relative to some standard E mapped onto judgments by some function F for some purpose G". (Chesterman, 1998: 12)

从上面的话我们可以得出两点结论，第一，绝对的"同"或"相似"是没有的，"同"要受到许多条件的制约，而每一个条件的变化就会造成"异"。从这方面说，"异"才是世界的本质。第二，求"同"只能通过分析产生"同"的条件来进行，也就是说，只有通过分析"异"才能达到"同"。这样看来，没有单纯的求"同"的研究，更不存在为"同"而"同"的研究；不论求"同"或求"异"，都要从承认"异"、分析"异"开始，否认研究"异"的价值，实际上也就是否认求"同"研究本身。对比语言学尊重"异"、强调"异"、以对"异"的分析为研究的重点，这是无可非议的。

The above serves to reiterate two points. There is no similarity in absolute terms, as it is heavily conditioned and one change in condition would lead to some point of departure. In this sense, the nature of the world is "difference". Next, the "similarity" quest is dependent on the analysis of the relevant conditions, which is to say we see through "differences" the similarities. Taken in this light, all research on similarities and differences must begin with analysis of differences. Without due respect to the value of differences, there are no similarities to talk about. This is where contrastive linguistics stands.

另一方面，对比语言学从洪堡特开始，从来也没有否认过"同"的问题。洪堡特的观点已如上述，这句话里充满了辩证法的思想，在某种程度上正是德意志民族思想的产物，是别的西方民族所缺乏的。大约也只有在老子传统熏陶下的中国人最容易对他有同情的理解。例如戴浩一说：

On the other hand, no one has ever denied "similarity", even Humboldt. His dialectic quotation above is perhaps a showcase of the spirit of the Germans and is not easy to follow. Perhaps only those followers of Chinese philosopher Lao Zi could empathize with him. James H-Y Tai aptly pointed out that:

> 我们着重汉语和英语的异，并不意味着否认语言共性、否认探寻共性的研究有重要意义。相反，我们要通过系统地穷尽语言的特殊性，从容、谨慎地采取归纳的方法来达到语言的共性。（戴浩一，1987：192）

> When we focus on the differences between Chinese and English, it is not to say that we are denying language universal or the significance of language universal research. On the contrary, the systematic and exhaustive research on the peculiarities of languages would allow us to deduce in a composed and prudent manner, the universality of language. (James Tai, 1987: 192)

伍铁平和姚小平在分析洪堡特的思想时说：
Introducing Humboldt's philosophy, Wu Tieping and Yao Xiaoping (1998: 58) says:

> 洪堡特提出，Sprache（语言）这个词应包含两种相互联系的涵义，一是指die Sprache "语言"（单数），即人类语言；二是指die Sprachen "语言"（复数），即具体的、个别的语言，民族语言。他特别强调，作出这样的区分决不是咬文嚼字。一方面，人类的语言应该是统一的，因为人类本身就是一个统一体，个人与个人、民族与民族有共通之处；所有民族都具有语言，语言是"自动、自发地"从人

类的内在本性中产生出来的，它是全人类的共同财富，反映了人类统一的存在本质。另一方面，语言是一种民族现象，各民族的语言在结构形式、意义内涵上有所不同，一定的民族语言与一定的民族性和文化特征相维系。人类语言与民族语言的关系，是一般与个别或本质与现象的关系。（伍铁平、姚小平，1988：58）

According to Humboldt, the word Sprache (language) comprises two senses in connection. die Sprache (language, singular form) refers to human language; and die Sprachen (languages, plural form) refers to specific, individual languages, national languages. He made special qualification that the division was not excessive or pedantic. On one hand, mankind as a unity finds common points between individuals and between nations and its language should be unitary. Every nation speaks a language. Language, being autonomous, is automatically generated from the inner self of mankind. It is the common asset shared by mankind reflecting the nature of human existence. On the other hand, language is a national phenomenon. Each nation carries a different language structure differing in meaning and connotation. Specific native tongues are linked to the specific ethnicity and cultural traits. The relation of human language and national languages is akin to general and particular; nature and phenomena.（Wu and Yao, 1988：58）

在这个基础上，潘文国指出：从根本上说，共性和个性互相依存，脱离个性的共性，与脱离共性的个性一样，都是不存在的。从来没有什么个性研究者会完全否认共性，也没有什么共性研究者会完全无视个性。但是，强调共性，还是强调个性，却体现了一种价值取向，体现了理论研究追求的终极目标。（潘文国，2000：7）

As such, universality and particularity are dependent upon each other, and thus inseparable. No researcher of universalism would deny individualism, and the opposite is also true. However, placing weight on universality or particularity demonstrates the value judgment in the ultimate concern of theoretical studies (Pan Wenguo, 2000: 7).

从实际上来看,"差异派"与"共性派"的分歧,或"对比派"与"比较派"的分歧,并不在于理论研究的最终目标(人类语言的共性),而在于达到这一共性的途径:"差异派"或"对比派"主张通过研究"异",最后达到"同",其表现就是对"异"的不厌其详的寻找与分析;"共性派"或"比较派"主张从"同"出发,最后走向"同",其方法就是"解释":举出一条"有普遍意义的""西方现代语言理论",然后"用汉语事实加以验证或证伪"。关于这一点,前文引过的伍雅清的话里说得非常清楚:我们的比较研究就应该用汉语的语料对建立在英语和其他欧洲语言基础上的理论原则加以验证或证伪。(伍雅清,2000/2004:35)

In the case of China, the point of contest is not the ultimate concern of the language universal; rather, it is the method to achieve it. Contrastivists would depart from "differences" for "similarity" through detailed analysis. The comparative or universal camp would set off from "similarity" for "similarity" through explanation——to validate or falsify some "universal patterns" derived from "modern western linguistics", as illustrated by Wu Yaqing's quotation above.

问题在于,为什么这些"理论原则"(说穿了只是西方语言学某一派提出来的"原则",并没有得到西方语言学的公认)能够作为共性研究的基础呢?几年前我们说过:

The question is why should some "principles" derived from a particular linguistics school of the West be taken as the basis for language universal studies? As Humboldt said, language universal is a common asset of mankind. Only theory whose explanatory power covers world languages fits to be a universal theory. Pan Wenguo elaborates:

只有对世界上各种语言都有解释力的理论,才是具有普遍性的理论。共性的研究有两条途径,根据研究一部分语言得出的规律向别的语言推绎是一种,从各语言的具体语言事实出发去归纳是另一种。相比于印欧语各种语言,汉语是远远没有研究透的语言,在这种情况下，拿从西方语言研究中归纳出来的规律去指导寻找汉语的规律，恐怕不如从汉语自身的事实出发去归纳。（潘文国，2002b：78）

There are two methods to universal studies. To deduce from the rudiments derived from some languages and apply it to other languages; or to generalize from the facts of specific languages. Relative to Indo-European languages, Chinese is less than a thoroughly researched language. Under such circumstances, in the search of Chinese characteristics, it would be better to fall back on the facts of Chinese instead of being guided by rules deduced from Indo-European languages. (Pan Wenguo, 2002b: 78)

这是我们坚持要在对比研究中注重找差异的原因。那么"同"在对比研究中处于什么地位呢？我们认为，由于"同""异"是一对基本矛盾，你中有我，我中有你，两者缺一不可，因而如同"异"回避不了一样，"同"也回避不了。认识"同"的地位，切斯特曼的观察很有启发性，他把similarity（我们称之为广义的"同"）分成两种，一种叫做"分的相似"（divergent similarity），是从"类"（type）到"例"（token），一种叫"合的相似"（convergent similarity），是从"例"到"类"。前者适用于翻译学，后者适用于对比语言学（切斯特曼，1998：12—15）。仿此，我们可以认为有两种"同"：初始的"同"和归终的"同"：

This is why there should be no compromise in underlining the "differences" in contrastive studies. How then, should "similarity" be regarded? As mentioned earlier, they are the two sides to a coin, mutually encompassing and cannot be neglected. A more expressive description is from Chesterman (1998: 12—15). In the insightful observation of Chesterman, similarity is a binary concept: Divergent similarity resulting from a process that moves from type to tokens; and convergent similarity resulting from a process that moves from tokens to type. Drawing from Chesterman, sameness or oneness is to be found at both the starting and finishing points:

（1）初始的"同"就是"可比性"，是对比的出发点。拿两样东西作比较，总得有个基础，有个值得比的地方，这就是"可比性"，而"可比性"就是"同"。没有这一层次的"同"，可说对比研究无法开展。因而，这个"同"，存在于所有的对比研究里，特别是在起始的时候。至于这个"同"是什么，除了与"共性派"的根本差异之外，也还有方法论上的选择。我们将在下一章对此进行讨论。

(1) Sameness at the starting point refers to contrastability——the common platform or value proposition of contrastive studies without which there will be no ground for contrasting. As to the question of what constitutes this sameness, apart from the fundamental differences with "universal", it is really methodological issues; we shall touch on this in the next chapter.

(2) 归终的"同"就是语言的"共性"，是对比研究的终极目标。而这个目标，按照我们建议的对比语言学体系，主要存在于第一层级即语言哲学层级。它并不是或主要不是其他三个层级对比研究的目标。相反，在这些研究里，我们还是要积极地寻找差异、分析差异，以为最终的语言哲学思考提供基础。直到这一层级，我们才能达到语言研究最高层次的"共性"或"同"。说到底，"共性"的研究只有在这一层级才需要和可能得到实现。而对比语言学者必须时时在心中存有这个终极目标，才能使自己的研究在理论上和深度上更上一个层次。

(2) Sameness at the finishing point refers to the "universality" in languages———the ultimate concern of contrastive studies. This is the philosophical guiding principle of contrastive linguistic sitting on the foundation of the discipline. It is not to be equated to some universal objective in theoretical or applied studies. However those studies are useful for exhausting the differences and having them thoroughly analysed for their ultimate contribution to "language universalism" at the philosophical level. This is the highest level of sameness to be achieved and only at the philosophical level can it be illuminated. With this aim in mind, we would then progress further in the discipline.

4.5 对比语言学的再定义
4.5 Redefining contrastive linguistics

下定义是在学科发展、走向成熟过程中提出的要求，只有学科理论建设到了一定的阶段，才能在总结以往理论与实践的基础上，集中众人的智慧，给学科下出一个比较满意的定义。从这个意义上说，下定义和不断对定义进行修改的过程也是学科理论建设的一部分，是学科发展过程中不可缺少的一部分。

At this point in the discussion, it would be natural to revisit the definition of contrastive linguistics. Defining and redefining are part and parcel of a growing process leading to maturity.

洪堡特等早期学者给对比语言学下的定义其实并不是严格意义上的定义，只能是一种"准定义"，因为其时学科尚未发展成熟，他们只能对拟想中的学科的研究目标作出一种构想。至于能否实现这一构想，则要靠后人的努力实践。如前所述，他们的"定义"体现了对这个学科最终目标的追求：研究人类语言和人类思维的关系、民族语言和民族精神的关系。

The early concepts of Humboldt and others are not definitions in the strict sense, since contrastive linguistics as a discipline has not taken shape. However, they have stated in their conceptualizations the desirable ultimate outcome in getting at the relations between human language and thought patterns as well as the relations between national tongues and national spirit.

后来拉多下的"准定义"也是表达他的研究想要达到的目标：找到第二语言学习者在学习过程中遇到的困难及解决办法。

Lado's "definition" was also an expression of the desired outcome which is to predict and resolve problems in second language learning.

真正试图给对比语言学下一个学科性的定义，在西方似乎始于菲齐亚克：

A real attempt at a scientific definition came from Fisiak:

> 对比语言学可以大体上定义如下：这是语言学的一个分支学科，它通过对两个或两个以上的语言或其分支系统比较，来确定其相同点和相异点。（菲齐亚克等，1978：1）

> Contrastive linguistics may be roughly defined as a subdiscipline of linguistics which is connected with the comparison of two or more languages (or subsystem of languages) in order to determine both the differences and similarities that hold between them. (Fisiak et al. 1978: 1)

这个定义只强调通过比较来确定两个语言间的异同，却回避了以往学者都强调的对比目的性问题。

This definition places stress on the contrastive methodology in ascertaining similarities and differences between two languages but avoids the question on objectives highlighted by most in the past.

詹姆斯在认真考虑了普遍和特殊、单一和比较、历时和共时三对矛盾以后，给出了一个新的定义：

After careful consideration on the three pairs antonyms of "universal *vs.* peculiar", "singularity *vs.* comparative" and "synchronic *vs.* diachronic", Carl James arrived at the following definition:

> 对比分析是是一种语言学方法，它在承认语言可比性的基础上，通过对两种语言的对比而非比较，得出具有（共时和历时）双重价值的语言类型。（詹姆斯，1980：3）
>
> CA is a linguistic approach aimed at producing inverted (i.e. contrastive, not comparative) two-valued typologies (a CA is always concerned with a pair of languages), and founded on the assumption that languages can be compared. (James 1980: 3)

詹姆斯所说的三对矛盾，其实与我们分析过的共性与个性、对比与比较等类似，他认为人类学家和语文学家（本书著者按：原文philologist，詹姆斯用此词实际指欧洲的历史比较语言学家）常倾向于个性论者，哲学家常倾向于共性论者；单一论者注重研究某一语言的特殊性，比较论者关注语言的类型性；类型学家常是共时论者，语文学家常是历时论者。詹姆斯拿这三对矛盾来考察对比语言学，结果却发现它不属于任何一种，而往往介于矛盾着的双方的中间：

James considers that anthropologists and philologists (author's note: referring to historical comparative linguists of Europe) are inclined towards particulars while philosophers gravitate towards generals. Supporters of singularity are single minded on the peculiarities of a particular language while comparative scholars are occupied with language typology. Typologists are often working on synchronic study, whereas philologists focus on diachronic. Surveying contrastive linguistics from these contradictions, James discovered that contrastive linguistics belonging to none, more often than not, stands in mediation:

> 首先，对比学者既非共性论者又非个性论者，而似乎介于两个极端之间。同样，对比学者既对某一语言的内在智慧感兴趣，又对语言间的可比性感兴趣，但他对分类却没有兴趣，而且从"对比"这个名词可知，他更感兴趣的是语言间之"异"而非"同"。最后，对比学者既不

> 关心语言谱系或其他与语言史有关的因素，又不完全是从事"静态"的研究以至可被贴上"共时"的标签。（詹姆斯，1980：2—3）

> First, CA is neither generalist nor particularist, but somewhere intermediate on a scale between the two extremes. Likewise, CA is as interested in the inherent genius of the language under its purview as it is in the comparability of languages. Yet it is not concerned with classification, and as the term contrastive implies, more interested in differences between languages than in their likenesses. And finally, although not concerned either with language families or with other factors of language history, nor is it sufficiently committed to the study of "static" linguistic phenomena to merit the label synchronic. (James, 1980: 2—3)

可见他在下定义的同时也为对比语言学与其他语言研究划定了一条界线和范围。他第一个在定义里强调了对比而非比较的原则，同时指出对比的结果具有共时和历时双重的类型学意义。

Obviously, James has drawn a line between contrastive linguistics and other linguistic studies, placing stress on contrastive principles and the significance of two-valued typologies in synchronic and diachronic dimensions.

在中国，第一个给对比语言学下出严格定义的是许余龙：

In China, we should introduce the first scientific definition from Xu Yulong incorporating the principles of synchronicity, contrast and difference-seeking:

> 对比语言学是语言学中的一个分支，其任务是对两种或两种以上的语言进行共时的对比研究，描述它们之间的异同，特别是其中的不同之处，并将这类研究应用于其他有关领域。（许余龙，1992：4）

> Contrastive linguistics is a branch of linguistic studies whose aim is to contrast synchronically two or more languages for description of their similarities and differences, particularly the differences to aid application in relevant fields. (Xu Yulong, 1992: 4)

这一定义强调了"共时"、"对比"、"求异"几个原则。但对其中的"共时"原则其他人未认同。王宗炎早就指出：

However, the synchronic principle invited disagreement as mentioned earlier by Wang Zongyan (1983/1996: 4) that:

对比分析或对比语言学不同于比较语言学。比较语言学是历时性研究，它要追溯语言之间的谱系关系；对比分析是共时性研究，它要揭示语言之间的一致性和分歧性——尤其是分歧性。但是为了说明问题，对比分析有时也不能不谈词源和语言的某些历史演变，这是不难理解的。（王宗炎，1983/1996：4）

Contrastive analysis or contrastive linguistics is not comparative linguistics. Comparative linguistics is a diachronic study tracing the ancestry of languages; contrastive linguistics is synchronic and aims at revealing the uniformity and diversity, particularly the diversity. However, in illustration, it is understandable that it is sometimes required to bring in diachronic changes in languages or etymology. (Wang Zongyan, 1983/1996: 4)

其后对下定义最关注的学者是杨自俭。杨自俭是中国英汉语比较研究会的会长，对学科建设的意识特别强。在许余龙的定义的基础上，他在几年时间里反复思考，数易其稿，最后为英汉对比语言学（也可推而广之到一般的对比语言学）提出了下面这个定义：

And then, there is Yang Zijian, the president of the CACSEC, who is most concerned with the institutional growth of contrastive linguistics. After years of pondering and several revisions, Yang Zijian proposed on the basis of Xu Yulong's definition, to define English-Chinese contrastive studies (applicable to general contrastive linguistics) as follows:

英汉对比语言学是语言学的一个分支学科，它兼有理论语言学和应用语言学的性质，其主要任务是对英汉两种语言进行共时和历时的对比研究，描述并解释英汉语之间的异和同，并将研究成果应用于语言和其他相关的研究领域。（杨自俭，2004：6—7）

English-Chinese contrastive linguistics is a branch of linguistic studies incorporating the natures of both theoretical and applied linguistics whose aim is to contrast synchronically and diachronically, English and Chinese for description of their similarities and differences and for findings to be applied to language or other relevant fields. (Yang Zijian, 2004: 6—7)

这个定义有几个特点。第一，它总结了近年来对比语言学学科建设的成果，注意将理论和应用并重、共时和历时并重、异同并重、描写和解释并重。可见这是非常全面和周到的考虑；第二，这一定义的前一稿最后一句是这样的："并将研究成果应用于语言理论研究和语言应用领域"（杨自俭，2000：13）。我们猜想作者改变成现在的面貌，是因为觉得对比语言学的研究成果不光可以为语言学和应用语言学领域（如二语教学、翻译、双语词典编纂等）所利用，还可为其他领域如对比文化学等所利用。这样的认识无疑比原来又高了一个境界，扩大了对比语言学的应用范围。

The definition, absorbing the findings of recent years, is balanced and comprehensive in terms of theory and application, synchronicity and diachronicity, similarity and difference, description and explanation. In the version before this, Yang was considering the last sentence to be "for findings to be applicable for the study of linguistic theory and adoption in applied linguistic fields" (Yang Zijian, 2000: 13). We imagine that Yang had it revised on second thought that the findings from contrastive linguistics need not be confined to applications in linguistics and applied linguistics (such as second language teaching, translation, bilingual dictionary compilation and more). It is beneficial to other areas such as comparative cultures and the like. This standpoint does help to elevate the discipline and expand its scope of application.

杨自俭的定义已为中国多数对比学者所接受，本文作者也是同意的。但经过本章对一些原则问题的讨论，我们对这个定义又感到有一些不满足，主要是：没能反映学科的哲学基础；没能区分"同""异"在不同阶段的侧重性；同时，也没有反映赵元任"对比语言学就是普通语言学"的思想，其定位容易引起歧义。

Yang's definition has gained wide acceptance among Chinese contrastivists. While we agree, we also have some concerns after the deliberation of this volume. There could be some reflections on the philosophical groundings; more explicit on the different emphases on the importance of "similarity" and "difference" in the various stages and to avoid any misconstrual of its status, the positioning of contrastive linguistics as general linguistics, as suggested by Chao Yuen-ren.

根据这些想法，我们尝试提出一个对比语言学的新定义，以作为进一步深入研究的基础：

With these in mind, we would like to suggest the following definition as a base for further advancement:

> 对比语言学是在哲学语言学指导下的一门语言学学科，具有理论研究和应用研究的不同层面，旨在对两种或两种以上的语言或方言进行对比研究，描述其中的异同特别是相异点，并从人类语言及其精神活动关系的角度进行解释，以推动普通语言学的建设和发展，促进不同文化、文明的交流和理解，促进全人类和谐相处。
>
> Contrastive linguistics is a branch in linguistics maintained by foundations in philosophical linguistics, comprising aspects in theoretical and applied studies with an object to contrast two or more languages or dialects to describe the similarities and, particularly, the differences for an explanation in view of the relations between human language and its spirit, so as to promote advancement in general linguistics and facilitate the exchanges and understandings of cultures and civilizations for human harmony.

提"哲学语言学"而不直接提语言世界观，因为定义需要包容的范围更大，而"哲学语言学"一词已足以使人想起洪堡特；讲"不同层面"，是因为考虑到"理论对比语言学"与"应用对比语言学"都不只是一个层面；包括了"方言"，是希望对比语言学能扩大到更多的方面，再则语言和方言的界线并不清楚；"语言及精神活动的关系"比"语言与思维"、"语言与心理"、"语言与逻辑"、"语言与文化、历史、民族"等范围都要广，而且更空灵，同时也更接近洪堡特的原意。

Philosophical linguistics is used instead of language worldview for the broad and encompassing sense required in any definition. And philosophical linguistics leads directly to Humboldt. The use of "aspects" indicates the many faces of theoretical and applied contrastive linguistics. Dialects are included for the vague line between language and dialect as well as considerations in expanding the scope of studies. The phrase "relations between human language and its spirit" gives more space for choices in language and thoughts, language and psychology, and language and logic, as well as language and culture, history and ethnicity, to mention a few, perhaps closer to the intention of Humboldt.

最后两句话是我们特意加上去的,一方面诚然是因为"促进不同文化、文明的交流和理解"的范围,比二语教学、翻译、词典编纂、文化对比等等加起还要大,而更重要的是我们觉得这样才能真正体现前辈们创始对比语言学的良苦用心。我们非常强烈地希望学术研究不要过于学术气,似乎不食人间烟火,不要距离人类的生活过远,特别是作为人文科学的研究者更应该有博大的人文关怀。我们甚至感到,对比研究也好,别的语言研究也好,"描写"固然不是目的,"解释"也不是最终目的。世上的一切,"同"是相对的,"异"是绝对的,但如果仅有"描写"和"解释",说明了什么是"异"、为什么会"异",作为人文主义者,我们尽到责任了吗?"异"有两面性,一面是争斗性,适者生存,残酷斗争,你死我活;而另一面是互补性,不同的语言、不同的文明之间彼此可以互通有无、取长补短,达到共同发展的目的。跨语言研究的根本目的是要在世人中架起一道理解的桥梁,以便使地球上的人类更和谐地相处。对比研究作为一种重在找差异的研究,尤其要特别注意其中的互补性,要通过它来丰富人们的语言生活和精神生活。

The purpose of adding the last portion of the definition is two-fold. For one, the facilitation of exchanges and understandings of cultures and civilizations is a larger scope than second language teaching, translation and dictionary compilation, and more importantly, we find in it the painstaking efforts of our forerunners in putting forward contrastive linguistics. It is our passionate hope for academic studies not to be confined within an ivory tower, particularly for humanity studies, which should demonstrate unstinting magnanimity towards humanity. Be it in contrastive studies or other linguistic studies, as much as description is not the objective, so is explanation not the ultimate concern. In all things, we see similarity as relative and differences as absolute. Are we done just showing what leads to the differences and why? As humanists, we should see the two sides to "difference": on the one hand, it implies struggles and survival of the fittest; one the other hand, it signifies complementary efforts between various languages, cultures and civilizations to achieve total progress for all. Fundamental to cross-linguistic studies is bridging the opinion gaps for human harmony. Focusing on the differences, contrastive studies ought to emphasize areas requiring complementing efforts upon which the linguistic and mental life of humans would be enriched.

我们的这个想法，说到底还是受到了洪堡特、高本汉和沃尔夫等人的启示。洪堡特说：

On this note, we would like to share the supporting thoughts from Humboldt, Karlgren and Whorf. From Humboldt:

> 然而，语言正是通过接触有巨大差别甚至尖锐对立的语言而变得有力、充实，首先是形式变得更多彩，因为在那些语言里已经组织进了人类的丰富生活。它真正得到的只是：更充实的内容、无穷无尽的创造力、观察力、想象力，以及感知力。（洪堡特，1824：88）

> However, languages gain in strength, richness, and form above all through the encounter of greater and even contrasting diversities, since a richer content of human existence already formed into language goes into them. This alone is their real gain: an enrichment produced in them, as in nature, from the fullness of creative forces (whose creativity reason cannot fathom), from observation, from imagination, and from feeling. (Humboldt, 1824: 88)

高本汉也说：

From Karlgren:

> 人们常说，每学会一种语言，就多得到了一个灵魂。这句话的正确性，并不仅仅是指那个语言的文学或是作品向你打开的新鲜观点和美丽世界——这些通过好的翻译毕竟也能得到——而且是指或者更重要的是指，你的思想将被迫离开由于你自身的语言而造成的熟悉的轨道，从而将自己提升到一个更高的视界。你会发现，原来根本上相同的观点，可以用非常不相同的方式，用跟你的母语完全不相同的语言范畴表达出来。（高本汉，1949：3—4）

> It is a well-known saying that with every language you learn, you acquire one more soul. This is true, not only with respect to the literature of that language, with its new world of ideas and beauty that is thereby opened up—this might, after all, be made accessible in good translations—but also, and above all, because your thoughts are compelled to leave the tracks made familiar to you by your own language and you are enabled to raise yourself to a higher vantage point. You can come to realize that fundamentally identical

ideas may be given form in widely varying ways and expressed in completely different language categories from those you are accustomed to in your mother tongue. (Karlgren, 1949: 3—4)

至于沃尔夫的话，我们已在第一章引过了。谁读过了那段话都会难以忘怀。这里我们只想再引其中的一句：

And again from Whorf as we covered in Chapter 1:

> 我们不会再认为这些语言（按：指印欧语言）以及与之相伴的我们的思维过程囊括了全部理念和知识，而会认为它们只是广袤星系中的一个星座。当我们充分地认识了全球语言系统惊人的多元性，我们就会不可避免地感到，人类的精神令人难以置信地古老；我们以文字记录的几千年历史，在衡量我们在这个星球以往经验的尺度上，不过是细细的一道铅笔痕。……（沃尔夫，1940a: 218）

> They [Indo-European languages], and our own thought processes with them, can no longer be envisioned as spanning the gamut of reason and knowledge but only as one constellation in a galactic expanse. A fair realization of the incredible degree of diversity of linguistic system that ranges over the globe leaves one with an inescapable feeling that the human spirit is inconceivably old; that the few thousand years of history covered by our written records are no more than the thickness of a pencil mark on the scale that measures our past experience on this planet. (Whorf, 1940a: 218)

那些在对比研究过程中念念不忘印欧语中心的人，读了真正的人文主义者的这种肺腑之言，应该感到脸上羞红。

We dedicate these true words from the hearts of great humanists to all contrastivists, particularly to those who make every effort to straight jacket Indo-European languages over other ethnic languages.

第五章
对比语言学的方法论
Chapter 5 Methodological Considerations in Contrastive Linguistics

5.1 方法论研究的回顾
5.1 Methodological studies in retrospect

在学科建设中,本体论之外,最重要的就是方法论。本体论与方法论的关系是"体"与"用"的关系,"方向"与"路线"的关系。本体论决定方向,而方法论决定路线。一个没有本体论的学科是不可想象的,一个只有本体论而没有方法论的学科同样是不可想象的。

The importance of methodology in building a new discipline is next only to ontology. Ontology and methodology go hand in hand like body and function. To understand the relationship between ontology and methodology, we may think of a theory and its application, or in terms of direction and approach. Ontological studies give direction to a subject matter whereas methodology determines the various approaches that can be adopted in order to align with the set direction. There is no discipline without a part of ontology, just as there is no discipline without a part of methodology.

对比语言学的先驱洪堡特、叶斯柏森、沃尔夫等都是既重视本体论,又重视方法论的。洪堡特(1836:54)的"语言如何从精神出发,再反作用于精神,这是我要考察的全部过程"一语,就是他的对比语言学(或普通语言学)方法论的精髓,这句话里体现了辩证法的智慧,是德意志民族精神的表现。乔姆斯基自称从笛卡尔和洪堡特两位先辈身上受益最多，但并没有真正理解洪堡特博大精深的语言学思想，也没有学到洪堡特的辩证法精神，他只从洪堡特那里获取自己需要的东西，如"以有限的形式表达无限的内容"[1]等，便一头钻进牛角尖，再也出不来了。这种辩证法精神的缺乏同样体现在沃尔夫身上，因此同样主张语言世界观，沃尔夫受到的质疑和批评就比洪堡特要多得多。

The forerunners of contrastive linguistics, Humboldt, Jespersen and Whorf all laid emphasis on both ontology and methodology. Humboldt's (1836: 54) words that "we are to consider the whole route whereby, proceeding from the mind, it reacts back upon the mind" reflect what he considers to be the essence of methodology in CL, which in some sense a manifestation of German dialectic wisdom. We are reminded that Chomsky in the twentieth century claimed to have derived much insights from two respectable antecessors, René Descartes (1596—1650) and von Humboldt. However, Chomsky's understanding of Humboldt's broad linguistic thinking as well as the essence of the German dialectics is highly questionable. What he gets from Humboldt is only those highly selective points seemingly useful to the construction of his own theory, such as 'to use finite means to perform infinite variety of acts' and then goes into a blind alley and never returns. Deficiency in dialectical thinking is also witnessed in Whorf, who receives a much larger share of criticism than Humboldt although both advocate linguistic relativism.

叶斯柏森的方法论主要体现在他的"从外到内"、"从内到外"两条路线，而他的"由C（意念）通过B（功能）达到A（形式）"更是他的对比语言学的完整的研究路线。

The methodology advanced by Jespersen involves two ways of research, i.e. "from

---

[1] "换句话说，我们看不出哈里斯理解了洪堡特的见解，即语言不仅仅是各类成分的型式化组织，要充分对它进行描写，必须将这些成分与有限的生成原则的系统联系起来，正是这些系统决定了个别语言成分及其互相关系，并使人们能行使无限多种类的有意义的语言行为。"（乔姆斯基，1966：22）
"(Harris) does not, in other words, give any indication of grasping Humboldt's insight that language is far more than 'patterned organization' of elements of various types and that any adequate description of it must refer these elements to the finite system of generative principles which determine the individual linguistic elements and their interrelations and which underlie the infinite variety of linguistic acts that can be meaningfully performed" (Chomsky, 1966: 22).

O to I" and "from I to O", while his proposition of going "from C (notion) through B (function) to A (form)" suggests a complete line in doing contrastive study.

沃尔夫的方法论则体现在他关于"语法范畴"的论述上,因为他认为建立在印欧语基础上的那些语法术语,不足用来作研究印欧语以外的语言的凭据。这也是在对比语言学史上第一次对"中间项"的相关讨论。

The methodology presented by Whorf can be seen in his discussion of grammatical categories where he opines that grammatical concepts based on European languages are not suited for analysing languages other than the Europeans. That can well be regarded as the first discussion in the history of contrastive studies related to a possible *tertium comparationis*.

从拉多开始的对比语言学,在方法论研究上却表现出惊人的薄弱。这也难怪,因为在相当长一段时间里(甚至直到现在)许多人都不敢将对比研究称为对比语言学,连研究对比语言学本体论的问题都觉得超出了他们的视野,"皮之不存,毛将焉附"?

Contrastive studies since Lado, however, reveal a surprising weakness as far as methodology is concerned. It is understandable that for a very long time—even up to this day—many researchers are reluctant to use "contrastive linguistics" in the titles of their studies. More alarmingly, study on ontology has never entered their research horizon. If the ontology of contrastive linguistics fails to hold, how can one expect a place for methodology?

在西方对比语言学史上首倡并特别重视理论对比语言学的菲齐亚克谈到了要研究方法论问题,但他的方法论却归结为对比研究的"模式"。我们下面将看到,"模式"研究与方法论研究还是有区别的。

Fisiak, being the first in the West to emphasize the importance of theoretical contrastive linguistics, also calls on the study of methodology. However, his "methodology" turns out to be a contrastive "model", which is clearly not the same thing, as we shall soon see below.

另一位重视理论研究的学者自然非克尔采斯佐斯基莫属。他对"对比中立项"(*Tertium comparationis*)的概念作了最持久、最全面的研究。只是他过于贪大求全。如果将他的体系看成了历史观的记录倒是挺好的,但要看成"一家之言"未免有些庞杂而且自相矛盾。不过他在方法论研究上的贡献是毋容置疑的。

Another scholar who pays attention to theoretical study is none other than Krzeszowski. Krzeszowski fell into disfavour because his proposal was complicated and at times contradictory. Nonetheless, his continued effort in the holistic study of *tertium comparationis* remains a noticeable contribution to the study of methodology.

另两位对方法论研究提出很多真知灼见的学者是利宾斯卡（Maria Lipińska，1980）和切斯特曼（1998）。利宾斯卡是西方对比学者中少见的有哲学头脑的人，对一些问题的意见非常启人思考，尽管我们并不赞同她对转换生成语言学近于迷信般的推崇。切斯特曼堪称是西方对比语言学的思想家，在方法论上也是如此。可惜他的位置似乎没有摆正，在不是谈方法论的章节里有很多关于方法论的深刻见解，在方法论的标题下谈的却是对比研究的操作程序。这似乎是他的书美中不足的地方。

Two other philosophically-minded western scholars, Maria Lipińska (1980) and Chesterman (1998), also contributed to the study of methodology. Many of Lipińska's ideas are worth pondering, although we do not accept her religious belief in generative and transformational grammar. Chesterman is the master-thinker for the discipline and its methodology in the West. His discourse on methodology is scattered throughout his writings apart from the section on "methodology", where he concentrates on steps and procedures instead.

在中国，重视对比研究方法论的首推黎锦熙和林语堂。黎锦熙（1933：13）提出"'不迷其所同，而亦不失其所以异'，可借用为比较文法研究的原则"；又说："所谓比较，重在异而不在同：同则因袭之，用不着一一比较；唯其异，才用得着比较，或大同而小异，或小同而大异，或同中有异，或异中有同"。对于对比语言学而言，异同问题既是本体论问题，又是方法论问题。林语堂则提出并实践了叶斯柏森的由内到外的对比研究路线，并取得了不俗的成绩。

Among the Chinese scholars with a keen interest in methodology, we may first mention Li Jinxi and Lin Yutang. Li (1933: 13) said, "The saying 'Don't get puzzled by their likeness while mindful of their differences' can be adopted as a principle for the study of comparative grammar." He further remarked that "In comparison emphasis should be laid on differences rather than similarity. For if two things are similar, they are linked by conventions; the need to compare and contrast only arises when there are differences. It may be similar for the large part and different for the small part; or similar for the small part and different for the large part; or there may be differences amongst similarities and similarities amongst differences". The discussion on similarity and difference is indeed of ontological as well as methodological significance in contrastive study. Lin Yutang, on the other hand, was one of the earliest western-trained Chinese linguists to have put into pracice Jespersen's suggestion of the "I to O" method in English-Chinese analysis and achieved remarkable success.

其后，王力、吕叔湘等都很重视对比研究的方法论。吕叔湘尤其具有辩证的眼光，他的《中国方法要略》（1942）上卷"词句论"，下卷"表达论"，开创了同时进行"从外到内"、"从内到外"研究的先例。他的"一句中国话，翻成英语怎么说；一句英语，中国话里如何表达"，实际上提出了一种双向对比的原则。

Picking up the baton, both Wang Li and Lü Shuxiang put in great effort to iron out issues in contrastive methodology. Lü was especially full of dialectic insight. His masterpiece, *Essentials of Chinese Grammar*, divided into "syntax" and "expression", attests excellently to the synthesis of going from "I to O" and from "O to I". By considering "what is to be said in rendering a Chinese utterance into English, and how to express an English representation in Chinese…", Lü raised as a matter of fact the principle of double track contrasting.

20世纪90年代以来的学者中，重视方法论的往往是那些对语言哲学比较关注的人，如张志公、徐通锵、杨自俭、刘宓庆、丁金国、钱冠连、潘文国等。杨自俭在许多场合大声疾呼要重视方法论的研究，刘宓庆提出了"层面透视法"，徐通锵和潘文国都主张从西方语言学的"立论精神"出发来研究语言，并在与印欧语"词本位"对比的基础上提出了汉语的"字本位"理论，潘文国（1997c）还专门提出了"从汉语出发"的汉英对比方法论原则，等等。但总的来说，关注方法论的，没有关注本体论的人多，专门研究方法论的论著更是非常稀有。这说明，这门学科的建设还大有可为。本书也许是在这个领域的第一次比较集中而专门的讨论。我们将首先对方法论研究的一些原则问题进行探讨，再就一些具体的方法论问题进行较深入而细致的分析。

Since the 1990s, scholars interested in methodology are confined amongst those who have a flair for language and linguistic philosophy, such as Zhang Zhigong, Xu Tongqiang, Yang Zijian, Liu Miqing, Ding Jinguo, Qian Guanlian and Pan Wenguo. Yang Zijian endeavoured to encourage contrastivists to be committed to the study of methodology on numerous occasions by taking pain to explain the concept of methodology. Liu Miqing (1991) proposed a three-pronged stratification comparison schema, namely, surface stratum (surface structures of sound, writing, lexicology and syntax), intermediary stratum (effective models in representation) and deep stratum (thought patterns demonstrative of the humanity in language development as well as the dialectical relations between thought and language). Both Xu Tongqiang and Pan Wenguo precipitated discussion on a linguistic programme that draws heavily on the schemes of argument underpinning western theories while putting forward a "sinigram-based" linguistic theory parallel to the European "word-based" theory. Pan (1997c) even suggested a methodological principle to perform comparison with "the Chinese language as the locus". These big names though did not change the culture around. On the whole, there are far fewer scholars interested in contrastive methodology (as compared to, say ontological study), and publications dedicated to the study of methodology are rare. This leaves much ground to be covered in this area. The present chapter could be the first attempt to present a comprehensive survey. We will first discuss the fundamental principles of methodological study before we delve into more details.

5.2 方法论研究的原则
5.2 Principles of methodological study

5.2.1 方法与方法论
5.2.1 Method and methodology

首先我们要区别方法与方法论，这两者尽管有联系但却是两个不同的概念。丁金国说：

Before we move on, it is important to distinguish between method and methodology—a pair of subtly different but yet related concepts. Ding Jinguo offered an explanation below,

方法论（methodology）与方法（method or approach）不同，方法论是形而上的，是为研究某一特定学科所使用的指导原则与规则。方法论有的跨学科，有的则只适应于特定的学科，而方法是为解决某一特定问题采用的具体方式与做法。（丁金国，1996/2004：8）

Methodology differs from method or approach in the sense that it is metaphysical. It is the guiding principles or rudiments behind a specific discipline. It may be specific to a discipline or applicable across several disciplines. Methods, on the other hand, are some specific ways or procedures deployed to investigate and counter a given problem. (Ding Jinguo, 1996/2004: 8)

他指出了方法论的三个特点。第一，方法论是形而上的，即具有哲学性。在哲学上，方法论是相对于本体论而言的，是完成本体论所规定的目标的指导性原则。对本体论的认识不同，就会导致不同的方法论。例如，西方哲学研究的本体始终是"存在"（Being）的问题，由于对本体的认识不同，导致了研究方法的变更，出现了西方哲学史上的三次大转向。这些转向，包括从20世纪初以来的语言转向，从本质上来说，都可以看作是方法论的转向。第二，方法论是"为研究某一特定学科使用的"，即具有针对性。在一门学科的研究中，我们可以使用许多方法，但并不是所有的方法都具有方法论的意义。一些一般性、并非为这一学科量身定制的方法就不一定具有学科方法论的意义。例如分析与综合。从事任何学科的研究都有采用分析与综合方法的需要和可能，这是个普遍适用的方法，但对于某一具体学科（如对比语言学）来说，并不具有方法论的意义。第三，方法论是"指导原则"，[1]因而具有宏观性。方法论必须是对学科的总体研究具有指导意义的原则，而不是在个别的、局部的问题上的具体研究方法，"解决某一特定问题采用的具体方式与做法"是"方法"。这三个特点对我们理解和研究方法论有重要的意义。我们研究方法论，先要学会区别什么是方法论，什么不是方法论而只是一般方法。这才能使我们对方法论的研究和运用更具有自觉性。下面我们就对比语言学的学科性质（本体论）来看，

1　丁氏的原文是"指导原则与规则"，但我们不知道他的"规则"指什么，他在举例中也没有提到，因此我们不取。我们认为，从宏观上来看，"规则"没有指导意义。

Ding's original text penned in "rules" in addition to "principles". But we are unsure what he meant by "rules" since no illustration was given. So we decided to lift out "rules", also because we do not think that macroscopically, "rules" offer any "guiding" role.

我们平常所经常谈到的一些概念，哪些是方法论？哪些只是方法？

The above quotations invoke considerations on three characteristics of methodology. To begin with, methodology is metaphysical or philosophical. In Philosophy, methodology takes bearing from ontology and formulates investigative guiding to bring about outcomes aligned to ontological direction. Different understandings in ontology give rise to different methodology. For instance, the key concept of Being and the problem of Existence have been the ontological preoccupation, or center of western philosophical research inquiry since the pre-Socratic. That said, history of western philosophy witnessed three big turns, of which the linguistic turn at he beginning of the 20th century was a major development. Each turn signifies a different ontological direction and therefore a shift in methodology. Secondly, methodology is used by "a specific discipline", put in other words, with pertinence. A number of methods may be applicable in every research project, but not all methods are of methodological significance. Universally applicable generic methods may not be of methodological value to certain disciplines. Synthesis and analysis, for instance, can and will be used in all kinds of research in any discipline, but cannot be said to be of methodological importance in a specific discipline, say, contrastive linguistics. Thirdly, since methodology benefits a discipline as "guiding principles", it must be macroscopic in nature and cannot refer to specific approaches applicable only to isolated cases or partial problems. As such, "specific ways or procedures to investigate and counter a given problem" are nothing but "methods". Our understanding and study of methodology shall take pointers from the above-mentioned characteristics. That would help in discerning what is and what is not "methodology" and keep our study on methodology sharp. In the following sections, common scientific methods frequently mentioned in contrastive studies are deliberated to distinguish methods from methodology.

5.2.1.1 不宜看作本学科方法论的方法

5.2.1.1 Methods which are not methodology in CL

5.2.1.1.1 分析与综合

5.2.1.1.1 Synthesis and analysis

上面已经指出，分析与综合是一般的方法，在任何学科的研究里，都既需要用分析方法，又需要用综合方法。只会分析不会综合，和只会综合不会分析，在当代社会里，都不是一个合格的研究人员。有人在进行中西文化和思维方式对比的时候，说，西方人长于分析，东方人长于综合；[1]西方人喜欢分析，不断地把事物一分为二、一分为二地分析下去，到头来只见树木，不见森林。而中国人喜欢综合，从整体上、系统上看问题，天人合一，所谓宇宙大舞台、人体小宇宙等等。这些作为思维方式的总体特征进行对比是可以的。但即使这些都是事实，也不能因此把分析或综合单独或共同用来当作对比研究的方法论。

Synthesis and analysis are general scientific methods applicable to all disciplines. In any kind of research one must have a good blend of both processes. No qualified research can be completed with the single use of synthesis or analysis alone. In contrasting Chinese and Western cultures and thinking modes, some suggest that westerners are more analytic while the Chinese are better at synthesis. Leaning towards data analysis, westerners prefer dividing things into smaller and smaller constituents, so much so that they may fail to "see the wood for the trees." On the other hand, the Chinese prefers inspection of the entirety or approaching from a systemic view, to the extent that sometimes, only a general picture and a vague impression were left. These are of course very interesting comparisons acceptable as a way to characterise thinking modes. Nonetheless, the truth to this recognizes neither analysis nor synthesis as a methodology in CL.

从语言学的角度看，有人认为西方形态性的语言因为对象的形式丰富，因而比较适合用分析的方法去研究；而语义型的语言因为对象是个混沌，因而适

---

1 见林语堂：1938:76。
e.g. Lin Yutang 1938: 76.

宜用综合的方法去研究。这个观点即使能成立，其实也只是语言对比过程中的具体的研究方法，并不具有学科方法论的性质。

It has also been suggested that in linguistic study, analytic method is most suited for rule-bound European languages; whereas synthetic method is more appropriate for semantic-based Chinese language devoid of formal properties. This viewpoint, even if it stands, is nothing more than specific "methods" employed for comparing language structures and does not serve methodological purposes.

5.2.1.1.2 宏观与微观
5.2.1.1.2 Macroscopic and microscopic studies

与上条有关，宏观与微观这一对方法也不宜看作对比研究的方法论。在第四章里，我们曾指出宏观与微观可以有三种理解：一、微观指句以下层面的研究，宏观指大于句的语言形式的研究，常用来指篇章研究与话语研究；二、微观指所谓的"内部语言学"，宏观指跟其相对的"外部语言学"，即结合文化、社会、心理因素的语言研究；三、宏观与微观均作为研究方法。前两种理解涉及到学科的研究范围和目标，因而在对比语言学里具有本体论的重要性。我们（2002a）在谈到新时期对比研究八大趋势之一"从微观走向宏观"时主要也是指这两个含义，所具体指明的两个变化（a. 语言层面的提升；b. 从结构走向思维）也清楚地表明了这一点。

Likewise, it is inappropriate to accord methodological importance to macroscopic and microscopic methods. In the previous chapter, we explained three ways of interpreting the terms "macroscopic" and "microscopic". For one, using sentence level as the divider, microscopic study covers those scopes below the sentence level, while macroscopic refers to those above, usually discourse or textual analysis. Next, with Saussure as the point of reference, what he called "internal linguistics" is microscopic, while "external linguistics" is macroscopic. (Saussure, 1916: 41) In this sense, macroscopic language study takes as its object of study the role of language in socio-political history, ethnology, psychology, geography etc. Last but not least, both macroscopic and microscopic are scientific methods of research. The first two interpretations are related to the scope and object of contrastive study and are hence of ontological significance. Pan (2003b) singled out eight developmental trends in contrastive study in the last decades, one of which was the shift "from microscopic to macroscopic" study in the context of the first two interpretations above. It was highlighted that this particular trend is marked by (a) the raising of linguistic units under study; and (b) the shift in emphasis from structural to thought pattern and psychology.

  作为研究方法，宏观和微观各有其特征。宏观是一种大处着眼，从总体、全局上着手的以大观小的研究；微观是一种着重局部细节，条分缕析，以小观大的研究。就英语和汉语的语序对比而言：

  As research methods, macroscopic and microscopic techniques are distinctively different. Macroscopic method is concerned with the gross, on the whole event by which the behaviour of constitutents may be interpreted against. On the contrary, microscopic method deals with the discrete elements or parts where projection to a higher plane may then be allowed. For instance, in contrasting English and Chinese word orders,

> 微观的对比是就一个个具体项目进行对比，找出其中的相似点和不似点，宏观的研究是从整体上对两种语言的语序进行考察，找出造成其差异的原因，并从语言特点上作出解释。微观对比是一种差异的研究，其目的是为了找出两种语言语序在表层上的不同表现，为教学和翻译的实践服务；宏观对比不仅是一种差异的研究，而且是一种本质的研究，目的是透过表层的差异来探索其在深层反映的本质，并以此来检验我们对两种语言各自特性的认识并使之更加深化。用一句通俗的话来说，微观对比是一种"知其然"的研究，而宏观对比是一种"知其所以然"的研究，两者可以互相补充，互相阐发。（潘文国，1997a/2002：226）

  Microscopic study is to contrast specific linguistic items, one after another, to find the similarities and differences of the two languages; whereas the macroscopic method is to contrast the word orders in the two languages in general, look for the causes behind the differences and try to explain them from the linguistic features of the two languages. Microscopic contrasting aims at finding the differences in word order of the two languages and their surface representations, so as to provide solutions to practical problems in teaching and translation. Macroscopic contrasting, on the other hand, goes beyond surface differences to search for differences at the deep structure of the languages so as to gain a better understanding of the nature of the language and languages. In other words, microscopic contrasting inquire into the whats, whereas macroscopic contrasting, the whys. The two can complement and explain each other. (Pan Wenguo, 1997a/2002: 226)

由于写作时的历史原因，[1]这里对宏观研究的长处讲得多了一点。其实两者各有短长。宏观难在不易做得细大不捐，容易忽视细节；微观难在视野狭窄，不能做到小中见大。比较理想的是两者能够兼顾，我们觉得每一个对比研究者都不妨试试两种研究法，当然不排除一个人在某个时期以某种研究方法为主。但不管怎样，微观和宏观的研究方法都具有一般性，不论是哪一种，都不宜看作是对比语言学的方法论原则。

Compelled by realities at the time of writing, the author had given more weight to macroscopic study. In fact, both ways have their strengths and weaknesses. Macroscopic study falls short in being difficult to go into great detail and thus lose tracks of many specific facts; whereas microscopic study is disadvantaged by a narrower-perspective and often ended up in splitting hairs. Ideally, marrying the two would possibly yield the best result. It is our hope that contrastivist should seek out both ways, though the preference towards one may be more obvious at certain window period. That said, both macroscopic and microscopic study are general in nature, and none should be regarded as a principle of methodology in contrastive study.

5.2.1.1.3 定量与定性
5.2.1.1.3 Qualitative and quantitative analyses

近些年来，随着语料库语言学的发展和统计分析方法的不断完善，定量研究越来越受到重视。其实这一趋势不自今日始，早就有人指出，由定性向定量

1　当时从事宏观对比的人不多，作者觉得需要大声疾呼，以引起人们的重视。
There were far more people doing microscopic than macroscopic study in the said period so much so that the author thought it necessary to stress more on the latter way of research.

发展是二十世纪科学研究的重要特点之一，只不过近来由于计算机手段的便利，呼声更高而已。

Recent development in corpus linguistics and advancement in statistical analysis saw quantitative approach attracting more and more attention. As a matter of fact, this is by no means a "new" movement. As early as several decades ago, there were already arguments for quantitative approach as a critical development in scientific research in the twentieth century. And the growth and deployment of composite computational tools and treatments add strength to quantitative measures.

但是我们仍然认为，不宜将定量或定性研究作为对比语言学的方法论原则。理由同样是因为，这是各门学科所普遍适用的两种研究方法，不具有对于对比语言学学科的独特的针对性，也并不影响对比语言学的学科性。

Albeit the swing in the direction, neither qualitative nor quantitative analysis should be regarded as broad methodological approaches in contrastive linguistics. The reasoning runs along the same vein: they are universal research methods and may be applied across disciplines, not specifically to contrastive linguistics. The adoption of either of the two methods has no direct influence on the nature of the discipline.

近年来对定量分析法比较关注并作出重要成绩的学者有克尔采斯佐斯基（1990）、许余龙（2001；2002）等。从他们的论著中可以看出，定量与定性都是一般性的研究方法，各门学科都可以用，即使在语言学中也适用于多种学科和不同目标的研究：

By way of quantitative methods, two scholars in the discipline have in recent years achieved remarkable results. They are Krzeszowski (1990) of Poland and Xu Yulong (2001, 2002) of China. Their research proves that both qualitative and quantitative analyses are general methods applicable to all disciplines. Even in linguistic study, they can be used in many branches for different purposes, remarked Xu Yulong:

> 语言研究中的历史研究和人种学研究大致可归入……理论阐释研究，而实验研究、准实验研究和调查研究大致可归入实证研究。理论阐释研究含有较多定性成分，而实证研究含有较多定量研究成分。
> （许余龙，2001/2004：68）

In linguistic study, historical and ethnological research may generally be included in theoretical interpretation, while experimental, quasi-experimental and investigation approaches may be included in experimental study. Theoretical interpretation is more qualitative in nature whereas experimental study is more quantitative in nature. (Xu Yulong, 2001/2004: 68)

看来定量与定性跟上面的微观与宏观有一定程度上的重叠之处：微观研究可以更多地采用定量方法，而宏观研究可以更多地采用定性方法。也与宏观与微观一样，定性与定量也各有短长。有的问题是定量研究解决不了的，例如世界上的形态型语言有成千上百种，非形态语言即使只有汉语一种，也不能因此而否定汉语的类型学意义。但定量研究可使得出的结论更具说服力，是定性研究的有力补充。作为对比学者，我们有必要学会使用多种跨学科的方法来为我所用，而不又被方法所牵制。

In a way, qualitative and quantitative techniques are rather closely knitted with macroscopic and microscopic methods. More often than not, microscopic analysis tends go with quantitative method whereas macroscopic analysis, qualitative method. But as with any other methods, both qualitative and quantitative analyses have their merits and demerits. Certain problems are not suited for quantitative study. For instance, thousands of languages featured morphological inflections except for a handful, such as Chinese. Yet in no way would this very piece of statistics deny the Chinese language of its place in linguistic typology. However, in most other cases, quantitative study speaks convincingly with figures and proofs to be a good and necessary complement to qualitative analysis. Contrastivists ought to be able to use various kinds of cross-disciplinary methods while at the same time not confined to certain methods.

定量方法有调查法、统计法、语料库方法等。定性方法人们常用的有形式逻辑的三段论法，以及实证法，即用经验性事例来证明某一理论的正确或不正确。其实还有一个重要的甚至更有效的定性研究方法值得推荐，这就是德国哲学家波普尔（Karl Popper，1982）提出的证伪法（falsification），切斯特曼以之作为他的对比研究方法论的基础（Chesterman，1998：53—54）。钱冠连（2005：246—253）也运用这个方法从理论上证明了萨丕尔-沃尔夫假设。

Quantitative methods involve survey investigation, statistics, corpus and other measurements while qualitative methods employ syllogism in formal logic, deduction, analogy, positivism, etc. To this list, we may add one important and effective method: falsification test by way of hypothetico-deductive method advocated by the German philosopher Karl Popper (1982). It is by way of falsification that Chesterman (1998: 53—54) built his contrastive methodology; and Qian Guanlian (2005: 246—253) established the logical sufficiency of the Whorf-Sapir hypothesis theoretically.

5.2.1.1.4 描写与解释
5.2.1.1.4 Description and explanation

　　描写与解释也不是我们的方法论原则，这话恐怕有点骇人听闻，特别是对那些惯于高唱"解释"是语言学研究最高阶段的人来说更是如此。但是我们只要冷静下来想一想就会发现，描写与解释同样是许多学科包括语言学各门学科都运用的方法，具有一般性方法论的意义。没有一门实证性学科不需要对客观事实进行描写，也没有一门学科不需要对描写出来的事实进行分析和解释。即使我们看作伪科学的那些"学问"例如看相算命，也有它们的描写和解释，例如它们需要收集大量的人的面相和手相的资料，并与有关人们的祸福遭际联系起来，分门别类进行保存和强记，这就是"描写"；到后来再给别人看相时，按照以前收集的资料一一对号入座，这就是"解释"。"描写"与"解释"之成为语言学的专门术语，成为某家某派的特色，这完全是历史造成的偶然。始作俑者是美国的结构主义者。本来，"描写"一词原是欧洲语言学家使用的，如英国的斯威特（Henry Sweet）及丹麦的叶斯柏森等，他们针对传统学校语法的规定性（prescriptive），而把他们自己注重语言实际使用情况的研究叫做"描写性"（descriptive）。但曾几何时，美国的结构主义者把这个词接过去，用来专门指他们调查记录印第安人语言的工作，并自称为"描写主义者"（descriptivist），同时把"描写"的精神发挥到极致，例如霍凯特就公然宣布"语言学是分类的科学"（Hocket，1942：97），分类是其最终目标；裘斯则认为"解释不是语言学的任务"（Joos，1950：349）。这就在历史上第一次出现了一个把"描写"和"解释"分开，并且只致力于"描写"的语言学流派。"描写"也就成了他们最重要的方法论原则。1957年的"乔姆斯基革命"反对结构主义，其中一个内容就是反对他们的光"描写"不"解释"。但同时这个学派却走到了另一个极端,就是只"解释"不"描写"。乔姆斯基曾经公开表示语言研究的田野工作没有用,他将这种田野调查(描写语言学家视为性命的"描写"工作)比作采集标本,说:

Disqualifying both description and explanation as methodology in CL study may be surprising, especially to those who believe in the dogmatic status of "explanation" in linguistic research. Upon careful examination, that these two methods are of a universal nature applicable to many different disciplines or sub-disciplines must be admitted. No positive research can be carried out in a discipline, without adequate description of objective facts, and no research can be done without providing adequate analysis and explanation to the facts collected and described. Even those pseudo-scientific enterprises such as fortune-telling or physiognomy need their "description" and "explanation" as well. A large databases of people's faces, palm line, etc., connect them with the happenings and events in people's lives, and these materials are subsequently classified in their minds. That is as good as a "description". And when they later start to tell fortunes for other people, relevant information will be retrieved them from memory, and necessary connections will be made for the present purpose. That is similar to "explanation". It is only by chance or by purpose that "description" and "explanation" become specific linguistic terms or even the characteristics of certain linguistic schools. And it all began with the American structuralism. Initially, "description" was a common term used by European linguists such as Henry Sweet or Otto Jespersen. Criticising the traditional grammar school as being "prescriptive", they named their way of acknowledging the objective reality of language use or actual language usage as "descriptive". The American structuralists conveniently borrowed the term to refer to their work of transcribing the American Indian languages. The Americans called themselves, rather exclusively, as "descriptivist", bringing into full play "descriptivism". For instance, Charles Hocket announced that "linguistics is a classificatory science" and that classification was the final aim of linguistic study (Hocket, 1942: 97). Martin Joos rejected explanation, saying, "We try to describe precisely; we do not try to explain" (Joos, 1950: 349). A particular school of thought thus appeared in the history of linguistics, clearly demarcating description from explanation and engaging only in the former. Description henceforth became the first principle of methodology in descriptive research. In 1957, The Chomskian revolution was launched chiefly against American structuralism. Part of their criticism was that the structuralists were doing taxonomy without explanation. But the Chomskian school pushed to another extreme to emphasise explanation at the expense of description. Chomsky openly dismissed "field work" as useless, "...it is obvious that the set of grammatical sentences cannot not be identified with any particular corpus of utterances obtained by the linguist in his field work" (Chomsky, 1957: 15). And he compared such "field work" to "collecting samples", saying,

> 你可以去采集蝴蝶标本，写下许多观察记录。你要是喜欢如此，那也无伤大雅。但这种工作不宜与研究工作混为一谈，研究工作关心的是发现解释性原理，而且要有一定深度，否则要失败的。（乔姆斯基，1977: 57）[1]
>
> You can also collect butterflies and make many observations. If you like butterflies, that's fine; but such work must not be confounded with research, which is concerned to discover explanatory principles of some depth and fails if it does not do so. (Chomsky, 1977: 57)

这一派后来的一些追随者更是无比夸大"解释"的意义，把上述的这些历史事实串起来，提出了一个语言研究发展三阶段论，第一个阶段是"规定性"，第二个阶段是"描写性"，第三个也是最高阶段的就是他们的"解释性"。这种自我抬高的神话经过一些人的推波助澜似乎真成了语言研究的什么规律，结果研究语言的人要是不讲自己在从事"解释"性的工作，仿佛就意味着落伍或者处在初级阶段似的。

Followers of the school went even further to strengthen the importance of "explanation". They connected the historical facts we mentioned above and suggested "three stages in linguistic evolution": "prescription" being the first stage, "description" the second and "explanation" the third and most advanced stage. So much for self-praise, the mythical three-stage theory turned into a linguistic law for some. Under the pressure, even the non-Chomskians had to proclaim they were doing "explanation" in order to get a place for their work as current and advanced.

---

[1] 译文见许国璋（1997: 63）。
Chinese translation see Xu Guozhang (1997: 63).

从这段历史可以看出两点：

Two conclusions may then be derived:

第一，"描写"和"解释"对于某一学派来说，确实具有方法论的意义。例如"描写"是美国结构主义语言学的基本方法论原则，"解释"是转换生成语言学派的基本方法论原则。但对于别的语言学研究者来说，如果他们不想使自己归入这两家中的任一派的话，就没有必要把"描写"或"解释"视作自己的方法论原则。对比语言学在拉多时代曾以结构主义为其理论支柱，在迪·皮德娄时代又曾以转换生成语言学为其理论支柱，因此有关研究者提及这两个关键术语是可以理解的。但对比语言学发展到现在，如果我们同意对比语言学是门独立的语言学学科，不需要依附其他学派的理论才能生存的话，我们自然也就理所当然地要否定"描写"或"解释"对本学科的方法论意义。

First, to specific schools of linguistics, "description" and "explanation" are of methodological significance, categorically. Essentially, "description" is the principal methodology for American structuralism and "explanation", the principal methodology for transformational and generative grammar. However, the case differs for other research disciplines. For research study adopting other approaches, there are no compelling reason to regard either description or explanation as the methodology. In the history of contrastive linguistics, Lado and his contemporaries based their research on structuralism, whereas Di Pietro and others based their study on transformational grammar. It is therefore understandable that both these terms are referred. But at a time when contrastive linguistics is to be understood as an independent discipline not subordinative to some linguistic schools of thought, description or explanation cannot be accepted as of methodological significance.

第二，"描写"和"解释"本来是不可分开的两种研究方法，我们不能只管描写不管解释，也不能只管解释不管描写，像上述两个学派那样各自偏执一方的做法是不可取的。我们不赞成将"描写"或"解释"作为对比语言学的方法论原则，但我们仍然承认"描写"和"解释"作为语言学研究方法本身的价值。在对比研究中，我们提倡的是"描写"和"解释"并重的方法。

Secondly, "description" and "explanation" are two inseparable techniques that should not be carried out separately as the two above-mentioned schools did. We cannot merely undertake description without explanation, nor explanation without description. While "description" and "explanation" do not carry methodologically significance for contrastive linguistics, they are indispensable in linguistic study and ought to receive equal attention.

此外,我们还要知道有两种"描写"和两种"解释",在运用这对方法时我们还要坚持其中一种而防止另外一种。

It must be further noted that there are two types of "description" and two types of "explanation" in linguistic research. In applying these pairs of techniques, we must be mindful enough to choose one over the other.

两种描写:一种是对客观事实的描写;一种是有主观框框的描写。所谓描写,就是要为语言研究收集足够多的实际使用的语料。结构主义在这些方面是颇有所长的,他们重视调查,重视收集第一手材料。但在结构主义遭到否定之后,继起的语言学理论就在倒洗澡水的时候将孩子一起倒掉了。一些人不想像结构主义者那样辛辛苦苦地收集材料,那么在需要语料的时候怎么办呢?有人就提出了一种"内省法",相信自己作为母语者的语言"本能",于是就随意自造例子,冒充调查来的语料。但是为适应某种理论而造出来的句子未必是真实使用的,于是又有人提出了一种说法:只要你把这句话连读十遍,那么原来似乎不通的话听起来也会"通"了。在对比研究中也会遇到类似的状况,即在对比一种语言现象时,正好缺少某种语料,于是有人就会将第一种语言的例子生硬地译成第二种语言,以此来造成对比的等价物。我们要坚持前一种"描写",防止和反对后一种伪"描写"。

The two types of description are description of objective facts and description of subjective facts. Description, as the name implies, requires a bulk collection of real-life linguistic data. The structuralists are all experts in field study and collection of first hand data. But at the same time as structuralism was repudiated, that tradition of description was also abandoned. Collection of linguistic data can be tedious and the spirit of our structuralist predecessors is therefore not followed by many. When examples are needed for illustration, a so-called "introspection" method was used to make sentences out of their own "mother tongue instinct". Very often sentences created this way do not sound natural, so the joke was that if one were to read those sentences aloud ten times in succession, what deemed to be "unnatural" sentence begin to sound "natural". Similar practice is also found in language comparison. When certain data is missing for attestation during comparison, some will simply do a word-for-word translation so as to make up an equivalent for comparison. These, of course, are far from genuine "description". Linguistic description must therefore stand on objective data unless we are prepared to accept pseudo description.

两种解释：一种是描写基础上的解释；一种是从原则到原则的解释。前一种情况如中国学者邵敬敏所说：

The two types of explanation refer to one based on description, and the other revolved around some guiding principles. On the former, Shao Jingmin said:

> "解释"的前提和基础是"描写"，没有客观的科学的描写，任何解释都是毫无意义的；但是，只有描写，没有进一步的解释，则我们的认识不可能深化，不可能上升到理论的高度。显然，这两者是相辅相成，缺一不可的。（邵敬敏，1996）
>
> The prerequisite and foundation of linguistic explanation is description. Without a scientific and objective description, no meaningful explanation can be expected. On the other hand, description without accompanied explanation fails in deepening our understanding, and uncertainly unhelpful in raising our understanding to a higher, theoretical level. Obviously, the methods complement each other and cannot exist without the other. (Shao Jingmin, 1996)

后一种"解释"则是某一派学者的做法。因为他们否定了以"描写"作为"解释"的基础，因而就只能从"普遍"的原则出发，在各种语言里边寻找例子，通过"解释"，证明了原先说的"原则"确实是"普遍"的原则。一个手边的例子便是所谓"在没有WH-移动的语言里移动WH-"的观点（参见伍雅清，2000/2004：32）。对这个结论本身我们不予置评，但从其方法本身来看，我们却觉得有循环论证或"乞贷论证"之嫌。这显然不是一种科学的研究方法，是不应提倡的。

The latter in fact is the practice of a certain linguistics school. Having defied description as the basis for explanation, and starting from some supposedly "universal" principles, this school would look for appropriate examples in other languages, and through "explanation" fit them into the "universal" principle and in so doing, arrive at the conclusion that the principle is indeed "universal". An example can be found in a paper attempting to "move WH- in a language without WH- movement" (cf. Wu, 2000/2004: 32). We reserve our comments on the findings, but we may contest the method used because it seems somewhat circular and that should be discouraged.

5.2.1.1.5 翻译法
5.2.1.1.5 Translation method

翻译法是对比研究中广泛使用的方法，也是一种非常重要的方法。吕叔湘先生就很主张使用翻译法，他在1942年说的一段话就是这一主张的明确表达：

Translation method is widely used in language comparison. In China, this method appears to have the endorsement of Lü Shuxiang. Lü (1942) so expressed:

> 文言里一句话，白话里怎么说白话里一句话，文言里怎么说，这又是一种比较。一句中国话，翻成英语怎么说；一句英语，中国话里如何表达，这又是一种比较。（吕叔湘，1942：前言）

> How do we put a literary Chinese expression (*wenyan*) colloquially and conversely, a colloquial expression (*baihua*) into literary Chinese? How can we render a Chinese utterance into English, or express an English utterance in Chinese? All these are but some sort of comparison. (Lü Shuxiang, 1942: Preface)

1977年《通过对比研究语法》一文中的实例，更是翻译法的具体应用。但尽管如此，我们仍觉得不宜将翻译法作为对比研究的一种方法论来提倡。理由是：

And what he provided as examples in his 1977 talk demonstrated the application of this method. While it can be a useful method, it is overstretched to attach methodological importance to the translation method in contrastive study. The reasons are:

第一，还有不少人反对使用翻译法。如王力就是很坚决的一个，他（1944—1945/1984：5）曾断然说过，"一切的对译都是不能帮助词性或用途的确定的"。戴浩一是另外一个，他说：

1. This method is met with strong opposition from amongst contrastivists. Wang Li clearly stood firm on his opposition. He said categorically that "No equivalent translations can help to decide neither parts of speech nor functions" (Wang Li, 1944–1945/1984: 5). James H-Y Tai also voiced his doubts. He said,

> 用翻译作为一种启发，没有什么不对。要不得的是研究汉语语法的人，包括当前的管约派在内，只是把英语的结构架在被看成英译的汉语句子上面。难怪结果是汉语呈现出与英语基本相同的特点。（戴浩一，1987：191）
>
> There's no problem using translation as something referential. What is problematic is that some Chinese grammarians, GB scholars included, just place the English structure over the Chinese sentences as if they were translated from English. No wonder Chinese grammar appears fundamentally the same as the English Grammar. (James H-Y Tai, 1981: 191)

翻译法诚然是使用得很广泛的一种方法，但如使用不当，很容易产生戴浩一等所担心的误导作用。克尔采斯佐斯基曾明确主张在对比中采用直译得到的语料：

Popular as the translation method is, its improper use may be misleading, as Tai noted. On the contrary, Krzeszowski argued for the use of grammatical word-for-word translations in contrastive study:

> 如果存在着语法上逐字翻译和意义上逐字阐释的最接近材料，那么这就是对比研究最主要的资料。（克尔采斯基，1990：19）
>
> A contrastive grammar will take as its primary data the closest approximations to grammatical word-for-word translations and their synonymous paraphrases, if such forms exist. (Krzeszowski, 1990: 19)

最方便但是也是最容易出问题的方法，作为方法论原则是不妥的。

As a most convenient yet most problematic approach, it is certainly inappropriate for the translation method to be accepted as a methodology principle.

第二，翻译又是最复杂的。一句话翻译成另外一种语言，常常有不止一种的译法。撇开翻译界说的直译、意译、死译、胡译等不说，我们在上一章也曾提到过三种翻译：教学翻译、实用翻译和文化翻译，分别适用于结构层、交际层和认知层的对比研究。这里我们举一个英语例子及其三种汉译法来说明这个问题：

2. Translation is complex. There exist many ways to translate a sentence into another language. In the previous chapter, we mentioned three kinds of translation:

pedagogical translation, practical translation and cultural translation, to be applied respectively in contrastive studies at structural, communicational and cognitional levels. Below is one English sentence with three translations in Chinese to illustrate the point.

【原　文】The man must be killed.
【译文一】这个人必须被杀。
【译文二】这家伙该杀。
【译文三】非杀了这厮不可。

[original] The man must be killed.
[tr. 1] 这个人必须被杀。
[tr. 2] 这家伙该杀。
[tr. 3] 非杀了这厮不可。

第一种翻译完全符合上述克氏的标准，但这种译法只能用于第一层面的对比（即使如此也会有不同意见，因为有人会说这句话中国人实际上是不说的。但按照某些人"不通的句子读它十遍就好像通了"的逻辑，这句话也并非完全不能接受，至少在"现代汉语语法"里它是正确的），用于第二、第三层面就有问题。为什么用在第一层面可以？因为教学语法、教学翻译以帮助学生理解掌握外语的基本结构为目标，是只讲实用不讲理性的（即是所谓的"规定性"的），某些半通不通的直译式句子在这里是可以容许存在的。而第二、第三层面要求人们真实使用的语料，它就用不上了。

Translation 1 fully achieves the standard as suggested by Krzeszowski. But such word-for-word translation can only be used at the structural level. Even then, different opinions may arise, for people would say that native speakers would never use such representation. Of course, after reading the sentence aloud ten times in succession, what sounds unnatural becomes natural—the sentence is not entirely unacceptable, at least it is "correct" in modern Chinese grammar. Nevertheless, this translation cannot be used at the practical and cultural levels. Why? Because the aim of both pedagogical grammar and pedagogical translation is to help a learner master the basic structure of a foreign language. For this purpose, the translation method is practical rather than rational. Certain unnatural or awkward sentences resulting from word-for-word translation can be allowed at this stage. When it goes to the second and third stages where communicable real-life language is required, such sentences are of course out of place.

　　第二种翻译以在译文语言中真实、通顺、适用、得体为目标。如果说在上一种翻译里，因为要紧贴原文的句式、词义（常常是词典上的），译文常常是惟一性的，这一种翻译的开放度很大，译法可以五花八门（包括第三种译文），而都可以接受。关键是哪一种最适合特定的上下文。

　　Translation 2 aims at making a sentence sound more natural, fluent, and appropriate and to the point in the target language. Its meaning is relatively open ended as compared to the first one which is rather exclusive for the purpose of exact equivalence in both syntax and most often then not, dictionary meaning. The choice is between those that are closely suited to the context.

　　第三种翻译强调译文语言的"地道"性。我们指的不是"这厮"，因为它完全可换成"这家伙"、"这人"、"这匹夫"等，以适用于不同的语境；我们指的是"非……不可"这个句式，这是汉语中道道地地而在英语中绝对不可能有的句式。这在英汉语的"语言文化"的比较上就用得上了。

　　Translation 3 lays emphasis on the idiomatic character of the translated sentence. We do not mean vocabulary of local-flavour such as "这厮" (this chap), for it can be replaced by other vocabulary like "这家伙" (this fellow), "这人" (this guy), "这匹夫" (this chip), etc. We mean, rather, the construction "非……不可" which is unique to the Chinese language in comparison with the English language. And that will lead us to the contrast of "language culture".

　　把翻译分成这么三种，分别对应于三个层面的比较，在我们看来当然是颇为得意的。但首先，未必人人同意这种分法；其次，未必每句话每个词都正好有这三种译法；再次，对译出来的句子的归类每个人也未必相同。因此，在对"三种翻译论"取得共识之前，将翻译作为对比的方法论原则尚为时过早。

　　Surely we can flatter ourselves for classifying translations on three planes to serve the different purposes of contrastive study, but we are mindful that not everyone agrees with this classification; and not every word or every sentence can be translated in all three ways; and finally, not everyone will agree to group translations in the same way. So, unless a general consensus on this theory of "three-translations" can be reached, it may be too early to talk about translation as a principle of methodology in contrastive study.

　　最后，第三，翻译毕竟只是一种具体的方法，而"方法论"讲的是"原则",更具有抽象的意义。

3. Translation is, after all, a concrete method, whereas methodology deals with principles which are more abstract in nature.

不同意翻译作为方法论,不等于说我们不赞同在对比中使用翻译方法。相反,我们还是主张在对比中要大量使用翻译的方法。

To exclude translation in contrastive methodology does not mean that it is not regarded as a useful tool in contrastive study. In fact, we like to suggest using this method on a larger scale particularly on the cultural plane when contrasting heterogeneous language pair for it is in there that vivid nuances on similarities and differences are highlighted.

5.2.1.1.6 研究模式
5.2.1.1.6 Research models

在菲齐亚克的"理论对比语言学"里,他非常重视对比研究模式的研究。在一定程度上,我们觉得他恐怕误把对比研究模式当作对比研究的方法论了。其实这还是两回事。"对比模式"所研究的还是具体的方法,而不是研究的指导原则。只不过它不是孤立地对方法进行一个一个的研究,而是成系列、成套地研究。对于某一位具体的研究者来,"模式"常有一以贯之的整体性、全面性,对建立某位学者自身的学术体系有重要的作用。我们往往可以从某位学者的研究模式中看到这位学者研究的"个性"。由于研究模式里的方法是成系列、成套的,我们可以称之为"方法集"。"方法集"比"方法"要高一个层次,但"方法集"还是"方法",不是"方法论"。

In Fisiak's "theoretical contrastive linguistics", the attention paid to contrastive models has to a certain extent confused contrastive models with research methodology, which is certainly fallacious. "Contrastive models" deals with concrete methods but not guiding research principles. Instead of treating and examining generic methods in isolation, models consider them as a structured whole and a problem solution may be interpreted with a sequence of activities aimed at development of results. Individual researchers almost often keep to a desired model and allow it to play a pivotal role in establishing one's own academic research character. Methods comprising a model may form into integrated or synchronous modules and may be called "set of methods". However, "set of methods" are still methods, not methodology.

在对比研究史上,我们看到了四种对比研究模式:

Over the course of development, four models for contrastive study have been proposed.

第一种是拉氏模式,可称为"一贯模式"。这是拉多创造的。在他的《跨文化语言学》一书里,他对比了语音、语法、词汇、文字、文化五个方面,但每一种对比,他都坚持采用同一种方式,即从形式、意义以及形式和意义的分布三个方面进行对比,尽管有的做得较好,有的不尽如人意(参看本书第一章的分析)。这就形成了一种模式,也就是拉多进行对比研究的独特思路。否则,要是光就语音、语法等方面进行比较,那几乎人皆如此,就没有自己的风格了。拉氏模式可图示如下:

The first one is Lado's Model or "consistent model". In *Linguistics across Culture*, Lado sets out five aspects of contrastive study: phonetics, grammatical structures, vocabulary, writing systems and culture. He persists in applying the same method throughout all five aspects by comparing the form, meaning, and the distribution of form and meaning. Better results may be seen in some aspects than others (refer to Chapter 1). The consistency becomes a hallmark of Lado's contrastive study and sets him apart from common practice of examining the languages and syntax concerned. Lado's Model can be illustrated as follows:

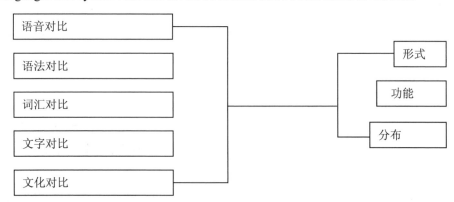

图5.1 拉多模式

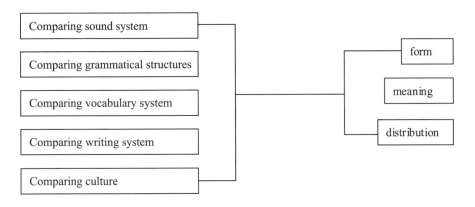

Figure 5.1 Lado's model

第二种是恩氏模式，可称为"递进模式"。这是语篇对比学家恩克维斯特创造的。恩氏是篇章对比研究的专家，经十余年研究，于1984年发表《对比语言学与篇章语言学》一文，提出了他的篇章对比思路。他把篇章对比分成四步：（1）基于句子的篇章研究；（2）基于述说的篇章研究；（3）认知篇章研究；（4）互动篇章研究。但这四种研究又不是各自孤立的，而是一环扣一环、一环深于一环，一步解决不了，就很难到下一步。每步都有各自的对比策略，就这样建成了一个内部联系紧密的研究体系。恩氏把他的四种研究都叫做"模式"，但我们觉得，只有把它们合起来看，才更能体现恩氏的研究模式和他所建立的独特研究体系。恩氏的模式可图示如下：

The second model, by textual linguist Enkvist, may be called a "progressive model". Enkvist's *Contrastive Linguistics and Text Linguistics* (1984) proposes a way of contrasting texts in four modules: (1) sentence-based text module; (2) predication-based text module; (3) cognitive text module; and (4) interactional text module. The four interwoven modules form a continuum to take on issues unresolved at the previous module and go on to solve further problems. While each module deploys a different strategy, when put together, the four forms an organic, self-contained research system. Enkvist actually sees each module as a separate 'model', but in our opinion, only when the four 'models' function as one can the general system and peculiarity of Envist's research be more vividly understood. Enkvist's model can be illustrated as follows:

图5.2 恩氏模式

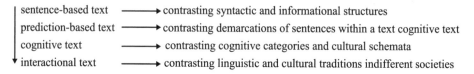

Figure 5.2 Enkvist's model

第三种是克氏模式，可称为"综合模式"。这是克尔采斯佐斯基创造的。克氏是专门研究"对比中立项"的，为此进行了长达十余年的研究。最后他将所有他见到的和所能考虑到的"对比中立项"兼收并蓄，全部纳入了一个庞大的体系。由于内容繁多，需要进行整理，因而他想出了一个以"对比中立项"为横轴，以句法语义的从抽象到具体为纵轴，纵横交错而成的一个庞大的体系。克氏的不足在于过于贪多求全，因而造成一些内部混乱和自相矛盾之处。撇开这不谈，他对"对比中立项"的这种穷尽性讨论的努力却使他在这个问题上成了后人绕不过去的一道风景。以后切斯特曼（1998）、许余龙（1992/2002）等对这个问题的批评和发展都是在他的基础上进行的。

The third, by Krzeszowski, is entitled "synthetic model". Krzeszowski studied *tertium comparationis* for over a decade and finally organized all the "*tertia comparationis*" found or under consideration into a large system. The entire model is upheld by *tertium comparationis* at the horizontal axis and semanto-syntactic equivalence at the vertical axis and is so exhaustive that anyone on the subject of "semanto-syntactic equivalence" cannot do it without referencing the synthetic model notwithstanding the fact that the massive system plays itself out somewhat being confusing and contradictory in certain respects. The discussions of *tertium comparationis* by Chesterman (1998) and Xu Yulong (1992/2002) are exactly based on this model.

第四种是切氏模式，暂且称之为"立体模式"。这是切斯特曼创造的。第一章曾介绍说切氏建立了一个迄今为止最为庞大的对比研究体系，这是有根据的。根据就是我们曾将他的体系归纳成一个表格形式，结果居然要占4页的篇幅。由于太长无法全部转引，我们只将最主要的内容列成下表：

The fourth model came from Chesterman and may be called a "cubic model" for lack of better term. In the opening chapter of the present book, Chesterman's system for contrastive linguistics was hailed as the largest ever: To include all the items he has discussed into a table would extend the table to four pages! Here, we attempt to sum up the main contents as follows:

表5.1 切氏模式

句法语义结构		篇章语义结构		话语语义结构	
陈述	陈述类型	信息	篇章类型	交流	交流类型
	角色		事件		话段
特指		特指		特指	
复杂化					
评论		诉求		地位关系	
句间连接		篇间连贯		话语控制	

Table 5.1 Chesterman's model

Semantic Structure		Macrostructure		Interstructure	
Predication	Predicate	Message	Text	Exchange	Exchange
	Actant		Episodes		Move
Specifiers		Specifiers		Specifiers	
Complicators					
Commentators		Appeals		Status Relations	
Conjunctors		Coherence		Controls	

从表中可以看出，他的模式既具有拉氏模式"一贯性"的特点，每个纵栏都分成四个组成部分，彼此对应（分别指向基本单位、概念意义、语用意义和语篇意义）；又具有恩氏模式"递进性"的特点，随着由句法语义结构向篇章语义结构和话语语义结构发展深入，四个组成部分也相应变化，有的还采用了

不同名称；还具有克氏模式"综合性"的特点，纵横合成一个矩阵。而且其内部比较一致，不像克氏那样凌乱。

It is noteworthy that Chesterman's model encompassed the hallmark features of all three other models. It is as "consistent" as Lado's for each column is divided into four main components (semantics, specifiers, pragmatics, textual) and items in each column correspond with each other. It is as "progressive" as Ekvist's in that it evolves from semantic structure, macrostructure to interstructure with relevant adjustments made to components of each column. Being as "synthetic" as Krzeszowski's and yet devoid of its shortcoming, Chesterman's model can also be represented in the matrix form.

这四种模式，有的用于实践，如拉氏模式；有的用于理论，如克氏模式；有的兼有两者，如恩氏和切氏模式。从理论上来说，四种模式都可用于各个层次的对比研究。

Of the four models, Lado's is applicable in practice while Krzeszowski's is for theoretical study. Ekvist's and Chesterman's cover both ends. And all are suitable, at least in theory, for all levels of contrastive study.

国内的学者，似还没有认真考虑过研究模式的问题。因而各人研究的独特风格、独特体系还不明显。本书上一章关于对比语言学的学科定位，也许可说是克氏模式的一个尝试。

Across the hemisphere, research modeling is less well received. Few Chinese scholars have yet to consider building research models. It is probably for this reason that Chinese research in the discipline has yet to stand out in style and approach. With this in mind, the present work presented a map giving contrastive linguistics its place as an independent discipline in the last chapter and that is a closest shot to establish a system along the line of Krzeszowski's model.

但显然，研究模式的建立有助于个人研究风格的建立，对于任何学科都是适用的。因而我们要鼓励对比研究者在研究中探索自己的模式，但却不能将这种模式研究看成是对比研究的方法论原则。

It is quite obvious that research models have the benefit of strengthening the discipline. Models are much like scaffolding marking out the boundaries so that guiding principles provided by methodology may maneuver in the specific direction with ease.

5.2.1.2 可看作本学科方法论的方法
5.2.1.2 Methodology in CL

那么，什么是本学科的方法论呢？在排除了一般化的方法之后，我们认为下面这些方法对于对比语言学来说，具有学科方法论的意义。也就是说，这是些对比研究者无法回避，在对比过程中必须考虑，而且如果有一个以上选择项的话，必须有所选择的方法。否则对比研究就无法顺利进行乃至根本无法进行。

Which methods in CL are of methodological importance? We shall discuss them below. By regarding them as methodology in CL, these methods are deemed to be necessary and must be taken into consideration in the process and, where there are several parameters, a decision must be made to approach one.

我们把这些方法分为两组，一组兼有本体论又有方法论的意义。另一组主要具有方法论意义。在这一节里先略作叙述。重要的我们在后面再作专题讨论。

Such methods fall into two groups. One has both methodological and ontological importance, and the other has methodological importance. The present section shall give an overview of these methods and important issues will be taken up in later sections.

5.2.1.2.1 兼具本体论与方法论意义的方法
5.2.1.2.1 Methods of both ontological and methodological importance

这一组方法都是既具有本体论意义，又具有方法论意义的。所谓本体论意义，是指它们在一定程度上参与确定对比语言学的学科性质；所谓方法论，是说它们在研究过程中具有实际可操作性，是建立研究模式、设计研究程序的依据。对比与比较、求异与求同、共时与历时这三种就属于这样的方法。

Methods discussed in this section are of both ontological and methodological importance. By ontological importance we mean that to a certain extent they aid in shaping the nature of contrastive linguistics as a discipline; by methodological importance we mean that they are functional in practice, and form the bases for establishing research models and designing research procedures. These methods include contrast as oppose to compare, similarity within difference, and synchronic within diachronic.

5.2.1.2.1.1 对比与比较
5.2.1.2.1.1 Contrast *vs.* compare

　　对比与比较的问题我们在上一章已经论述过。对比语言学之所以叫做对比语言学而不叫比较语言学是由"对比"这一术语的学科性所确定的。有的人不喜欢"对比"这个字眼而爱用"比较"这个字眼，这当然是他们的自由。但是经过半个多世纪的发展，"对比语言学"与"比较语言学"各自的学科畛域已经明确，在学术界也已得到了比较广泛的认可，在这种情况下就最好不要以一己之愿而滥用术语。如果你愿意的话，尽可把自己的研究称作"比较语言学"而建立与"对比语言学"不同的学科体系（当然这个时候又得认真区分这个新的"比较语言学"与语言学史上的"比较语言学"或"历史比较语言学"，不要造成新的混淆）。孔子主张的"正名"在学术研究中也有其积极意义，那就是在学术讨论中论辩的双方要确定是在一个共同的基础上，例如在讨论对比语言学的时候，要确定讨论的对象是对比语言学，最好不要从比较语言学的立场来进行批评，那就说不到一起去了。

　　Concept of contrasting *vs.* comparison has been discussed earlier. The ground for adopting "contrastive linguistics" thereby differentiating it from "comparative linguistics" is decided by the academic connotation of the term "contrast". To this day, some preference still goes to the term "comparative" and though personal choice is respected, the act of it is not encouraged for stiring up confusion and do damage to comparative linguistics of the nineteenth century. Given that the distinction between contrastive linguistics and comparative linguistics has been well established and generally accepted, it is better to stick with reality. In the wise words of Confucius, having a title/name that commemsurates with the object and content stands the subject on moral high ground. On this note, contrastive linguistics should be dealt within the scope of contrastive linguistics and criticism seen through the lens of "comparative (historical) linguistics" has no place.

　　除了这一本体论意义，对比与比较还具有方法论的意义。就是说，对比语言学在研究的时候必须采用"对比"的方法，而不是"比较"的方法。这两种方法在形式上有点相似，即都是对两种或两种以上的事物（在我们的例子里是语言）进行比较，以找出它们的异同。但由于这两个词的西文字源意义，[1] 以及比较语言学与对比语言学发展的不同历史背景，实际上在语言学研究中已形成了相对固定的含义，即在异同的问题上，尽管双方都不会有只要找"同"或只要找"异"的极端主张，但却有明确的倾向性。"比较"作为方法论来说，是一种侧重求"同"的研究；而"对比"作为方法论来说，是一种侧重求"异"的研究。此外，"对比"由于词义所限，往往是在两种事物间进行，如汉英对比，不大能在两种以上的事物间进行，如说汉英日对比。这个时候尽管人们仍有找差异的目的，但一般却只能叫作"比较"而不叫作"对比"。这恐怕也是洪堡特和叶斯柏森没有用"对比"去命名他们的"新的比较语言学"的原因之一吧？

Besides the ontological role discussed above, drawing a line between "contrastive" and "comparative" is methodologically significant, by which we mean contrastive linguistics favour the method of contrasting over the method of comparison. In appearance, the two methods are similar, for both examine two or more items (units in languages) side by side for similarities within differences. Nonetheless, in terms of academic notion, they are quite different in present days, partly because of the etymological meanings of the two words, and partly because of disciplinary traditions widened in the course of development. Although neither carries an extreme demand to look for "similarity" or "difference" only, both nevertheless tend to lean towards either similarity or difference, i.e. methodologically, the "comparative" method foreground similarity, while the "contrastive" method, differences. Besides, as the definition implies, "contrast" is usually carried out between, and seldom more than two items. For instance, we may contrast English and Chinese, but it is quite unlikely to "contrast English, Chinese and Japanese", even if our aim is indeed to find differences. Under such

---

1　根据 *The Concise Oxford Dictionary*，"compare" 的意义是 "to observe the similarity or relation between"；"contrast" 的意义是 "to set two things in opposition, so as to show their differences"。

According to *The Concise Oxford Dictionary*, "compare" means "to observe the similarity or relation between" and "contrast" means "to set two things in opposition, so as to show their differences".

circumstances, the term "compare" in its general sense is used. This may explain why neither von Humboldt nor Jespersen uses "contrast" as the name for their novel idea in "comparative linguistics", as the set of languages under their surveillance was far more than two.

5.2.1.2.1.2 求异与求同
5.2.1.2.1.2 Similarity *vs.* differences

　　如上所说，对求"异"求"同"的不同倾向性，是对比语言学的学科性质决定的，因而求"异"求"同"本身就具有本体论的意义，是方向性的问题。有人以为可以"异""同"并重，这在逻辑上显得很公允，而实际上是办不到的。因为这会模糊学科的界限，使学科的追求目标变得不清晰。而且"异""同"并重在实践中也没有可操作性。在对比（或比较）时将两种语言的异同都罗列出来，这是可能的，也是必要的，但这并不意味着"异""同"并重，而只是找"异"找"同"过程中的一个必要步骤。在异同点罗列出来以后，下一步怎么走？是在"同"中求"异"，还是在"异"中求"同"，这就成了两大研究法的分野。比较研究会在"异"中去找"同"；而对比研究会在"同"中去找"异"。这就造成了两大学科的不同发展路线。因而求"异"求"同"又是路线性的问题，具有方法论的意义。在确定了"同中求异"的基本原则之后，怎样看待"同""异"？怎样求"异"？怎样看待对比语言学在发展到语言哲学层次时的求"同"问题？就是对比研究方法论需要认真考虑的。这个问题我们将留到后面作进一步讨论。

　　Methods used to single out similarities or differences have a bearing on the nature of contrastive linguistics and are therefore of ontological significance. While logically speaking, equality principle should apply to both similarity and difference in contrastive study, in reality, this reconciliation can be difficult. Research object will become unclear; the line to be drawn between similarity and difference becomes ill-defined, invalidating research effort in this lofty direction. Notwithstanding, it is possible to and probably should make a list of all similarities and differences between the two languages in question, and that is not the same as giving equal attention to both. The more important question is "what next", what shall we do after the list is made? To look for similarities out of differences, or to look for differences out of similarities? That shall be the point for demarcation. Usually, titles using "comparative study" will cover the former, whereas "contrastive study" will take on the latter, and two parallel lines of research are thus formed. In this light, emphasis on either similarity or difference carries methodological significance. When the fundamental principle of "seeking differences within similarities" is settled, more complex and more abstract questions await: such as "what is 'difference'?", "what is 'similarity'?", "how do we seek difference within similarity?", "how to handle the notion of 'similarity' at the philosophical level?", etc. Follow-up discussions are found in the upcoming section.

5.2.1.2.1.3 共时与历时
5.2.1.2.1.3 Synchronicity *vs.* diachronicity

共时与历时对于对比语言学来说，也兼具有本体论与方法论的意义。在20世纪五十年代对比分析兴起以后，拉多、詹姆斯等人都非常强调对比语言学的共时性，并作为其一条基本特征，以与"比较语言学"相区别。中国学者在引进这个学科时也曾强调过这一点。但随着学科研究的深入，尤其是，当对比语言学的目标发展到吕叔湘（1990）所提出的两个层次（即1. 指明事物的异同；2. 追究它们何以有此异同）后，学者们普遍感到，前一个层次的问题也许还能在"共时"的格局内解决，而后一个层次的问题却必须联系历时的因素，因此一些学者如杨自俭、潘文国等都指出，必须加强对语言史和语言研究史的研究，熟悉和了解有关的历史文化知识。杨自俭在反复琢磨对比语言学的定义时，也毫不犹豫地把"进行共时和历时的对比研究"写了进去，从而使这个问题具有了本体论的意义。

"Synchronic" and "diachronic" methods of contrastive research are also of both ontological and methodological significance. In the 1950s, contrastive analysis came into being with Lado, James and many others holding the fundamental principle of synchronicity as the feature of contrastive linguistics, and a marked distinction from comparative linguistics. Chinese scholars shared exactly the same perception when CL was first introduced to China. However, development footprints in the two regions soon parted ways. The watershed moment came when Lü Shuxiang (1990) of China set two targets for the discipline: "finding" and "explaining" differences and similarities. Many Chinese researchers were confident of meeting the first target with synchronic study, but opined that the second target could not be met without considering diachronic factors. Knowledge in histories of languages and linguistics grew in importance with Yang Zijian and Pan Wenguo taking the lead in the CL community. Yang Zijian, for example, did not hesitate to revise his definition for contrastive linguistics to explicitly promote "synchronic and diachronic contrasting study", henceforth projecting an ontological dimension to the issue.

然而同时，共时与历时也是个方法论问题。怎样"进行共时和历时的对比研究"呢？是共时管共时、历时管历时？还是"描写"时管共时、"解释"时用历时？还是描写和解释时都共时、历时并举？共时的原则如何体现？历时的原则如何体现？历时的研究又如何与对比基础的"共时性"要求相结合？丁金国在讨论"汉英对比的方法论原则"时把"共时性"（synchronicity）作为第一条原则：

At the same time it must be made clear that "synchronic" and "diachronic" are also a matter of methodology. How should we do "synchronic and diachronic contrasting study"? Should they be carried out separately? Or should "synchronic method" be adopted in description and "diachronic method" be adopted in explanation? Or should both "synchronic" and "diachronic" methods be employed for description and explanation? How are "synchronic" principles realized? How are "diachronic" principles realized? How do we conjoin diachronic study with "synchronicity", the underlying feature of contrastive linguistics? In respond, Ding Jinguo (1996) sets "synchronicity" as the first principle with reference to his discussion on the methodological principles of Chinese-English contrastive study:

> 共时研究的基本特点是把特定历史时期相对稳定的语言事实作为研究对象。需要说明的是，"共时"绝非指"当代"或"现代"，而是指在历史发展中所截取的任一横断面作为研究对象的事实。所以我们在对比过程中，不能拿上古汉语的某一语言事实与当代英语进行比较，当然也不能拿中古英语与现代汉语进行比较。但这并不排斥为了说明某一共时事实，而使用历时性材料。（丁金国，1996/2004：8）
>
> The fundamental feature of synchronic study is to examine those relatively stable linguistic facts pertaining to specific historical stage. We must underline

the fact that "synchronicity" has nothing to do with "present" or "current". Instead it refers to the linguistic facts of any crosscut section in historical development. Thus, in our contrasting practice, we do not contrast ancient Chinese with contemporary English, nor do we compare Middle English with modern Chinese. But that does not preclude the use of historical material to offer explanation on a synchronic fact. (Ding Jinguo, 1996/2004: 8)

丁氏此文是难得的一篇专门提及对比研究方法论的专文，很值得理论研究者重视。但我们觉得这段话在逻辑上是有矛盾的：既然"'共时'绝非指'当代'或'现代'，而是指在历史发展中所截取的任一横断面作为研究对象的事实"，而对比研究又可在任两种语言间进行，那为什么"不能拿上古汉语的某一语言事实与当代英语进行比较，当然也不能拿中古英语与现代汉语进行比较"呢？因为这四种"语言事实"不都是"历史发展中所截取的任一横断面"吗？实际上，我们之所以没有将上古汉语与当代英语进行比较，或将中古英语与现代汉语进行比较，是因为没有这种需要。如果一旦有了这种需要，我们完全可以在这些"语言事实"间进行对比研究，这一点也不违背"共时性"的原则。"共时性"是指对比一方所使用的语言事实自身的共时性，例如"上古汉语"里不应夹杂有现代汉语的流行语，"中古英语"里不应有嬉皮士唱的歌词。否则的话，如果要求历史材料在时代上的同一性，那除了"当代英语"与"当代汉语"之外，就没有什么其他材料具有"可比性"了，须知，最早的"古英语"，对于汉语来说，已经处于"近古"时代了。

Ding (1996) was one of the few rare papers ever written exclusively on methodology in contrastive linguistics and should be given due attention. And we note something paradoxical in the above quote: if "synchronic" does not mean "present" or "current", but refers to the linguistic facts of any crosscut section in the historical development, and if we all agree that contrastive analysis can be carried out between any two languages, then, why are there out of bound areas such as those between ancient Chinese and contemporary English, Middle English and modern Chinese? "Ancient Chinese", "modern Chinese", "Middle English' and "contemporary English" are legitimate language varieties and the true reason for not putting them together for comparison is that we do not feel it necessary. Once the need arises, there are no off-limits zones and it does not in the least violate the principle of synchronicity.

"Synchronicity" refers solely to the synchronic nature of the language to be compared, for instance, modern Chinese slang should not crisscross with ancient Chinese data and Middle English data must not include traversed input of songs sung by contemporary hippies. Otherwise, if the scope is confined to the same historical period, few comparisons could meet the mark besides contemporary English and contemporary Chinese, for even the earliest "Old English" emerged much later than the latest "Middle Chinese".

可见共时和历时的问题，说起来容易，真要操作起来问题还不小。这些都有待于人们从理论上进行认真深入的研究。

In practice, research issues relating to "synchronic" and "diachronic" are many. In terms of methodology and specific ways of contrastive treatment, serious further study is much needed.

5.2.1.2.2 主要具有方法论意义的方法
5.2.1.2.2 Methods mainly of methodological importance

我们把下列这些方法列为主要具有方法论意义的方法，就是说，它们对于对比语言学的学科性质没有决定性的意义，但是在具体从事对比研究时却不能不考虑的问题。在一定程度上，它们可以决定对比研究的成败。这些方法是：对比的出发点、对比的方向、归纳和演绎、静态与动态。

The following are methods whose main contribution serves the purpose of methodology. They are indispensable in contrastive studies, often affecting the final results but do not play a major role in deciding the nature of the discipline. These methods include deduction vs. induction, and static *vs.* dynamic. The discussion shall begin with the point of contention (or "starting point/primary premises") and the similarity-difference preference.

5.2.1.2.2.1 对比的出发点
5.2.1.2.2.1 Starting point

出发点，或starting point，这个在中文听起来有点"俗"，不像学术术语的词，在西方却颇有历史渊源，因为这是亚里士多德首倡的哲学用语。亚里士多德认为：

> All study begin with a point of contention, or what used to be called starting point. The term "starting point" also translated as "primary premise" (for practical reasoning) was first used by Aristotle in his philosophical study:
>
> 出发点不可能是科学知识，而比科学知识更真实的只能是本能，因而只能本能才能获取出发点。（亚里士多德，330 BC/1996: 21）
>
> There cannot be scientific knowledge of the starting-points, and since nothing can be more true than scientific knowledge except intuition, it is intuition that grasps the starting-points. (Aristotle, 330 BC/1996: 21)

亚里士多德否认"出发点"的科学性，这大概是西方许多学者不爱用这个词，而偏爱用 Tertium comparationis 一词的原因吧？Tertium comparationis 一词，我们译作"对比中立项"，但对比的出发点未必全是不偏不倚的"中间项"，单向性的对比研究就不是从"中间项"出发的。许余龙（1992：43）把 Tertium comparationis 译作"对比基础"，"基础"一词的含义又太宽泛了一点，对比的哲学基础、语言学基础、可比性问题，甚至两种语言的有关知识等等，都可以是"对比的基础"。因此我们还是回到这个最老的术语——出发点。

Aristotle denies the scientific nature of starting points, which may explain the reason why so many western scholars eagerly drop and replace this term with *tertium comparationis* instead. In Chinese, *tertium compa- rationis* is commonly known as *duibi zhongjianxiang* (对比中间项), literally meaning "neutral item in language comparison", but not all points of contention are items in the middle ground absolutely free of deviation. Unidirectional contrasting (either for similarity or difference), for instance, does not specify a 'neutral item' to begin with. Alternatively, Xu Yulong (1992: 43) interprets *tertium comparationis* as *duibi jichu* (对比基础), literally meaning "base for comparison". A lot of thought has been put into this interpretation even as we found "base" covers too much in the range—Philosophical ideas, linguistic knowledge, comparability, or even background of the languages. From where Xu is coming from, "base" really should be read as "premise" for a lack of adequate equivalent in Chinese. For a more neutral position, we suggest keeping it to point of contention or starting point.

从事对比研究的人也许未必人人都一天到晚在考虑对比的性质啊、对比的目标啊等等理论问题，但却必须考虑"从哪里出发进行对比"这一非常现实的问题；他也许未必认真想过从不同的地方出发，会给他的对比过程和对比结果带来什么影响的问题，但实际上这个问题却必然存在。因而，出发点问题也是一个事关对比全局的一个重要的方法论问题，我们将在后面进行稍深入的专题讨论。

Not everyone engaged in contrastive study shares the burden of theoretical concerns such as nature and object of language comparison, yet practially all in the field need to consider the question of where to begin? Oblivious to many, their choices of the bone of contention often lead to very different ways of contrasting and findings. Sitting right at the top of the whole issue of methodology is none other than the point of contention, the starting point. We will delve more deeply into that later.

5.2.1.2.2.2 对比的方向
5.2.1.2.2.2 Direction

出发点之外，进行对比的另一个非常现实的问题是对比研究的方向性问题。对比究竟应该是单向性的？双向性的？无向性的？不同的处理又出自何种不同的目标，会造成怎样的后果？这些也是从事对比研究必须解决的方法论问题。也值得花专门的篇幅进行讨论。

Pertinent to the point of contention is the crucial decision on the direction of contrastive research. Should contrastive study be uni-directional, bidirectional, or multidirectional? What dictates which of these preferences one would chose and what would result as a consequence? Such considerations and related assumptions are impactful on methodology and worthy of in-depth dedicated discourse.

5.2.1.2.2.3 归纳和演绎
5.2.1.2.2.3 Induction *vs.* deduction

归纳与演绎，跟上一节提到的描写与解释相关，本来归纳应属于一般的方法，是哪门学科的研究都可以用的，而且也不存在着哪种研究只能用归纳、哪种研究只能用演绎的问题,并不只是跟对比语言学有关。[1]但是自从转换生成语言学把"解释"变成它的"独门之秘"之后,"演绎"也成了这一派的独门兵器。他们声称归纳的方法是不科学的,只有演绎的方法才是科学的方法。"真正的"语言研究只能用演绎法。由于对比语言学在拉多之后只有极短的一个时期受到结构主义影响,多数是在这一语言学派的影响下发展起来的。因此这一方法对于对比研究的影响是不容忽视的。而中国当前有一些学者呼吁用汉语的事实去"证实"或"证伪"西方的"现代语言理论",其实这一方法也就是演绎法,要用西方的语言理论"演绎"出汉语的规律来。他们心目中的"西方语言理论"其实仅此一家,就是生成语言学,西方的其他语言理论是并不包括在内的。因而归纳和演绎这一本来一般性的方法问题对于对比语言学来说,就突然有了学科方法论的意义。是主张归纳?还是演绎?还是先归纳再演绎?先演绎再归纳?演绎和归纳同时进行?……就成了对比研究者必须作出抉择的方法论之一。

As principles of reasoning and inference, induction and deduction are broad, generic methods applicable to all disciplines and neither is exclusive to any one discipline, including contrastive linguistics. To regard them as methodological principles for contrastive study seems puzzling. The story begins with transformational grammar. TG proclaims explanation as the method unique to itself and in the process, monopolizes the use of deduction too. They denounce inductive method as unscientific and prize deduction as the only "scientific" method that should be adopted by all "genuine" linguistic studies. If we recall, CA was popularised and was influenced by a structuralist R. Lado for a short period, but was for most of the time under the dominance of transformational grammar, the overwhelming power of which is not to be neglected anyway. The extent of the influence led some Chinese scholars today suggests that the only constructive

---

[1] 美国逻辑学家皮尔斯(1958)提出三种普遍试用的逻辑方法:归纳、演绎和溯因。虽然没有特别提起,溯因在对比语言学中也有方法论的意义,特别是对于处理动态共时的语料。许余龙(2014)论及这三种逻辑推理在语言学中的应用,有兴趣者可进一步阅读。
C.S. Pierce (1958) brought forward three types of scientific reasoning for general use. Besides induction and deduction, there is abduction. While we did not go into abduction, we must not fail to notice its methodological significance in contrastive linguistics, particularly when dynamic, synchronic data are concerned. Readers may be interested to read Xu Yulong (2014) for application of these three methods in linguistic studies in general.

purpose of contrastive linguistics is to use facts in Chinese language to verify or falsify "modern western linguistic theory". "Modern western linguistic theory" points specifically to generative linguistics, and the contrastive method proposed, as can be expected, is deduction. Their real intention is to deduce rules of Chinese grammar from GL's universal grammar. All of a sudden, general interest in deduction and induction unexpectedly assumes methodological importance in contrastive linguistics. A contrastivist is forced to make a choice before everything else: to use deduction only? Or induction only? Or deduction followed by induction? Or vice versa? Or two methods to be used alternately? Taking into account synchronicity and diachronicity description and explanation in contrastive study, truth be told that both induction and deduction must complement each other for data to fall into place. Precisely on this holistic perspective at theoretical level that induction and deduction hold grounds as contrastive methodological principles.

5.2.1.2.2.4 动态与静态
5.2.1.2.2.4 Dynamic *vs.* static

跟"历时与共时"相关的是"动态与静态"的问题。由于我们觉得"动态与静态"并不像"历时与共时"那样，还具有对比语言学的本体论意义，因而将它放到了这个位置，也就是说，我们认为这也是进行语言对比时必须考虑的一个方法论问题。

The "dynamic *vs.* static" pair is pertinent to the "synchronic *vs.* diachronic" pair with presence in ontology but offers methodological considerations in the contrastive study.

"动态与静态"从表面上看来，跟"历时与共时"相仿，似乎是一个问题的两种说法。其实不然。"动态"所包括的范围比"历时"要广，它不但包括"历时"的变化，还包括"同时"的变化，还包括所比两种语言彼此间的渗透和影响，以及由此带来的关系的变化。一个显著的例子是汉英色彩词所包含的文化含义。从历时的角度看，我们会想到"红、黄、白、黑"这些词在汉语中古今不同的含义；但从"共时"的角度看，我们又要看到这些含义在英、汉语中的相互渗透关系，有些含义的产生正是翻译、借用对方语言的结果。将这些因素考虑在内，我们就会有一种崭新的视角来看这个问题。又比如，在将现代汉语的组织法与其他语言作对比时，我们一定要有动态的眼光，要看到现代汉语语法的不稳定性和过程性，它既不如古汉语语法那样相对稳定，也不如现代英语语法那样相对比较稳定，而是还处在发展、成熟过程中。因而，从我们对语言性质的新的认定——人类认知与表述世界的方式与过程——出发，我们觉得动态性应该成为新一代语言对比研究的一个方法论特征。

It could easily be mistaken that the dynamic-static pair and the synchronic-diachronic pair are but two sides of a coin. In fact, dynamic study covers a wider scope than diachronic study and includes not only the historical changes but synchronous and ongoing changes as well. It also includes the infiltration and induced-shift, transfer and copying arising from language contact and the resultant change in relation. One prominent example is the cultural implication of colour words in Chinese and English. Diachronically we think of the different connotations of colours like red, yellow, black or white in classical and modern Chinese, but synchronically, we see mutual influence of cultural senses in English and Chinese: some new implications are nothing but the result of translation and borrowing from the opposite language. Giving all relevant factors due consideration opens up an entirely new perspective on dynamic, static, synchronic and diachronic. A further example has to do with contrasting modern Chinese grammar with other languages. Dynamic viewpoint has to be adopted in such cases given that modern Chinese grammar, still evolving and maturing, is not as stable as either classical Chinese grammar or modern English grammar. With a renewed understanding of the nature of language in mind, i.e. language is the fashion and process in which man cognizes and states the world, we felt strongly for dynamism to be recognized as a key feature in contrastive methodology.

5.2.1.3 对比的程序问题
5.2.1.3 Procedural issues

下面我们要讨论一个既非方法论原则又不是一般方法，却又为许多对比学者所关注的问题——对比的程序。程序不是方法，但又与方法密切相关，这是有关研究者从他的研究目标出发,将他的方法论和方法付诸实践的过程,往往是研究者经验的可贵总结。从程序我们有时可能更清楚地看出研究者的成就以及可能有的局限。对于后来者来说,程序往往是最直接的启示,越是具体的"程序"越是能够帮新手入门。因此我们真该鼓励有经验的学者都来介绍他们的"研究程序"。

Next we are going into the procedure of going about contrasting. Procedures are not guiding principles per se, but it has something to do with concrete methods and is really the process whereby research methods and principles are put into practice to fulfill the targeted task. By scrutinizing the procedure, research achievements and limitations can clearly be seen. To junior researchers, procedure serves as the best teachers, providing them with the rope to learn the necessary techniques. It is certainly beneficial to have experienced researchers come forward to share the procedures they adopt.

在对比研究史上,有几位学者谈到了程序问题。第一位有名的便是拉多。他的程序分四步:

Several scholars did exactly that. One of them, Robert Lado, put forward a four-step procedure in doing language comparison:

(1) 找到对所要对比语言的最好的结构描写;
(2) 把这些结构简约化成大纲;
(3) 依大纲进行一一对比,发现难点;
(4) 把小难点集中成大难点,便能发现学习中的所有问题。

(拉多,1957: 67—70)

> First step: *Locate the best structural description of the languages involved.*
> Second step: *Summarize in compact outline form all the structures.*
> Third step: *Actual comparison of the two language structures, pattern by pattern.*
> Fourth step: *Regrouping single problem patterns into larger patterns of difficulty.*

(Lado, 1957: 67—70)

我们很快便能从程序中发现他的方法的局限和问题:第一,他进行对比的前提是两种语言都已经有了很好的结构描写(如果没有就要先进行这样的描写),但实际情况是,除了英语及少数印欧语之外,其他语言(比如汉语)都没有这样的条件。在这样的条件下,如果要按拉多的标准,研究者要么就首先回去研究好汉语的结构描写(但他未必有这样的耐心和能力),要么就硬着头皮,把没有充分描写好的汉语结构(如"暂拟系统")当作已经描写好的结构去对比。第二,拉多的这一方法只适合于结构系统的对比,对于别的出发点则无能为力。第三,上述(3)、(4)两条表明拉多把两种语言的"差异"当作"学习难点"的代名词,这并没有经过证明。

The documented procedure exposes limits and design flaws. First, on the pre-requires for "best structural description of the languages involved": if the form, meaning or distribution of a pattern is found missing or adequately described, an attempt must be made to complete the description as accurately as possible before moving forward. Harsh is the fact that apart from English and some other European languages, few languages, Mandarin Chinese included, can fulfill that pre-requisite. Under such circumstances, only two things can possibly be done: do up an adequate description of Chinese first even if it meant a long wait; otherwise, proceed from an "inadequately" described system, such as the "provisional grammar". It is not difficult to expect that neither will produce a satisfactory outcome. Secondly, Lado's procedure appears to be applicable only to the comparison of "structures". Does it work for study involving other starting points? Thirdly, we know that to Lado, differences in languages is just another way of articulating the difficulties in learning a language—a perception yet to be proven.

第二位是迪·皮德娄,他(1971/1978: 29—30)的对比过程分为三步:
A markedly different procedure is suggested by Di Pietro in three steps:

(1)观察两种语言表层结构上的不同,前提是假设不管其表面上如何不同,背后总有什么普遍性东西可解释;
(2)假定这背后的普遍性东西;
(3)找出从深层实现为表层的规则。(皮德娄,1971/1978: 29—30)

The first step is to observe the differences between the surface structures of two languages. Such differences may range from total absence of some surface feature in one of the two languages to partial sharing of a feature

.... However great the contrasts, we assume, in this first step, that they are explainable in terms of some underlying universal. (*e.g.* number)

The second step is to postulate the underlying universals… (*e.g.* number)

The third step is to formulate the deep-to-surface (realization) rules concerning the various expressions of NUMBER in each of the languages involved in our CA. (Di Pietro, 1971/1978: 29—30)

这大概可说是最典型的生成语法派的"对比":实际上是先有结论再来证明,之后将其"转换"过程"规则"化就算完成了任务。这种对比除了"证明"本来就已"存在"的"共性"并没有提供什么新的东西。

That is probably what a generalist would typically go about comparing languages. Consistent throughout the three steps is so called "underlying universals" that ought to be identified right from the start. There lies the biggest loophole in the design because the outcome proves nothing but the "universals" already exists.

第三位提出对比程序的是詹姆斯,詹姆斯提出了一个四步法(1980:63):

Next, Carl James draws up two basic processes: description and comparison, demonstrated in his example as a four-step algorithm: (1980: 63)

(1)汇总资料;(2)进行描写;(3)根据需要补充资料;(4)进行对比。(詹姆斯,1980:63)

(1) assemble the data; (2) formulate the descriptions; (3) supplement the data as required; (4) formulate the contrast. (James, 1980: 52)

与拉多相比,第一,他不是找对象语言已经描写好的结构,而是要研究者自己进行描写,这就对研究者提出了更高的要求,但同时也给了他自主性,他可以按照他自己熟悉的理论或体系(如生成语法)去进行描写。问题是,这样的描写主观性可能很大。第二,他要搜集的"资料"没有强调是"结构",因而可以容纳多种基础(如意义等)的对比,开放性比拉多大。第三,他把"进行对比"放在最后一步,但"如何对比"却没有说,对于初学者来说就等于什么也没有说。

Description, the common feature in both James's and Lado's procedure, is handled differently: forgoing descriptions already on the shelf, Carl James would rather that the data can be described personally. While that places high expectation on the researcher, it also allows for the use of a theory more familiar to the researcher. The problem that follows may be a highly subjective description. It is also disturbing that the procedure stop short at "doing contrast" without filling in on how to go about doing it. A plus point though is that data collection in this case is not limited to "structures" but open to more varieties of practices based on more items such as semantics.

第四位是克尔采斯佐斯基。我们在第一章引过他（1990：101）提出的一个语用对比程序，这里我们去掉他那令人眼花缭乱的符号，简化成下面一个流程图：

The most elaborate procedure came from Krzeszowski (1990: 101) whose pragmatic contrasting procedure we introduced in Chapter 1. To the benefit of the general reader, we simplify the very complicated description in the following flow chart:

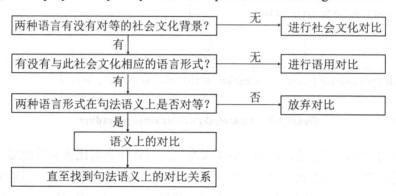

图5.3 克氏的对比模式

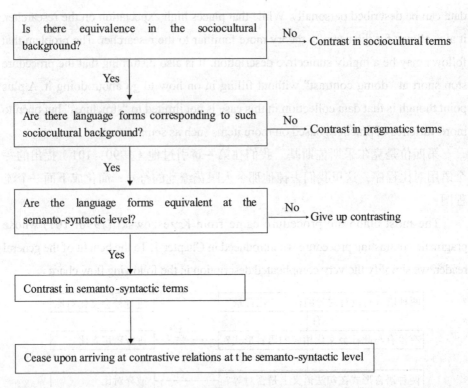

Figure 5.3 Krzeszowski's contrastive procedure

我们发现的问题是，他把"对等关系"的存在作为对比研究的前提，如没有就进行对比，如有就再找下一层"对等关系"。问题是我们怎么知道事先两件事物间有对等关系呢？如果知道有还需要进行对比吗？因而这一"对比"实际上成了循环论证。

The most troubling part of this procedure is the imposition of "equivalence" as the premise for language contrast: Absence of equivalence legitimatised the proceeding of language comparison; if some form of equivalence is being found at one level, move on to a lower level. Here comes the question: how do we know whether there is equivalent or not right at the beginning? And if the knowledge of equivalent is hitherto established, the motion for contrast would have been killed. The elaborate scheme is than reduced to a circular argument.

在中国，首次讨论对比程序的是许余龙（1992：59—66），恐怕也是迄今惟一的一位。他把对比分为六个步骤：

Over in China, the first scholar to have deliberated on contrasting procedure is Xu Yulong (1992: 59—66), who proposed a six-step procedure:

（1）确定对比范围，包括语言层面（语音、语法等）、语言单位或现象（句子、篇章、衔接等）及语言学内容（结构、功能等）；

（2）文献收集与研究，其中"文献"指已有的对比研究，"研究"指对两种语言分别作的分析研究；

（3）确定理论框架；

（4）搜集语言材料（注意时代、语体、风格等）；

（5）分析对比；

（6）总结。

(1) Define the scope of contrasting including linguistic levels (phonetics, grammar…), linguistic phenomena or units (sentence, text, cohesion…), and linguistic content (structure, function…);

(2) Collect and collate literature on the chosen topic and conduct preliminary study of the languages involved;

(3) Decide on a theoretical frame;

(4) Gather linguistic data with special reference to time, register and style;

(5) Perform analysis on the comparison;

(6) Conclusion.

将许氏的程度与克氏作比较，我们会发现克氏还是停留在从理论到理论，其程序有点空想性；而许氏的可操作性大得多，相信是个人实践经验的总结。然而相对于前四条，第五条的内容还是较空，跟詹姆斯一样，他还是没有告诉我们"对比"本身到底该如何进行。更令人费解的是第三条"确定理论框架"，据我们所知这也是中国高校外语系许多教授对博士生写作论文的要求，似乎不这样做就不足以显示论文的"理论性"。我们不解的是：

Xu has likely drawn from his own practice in the field and does not end up in theory like Krzeszowski's. Comparing Xu's procedure against Krzeszowski's framework reveals strikingly it's more feasible than merely being ideal in theory. However, like Carl James, Xu Yulong breaks off without telling us HOW to go about contrasting. Xu also keeps us musing over his Step 3, "Decide on a theoretical frame". For a moment, it sounds like the perceived requirement of a doctoral thesis many supervisors in Chinese universities would demand of their students as they set about writing their dissertations. The perception takes the view that something is plucked from the air without an underpinning theoretical framework or scientific justification. We cannot help but think through the following:

一、为什么事实的分析必须以某种理论为指导？没有理论就不能进行分析吗？平心而论，我们都接受理论的训练，理论也有指导的意义。但是，囿于一家一派的说法未免狭隘，犹有甚者，削足适履，编造语料来迁就某个理论框架，实不足取。总而言之，对比研究中，理论的指导意义固然可取，墨守成规则不可行。对比研究中必须尊重语言事实，根据对比结果对理论作出调适和修订是必然的。

1. Why ought analysis of facts to be based on a specific "theory"? Should analysis conducted without the auspices of a theory be invalidated? To be fair, we reckon that we are all trained in theories and theories serve useful guidance too. Nonetheless, it may be narrowly particular if we were to stick religiously to one school of thought and it would be worst to the extent of distortion if data are made to fit a certain framework. In essence, while some form of theoretical guidance is desirable, fixated form on a rigid idea is not. Respecting linguistic data as it is and fine tuning or modifying the theory as necessary is the way to go.

二、难道理论不同，分析的结果就会不同吗？如果同样的材料，用一种"理论"分析出来是"异"，用另一种"理论"分析出来是"同"，那究竟是理论有问题还是材料有问题？如果是材料有问题，我们就回到了"理论决定材料"的怪圈；如果是理论有问题，那我们寻求某种理论支撑的意义又何在呢？

2. Would different "theoretical frames" lead to variations in research findings? Take for instance, outcome from one "theoretical frame" points to a "difference" between a pair of languages; and another "theoretical frame" results in a "similarity" from the same data. How do we choose between these two true outcomes? And do we lay blame on theory or data for the dichotomy? If data is the culprit, then that is probably a weir case where data are feed to conform with the theory. If on the other hand, theory is at fault, wouldn't that defeat the purpose of having a theory to guide the way?

三、这种对"理论"的渴求症显然来自西方，西方的某些对比学者总对学科自身缺少自信，想要寻求某种"理论"的支撑，来提高自己的"理论"性，如迪·皮德娄及利宾斯卡等人，而且都不约而同地选中的转换生成语言学。所不同的是，西方某些学者对"理论"的选择是作为其整个研究体系的支撑，是在全部对比开始之前；而中国学者如许氏的安排却是在对比开始之后（已确定了对比范围及完成了文献收集），这就有点"看菜吃饭"的实用主义味道。而要求研究者能针对不同的研究范围、对象选用不同的理论模式，例如想对比结构就用结构主义或生成语法模式，想对比篇章就用功能主义模式，这就等于要求每个对比者都成为精通各门各派十八般武艺的武林高手，面对不同对手，既会打少林拳，又会使太极剑，必要时还能挥出降龙十八掌！而这样的"武林高手"一般是不会有的，这样用出来的"理论"也只能是花拳绣腿而已。

3. The quest for support in linguistic theory mirrored some unhealthy development in the West. Some western scholars being uncertain of contrastive linguistics as a full-fledged branch of linguistics, borrowed support from other theoretical frames. Coincidentally, both Di Pietro and Lipińska went for the more theoretical-sounding transformational grammar for this purpose. Normally, the choice of theory is made right from the beginning so that the chosen theory underpins the entire contrasting framework. Chinese scholars mimic this process with a twist: the selection of theory is made mid way through when research scope and literature collection are done. We cannot help wondering a pragmatic selection of theory as such is not an attempt to adapt the theory to serve the purpose. At the same time, it would be incredible for one to have mastered the various theories to suit different targets and purpose. We cannot expect one to use structuralism or transformational grammar when structures are involved, and to use systematic functionalism when texts are to be contrasted. That would be harmful to both theories and practices since proficiency in a whole basket of theories would be a tall order.

年轻中国学者王蕾（2014）在厘清前人所提的各种对比程序后，基于语料库，并以语言事实为出发点，提出"对比五步法"，在处理语料和理论框架时，谨慎避免循环论证，提出要以事实修订理论。其五步法为：

Standing on the shoulder of giant predecessors and obviously well acquainted with the criticism of various procedures, Chinese scholar Wang Lei (2014) did a pilot study on a 5-step procedure embracing corpus study and was careful in handling linguistic facts and theoretical framework to avoid circular argument or tailoring facts to suit theory while giving due considerations to the refinement of theory through the process:

1. 确定可比对象：通过观察语料，尤其是可以利用平行语料库或可比语料库，捕捉到两种语言间的某种相似之处，并将相似之处提炼为两种语言系统中的语言现象或用法X_a和X_b，从而确定可比对象；

2. 提出初始假设：X_a和X_b是等同的；

3. 确立理论框架，用以描述语言现象，并设计实证研究检验初始假设；

4. 分析检验结果：初始假设成立/不成立，如若不成立，则要修正假设，并进一步验证修正假设；

5. 结合对比结果，反观理论框架，进行理论探究。

1. Identify target for comparison: through observing linguistic data, particularly using parallel corpus or other corpuses, capture similarities and abstract them as phenomena or function X, and Y in the respective language system. Target for comparison may therefore be pin down;

2. Formulate preliminary hypothesis: X_a and X_b being the same;

3. Determine the theoretical framework to be used for description and design empirical study for hypothesis testing;

4. Perform analysis on the testing: If preliminary hypothesis stands, proceed to the next step. If it does not stand, go back to step 2, modify the hypothesis and go through the testing again;

5. Reflect on the outcomes and make necessary tweak to the theoretical framework.

王蕾（2014）希望通过语言事实验证和修订理论的用心可以体会。然而上述步骤依然存在陷阱，特别是初始假设和所选择的理论可能相矛盾。和西方学者一样，中国研究者必须突破对于理论的执著。

We can understand where Wang (2014) is coming from and his attempts to revise theory with real world linguistic data. Yet there is a catch in the proposed procedure when the hypothesis stands contradictory to the assumption of the chosen theoretical framework. It seems that like most of their western counterparts, Chinese scholars need to break the spell on theory.

所幸在西方也并不是所有的对比研究者都这样乞求"理论"的支撑，如斯奈尔·杭贝（1983）和切斯特曼（1998）就断然拒绝以什么现成理论作为自己研究的支撑。

Fortunately, not all western scholars buy in to "theoretical frames". Snell-Hornby (1983) and Chesterman (1998) stood out amongst those who refused to be bound by any existing linguistic theory in their contrastive study!

而切斯特曼（1998：54）也是真正对"对比"自身提出了操作程序的学者，他的没有结尾的"七步曲"[1]是对前此各家一语带过的"对比"过程的真正描述。当然，切氏的程序有他的独特性，而且非常符合他的从意义出发进行对比的要求。我们可以把他的程序称作模式，甚至也可同意他自己的说法，叫做"方法论"。这一程序模式的出现确实是对比方法上的一个大进步，对促进对比研究的深入无疑有很大意义。

In Chapter 1, we have introduced the procedure by Chesterman (1998: 54). That is by far the most fool-proof procedure for contrastive study. His seven-step procedure confronted head-on the pertaining question on HOW to conduct language contrast step by step. Of course, Chesterman's procedure is idiosyncratic and lean towards his preference over a semantic approach. His procedure, more like a "model", or to use his own words, a "methodology", blazed a trail in contrastive studies.

5.2.2 方法论的原则
5.2.2 Principles of methodology

分清了什么是方法，什么是方法论，下面我们要进一步讨论方法论研究的原则，亦即探讨方法论的采用受到哪些条件的制约。

Following the differentiation of methods from methodology, we will further discuss the principles of methodology, or rather, the conditions for adopting methodology.

综观对比语言学发生发展的历史，我们可以发现，不管是否自觉意识到，方法论的采用是受到制约的，我们把它称作方法论的原则。主要有三个原则，分别是方法论的背景性原则、选择性原则和同一性原则。

---

[1] 即1. 观察实例；2. 发现"相似"；3. 提出问题；4. 初步假设；5. 初步验证；6. 修正假设；7. 再次验证……（参见本书第一章）

1. Primary data: instances of language behaviour; 2. Comparability criterion: perceived similarity; 3. Problem: What is the nature of this similarity? 4. Initial hypothesis; 5. Test; 6. Revised hypothesis; 7. Testing of revised hypothesis. (refer to Chapter 1)

The history of contrastive study shows that the adoption of methodology is indeed conditioned by certain factors whether one realizes it or not. We think of these conditions "principles". These principles are grounded on three main aspects, namely, background, selection criteria and homogeneity.

5.2.2.1 背景性原则
5.2.2.1 Principles of background

背景性原则指的是在方法论背后起作用的东西。就对比语言学而言，下面三个因素对方法论有着决定性的作用。

Principles grounded on background factors refer to those decisive factors behind methodology. For contrastive linguistics, there are three.

5.2.2.1.1 本体论决定方法论
5.2.2.1.1 Ontology-decisive

对于任何学科来说，最重要的事是本体论的建设。没有本体论就谈不上方法论，如果连对比语言学是一个独立的学科都不敢承认，只敢自称为"对比分析"；或者即使自称是一门"学科"，却又拼命寻求什么更成熟的"语言学"作依靠，甘居"应用语言学的分支"、"比较语言学的分支"等地位，那就不会有什么方法论的考虑，也不需要有这种考虑。利宾斯卡说得好：

Any academic discipline would first consider its relevance in ontology. There is no methodology without ontology. But both ontology and methodology rest on the premise that contrastive study is a recognised independent discipline. Were it to be merely "contrastive analysis", or its disciplinary value is confined to be a "branch" of other linguistics such as applied linguistics or comparative linguistics, and therefore subject to theories applicable to the trunk, then there is no talk on methodology possible. Just as Lipińska puts it:

> 要是在总体上只把对比分析看作一种方法，能使我们能对两种语言间的异同有更清晰的了解，那这个任务很多方法都可以完成，就看研究者喜欢什么理论了。（利宾斯卡，1980：127）
>
> If Contrastive Analysis (CA) is defined generally as a method which

enables the differences and similarities between languages to be stated explicitly,[1] its task can be approached in many different ways depending upon the theory of language to which the investigator adheres. (Lipińska, 1980: 127)

要是对比分析本身只是"方法",那它所需要考虑的问题就是找个什么"理论"去依赖,就根本不存在方法论的问题。而西方的对比语言学地位长期未定,直至现在,仍处于"妾身未分明"的状态,难怪方法论始终没有人认真予以考虑和研究。

If contrastive analysis is itself a "method" and lives on other linguistic theories, the study of methodology is totally out of question. Looking at the West where the status for contrastive linguistics remains ambiguous to this day, it is understandable that seriously study on methodology is sparingly few.

中国是另外一种情况。八十年代以来,承认对比语言学是一门独立的学科的呼声倒是越来越高,但学科建设的进展不快。一些人受西方同行的影响,对学科的定性拿不定主意;还有一些人则较多地考虑本体论的问题,还来不及关注到方法论。而总体来讲,是中国学者对学科建设的哲学性一向考虑较少,对纯"形而上"问题思索的热情不高。表现在对"方法"和"方法论"的概念也不善于区别,有时误把对具体方法的研究误当作方法论研究,而没有考虑方法论与本体论的密切关系。

The contrastive environment in China is not any better. Although voices advocating contrastive linguistics as an independent discipline have been strong since the 1980s, yet the progress as a full discipline did not happen as expected. This was partly because some scholars showed little confidence in the nature of the discipline; after all, western endorsement has not been forthcoming. By and large, Chinese scholars appear to be less interested in philosophical consideration, and are weaker in handling metaphysical issues. Amongst those who are interested, most are totally absorbed inontological matters and overlook methodology. For this matter, it is not uncommon that methods are mistaken to be methodology while studies on specific methods are taken as studies on methodology.

1　This is the most generally accepted definition of CA (see Di Pietro, 1970). He does not, however, mention "similarity".
这是人们通常接受的关于对比分析的定义,见迪•皮德娄(1970)。不过他没有提到"同"。

5.2.2.1.2 目的论决定方法论
5.2.2.1.2 Teleology-decisive

在本体论中，对方法论影响最大的是学科的目标论。方法都是为目的服务的，想达到什么目的就会采用最容易达到这个目的的方法。如果目的只是要能说出两种语言的异同，帮助外语教学，那就会采用结构主义的方法（描写）；如果目的是为了语言表面"异同"背后的"普遍语法"，那就会采用转换生成语言学的方法（解释）。利宾斯卡曾指出：

Teleology, or the study of purposes, is impactful on methodology. Methods are adopted to serve purposes, and different purposes will naturally require a method closest to its realization. If the purpose is to seek out the differences and similarities between the pair of languages involved to ultimately provide better solutions in foreign language teaching, naturally the structural method of description will be the choice. If our aim falls on a "universal grammar" governing the differences and similarities of languages, the TG method of explanation could be a way out. Lipińska's early insight serves well:

> 评价一种理论必须联系其想达到的目标。如果对比研究的目标是为了直接有助于外语教学，而语言又被看作是一套系统，那么用结构主义方法列举出两种语言的异同点就已足够；但如果对比的目的不仅是为了教学，而是还想有助于研究人类语言的普遍理论，而各种不同的语言又被看作是某种共同的"普遍语言"的表面呈现，语言的性质与人类思维的性质密切相应，那么就会采用转换语法的分析框架。（利宾斯卡，1980：129）

An evaluation of a linguistic theory can be made only with reference to its goals. If the primary object of CA is taken to be immediate help in foreign language learning and teaching and language is conceived of as a system of various items, then the structural method of systematic enumeration of the similarities and differences between two language systems is sufficient. If, on the other hand, CA is to serve not as a basis for language teaching, but also as a contribution to the general theory of what a human language is, and if languages are viewed as surface realizations of one common "universal language" whose properties are in strict correlation with the properties of the human mind, then the analysis has to be performed within the framework of transformational grammar. (Lipińska, 1980: 129)

七十年代末的时候可供选择的普通语言学理论还不多，因此利宾斯卡只举了结构主义和转换语法两家。七十年代后语言学流派纷出，目标、内容各不相同，可选择的余地就更大了。即以研究语言与思维的关系，认知语言学可能就是比生成语言学更好的选择。

During her time, researchers were not spoiled for choices in linguistic theories, so Lipińska had to settle for structuralism and transformational grammar. Starting from the 1970s, various schools of thought, obviously armed with different goals, blossomed and opened up a new horizon for contrastive study. The danger at present though lies in the fact that many may be applying theory for the sake of it, having no relevance to and taking no bearing from ontology, purpose or most importantly, language perspective.

5.2.2.1.3 语言观决定方法论
5.2.2.1.3 Language-perspective-decisive

而在本体论、目的论之外，决定方法论的更重要甚至是决定性的因素是语言观。因为说到底，连对学科本体论和目的论的认识都是由语言观决定的。语言观是在学科性背后起作用的东西，不同的语言观导致了不同的语言理论，以及对于对比语言学学科性质的不同定位，从而决定对学科研究方法论的选择。还是来看利宾斯卡是怎么说的：

Even more important than ontology and teleology is the view on language. Language perspective forms a more fundamental basis for methodological study. After all, both ontology and teleology of contrastive study are decided by our fundamental understanding of language. A different take on language gives rise to a variety of linguistic theories and differing understandings of the nature of contrastive linguistics, which is consequential to the formulation and choice of research methodology. Again, Lipińska shared her forsight:[1]

不同的研究目标造成了不同的语言研究方法论,除此之外,不同党派的哲学观也造成了差异。而这种差异会影响到最终的研究目标。可以预想得到结构主义派强调的是语言间之异,而转换派会努力设法证明语言在本质上是"同一模子里浇出来的"。由于美国描写主义植根于人类学,因而不仅沿用了前者的一些研究方法,而且也接过了人类文化的差异多多少少反映在语言中这样的总体观点。结构主义者的主体哲学观是相对主义,他们通常接受沃尔夫-萨丕尔假说的弱式(甚至强式)。另一方面,转换派与当代哲学逻辑的发展趋势密切相关,它采用的是演绎法而不是结构主义派的归纳法,其哲学基础沿着笛卡儿的思维路线,是绝对主义:在高度抽象的层面,不同的语言都是一样的。因此其研究的主要目标就是寻找语言的普遍特点。(利宾斯卡,1980:128)

Apart from the divergence resulting from opposite methodological approaches to language and reflected in different formulations of the immediate goals of the analysis, differences can also be found in the philosophical assumptions underlying each school. These differences will influence the final goal of the investigations. It may be expected that structuralists will emphasize the differences among languages, whereas transformationalists will look for the evidence that languages are, after all, "cut to the same pattern". Since American descriptivism has its roots in anthropology, it not only retained some of the methods of this discipline but also the general view about the diversity of human cultures reflected at least to some extent in languages. The structuralist's philosophical outlook is mainly relativistic: the weaker (if not the stronger) version of the Sapir-Whorf hypothesis is usually accepted. On the other hand, the transformational school has close connections with some trends of modern philosophy and logic. The method is deduction rather than induction employed by the

---

1 Lipińska confused American structuralists with anthropologists. In fact early Chinese textbooks on general linguistics taught something like "both Sapir and Bloomfield are forerunners and representatives of American structuralism"—It now seems that the misconstrue stemmed from the West.

structuralists, and the philosophical basis, stemming from the Cartesian line of thought, is absolutist: when analyzed at a high level of abstraction, languages are all alike. The search for universal linguistic features is the primary objective of transformational grammar. (Lipińska, 1980: 128)

我们在本章开头曾指出利宾斯卡是西方对比学者中对方法论研究提出很多真知灼见的少数学者之一，这一节的三个方面都引用了她的话可以为证。因为我们找不到别人，包括在国内的学者，比她说得更透彻。尽管如此，我们还是要指出，她对有的事实的理解并不正确。例如把美国结构主义与人类学家混为一谈。多年前我们自己在学习普通语言学时，教科书上告诉我们的也是"萨丕尔与布龙菲尔德同为美国结构主义的鼻祖和代表"，想来这观点也是来自西方像利氏这样的语言学家。现在我们已看得很清楚，结构主义语言学与人类学语言学完全建立在对语言的不同理解上，一是自然科学式的理解，一是人文科学式的理解。而转换派在将语言当作自然科学研究对象时却与结构主义毫无二致。此外，利氏认为转换派研究的主要目标是寻找语言的普遍特点（features），那也是错误的。转换派想要找到的不是"特点"而是"规则"（rules）和"原则"（principles）。想寻找共同"特点"的反倒是她所批评的人类学语言学始祖之一、人文主义语言学家洪堡特。由于她有这些错误理解，加上她所处的时代，因而我们对她的过度拔高转换生成语言学也就可以理解了。当然，这更不影响我们对她有关方法论的精彩论述的赞赏。

At the beginning of the present chapter, Lipińska was mentioned as a remarkable few and far between scholars who had shed brilliant lights on the study of methodology in contrastive linguistics evident by the three citations in this section. However, her observations are not without flaws. It is beyond question that American structuralists and anthropologists hold entirely different views on language with the former coming from a naturist perspective and the latter, humanist perspective. In this sense, transformationalists and structuralists agree as they both regard language as the subject of natural science. In retrospection, Lipińska's comment that "the search for universal linguistic features is the primary objective of transformational grammar" needed qualification. Transformational linguists pursue universal rules or principles as "universal features" of languages, in common with von Humboldt, one of the forerunners of humanist linguistics and anthropological linguistics she criticized. However, limited by her time, that transformation grammar was actually moving further and further away from their purpose was not immediately clear. Notwithstanding, that is not a blemish that would outweigh her contribution on the subject of methodology.

　　进一步说，语言观和语言理论是在两个层面上操作的。语言观是基础，在其上层是语言理论和语言学。语言观从本质上来看有三种：（1）着重语言的自然属性，把语言看作自然科学研究的对象；（2）着重语言的社会属性，把语言看作社会科学研究的对象；（3）着重语言的人文属性，把语言看作人文科学研究的对象。如果再细致地分下去，那同一种语言观的细分、排列和组合，可以形成形形色色的语言学理论。例如同样强调语言自然属性、侧重于系统性的，形成了结构主义理论；侧重于生物性的，形成了神经语言学或生物语言学。又如，同样强调语言社会属性、侧重人际交往性的，形成了交际语言学；而侧重语言不同阶段变化的则形成了文化语言学、人类语言学中的各种理论。当我们同时注意到语言的两种或三种属性时，就会因应侧重点或综合先后的不同而形成了不同的语言学流派。

　　To go a step further, language perspective and language theory function on two planes. Language perspective governs the primary level. Language theory or linguistics serves the secondary level. Fundamentally speaking, there are three broad perspectives of language: (1) the naturalistic approach to language regarding language as the object of natural sciences; (2) social approach to language regarding language as the object of social sciences; and (3) humanistic approach to language regarding language as the object of humanities. Upon finer classification, different loci in the respective language perspectives served as the basis for different linguistic theories. For instance, within the naturalistic approach, emphasis on the systemic nature leads to the theory of structuralism whereas emphasis on the biological nature leads to the theory of neurolinguistics or biolinguistics. On the other hand, sharing the same social approach to language, emphasis on the communicative nature evolved into the theory on communicative linguistics; while emphasis on different phases of change brought about theories in cultural linguistics, anthropological linguistics, etc.. Sometimes researchers may hold an integrated view of language and branch into a linguistic school or put forward a linguistic theory consistent to the view.

对比语言学在本质上属于语言学的一个分支，与其他分支处在同一层次，对比语言学在形成过程中首先受语言观的指导，但同时也会受到既有的种种语言学理论的不同影响。但是，有些语言学者不一定认同这个观点。这样的分歧导致对比研究被各种理论瓜分，有些理论还是互相矛盾的。有志于从事语言对比研究的工作者必须认清当前这个局面，认识语言观的重要性，首先要清楚地识别和确认语言对比应有的语言观。对语言观缺少了深度认识，也就无从把握对比语言学的本体论和方法论。

By nature, contrastive linguistics is like any other branch of linguistics and being grounded on a language view. Not all scholars of linguistics are convinced nonetheless. The contrastive study is divided into a wide range of theories championing conflicting approaches to language. The present circumstances should set Contrastivists ahead in their understanding of the role played by language perspective and permit a mindful choice in language perspective. Unless there is a solid grounding on the language view, no ontological or methodological questions can be taken meaningfully.

5.2.2.2 选择性原则
5.2.2.2 Principles grounded on selection criteria

上面说的背景性原则可以说是一种强制性原则，如果背景确定，研究者几乎没有选择的余地。这种强制性最容易在对别的研究者所使用的方法论的观察上看出来。如果我们知道某一研究者的语言观属于我们在上一章所分析的四种中的某一种，他所信奉的又是某一家的语言理论，那我们几乎可以断定他在研究中大致会采取什么方法论路线；甚至看了题目就可以预见他想达到什么结论。而这里要说的选择性原则可以说是一种主观性原则，指的是研究者在开始研究前还有一定程度的选择自主性。

Principles grounded on background and discussed above are definitive—once formulated, must be adhered to. By examining the methodology adopted in contrastive studies, the definitive nature of these principles cannot be clearer. With the broad language perspectives at our finger tips, preferred linguistic theory in contrastive studies decides almost at once the methodology to be taken. In most cases, the title of the research is enough to foretell the anticipated conclusion. The next set of principles on selection criteria, however, is subjective, allowing freedom of choice to be exercised. Six such principles are as follows:

- 语言观和语言理论的选择性
- choice of language view and linguistic theory

前文从方法论回溯到本体论，最后落实在语言观，重点就是要指出语言对比工作首先必须确认语言观和相应的语言学理论，从而奠定具体贯彻对比研究的大框架。理论上来说，由上而下，从语言观到理论到实践操作虽然最为理想，从反方向，基于某个语言问题，选择适当的理论解释以配合研究主旨也许更为实际，惟必须尊重语言事实，不能把语料生搬硬套。应该说明的是，理论不能囿于一家一派，必须就语言事实考虑各种适用层面，比如以汉语为目标的英汉对比中，英汉相似的句子结构问题，纳入语义、语用的考虑，更能发挥解释力度，但要选取哪个语义、语用的观点才能突显同中之异，就要求研究者博关经典，博采众长。由上而下或者由下而上都不是一个直达的程序，而是不断调适的过程，基于所对比的材料，不断把理论修订得更细致，而多种差异大的语言材料对比之后，也会帮助我们重塑更为理想的语言观。这就是对比语言学以普通语言学为宗旨的重大意义。

Following the discussion above tracing methodology to ontology and finally language perspective, the first selection confronting a researcher is none other than the selection of language view and linguistic theory. The decision on a language view would have laid down the general policy for performance in contrastive study. While a top-down approach from language perspective to theory to application is favoured theoretically, it is perhaps more practical to adapt appropriate theory on specific linguistic data to the chosen theme of a research on the condition that data are not massaged to fit the theory. It should be clear by now that by theory, we are not confining to a particular school of thought, in fact, we need to open up to a wider spectrum of possibilities relevant to the pair of language under consideration. For instance, in English-Chinese contrastive study with the Chinese language as the target, a similar construction found in the language pair would be most likely to be arrived at a more convincing explanation taking into account considerations in semantics and pragmatics. But exactly which finer theories in semantics and pragmatics would shed light on differences in similarity? That would demand a more accommodative understanding of available viewpoints on the part of the researchers to make informed and intelligent selection. We cannot emphasize more that top-down or bottom-up, there is no through road access. It is a continual adaptation of theories based particularly on comparing languages that are poles apart to ultimately shape a most ideal language view. Unmistakably, nothing illustrates the essence of contrastive linguistics for general linguistics more than that.

- 研究层级的选择性
- Choice on research facets

语言观一旦选定，可说方向性的问题已经确定，以下的选择都是具体"路线"上的。研究者首先可以在研究层级上做出选择，即在"理论"、"应用"、"实践"三个层级上（包括语言哲学是四个层级）确定自己的主攻方向，是侧重理论呢，还是侧重应用？如此等等。因为理论研究与应用研究、实践研究的方法是不同的，如理论研究可以用宏观方法，而应用性研究和实践性研究一般多用微观方法。

The next option to be considered concerns the "lines" along which to carry out the policy with ontological factors in sight. Upon the basis of earlier discussion, research facets are grouped under "theory", "application" and "practice", or even "philosophy". As a matter of fact, approaches for theoretical, applied theoretical and practical studies widely differ in scope and method—say, macroscopic methods for theoretical studies, microscopic methods for practical studies—the researcher's decision may become his or her main area of study over a period of time.

- 研究层面的选择性
- Choice on linguistic levels

其次可以在研究层面上做出选择。本书提出的语言定义的特点是包容性大，因而对比语言学所容纳的范围也大。把语言当作符号系统（自然属性）、交际工具（社会属性）、民族精神的体现（人文属性）进行对比是大的划分，下面还可进一步划分成语音层面、语法层面、话语层面、语篇层面、文体层面、风格层面等等进行对比。当然还可分得更细，如语法下划出句法和词法等等。研究者在这些方面都有进行选择的自由。而不同层面的选定相应也就确定了不同的研究方法。例如从大的三个层面来看研究方法显然不同，而即使在小的方面如语音和语法的研究方法也不相同。如考虑到对同一对象（如语法）从三个不同层面（自然、社会、人文）的角度去进行对比研究，方法上更会有差异。

The refined definition for language proposed in the present book is highly inclusive, so is the scope of contrastive linguistics based on such understanding. At a broader level, language can be taken as a symbolic system, a means for communication and embodiment of national spirit present a rich reservoir of data for study. Traditional sub-levels of language deal with units in phonology, grammar, discourse, text, genre and style and further divisions can be expected, such as dividing grammar into morphology, syntax, phonetics etc.. Choices in linguistic units intrinsically associate with the method to be employed.

·语言方向和异同倾向的选择性
· Choice on language direction and "similarity-difference" preference

再次，研究者在研究的向度上可以做出选择。对比研究的向度大体有单向、双向和无向（即从"中间项"出发）的区别；单向还有从A语言到B语言，及从B语言到A语言的区别；无向还有双语和多语的区别。研究者对这些都有选择的自由。但这种选择与研究者自身的知识结构有关（如只懂双语者自然无法进行多语种间的对比），也与研究目的有关（如进行汉英对比是为英语教学还是汉语教学服务），更与对学科本体论的认识有关。后面我们对此还要讨论。

Almost sequentially, preference for direction came up next. In terms of language direction, there are in general three directions contrastive study may be undertaken: unidirectional, bidirectional, and multidirectional. In the case of unidirectional study, further considerations on whether the direction is from language A to language B or vice versa are needed. The knowledge and skill-set of the researcher naturally preclude or confine his/her option; a bilingual scholar cannot be expected to undertake multidirectional study, for instance. Beyond personal preference, considerations must relate to the goal of contrastive study (e.g. is an English-Chinese contrastive study to serve the teaching of English, or the teaching of Chinese?), and most of all, the understanding of contrastive linguistics itself. In terms of similarity-difference preference, we may proceed from universality to particularity or vice versa. We will take on the discussion further later.

- 研究方法的选择性
- Choice of research methods

在研究方法上,研究者可以选择的余地就更大。我们之所以在本章中要严格区分方法与方法论,就是为了方法的多元性和开放性。因为方法论是受限的,方法是不受限的。属于学科的方法论,则本学科的每位研究者都得考虑和做出选择,回旋余地很小;而不属于学科方法论的一般方法,研究者就可以完全从自己的角度考虑是否要采取以及怎样采取。如本章前面提到的分析与综合、宏观与微观、定量与定性、翻译法等等,研究者都可以根据自己的需要或取或否,或取此弃彼。

Researchers are spoilt for choice when it comes to research methods. The present chapter took pain to mark a strict distinction between method and methodology to rewire misconceptions obstructing the healthy growth of the discipline. That methodology is closely related to the nature of the discipline, it has to be taken into account in deciding on the method(s) to be used to ensure alignment with the ultimate goal of contrastive linguistics. To this end, there should be a good mix of generic and specific contrastive methods to serve research purposes.

- 研究模式的独创性
- Formulation of research model

我们把研究模式定义为方法集,这是研究者在大量实践基础上对前人,特别是自己的经验体会的总结和提升,对学科的发展和深入,及后继者的培养和启示,有着重要的意义。这是中外对比语言学发展史上比较薄弱的方面,有待于在今后加强。在这方面,所有的研究者都大有可为。

Inevitably, contrastive study involves intuitive integration of available methods guided by language perspective, methodology and teleology. When an integration of methods found application across the language facets, invariably, a research model is formed. Formulation of research model draws heavily on the versatility of individual researcher, but once an ideal model is in place, any one may apply the model to any sub area of contrastive study.

或许对比的方向和程序引起了较多的注意，然而最关键的并不在于此。昆士兰大学中文教授陈平（2017）的文选《汉语的形式、意义和功能》把过去发表的文章结集，虽然不都运用对比方法，但是从对比的角度审视，也颇有启发。（1）还在建立自己的分析体系的语言如汉语者，借助于成熟的印欧语言体系的多样化理论也不是一无可取的，我们如今已经有较高的印欧语眼光的意识，可以比较持平地采用对比来透视汉语特点，点点滴滴地拼凑起完整的汉语图像。这个过程是崎岖的，也要求研究者对各种理论有较强的认识。比如陈平（2017）探讨汉语句子成分和语义关系以及汉语的结构话题综合运用了语义和语用学理论，观察到一些很有意思的分布情况并给予解释。（2）文选以形式、功能和意义为题，似乎与叶斯柏森的哲学眼光遥相呼应。陈平所选取的共性视角精当，语料与理论的配合非常贴切，兼顾形式、功能和意义，所以解释也比较到位。该论文集解释共性视角的选择其实很关键。饶有趣味的是，在众多视角中，陈平所选择的共性往往具有哲学含意，比如时间系统中的逻辑分类，这对于系统化的比较大有裨益。沃尔夫从时间系统考察了霍皮语，陈平（2017/1988）也提出汉语有三个时间子系统，对于其中的时态子系统，也许有学者持异议，但是时态不只是形式变化的时态，也是哲学时态，汉语确实以不同的手段来表达时态的意义。就如汉语形式上没有印欧语的语气，但是可以以其他手段来表达虚拟和条件境况。无论是从共性到个性，抑或从个性到共性，陈平筛选的理论有较强的解释力度，突出汉英对比的同中之异，有利于整理汉语的个性系统。（3）尽管我们还没有提出研究模式，如果继续往这个方向努力，必能形成几种合理的研究模式。根据我们在4.3章所提出的体系，如果把有哲学意义的共性纳入对特定语言之对比研究合宜的理论，也许会有所发明。

Before we move on, current attention on language direction and procedure for comparison though important, is not overriding. A collection of articles by Chinese linguist Chen Ping (2017) of the University of Queensland, though all not using contrastive methods, may be examined through the contrastive len to shed light on a few points. (1) For languages yet to establish their own system, such as Chinese, it may not be entirely a bad idea, even as we are watchful of a SAE tint, to take advantage of the variety of theories in the more matured western linguistic system from a balanced contrastive perspective to sieve out the particularities before piecing them together to complete the jigsaw puzzle. It is by no means an easy endeavor requiring a mastery of an array of theories. For example, articles in Chen (2017) show that semantics, pragmatics are employed to study subject and structural topic in Chinese to offer a series of interesting observations. (2) In giving his collection the title "form, function and meaning", Chen came across as aspiring to ride on the same philosophical plane as Otto Jespersen as can be seen in his choice of universals and clever fitting of data to theories to truly account for form, function and meaning in a holistic way. Given that his choice of universals is pivotal, it is interesting to find that although there are seemingly many universals to choose from, Chen picked those that reflect language philosophy, e.g, the logical classification of temporal system etc. that would allow systemic comparison. Benjamin Whorf drew conclusions on Hopi language on time, while Chen (2017/1988) formulated a triplex structure for temporal system in Chinese with tense as a sub-system. Some may disagree with Chen on tense, but we should look at tense as a philosophical concept rather than a morphological concept. Just as although Chinese does not have morphological changes to indicate mood, there are other means to express similar meaning in subjunctive or condition with other forms. Be if from particularity to universality or vice versa, what is noteworthy is the flexibility in Chen's intelligent selection of theories to provide a fuller explanation that highlight the differences demonstrated by the Chinese language against western languages such as English. (3) While there is no research model yet to be proposed, effort in the same direction could possibly point the way forward to assemble reasonable models. It would be interesting to see how the matrix we brought forth in Chapter 4.3 would work out if we plug in universals with philosophical significance and assemble a series of theories functionable for a particular language pair.

5.2.2.3 同一性原则
5.2.2.3 Principles grounded on homogeneity

如果说方法论三原则中，背景性原则是客观的强制性原则，选择性原则是主观的自主性原则，则同一性原则是主观的约束性原则。在某种程度上这是对选择性原则的一种约束，即研究者在研究中的选择实际上没有绝对的自由，而必须受到一些约束。

If principles grounded on background are mandatory, principles grounded on selection criteria are subjective, then the principles of homogeneity may be said to be restrictive. Homogeneity principles impose restrictions on the principles grounded on selection criteria, that is to say, the hands of researchers are tied although choices seem aplenty.

5.2.2.3.1 理论的一贯性

5.2.2.3.1 Consistency in theory

说到理论的一贯性，有人马上会想到运用某种现成语言理论时的前后一致性。例如，不要一会儿用结构语言学，一会儿用生成语言学，一会儿用认知语言学，一会儿又用功能语言学、话语分析理论等等，最好用一种理论就始终坚持到底，用功能语言学就自始至终是功能语言学，用形式语言学就自始至终是形式语言学。这当然是对的。因此我们不赞同前面某位学者提出的先定课题再找理论的观点，因为这有可能造成机会主义的研究态度。而且从单篇文章来看也许还看不出，把同一作者的几篇文章放在一起就有可能造成理论上的前后矛盾。

What comes easily to mind upon reading this subtitle is the consistency in theory application in research. It is a basic rudiment to keep to a theory throughout the whole research process rather than jumping opportunistically from one theory to another. It is all the more relevant today as numerous linguistic theories are seen contradicting one another. We cannot, for instance, explain the facts of language A with one theory, and the facts of language B with another, nor can we use facts proven by theory A to criticize facts proven by theory B. All theories must be examined and verified within their own scopes.

但是我们主张的要点还不在此。我们认为，既然对比语言学在性质上就是普通语言学，它不是任何一个二级学科语言学（如应用语言学）的分支，也不从属于普通语言学的某一理论学派（如生成语言学），它就不存在对某一派的语言学理论的"从一而终"的问题。对比语言学在自身的学科建设中应该敞开胸襟，博采众长，对各种语言学理论中能够为我所用的部分兼收并蓄。这也就是我们（潘文国，2002a）支持和鼓励"理论和方法的多元化"的原因。"理论和方法的多元化"不仅是整个学科的前景，也值得每一位研究者积极尝试。

因此在不同层级、不同层面、不同对象、不同目标上采用多家理论和方法来进行对比研究可以说是必然的事。但是，这种多元化，是各家理论、学说的有机融合，不是头痛医头、脚痛医脚式的杂凑拼合，各种理论要经过研究者头脑的消化，在新的基础上，形成为新的学科目标服务的新的内部一致的体系。这才是"理论的一贯性"的真正意义。

However, that's not the point of contention here. In fact, that contrastive linguistics is part of general linguistics and not merely a sub-branch of any linguistic school or linguistic theory, and consistency within the theory of one existing school is not the issue. Truth be told that contrastive linguistics is wanting in a theory of its own: what ought to be done is open its bosom to welcome all kinds of linguistic theories, take in what is useful and construct a theory of its own. Verily, attempts of various sorts using diversified range of methods on an array of linguistic units would eventually prove to be beneficial to the discipline moving forward. So at least at this stage, an assortment of linguistic theories and methods to suit different purposes is something to be expected. It is against this background that we call for consistency in formulating a contrastive theory. Under this principle, individual research efforts are pooled together for assimilation and integration into a theory consistent with the objective of contrastive linguistics.

要做到理论的一贯性，我们要一方面支持一以贯之地引进、运用国际上最新语言学理论的人，鼓励他们从事对比研究；另一方面更要大力支持能"化入、创生"国际语言学理论、积极创新对比语言学以及包括汉语在内的普通语言学理论的人，大兴重视理论研究之风，大兴创新研究之风。

To construct a consistent theory for the discipline, on the one hand, persist in studying and introducing novel ideas from linguistic theories abroad and test their application in contrastive study; on the other hand, encourage Chinese scholars to transfigure and create contrastive theories drawing inputs from general linguistic theories that acknowledge the place of Mandarin Chinese as well as Chinese linguistic facts.

5.2.2.3.2 材料的同质性
5.2.2.3.2 Homogeneity of linguistic data

材料的同质性是研究过程中对选用材料的约束。前面我们曾对"共时"和

"历时"的区分颇有一些微辞。从本质上来说，索绪尔的"共时"、"历时"之分是为其建立"共时语言学"服务的，因此只有"共时"是相对清晰的，"历时"的概念却相对含混，实际上"历时"是相对于"共时"而言的，只是"共时"的陪衬。这才出现了上面有的学者说的"不能拿中古英语与现代汉语比，也不能拿上古汉语与汉代英语比"这样似是而非的话。在语言学上，由于历史发展的差异性，除了"当代"之外，几乎不存在历史上的"共时"对比的可能性。比方说，我们既不能拿严格的历史年代作标准，如八世纪、十五世纪等（要那样的话，莎士比亚的英语也许还能同汤显祖的汉语作比较，但大部分时期的古代汉语就失去了比较的对象）；也不能拿相对的"历史时期"作标准，如"同在中世纪初期"、"同在资本原始积累时期"（要那样的话，拿来与"现代汉语"比的，不该是"当代英语"，而该是培根时代甚至更早的英语）。同时，"共时"的语言材料也是"历时"堆积的结果，"现代汉语"里的成语有的可追溯到一、两千年以前；"当代英语"中，也有大量几百年前"钦定圣经"英文的遗留，这些都已经熔化在两种现时语言里，我们很难再在里面区分出"共时"、"历时"来。因而我们主张，在对比研究中，要严格控制这对概念的使用，把"共时"确定为某一语言在某一时期的现存状态，把"历时"用来指某一语言本身发展和演变的过程。"共时"与"历时"都是就某一语言自身而言，而在语言对比中，我们以"同质"来取代之，以"同质"材料作为对比的材料。这个"同质"，既可能是相对的"共时"，也可能是相对的"历时"。根据前者，我们就既可以把"当代英语"与"现代汉语"比，在需要的时候，也不妨跟几百、几千年前的汉语比；[1]根据后者，我们就可以把三千年的汉语发展史，跟一千年的英语发展史作对比。而不用担心在方法论上出什么问题。

Linguistic material in research has to pass the homogeneity test. Readers may recall reservations in earlier deliberation on synchronic and diachronic studies. 19th century linguists like Baudouin de Courteney, Ferdinand de Saussure and those of the Prague School saw the need to draw distinction between "dynamic"

---

1 马建忠不就是把唐以前的汉语与十九世纪的欧洲语言作比较而写出了他的《马氏文通》吗？谁说古代汉语不能与现代英语比呢？
It is wrong to suppose that modern English cannot be compared with ancient Chinese. The famous *Mashi Wentong*, written by Ma Jianzhong a century ago, is the result of comparison between the 19th century's European languages with Chinese of the 8th century or earlier.

and "static", "synchronic" and "diachronic" at a time when synchronous data was given heightened attention. (refer to Chapter 1) At that time, the relative sense of these two pairs of concept was clear, separating comparative linguistic data and data of currency. As time evolves and a longer historical horizon comes into the picture, Baudouin's concept on dynamic and static was buried under stone and the relative sense of synchronic and diachronic becomes rather vague and perilous of being misconstrued. This explains paradoxical argument against comparing Middle English with modern Chinese, or ancient Chinese with contemporary English. While diachronic clearly refers to linguistic data over time, the "currency" of synchronic could refer to any specific period of time. So, the English of Shakespeare's (1564—1616) may be contrasted against the Chinese used by Tang Xianzu's (1550—1616) in a synchronic study. And it should be noted that the synchronous nature of such study comes with a diachronic dimension that highlights the stages of development concerning the languages involved. Contrariwise, it is common knowledge that expressions currently in use may be dated back to antiquity—that strength of live has no impact on the synchronicity or diachronicity of linguistic data of a particular period of time. For instance, many idioms passed down from days of yore remained relevant in modern Chinese in the same way as contemporary English witnessed the use of numerous expressions traced to the "authorized version of Bible" of classical times. In any case, expressions from the good old days constitute part of the data in a synchronic study although any variation in current usage may be part of a diachronic study. In retrospect and for the benefit of contrastive studies, it may be useful to confine the use of "synchronic" and "diachronic" with reference to a language in discussion such that "synchronic" describes existing status of a language at a specific period of time; and "diachronic", the process of evolution and change within one language. Whereas in contrasting two or more languages, the term "homogeneity" may be more useful: only homogeneous linguistic materials can be used for contrasting. Homogeneous material may be relatively "synchronic", or relatively "diachronic". In the first instance, modern English may be compared with either modern Chinese, or Chinese of hundreds or thousands of years ago.[1] In the second instance, comparison may be made between the historical development of Chinese over 3,000 years and that of English over just 1,000 years and feeling safe that methodological wise, it is sound.

　　"同质"的对立面是"异质"。坚持同质材料的对比研究,当然就要反对异质材料的对比研究。那么什么是异质呢?从上面分析可知,相对的"共时"和相对的"历时"分别相比较都属于"同质",那异质就只能是相对的"共时"跟相对的"历时"直接相比。凡是"共时"都带描写性,凡是"历时"都带解释性,因此,凡是将描写的材料与"解释"的材料作对比那就是异质。比如说现实英语中有某种现象,但在现实汉语的描写中找不到,于是经过一番"解释",说在汉语的历史上可能有,或将来可能有,或"按理"可能有,然后造出一些"读十遍就能读通"的例子来与现实的英语例子对比,这样的研究就是异质的研究。例如为了证明汉语与英语"同源",找来一对词"say"和"说"(shuo),要证明shuo就读[sei],第一步是说汉语的卷舌不卷舌历史上可以相通,第二步是说"说"与"税"声符相同,都是"兑"([duei]),第三步是汉语发展过程中中介音是后起的,[uei]原来应该是[ei],这样"说"的"古音"就应该念[sei],与英语"say"相同。

　　The opposite end of homogeneity is heterogeneity, something to avoid in contrastive study. Following the discussion above, language contrast between two sets of relatively synchronic or diachronic data both considered "homogeneous". However, to conduct contrastive study between a set of relatively synchronic data with a set of relatively diachronic data will be considered as "heterogeneous". As a matter of fact, the treatment of synchronous data is descriptive, so is the nature of synchronic study; whereas, diachronous data may be descriptive or explanatory with the nature of diachronic study mainly explanatory. For this matter, contrastive project needs to exercise care in handling data to avoid ending up with a heterogeneous pair of data, one being descriptive and the other, explanatory. For example, for a particular phenomenon in modern English (as a result of description), we may like

---

1　It is a mistake to suppose that modern English cannot be paired with ancient Chinese for comparison. The prominent *Ma's Grammar*, written by Ma Jianzhong a century ago, is the result of comparing European languages of the nineteenth century with Chinese of the eighth century.

to find a similar phenomenon in modern Chinese or older Chinese (also as a result of description) for comparison. That data set is homogeneous. Questions arise when a similar phenomenon fails to be found in existing Chinese data and yet there is still a wish to set up a relation between the two languages. The study may go on to use method of deduction or analogy ("explanation") to prove that some Chinese dialect or some point in time in the development of the Chinese language, traces of such a phenomenon may be found to fulfill the aim of the study. Those data sets are heterogeneous. To illustrate the point, below is a fabricated example. Now a study wishes to show that English and Chinese are two cognate languages. Using an English word "say" [sei] and its Chinese equivalent 说 (shuo), the study claims that 说 "originally" was pronounced as [sei]. The "explanation" goes along the following line: (1) Historically and even in some dialects today, the consonants s and sh are interchangeable, so say and shuo in fact share the same consonant; (2) The two Chinese characters 说 (shuo) and 税 (shuei) share the same phonetic component 兑 (duei) and all ended with a final [uei]; (3) In Chinese phonological history, medials like (i, u, ü) appear rather late, so [uei] should originally have been pronounced as [ei]; (4) Putting together (1) and (4), that 说 was originally pronounced as [sei], the same as the English synonym "say" is proven.

上面这个例子是我们杜撰的。但据我们所知，确实有人在做这样的"研究"。语法上做这种尝试的人更多。这样的对比研究或"比较"研究是令人为他们捏一把汗的。

The above example may be fabricated, but there are studies that were conducted along the same line of thought, particularly at the grammatical level. All these ought to be discouraged.

作为本节的小结，我们不妨统揽对比语言学的研究现状。我们在第四章第三节提出了对比语言学的学科体系，将对比研究分成若干个层级，如理论、应用等，又分为若干个层面，如结构、交际等，纵横交错加上语言哲学形成八个研究领域。对比研究者从事对比研究当然有充分的选择余地，但他同时也必须受到某种约束。表现在领域上，对比必须在对应的领域范围内进行。也就是，理论对理论、应用对应用、实践对实践。更进一步，结构理论对结构理论、交际应用对交际应用。一般来说，领域不能交叉，比方说不能用一方的结构理论研究成果来对比另一方的交际应用，指责后者所存在的"问题"。甚至在对比中所运用的理论也是如此，都应该控制在相应的范围。在同一个领域内，研究"同质"的语言材料，应该运用同一个理论。不能对甲语言材料用一种理论去解释，对乙语言材料用另一种理论去解释。也不能用甲理论的证据去批驳乙理论的证据，每一种理论都只能在本理论自身范围之内检验其适应程度的高低。另一方面我们也必须强调指出，这十个领域共同组成对比语言学的学科体系，不只是纵横交错的简单结果，不是一个贪大求全的大杂烩，而是具有严密的体系性的。这个体系性体现在两个方面，一个是包容性，一个是层次性。

To close off the section, it is worthwhile to take an overarching view on research in contrastive linguistics. Chapter 4.3 proposed eight domains in the matrix of contrastive linguistics on several facets and levels including language philosophy, communication and structure. It goes without saying that contrastive studies have to be conducted within corresponding domains, i.e. comparing structure with structure, theory with theory, keeping in mind consistency in theory and homogeneity of data. These eight domains are not pieced together haphazardly as a compromise to accommodate various ideas. It forms a water-tight system after careful deliberation to encompass the necessary and take into account the progressive nature of language as a natural science, social science and human science. In this regard, the eight domains do not spread out in a single file or dimension. Moving from one domain to another suggest movements between dimensions. Essentially, the movement could be from specific linguistic units towards theory and ultimately language philosophy or going from top down in the opposite direction. In this sense, even as we mention "choices" above, the whole system has imposed restrictions. A researcher must be familiar enough to know exactly where he/she is coming from in the entirety of the contrastive linguistics blueprint.

5.3 对比研究的出发点
5.3 Primary premise or starting point in contrastive study

在本章的最后几节，我们将具体讨论几个在对比研究中比较重要的方法论问题，从历史和哲学的角度对它们作比较细致的探讨。

The remaining sections of this chapter are devoted to some of the most important methodological issues in contrastive linguistics, both from the perspectives of history as well as philosophy.

第一个便是对比研究的出发点问题。这是每一位从事对比研究的人所遇到的第一个问题。研究这个问题的意义在于，它虽然只是个"起点"问题，但却影响到全局，几乎从一开始就已经可以预示到最后的结局。人们不得不对它慎之又慎。

Topping the list is the issue concerning primary premise or starting points—the stumbling block every researcher will encounter right from the start before anything else. From the starting point, it has a far-reaching influence over the whole process of the study, and may even forecast the final results. One can never be too careful in this regard.

我们来看历史上有过的，或有人主张过的比较研究出发点。

First let's examine the known "starting points" in the course of development.

5.3.1 从体系出发
5.3.1 Premised on systems

这可以说是结构主义的特色。我们看只要看拉多提出的对比模式，就可知道这在五十年代以后对比分析的初期曾是个重要的、主要的（如果不是惟一的）、并被寄予厚望的模式。拉多模式的要点就在于：（1）认为结构是语言研究的核心，也是外语学习的核心，因此语言间一切异同问题可以通过结构对比来解决；（2）对比只要将两种语言的结构拿出来，进行平行比较就可以了；（3）这样发现出来的"同"无足轻重，而"异"对语言学习就有着切实指导意义，是编写外语教材的依据。事实证明，这一理解从理论上说是错误的，从实践上说是不可行的。

Premised on systems is the hallmark of structuralism. In the 1950s, Lado's contrastive model bears evident as the most important, if not the only, model upon which much hope on CA has been pinned. The salient points of Lado's model may be summed up as: (1) Structure is at the core of linguistic study and language education. All questions pertaining to similarities and differences between languages can be resolved through structural comparison; (2) It is sufficient to presents two linguistic structures side by side for language comparison; (3) Similarities thus found are of little importance while differences discerned are of great value and should be compiled in textbooks for foreign language teaching. However, these points have been proven to be theoretically unsound and impractical.

理论上的错误在于学习语言的核心并不完全在语言表面的结构。从表层讲，语言学习是为了说不同语言的人们之间的交流；从深层讲，语言学习是为了学习不同民族的人认知和表述世界的方式。在这过程中，语言的结构是重要的，但不是决定性的，学习外语时发生的错误有的与结构有关，更多的未必跟结构有关。仅从结构着手，只能达到事倍功半的效果。对比研究的实践证明了这一点。西方第二期与中国第四期对比研究的最终淡出，主要原因就在于这一模式未能达到预期的目标，它以热心地宣告要为外语教学服务始，却以在教学中的作用"极其有限"终。因而整个第方第二期对比研究的失败不是对比语言学的失败，而是以拉多为代表的这一对比模式的失败。

Lado's mistake, theoretically speaking, lies in the fact that foreign language learning is not dependent on the structure alone. On the surface, foreign language learning is to facilitate communication with another tongue. Fundamentally, it means learning the fashion another ethnic group uses to cognate and represent the world. It is certainly important to learn the structure but that is not everything. Part of the errors made in learning a foreign language may be explained from the structural point of view but a large part of it is unrelated to language structure. Focusing on structure alone may be counter productive as the development of CA has already proven. That CA ultimately bowed out in both the West and in China is telling that its intended target—to serve foreign language teaching failed. It could well be said that the failure of CA is not so much the defeat of contrastive linguistics per se as the breakdown of Lado's model.

更致命的还在实践上，这一点很多人可能还没看出来。拉多说得很清楚，这一对比的前提是必须有对所要对比的两种语言结构的充分的描写；如果没有这样的描写，就必须先进行这样的描写。而这一点常被人忽略了。世界上有几个语言的结构系统是得到了充分的描写的？绝大多数语言的结构至今没有进行过充分的描写，人们之所以能将它们归入不同的"语系"、"语族"、"语支"……是依靠语言学家们对它们的"特点"的一些非常有限的描述或归纳。在一些似乎得到过"充分"或比较"充分"的描写的语言里，我们看到的是"希腊—拉丁"式语法病毒式的扩散过程，按照帕麦尔的说法，连英语这种非拉丁系语言的语法都深限于拉丁语法的范式不能自拔，何况世上极大多数非印欧系语言？沃尔夫等西方有识之士早就说过，印欧语的模式只是人类语言结构的一种可能的模式，它需要有与非这样的模式作比较才能更好地发展自己，然而在世界语法研究模式"拉丁化"的过程中，这种模式已成了"惟一"的模式，有多少按照这种模式描写得"充分"的语言是真正符合本族语言特色的"描写充分"？在这样的前提下，所谓的"比较"或"对比"，只能在拉丁语法的框架内修修补补、拾遗补缺，在初级阶段的外语教学中也许还有点用处（这是我们不反对作这种比较的原因），对于达到对比研究的真正目的（沃尔夫或吕叔湘所说的）可能毫无用处。

Nonetheless, few noticed the more fatal blow to the model is impracticality. Lado states very clearly that the prerequisite for structural comparison is the adequate description of the two languages involved, and if there isn't one, work has to begin from there. Yet that statement is grossly neglected by many if not all. Probing further, how many languages have their structures had adequately described? Not many. Majority of world languages are deprived of an adequate description. That world language family tree is drawn up is based only on some very limited observation or generalization of "features" in place of adequate description. In some seemingly adequately described languages, what we see is the rampant expansion of the Greek-Latin model of grammar. So remarked Palmer, if even the grammar of English, a non-Latin language, is so deeply rooted in the Latin pattern and can find no way out, how shall we judge the grammars of most other non-European languages? Sober western scholars like Whorf long recognised that European language pattern is but one mould in human language structures and can better develop itself only by comparison with other existing patterns. But unfortunately this pattern has domineered over other patterns in the Latinization process of world grammars. One may wonder if a native language grammar may be considered adequately described after this comprehensie pattern. The answer may be arguable. What we do find at this stage is that any contrast or comparison findings based on the European mould may be of some use initially but are far from accomplishing the fundamental task of contrastive linguistics set by Whorf or Lü Shuxiang.

而这种方法对于还没有"语法"的语言建立语法系统就更加有害。马建忠建立汉语语法系统，在本质上用的就是这样一个方法：他从西方"葛朗玛"的体系出发，将汉语的语言事实尽量纳入这一框架，实在纳不下的（如"助字"）就称之为"华文所独"，汉语语法史上的百年公案，就是由这第一步造成的。

The Latinisation method is especially harmful to languages awaiting for a more ideal description that would acknowledge and install a grammar they can call their own. As a case in point, chapter 2 mentioned the effort of Ma Jianzhong in establishing the first written Chinese grammar modeled after Latin grammar and adapting the Chinese language into the system. Only those linguistic facts with no matching equivalent were recognized by Ma as unique to Chinese. This very first step made by Ma premised on systems left an indelible mark in Chinese linguistic research in the century that follows. Till this day, while many academics are being fed following along this line of research, the real face of Chinese linguistics remains largely behind mask.

体系对比的扩大就是语言学体系的全面对比，这也是拉多开的头。他在薄薄的一本书里对比了语音、语法、词汇、文字、文化等五个方面。以后不少对比著作也都学他的样，一本书里面面俱到，什么都要比较，什么都不拉下。由于"体系"总是浮在语言现象的表层，因而这样的比较往往流于浮浅，"同"既未必真"同"，异也不能讲透。作为入门性质的教科书有时还有点用，但作为真正的研究是谈不上的。

Expanding from structural comparison, linguistic systems as a whole may also be compared, and again, Lado took the lead. In his thin book of merely a hundred pages, Lado touched on five aspects of the language systems: phonetics, grammar, vocabulary, scripts and culture. Many later books took after his. To attempt too much at one go always leaves much to be desired in the end. That may be something that we want to think about. As the closing remark of Chapter 5.2 suggests, moving from one domain to another and from one dimension across another to gradually build up a whole system of comparison may allow for deep insight.

5.3.2 从规则出发
5.3.2 Premised on rules

1957年"乔姆斯基革命"造成了美国结构主义的失势，转换生成语法迅速成了美国、以及在一定程度上国际语言学的"主流"。"对比分析"失去了原来的理论依托，要想继续生存和发展就必须改换门庭。尽管从理论上看，新的语言学所主张的"普遍语法"说从根本上动摇了对比研究存在的必要性（既然语言在本质上都是相同的，只要学会了普遍语法就自然能解释语言间在表层上微不足道的差异），然而，处于困境中的西方对比研究者几乎还是义无反顾地"集体"倒向了生成语言学，从迪·皮德娄到利宾斯卡，从凡·布伦到克尔采斯佐斯基，还有许多其他人莫不如此。

The Chomskyan revolution of 1957 replaced structuralism almost overnight to become the mainstay of linguistics in the United States, and to a certain extent, in the international linguistic community. With structuralism fading out, contrastive analysis soon found itself "groundless" in theory and would have to turn to another theory to live on. Ironically, the emerging generative grammar offered no help to CA, for many of its basic concepts, especially those of "universal grammar", were shackles to the foundation of CA—since all languages are the same in nature, and comparison is redundant. And surface differences are but results of different processes in transformation, all one has to do is to study the grammar of one language and its transformational rules – yet the deeply trapped CA could find no other way out except falling, almost unanimously, head over heals before the new despot. Di Pietro, Lipin'ska, van Buren, Krzeszowski and many others were no exception.

倒向生成语言学的一个积极成果是使对比分析摆脱了为教学服务的狭隘范围，强化了理论诉求。要求"对比分析"改称"对比语言学"、要求对比语言学摆脱"应用语言学"、要求"对比语言学"分为"理论对比语言学"和"应用对比语言学"并加强对后者的研究等等，这些呼声差不多都是在这个时候同时发出的。原因今天看来非常简单，因为生成语言学是个纯得不能再纯的纯理论语言学，"对比分析"要靠向它，只能修改自己的定性和理论追求目标。对比语言学的目标被改变为"解释人类语言的本质和人类语言的共性"，而在研究方法和思路上也有了变化。最显著的首先表现在对比研究的出发点上。

There were positive outcomes though in taking shelter under generative linguistics. Language comparison was liberated from the narrow goal in foreign language teaching and began to recognise the importance of a theoretical foundation. It is not difficult to envisage new appeals such as re-naming of CA to contrastive linguistics poured in immediately following that saw CL pulling out of the applied linguistics branch with two new arms in theoretical CL and applied CL etc.. That development is understandable in retrospect. Under the auspices of generative linguistics—an extremely "pure" linguistics interested only in its theoretic pursuit—CA had no future but to evolve along and restate its target to suit the new landscape. Following which, the goal for contrastive linguistics was adjusted to "explaining the nature of human language and its universality", reflected in change of research methods thereafter, most prominently reflected in the so-called "starting point".

　　"从体系出发"肯定不行了,因为这是结构主义的;而且这个说法隐含着人类语言的结构是不同的,那是语言相对论的观点,哪能再用？"从事实出发"也不行,这种老掉牙的"归纳法"又是结构主义的老路；"从功能出发"也不行,语言学研究的是"competence",不是"performance","应用"不是语言研究的目的。因而这一派所主张的,只剩下"从形式出发"、"从规则出发"、"从原则出发"。这三者其实是一回事。"原则"（principles）相对于"参数"（parameters）是人类语言的"共性"；"规则",因为普遍语法是由一系列"规则"（rules）组成的；"形式",因为语言研究的最终目标,要能对规则进行形式描写,人类的普遍语法应该是个"形式化"的语法。也许"从规则出发"用得多一些。

　　From the perspective of generative grammar, premised on systems with its structuralist-bias can never work out since the agenda, also supported by linguistic relativism that languages are mapped onto different structures contradicts. Even premised on linguistic facts is also out of question because it involved old-fashioned induction method structuralists uses. Using "function" as the starting point won't do either because linguistics study is about competence rather than performance. Anything that has to do with the "applied" side has no place. So, contrastive linguistics reined by generative grammar is only left with a few premises: "forms", "rules", and "principles", which eventually converged to rules. "Principles" as against "parameters", are "universal" in human languages; and universal grammar is form by a series of "rules"; and "forms" are in fact 'rules' in linguistic descriptions, and the universal grammar of humankind ought to be "formalized". Among the three, premised on rules is most common.

　　这些主张以迪•皮德娄表述的最直接和明白。例如他说：
　　Di Pietro expresses the same in a most straightforward and candid manner. He said:

　　　　如果所有的语言之间有共性,那么任何差异点只是共性在各别语法中实现的不同方式而已。……本书的语言观是一种规则观，即认为所有语言的语法都是由一套可以形式化的解释组成，将它们付诸实施，就可以造成该语言的句子。这些解释或者规则的排列次序，是从普遍到具体。（皮德娄，1971/1978：5—6）

If all languages share universals, then any differences are to be found in the ways these universals are realized in particular grammars... The view of language in the present book is rule oriented. That is to say, the grammar of each language is interpreted as consisting of a set of formalized explanations which, when put into operation, yield the sentences of that language. These explanations, or rules, are ordered so that the progression is from the general to the specific. (Di Pietro, 1971/1978: 5—6)

如果将这种观点与上一条加以比较，我们就会发现生成语法在一点上与结构主义是完全相同的，即把语言看成一个自然形态的系统。所不同的是结构主义认为不同语言有不同的系统，而生成语法认为人类语言只有一个系统，即所谓普遍语法。而且在强调语言的自然属性上走得比结构主义更远，主张也更机械、更僵硬。如强调语法只能是一套可以形式化的规则。

Compare this viewpoint with the previous primary premise, generativists in fact share at least one point in common with the structuralists, that is, both regard language as a natural system. Their major point of departure lies in whether there are different structural systems as suggested by the structuralists or there is only one system, i.e. the universal grammar, for all human languages. Albeit the commonality in upholding language as a natural science, the generativists go even further with a viewpoint that is even more rigid and mechanical. Their insistence that grammar is only a set of rules which can be formalized is a case in point.

在这种前提下，语言对比确实无法进行。所谓的"对比"，只能是通过如此这般的一番操作，"证明"原来所设想的普遍性"规则"的正确，的确具有"普遍性"。"对比"成为解释"普遍语法"的一个手段。这样，好不容易从结构主义那里解放出来的对比语言学，尽管"理论性"得到了重视，但仍无可奈何地沦为生成语言学的一个分支——甚至连分支都谈不上，分支还会有自己的研究体系和方法论，而在生成语言学下，对比分析本身只是可有可无的一个方法，其"分析"过程与生成语言学现在在走的路（用世界各种语言的例子来证明"普遍语法"的普适性）没有什么两样。跟着生成语言学走，对比语言学就等于取消了自己。因而八十年代以后，西方的对比语言学几乎没有再跟普遍语法派走的。

As one may have gathered, there is hardly room for contrastive study under these suppositions. Language comparison, if at all, only served as a means to verify "universal grammar" with such "proofs" that the assumed universal "rules" are indeed correct and "universal". Like jumping from fire into frying pan, after a long winding path with the structuralists, contrastive study instead of setting itself free, resigned to become merely a method of trivial importance, not even fit to be a sub-branch of generative linguistics (GL). In fact it needs no foreshadowing that the procedure of "contrastive study" does not differ significantly from the general method GL is applying, i.e. to prove the universality of universal grammar with examples from other languages. Therefore, attachment to generative linguistics is as good as consuming CL itself. For this reason, no contrastivists in the West would like to be tagged with generative linguistics since the 1980s.

奇怪的是，在生成语言学本来没有多少市场、跟对比研究更没有什么瓜葛的中国，最近几年却出现了一些鼓吹对比研究要走普遍语法路子的声音，而且打的是要跟国际接轨的名义。这值得我们深思：要跟国际接轨，先要知道国际上本学科当前的发展趋势。我们是要跟当前的国际接轨呢？还是要跟二十多年前的国际接轨？把已经成为夕阳的国外语言学一些东西改头换面再"介绍"到中国来，对发展中国和国际语言学有什么好处？

In which case, what is happening in China seems more bizarre. Where GL has had little influence and CA not really within sight, there has been advocation in China in recent years urging CA to follow the pathway of GL. These are seemingly attempts for China to "reconnect with the world" but done without consideration to the development trend. We like to caution against putting things backward and hinder positive developments.

5.3.3 从范畴出发
5.3.3 Premised on categories

由于认识到各种语言的结构方式各不相同，而除英语等印欧语之外多数语言还缺乏自己的结构描写，因此对比语言学的先驱们很早就认识到了从体系或形式出发进行对比的不可靠。叶斯柏森提出的解决方案是采取"从I到O"的办法，即从"意义"经过"功能"再到"形式"；沃尔夫的解决方案则是从"范畴"出发。由于他们当时考虑的都是语法问题，因此，所谓"意义"、"功能"，其实是指"语法意义"、"语法功能"；所谓"范畴"，当然也是"语法范畴"，因而这两者其实是一致的。而"功能"后来在林语堂和吕叔湘的书里都称为"表达"。因而，这里所说的"从范畴出发"，与"从（语法）功能出发"和"从表达法出发"从某种角度看是一致的，我们也就放在一起讨论。

The forerunners of contrastive linguistics long realized the unreliability of the primary premise on systems or forms since they reckoned that languages came in different structures and most languages other than the Euro-Indo family were deprived of an adequate description. Another path was carved out. Jespersen's proposed to proceed from "I" to "O"; that is, beginning with deep structure "meaning", through "function" to "forms" on the outward; whereas Whorf's solution uses categories as the primary premise. Given that grammar was taking centerstage at the time, by "meaning", "function" or "categories", they meant "grammatical meaning", "grammatical function" and "grammatical categories", and essentially, the two scholars were not on different grounds. Over in China, "function" was known as "expression" in Lin Yutang's and Lü Shuxiang's books. On the above account, what we call "premised on categories" are in approximity to "premised on function" or "premised on expression" to an extent.

尽管叶斯柏森直到他的书《语法哲学》的最后一页才提到了这一新的语言比较研究的方法，然而这只是从学科及学科方法论的角度来看是如此。从实际内容来看，其实《语法哲学》一书本身就是按这一思路写的，他提出了一些语法学中最常见的范畴：人称、性、数、格、时态、否定、语气，乃至最常见的一些语法概念，如词类、句子等等，探讨了它们在二十多种语言里的表达方法，从而对这些语法术语、语法范畴本身进行了哲学的探讨。他的书没有以对比语言学命名，后人似乎也没有把它当作对比语言学著作看，然而这本书是最符合对比语言学精神的，因为他探讨的就是人类语言，特别是语法的本质。

Although Jespersen saved mentioning his method in "new comparative grammar" to the last page, his enterprise *The Philosophy of Grammar* was a shining living example written exactly to map out his thinking. In this title, Jespersen investigated common grammatical categories such as person, gender, case, tense, aspect, negation, mood alongside common notions like sentence, word class, etc. and discussed how they were being expressed in over 20 languages and finally outlined a beautiful philosophical insight. Even though the words "contrastive linguistics" were missing in the title and few recognised the status of this title in the discipline, but no other title ever came so close to the spirit of contrastive linguistics, devoting the entire content to probe into the nature of human languages, especially the nature of grammar.

叶斯柏森之外，成功运用这一方法的是中国学者。林语堂在1933年出版了《开明英文文法》，这是第一次将叶斯柏森的方法用于双语对比，同时密切结合了外语的教学与研究。林语堂同样从语气、替代、指示、修饰、性、数量、比较、体貌、时间、虚实、关系等范畴出发，探讨了英语和汉语在表达这些意义时的特点，特别是指出了中国人在学习英语时容易犯的错误。这本书是对比结合实用的一次成功实践。由于林语堂采取了从表达出发的方法，从表面看来与一般语法书反其道而行之，实际上最符合外语学习的实际需要和规律，结果取得了教学上的极大成功。

Following Jespersen, Chinese scholar Lin Yutang successfully applied the same method in his *Kaiming English Grammar* published in 1933. For the first time, Jespersen's method has a huge bearing on English-Chinese contrasting, incorporating practical thoughts on foreign language teaching and learning. Like Jespersen, Lin set off from grammatical categories such as mood, substitution, demonstrative, qualifier, gender, number and classifier, comparative, aspect, tense, functional and substantiative classes, and relation to compare representations in English and Chinese for characteristics and with special reference to the errors made by Chinese learner of English. It was a successful attempt at integrating theory and practice. Lin's bold decision to proceed from expression may have broken new ground against rule-based foreign language textbooks flooding the market. The great success so enjoyed testified to the way forward.

另一位学者吕叔湘则同时运用了叶斯柏森提到的两个方法，既采用了"从O到I"的方法，又采取了"从I到O"的方法。他出版于1942年的《中国文法要略》分为两个部分，第一部分用前法，称为"词句论"，后一部分用后法，称为"表达论"，从而建立了在汉语语法史上有着重要影响的一个语法新体系。其中后一部分尤为人所称道，实际上建立了一个语法研究"表达论"的体系。不过吕叔湘在这里对比的主要是古代汉语与现代汉语，英语只是偶尔涉及。1998

年，赵世开主编了一本《汉英对比语法论集》，完全沿着这一体系的路子甚至标题，从"指称"、"方所"、"时间"、"比较"、"数量"、"正反"、"关系"七个方面出发对汉语和英语进行了深入的对比，并把这些概念重新命名为"认知范畴"，这就比沃尔夫的"语法范畴"在理论上又深了一层。

Another Chinese scholar, Lü Shuxiang, put into practice both the ways suggested by Jespersen. His prominent work, *Essentials of Chinese Grammar* comprises two parts. The first part "Ciju lun" (On constructions) applies the method from "O" to "I", and the second part "*Biaoda lun*" (On expressions) applies the method from "I" to "O", thus establishing an unique system of grammar which has a lasting influence even today. The second part is critically acclaimed with its insightful treatment of "expression" covering both functional (grammatical and semantico) and philsophical aspects. With his wisdom, Lü could have set high benchmark for contrastive study in China were he to work on Chinese-English comparison instead of classical and modern Chinese. That said, Lü's effort is still eye opening. Half a century later, Zhao Shikai edited a book (Zhao 1998) following exactly LÜ Shuxiang's line of research to details like subtitles (indication and substitution, direction and location, time, comparison, classifier and qunatifier, affirmation and negation and relation), and renaming these concepts as "cognitive categories", which may be a further development of Whorf's "grammatical categories".

林、吕之外，张今和陈云清（1981）、刘宓庆（1991）、连淑能（1993）等，都从表达法出发，对汉英语进行了卓有成效的对比，以致"表达法"被确认为汉英对比三个层次中的一个重要层次。

Subsequently, Zhang Jin and Chen Yunqing (1981), Liu Miqing (1991) and Lian Shuneng (1993) have all made remarkable contributions to contrastive studies between English and Chinese premised on ways of expression. All these efforts laid good foundation for contrastive studies premised on ways of expression which is one of the three important levels in contrastive linguistics.

反观西方，叶斯柏森之后，似乎很少有人沿着这个路子继续往前走。在英语教学上，英国后来出现了"功能教学法"、"情景教学法"，1976年，威尔金斯（D. A. Wilkins）出版了一本《意念大纲》，也出现了一些意念语法、功能语法、交际语法等，但只是英语自己在唱独脚戏，很少见到什么人用这个原则来从事对比语言学研究。这未免是一个遗憾。

Back to the West, we find very few researcher picks up the baton from Jespersen. Although we notice the invention of a "functional method" and "situational method" in English language teaching in Britain, a "notional syllabus" by Wilkins (1976), and some publications in "notional grammar", "functional grammar" and "communicational grammar", but all these were confined within English itself. No one seems interested in applying Jespersen's principle to contrastive study. That is a real shame.

不管从结构出发还是从范畴出发，着眼点都还是语法，特别是句法。随着对比语言学的研究对象扩大到语篇和话语，这些显然都不够用了。相应的"篇章"、"话语"成了新对比研究出发点。出现了一些新的功能范畴，如礼貌原则、拒绝策略、衔接策略等等。对比研究出现了新的面貌。但是，从总的来说，还没有突破"结构"、"范畴"以及更广的"表达"的大范围。相对于吕叔湘的表达论体系，目前的话语对比和篇章对比，视野似还较局促。

In both premises on structures and categories, the focus inevitably falls on grammar, especially syntax. That scope is obviously limited when contrastive linguistics develops to include texts and discourses which become new starting points with added functional categories such as the principle of politeness, strategy of refusal, strategy of cohesion, etc. All in all, research efforts have not escaped the confinement of structures and categories to explore broader scope in expressions. The depth and breadth of Lü Shuxiang's framework has not been surpassed thus far. We can only hope for breakthrough to be within sight.

5.3.4 从意义出发
5.3.4 Premised on semantic

比范畴和表达的范围更大，就是从意义出发的对比。这个"意义"不再是"语法意义"，而是更一般意义上的"意义"。因为如上所说，范畴和表达基本上还在语法范围之内（话语和篇章只是在组织形式上的扩大），但比较的对象毕竟不限于语法。在词汇这一领域，一旦突破了结构（如构词法）和范畴（如成语、谚语），直接深入到词义，则可比范围就无限之广。比词语大的句义、篇义等等也是如此。因为语言所有的结构形式、所有的范畴，归根到底都是要表现语义的。从语义出发，可说是抓住了对比的一个核心。特别是当词语的对比从个别词发展到词语群（如色彩词、亲属词、动物词、植物词等），从词语意义发展到命名理据和词义引申过程，更为人们打开了一个异常广阔的天地，发现意义不同的背后是人们认知世界的方式不同，因而民族心理和民族文化便不可避免地引入到了对比研究的内容之中。以这个精神再回过头来看语法乃至语音等其他本来觉得似乎纯属"形式"的部门，其实也深受民族文化的影响。可以说，正是意义出发的对比，才使对比研究者更加领略到了洪堡特思想的伟大和深刻。对比研究才能发展到今天这样的局面。

Beyond category or expressions, semantic is an important primary premise. "Semantic" takes on a more general sense than grammatical meaning. Categories, expressions, and even larger units in discourse or text, remained in the scope of grammar, but the subject of contrastive study can not be confined to grammar. Take lexicology for instance, beyond structures (e.g. word-formation) and categories (idioms, proverbs, etc.), contrastive study has a huge ground to cover delving down right into sense and meaning in word, sentence and text. After all, there is no structure and category without semantic aspect. On this ground, contrastive study premised on semantic grasped contrastive linguistics at one of its core. In particular, proceeding from word level or the Chinese unit of Ci, study can take closer look at word-group (e.g. words for colour, for kinship, for animals or plants); or advance from logical meaning to the motivation behind nomenclature and derivation of senses. So, there is indeed a huge ground to be covered before us for we will soon realize that ethnic psyche and culturally-rooted cognition govern semantic differences across tongues. You might just realize the champion of von Humboldt on national psyche and culture is inevitably brought into the spheres of contrastive studies. In the same way, we could trace "purely" formal, grammatical and phonetical differences to the deep underlying influence of ethnic psyche and cognitive culture. The premise on semantic shed lights on the profoundness of Humboldt's thought and help anchored contrastive study in China at where we are.

而且更不可思议的是，从语法出发，不管从结构还是从范畴（更不要说从"规则"）出发，总使人越比越觉其"同"；而从意义出发，总使人越来越看到其"异"。如果从"求异"的目标出发，也许从意义出发是更便捷的途径。

What is the most noteworthy is the fact that contrastive studies premised on grammar, be it structure or category, and not to mention grammatical rules, the findings almost invariantly point towards "similarities"; whereas those premised on semantic tend to single out more "differences". If the aim of contrastive linguistics is indeed to look for differences, the premise on semantic would make more sense.

　　同样难以置信的是，从意义出发这个简单的办法，西方却隔了很长时间才真正领会到。这也许跟西方语言形态性强有关，这么多的形态和形式，便语言研究者形成了一个"形式情结"，什么研究不跟形式挂起钩来，总觉得不踏实。甚至连最早提出从意义出发的叶斯柏森，也要通过"功能"落实到"形式"，而没有主张就意义本身进行对比（当然，这可能与他写的是"语法哲学"，不是"语言哲学"有关）。而中国的林语堂和王力，就比较明确地提出从意义出发和从语言事实出发进行对比。进入五十年代以后，我们发现西方的对比研究几乎都是围着这样那样的形式进行，语义的对比非常薄弱，尽管语义学界出现了语义场理论，如德国学者魏斯格伯尔（L. Weisgerber，1953/54）在五十年代出版了《论德语的世界》一书，用语义场理论分析了空间、时间、植物、动物、亲属、人体、颜色等，产生了很大影响，但这个方法基本上没有影响到对比学界。当代西方最早提出从意义出发的，是最重视对对比进行哲学思考的利宾斯卡，她甚至以从意义出发的想法否定了乔姆斯基的句法说，考虑到她又是以坚持支持转换生成语言学著称的学者，这确实值得我们深思。她说：

　　While premised on semantic come across as a method most simple and natural, it took a seriously long time to attract the attention of western scholars. We could possibly blame it on the form-over-meaning nature of western languages. With so many inflections and other forms of agreement to take care of, it is understandable if researchers somehow feel unsecured not to fall back on forms. Even Jespersen who took the lead to campaign for contrastive study to look to semantic, held that semantic is too arrived at "forms" via "function". Chinese scholar Lin Yutang took after Jespersen with a tweak, adhering to the premise on semantic and pure language facts more resolutely, so is prominent linguist Wang Li. Development in the 1950s saw most contrastive studies in the West centred round forms, sparingly few were interested in contrast by way of semantics. The ground was not shaken even as the influential theory of semantic field developed by German philosopher Weisgerber (1953/54) to analyze words grouped according to space, time, plants, animals, kinship, human body and colours created quite a wave. Among modern scholars, the philosophically minded Lipińska once again be among the first to move motion on semantic-based contrastive studies. As an ardent supporter of generative grammar, she even went on further to repudiate Chomsky's syntax-based model on semantic grounds and that was certainly provocative. Here was what she said:

> 对比分析必须建立在意义基础上,我们所要比较的只是同一意义在不同语言中的表达方式……以句法为基础的模式,如《面面观》所示的,我们在上面已证明其不能处理很多语法现象。句法上的深层结构其实是个非常肤浅而且依赖于某一语言的分析方法。乔姆斯基(1965)所论的句法基础还有待证明,因此不能用来作为比较研究的一个层面。而我们却可以非常放心地、非常合理地假设同一意义在不同语言中进行表达这一的可能性。(利宾斯卡,1980:169—170)

> CA has to be meaning-based. What is to be compared are the ways of expressing the same meaning in different languages...The syntax-based model, such as that of Aspects, as it was proved and pointed out above, cannot cope with a number of grammatical phenomena. Syntactic deep structure is in fact a very shallow and specific language dependent level of analysis. The common syntactic base (in the meaning of Chomsky 1965) is something which would have to be proved and, thus, could not be used as a level of reference in the comparisons of languages. On the other hand, the possibility of expressing the same meaning in different languages can be reasonably safely assumed. (Lipińska, 1980: 169—170)

而在这对比中做得最成功的是德国学者斯奈尔-杭贝(Mary Snell-Hornby)。她更进一步提出了从事实出发而不要从现成理论出发的主张:
On the other hand, it has to be Snell-Hornby of Germany whose contrastive studies premised on semantic had been most successful. She further suggested for research to be fact-based rather than theory-based. She said,

> 本研究是建立在直接的观察上而不是别的语言学家的理论上,也就是说,它不采用任何现成的理论,而采取一种从经验到理论概念的研究方法。(斯奈尔-杭贝,1983:13)

> The study is based on direct observation of language and not on the

theoretical considerations of other linguists; in other words, instead of applying already existing theories to the language, it proceeds from empirical research to a theoretical concept. (Snell-Hornby, 1983: 13)

她的《德英语描写性动词的语义对比》（1983）是西方对比语言学少见的扎实的著作。中国近年出版的王逢鑫的《英汉比较语义学》（2001）在性质上及成就上与之相似。

Her book title, *Verb-descriptivity in German and English: A Contrastive Study in Semantic Fields* (1983) exemplified a very solid contrastive study on semantics. A close comparison came from Chinese scholar Wang Fengxin's *A Comparative Study between English and Chinese Semantics* (2001) 20 years later.

另一位做得非常成功的学者是澳大利亚的维尔茨皮卡，她还在"自然元语义"（natural semantic metalanguage）理论的基础上，提出了"普遍初义"（universal semantic primitives）假设，作为进行语言文化比较的基础。详见第一章的介绍，此处不赘述。

And of course we cannot afford to miss out Wierzbicka of Australia who has done amazing work in this regard. On the basis of her theory on "natural semantic metalanguage", she proposed using "universal semantic primitives" as the hypothesis for comparative study of language and culture. Please refer to Chapter 1 for greater details.

而从对比语言学的角度看，在这方面集大成的学者是切斯特曼。由于从意义出发必然涉及到翻译问题，从意义出发也就是从翻译出发，因而切斯特曼非常通达地论述了形式、意义与翻译的关系：

As far as contrastive linguistics as a discipline is the concern, Andrew Chesterman of Finland stood out as someone who best synthesizes various attempts in a wholesome approach. Considering the fact that semantic comparison has to be done in relation to translation, premised on semantic is akin to premised on translation, Chesterman did a remarkable job expounding on the relation between meaning, form and translation. He said:

在对比研究中，形式关系与意义关系彼此制约。考察形式时，我们总假定两个语法术语在意义上是等值的，最简单的理由就是我们之所以会将芬兰语的*passiivi*与英语的*passive*作比较，就是因为觉得这两个词可以互相翻译。另一方面，当我们考察通过翻译建立的意义联系时，我们又总倾向于不用那些"译错"的资料，也不用那些过于"意译"（即与原文在形式上及字面意义上相距过远）的资料。（切斯特曼，1998：30）

In contrastive studies, formal relations and semantic relations in fact constrain each other. When looking at form, for instance, we assume a semantic equivalence between grammatical terms: an initial reason why we compare the Finnish "passiivi" to English "passive" is because the two terms seem translations of each other. On the other hand, when looking at meaning relations as manifested through translation, we have tended to omit data that seem to be "too freely" translated—i.e. which differ too much from the original form, as well as its meaning—in addition to data that have been "wrongly" translated. (Chesterman, 1998: 30)

这可以说是从形式出发、从意义出发和从翻译出发的一个颇有意思的总结。
The observation above neatly summed up various discussions on premising on form, on meaning and on translation.

5.3.5 从问题出发
5.3.5 Premised on research question

上面我们讨论了四种对比出发点，第一、二种我们可说持有保留意见，原因其实从亚里斯多德对"出发点"的要求就可以看出来，它过于追求"科学性"，反而变得不可靠。第三、第四种可以用于结构与交际两个层面，如范畴适用于结构层面，功能适用于交际层面，意义则可兼用于两个层面，还可用于文化层面。但主要用于文化层面或大宏观层面的对比出发点，学界讨论得还不多。从这方面进行研究的比较有影响的著作主要是潘文国（1997）《汉英语对比纲要》，这本书对比了英语和汉语史、英语与汉语的语法研究史，以及英汉语各自的基本特点、基本结构单位、句子、语序、虚词、话语组织法、语言心理等几个方面，涉及内容很多，读时的感觉一方面觉得其中隐隐有个系统，一方面又好像说不清是个什么系统，甚至对作者对比研究的出发点也难以归纳。好像无法纳入我们上面讨论过的任何一种。经过反复考虑，我们想提出一个不成熟的想法：是否能把这样的研究角度叫做"从问题出发"？因为宏观研究总是从一些比较大的、有时甚至是关系到全局性的问题着手的，很难用具体的范围去框定。提出"从问题出发"这个方法，也许有助于研究者打开思路，推动宏观研究的展开和深入。

Four "starting points" for contrastive study were discussed above. Reservations were on the first two, being far too "scientific" to be reliable, according to Aristotle's requirement on "starting-points". The third and forth are applicable to both the facets of structure and communication. For example, premised on category can be used in the contrast of structures; that on function can be employed to compare the nitty-gritty in communication; while those on semantic is not only applicable to the above both but also in the contrast of culture. A more macroscopic contrastive study can be seen in Pan Wenguo's *An Outline of Contrastive Study between Chinese and English* (1997). This title deals broadly with the contrast between the history of the English and Chinese languages, history of English and Chinese grammatical studies, the basic features of the two languages, the basic units, syntax and word order, "empty words", the organization of discourse and texts and language psychology. While there was an attempt to put everything under a system, that system is rather obscure to the readers, and it is not even possible to conclude what premised is the title based on. After much consideration, we would like to make a tentative proposal here that it is also possible for the premise to fall on specific "research question", since macroscopic study usually involves the larger picture and less pin-pointing. This suggestion to have a primary premise on specific research question may help to broaden our perspective to push forward macroscopic contrastive studies.

5.3.6 从"中立项"出发
5.3.6 Premised on tertium comparationis

最后，我们简单谈谈从"对比中立项"出发的问题。"对比中立项"（*tertium comparationis*）是西方理论对比研究的一个重要概念，对有的人（如克尔采斯佐斯基）来说更是一个核心概念，他花了十多年的时间来完善他的"对比中立项"体系。这个体系庞大芜杂，切斯特曼批评说如果将之作为"对比中立项"研究史的一个小结倒挺好，但作为一个体系就有点自相矛盾。克氏设立了七个"对比中立项"，多数我们上面提到过。下面我们结合切斯特曼的

评论 (Chesterman, 1998: 31—35) 略作介绍:

Finally, study premised on *tertium comparationis,* an important concept in theoretical contrastive studies in the West. Krzeszowski, a major anchor man in contrastive linguistic, spent over a decade to establish a system of *tertium comparationis*. Unfortunately, it ended up far too huge and disorderly to forge into a system, and so Chesterman suggested that it be regarded as a summary of the development history on *tertium comparationis*. Krzeszowski sets up seven "equivalences" (*tertium comparationis*) in his system (refer to Chapter 1). Below, we shall incorporate Chesterman's (1998: 31—35) comments as we go through each of them.

（1）统计对等（statistic equivalence）

克氏要求所比对象有最大限度的相似出现频率，切氏认为出现频率的高低背后是其他的因素，因而更应关注这些"其他因素"，如形式或意义。

(1) Statistic equivalence

Krzeszowski demanded the objects of study must have frequency of occurrence in close proximity. Chesterman argued that frequency of occurrence may be affected by other factors, and it is those "other factors" like form and meaning that should hold our attention.

（2）翻译对等（translation equivalence）

由于克氏允许接受各种翻译文本，包括考虑到语用和交际因素的译本，切氏评论说这样的情况下翻译对等与语义对等就不是一件事，翻译对等研究就成了对翻译家工作的研究。而且翻译对等只能是在一定上下文中的对等。

(2) Translation equivalence

Krzeszowski allowed for all kinds of translated texts, including those with a pragmatic and communicational slant. In so doing, criticized Chesterman, translation equivalence and semantic equivalence will become two, and translation equivalence could well turn into the study of how translation was being done. Besides, translation equivalence can only be defined by the specific context.

（3）系统对等（system equivalence）

这是我们上面讨论过的"从体系出发"。切氏对此也不赞成，认为这实际上是在作"语法标签"（grammatical labels）比较，而"语法标签"往往会误导。

(3) System equivalence

This was discussed above under the heading "premised on systems". Chesterman disagreed with this, saying that was in fact a comparison between "grammatical labels" which never failed to mislead.

（4）句法语义对等（semanto-syntactic equivalence）

这是克氏提倡的"对比生成语法"（Contrastive Generative Grammar）的基础。克氏的"生成"是从语义深层结构生成句法表层结构，而且认为辨认出句法语义对等是说双语者的本能。切氏认为句法语义对等与翻译对等是冲突的，而"本能"各人并不一定相同；再说句法—语义对等本身有循环论证之嫌。

(4) Semanto-syntactic equivalence

This is the foundation of Krzeszowski's Contrastive Generative Grammar. By "generative", Krzeszowski means to generate from semantic deep structure, surface syntactic structure. To Krzeszowski, it is in the instinct of a bilingual speaker to differentiate semanto-syntactic equivalence. Disagreeing, Chesterman opined that semanto-syntactic equivalence contradicts with translation equivalence and that "instincts" differ from individual to individual. Most of all, semanto-syntactic equivalence per se is suspicious of circular argument.

（5）规则对等（rule equivalence）

这条来自转换生成语法，我们上面讨论过。

(5) Rule equivalence

As discussed above, this clearly comes from transformational generative grammar.

（6）实体对等（substantial equivalence）

克氏的实体对等是"语言外"（extra-linguistic）的实体，如语音学中的发音和听觉、词汇学中的词外语境等。切氏认为在这问题上的"相似度"是个问题。斯奈尔-杭贝（1983）将语义分为"全等"（total equivalence）、"临时相等"（working equivalence）、"部分重合"（partial coverage）、"完全不合"（nil-coverage）四级的办法可以参考。我们在上面的讨论中只讨论了"出发点"的问题，在具体对比词义时切氏的建议是可以参考的。

(6) Substantial equivalence

Krzeszowski refers to "substances" as extra-linguistic substances such as articulation and audition in phonetics and context in support of vocabulary. Chesterman points out that the obstacle here concerns the degree of similarity. For this purpose, Snell-Hornby's (1983) classification frame for semantic meaning as: total equivalence, working equivalence, partial coverage and nil-coverage is worthy of reference. What has been discussed pertains to semantic as a premise. In practice, Krzeszowski's idea on contrasting word sense is a good reference.

（7）语用或功能对等（pragmatic or functional equivalence）

这是克氏体系惟一涉及语篇的内容，我们在上面讨论过。切氏引了在这问题上的一些争论，特别是维尔茨皮卡对语用对等的根本否定，认为说到底，"对等"是个相对的概念。

(7) Pragmatic or functional equivalence

This is the only part in Krzeszowski's system dealing with text. Chesterman sided with some of the arguments, especially Wierzbicka's total disapproving of pragmatic equivalence. After all "equivalence" is something relative.

1992年，许余龙出版《对比语言学概论》时引用了克氏和艾立斯（J. Ellis）的理论，并把"对比中立项"改称为"对比基础类型"，共立出了九项，为：物质实体；语言环境；交际情景；语言系统；语言结构；语言规则；语法功能；篇章功能；功能负荷量。其中最后一项即克氏的"统计对等"，其余我们上面都讨论过，这里不再重复。就理论意义而言，克氏的历史追溯，有助于我们思考能推动持平的对比研究的对比中立项；许余龙的"对比基础"则立足于实践，列举出对比研究中的制约因素。

Xu Yulong (1992), *An Introduction to Contrastive Linguistics,* cited Krzeszowski's and Ellis' theory but interpreted *tertium comparationis* into "bases of contrastive". (refer to 5.2.1.2.2) He listed nine such bases or primitives: material entity, linguistic environment, situation in communication, linguistic systems, linguistic structures, linguistic rules, grammatical functions, textual functions and functional load capacity, the last being another term for Krzeszowski's statistic equivalence. While Krzeszowski, from a more theoretical sense, traced through history for *tertium comparationis* required for a more balanced approach in contrastive studies, Xu Yulong, with a practical outlook, listed conditioners in conducting contrastive survey.

所以，对克氏的批评并不等于说对比中立项毫无用处。实则，洪堡特和叶斯柏森都使用了对比中立项——洪堡特以民族精神为基；叶氏的"范畴"立意宽广，概括了形式、功能和意义——都搭建在哲学层面上。洪堡特与叶斯柏森以其不朽论著清楚地揭示，对比中立项必须立足于哲学层面，如此方能由上而下地指导语言对比，同时兼顾动态和共时语料。这样的要求无疑远远超出某种"对等"或者比较实际的对比基础，事实上，意义实在的对比中立项无一不遭受批评。

The critical comment on Krzeszowski's however, does not discredit the usefulness of *tertium comparationis*. In comparing across languages, von Humboldt and Otto Jespersen are using *tertium comparationis* on the philosophical plane. While Humboldt uses ethnic spirit, Jespersen uses category on a broader sense involving form, function and meaning. The essence of *tertium comparationis* is loud and clear in the outstanding works of Humboldt and Jespersen: it has to be an entity with a philosophical dimension allowing for a top-down approach in comparison, accommodative to dynamic, synchronic data. The requirement far surpasses those of equivalent or some practical primitives for *tertium comparationis* grounded on practicality tend to draw flakes.

5.4 对比的方向性
5.4 Direction in contrasting

第二个要讨论的对比研究方法论问题是对比研究的方向性问题。这个问题表面上看来比较简单。方向性无非是三类情况：

Yet another methodological problem to be addressed concerns the direction in which contrastive studies are conducted. From the look of it, there are three ways:

（1）单向性。又有两种情况：
　　①A→B（如从英语到汉语），或
　　②B→A（如从汉语到英语）
（2）双向性。也分两种：
　　①回向性（A→B→A，或B→A→B）
　　②同向性（0　↗A
　　　　　　　　↘B　）

（3）多向性。也有两种：
　①从一到多，或
　②从零到多

(1) Unidirectional, comprising two sub-directions:
　① A→B (e.g. from English to Chinese)
　② B→A (e.g. from Chinese to English)

(2) Bidirectional, also comprises two sub-directions:
　① Round trip (e.g. A→B→A, or B→A→B)
　　　　　　↗A
　② Single way (0　　　) (starting from certain *tertium comparationis*)
　　　　　　↘B

(3) Multi-directional, again comprises two sub-directions:
　① One to many (A→B, C, D…e.g. from English to Chinese, French, Japanese)
　② Zero to many (0→A, B, C, D…e.g. from *tertium comparationis* to Chinese, English, French…)

其实也有一些可讨论的，有的还非常重要。

Straight forward enough, yet some underlying problems are worthy of discussion, some of which are significant.

5.4.1 单向性

5.4.1 Unidirectional

语言对比的方向如果是从一种语言到另一种语言，最大的可能性是从强势语言出发来观照弱势语言。这个强势弱势不是数量概念，而是国际影响力及语言学上的描写成熟度。毫无保留，英语是当今世界上的惟一强势语言，往日的敌手法语和俄语早已不在话下，何况其他研究欠成熟的语言（如汉语）？因而在单向性的对比研究中，只要对比双方有一方是英语的，从英语出发几乎是人们不假思索的选择。

In contrasting two languages, it is highly probable that the movement goes from the language of higher status to the language of lower status. The status of a language has nothing to do with the number of people speaking the language but has everything to do with its international influence and its adequacy of description. Undoubtedly, English is the "super language" of the world today. Her former rivals, French and Russian, no longer enjoy their past glory, not to mention other less than adequately described languages such as Chinese. On this account, many unidirectional contrastive studies involving the English language automatically use it as the default starting point without even a moment of hesitation for most cases. That said, it is by no means that the English language should always be as the base language for comparison.

但是这一选择恰恰是违反对比语言学的基本宗旨的。

In fact, this default setting of using English as the base language for comparison, in our view, runs against the fundamental aim of contrastive linguistics.

如果我们对比的宗旨是要用英语的语法、英语的组织规律去"统一"全世界各语言的语法，或使全世界的语言组织规律都能用英语语法的术语来进行解释，那么这样做无可厚非；如果对比的宗旨是了解各民族语言的异同，以便更好地进行跨文化交流，那么这样做的后果可能适得其反。

If it is the ultimate aim of contrastive study to unify the grammars of world languages with English grammar, or to explain structures of all other languages with the set of terminology for English grammar, there is no one to blame for this default setting; if however, it is the aim of contrastive study to understand the similarities and differences between different ethnic tongues to improve efficacy in cross-cultural engagements, that default directional setting will lead to the very opposite.

从英语出发去进行对比，一般有两种做法：

Starting with the English language, there are generally two approaches.

第一种做法，从形式出发或从范畴出发，即从英语的语法形式或语法范畴出发，去寻找另一语言中的"对等物"。上面说过，另一语言是描写欠成熟的语言，语法术语等本来就不够用，英语如果提供了一些它原来所没有的术语，那就正好中其下怀，愉快接受了。要是这另一种语言又正好是像汉语这样的形态欠发达甚至根本谈不上有什么形态的语言，那么英语语法中任一新术语，都可以很容易地在汉语中找到相似物。例如英语有主语谓语，那汉语也可找出主语谓语来一一对应；英语动词可分及物不及物，汉语也可找出相应的及物不及物动词；英语语法讲深层结构表层结构了，那么汉语中也可找出深层和表层结构来；英语现在讲"空语类"、讲"移位"了，汉语中也可很方便地找到"空语类"和"移位"的例子。至于汉语中找到的这些主语、谓语等等是不是真正的主语谓语、跟英语的主语谓语是不是一件事,人们很少去问。一百多年来汉语语法研究始终跟着英语转,甚至到了亦步亦趋的地步,就是这种"对比"的结果。这种对比的结果,就使汉语语法的面貌完全呈现出英语语法的面貌,这是对比希望达到的目的吗?

The first based on forms or categories, that is, with the grammatical forms or categories in English in mind, looks for their equivalents in another language. As iterated, the other language is most probably inadequately described, and wanting of a set of fitting grammatical terms. Given that English has a rich library of terms, any loan would be gladly accepted without a second thought. If the "other language" is a language like Chinese poor in inflectional forms, than almost any grammatical label in English can match with an "equivalent" in Chinese and be justified. For instance, "subjects" and "predicates" in English are easily mapped to their counterparts in Chinese; transitive and intransitive verbs in English, soon found their friends in Chinese verbs. Subsequently, the deep structure and surface structure in English are happy with their correspondence in Chinese. Recently, grammarians are on "empty category" and "movement" in English, and it will not surprise any one to see examples in Chinese. It bothers few whether those so called "subject", "predicate" and other labels you name it in Chinese are "genuine" or shall we say, share the same definitions or features as their counterparts in English. For over a century, the grammar of the Chinese language has been learned through this approach following closely every step the English grammar took. The result? We now have a Chinese grammar amazingly similar to the English grammar. We cannot but wonder if that is expected of contrastive linguistics?

第二种做法,从意义出发,最常见的是翻译法,把一句英语句子译成汉语。我们知道,翻译从逐字直译到自由意译有许多层次,最偷懒、最方便的是逐字直译;碰到翻译出来的句子在目的语里又很清通,那译家更是乐此不疲了。汉语由于形态欠发达,词句的组合非常灵活,因此,一般直译的句子汉语大多能接受。一时不习惯的,反正理解没有问题,也就让它存在了,久而久之对许多外来的句式也就安之若素,并让它在汉语中安下家来了。拿这样直译得来的汉语句子与英语原文一"对比",不用说,又是"同大于异"。例如下面这一句句子:

The second approach begins with semantic, usually through translation. As we know, there can be a variety of translation versions of a same text, ranging from very literal to extremely free with word-for-word translation as a most convenient easy way out. If the resulting "translated" sentence manages to get its way in the target language, then more and more translators will take benchmark from there, for good or for bad. Fortunately or not, as Chinese is free from inflection and exhibits great flexibility in sentence formation, most literally "translated" sentences are more or less passable. Even awkward expressions will finally get to stay so long as they do not hinder communication. As a result, English-like sentences are aplenty in Modern Chinese. Were we to compare such Chinese sentences with the English language, it almost goes without saying that "similarities" rule over "differences". Let's consider a back translation example:

英语：What matter if we have to face some difficulties? Let them blockade us! Let them blockade us for eight or ten years! By that time all of China's problems will have been solved.

汉语译文：如果我们必须面对一些困难有什么关系呢？让他们封锁我们吧！让他们封锁我们八年或者十年吧！到那个时候，所有中国的问题都将会得到解决了。

English "source" text: What matter if we have to face some difficulties? Let them blockade us! Let them blockade us for eight or ten years! By that time all of China's problems will have been solved.

Chinese back translation: 如果我们必须面对一些困难有什么关系呢？让他们封锁我们吧！让他们封锁我们八年或者十年吧！到那个时候，所有中国的问题都将会得到解决了。

(Literally: if-we-have to-face-some-difficulties-there is-what-relation-ne? let-them blockade-us-ba! Let-them-blockade-us-eight-years-or-ten-years-ba! By-that-time, all-china's-problems-all-will-get-solved-le.)

如果把两句子加以"对比"，除了汉语多了几个"助词"我们确实发现不了什么汉语的特色了。至于这一句英语句子，汉语还有哪些译法，有没有跟英语很不一样，而又是非常地道的汉语的译法呢？一般人是懒得考虑的。

Comparing the English "source" text and its back translation, we can find little differences except for some particles—that is exactly what Ma Jianzhong told us a century ago. The translation is so readable that no one will care to attempt for variety and more idiomatic Chinese representations.

因而这两种"对比"的结果,都是造成一批英语式的汉语句子。我们不能说这些句子不是汉语的,但这只能是一部分,更多的因为"对比"时没有涉及到,就有意无意地隐藏起来了。这是我们通过对比希望得到的真相吗?

It seems that both approaches end up with the same result—the creation of English-like Chinese sentences. Of course they are Chinese sentences, but a minor part of all Chinese sentences. A great many more sentences remain obscure because they have no chance of surfacing in these approaches. Is it the "truth" of Chinese language (not to say culture) we are seeking through contrastive study?

在九十年代以来的翻译学研究里,美国翻译理论家凡努蒂痛感从非英语译成英语的文学作品里,由于一直倡导"归化"(domestication)的译法、"流利"(fluent)的英语,结果完全失去了原作中的民族文化特色,他愤慨地说,翻译成了帝国主义推行殖民统治的武器。为了对抗这一势力,他(1992)提倡进行"异化"(foreignization)的翻译。

In the field of translation studies, American theorist Lawrence Venuti (1992: 5) investigated what happened to literatures in other languages when they get translated into English and painfully pointed out that "a fluent strategy effaces the linguistic and cultural difference of the foreign text", and charged that translation has become a weapon for ethno-centrism and imperialism. He then proposed a strategy of foreignization to fight against it:

> 我想指出,考虑到异化翻译以抗拒种族中心主义的翻译暴力为目的,在当前的世界局势下,异化翻译更应该作为战略性的文化干预手段,对抗那些霸道的英语国家,抗议他们以不平等的方式和世界其他国家进行文化交流。在英语中出现的异化翻译就是抗拒种族中心主义和种族歧视、文化沙文主义和帝国主义的一种形式,全然以民主的地缘政治关系之利益为出发点。(韦努蒂,1992:20)

I want to suggest that insofar as foreignizing translation seeks to restrain the ethnocentric violence of translation, it is highly desirable today, a strategic cultural intervention in the current state of world affairs, pitched against the hegemonic English-language nations and the unequal cultural exchanges in which they engage their global others. Foreignizing translation in English can be a form of resistance against ethnocentrism and racism, cultural narcissism and imperialism, in the interests of democratic geopolitical relations. (venuti, 1992: 20)

几年后，为了避免"异化"引起的歧义，他（1998）更改为"少数化"（minorization）。这使我们联想到，对比研究中处处从英语出发，也会在客观上造成或助长英语的语言和语言学霸权主义。在对比中，我们也应该倡导一种"minorization"，从非英语和弱势语言出发，一定能更多地发现非英语语言的特色。

Later in 1998, he replaced the word "foreignization" with "minorization" to avoid ambiguity. Venuti reminded us that in contrastive studies the default strategy of using English as the base will inevitably promote the hegemony of the English language and English linguistics, and that in contrastive studies, a strategy of minorization should also be encouraged. If we use a language of lower status as the base, and compare it with English, we may delve deeper into the traits of that language.

而事实也是如此，从汉语出发，我们就会发现一些从英语出发想也想不到的问题。例如鲁迅《狂人日记》的第一句：

For instance, taking reference from the Chinese language may reveal a range of issues which will never get surfaced if the reference point rests on the English language. Below is the opening sentence in Lu Xun's *A Madman's Diary*:

> 今天晚上，很好的月光。
> 今天晚上，很好的月光。（鲁迅，1974：2）
> The moon is extremely bright tonight.
> The moon is extremely bright tonight. (Lu Xun, 1974: 2)

英语中有对应的句式吗？"Today's night, very good moonlight"成话吗？如果不成话，译成流畅的英语例如：
The literary equivalent, "today-night, very-good-moonlight" makes no sense in English. A fluent translation read as follows:

再拿来与汉语原文对比就有很多内容可比了。而英语中不可能有的汉语造句和用词特色也就反映出来了。再举一个例子，是《水浒》里的一个句子：

Now, more observations can be made on the characteristics of Chinese sentences in terms of subject, topic, passivity, word formation and more, fully exposing some of the features apparently not found in English.

Here is another example from the Ming dynasty classic *Water Margin* (also known as *The Outlaws of the Marsh)*:

> 那一阵风起处，星月光辉之下，大吼了一声，忽地跳出一只吊睛白额虎来。（《水浒》四十三回）。

> 那 一 阵 风 起 处 ， 星 月 光 辉 之 下 ， 大 吼 了 一 声 ， 忽 地 跳 出 一 只 吊 睛 白 额 虎 来 。(Chapter 43)

> (word-for-word: that-a-gust-wind-start-place, star-moon-light-under, big-roar-le-one-sound, suddenly-jump-out-one-lift-eyes-white-forehead-tiger-(out))

> literal: With a gust of wind, under the light of stars and the moon, with a loud roar, suddenly jumps out a upward-slanting eye, white-forehead tiger.

沙博理译文供比较：

Fluent translation for comparison: "…a sudden gale arising among the tress…From the place where the wind blew, a roaring tiger leaped out. It had upward-slanting eyes and a white forehead." (tr. Sidney Sapiro)

郭绍虞先生分析说，如果按照现行来自英语的语法体系：

Apparently, from syntactic organization to narrative structure, there is a series of topics strikingly different from English and worthy of further exploration. Guo Shaoyu had a good summary on the above example. He said, going by the present Europeanised Chinese grammar,

> 假如以动词为重点，那么，在这一句中就要以白额虎为主语，说成"一只吊睛白额虎在星月光辉之下，随着一阵风，大吼一声，忽地跳了出来了"；如果以李逵为主语，说成"李逵在星月光辉之下，猛觉一阵风起，听到一声大吼，看到一只吊睛白额虎跳了出来"。这样说，语法上都是通的，也表达了同样的意思，但都失掉了汉语的精神，变得干瘪而无生气了。（郭绍虞，1979：144）

If the focus is on the verb, then the tiger is the subject, and the sentence in Chinese would become "In a starry night and where the moon is shinning, a white-forehead tiger follows a gust of wind, gives a thunder roar and leaps out suddenly". If Li Kui is to be the subject, then the sentence becomes "In the lit from stars and the moon, Li Kui felt a gust of wind, heard a startling roar, and saw a white-forehead tiger jumping on him". Both sentences are grammatically correct in Chinese and express the same meaning. What is lost though, is the spirit of Chinese and the whole sentence is so dry and lifeless. (Guo Shaoyu, 1979: 144)

如果我们通过对比，还想保留"汉语的精神"，造出生气勃勃、丰富多彩的句子的话，就只有改弦更张，换一条路子，试着真正从汉语出发。

To keep the "spirit of Chinese" and preserve the ability to form vivid and colourful sentences, it would be wise to make a U-turn and start taking reference from Chinese, the language of a lower status in this case.

5.4.2 双向性
5.4.2 Bidirectional

双向性的对比研究也有两种。第二种是从第三者的立场出发，同时面向两种语言。这就是上一节说的"对比中立项"的内容，可以参看。

Of the two cases of bidirectional contrasting, the second one is the same as to start from *tertium comparationis* as discussed above.

第一种回向性的对比，指的是翻译中的回译法。这是吕叔湘主张的方法。他也是经常这样实践的。我们排成"A→B→A"与"B→A→B"两种形式，也是为了强调这里也可以有两种选择。而我们的主张，不用说，也是"少数化"，即以弱势语言开始，译成强势语言，再回译成弱势语言来进行对比。

Of the two modes of bidirectional contrasting, the first one, or the round-trip bidirectional contrasting, is actually the back-translation method suggested by Lü Shuxiang. It involves two paths, "A→B→A" and "B→A→B". And in line with our discussion above, starting from the relatively lower status language is recommended in order for a fuller review of the traits of the lower status language.

把强势语言译成弱势语言再回译，以英译汉为例，由于在第一次翻译时造成的已经是英语式的汉语（由于事先考虑到要回译，这种趋势还更强烈），因此回译时可说毫无困难，基本上就是原来句子的样子。这时来进行"对比"，可说已没有什么意思了。

Most importantly, for contrasting through back-translation, taking reference from the higher status language such as English when comparing with a lower status language such as Chinese will hardly yield any positive results. The first example on Mao Zedong's quote given in the section above speaks volumes. Since the back-translated sentence in Chinese already sounds very "English", and in close proximity to the English sentence, there is virtually nothing to do for the contrastivists.

而从汉语出发先译成英语再回译，情况就不同了。其实上一节开头的第一个句子，英文"原文"原来是从《毛泽东选集》第四卷的《别了，司徒雷登》一文中的一个句子翻译过去的：

多少一点困难怕什么？封锁吧，封锁十年八年，中国的一切问题都解决了。

我们没法逐字直译，因为这几乎不可能。我们仔细将这两种汉语加以对比，再看看英语译文，是会受到很多启示的。

But if we go the other way round, things will be totally different. We already know that the English sentence at "source" turns out to be a translation of a Chinese sentence lifted from *Mao Zedong's Works* which reads,

多少一点困难怕什么？封锁吧，封锁十年八年，中国的一切问题都解决了。

(word-for-word: more or less—a bit—difficulty—fear—what? Brockade—*ba*, brockade—ten—years—eight—years, China's—every—problem—all—solve—*le*.)

Comparing the Chinese original, its English translation and its back translation in Chinese, more observations can be made, including among others, the use of pronounce in the two languages involved, and obviously, taking reference from the Chinese language in this case serves the contrastive purpose well.

另两个例子也是如此。例如《狂人日记》那一句，既然译成"Today's night, very good moonlight"是不可能的，就只有译成"The moon is extremely bright tonight"。而回译的时候，按照一般人的做法，肯定是译成最贴近英语面貌的"今夜的月光特别明亮"之类。把这两种汉语句子与英语句子一起对比，那对比的内容也就丰富了。

The same applies to the other two examples that follow. As Lu Xun's original sentence (Today's night, very good moonlight) cannot be translated into English literally, it has to be translated into a form closest to its original yet acceptable in English, something like "The moon is extremely bright tonight". Then, when back-translated into Chinese, a more or less acceptable English equivalent will be given, such as "今夜的月光特别明亮" (tonight's-moonlight-especially-bright). On closer examination on the two Chinese sentences and comparing them with the English equivalent, we could gain more insights. The second mode starts from a *tertium comparationis* discussed above and apply in single direction on a pair of languages for comparison. Issues with the different types of equivalent associated have been chewed over.

5.4.3 多向性
5.4.3 Multi-directional

多向性中的"从零到多"没有什么可多说的，这也是从"对比中立项"出发进行的对比。由于从"中立项"出发，不受语言多少的约束，因此可以在一个大题目下，多种语言共同对比。这种对比的最光辉例子，就是从洪堡特到叶斯柏森的哲学语言学。事实上，这也就是普通语言学建立的过程。因此我们说，对比语言学与普通语言学本质上是相通的。只要有了足够多的各种语言的知识，人们就能从双语对比，逐步走向"从零到多"的多语式对比（或"比较"），"中立项"这时就会起语言类型学的区别标准的作用。普通语言学的大家，几乎都是多语言的精通者，就是一个最好的证明。

The second mode of multi-directional contrastive study, i.e., from zero to many, is as good as starting from a *tertium comparationis* with a philosophical dimension as mentioned above. There is no restriction to the number of languages to be contrasted when starting from a neutral *tertium comparationis*. Brilliant examples had been illustrated in the works on philosophical linguistics from Humboldt through Jespersen. As a matter of fact, this process matches exactly with the process in establishing general linguistics. That's why we are adamant that contrastive linguistics and general linguistics share the same aim and objectives. So long as one possesses knowledge of different languages, one can eventually move from bilingual contrastive study to multilingual contrastive study (the zero to many patterns) or general linguistic study. Then the *tertium comparationis* in contrastive study shoulder on the role as a standard divider in linguistic typology.

多向性中的"从一到多"人们可能未必意识到,其实生成语言学的一些信奉者在做的就是这么一件事。在美国,在20世纪80年代以前很长一段时间里,对句法的理论研究几乎一直限于对英语的分析,以乔姆斯基为代表的一些语言学家认为,了解语言共性的最好方法是对一种语言作详尽的研究,他们还提倡用抽象的结构(例如转换生成语法里的深层句法结构)来表述语言共性(Comrie, 1989: 1—2)。这种情况直到八十年代才有所改观,开始强调共性研究最有效的方法是根据对一系列广泛语言材料的考查。而这种考查的办法,就是用生成派从英语中研究出来的"原则"和"规则",放到各种语言里去证实或证伪(其实"证伪"是说说的,多数情况下,经过如此这般的"解释",一般都能得到证实)。这就是"从一到多"的实际例子。这种研究无非是把双语对比中的"从英到X"扩大化,由于可以涉及到任何语言,因此也是一种普通语言的研究。但是我们要清楚,这一路子与洪堡特创始的普通语言学是没有什么共同之处的。

Next, on the one to many multidirectional approaches, not many people realize that was exactly what followers of generative linguistics adopted. For a long time before the 1980s, the generativists represented by Chomsky believed that the best way to study the universals of human languages is to make an exhaustive study of one language (often English), and that universalities are best be expressed by abstract forms such as deep structure (cf. Comrie, 1989: 1—2). Since the 1980s, their strategy changed. A more effective way to study universals was found to be through the investigation of a vast number of language samples premised on "principles" or "rules" summed up from the English language for verification or falsification in other languages (needless to say, verification is almost always successful through various kind of explanation, and example of "falsification" is rare). These are practical examples of comparative study from one to many. As it involves many languages, it is also a type of general linguistics research, but its goal has little to do with the general linguistics advocated by Humboldt.

5.5 求同求异的方法论
5.5 Issues in seeking differences and similarities

最后，我们从方法论的角度再来考察一下"求同"和"求异"的问题。同异问题是对比语言学学科的核心，再怎么重视也不过分。它既是本体论的问题，又是方法论的问题。本体论要解决what和why的问题，方法论则要解决how的问题。当然这两者是有联系的，本体论会涉及到方法论，方法论也会折射出本体论。

Last but not least, the issues involved in seeking differences and similarities from the methodological point of view. These issues sat at the core of contrastive linguistics, specifically associated with ontology and methodology, cannot be emphasized enough. Ontologically the questions are WHAT and WHY; methodologically the question is HOW. Of course the two aspects are interrelated.

首先要说明的是，"同"除了等同，也包含"相似性"。有些学者打着普通语言学的旗号，致力于求证语言的"同一性"，与对比语言学强调"同中之异，异中之同"大相径庭，因此对比研究中需要区分"等同性"和"相似性"。

Before going into the details, it may be necessary to highlight a caveat. The word "similarity" expressed as Chinese in the character "同" (tóng), literally means "the same". It may soon be found that while contrastive study seeks to find similarities and differences, some "universal grammarists" are devoted to proving "sameness". So, it may warrant effort to distinguish sameness and similarity.

从方法论的角度看，求同求异无非是四条途径：

Methodologically, there are typically four approaches in seeking differences or similarities (or sameness).

（1）由同求同；
（2）由异求异；
（3）由同求异；
（4）由异求同。

(1) Seek sameness with sameness (from S to S);
(2) Seek differences with disparity (from D to D);
(3) Seek differences with similarity (from S to D);
(4) Seek similarity with disparity (from D to S).

5.5.1 由同求同
5.5.1 From S to S

第一种"由同求同",其实就是"普遍语法派"在走的路子,他们从"同"(不管是叫"深层结构"、"共同原理"、"共性"、"原则",还是叫"规则")出发,经过比较或是研究,最后还是达到"同"。这个"同"往往还是原先那个"同",尽管从理论上来说,可以有"修正"或"补充"的可能。但从实际情况来看,"补充"是有的,因为又增加了一些语言的"证据";"修正"对多数人来说可能是未必,特别是那些从事以汉语材料来研究"共性"的人。这种方法为对比语言学所不取。因为在这种研究中,"异"只是个幌子,在整个研究过程中,其实研究者从未真正把"异"当作一回事,他们急切地想证明的,是"共性"、"规则"的正确性、普适性。而对比研究者所关心的另外一个方面,对比研究的实际应用方面,不论是语言教学、是翻译,还是词典编纂等等,从来没有进入过他们的理论视野。对比语言学是一门理论和应用并重的学科,对于完全拒绝考虑应用层面的理论和做法,对比语言学也有理由拒绝它们。

In the first approach "From S to S", the two "S"s are better read as "sameness" instead of "similarity". This is in line with the general practice of "universal grammar" followers. Whether the "S" is to be understood as "deep structure", "language universals", "universal principles" or "rules", this group of researchers start from a certain S, and through comparison or rather, verification, reach the same S in the end. Theoretically, there are supposed to be some supplementation and revision during the process, but in the eagerness to verify "universal principles" with examples, particularly from the Chinese language, if any at all, there are more supplementations than revisions. "Differences" are mentioned, if ever, only to be proven of little importance against the larger backdrop of sameness. As an independent discipline, contrastive linguistics will not endorse this approach for that approach has forsaken the seeking of differences altogether. Besides, researchers for this approach concerned themselves merely with theoretical issues, and do not bother with practical application of theories in areas such as language teaching, translation or dictionary compilation, which do come under the purview of the contrastivists.

5.5.2 由异求异
5.5.2 From D to D

第二种"由异求异",是一种走极端的研究方法。我们在上文说过,对比研究的第一步是发现两种语言间的有异有同,再下一步就是两大语言学的分野:比较语言学会刻意走"由异求同"的路子,而对比语言学会努力走"由同求异"的路子。"由异求异"是一条什么路子呢?那就是绝端夸大两种语言的差异性,否认两种语言之间的互通性、可交流性、可译性,极端否定两种文化之间的通约性。洪堡特曾经高瞻远瞩地指出,"每个人都有一种语言","全人类只有一种语言",这两者是统一的。而刻意夸大差异并将之绝对化的人是只理解了前一半而忘了或不懂得后一半。"沃尔夫-萨丕尔假说"的"强式"(strong form)很容易使人引起这样的联想,这也是它不断遭到人们批评或将信将疑的缘故(其实这未必是沃尔夫的原意)。

The second approach, from D to D, goes to the other extreme. To recall, identifying differences and similarities between the pair of languages involved is the first thing to do in both comparative and contrastive study. The next step will then mark the departure of the two camps: the contrastivists will look further for differences within similarities; whereas the comparativists will tend to look for similarities within differences by way of tracing back history. The curious thing about looking for differences from disparity is then an attempt to magnify the differences between languages to such an extreme as to deny the possibility of mutual intelligibility, communicability and translatability to the point of rejecting the commensurability of two cultures. The early wisdom of von Humboldt is certainly more comforting by any measure: "we may say with equal correctness that the whole of mankind has but one language and that every man has one of his own" (Humboldt 1836: 53). The extremists rip Humboldt's quote in half and took only what fits their purposes. For commensurability has to be the cornerstone of linguistics, the strong form of Sapir-Whorf hypothesis felt the need to come under fire for this reason even though Whorf, far from being an extremist, was merely on differences within similarities.

对比语言学对于"求异"原则的反复强调,也会被人不恰当地联想为主张"以异求异"。但对比语言学从来没有主张过,我们一向主张对比研究异同并重,但任务有阶段性,各阶段的任务和侧重点并不相同。简单地说,在理论和应用层面侧重"由同求异",在哲学层面侧重"由异求同"。

It is commonly mistakenly that contrastivists are doing from D to D because of the emphasis on the necessity to seek differences. That is pure assumption. Contrastive linguistics seeks both similarities and differences, at different stages. At the theoretical and application planes, there is more emphasis on seeking differences, but at the philosophical plane, similarity is the ultimate goal.

5.5.3 由同求异
5.5.3 From S to D

第三种"由同求异",这是对比语言学的基本的方法论。必须强调指出,"由异求异"是一种极端的思维方式,不可能是一种方法论。因为彻底的"由异求异",如同彻底的"由同求同"一样,本质上是不需要什么论证过程的,一句话就说到底了,也没有回旋的余地,剩下的只有对不同意见的反驳。"由同求同"者:我说某条规则是人类语言的共性,你说不是,举出某语言中某例是例外,我就通过"解释",证明这个"例外"归根到底并不是例外,我的"规则"还是成立的。"由异求异"者:我说某两种语言截然不同,你说不是,举出某对相似的例子,我就通过寻找反例,证明你这个例子不成立,我的观点还是对的。而对比语言学主张的"由同求异"却有两个特点:第一,它具有方法论的意义,指导着研究的过程;它不是一个强词夺理、以反证取胜的论证方法,而是一个细心的、不断的研究过程。第二,求"异",甚至是彻底的"异",对于对比语言学来说,只是一个阶段性的成果。"求异"的成果可以有效地应用到语言教学、语际翻译、词典编纂等实践中去,但求"异"并不是对比语言学在理论上最终的追求目标。在最终的目标上,对比语言学主张"异中求同"。

If the extremist thought behind from D to D disqualifies it to be even considered as of methodological significance, from S to D is the basic methodological approach in contrastive linguistics. There are two features in this approach. First, its methodological importance guides the whole argument process of contrastive study demanding meticulous and continuous effort requiring not just opposing examples. Secondly, the "differences" found at various stages can never be the end result. All the disparities found can be put into good and effective use in foreign language teaching, interlingual translation and bilingual dictionary compilation, but because to seek differences is not the ultimate goal of contrastive linguistics, all differences surfaced served the ultimate purpose of singling out universal similarities, i.e. some sort of "from D to S".

"由同求异"不仅是一个原则,而且是具体的方法,具有实际的可操作性。在实践中,它总是兼顾"同""异"两个方面,而侧重点却始终在"异",或者说,"同中之异"上。对比研究深入的过程,就是持续不断地找"异"的过程、不断地在"同"的表象中看出"异"的内涵的过程。这过程可以图示如下:

Moreover, "from S to D" does not only function as a principle for contrastive study, and it doubles up as a concrete, practical method. In the process, though similarity and difference are both under consideration, the emphasis is placed on seeking differences, or rather, on understanding the weight of these differences within similarities. This iterative process is illustrated as follows:

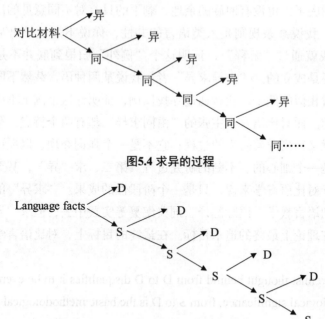

图5.4 求异的过程

Figure 5.4 The process of seeking differences

也就是说,在对比研究过程中,我们不轻易相信所谓的"同",凡是

"同",都要作进一步分析,看看里面是不是存在着实际上的"异"。这也就是黎锦熙(1933:13)说的"所谓比较,重在异而不在同:同则因袭之,用不着——比较;唯其异,才用得着比较,或大同而小异,或小同而大异,或同中有异,或异中有同"的意思。只有不断地找"异",对比研究才具有理论和应用上的价值。这就是对比语言学反复强调"求异",或给人造成的印象只是"求异"的原因。

The diagram shows that in practical contrastive study, we do not take the "similarities" for granted and accept them readily. Each "similarity" needs to be further scrutinized to check out obscure "difference" underneath the surface. This was what Li Jinxi (1933: 13) meant when he contended that "In comparison emphasis should be laid on differences rather than similarity. For if two things are similar, they are linked by conventions; the need to compare and contrast only arises when there are differences. It may be similar for the large part and different for the small part; or similar for the small part and different for the large part; or there may be differences amongst similarities, and similarities amongst differences". It is perhaps such reiteration to seek differences that leaves an impression that contrastivists are only interested in differences.

5.5.4 由异求同
5.5.4 From D to S

第四种"由异求同",这是对比语言学在理论上或在哲学层面上的最终追求目标。必须指出的是,这里的"同"与上面各条讲到的"同"不同。如果说上面讲到的"同"都是具体的"同"的话,这里的"同"却是个抽象的"同",是高层次的"同"。洪堡特的下面这段话也许对我们会有某种启示:

From D to S is another approach of methodological importance in contrastive linguistics. And it is also the way to reach the ultimate theoretical or philosophical goal for contrastive study. It should be highlighted that the "S" here is different from the "S" in the above three where it refers to concrete "sameness" or "similarities". The "S" here refers to an abstract concept at a higher level of human understanding, cultural commsumerability and language universals. The following quote from von Humboldt may help deepen understanding in this respect.

要想充分认识到结构的差异，便需要采取第三种做法，即对本族语言和异族语言的形式具有同样强烈的意识。显然，这种意识需要有一个前提，那就是达到某种更高层次的、统辖起本族语言和异族语言的视点，并且恰恰是在初看起来差异极大、两种语言似乎不可能相互同化的情况下有所醒悟。（洪堡特，1827—1829/2001: 237）

A third approach to the full knowledge of the difference of structures is to cultivate a sense for the forms of the foreign language as strong as that of the native language. The sense is obviously based on the realization of a viewpoint at a higher level embracing the native and the foreign language, however great their difference at a first glance and the impossibility for their mutual assimilation. (Humboldt, 1827—1829/2001: 237—the English translation is ours.)

我们知道，在哲学上，越是高层次的概念就越是抽象，有时很难进行具体的描述。例如"人"，相对于"男人、女人、中国人、英国人、好人、坏人……"就是个非常高的抽象（"男人、女人……"也是抽象，但比"人"层次要低），我们很难描述"人"是个什么样子，只有具体的男人、女人……。同样，在语言研究上，最高层次的"同"，或是语言共性，也必然是个高度的抽象，绝不是某些人、某些学派所相信的可以用数学公式加以具体描述的规则。凡是把共性解释为"规则"的观点，可以说在哲学上就是难以成立的。语言学上的共性只能是些抽象的原则、共同的原理、基本的规律。对之的描述只能是粗线条的、难以数学化的。对比语言学的最终任务就是要在所对比的具有或大或小的差异背后的、作为人类语言的共同性，以此来作为不同民族、不同文化的人们共同友好相处并进行互相交际的基础。我们一再强调对比研究重在求"异"，我们也一再强调，对比研究的最终追求目标不是"异"，而是"同"。我们不能为"异"而"异"，找"异"的目的不是为了制造不同民族、不同文化、不同语言之间的人的对立甚至敌对，而是为了在承认"异"、了解"异"的基础上实现互补，更好地促进整个人类的共同健康发展。对比研究，乃至整个跨文化语言研究，追求的应该是语言与语言、文化与文化、民族与民族、人民与人民之间的高度和谐和共同发展。从这个意义上说，我们追求的不是"同"，而是"和"。孔子说："君子和而不同。"具体的、绝对的"同"是不可求也不可能求得到的。绝对的求"同"，只能是消灭差异、消灭分歧，只能意味着一种语言、一种语言观、一种语言分析方法，凌驾于其他一切语言之上，取代其他一切语言。这就意味着语言世界的纷争和人类社会的不太平。有人会以为这些话未免言之过重，但逻辑的推理只能如此。

As we are all aware, the higher a concept rise on the philosophical ladder, the more abstract it is for description. This particular "S" (similarity, sameness, universality...) at the highest level is so highly abstract that it is beyond any concrete form of expression including rules in mathematical formula. Linguistic universals can be aptly understood as abstract principles, general tendency or common linguistic laws, describable only in plain and general terms. Contrastive linguistics, as an academic discipline, works categorically and untiringly at sorting out the differences among languages save from stopping just there. To be exact, it will press on to find the common principles of human languages governing the major and minor differences amongst languages so as to raise that as a base for peaceful co-existence and friendly communication between ethnic groups and cultures. Differences are important and must never be neglected, but differences must not be led to opposition and even antagonism. Recognition of differences should only lead to mutual understanding and respect, upon which mutual development can be promoted. Ultimately, the final goal for contrastive linguistics and the whole cause of cross-lingual, cross-cultural studies, is to advance a high level of harmony where languages, cultures, nations down right to the peoples would enjoy co-development. In this sense, the "S" specifically in "from D to S" is no longer a simple "S" standing for similarity or sameness, but "harmony in principles" represented by the Chinese character 和 (he), a complementary concept to 同 (tong). Illustrious ancient Chinese sage Confucius remarked, "A true gentleman seeks harmony in principle rather than convoluted sameness". Absolute, concrete sameness or similarities between languages does not exist. To work towards one unique "sameness" or "universality" can only mean one thing: one language, one linguistic view, one culture, to ride roughshod over all other variety of languages, linguistic views and cultures.

因此，对比语言学的终极目标是求"和"，这也是本书的最终结论。

The ultimate aim of contrastive linguistics is to seek harmony in principles within variations and differences. On that, concludes the present book.

参考文献
Bibliography

Adamska-Salaciak, A. "Jan Baudouin de Courtenay's Contribution to General Linguistics". In *Towards a History of Linguistics in Poland: From the Early Beginnings to the End of the 20th Century*. Amsterdam and Philadelphia: John Benjamins, 175—208, 2001.

Agard, F. and R. Di Pietro. *The Grammatical Structures of English and Italian*. Chicago: The University of Chicago Press, 1965b.

Agard, F. and R. Di Pietro. *The Sounds of English and Italian*. Chicago: The University of Chicago Press, 1965a.

Alatis, J. E. (ed.). "Contrastive Linguistics and Its Pedagogical Implication", Report on the 19th Annual Round Table Meeting on Linguistics and Language Studies. Washington DC, 1968.

Anderson, S. R. & A. D. Andrews. "Syntactic Typology and Contrastive Studies". *Research on Syntactic Typology*. vol. 1 of 3 vols, retrived from ERIC database, 1972. [ED067961]

Anderson, Wallace L. & N. C. Stageberg. *Introductory Readings on Language*. New York: Holt, Rinehart and Winston, Inc. 1962.

Aristotle. *Analytica Hystera*. Translated into English by John Cottingham, in John Cottingham (ed.). *Western Philosophy: An Anthology*. Oxford: Blackwell, 330 BC.

Austin, John. *How to Do Things with Words*, ed. by J.O. Urmson. New York: Oxford University Press, 1962.

Barthes, Roland. *Elements of Semiology*. Translated from the French by A. Lavers and C. Smith. London: Cape, 1964/1967.

Baudouin de Courtenay Jan. *Pol'skij jazyk sravnitel'no s russkin I drevnocerkevnoslovanskim*. St. Petersburg: N. P. 1912.

Beaugrande, Robert de & Wolfgang Dressler. *Introduction to Text Linguistics*. London and New York: Longman, 1981.

Birnbaum, Henrik. "Contrastive Linguistics and Language Typology: The Three-Way Approach" in Kastovsky, D. and A. Szwedek (eds.). *Linguistics across Historical and Geographical Boundaries: In honour of Jacek Fisiak on the Occasion of His Fiftieth Birthday*. Berlin:

Mouton de Gruyter, 1986, II: 1133—1146.

Bloom, A. H. *The Linguistic Shaping of Thought: A Study in the Impact of Language on Thinking in China and the West.* Hillsdale, NJ: Lawrence Erlbaum, 1981.

Boas, Franz. "Introduction", in F. Boas (ed.). *Handbook of American Indian Languages.* Lincoln: University of Nebrsaska Press, 1911, 1—79.

Bogordickij, V. A. *Fizjologia proiznošenija jazykov francuzkogo, anglijskogo I nemeckogo srvnitel'no s russkom.* Kazan: Izd. Kazanskogo Universiteta, 1915.

Bolinger, Dwight. "Introduction", in Di Pietro, *Language Structures in Contrast.* Massachusetts: Newbury House Publishers, 1971.

Brown, Penelope and Stephen Levinson. Politeness: Some Universals in Language Usage. Cambridge: Cambridge University Press, 1988.

Brunot, Ferdinand. *La pensée et la langue, Méthodes, principles et plan d'une théorie nouvelle du language appliquée au français.* Paris: Masson, 1922.

Burgschmidt, E. and D. Götz. *Kontrastive Linguistik Deutsch/English,* Hueber Hochschulreihe 23. München: Hueber, 1974.

Campbell, Lyle. "The History of Linguistics", Blackwell Reference Online, http://www.mapageweb.umontreal.ca/tuitekj/cours/chomsky/Campbell-History-of-linguistics.pdf [assessed Dec 2011], also in Aronoff, Mark, Janie Rees-Miller (eds.), 2002, *A Handbook of Linguistics.* Oxford: Blackwell, 2007.

Candlin, C. N. "Preface", in James Carl, 1980, *Contrastive Analysis.* Amsterdam and Philadelphia: John Benjamins Publishing Co. 1980.

Chao, Yuen Ren. "A preliminary Study of English Intonation and Its Chinese Equivalents", in *Studies Presented to Ts'ai Yuan P'ei on His Sixty-Fifth Birthday.* Peiping: Academic Sinica, 1933.

Chao, Yuen Ren. "Rhythm and Structure in Chinese Word Conceptions", 1975/1992, in Chao, *Aspects of Chinese Sociolinguistics*, translated into Chinese by Wang Hongjun, in Yuan Yulin (ed.), 1992, 《中国现代语言学的开拓和发展——赵元任语言学论文选》, Beijing: Tsinghua University Press, 1992年, 231—248。

Chao, Yuen Ren. *A Grammar of Spoken Chinese.* Berkeley, Los Angeles and London: University of California Press, 1968.

Chao, Yuen Ren. *Mandarin Primer: An Intensive Course in Spoken Chinese.* Cambridge: Harvard University Press, 1948.

Chase, Stuart. "Forward", in B. L. Whorf, 1956, *Language, Thought and reality: Selected Writings of Benjamin Lee Whorf,* edited by John. B. Carroll. Cambridge, Massachusetts: The MIT Press, 1955.

Chesterman, A. *Contrastive Functional Analysis.* Amsterdam: JBPC, 1998.

Chesterman, Andrew. *Contrastive Functional Analysis*. Amsterdam/Philadelphia: John Benjamins Publishing Company, 1998.

Chomsky, Noam. *Aspects of the Theory of Syntax*. Cambridge and Massachusetts: The MIT Press, 1965.

Chomsky, Noam. *Cartisian Linguistics*. New York and London: Happer & Row, 1966.

Chomsky, Noam. *Language and Problems of Knowledge*. Cambridge, Mass.: The MIT Press, 1988.

Chomsky, Noam. *Language and Responsibility*. Sussex: The Harvester Press, 1977.

Chomsky, Noam. *Powers & Prospects: Reflections on Human Nature and the Social Order*. Boston, MA: South End Press, 1996.

Chomsky, Noam. *Syntactic Structure*. The Hague: Mouton & Co, 1957.

Comrie, Bernard. "Contrastive Linguistics and Language Typology" in Kastovsky, D. and A. Szwedek (eds.). *Linguistics across Historical and Geographical Boundaries: In Honour of Jacek Fisiak on the Occasion of His Fiftieth Birthday*. Berlin: Mouton de Gruyter, 1986, II: 1155—1163.

Comrie, Bernard. "Linguistic Typology", *Annual Review of Anthropology.* 1988, 17: 145—159.

Comrie, Bernard. *Language Universals and Linguistic Typology*. Oxford: Blackwell, 1981/1989. Translated into Chinese as 《语言共性和语言类型》, Beijing: Huaxia Publishing House, 1989年。

Connor, Ulla & R. B. Kaplan (eds.). *Writing across Languages: Analysis of L2 Text*. MA: Addison-Wesley, 1987.

Connor, Ulla. *Contrastive Rhetoric*. Shanghai: SFLEP, 2001.

Connor, Ulla. *Contrastive Rhetoric: Cross-cultural Aspects of Second-language Writing*. Cambridge: Cambridge University Press, 1996.

Corder, S. P. "Idiosyncratic Dialects and Error Analysis", *International Review of Applied Linguistics*. 1971, 9(2): 147—159.

Corder, S. P. "The Significance of Learner's Errors", *International Review of Applied Linguistics*. 1967, 5: 161—169

Corder, S. P. *Error Analysis and Interlanguage*. Oxford: Oxford University Press, 1981.

Corder, S. P. *Introducing Applied Linguistics*. Harmondsworth, Middlesex: Penguin Books Ltd, 1973.

Crystal, David. *The Cambridge Encyclopedia of Language*, second edition. Cambridge: Cambridge University Press, 1997.

D'Andrade, Roy. *The Development of Cognitive Anthropology*. Cambridge: Cambridge University Press, 1995.

Dezso, Laszlo. "Theoretical Contrastive Linguistics and Typological Characteriszation", in Vladimir Ivir and Damir Kalogjera (eds.). *Languages in Contact and Contrast: Essays in Contact Linguistics*. Berlin and New York: Mouton de Gruyter, 1991, 115—132.

Di Pietro, R. J. *Language Structures in Contrast*. Rowley, Massachusetts: Newbury House Publishers.

Duranti, Alessandro. *Linguistic Anthropology*. Cambridge: Cambridge University Press, 1997.

Eckman, F. R. "Universals, Typologies and Interlanguage", Retrieved from ERIC database, 1981.

Edelman, Gerald. *Bright Air, Brilliant Fire: On the Matter of the Mind*. Harmondsworth: Penguin, 1992.

Edelman, Murray. *The Symbolic Uses of Politics*. Urbana, Ill.: University of Illinois Press, 1964.

Enfield N. J. (ed.). *Ethnosyntax: Explorations in Grammar & Culture*. Oxford and New York: Oxford University Press, 2002.

Enkvist, Nils Erik. "Contrastive Linguistics and Text Linguistics", in Jacek Fisiak (ed.). *Contrastive Linguistics: Prospects and Problems*. Berlin/New York/Amsterdam: Mouton Publishers, 1984, 45—67.

Enkvist, Nils Erik. "Kontrastive Textlinguistik und Übersetzung", *Grazer Linguistische Studien* 5, 1977, 47—73.

Enkvist, Nils Erik. "Why We Need Contrastive Rhetoric", *Alternation* 4: 188—206, 1997.

Fillmore, Charles J. "Remarks on Contrastive Pragmatics", in Jacek Fisiak (ed.). *Contrastive Linguistics: Prospects and Problems*. Berlin/New York/Amsterdam: Mouton Publishers, 1984, 119—141.

Fisiak, Jacek (ed.). *Contrastive Linguistics and the Language Teacher*. Oxford: Pergamon Press, 1981.

Fisiak, Jacek (ed.). *Contrastive Linguistics: Prospects and Problems*. Berlin/New York/ Amsterdam: Mouton Publishers, 1984.

Fisiak, Jacek (ed.). *Contrastive Linguistics: Prospects and Problems*. Berlin: Mouton, 1984.

Fisiak, Jacek (ed.). *Further Insights into Contrastive Analysis*. Amsterdam and Philadelphia: John Benjamins, 1990.

Fisiak, Jacek (ed.). *Theoretical Issues in Contrastive Linguistics*. Amsterdam: John Benjamins, 1980.

Fisiak, Jacek et al. *An Introductory English-Polish Contrastive Grammar*, 1978, Warszawa: PWN. In Fisiak (ed.). 1980, 1—4.

Fisiak, Jacek. "Introduction". In J. Fisiak (ed.). *Theoretical Issues in Contrastive Linguistics*. Amsterdam: John Benjamins, 1980, 1—7.

Fisiak, Jacek. "Introduction". In J. Fisiak (ed.). *Theoretical Issues in Contrastive Linguistics*. Amsterdam: John Benjamins Publishing Co. 1980, 1—7.

Fisiak, Jacek. "On the Present Status of Some Metatheoretical and Theoretical Issues in Contrastive Linguistics", in J. Fisiak (ed.). *Further Insights into Contrastive Analysis*, Amsterdam and Philadelphia: John Benjamins Publishing Co., 1990, 3—22.

Fisiak, Jacek. "On the Roots of Contrastive Linguistics", Folia *Linguistica*. 1984, 18 (1—2): 139—153.

Fisiak, Jacek. "Some Introductory Notes Concerning Contrastive Linguistics", in J. Fisiak (ed.). *Contrastive Linguistics and the Language Teacher*. Oxford: Pergamon Press, 1981, 1—11.

Fisiak, Jacek. "The Contrastive Analysis of Phonological Systems", *Kwartalnik Neofilologiczny*

22, 1975, 341—351.

Fisiak, Jacek. "The Poznań Polish-English Contrastive Project", in R. Filipović (ed.). *Zagreb Conference on English Contrastive Projects*. Zagreb University, 1971, 87—96.

Foley, W. A. *Anthrolopological Linguistics*. London: Blackwell, 1997.

Forrest, R. A. D. *The Chinese language*. London: Faber and Faber Ltd. 1948.

Frank, Arimin P, Harald Kittel, Norbert Greiner (eds). *Übersetzung: ein internationales Handbuch zur Übersetzungsforschung, Part 1, Volume 1*. Walter de Gruyter, 2004. http://books.google.com.

Fries, C. C. *Teaching and Learning English as a Foreign Language*. Ann Abor: University of Michigan Press, 1945.

Fromkin, Victoria. et al. *An Introduction to Language*. Sidney: Harcourt Australia Pte Ltd. 1999.

Gipper, Helmut. "Understanding as a Process of Linguistics Approximation: The Discussion between August Wilhelm von Schlegel, S. A. Langlois, Wilhelm von Humboldt and G. W. F. Hegel on the translation of the Bhagavadgita and the Concept of 'Yoga'", in Bynon, Theodora, F. R. Palmer (eds.). *Studies in the History of Western Linguistics*. New York: Cambridge University Press, 1986, 109—128.

Goodenough, W. H. "Cultural Anthropology and Linguistics", in Paul L. Garvin (ed.). Report of the Seventh Annual Round Table Meeting on Linguistics and Language Study. Washington D. C.: Georgetown University, 1957.

Goodman, Nelson. "Seven Strictures on Similarity", in N. Goodman, *Problems and Projects*. Indianapolis, IN.: Bobbs-Merrill, 1972, 437—447.

Graffi, Giorgio. *200 Years of Syntax*. Amsterdam and Philadelphia: John Benjamins. 2001.

Grandgent, C. H. *German and English Sounds*. Boston: Gin, 1892.

Grucza, Franciszek. "Origins and Development in Applied Linguistics in Poland", in Koerner, E. F. K and A. J. Szwedek (eds.), 2001, *Towards a History of Linguistics in Poland: From the Early Beginnings to the End of the 20th Century*. Amsterdam & Philadelphia: John Benjamins. 2001, 53—100.

Gumperz, John. "The Speech Community", in Sills, D. L. (ed.), *International Encyclopedia of the Social Sciences*. New York: McMillan, 1968, 381—386.

Gutt, Ernest-August. *Translation and Relevance: Cognition and Context*. Oxford: Blackwell, 1991.

Halliday, M. A. K. & Ruqaiya Hasan. *Cohesion in English*. London: Longman, 1976.

Halliday, M. A. K. et al. *An Introduction of Functional Grammar*. London: Edward Arnold, 1985.

Halliday, M. A. K. et al. *The Linguistic Sciences and Language Teaching*. London: Longman, 1964.

Hartmann, R. K. *Contrastive Textology: Comparative Discourse Analysis in Applied Linguistics*. Heideberg: Julius Groos Verlag, 1980.

Hatim, Basil, *Communication across Cultures: Translation Theory and Contrastive Text Linguistics*. Exeter, Deven: University of Exeter Press, 1997.

Hocket, Charles F. "A System of Descriptive Phonology", 1942, in M. Joos (ed.), *Readings in Linguistics*. New York: American Council of Learned Societies, 1957, 97—108.

Hocket, Charles F. *Refurbishing Our Foundation: Elementary Linguistics from an Advanced Point of View*. Amsterdam and Philadelphia: John Benjamins, 1987.

Hoenigswald, Henry M. "On the History of Comparative Method", *Anthropological Lingsuitics* 5:1, retrieved from Jstor database, 1963.

Humboldt, Wilhelm von. "On Alphabetic Script and Its Relation to the Structure of Language", 1824, in T. Harden and D. Farrelly (eds), *Essays on Language/Wilhelm von Humboldt*. Frankfurt am Main: Lang, 1997, 68—94.

Humboldt, Wilhelm von. "On the Comparative Study of Language and Its Relation to the Different Periods of Language Development", 1820, in T. Harden and D. Farrelly (eds), *Essays on Language/Wilhelm von Humboldt*. Frankfurt am Main: Lang, 1997, 1—22.

Humboldt, Wilhelm von. "On the Grammatical Structure of the Chinese Language", 1826, in T. Harden and D. Farrelly (eds). *Essays on Language/Wilhelm von Humboldt*. Frankfurt am Main: Lang, 1997, 95—110.

Humboldt, Wilhelm von. "On the National Character of Languages", 1822, in T. Harden and D. Farrelly (eds). *Essays on Language/Wilhelm von Humboldt*. Frankfurt am Main: Lang, 1997, 52—67.

Humboldt, Wilhelm von. "Ueber die Verschiedenheiten des menschilichen Sprachbaues", 1827—1829, translated into Chinese by Yao Xiaoping, in《洪堡特语言哲学文集》, Changsha: Hunan Education Press 2001年, 226—422.

Humboldt, Wilhelm von. "Thesen zur Grundlegung einer Allgemeinen Sprachwissenschaft", 1810-1811, translated into Chinese by Yao Xiaoping in《洪堡特语言哲学文集》, Changsha: Hunan Education Press. 2011. 4—10.

Humboldt, Wilhelm von. *On Language: The Diversity of Human Language-Structure and its Influence on the Mental Development of Mankind*. 1836, Michael Losonsky (ed.), Peter Heath (trans.). Cambridge and New York: Cambridge University Press, 1999.

Hymes, Dell (ed.), *Language in Culture and Society: A Reader in Linguistics and Anthropology*, New York: Harper and Row, 1964.

Hymes, Dell. "On Typology of Cognitive Styles in Language", *Anthropological Linguistics* 1961, 3: 22—54.

Hymes, Dell. "Two Types of Linguistic Relativity", in William Bright (ed.), *Sociolinguistics: Proceedings of the UCLA Sociolinguistics Conference*. Hague: Mouton, 1966, 114—167.

Issacs, H. R (ed.), *Straw Sandals*. Cambridge, Massachusetts: The MIT Press, 1974.

Jackson, Howard. "Contrastive Linguistics—What Is It?", *ITL* 1976, 32: 1—32.

James, C. *Contrastive Analysis*. Qingdao: Qingdao Publishing House, 2005.

James, C. *Contrastive Analysis*. Harlow, Essex: Longman Group Ltd., 1980.

Jespersen, Otto. *Growth and Structure of the English Language*. Oxford: Basil Blackwell,

1938/1978.

Jespersen, Otto. *Mankind, Nation and Individual: From a Linguistic Point of View.* London: George Allen & Unwin Ltd., 1946.

Jespersen, Otto. *The Philosophy of Grammar.* London: George Allen and Unwin, 1924/1951.

Joos, M. "Description of Linguistic Design", in M. Joos (ed.). *Readings in Linguistics*. New York: American Council of Learned Societies, 1950/1957, 349—356.

Joseph, John. "A Matter of Consequenz: Humboldt, Race and the Genius of the Chinese Language". *Historiographia Linguistica* 26 (1999), 89—148.

Kaplan, R. B. "Cultural Thought Patterns in Intercultural Education", *Language Learning*. 1966, 16: 1—20.

Kaplan, R. B. "Foreword: What in the World is Contrastive Rhetoric?", in C. G. Panetta (ed.), *Contrastive Rhetoric Revisited and Redefined*. Mahwah, New Jersey and London: Lawrence Erlbaum Associates, Inc., 2001.

Kaplan, R. B. *The Anatomy of Rhetoric: Prolegomena to a Functional Theory of Rhetoric*. Philadelphia: Center for Curricula Development, 1972.

Karlgren, Bernhard. *Sound and Symbols in Chinese.* revised edition, 1923, Hong Kong: Hong Kong University Press, 1962.

Karlgren, Bernhard. *The Chinese Language: An Essay on Its Nature and History.* New York: The Ronald Press Company, 1949.

Katzner, Kenneth. *The Languages of the World.* New York: Funk & Wagnalls, 1975. Translated into Chinese by Huang Zhangzhu and Lin Shuwu, 黄长著、林书武中译,《世界的语言》, Beijing: Beijing Publishing House, 1980年。

Kluckhohn, Clyde. *Mirror for Man.* New York: McGraw-Hill. 1949.

Koerner, E. F. K. "Jan Baudouin de Courtenay: His Place in the History of Linguistic Science", in *Canadian Slavonic Papers*. 1972a, 14 (4): 663—683.

Koerner, E. F. K. "Towards a Historiography of Linguistics: 19th and 20th Century Paradigms", *Anthropological Linguistics*. 1972b, 14 (7): 255—280.

Koerner, E. F. K. and A. J. Szwedek (eds.). *Towards a History of Linguistics in Poland: From the Early Beginnings to the End of the 20th Century*. Amsterdam: John Benjamins. 2001.

Koerner, E. F. K. *Linguistic Historiography: Projects and Prospect*. Amsterdam: John Benjamins. 1999.

Krzeszowski, T. P. "Tertium Comparationis". in Fisiak (4).

Krzeszowski, T. P. "Fundamental Principles of Structural Contrastive Studies", in *Glotto-didactica*, 1967, 2: 33—39.

Krzeszowski, T. P. "Toward a Typology of Contrastive Studies", in W. Oleksy (ed.). *Contrastive Pragmatics*. Amsterdam and Philadelphia: Benjamin, 1989, 55—72.

Krzeszowski, T. P. *Contrasting Languages: The Scope of Contrastive Linguistics*. Berlin and New

York: Mouton de Gruyter, 1990.

Krzeszowski, T. P. "Contrastive Generative Grammar: Theoretical foundations", in *Studies Anglica Posnansienie*, 1974b, 5: 105—112, reprinted in Fisiak (ed.) 1980, 185—192.

Krzeszowski, T. P. "Tertium comparationis". In J. Fisiak (ed.). *Contrastive Linguistics. Prospects and Problems*. Berlin/New York/Amsterdam (*Trends in Linguistics Studies and Monographs* 22), 1984, 301—312.

Krzeszowski, T. P. *Contrastive generative grammar: Theoretical foundations*. Łódź: Uniwersytet Łódźki, 1974a, Tübingen: Gunther Narr Verlag, reprinted in 1979.

Kufner, H. *The Grammatical Structures of English and German*. Chicago: The University of Chicago Press, 1962.

Kurteš, Svetlana, "Review: Contrastive Linguistics: Pan & Tham", 2007, The Linguist List (vol. 19. April) 2008.

Lado, R. *Linguistics across Cultures*. Ann Arbor: UMP, 1957.

Lado, R. *Language Teaching: A Scientific Approach*. New York: McGraw Hill, 1964.

Lado, Robert. *Linguistics across Culture*. Ann Arbor: University of Michigan Press, 1957.

Lakoff, George & Mark Johson. *Metaphors We Live By*. Chicago: University of Chicago Press, 1980.

Lasswell, H. D. et al. *Language of Politics: Studies in Quantitative Semantics*. Cambridge, Mass.: The MIT Press, 1949/1968.

Lee, Penny. *The Whorf Theory Complex*. Amsterdam and Philadelphia: John Benjamins, 1996.

Lehmann, W. P. *Historical Linguistics: An Introduction*. New Delhi: Oxford & IBH Publishing Co. 1966.

Lewis, M. M. *Infant Speech: A Study of the Beginnings of Language*. London: Kegan Paul, 1936.

Li, Charles and Sandra Thompson. "Subject and Topic: A new Typology of Language", in Charles Li (ed.). *Subject and Topic*. New York: Academic Press, 1976.

Lin, Yutang. *My Country and My People*. London: William Heinemann, 1938.

Lipińska, Maria. "Contrastive Analysis and the Modern Theory of Language", in Fisiak (ed.). 1980, 127—184.

Lucy, John. *Grammatical Categories and Cognition: A Case Study of the Linguistic Relativity Hypothesis*. Cambridge: Cambridge University Press, 1992b.

Lucy, John. *Language Diversity and Thought: A Reformulation of the Linguistic Relativity Hypothesis*. Cambridge: Cambridge University Press, 1992a.

Malinowsky, Bronislaw. "The Problem of Meaning in Primitive Language", supplement 1 in Ogden, C.K. and I. A. Richards, 1960, *The Meaning of Meaning: A Study of the Influence of Language upon Thought and of the Science of Symbolism*. London: Routledge & Kegan Paul, 1923, 296—336.

Martin, J. R. *English Text: System and Structure*. Philadelphia: John Benjamins. 1992.

Martinet, André. *A Functional View of Language*. Oxford: Oxford University Press, 1962.

Matasovic, R. "Comparative and Historical Linguistics", in *Encyclopedia of Life Support Systems* (EOLSS), Developed under the Auspices of the UNESCO, Eolss Publishers, Oxford, UK. (http://www.eolss.net)

Mathesius, V. "On Some Problems of the Systematic Analysis of Grammar", *Traveaux de Cercle Linguistique de Prague* 6, 95—107, Prague, Czechoslovakia, 1936.

Mathesius, V. "On the Linguistic Characterology of Modern English", *Actes du Premier Congrès International de Linguistes á la Haye*. The Hague, 1928, 50—67.

Mathiot, Madeleine (ed.). *Ethnolinguistics: Boas, Sapir and Whorf Revisited*. The Hague: Mouton, 1979.

Medin, D. L. & R. L. Goldstone. "The Predicates of Similarity", in C. Cacciari (ed.). *Similarity in Language, Thought and Perception*. Turnhout: Brepols, 1995, 83—110.

Mey, J. L. *Pragmatics: An Introduction*. Oxford: Blackwell, 1993.

Morris, C. W. *Foundations of the Theory of Signs*. Chicago: Chicago University Press, 1938.

Moulton, W. *The Sounds of English and German*. Chicago: The University of Chicago Press, 1962.

Mustajoki, Arto. *Mielestä kieleen*. Helsinki: Helsinki University Press, 1993.

Mustajoki, Arto. "Is a Meaning-based Syntax Model Possible?" Paper read at the conference "Linguistcs by the End of the Twentieth Century: Achievements and Perspectives", Moscow, February 1—4, 1995.

Niemeier S. and R. Dirven (eds.). *Evidence for Linguistic Relativity*. Amsterdam and John Philadelphia: Benjamins, 2000.

Oleksy, Wiesław (ed.). *Contrastive Pragmatics*. Amsterdam and Philadelphia: John Benjamins, 1989.

Oleksy, Wiesław. "Towards Pragmatic Contrastive Linguistics", in J. Fisiak (ed.) *Contrastive Linguistics: Prospects and Problems*. Berlin/New York/Amsterdam: Mouton Publishers, 1984, 349—364.

Olmsted, D. L. and L. A. Timm. "Baudouin de Courtenay as Sociolinguist", in Frederick B. Agard (eds.). *Essays in Honor of Charles F. Hockett*. Leiden: EJ Brill, 1983, 430—443.

Palmer, Frank. *Grammar*. Harmondsworth, Middlesex: Penguin Books, 1971.

Pan, Wenguo and Tham Wai Mun. *Contrastive Linguistics: History, Philosophy and Methodology*. London and New York: Continuum, 2007.

Pan, Wenguo. "English-Chinese Contrastive Studies in China: A Century's Retrospect", in Tham Wai Mun & Lim Buan Chay (eds.). *Translation and Contrastive Studies: Collected papers*. Singapore: Centre for Chinese Language & Culture, Nanyang Technological University, 2003.

Panetta, Clayann Gilliam (ed.). *Contrastive Rhetoric Revisited and Redefined*. Mahwah, New Jersey and London: Lawrence Erlbaum Associates, Inc. 2001.

Passy, Paul. *Petite phonétique comparée des principales langues européennes*. Leipzig: Teubner, 2nd rev. ed. (1st edition 1901) 1912.

Pietro, R. J. D. *Language Structures in Contrast*. Rowley, Massachusetts: Newbury House

Publishers, Inc. 1971/1978.

Pinker, Steven. *The Language Instinct.* New York: William Morrow and Company, Inc. 1994.

Popper, Karl. *Objective Knowledge. An Evolutionary Approach.* Oxford: Clarendon Press, 1972.

Preston, D. R. "Contrastive Analysis—the Outlook from Modern Grammar", *Papers and Studies in Contrastive Linguistics.* 1975, 3: 63—72.

Purves, A. C. (ed.). *Writing across Language and Cultures: Issues in Contrastive Rhetoric.* Newbury Park: Sage, 1988.

Pütz, Martin and Marjolijn Verspoor (eds.). *Explorations in Linguistic Relativity.* Amsterdam and Philadelphia: John Benjamins. 2000.

Radwanska-Williams, Joanna. *A Paradigm Lost: The Linguistic Theory of Mikolaj Kruszewski.* Amsterdam & Philadelphia: John Benjamins. 1993.

Richards, J. C. "A Noncontrastive Approach to Error Analysis", *English language Teaching.* 1971a, 25, 204—219.

Richards, J. C. "Error Analysis and Second Language Strategy", *Language Sciences.* 1971b, 17, 12—22.

Riley, Philip. "Towards a Contrastive Pragmalinguistics", 1979/1981, in J. Fisiak (ed.) *Papers and Studies in Contrastive Linguistics*, Adam Mickiewicz University, Poznań, Poland and Washington, DC, USA; reprinted in J. Fisaik (ed.), *Contrastive Linguistics and the Language Teacher.* Oxford: Pergamon Press, 1984, 121—146.

Robins, R. H. *A Short History of Linguistics.* Beijing: FLTRP, 2001.

Robins, Robert H. "Leibniz, Wilhelm von Humboldt and the History of Comparative Linguistics," in De Mauro, Tullio, Lia Formigari (eds.) *Leibniz, Humboldt, and the Origins of Comparativism.* Amsterdam and Philadelphia: John Benjamins Pub, 1990, 85—102.

Rousseau, Jean-Jacques. "Essai sur l'origine des langues", 1772, translated into English by John H. Moran, in Peter H. Salus (ed.), 1969.

Sajavaara, Kari & Jaakko Lehtonen (eds.). "A Bibliography of Applied Contrastve Studies", in J. Fisiak (ed.), *Contrastive Linguistics and the Language Teacher.* Oxford: Pergamon Press, 1981.

Sajavaara, Kari. "Contrastive Linguistics Past and Present and a Communicative Approach", *Jyvaskyla Contrastive Studies.* 1977, 4: 9—30.

Sajavaara, Kari. "Contrastive Linguistics Past and Present", in J. Fisiak (ed.). *Contrastive Linguistics and the Language Teacher.* Oxford: Pergamon Press, 1981.

Salmon, Vivian. "The Study of Foreign Languages in 17th Century England", *Histoire Epistemolognie Language.* 1985, 7 (2): 45—70.

Salus, P. H., (ed.). *On Language: Plato to von Humboldt.* New York: Holt, Rinehart and Winston, Inc. 1969.

Sapir, Edward. *Language: An Introduction to the Study of Speech.* 1921, New York: Harcourt, Brace & World, Inc. (Reprinted in 1949)

Sapir, Edward. *Selected Writings*. Berkeley and Los Angeles: University of California Press, 1949.

Saussure, F. de. *Cours de linguistique générale*. 1916, translated into English by R. Harris as *Course in General Linguistics*. La salle, Illinois: Open Court Publishing Co. 1986.

Sayce, A. H. *Introduction to the Science of Language*. London: C. Kegan Paul & Co. 1880.

Schleicher, A. *Die Darwinische Theorie und die Sprachwissenschaft*. 1863, translated as *Darwinism Tested by the Science of Language*. London: Hotten, 1869.

Scollon, Ron. et al. *Contrastive Discourse in Chinese and English: A Critical Appraisal*. Beijing: Foreign Language Teaching and Research Press, 2000.

Selinker, Larry. "Interlanguage", *International Review of Applied Linguistics*. 1972, 10: 209—231.

Selinker, Larry. "Language Transfer", *General Linguistics*. 1969, 9(2), 67—92.

Selinker, Larry. *Rediscovering Interlanguage*, London and New York: Longman, 1992.

Sinclair, John & Coulhard, Malcolm. *Towards an Analysis of Discourse: The English Used by Teachers and Pupils*. London: Oxford University Press, 1975.

Skalicka, Valdimir & Petr Sgall. "Praguian Typology of Languages", in Philip A. Luelsdorff (ed.). *The Prague School of Structural and Functional Linguistics*. Amsterdam: John Benjamins, 1994, 333—356.

Snell-Hornby, Mary. *Verb-descriptivity in German and English: A Contrastive Study in Semantic Fields*. Heidelberg: Carl Winter Universitätsverlag, 1983.

Sovran, Tamar. "Between Similarity and Sameness", *Journal of Pragmatics*. 1992, 18, 4: 329—344.

Sperber, Dan & Deirdre Wilson, *Relevance: Communication and Cognition*. Oxford: Blackwell, 1986.

Stankiewicz, Edward. "Baudouin de Courtenay: Pioneer in Diachronic Linguistics", in Aarsleff, Hans, L. G. Kelly, Hans-Josef Niederehe (eds.). *Papers in the History of Linguistics*, Amsterdam: John Benjamins, 1987, 539—549.

Stankiewicz, Edward. "Slavic Morphophonemics in Its Typological and Diachronic Aspects" in Sebeok, Thomas Albert (ed.), 1966, Current Trends in Linguistics vol 3: *Theoretical Foundations*. The Hague: Mouton & Co.1966, 495—520.

Stankiewicz, Edward. *A Baudouin de Courtenay Anthology: The Beginning of Structural Linguisticss*. Bloomington: Indiana University Press, 1972.

Steinfatt, Thomas M. "Linguistic Relativity: Toward a Broader View", in Stella Ting-Toomey and Felipe Korzenny (eds.). *Language, Communication, and Culture: Current Directions*. Newbury Park, London and New Delhi: Sage Publications, 1989, 35—75.

Stockwell, R. and J. Bowen. *The Sounds of English and Spanish*. Chicago: The University of Chicago Press, 1965.

Stockwell, R., J. Bowen, and J. Martin. *The Grammatical Structures of English and Spanish*. Chicago: The University of Chicago Press, 1965.

Stubbs, Michael. *Discourse Analysis: The Sociolinguistic Analysis of Natural Language.* Oxford: Blackwell, 1983.

Sweet, Henry. *A New English Grammar, Logical and Historical*, Part I. London: Oxford University Press, 1891.

Toman, Jindrich. *The Magic of a Common Language: Jakobson, Mathesius, Trubetzkoy and the Prague Linguistic Circle.* Cambridge, Mass.: The MIT Press, 1995.

Toury, Gideon and J. Laffling. "Translation of Literary Texts vs. Literary Translation: A Distinction Reconsidered", in S. Tirkkonen-Condit (ed.). *Recent Trends in Empirical Translation Research* (Studies in Languages, NO. 28), University of Joensuu, 1993.

Toury, Gideon. *In Search of a Theory of Translation.* Tel Aviv: The Porter Institute, 1980.

Trager, G. L. "The field of Linguistics", *Studies in Linguistics. Occasional Papers* 1. Norman, Okl.: Battenburg, 1949.

Tversky, Amos. "Features of Similarity", *Psychological Review.* 1977, 84: 327—352.

Vachek, Josef. "Vilem Mathesius as Forerunner of Contrastive Linguistic Studies", in J. Fisiak (ed.). *Papers and Studies in Contrastive Linguistics* vol 11: *The Polish-English Contrastive Project.* Washington D. C: Centre for Applied Linguistics, 5—16. Retrieved from ERIC database, 1980. [192616].

Van Buren, Paul. "Contrastive Analysis", in J. Fisiak (ed.). 1980, 83—117.

Varo, Francisco. *Arte de la lengua Mandarina*, (ed.). 1703 (Ms 1682), by Petro de la Piñuela, Canton (publisher unknown). Translated into English by W. South Coblin (柯蔚南) and Joseph A. Levi, *Francisco Varo's Grammar of the Mandarin Language.* Amsterdam and Philadelphia: John Benjamins, 2000. Translated into Chinese by Yao Xiaoping and Ma Youging, 2003, as《华语官话语法》，Beijing：Foreign Language Teaching and Research Press，2003年。

Venuti, Lawrence. (ed.). *Rethinking Trasnslation: Discourse, Subjectivity, Ideology.* London and New York: Routledge, 1992.

Venuti, Lawrence. *The Scandals of Translation.* London sand New York: Routledge, 1998.

Viëtor, Wilhelm. *Elemente der Phonetik des Deutschen, Engkischen und Französischen.* Leipzig: Reisland, 1894.

Vinay, Jean-Paul and Darbelnet, Jean. *Stylistique Compare du français et de l'anglais: Méthode de traduction.* Paris: Didier, 1958/1966.

Vossler, Karl. *Positivismus und Idealismus in der Sprachwissenschaft.* Heideberg: C. Winter, 1904.

Warren, James Perrin. "Organic Language Theory in the American Renaissance" in Aarsleff, Hans, Hans-Josef Niederehe, Louis G. Kelly (eds.), *Papers in the History of Linguistics.* Amsterdam: John Benjamins. 1987, 513—522.

Wasik, Zdzislaw. "General Linguistics in the History of the Language Sciences in Poland: Late

1860s-late 1960s", in Koerner, E. F. K. & Aleksander J. Szwedek (eds.), *Towards a History of Linguistics in Poland—From the Early Beginning to the End of the Twentieth Century.* Amsterdam/Philadelphia: John Benjamins Publishing Co. 2001, 3—51.

Weinreich, U. *Language in Contact.* New York: The Linguistic Circle, 1953.

Weisgerber, Leo. *Vom Welbild der deutschen Sprache.* Düsseldorf: Pädagogischer Verlag, 1953—1954.

Werlich, Egon. *A Text Grammar of English.* Heidelberg: Quelle & Meyer, 1976.

Whitney, W. D. Nature and Origin of Language, in Roy Harris (ed.), *The Origin of Language.* Bristol: Thoemmes Press, 1996, 291—313.

Whorf, B. L. "Gestalt Technique of Stem Composition in Shawnee", in John B. Carroll (ed.), *Language, Thought and Reality: Selected Writings of Benjamin Lee Whorf.* Cambridge, Mass.: The MIT Press, 1939b, 160—172.

Whorf, B. L. "Grammatical Categories", in John B. Carroll (ed.), *Language, Thought and Reality: Selected Writings of Benjamin Lee Whorf.* Cambridge, Mass.: The MIT Press, 1937, 87—101.

Whorf, B. L. "Language and Logic", in John B. Carroll (ed.), *Language, Thought and reality: Selected Writings of Benjamin Lee Whorf.* Cambridge, Massachusetts: The MIT Press, 1941a, 233—245.

Whorf, B. L. "Language, Mind, and Reality", 1941b, in John B. Carroll (ed.), *Language, Thought and Reality: Selected Writings of Benjamin Lee Whorf.* Cambridge, Mass.: The MIT Press, 1956, 246—270.

Whorf, B. L. "Linguistics as an Exact Science", in John B. Carroll (ed.), *Language, Thought and Reality: Selected Writings of Benjamin Lee Whorf.* Cambridge, Mass.: The MIT Press, 1940b, 220—232.

Whorf, B. L. "Science and Linguistics", in John B. Carroll (ed.), *Language, Thought and Reality: Selected Writings of Benjamin Lee Whorf.* Cambridge, Mass.: The MIT Press, 1940a, 207—219.

Whorf, B. L. "The Relation of Habitual Thought and Behavior to Language", in John B. Carroll (ed.). *Language, Thought and Reality: Selected Writings of Benjamin Lee Whorf.* Cambridge, Mass.: The MIT Press, 1939a, 134—159.

Whorf, B. L. *Language, Thought and Reality: Selected Writings of Benjamin Lee Whorf.* Edited by John B. Carroll, Cambridge, Mass.: The MIT Press, 1956.

Wierzbicka, Anna & Jean Harkins. "Introduction", in Jean Harkins and Anna Wierzbicka (eds.), *Emotions in Crosslinguistic Perspective.* Berlin and New York: Mouton de Gruyter, 2001.

Wierzbicka, Anna. *Lingua Mentalis: The Semantics of Natural Language.* Sydney: Academic Press, 1980.

Wierzbicka, Anna. "Contrastive Sociolinguistics and the Theory of 'Cultural Scripts': Chinese vs. English", in Marlis Hellinger and Urich Ammon (eds.), *Contrastive Sociolinguastics.* Berlin:

Mouton de Gruyter, 1996, 313—44.

Wierzbicka, Anna. "Cultural Scripts: A New Approach to the Study of Cross-cultural Communication", in Pütz, Martin (ed.), *Language Contact and Language Conflict*. Amsterdam and Philadelphia: John Benjamins, 1994, 69—87.

Wierzbicka, Anna. "Ethno-syntax and the Philosophy of Grammar", *Studies in Language*, 1979, 3(3): 313—383.

Wierzbicka, Anna. *Cross-Cultural Pragmatics: The Semantics of Human Interaction*. Berlin and New York: Mouton de Gruyter, 1991.

Wierzbicka, Anna. *Emotions across Languages and Cultures*. Cambridge: Cambridge University Press, 1999.

Wierzbicka, Anna. *Semantics, Culture, and Cognition: Universal Human Concepts in Culture-specific Configurations*. New York and Oxford: Oxford University Press, 1992.

Wilkins, D. A. *Notional Syllabuses*. Oxford: Oxford University Press, 1976.

Yip, Po-Ching. "Linguistic Dispositions: A Macroscopic View of Translating from English into Chinese", *Journal of Chinese Language Teachers' Association*, Volume XXVIII, No. 2, 1993.

白　珊：《导论：弗朗西斯科·瓦罗的<华语官话语法>》，2000，见Varo Francisco. (Ms 1682) *Arte de la lengua Mandarina*. ed. by Petro de la Piñuela, Canton (publisher unknown), 1703. Translated into English by W. South Coblin (柯蔚南) and Joseph A. Levi, Francisco Varo's *Grammar of the Mandarin Language*. Amsterdam and Philadelphia: John Benjamins, 2000. 姚小平、马又清中译《华语官话语法》，北京：外语教学与研究出版社，2003年，F19—F65。

贝罗贝：《二十世纪以前欧洲汉语语法学研究状况》，见侯精一、施关淦主编《<马氏文通>与汉语语法学》，北京：商务印书馆，2000年，149—161。

蔡基刚：《英汉词汇对比研究》，上海：复旦大学出版社，2008年。

蔡勇飞，王之光：《汉英文字比较研究》，杭州：浙江大学出版社，2005年。

陈　虎：《英汉语调音系对比研究》，开封：河南大学出版社，2006年。

陈保亚：《20世纪中国语言学方法论》，济南：山东教育出版社，1999年。

陈承泽：《汉语语法丛书》，北京：商务印书馆，1982年。

陈定安：《英汉比较与翻译》，香港：商务印书馆（香港）有限公司，1985年。

陈平：《汉语的形式、意义与功能——陈平语言学文选》，北京：商务印书馆出版，2017年。

陈其荣，曹志平：《科学基础方法论》，上海：复旦大学出版社，2004年。

陈望道等：《汉语语法丛书》，北京：商务印书馆，1987年。

陈寅恪："与刘叔雅论国文试题书"，载陈寅恪《金明馆丛稿二编》，上海：上海古籍出版社，1980年；又载胡道静主编《国学大师论国学》（下），上海：东方出版中心，1998年，243—249。

程雨民：《汉语字基语法》，上海：复旦大学出版社，2003年。

褚孝泉：《语言哲学：从语言到思想》，上海：三联书店，1991年。
戴浩一："以认知为基础的汉语功能语法研究刍议"，1987，载戴浩一、薛凤生（主编）《功能主义与汉语语法》，北京：北京语言学院出版社，1994年。
道安："摩诃钵罗若波罗密经钞序"，载罗新璋编《翻译论集》，北京：商务印书馆，1984年。
丁金国："对比语言学及其应用"，《河北大学学报》第2期，1981年。
丁金国："汉英对比研究中的理论原则"，载《外语教学与研究》1996年第3期，又载王菊泉、郑立信（主编），2004，2—11。
丁声树等：《现代汉语语法讲话》，北京：商务印书馆，1961年。
方梦之："加强对比语言学的研究"，《语言教学与研究》1983年第4期。
冯胜利：《汉语的韵律、词法与句法》，北京：北京大学出版社，1997年。
高本汉：《中国语和中国文》，张世禄译，台北：文史哲出版社，1930/1977年。
高名凯："关于汉语的词类分别"，《中国语文》1953年10月号，后收入《高名凯语言学论文集》，北京：商务印书馆，1990年，262—272。
高名凯："关于汉语实词分类问题"，《语言学论丛》第四辑，1960年，后收入《高名凯语言学论文集》，北京：商务印书馆，1990年，302—307。
高名凯：《汉语语法论》，北京：商务印书馆，1986年。
高名凯："汉语语法研究中的词类问题"，《安徽大学学报》1963年第1期，后收入《高名凯语言学论文集》，北京：商务印书馆，1990年，308—335。
高名凯："三论汉语的词类分别"，《中国语文》1955年1月号，后收入《高名凯语言学论文集》，北京：商务印书馆，1990年，287—301。
高名凯："语言的结构与哲学的思想"，《学原》第1卷第12期，后收入《高名凯语言学论文集》，北京：商务印书馆，1990年，1—14。
高名凯："再论汉语的词类分别"，《中国语文》1954年8月号，后收入《高名凯语言学论文集》，北京：商务印书馆，1990年，273—286。
高一虹等（译）：《论语言、思维和现实》，长沙：湖南教育出版社，2001年。
辜正坤：《互构语言文化学原理》，北京：清华大学出版社，2004年。
桂诗春，宁春岩：《语言学方法论》，北京：外语教学与研究出版社，1997年。
郭绍虞："中国语言所受到的文字的牵制"，原载1946年4月22日《新闻报》，载郭绍虞《照隅室语言文字论集》，上海：上海古籍出版社，1985年，112—114。
郭绍虞："汉语词组对汉语语法研究的重要性"，载郭绍虞《照隅室语言文字论集》，上海：上海古籍出版社，1985年。
郭绍虞："中国语词的弹性作用"，载郭绍虞《照隅室语言文字论集》，上海：上海古籍出版社，1985年，73—111。
郭绍虞：《汉语语法修辞新探》，北京：商务印书馆，1979年。
郭绍虞：《语文通论》，上海：开明书店，1941年。

郭绍虞：《语文通论续编》，上海：开明书店，1948年。

郭绍虞：《照隅室语言文字论集》，上海：上海古籍出版社，1985年。

何　容：《中国文法论》，北京：商务印书馆，1985年。

何九盈：《中国古代语言学史》，广州：广东教育出版社，2000年。

何九盈：《中国现代语言学史》，广州：广东教育出版社，2000年。

何善芬：《英汉语言对比研究》，上海：上海外语教育出版社，2002年。

何晓炜：《英汉双及物结构的生成语法研究》，北京：外语教学与研究出版社，2011年。

洪堡特：《洪堡特语言哲学文集》，姚小平译，长沙：湖南教育出版社，2001年。

胡明扬：《试评我国语言学界目前存在的资产阶级思想》，《中国语文》1955年3月号，收入中国语文编辑部编《汉语的词类问题》（第二集），北京：中华书局，77—87。

胡明扬：《现代汉语词类研究综述》，载胡明扬主编《词类问题考察》，北京：北京语言学院出版社，1996年，22—55。

胡曙中：《英汉修辞比较研究》，上海：上海外语教育出版社，1993年。

胡以鲁："国外汉英对比研究杂谈"（二、续完），《语言教学与研究》第2期。

胡壮麟："国外汉英对比研究杂谈"（一），《语言教学与研究》第1期，1982年。

黄　勤：《英汉新闻语篇中的元话语对比研究》，武汉：武汉大学出版社，2014年。

康拉德：О китайском языке，1952年，彭楚南中译《论汉语》，上海：中华书局，1954年。

赖　彦：《英汉新闻转述话语比较研究》，北京：中国社会科学出版社，2016年。

黎锦熙：《今序》，1924年，载《汉语语法丛书》本黎锦熙《新著国语文法》，北京：商务印书馆，1992年，8—16。

黎锦熙：《新著国语文法》北京：商务印书馆，1992年。

黎锦熙：《比较文法》，1933、1973年修订本，北京：中华书局，1986年。

李　荣（编译）：《北京口语语法》，北京：开明书店，1952年。

李　雪：《英汉移动动词词汇化模式的对比研究》，北京：外语教学与研究出版社，2011年。

李葆嘉：《理论语言学：人文与科学的双重精神》，南京：江苏古籍出版社，2001年。

李国南：《英汉修辞格对比研究》，福州：福建人民出版社，1999年。

李临定：《句型范畴》，1990年，收入《李临定自选集》，郑州：河南教育出版社，1994年。

李临定：《汉语比较变换语法》，北京：中国社会科学出版社，1988年。

李临定：《现代汉语句型》，北京：商务印书馆，1986年。

李瑞华（主编）：《英汉语言文化对比研究》，上海：上海外语教育出版社，1996年。

李晓红：《双语语料库界面下英汉语义韵对比研究》，上海：上海交通大学出版社，2015年。

连淑能：《英汉对比研究（增订本）》，北京：高等教育出版社，2010年。

连淑能：《英汉对比研究》，北京：高等教育出版社，1993年。

列　宁：《论民族自决权》，《列宁文选》两卷本，第一卷，北京：人民出版社，1916年。

林同济：《从汉语词序看长句翻译》，1980年，载杨自俭、李瑞华编《英汉对比研究论文集》,上海:上海外语教育出版社,1990年。

林语堂:"研究方言应有的几个语言学观察点",1933b,载林语堂著《语言学论丛》,上海:上海书店出版社,1989年重印。

林语堂:《开明英文文法(*Kaiming English Grammar*)》,1933a,上海:开明书店;北京:外语教学与研究出版社,1982年重印。

刘 复:《中国文法通论》,增补四版,1920年,上海:群益书社,1924年。

刘 新:"任著<汉英比较语法>简评",《中国语文》1983年第5期。

刘礼进、徐真华:《篇章视点回指语用论:一项以汉英长距离反身代词为中心的对比研究》,上海:上海外语教育出版社,2012年。

刘宓庆:"汉英对比研究的理论问题(上)",1991/1996,《外国语》1991年第4期,又载李瑞华(主编)1996年,23—33。

刘宓庆:《汉英对比研究与翻译》,南昌:江西教育出版社,1991年。

刘宓庆:《新编汉英对比与翻译》,北京:中国对外翻译出版公司,2006年。

刘兴华:《英汉语篇跨文化修辞研究》,北京:外语教学与研究出版社,2015年。

刘英凯、李静滢主编:《比较·鉴别·应用:英汉对比应用研究》,上海:上海外语教育出版社,2009年。

刘英凯:《英汉语音修辞》,广州:广东高等教育出版社,1998年。

刘元亮等:《科学认识论与方法论》,北京:清华大学出版社,1987年。

刘正埮:"语言学界也应该广泛展开学术上的自由讨论",1955年,《中国语文》1955年3月号,收入中国语文杂志社编《汉语的词类问题》(第二集),北京:中华书局,1956年,22—25。

刘重德(主编):《英汉语比较研究》,长沙:湖南科学技术出版社,1994年。

刘重德(主编):《英汉语比较研究》,青岛:青岛出版社,1998年。

刘重德:《前言》,1998年,载刘重德(主编)1998年,1—4。

龙果夫:*Исследования по грамматике современного китайского языка*,1952年,中文本《现代汉语语法研究》,北京:科学出版社,1958年。

鲁川:《汉语语法的意合网络》,北京:商务印书馆,2001年。

鲁健骥:"中介语理论与外国人学习汉语的语音偏误分析",1984年,《语言教学与研究》1984年第3期,收入鲁健骥《对外汉语教学思考集》,北京:北京语言文化大学出版社,1999年,21—32。

陆国强:《英汉概念结构对比》,上海:上海外语教育出版社,2008年。

吕叔湘:《中国文法要略》,北京:商务印书馆,1982年。

吕叔湘、朱德熙:《语法修辞讲话》,北京:中国青年出版社,1952年。

吕叔湘:*Editor's Note*,1982年,林语堂《开明英文文法》,1933年初版,1982年重印,北京:外语教学与研究出版社。

吕叔湘:"把我国语言科学推向前进",1980b,载中国语言学会编《把我国语言科学推向前进——中国语言学会成立大会学术报告集》，武汉：湖北人民出版社，1981年，8—20。

吕叔湘："关于汉语词类的一些原则性问题（下）"，1954年，《中国语文》第28期，收入中国语文杂志社编《汉语的词类问题》（第一集），北京：中华书局，1955年，130—173。

吕叔湘："漫谈语法研究"，1978年，《中国语文》第1期。收入《吕叔湘自选集》，上海：上海教育出版社，1989年，329—340。

吕叔湘：《通过对比研究语法》，1977年，《语言教学与研究》试刊1977年第2期，收入杨自俭、李瑞华编《英汉对比研究论文集》，上海：上海外语教育出版社，1990年，21—33。

吕叔湘："序"，1986年，龚千炎《中国语法学史稿》，北京：语文出版社，1987年。

吕叔湘："语法研究中的破与立"，《吕叔湘全集》第十三卷，北京：商务印书馆，2002年，402—404。

吕叔湘："语言和语言学"，1958年，《语文学习》第2、3期，收入《吕叔湘文集》第四卷，北京：商务印书馆，1992年。

吕叔湘：《汉语语法分析问题》，北京：商务印书馆，1979年。

吕叔湘：《语文常谈》，北京：三联书店，1980年。

吕叔湘：《语言和语言研究》，载季羡林等《中国大百科全书·语言文字》，北京：中国大百科全书出版社，1988年。

吕叔湘：《中国人学英文》，1947年，1962年再版，改名《中国人学英语》，北京：商务印书馆。

罗选民等：《话语分析的英汉语比较研究》，长沙：湖南人民出版社，2001年。

马建忠：《马氏文通》，1898年，《汉语语法丛书》，北京：商务印书馆，1983年。

马庆株：《汉语语义语法范畴问题》，北京：北京语言文化大学出版社，1998年。

苗东升：《系统科学精要》，北京：中国人民大学出版社，1998年。

苗兴伟，秦洪武：《英汉语篇语用学研究》，上海：上海外语教育出版社，2010年。

南　潮：《被动义视角下英汉受事提升构句研究》，北京：外语教学与研究出版社，2016年。

牛保义，徐盛桓："关于英汉语语法化比较研究"，2000，《外语与外语教学》2000年第9期，又载王菊泉、郑立信（编）2004年，52—61。

牛保义主编：《认知·语用·功能：英汉宏观对比研究》，上海：上海外语教育出版社，2009年。

潘文国，谭慧敏：《对比语言学：历史与哲学思考》，上海：上海教育出版社，2006年。

潘文国，杨自俭：《共性·个性·视角：英汉对比的理论与方法研究》，上海：上海外语教育出版社，2008年。

潘文国，叶步青，韩洋：《汉语的构词法研究（增订本）》，上海：华东师范大学出版社，2004年。

潘文国，叶步青，韩洋：《汉语的构词法研究：1898—1990》，台北：学生书局，1993年。

潘文国、黄月圆、杨素英：《当前的汉语构词法研究》，载江蓝生、侯精一主编《汉语现状与历史的研究》，北京：中国社会科学出版社，1999年12月。

潘文国："'两张皮'现象的由来及对策"，《外语与外语教学》2001年第10期，34—37。

潘文国："比较汉英语语法研究史的启示"（上），《语言教学与研究》第2期，1996a。

潘文国："比较汉英语语法研究史的启示"（下），《语言教学与研究》第3期，1996b。

潘文国："对比研究与对外汉语教学"，《暨南大学华文学院学报》2003年第1期。

潘文国："关于对比语言学理论建设和学科体系的几点意见"，《青岛海洋大学学报》第3期，1996d。

潘文国："汉英对比研究一百年"，《世界汉语教学》2002年第1期。

潘文国："汉语研究：世纪之交的思考"，《语言研究》2000年第1期。

潘文国："换一种眼光何如？——关于汉英对比研究的宏观思考"，《外语研究》第1期，1997c。

潘文国："换一种眼光如何？——关于汉英对比研究的宏观思考"，刘重德主编《英汉语比较与翻译》，青岛：青岛出版社，1998年。

潘文国："论中国语言学的'落后'"，上海市语文学会编《语文论丛》第七辑，上海：上海教育出版社，2001b。

潘文国："语言的定义"，载戴昭铭、陆镜光主编《语言学问题集刊》第一辑，长春：吉林人民出版社，2001年。

潘文国："语言对比研究的哲学基础"，《华东师范大学学报》第5期，1995年。

潘文国："语言哲学与哲学语言学"，《华东师范大学学报》2004第3期，96—102。

潘文国："语言哲学与哲学语言学"，《华东师范大学学报》2004年第3期。

潘文国："字本位和词本位"，载耿龙明、何寅主编《中国文化与世界》第四辑，上海：上海外语教育出版社，1996c。

潘文国：《汉英语对比纲要》，北京：北京语言文化大学出版社，1997a。

潘文国：《汉英语对比纲要》，北京：北京语言文化大学出版社，1997年。

潘文国：《韵图考》，上海：华东师范大学出版社，1997b。

潘文国：《字本位与汉语研究》，上海：华东师范大学出版社，2002b。

彭宣维：《英汉语篇综合对比》，上海：上海外语教育出版社，2000年。

启　功：《汉语现象论丛》，1991年，香港：商务印书馆（香港）有限公司；增订本，北京：中华书局，1997年。

钱　瑗："A Comparison of Some Cohesive Devices in English and Chinese"，《外国语》1983年第1期。

钱冠连："对比语言学者的历史重任"，载杨自俭主编《英汉语比较与翻译》，上海：上海外语教育出版社，2000年。

钱冠连："论外语学者对母语研究的建树——再论'两张皮'"，杨自俭主编《英汉语比较与翻译》（4），上海：上海外语教育出版社，2002年，63—76。

钱冠连："语言学理论框架的跨国对比"，刘重德主编《英汉语比较与翻译》，青岛：青岛出版社，1998年，38—50。

钱冠连："哲学轨道上的语言研究"，《外国语》1999年第6期，9—16。

钱冠连："中西哲学的不同语言走向"，《解放军外国语学院学报》2001年第6期，1—4。

钱冠连：《语言：人类最后的家园》，北京：商务印书馆，2005年。

任学良：《汉英比较语法》，北京：中国社会科学出版社，1981年。

邵敬敏，方经民：《中国理论语言学史》，上海：华东师范大学出版社，1991年。

邵敬敏："'语义语法'说略"，《暨南学报》2004年第1期。

邵敬敏："关于'功能'和'解释'的几点思考"，《华东师范大学学报》第4期，1996年。

邵志洪：《英汉语研究与对比》，上海：华东理工大学出版社，1997年。

邵志洪：《结构·语义·关系：英汉微观对比研究》，上海：上海外语教育出版社，2008年。

申小龙：《文化语言学》，南昌：江西教育出版社，1993年。

申小龙：《中国句型文化》，沈阳：东北师范大学出版社，1988年。

申小龙：《中国文化语言学》，长春：吉林教育出版社，1990年。

沈家煊："我国的语用学研究"，《外语教学与研究》第1期，1996年。

沈家煊：《名词和动词》，北京：商务印书馆，2016年。

沈家煊：《语法六讲》，北京：商务印书馆，2011年。

史有为："词类问题的症结及其对策"，载胡明扬主编《词类问题考察》，北京：北京语言学院出版社，1996年，56—92。

斯大林：《马克思主义和语言学问题》，1950年，北京：人民出版社，1971年重印。

孙中山：《建国方略》（"以作文为证"），1918年，收入《孙中山选集》上卷，北京：人民出版社，1956年，126—131。

谭慧敏："西方对比语言史的重新思考"，《英汉对比与翻译》创刊号，2011年，32—39。

谭鑫田等：《西方哲学范畴理论》，济南：山东大学出版社，1993年。

涂纪亮：《现代西方语言哲学比较研究》，北京：中国社会科学出版社，1996年。

万惠洲：《汉英构词法比较》，北京：中国对外经济贸易出版社，1988年。

王蕾："换一种路径如何——以致使范畴为例谈英汉对比的研究方法"，中国英汉比较研究会第十一次全国代表大会暨2014年英汉比较与翻译研究国际研讨会会议论文，另见王蕾、李涛，"以致使范畴为例谈英汉对比的研究方法"，《长春大学学报》2016年第6期，98—102。

王　还："有关汉外语法对比的三个问题"，载《第一届国际汉语教学讨论会论文选》，北京：北京语言学院出版社，1986年，322—328。

王　力："关于汉语语法体系问题"，载《教学语法论集——全国语法和语法教学讨论会论文汇编》，北京：人民教育出版社，1982年，18—24。

王　力："在第一届国际汉语教学研究会上的讲话"，《语言教学与研究》1985年第4期，收入《王力文集》第十九卷，济南：山东教育出版社，1991年，395—396。

王　力："中国古文法",1927年,后收入《王力文集》第三卷,济南:山东教育出版社,1985年,1—85。

王　力："中国现代语法",1943—1944年,上海:商务印书馆。后收入《王力文集》第二卷,济南:山东教育出版社,1985年。

王　力："中国语法理论",1944—1945年,上海:商务印书馆。后收入《王力文集》第一卷,济南:山东教育出版社,1984年。

王　力："关于汉语有无词类的问题",1985a,《北京大学学报》1955年第2期,后收入中国语文杂志社编《汉语的词类问题》(第二集),北京:中华书局,1956年,33—63。

王　力："我的治学经验",《高教战线》1984年5期;后收入《王力文集》第二十卷,济南:山东教育出版社,1991年,536—551。

王　力："中国文法学初探",1936年,《清华学报》11卷1期,后收入《王力文集》第三卷,济南:山东教育出版社,1985年,87—152。

王逢鑫:《英汉比较语义学》,北京:外文出版社,2001年。

王洪君:"汉语语法的基本单位与研究策略",《语言教学与研究》2000年第2期。

王菊泉,郑立信(编):《英汉语言文化对比研究(1995—2003)》,上海:上海外语教育出版社,2004a。

王菊泉,郑立信:《前言》,见王菊泉、郑立信(编),2004年,1—36。

王菊泉,郑立信:《英汉语言文化对比研究》,上海:上海外语教育出版社,2004a。

王菊泉:"从外语界现状看加强对汉语的学习和研究的必要性",杨自俭主编《英汉语比较与翻译》(4),上海:上海外语教育出版社,2002年,51—62。

王菊泉:"关于英汉语法比较的几个问题——评最近出版的几本英汉对比语法著作",《外语教学与研究》1982年第4期,收入杨自俭、李瑞华编《英汉对比研究论文集》,上海:上海外语教育出版社,1990年,63—78。

王宗炎:"对比分析和语言教学",《语言研究》第1期,1983年,又见李瑞华(主编)1996年,3—22。

魏在江:《英汉语篇连贯认知对比研究》,上海:复旦大学出版社,2007年。

魏志成:《英汉语比较导论》,上海:上海外语教育出版社,2004年。

沃尔夫:《论语言、思维和现实》,卡罗尔等编,高一虹等译,长沙:湖南教育出版社,2001年。

沃尔夫:《论语言思维和现实》,高一虹等译,长沙:湖南教育出版社,2001年。

吴洁敏:《汉英语法手册》,北京:知识出版社,1981年。

伍铁平:"论语言的类型对比",《外语学刊》第4期,1984年。

伍雅清:"英汉语比较的两个问题",《外语学刊》2000年第1期,又载王菊泉、郑立信(编)2004年,30—39。

熊文华:《汉英应用对比概论》,北京:北京语言文化大学出版社,1997年。

熊仲儒:《英汉致使句论元结构的对比研究》,上海:上海外语教育出版社,2015年。

徐烈炯："语言对比与对比语言学"，《外语语言教学资料报导》第4期，1983年。

徐士珍：《英汉语比较语法》，郑州：河南教育出版社，1985年。

徐通锵："'字'和汉语的句法结构"，《世界汉语教学》，1994年第2期。

徐通锵："'字'和汉语的句法结构"，《世界汉语教学》，1994年第3期。

徐通锵："对比和汉语语法研究的方法论"，《语言研究》2001年第4期，见王菊泉、郑立信编，2004年，79—90。

徐通锵："序"，载潘文国《字本位与汉语研究》，上海：华东师范大学出版社，2002年，1—6。

徐通锵："语义语法刍议"，《语言教学与研究》第3期，1991年。

徐通锵：《汉语研究方法论初探》，北京：商务印书馆，2004年。

徐通锵：《基础语言学教程》，北京：北京大学出版社，2001a。

徐通锵：《语言论》，长春：东北师范大学出版社，1997年。

许国璋：《许国璋文集》，北京：商务印书馆，1997年。

许余龙：《对比语言学（第2版）》，上海：上海外语教育出版社，2010年。

许余龙：《对比语言学》，上海：上海外语教育出版社，2001年。

许余龙：《对比语言学》，上海：上海外语教育出版社，2002年。

许余龙：《对比语言学概论》，上海：上海外语教育出版社，1992年。

许余龙："三种推理模式及其在语言学研究种的功用——以名词短语可及性研究为例"，载《现代外语》（双月刊），2014年第37卷第6期。

严学窘："中国对比语言学的兴起"，《中南民族学院学报》第2期，1984年。

杨衍春：《博杜恩德库尔德内语言学理论研究》，中央民族大学博士学位论文，2009年，第119页。

杨自俭，李瑞华（编）：《英汉对比研究论文集》，上海：上海外语教育出版社，1990a。

杨自俭，李瑞华："英汉对比研究述评"，载杨自俭、李瑞华编《英汉对比研究论文集》，上海：上海外语教育出版社，1990b，1—17。

杨自俭："《英汉语篇衔接手段对比研究》序"，载朱永生等《英汉语篇衔接手段对比研究》，上海：上海外语教育出版社，2001a。

杨自俭："《英汉语言文化对比研究》序"，载王菊泉、郑立信（编），2004年，1—11。

杨自俭："简论对比语言学中的几个问题"，见王菊泉、郑立信编《英汉语言文化对比研究》，上海：上海外语教育出版社，2004，40—51。

杨自俭："简论对比语言学中的几个问题"，载杨自俭主编《英汉语比较与翻译》（3），上海：上海外语教育出版社，2000年，9—18。

杨自俭："序"，王宏印：《中国传统译论经典诠释》，武汉：湖北教育出版社，2003年。

杨自俭："英汉对比研究管窥"，《外语研究》1992年第1期，又载李瑞华（主编），1996年，45—55。

杨自俭："英汉语言文化对比研究和翻译理论建设"，载刘重德主编《英汉语比较研究》，长沙：湖南科学技术出版社，1994年，12—25。

杨自俭："再谈'两张皮'问题"，《外语与外语教学》2001年第10期，29—33。

杨自俭：《英汉语比较与翻译》，上海：上海外语教育出版社，2004年。

杨自俭：《语言多学科研究与应用》，南宁：广西教育出版社，2002年。

姚小平，马又清（译）：《华语官话语法》，北京：外语教学与研究出版社，2003年。

姚小平："译序"，载洪堡特著、姚小平译《论人类语言结构的差异及其对人类精神发展的影响》，北京：商务印书馆，1997年，1—70。

张　今，陈云清：《英汉比较语法纲要》，北京：商务印书馆，1981年。

张　今，张克定：《英汉语信息结构对比研究》，开封：河南大学出版社，1998年。

张　黎：《汉语意合语法学纲要》，（日本）中国书店，2001年。

张　黎：《文化的深层选择——汉语意合语法论》，长春：吉林教育出版社，1994年。

张培基：《习语汉译英研究》，北京：时代出版社，1958年。

张培基：《英汉声色词与翻译》，北京：商务印书馆，1964年。

张志公："关于汉语语法体系分歧问题"，《语言教学与研究》1980年第1期，后收入《张志公文集》（一），广州：广东教育出版社，1991年，466—478。

张志公："汉语词类问题需要进一步研究"，《语文论集》（二），1986年，北京：外语教学与研究出版社，后收入《张志公文集》（一），广州：广东教育出版社，1991年，591—602。

张志公："汉语辞章学与汉语语法"，《语言研究》1983年第2期，后收入《张志公自选集》（下册），北京：北京大学出版社，1998年，621—633。

张志公："汉语语法的再研究"，《外语教学与研究》1990年第3期，后收入《张志公自选集》（下册），北京：北京大学出版社，1998年，413—420。

张志公："加紧开展英汉对比研究"，《中小学英语教学与研究》第4期，1985年。

张志公："谈《暂拟汉语教学语法系统》"，《语文建设》1995年第1—2期，后收入《张志公自选集》》（下册），北京：北京大学出版社，1998年，541—548。

张志公："削足适履？赤足废履？改履适足？——关于词类问题，为高名凯先生说几句话并略说个人的一点看法"，《张志公自选集》（下册），北京：北京大学出版社，1998年，474—477。

张志公："语法研究和语法教学"，《语文研究》1980年第1辑，后收入《张志公文集》（一），广州：广东教育出版社，1991年，479—499。

张志公：《传统语文教育教材论》，上海：上海教育出版社，1992年。

张志公：《张志公自选集》，北京：北京大学出版社，1998年。

章炳麟："国语学草创序"，载胡以鲁《国语学草创》，上海：商务印书馆，1923年。

章士钊：《中等国文典》，上海：商务印书馆，1907年。

赵　宏：《英汉词汇理据对比研究》，上海：上海外语教育出版社，2013年。

赵世开（主编）：《汉英对比语法论集》，上海：上海外语教育出版社，1999年。

赵世开："浅谈英语和汉语的对比研究"，《外国语教学》第3期，又见杨自俭、李瑞华（编）1990年，34—42。

赵世开："序"，载杨自俭、李瑞华（编），1990年。

赵世开："英汉对比中微观和宏观的研究"，《外国语文教学》1985年第1—2期，又见杨自俭、李瑞华（编）1990年，97—105。

赵元任："A Preliminary Study of English Intonation and Its Chinese Equivalents"，载中央研究院历史语言研究所集刊外编《蔡元培先生六十五岁庆祝论文集》，1933年。

赵元任："Rhythm and Structure in Chinese Word Conceptions"，1975年，王洪君中译为"汉语词的概念及其结构和节奏"，载袁毓林主编《中国现代语言学的开拓和发展——赵元任语言学论文选》，北京：清华大学出版社，1992年，231—248。

赵元任：《汉语口语语法》，吕叔湘中译，北京：商务印书馆，1979年。

赵志毅：《英汉语法比较》，西安：陕西人民出版社，1981年。

支　谦："法句经序"，载罗新璋编《翻译论集》，北京：商务印书馆，1984年。

朱德熙：《语法答问》，北京：商务印书馆，1985年。

朱德熙：《语法讲义》，北京：商务印书馆，1982年。

朱永生，郑立信，苗兴伟：《英汉语篇衔接手段对比研究》，上海：上海外语教育出版社，2001年。

左飙（主编）：《冲突·互补·共存：中西文化对比研究》，上海：上海外语教育出版社，2009年。